Nomos Universitätsschriften

Recht

Band 983

Ma. Angela Leonor C. Aguinaldo

East Meets West

Development of Mutual Legal Assistance in Criminal Matters between and within the Association of Southeast Asian Nations and the European Union

Nomos

The book processing charge was funded by the Baden-Württemberg Ministry of Science, Research and Arts in the funding programme Open Access Publishing and the University of Freiburg.

The Deutsche Nationalbibliothek lists this publication in the Deutsche Nationalbibliografie; detailed bibliographic data are available on the Internet at http://dnb.d-nb.de

a.t.: Freiburg, Univ., Diss., 2020

original title: East Meets West: Development of Mutual Legal Assistance in Criminal Matters Between and Within the Association of Southeast Asian Nations and the European Union

ISBN (Print): 978-3-8487-7983-3
ISBN (ePDF): 978-3-7489-2113-4

British Library Cataloguing-in-Publication Data
A catalogue record for this book is available from the British Library.

ISBN (Print): 978-3-8487-7983-3
ISBN (ePDF): 978-3-7489-2113-4

Library of Congress Cataloging-in-Publication Data
Aguinaldo, Ma. Angela Leonor C.
East Meets West
Development of Mutual Legal Assistance in Criminal Matters between and within the Association of Southeast Asian Nations and the European Union
Ma. Angela Leonor C. Aguinaldo
710 pp.
Includes bibliographic references.

ISBN (Print): 978-3-8487-7983-3
ISBN (ePDF): 978-3-7489-2113-4

1st Edition 2021

Published by
Nomos Verlagsgesellschaft mbH & Co. KG
Waldseestraße 3–5 | 76530 Baden-Baden
www.nomos.de

Production of the printed version:
Nomos Verlagsgesellschaft mbH & Co. KG
Waldseestraße 3–5 | 76530 Baden-Baden

ISBN (Print): 978-3-8487-7983-3
ISBN (ePDF): 978-3-7489-2113-4
DOI: https://doi.org/10.5771/9783748921134

Onlineversion
Nomos eLibrary

Abstract

The Association of Southeast Asian Nations ("ASEAN") and the European Union ("EU") have in 2019 entered into a strategic partnership, which includes a renewed commitment to pursue stronger cooperation in combating terrorism and transnational crime as well as improvements of their respective infrastructures. The present study is mainly interested on how mutual legal assistance ("MLA") in criminal matters could develop between and within the ASEAN and the EU. The study applied a comparative criminal law approach in answering the research question by comparing the regional frameworks with each other as well as with their respective member state frameworks, which includes not only a look into the law in books but also the law in practice.

Mutual legal assistance can be further developed within and between the ASEAN and the EU if considerable weight is given to the two regional organizations' distinguishing features which then become the basis to understand how they are as international actors in terms of their decision and policymaking: intergovernmentalism v. supranationalism, principle of non-intervention and the ASEAN Way v. normative and hegemonic power, and harmonization v. approximation. In sum, any interregional treaty would be successful if each would take into account the other's values and neither party would dominate the determination of terms. Further, one must note that any lack of harmonization does not necessarily result in inefficiency of the cooperation mechanism. Member states are able to make the cooperation mechanism or mutual legal assistance work. The existence of approximation or the acceptance of minimum standards as well as open communication helps in building and maintaining (almost) smooth operations with each other.

Taking these into account, the present study came up with different suggestions ranging from the MLA within the regional frameworks (involving their own member states), the groundwork for the development of MLA between the two regional organizations, and suggestions for both substantial and procedural provisions that could be included in the possible MLA regime between the ASEAN and the EU. These suggestions mainly start with the least common denominators and non-negotiables of each regional organization in efforts to find agreement between the regional and member state frameworks.

In summary, the comparative criminal approach used by the present study in comparing the regional frameworks of the ASEAN and the EU, and the respective member state frameworks of the Philippines, Malaysia, the UK, and Germany, including a comparison of the law in books and the law of practice, would ultimately show that a mutual legal assistance regime could indeed be developed between and within the ASEAN and the EU. There is no need for the imposition of will of one regional organization on the other on what it thinks the other should do or practice. Instead, by building a common understanding of their respective frameworks and that of the other, as well as a common acceptance of the minimum principles, ideals and norms based on their differences, a formal international cooperation mechanism is highly plausible.

Acknowledgments

> "We are like the little branch that quivers during a storm, doubting our strength and forgetting we are the tree deeply rooted to withstand all life's upheavals." – Dodinsky

Undertaking a doctoral research and producing a written manuscript thereafter has not been an easy process. It can bring you to the highest peaks of lightness but it can also bring you to the deepest crevices of darkness. It speaks to the core of your humanity – your human personality – and tests your mental acuity, faith, resilience and courage especially in the darkest hours. It can be a lonely endeavor because you feel that you are left alone within the sphere of your individual research and undertakings. But then again, after undergoing such process I am deeply grateful that I made it through this bittersweet and rewarding endeavor. I have found a new sense of self and also, I discovered that I have always been deeply rooted to withstand all the upheavals.

How deep my roots go to withstand all the challenges of this research would have not been possible without the grace from the Almighty God. Thus, my gratitude should first go to Him. As He promised in Psalm 32:8, He guides me along the best pathway for my life and He shall advise me and watch over me. This entire work is a testament of God's love and grace and it is only right that any glory should be given back to Him.

Through God's grace He sent forth angels and instrumentalities that helped me undertake all of this work. I would be forever grateful to Kevin who has been part of this process every step of the way. We weathered the storm together and you have always reminded me of who I am and what I can be, especially when I have questioned my own worth and work on numerous occasions. The same goes with my parents and family, who despite being miles away from me, have never lacked in loving and supporting me. Although I have never been truly open about the personal demons and ordeals I face, they never lacked in showing me love and pushing me further. This especially applies to my Papa, who would always be my idol and stark supporter, who supported me in my decision to pursue my doctoral research. I love you.

The same amount of thanks belongs to my close friends and sisters here in Europe: Leah, Vena, and Chinky. Your moral support has been priceless and being here in Europe has been less lonelier knowing that the three of you would always have my back. Thank you for being there and supporting me along the way. Finishing my work would have not been possible without your love and support.

I am forever grateful to Hanns Seidel Foundation Philippines, especially to the late Paul Schäffer and Ms. Carole Lee, for the support they have given me especially during my first year in Germany. As promised, I will pay forward the kindness and support you have given me. I am also deeply grateful and will be forever indebted to the Max Planck Institute for Foreign and International Criminal Law (now Max Planck Institute for the Study of Crime, Security and Law) and the International Max Planck Research School for Comparative Criminal Law for taking me in and trusting my capabilities as the first and only Filipino doctoral researcher in your institute. I extend this gratitude most especially to my doctoral supervisor, Prof. Ulrich Sieber, my day-to-day tutor, Mr. Thomas Wahl, and my research coordinator, Dr. Nandor Knust. Thank you very much Prof. Sieber for taking me under your wing. I believe it was fate that allowed me to meet you and Mr. Schäffer during that Criminal Code Meeting in the Philippines. It has been a privilege and honor to be under your tutelage. I always hope that I make you proud as your doctoral student. Thomas, thank you for the valuable inputs you gave for me to improve my work. Through the inputs and help you provided I learned to work past my limits and give more than what I thought I could only give. Through you and Prof. Sieber, I re-realized that I have the spirit of Arete in me: the virtue of excellence to always go stronger, faster, and higher.

I would also like to express my gratitude to those who assisted me in trying to understand better the practice of mutual legal assistance. Thank you to the Philippine Department of Justice and Department of Foreign Affairs, Atty. Mildred Bernadette Alvor, Atty. Arnold Frane, PNP NUP Josephine Quieta, Atty. Vida Soraya Versoza, Attorney General's Chamber of Malaysia, Ms. Sitti Maulana Malap, Mr. Azlan Aziz, Atty. Edmun Bon Tai Soon, the ASEANAPOL and its former Executive Director General Yohanes Agus Mulyono and former Director Superintendent Ferdinand Bartolome, Ms. Yuli Cahyanti, Mr. Till Gut, Mr. Christian Schierholt, Mr. Klaus Hoffman, Ms. Gabrielle Launhardt, Ms. Elise McGrath, Ms. Catherine Hanna, Mr. David Dickson, and Mr. Nick Vamos. Thank you for taking time out of your busy schedules to entertain my inquiries and grant my requests for interviews.

Lastly, I am grateful to the people who I have met during this journey. I am also thankful not only for the people who stayed by my side through the ups and downs but also the people who have been instrumental in influencing the person I become. Thank you for reminding me of my non-negotiables, of who I am and who I can become, and being deeply rooted for the years to come. May I make you proud in the actions and decisions I make. God bless you always.

Overview of Contents

Table of Contents

Abbreviations

ACC	ASEAN Coordinating Council
ACDM	ASEAN Committee on Disaster Management
ACTC	ASEAN Center for Combating Transnational Crime
ADGC	ASEAN Directors-General of Customs
AEC	ASEAN Economic Community
AEMM	ASEAN-EU Ministerial Meetings
AFAS	ASEAN Framework Agreement on Services
AFM	ASEAN Finance Ministers
AFSJ	Area of Freedom, Security and Justice
AFTA	ASEAN Free Trade Area
AHRD	ASEAN Human Rights Declaration
AIA	Asian Investment Area
AICCM	Act on International Cooperation in Criminal Matters
AICHR	ASEAN Intergovernmental Commission on Human Rights
ALMM	ASEAN Law Ministers Meeting
AMLC	Anti-Money Laundering Council
AMMTC	ASEAN Ministers' Meeting on Transnational Crime
ARC	Asian Relations Conference
ARF	ASEAN Regional Forum
ARGUS	Networking of Rapid Alert Systems
ARO	Asian Relations Organisation
ASA	Association of Southeast Asian
ASC	ASEAN Security Community
ASCC	ASEAN Socio-Cultural Community
ASEAN	Association of Southeast Asian Nations
ASEAN MLAT	Treaty on Mutual Legal Assistance in Criminal Matters among Like-Minded ASEAN Member Countries
ASEAN-6	Association of Southeast Asian Nations Members Indonesia, Malaysia, Singapore, Thailand, Philippines, Brunei
ASEANAPOL	ASEAN Chiefs of Police Association
ASEAN-CMLV	ASEAN Members Cambodia, Myanmar, Laos, Vietnam

ASEM	Asia-Europe Meetings
ASLOM	ASEAN Senior Law Officials' Meeting
ASOD	ASEAN Senior Officals on Drug Matters
ASP	ASEAN Surveillance Program
ASPAC	Asia and Pacific Council
BDSG	Federal Data Protection Act
CCP	Common Commercial Policy
CFI	Court of First Instance
CFR	Charter of Fundamental Rights
CFSP	Common Foreign and Security Policy
CICA	Crime (International Cooperation) Act of 2003
CIS	Customs Information System
CISA	Convention Implementing the Schengen Agreement
CIWIN	Critical Infrastructure Warning Information Network
CJA	Criminal Justice Act
CJEU	Court of Justice of the European Union
COMECON	Council for Mutual Economic Assistance
CPIB	Corrupt Practices Investigation Bureau
DEIO	Directive on the European Investigation Order
DFA	Department of Foreign Affairs
DG	Directorate-General
DGICM	ASEAN Directors-General of Immigration Departments and Heads of Consular Affairs of the Ministries of Foreign Affairs
DILG	Department of Interior and Local Government
DNA	Deoxyribonucleic Acid
DOJ	Department of Justice
DPP	Director of Public Prosecutions
DRET	Democratic Republic of East Timor
EAS	East Asia Summit
EAW	European Arrest Warrant
ECB	European Central Bank
ECHR	European Convention on Human Rights
ECJ	European Court of Justice
ECOFIN	Council of Economic and Finance Ministers
ECRIS	Criminal Records Information System
ECSC	European Coal and Steel Community

ECST	European Convention on the Suppression of Terrorism
ECtHR	European Court of Human Rights
ECU	European Currency Unit
EDC	European Defence Community
EEA	European Economic Area
EEC	European Economic Community
EEW	European Evidence Warrant
EFSP	European Foreign and Security Policy
EFTA	European Free Trade Association
EIO	European Investigation Order
EJN	European Judicial Network
EJTN	European Judicial Training Network
EMS	European Monetary System
ENP	European Neighbourhood Policy
EPC	European Political Community
EPC	European Political Cooperation
EPCIP	European Programme for Critical Infrastructure Protection
EPG	Eminent Persons Group
EU	European Union
EURATOM	European Atomic Energy Community
EUROPOL	European Police Office
FCC	Federal Constitutional Court
FIU	Financial Intelligence Unit
FOI	Freedom of Information
FRETILIN	Revolutionary Front for an Independent East Timor
FSP	Foreign and Security Policy
GDP	Gross Domestic Product
HMRC	Her Majesty's Revenue and Customs
HRA	Human Rights Act
HSU	Heads of Specialist Trafficking Units
IAD	International Affairs Division
IAR	International Authority for the Ruhr
IBP	Integrated Bar of the Philippines
ICAC	Independent Commission against Corruption
ICCPR	International Covenant on Civil and Political Rights

IGC	Intergovernmental Conference
IMF	International Monetary Fund
INTERPOL	International Criminal Police Organization
IRG	Gesetz über die internationale Rechtshilfe in Strafsachen (Act on International Cooperation in Criminal Matters)
JHA	Justice and Home Affairs
KPK	KomisiPemberantasanKorupsi (Corruption Eradicating Corruption)
MACC	Malaysian Anti-Corruption Commission
MACMA	Mutual Assistance in Criminal Matters Act 2002
MAPHILINDO	Regional Organization by Malaysia, Philippines and Indonesia
MLA	Mutual Legal Assistance
MLAT	Treaty on Mutual Legal Assistance
MOU	Memorandum of Understanding
NAM	Non-Alignment Movement
NATO	North Atlantic Treaty Organization
NBI	National Bureau of Investigation
NTS	Non-Traditional Security
OCSC	Office of the Chief State Counsel
OECD	Organization of Economic Cooperation and Development
OEEC	Organization for European Economic Cooperation
PACE	Police and Criminal Evidence Act 1984
PMC	Post-Ministerial Conferences
PNP	Philippine National Police
PNR	Passenger Name Record
RiVASt	Guidelines on International Cooperation in Criminal Matters (Richtlinien für den Verkehr mit dem Ausland in strafrechtlichen Angelegenheiten)
QMV	Qualified Majority Voting
SAR	Special Administrative Area
SEA	Single European Act
SEAC	Supreme Allied Command in Southeast Asia
SEANWFZ	Southeast Asian Nuclear Weapons Free Zone
SEATO	Southeast Asian Treaty Organization
SGP	Stability and Growth Pact
SIS II	Schengen Information System

SOMTC	Senior Officials Meeting on Transnational Crime
TAC	Treaty of Amity and Cooperation
TEU	Treaty on the European Union
TFEU	Treaty on the Functioning of the European Union
ToA	Treaty of Amsterdam
TOC	Transnational Organized Crime
TOR	Terms of Reference
TREVI	Terrorism, Radicalism, Extremism, and International Violence
UK	United Kingdom
UKCA	United Kingdom Central Authority
UNCAC	United Nations Convention Against Corruption
UNCOC	United Nations Convention on Corruption
UNTOC	United Nations Convention on Transnational Organized Crime
USA	United States of America
VAP	Vientiane Action Programme
VIS	Visa Information System
VOC	Dutch East India Company (VereenigdeOostindische Compagnie)
ZOPFAN	Zone of Peace, Freedom, and Neutrality

Introduction

I. Background of the Study

A. Towards a Strategic Partnership between the Association of Southeast Asian Nations ("ASEAN") and the European Union ("EU")

On May 2017 the senior officials of the Association of Southeast Asian Nations ("ASEAN") and representatives of the European Union ("EU") discussed matters involving transnational crime during the same time period when the ASEAN Senior Officials held their annual Senior Officials Meeting on Transnational Crime ("SOMTC").[1] During said meeting there was an assurance among the ASEAN Senior Officials (and later, the discussion with EU representatives) of continued cooperation, especially as regards counter-terrorism, cyber security, and human trafficking, as well as an expressed interest in increasing cooperation with the International Criminal Police Organization ("INTERPOL") and European Union Agency for Law Enforcement Cooperation ("EUROPOL").[2]

Thereafter, during the ASEAN-EU Post-Ministerial Conference on August 2017, after the ASEAN Summit commemorating the 50th Anniversary of the ASEAN, the two regional organizations agreed on their second EU-ASEAN Plan of Action (2018-2022). Among the many things included in said Plan of Action is to enhance the ASEAN-EU Cooperation in the ASEAN-led security architecture. This includes the ASEAN enhancing dialogue and promoting cooperation with the EU on defense and security matters, such as in the area of counter-terrorism.[3] Further, there is a plan of action to combat terrorism, transnational crimes, and address other non-traditional security issues, including, but not limited to, (1) reviewing the implementation of the ASEAN-EU Work Plan to Combat Terrorism and Transnational Crime (2014-2017), and prepare for the next generation work plan that takes into account new mutually agreed priority areas; (2) convening the ASEAN Senior Officials Meeting on Transnational Crime – EU Consultations in the margins of the annual ASEAN SOMTC

1 *European Council*, pp. 1-10.
2 *European Council*, pp. 1-10.
3 *European Council*, pp. 1-11.

on a regular basis, in accordance with SOMTC processes to promote dialogue and cooperation on ways to tackle different aspects of transnational crime of mutual concerns; and (3) promoting interaction between national law enforcement agencies in the ASEAN member states and EUROPOL, aimed at strengthening the cooperation among them by providing mutual support as well as facilitating the exchange of best practices and expertise in the areas of mutually agreed interests.[4]

On 21 January 2019, both regional organizations took the decision to elevate their relationship to a Strategic Partnership during the EU-ASEAN Ministerial Meeting. Cooperation on regional and international issues were discussed. In line with this, one of the priority areas for 2019 is enhanced security cooperation, including counter-terrorism, transnational crime, maritime security, and cybersecurity. This includes the commitment to strengthen connectivity between the two regional organizations, which is consistent with their agreement to take new steps in undertaking region-to-region agreements.

B. Long-Standing Relationship between the ASEAN and the EU

To put things in their proper context, the ASEAN gives primordial consideration to its external relations. The ASEAN believes in "inclusiveness" and espouses political and economic openness to the rest of the world.[5] It believes that it is necessary to remain open to constructive relations with the rest of the world and be inclusive in its approach to regional endeavors should one want stability and security in the Southeast Asian region.[6] ASEAN's dialogue partners include Australia, Canada, China, the European Union, India, Japan, the Republic of Korea, New Zealand, Russia, and the United States.[7] Dialogues between ASEAN and its external partners were initially economically motivated but later have evolved to include political and security dimensions, with such dialogues being held during the ASEAN Foreign Minister's Annual Post-Ministerial Conferences with dialogue partners.[8]

4 EU-ASEAN Plan of Action, § 1.3.

5 *Severino*, p. 5.

6 *Severino*, pp. 13, 25; *Severino*, ASEAN: What It Cannot Do, p. 5.

7 *Severino*, ASEAN: What It Cannot Do, p. 5; *Tiwari*, p. 31.

8 *Severino*, ASEAN, p. 25; *Tiwari*, p. 31.

With respect to the European Union, the ASEAN as early as 1972 – or only six years since its establishment – has fostered a dialogue partnership with the European Economic Community ("EEC"), the European Union's predecessor.[9] This dialogue partnership with the ASEAN was motivated by the economic and political interests of the EEC to be able to access prospering Asian economies and improve its foreign policy profile.[10] An added bonus was to minimize the participation of the United States and Soviet Union in the region during the peak of the Cold War.[11] Further, stimuli was further provided during the 1970's when Vietnam invaded Cambodia and the Soviet Union invaded Afghanistan: both condemned these invasions and supported each other's positions in the international fora.[12]

In spite of this, the differences in approaches between the two organizations started to unveil: while the principle of non-interference is the basis of the formation of the ASEAN, European integration was grounded on pooling of the sovereignty of its member states in some areas.[13] Di Floristella writes that the ASEAN institutional design is premised on the historical circumstances of the region where "because of the need to consolidate the independence of post-colonial states, and to preserve national sovereignty against external influences, ASEAN elites opted for loose modes of cooperative security and non-interference."[14] Considered likewise herein is the diversity among the ASEAN member states in terms of political and government systems, levels of economic development, religious and cultural traditions, as well as legal systems,[15] to which EU member states would have a difficult time internalizing because conversely they share more or less similar and common Christianity roots, socio-political systems, levels of economic development, and legal systems especially in continental Europe.[16] Therefore, there ought to be an expectation that the ASEAN and its member states would resist the idea of pooling each one's sovereignty and to adopt in general binding instruments of crises

9 *Flers*, p. 2; *Tiwari*, p. 31.
10 *Flers*, p. 2.
11 *Flers*, p. 2.
12 *Flers*, p. 3.
13 *Flers*, p. 3.
14 *Di Floristella*, p. 24.
15 *Di Floristella*, p. 24. See also *Pasadilla*, pp. 2-3.
16 See for example *Hirst*, pp. 11, 22-25.

management that tend to intrude or interfere on the other's domestic affairs.[17]

Other than the stark difference in applicable paradigms, it can be said that the beginning years of the dialogue partnership between the ASEAN and the EU were generally dormant and did not have any concrete or sizeable development in terms of true cooperation.[18] During the Cold War, the ASEAN showed great interest in the integrationist, economic, likewise external trade qualities of the EEC.[19] This great interest was seemingly not reciprocated however and it was only in 1974 when this partnership was rediscovered – or rather, the interest of the EU strengthened – when Hans-Dietrich Genscher was inaugurated as West Germany's Foreign Minister and the external dimension of European Political Cooperation went beyond the Middle East and focused on Asia, and with it, the ASEAN.[20]

The existing ASEAN-EU dialogue partnership paved way to a more formal relationship through the 1980 European Community-ASEAN Cooperation Agreement, which included enhanced cooperation in areas concerning community development, commerce, economic and cultural developments and exchanges.[21] It likewise institutionalized the ASEAN-EU Ministerial Meetings ("AEMM"), which occurs once every two years.[22] Notably, the ASEAN member states in the late 1980's were strongly seen as recipients of EC donations and financial aid due to the weaker economic position of most ASEAN member states.[23] This translated to an inevitably weaker bargaining position on the part of ASEAN member states in the negotiation table in terms of ASEAN-EC cooperation.[24] Imagining it differently, the financial dole outs given by the EC and thereafter the EU could have been used as the needed "carrots" attached to a stick of proposals and policies the EC/EU wanted to implement.

This did not mean however that the ASEAN member states were willing and able to give in easily to the demands of the EC/EU. After the end of the Cold War, the EC/EU shifted towards demanding the inclusion of human rights and democracy clauses in the EC/EU-ASEAN cooperation, including therein policies of conditionalities, while providing links

17 *Di Floristella*, p. 24.
18 *Flers*, p. 3.
19 *Maier-Knapp*, p. 80.
20 *Maier-Knapp*, p. 80.
21 *Flers*, p. 3.
22 *Weatherbee*, p. 113.
23 *Flers*, p. 3.
24 *Flers*, p. 3.

between trade and aid to issues of human rights and democratization.[25] This was not taken lightly by the ASEAN member states and were perceived as unacceptable interference in their domestic affairs.[26] While the EC/EU felt empowered with the obligation to promote human rights and if the circumstances call for it, to interfere in the domestic orders of other countries, the ASEAN member states remained adamant and unwilling to discuss issues of human rights and democratization, instead insisted on their norms of regional conduct and cooperation.[27] This is especially the case with the ASEAN primordial principle of non-intervention, which former Singapore Prime Minister Goh Chok Tong underlined its importance as follows: "We don't set out to change the world and our neighbors. We do not believe in it. The culture of ASEAN is that we do not interfere."[28]

The "interference" by the EU also runs conflict to the so-called ASEAN Way or consensus approach, which is reflected in the ASEAN processes and structures.[29] A signature form of diplomacy of the ASEAN,[30] the ASEAN Way is in stark contrast to the general formal legalism prevalent in its western counterpart, which follows a different decision-making model usually involving (qualified) majority voting in the Council or the supranational authority itself makes decisions in behalf of its member states.[31] In brevity, the ASEAN Way of diplomacy reflects the Malay cultural practices of *musjawarah* and *mufukat*, which respectively requires leaders to make decisions not by imposing their own will unto others "but by gently pushing a community decision to the appropriate direction" through consensus and requiring participants to consider the larger interests of the community.[32]

An integral component of this ASEAN Way is the utilization of quiet diplomacy in the ASEAN. Although the organization cannot often resolve issues of contention between its member states, it can compartmentalize and set them aside so that these issues and problems would not be stumbling blocks that would prevent cooperation in other areas.[33] Over time, the disputants ideally find these areas of contention become less con-

---

25 *Flers*, p. 3.
26 *Flers*, p. 4.
27 *Flers*, p. 4.
28 *Flers*, p. 4.
29 *See Narine, pp. 17-20.*
30 *Narine, p. 18.*
31 *Davidson*, pp. 165, 167. See also *Di Floristella*, p. 24.
32 *Di Floristella, p. 24; Narine, p. 18.*
33 *Narine, p. 19.*

tentious as other relationships, interests, and issues develop to offset the problem(s).[34] In the meantime, the ASEAN member states go their separate ways while concealing their differences behind ambiguous language.[35] Narine cites Antonik, who defines these qualities as "restraint, respect, and responsibility", which are three key principles imperative to the survival of the regional order.[36]

Considering the different and often conflicting values between the ASEAN and the EU, there is a paradox surrounding their continued cooperation and partnership. Amidst their clashing of values there remains peace between the two organizations. It is quite plausible that the ASEAN quiet diplomacy and the normative power of the EU has allowed the two regional organizations to continue their cooperation and partnership. One can look into the Asia Strategy of 1994, a comprehensive document that not only evinces the post-Cold War rediscovery of Asia and the ASEAN but likewise reveals details involving not only economic, political and security cooperation but as well as cultural cooperation reflected in the various dialogue fora in which both the ASEAN and EU meet.[37] Such was followed by the launching of the Asia-Europe Meetings ("ASEM"), which was launched in 1996 and conducted once every two years, alternating between Asia and Europe, with Asian and European ministers meeting each other in between summits.[38]

In the face of this continued, and beforehand "renewed" and "revitalized",[39] dialogue partnership and cooperation agreement between the ASEAN and the EU, their partnership did not escape criticism. Despite the existing interregional relationship between the two regional organizations, the quality of the relationship between the two regional organizations had allegedly changed and became sidelined, or rather occupied just a small puzzle piece in a pan-Asian approach.[40] A reading of the European Commission's ("EC") document on Southeast Asia of 2003 shows, as cited by Maier-Knapp, that in the cooperation between the ASEAN and the EU "the political dialogue should, to the extent possible, concentrate on

---

34 *Narine, p. 19.*
35 *Narine, p. 19.*
36 *Narine, p. 19.*
37 *Maier-Knapp,* p. 80.
38 *Weatherbee,* pp. 113-114.
39 *Maier-Knapp,* p. 80.
40 *Maier-Knapp,* p. 80.

region to region subjects of interest and concern, leaving global issues to ASEM."[41]

Additionally, Maier-Knapp mentioned that another critical issue left unanswered then, was the nature of EU's true colors in its partnership with the ASEAN, not least because of the EU's nebulous way of coining its normative and material interests. Especially considering that the EU's rhetoric of "stability, partnership, and friendship" towards the ASEAN and the multi-sectoral and multi-dimensional relationship between the two regional organizations "that echoes traces of a common lifeworld" were incompatible with how the two organizations tried to reach a deeper and meaningful cooperative relationship, and how the EU has manifested its actorness inconsistently, patchily, and on a case-to-case basis in the ASEAN and its member states.[42]

One can easily trace back how the EU acted as a "friend" to the ASEAN through different incidents that not only further obscures the picture of the EU as a value-lecturing economic actor in the Southeast Asian region but also raises doubts towards how the EU is truly willing to act on its commitments and undertakings in the region.[43] It is without doubt that the EU projects its normative core values in its partnership agreements with the ASEAN member states in accordance with the goals of its external actions (which as mentioned above the ASEAN and its member states believe to be undue influence).[44] This is despite the underlying tension existing due to the clash of values of each regional organization. In fact, the ASEAN and the EU truly clashed in the issue involving the admission of Myanmar to the ASEAN in 1997, which led to an impasse in ASEAN-EU relations. The EU and its member states found it utterly unacceptable that some are willing to give the time of day to Myanmar considering the various human rights violations and atrocities happening in the country. Henceforth, the EU and its member states imposed sanctions on Myanmar since its membership to the ASEAN for its failure to protect human rights and follow processes of democratization.[45] Contrastingly, the ASEAN viewed the political instability and human rights problems as a purely domestic matter with which the ASEAN should not interfere.[46] Further,

---

41 *Maier-Knapp*, p. 80.
42 See *Maier-Knapp*, pp. 77, 80, 97.
43 *Maier-Knapp*, p. 81.
44 *Maier-Knapp*, p. 81.
45 *Flers*, p. 5.
46 *Flers*, p. 5.

the ASEAN was of the position that denying Myanmar membership would have been a violation of the Bangkok Declaration of 1967 (the founding instrument of the ASEAN), which opens membership to all countries in the Southeast Asian region.[47]

Notwithstanding this constant push of the EU to put human rights and democratization in the agenda of its relationship with the ASEAN, there seems to be a want of meaningful, concrete engagement on the part of the EU to make true its commitment. In other words, the EU seemingly fails to deliver on its own undertakings in its reciprocal obligation arrangement with the ASEAN. For instance, when the ASEAN and its member states were confronted with non-traditional security ("NTS") crises, such as the 2003 Avian influenza outbreak, 2004 tsunami and political conflict in Aceh (province in Indonesia), 2005 Asian Financial Crisis, the direct support given by the EU through its different institutions was described as a "mere drop to the bucket" because regardless of any financial support it gave, the EU did not actively participated in providing the needed technology transfer or know-how to resolve these issues.[48] What it could have given, it did not give.

Moreover, one could look into how the EU reacted during the October 2002 terrorism attack in Bali, Indonesia. Terrorism and extremism was made top priority in the international and interregional security agenda since the 11 September 2001 terrorist attacks in the United States.[49] Although the ASEAN member states did not buy totally into the idea that Southeast Asia was the second front of the United States on its War on Terror due to certain sensitivities to its Muslim population and resentments toward foreign intervention,[50] there were some ASEAN member states that cooperated actively with the United States and Australia after the bombings in Bali, Indonesia especially on coordinated actions and counter-terrorism measures.[51]

Conversely, the EU adopted a lesser direct approach. The European Commission was the initial responder on behalf of the EU but due to the national-centric nature of the attacks, which falls under the competence of the European Council, as well as the varying degree of effects and consequences to the ASEAN member states, the breadth of regional assis-

47 *Flers*, p. 5.
48 *Maier-Knapp*, pp. 80-91.
49 *Maier-Knapp*, p. 91.
50 *Caballero-Anthony*, p. 213; *Weatherbee*, pp. 192-193.
51 *Maier-Knapp*, p. 92.

tance and/or response was limited.[52] Further, while the European Council in behalf of the EU made its conclusions immediately after the attacks, declaring its willingness to provide the needed assistance and support Indonesia and the ASEAN needs in its counter-terrorism measures, the actual response was limited and mostly declaratory.[53] The majority of the assistance afforded by the EU was a patchwork of individual efforts by its member states and anything else was deemed for long-term goals such as capacity building and the like, as well as construed as complementary to the assistance and cooperation given by the US and Australia to the ASEAN member states.[54] It also became apparent that attention was not wholly given to the Southeast Asian region because by then, not only did the counter-terrorism and extremism measurers employed by the EU focused on the Middle East and Central Asia, but moreover, the EU was confronted on terrorism attacks on its territory, starting with the attacks in Madrid in 2004, two years after the Bali bombings.[55]

These circumstances and interesting dynamics, together with the recently minted strategic partnership between the ASEAN and the EU, as well as the second EU-ASEAN Plan of Action that intends to enhance cooperation in defense, security, and criminal matters, (including counter-terrorism measures) altogether raises interesting questions. As a start, there is already the existing partnership and endeavor to further cooperate in criminal and security matters. There is also the knowledge of how this partnership has been in all points of cooperation between the two regional organizations. By having this baseline knowledge, it would be easier to discern strategy as to what steps ought to be taken next should these two regional organizations really intend in fostering enhanced cooperation in criminal matters with one another.

At the outset, it is known that the EU boasts of an intricate criminal justice architecture in its regional framework that facilitates both informal and formal cooperation in criminal matters. Among the many formal arrangements, there is the European Arrest Warrant for extradition requests between member states and the more recently European Investigation Order that tackles mutual legal assistance or cross-border and transborder access to information and evidence. Contrastingly, the ASEAN member states have not been remiss in pushing for enhanced cooperation in crim-

52 *Maier-Knapp*, pp. 92-93.
53 *Maier-Knapp*, p. 93.
54 *Maier-Knapp*, p. 93.
55 See *Argomaniz*, pp. 7-10.

inal matters within their regional framework.[56] As early as the Bangkok Declaration of 1967, there was a call already to have an ASEAN Extradition Treaty but until now, this is left to be desired. And yet, the pervasiveness and seriousness of transnational crime such as terrorism in the region continuously exists. Significantly, this is not mutually exclusive to the ASEAN region alone but has arguably spillover effects throughout the world, including the European continent. Having this in mind, the ASEAN so far only has the 2004 Treaty on Mutual Legal Assistance in Criminal Matters Among Like-Minded ASEAN Countries (hereinafter "ASEAN MLAT") as the only regional instrument for international cooperation in criminal matters that serves the purpose of improving the effectiveness of the law enforcement authorities of the treaty's parties in "the prevention, investigation, and prosecution of offenses through cooperation and mutual legal assistance in criminal matters."[57]

Despite the disparity in legal frameworks, as well as the undeniable disparity and clash in values, principles, and practices, the discussion of how to develop an interregional cooperation in criminal matters between the ASEAN and the EU becomes more interesting because should the two regional organizations pursue a meaningful and effective enhanced cooperation, MLA between the two regional organizations would undeniably have a great value added to the enhanced partnership. However, this needs to be done in a manner that takes into account the characteristics, non-negotiables, and needs of both parties. Further, it necessitates an understanding and consideration of what truly happens in the member state frameworks because, regardless of how intricate the interregional instrument the two organizations would come up with, if said instrument is unimplementable in the member state levels or impossible to operationalize therein, then the whole exercise would be futile and everything would be left in rhetoric and declaratory statements, which is the prevalent criticism not only against the European Union in terms of its cooperation with the ASEAN, but also the ASEAN as a regional organization itself.[58] In this respect, the

---

56 *Pushpanathan*, pp. 23-26.

57 *See* 2004 Treaty on Mutual Legal Assistance in Criminal Matters signed on 29 November 2004 in Kuala Lumpur, Malaysia, 29 November 2004, 2336 U.N.T.S. 271 (entered into force 01 June 2005), Preamble. [hereinafter "ASEAN MLAT"].

58 ASEAN has often been criticized due to the alleged mismatch of its political will with the actual response being given by the member states. Nguyen also notes the lack of harmonization of laws among the ASEAN countries as something negative for the ASEAN. See *Nguyen*, p. 387. In the same vein, Emmers mentions

present study is most interested in knowing how mutual legal assistance in criminal matters can be developed within and between the ASEAN and the EU considering that mutual legal assistance would be the perfect baseline agreement for enhanced cooperation in criminal matters as both regional frameworks have existing mutual legal assistance regimes already in their respective systems. Notwithstanding the general provisions stated in the EU-ASEAN Second Action Plan, development within and between the ASEAN and the EU would be a means to concretize the joint endeavor for cooperation. And interestingly, a study has yet to be made on this question, especially on comparing and contrasting the existing ASEAN and EU mutual legal assistance frameworks and providing possible consequences for development and cooperation on the basis of analyzing both.

II. Objectives of the Study

Taking the foregoing into account, the study "East meets West? The Development of Mutual Legal Assistance in Criminal Matters within and between the Association of Southeast Asian Nations and European Union" is interested in knowing **how could inter-regional mutual legal assistance in criminal matters develop between and within the Association of Southeast Asian Nations ("ASEAN") and the European Union ("EU").** In answering this question, the present study shall have the following five objectives:

1. To know the historical development of the ASEAN and the EU, including the historical development of their respective regions that influenced not only the establishment of these regional organizations but also their different principles and norms, as well as the historical development of the two regional organizations' international cooperation mechanisms in criminal matters, specifically on mutual legal assistance, and the respective legal frameworks applicable to these mechanisms;
2. To know the historical development of international cooperation in criminal matters, specifically mutual legal assistance, as well as the legal framework for it (including substantive and procedural provisions) in selected member states of the ASEAN and the EU, which includes a

that the ASEAN suffers from insufficient resources allocated to its designated agencies in the fight against transnational crime and terrorism, and domestically, there is the situation of gaps and disparities in the legal framework. *Emmers*, pp. 419-438; *Nguyen*, p. 387.

study of how a sample member state from each region implements mutual legal assistance through law and practical information (law in the books v. law in practice);

3. To compare and contrast the mutual legal assistance frameworks of ASEAN and EU on criminal matters with their respective member state frameworks by knowing the present state of the mutual legal assistance framework on criminal matters and its application in the ASEAN and the EU, including a study of how a sample member state from each region is implementing the same, formally and informally, through law and practical application;
4. To compare and contrast the ASEAN and the EU regional frameworks with each other, including a comparison of their respective historical developments, institutional frameworks, fundamental principles, norms and practices, and their existing mechanisms of mutual legal assistance vis-à-vis how the same is implemented in their respective member state frameworks;
5. To evaluate, analyze and anticipate the problematic issues and problems with respect to the respective frameworks and provide recommendations for improvement, harmonization, revision, etc., when appropriate, and whether there could be a (further) development of mutual legal assistance in criminal matters between and within the ASEAN and the EU.

In relation to the first objective, the respective historical developments of each regional organization include the historical development of their respective regions which could provide a better and holistic understanding of each regional organization's underpinnings vis-à-vis their respective principles, norms, practices, and decision and policymaking processes. Admittedly, historical development does not necessarily provide a barometer for predicting the future decisions and policies of both the ASEAN and the European Union, including its member states. Nevertheless, historical development starting from that of the region, expanding further to the establishment and development of the ASEAN and the EU would help understand the dynamics occurring within the regional organizations, between the member states, and how the said underpinning governs internal mechanisms and external relations with possible dialogue partners or cooperation mechanisms, because these decisions, policies, and/or developments arguably emerge "from unique historical circumstances and will likely evolve in its own particular way."[59]

59 See *Acharya*, p. 327; *Benda*, p. 111; *Evans*, p. 303; *Osborne*, p. 17.

III. Methodology

In view of the foregoing objectives, the present study adopts the following five main steps:

1. Regional-level analysis of ASEAN and EU vis-à-vis mutual legal assistance in criminal matters;
2. Member state level analysis, which refers to the respective member state frameworks of the ASEAN and the EU and likewise incorporates an evaluation and/or analysis of the member states' available legal frameworks and their practical implementation and/or application (law in the books v. law in practice);
3. Comparison of the ASEAN and the EU regional frameworks with their respective member state frameworks in terms of the available legal frameworks (substantive and procedural provisions), mainly addressing questions of implementation, transposition, and/or translation to the member states of regional level legal frameworks, as well as problems and issues encountered in relation hereto;
4. Comparison of the ASEAN and the EU with each other, incorporating herein the development of their respective principles, practices, and values, existing cooperation mechanisms, approach to regional security, and mutual legal assistance, as well as taking into account the transposition or implementation of regional policies in member state frameworks, efficiency and respect for human rights; and
5. Evaluation, analysis, and anticipation of problematic issues and problems with respect to the respective frameworks on mutual legal assistance in criminal matters of ASEAN and EU, and discussion of the (possible) development of mutual legal assistance in criminal matters between and within ASEAN and EU.

A. Regional-level analysis

In the regional-level analysis of ASEAN and EU, it is imperative to look into each regional organization's historical development, functional framework, and underlying institutional foundations and/or principles to have a better understanding of their legal initiatives vis-à-vis mutual legal assistance in criminal matters. To do so, desktop and literature review, study of available records, and content analysis was done to capture data without prejudice to the use of a longitudinal approach should there be a need to further elucidate the situation prior to and after the enactment of both the ASEAN and EU MLA framework on criminal matters. Qualitative interviews have additionally been done to capture the motivations behind the development of the ASEAN and EU mutual legal assistance in criminal matters regimes, respectively.

B. Member state level analysis

Member state level analysis focuses on the development, implementation, functioning vis-à-vis mutual legal assistance in criminal matters in both ASEAN and EU. Although the present study could have limited itself with a regional level analysis, it analyzed selected member state frameworks of each regional organization to have a clearer and sounder grassroots knowledge of how regional level policies, decisions, and legal frameworks translate on the member state levels. The present study likewise adopted this step to better discern and assess the better ways to pursue the development of mutual legal assistance between and within the regional frameworks.

1. Selection of member state samples

The present study concedes to the impossibility of gathering data from all of the member states of both the ASEAN and EU. Given this constraint, analysis was limited to two sample member states per regional organization.

As regards the ASEAN, focus was given to the Philippines and Malaysia, two of the original ASEAN member states and earliest signatories of the ASEAN MLAT. The Philippines has a unique legal system of both Anglo-Saxon common law and civil law. Further, it adopts a strong position against transnational crime within the ASEAN.

On the other hand, Malaysia is a predominantly common law country with a separate Islamic law system. It is through Malaysia's initiative that the ASEAN MLAT came into fruition. Hence, both the Philippines and Malaysia could provide good insights and examples as to the current state and practice of mutual legal assistance in criminal matters in the ASEAN region.

As regards the EU, focus was on the United Kingdom and Germany. Both Germany and the United Kingdom have domestic legislation on international cooperation in criminal matters, including mutual legal assistance and the application of the European Investigation Order as regards other EU member states. In line with this, Germany espouses a continental form of legal system and inquisitorial kind of criminal proceedings. On the other hand, the United Kingdom is the most important common law country in the EU. Like the Philippines and Malaysia, the United Kingdom follows the adversarial system, wherein two advocates represent their parties' positions before an impartial person or group of people, usually a judge or jury, who attempt to determine the truth of the case.

At this juncture it must be mentioned that the United Kingdom has been the first EU member state to engage Article 50 TEU and exit the European Union.[60] From 01 January 2021 the European Investigation Order shall cease to apply and new rules for judicial cooperation such as mutual legal assistance are provided for by the new EU-UK Trade and Cooperation Agreement.[61] The said Agreement shall provide the new legal basis in terms of surrender, mutual legal assistance, freezing and confiscation, and exchange of criminal record information.

These developments have not changed the fundamental aim of the present study, namely, to examine and analyse the development of mutual legal assistance within and between the ASEAN and the EU, including the legislative and practical implementation of the European Investigation Order in the member state level. The choice of the United Kingdom still remains relevant as not only because the new Trade and Cooperation Agreement contains earmarks of the principles and practices of the EIO, but also because UK as a common law country should be contrasted with a continental country in Europe to broaden the insights to be gained in pursuit of this study's objectives.

2. Historical development, legal framework, and implementation

Akin to the regional level analysis, desktop review together with agency records, and content and secondary analysis was applied to discover historical development, legislative evolution, and the existing legal framework vis-à-vis mutual legal assistance in criminal matters.

---

60 *Gordon*, p. 21; *van Wijk*, p. 155.

61 For specific provisions governing law enforcement and judicial cooperation in criminal matters, one can refer to Part Four of the Trade and Cooperation Agreement Between the European Union and the European Atomic Energy Community, of the One Part, And The United Kingdom Of Great Britain And Northern Ireland, of the Other Part dated 30 December 2020.

Given the importance of discerning the difference on what is provided in the books and how the law is applied in practice, interviews were conducted to ascertain practical application and/or implementation. In light of this, three to four authorities or experts were interviewed per member state. While a higher number of interviews would be desirable, there were time and communication constraints that prevented this. Nonetheless, the persons interviewed for the present study are either the main representatives and point persons for mutual legal assistance and/or international cooperation in criminal matters within their respective central authorities, administrative department and agencies, or law enforcement agencies, or they are practicioners directly involved or invested in the practice of international cooperation in their respective countries, i.e. judicial authorities, Eurojust representatives, central or executing authorities.

Moreover, it needs to be clarified that the present study is not empirical in nature. Rather, the interviews and personal communication are meant to be supplementary in nature and give out details in practice not necessarily disclosed in literature or in other academic studies. Moreover, the interviews were meant to analyze the grassroots of the situation to better grasp how the MLA frameworks work per regional and member state level.

C. Comparison of the Regional Frameworks with their respective Member State Frameworks

After analyzing the regional frameworks of the ASEAN and the EU, and of the respective member state frameworks under each one, the next step taken is to compare the regional frameworks with their respective member state frameworks. Through the exercise of comparing and contrasting the regional and member state frameworks, the study determined not only whether and to what extent the international requirements have been implemented in the national legal systems, but also the existing gaps, problems, and issues that ought to be addressed in the mutual legal assistance regime within each regional framework. This step was focused in comparing and contrasting mainly the historical development of the MLA frameworks, existing legal framework, and the different substantive and procedural provisions.

D. Comparison and Contrast of ASEAN and EU Frameworks

As a condition precedent in evaluating both frameworks on mutual legal assistance in criminal matters in terms of the different problems and issues they encounter, a neutral comparison of both frameworks is done. This entailed two components. The first component involved the regional frameworks by themselves. This involved looking into four (4) aspects drawn out from a comparison of the ASEAN and the EU: (1) the development of respective principles, ideals, and norms within each organization; (2) existing cooperation mechanisms; (3) approach to regional security; and (4) mutual legal assistance in criminal matters.

By understanding these features, there would be a better picture of the running mechanisms of each regional framework, including the motivations on what influences these mechanisms to run. Further, there is the understanding of how a particular regional framework views cooperation and how it would act and/or decide on a particular partnership or cooperation mechanism, such as mutual legal assistance in criminal matters.

The second component looks into the micro level, or the member state frameworks in relation to the regional framework. This included looking firstly into the transposition or implementation of the regional agreement to the domestic level. Similarities, differences, and even idiosyncrasies were highlighted to gauge not only how influential the regional frameworks are in influencing domestic policies but how member states remain true to the ideals or provisions being promoted on a regional level. This included a look into certain characteristics highlighted by the law in practice, which are not necessarily apparent in the law in the books.

Included likewise in the evaluation of the member state frameworks is a look into the efficiency aspect and protection of human rights. This mirrors the sword and shield function of criminal law and can thus be described as to how efficient member states are in fostering cooperation and how they respectively value the protection of human rights. Again, similarities, differences, and idiosyncrasies would be mentioned herein.

E. Evaluation, Analysis, and Anticipation; Lessons learned

The last portion of the present study proves to be the most crucial. In view of any development between and within the two regional organization of further cooperation in criminal matters through mutual legal assistance, there was the need to further internalize the results of the next preceding step and evaluate certain issues and problems surrounding the present regional and member state frameworks of mutual legal assistance in criminal matters in the ASEAN and the EU.

The first component of this analysis and evaluation was to identify lessons that could be learned. Herein three aspects or values of each regional framework were analyzed, on the basis of what has been previously learned: (1) intergovernmental v. supranational natures in relation to being formal v. informal; (2) the ASEAN principle of non-intervention v. normative power of the EU; and (3) harmonization v. approximation. Values would be considered against each other in efforts to discern what needs to be learned from each one. This is again in furtherance of the research question of how to develop mutual legal assistance between and within the ASEAN and the EU.

Based on the foregoing steps, the next component is to provide suggestions for the development of mutual legal assistance within and between the ASEAN and the EU. This last step includes four parts. The first part involves the mutual legal assistance within the respective regional frameworks. It considers what could be improved, what could be retained in the present framework, etc. This is to be followed by the needed groundwork: what ought to be kept in mind in moving forward with the development of the cooperation mechanism between the regional organizations. Thereafter, the third part and fourth part would be the substantive and procedural provisions, respectively, that could constitute the MLA agreement between the two regional frameworks.

IV. Structure of the Study

In view of the foregoing, the present study is structured into four (4) main parts. Part 1 and Part 2 focused on regional orders of the ASEAN and the EU respectively. Each part is composed mainly of four (4) parts: (1) regional framework, (2) member state framework of first sample member state, (3) member state framework of second sample member state, and (4) comparison of the regional framework with the member state frameworks. Anent the first part on regional framework, the historical development of the regional organization was incorporated along with the historical development of the region from where these organizations were established, including their respective institutional and legal frameworks, and framework on cross-border cooperation, in particular the one involving mutual legal assistance.

As regards the member state frameworks, it incorporated the historical evolution of international cooperation mechanisms and the existing legal framework on mutual legal assistance.

Thereafter, the regional and member state frameworks are compared with one another using the same parameters previously provided, i.e. historical development, substantive provisions and procedural provisions.

Part 3 focused on the comparison between the ASEAN and EU. This part is then divided into two components, with one focusing on the regional frameworks themselves while the other focuses on the member state frameworks. Included in the first component is the (1) discussion of how the principles, practices, and norms developed in each regional organization, (2) existing cooperation mechanisms, (3) approach to regional security, and (4) mutual legal assistance; whereas the second component on member state frameworks shall encompass (1) transposition of law in the member states, (2) efficiency, and (3) protection of human rights.

Part 4 is mainly the evaluation and analysis part of the study wherein using the results from the previous part, lessons learned were derived, including the values needed to be taken into account should one formulate proposals or suggestions for the development of mutual legal assistance within and between the ASEAN and the EU. On the basis of these lessons to be learned, the second step discussed the groundwork needed to be done to develop mutual legal assistance within the regional organizations. Following this are suggestions for the possible substantive and procedural provisions that can be taken into account should an interregional mutual legal assistance be made between the ASEAN and the EU.

Part 1: The Association of Southeast Asian Nations (ASEAN)

The first portion of the study focuses on the Association of Southeast Asian Nations ("ASEAN") and the discussion shall mainly be divided into three main portions.

First, there is a discussion of the historical development of the Southeast Asian region as well as the development of the ASEAN regional organization, including the development of international cooperation in criminal matters such as mutual legal assistance, which is the crux of the entire study. Though it is admittedly easier to overlook the historical development of the Southeast Asian region (which may go as far back as the pre-colonial times of the ASEAN member states) and focus instead mainly on how the regional organization was created and thereafter the legal framework that subsequently existed, the historical development of the region is necessary for one to understand the underlying motivations, reasons, and background as to how the ASEAN was shaped and continuously shapes and defines itself in its decisions, policies, cooperation mechanisms, etc. Without the underlying current of the region's historical development, any further analysis would be incomplete and bereft of the grassroot understanding imperative to knowing the mechanism on how the organization works. In the same vein, a complete and deeper understanding of the historical development will help in assessing and discerning how the ASEAN could and would foster external relations, build and maintain effective international cooperation mechanisms that would work for it and its member states. Therefore, this first portion – without necessarily going through the minute and explicit details – looks through the different changes and influences the region undertook before the ASEAN was finally established.

The second part of the discussion involves the institutional and legal framework, incorporated therein are the salient features of the ASEAN as a regional organization, its organizational structure, and its fundamental principles, norms, and practices. This portion, together with the exploration of ASEAN historical development, is meant to be an exercise in knowing the regional organization well and acquainting oneself with the underpinnings of the different processes, including decision-making, in the regional organization.

Third, discussion shall focus on the cross-border movement of evidence. This portion of the study includes the historical development of mutual legal assistance in the ASEAN through the ASEAN Mutual Legal Assistance Treaty, which is a product of the ongoing cooperation occurring within the ASEAN as regards criminal matters. Afterwards, the different defining substantive and procedural provisions of mutual legal assistance shall be examined. Substantive provisions focus on (5) main points: the applicability of the assistance available through the ASEAN MLAT; types of mutual legal assistance available; compatibility with other arrangements; designation of central authorities; and the different principles, conditions, and exceptions, which is further subdivided into different topics. On the other hand, procedural provisions mainly focus on aspects involving the preparation and execution of MLA requests.

After centering on the regional level, it shall be followed by a discussion of the respective member state level frameworks of the Philippines and Malaysia. The discussion of these respective member states shall follow the same exercise as what was done in the examination of the regional level framework.

Thereafter, the frameworks of the regional level and member state level shall be compared and contrasted with each other.

I. Regional Framework

A. Historical Development

The discussion of the historical development of Southeast Asia as a region is necessary to understand the ASEAN as a regional organization. The historical development and the experiences that are included herein is imperative in having a more holistic understanding of how the ASEAN and its member states approach decision and policymaking, which is not mutually exclusive to how they approach international cooperation in criminal matters.

There is admitted difficulty in subsuming ASEAN and/or its member states in terms of an integral civilization.[62] At the onset, the southeast region of the Asian continent has been geographically defined, divided, and delineated as nowhere else in any of the other parts of Asia.[63] In fact,

62 *Benda*, p. 107.
63 *SarDesai*, p. 6.

there came a time when there was no single answer as to how "Southeast Asia" should properly be geographically defined and delineated:[64] there only came a clearer geographical delineation and/or definition during the Second World War through the invention of Europeans, when identification and definition of the region became politically (and militarily) important.[65] Such geographical division in the subject Asian segment has successfully fractionalized its countries into diverse social, cultural, and political units, which could have resulted in the multi-centric historical development that further complicates the understanding and consolidating the region's historical development.[66] Hence, a step back is necessitated to have a more meaningful understanding of ASEAN's historical development. Prior to a discussion of how the regional organization ASEAN was established, a brief walk through the historical beginnings and/or circumstances surrounding the Southeast Asian region and the countries in it (which eventually became the ASEAN member states) shall be made to better understand the underpinnings of ASEAN. Understanding its history may not provide a barometer for the region's or ASEAN's future development (this is not history's task),[67] but a review of the Southeast Asian region's history could "illuminate the present," making clear internal dynamics within the region, and in relation to the establishment of the ASEAN, understand how its development and decisions arguably emerge "from unique historical circumstances and will likely evolve in its own particular way."[68]

1. From Early Southeast Asia to Modern Southeast Asia

a. Early Southeast Asia

Albeit interest in Southeast Asian history arguably started during its colonization by different European imperial powers, the history of Southeast Asia or the region's cultural, political, and social development could be traced earlier on and surely did not begin with the Europeans' arrival.[69]

---

64 *Benda*, p. 108.
65 *Beeson*, p. 18; *Hemmer/Katzenstein*, p. 575; *Tilman*, p. 16.
66 *Benda*, p. 108; *SarDesai*, p. 6; *Severino*, ASEAN, p. 4; *Wolters*, p. 39.
67 *Osborne*, p. 17.
68 See *Acharya*, p. 327; *Benda*, p. 111; *Evans*, p. 303; *Osborne*, p. 17.
69 *See Tilman, pp. 16-17.*

Southeast Asia as a region is highly diversified, created not only through human settlement by geographical fractionalization,[70] or successive migrations to the area, but also obstacles such as jungles, mountains, bodies of water, and the like, which later enabled the diversification of the peoples of Southeast Asia over time: "cutting them off from one another over time and promoting their distinctiveness in different parts of the region."[71] Amidst this diversification and differentiation however, Southeast Asian groupings, settlements and/or kingdoms interacted with another and subsequently developed amongst themselves common experiences, attitudes, and beliefs.

On a cultural and socio-political context, early Southeast Asia had an indigenous cultural and socio-political development which was not necessarily homogenous but could be described by common characteristics linking those in mainland and insular Southeast Asia.[72] Learning instead to reap the benefits and share the problems brought by the uniqueness of the region (for example, biological diversity and large bodies of water separating each country), countries progressively developed societies and organizations based on agriculture or irrigated cultivation and then maritime trade.[73] Agriculture and maritime trade contributed highly to such state formation and in turn, the development of various principalities and kingdoms across various parts of the Southeast Asian region.[74] There was a direct relationship between agricultural prosperity and rise of states; and there was more strength in those areas where there is equal access to both agricultural prosperity and sea (maritime trade).[75]

Furthermore, agriculture and maritime trade facilitated the ebb and flow of ideas, beliefs, customs, and traditions from one country to anoth-

---

70 Southeast Asia extends throughout an area bounded by Myanmar (formerly, Burma) in the northwest corner to Indonesia (formerly, West Irian) in the southeast. Within these boundaries, one could identify a mainland portion, which makes Southeast Asia penetrable through land from the northern direction. Mainland Southeast Asia is composed of Myanmar, Thailand, Laos, Cambodia, and Vietnam. One could also identify an insular portion of Southeast Asia, which generally makes Southeast Asia accessible through sea from all directions. Philippines, Brunei, Indonesia, East Timor, Malaysia, and Singapore composed this insular portion of the Southeast Asian region.*SarDesai,* p. 6; *Tarling,* p. 3; *Tilman,* pp. 16-17.

71 *SarDesai,* p. 6; *Tarling,* p. 3.

72 *Reid,* p. 8; *SarDesai,* p. 14.

73 *Reid,* p. 8; *SarDesai,* p. 14.

74 *Reid,* pp. 6-8; *SarDesai,* p. 22.

75 *SarDesai,* p. 22. 44.

er.[76] This resulted in cultural and socio-political transmission and assimilation in various states in the Southeast Asian region, with Arabic, Persian, Indian, and Chinese cultures being identified as key influences.[77] In the end, either culture or both were integrated in the culture and socio-political systems of many countries, more especially those in insular Southeast Asia, which received great influence from other countries' cultures, without necessarily discarding the indigenous ethnicity each country already had.[78] In particular, Myanmar and Vietnam (which was a former Chinese territory) were said to be vital conduits to the spread of Indian culture and Chinese socio-political systems, respectively.[79]

Religions likewise played an integral role. Various religions from external origins spread throughout the region, which subsequently influenced society's values and established manners in which Southeast Asians would identify themselves as members of universal cultures.[80] Early Southeast Asia witnessed the rise and proliferation of Islam in Malaysia, Indonesia, Brunei, and Southern Philippines, Theravada Buddhism in Myanmar, Laos, Cambodia, and Thailand (these countries have more cultural borrowings from India), and Mahayana Buddhism in Vietnam (which was highly Chinese-oriented).[81] Northern and central Philippines, on the other hand, lacked a strong "sacerdotal hierarchy".[82] Instead, there was a prominent belief in an indigenous "Southeast Asian religion," as others would otherwise refer to animism or shamanism, which believed more in animistic spirits and the importance of the spiritual realm.[83]

The foregoing notwithstanding, the history of early Southeast Asia also witnessed many political changes and interstate rivalries. As mentioned, there were different principalities and kingdoms that existed in the region. In both mainland Southeast Asia and insular Southeast Asia arose different kingdoms and/or empires such as, but not limited to, the Funan, Champa, the Khmers, Srivijaya, and Majapahit.[84] Understandably, political differences, power struggles, and territorial disputes ensued which led to conflicts and subsequent changes. Particularly, mainland Southeast Asia

76 See *Reid*, p. 96.
77 See *Reid*, pp. 130-133; *SarDesai*, pp. 14-18.
78 *Reid*, p. 26; *SarDesai*, pp. 16, 43.
79 *SarDesai*, pp. 32, 36.
80 *Christie*, p. 7; *Reid*, p. 96.
81 *SarDesai*, pp. 18-21. See also *Reid*, pp. 96-119; *Solidum*, pp. 4-5.
82 *SarDesai*, p. 71.
83 *Reid*, pp. 97-98.
84 *SarDesai*, pp. 22-62; *Tarling*, pp. 10-17.

underwent strong changes when there were movements for consolidation in Myanmar, Thailand, and Vietnam.[85] Interstate tensions ensued thereafter after disagreements as to territory and political control.[86]This soon after became ingrained in the socio-political development of cultures and determinant of their respective decisions and policymaking. Nonetheless, it did not take long before mainland Southeast Asian countries by themselves boasted of a "strong administration, well-recognized hierarchical social order, territorial divisions, a bureaucratic system, and a self-sufficient economy."[87]

b. Building empires and colonies: East-West Relationship

The shift to modern times in Southeast Asia arguably began with the colonization of the Asian countries.[88] Colonization brought significant changes during this period. Asia has long attracted the attention of Westerners, particularly the Europeans, through the lure of trade, economic gain, or establishing a power stronghold.[89] By the dawn of the 15th century, Southeast Asia has entered an "Age of Commerce" and strong economic, social, political intra-state exchanges were ongoing.[90] Commercial trade links existed between Southeast Asia and across Asia and between Southeast Asia and Europe through the Middle East, and by the time of 15th century, Asia and Europe found themselves in a new phase of economic expansion following recovery from the Black Death, the great plagues of the 14th century, and partially the effect of Chinese initiatives during the Ming Dynasty in so-called discovery voyages.[91] At the same time, Europe was broken down into nation-states with admittedly limited space for expansion that sought security and domination over each other, driving them to seek power and wealth overseas.[92] Colonizers were thus either motivated through trade competition, great wealth accumulation, cultural expression, or the need to secure and extend political power.[93]

---

85 *Christie*, p. 7; *Reid*, p. 175; *SarDesai*, pp. 74-81, 84.
86 *SarDesai*, p. 84.
87 *SarDesai*, p. 84.
88 *Cotterell*, p. 239; *Tilman*, p. 17.
89 *Cotterell*, pp. 240-268; *Ricklefs/Lockhart/Lau, et al.*, pp. 165-166; *Solidum*, p. 4.
90 *Reid*, pp. 74-95; *Solidum*, p. 5.
91 *Reid*, pp. 57-95; *Tarling*, p. 21.
92 *Healy/Dal Lago*, p. 4; *Sèbe*, p. 125; *Tarling*, p. 22. See also *Christie*, pp. 3-8.
93 *Christie*, p. 6; *Cotterell*, pp. 240-268; *SarDesai*, pp. 140-141; *Tarling*, pp. 22, 40-41.

It was the Portuguese who first colonized in the Southeast Asian region when they captured Malacca in 1511.[94] The former was followed by the Dutch and the Spaniards which later on superseded the Portuguese as strong European powers in the region. The Spaniards began to colonize the Philippines in 1559.[95] The Dutch followed in around 1606-1609 through the "Vereenigde Oostindische Compagnie" (VOC) or the so-called Dutch East India Company.[96] Then it was around the onset of the 19th century when the British, French, and Americans landed in Southeast Asian shores and colonized most of the territories.[97] By 1913 or shortly before the First World War began, the French colonized Indochina; the British, the Malay states and Brunei; and the Dutch, Indonesia.[98] Thailand, through good diplomatic strategies and geographical location, was the only Southeast Asian country that escaped imperialism and remained independent, albeit by paying the price of losing some of its territories to the British and French.[99]

By this same time period, the Philippines found itself, after declaring in 1868 independence from the Spaniards (which colonized the former for 333 years), a new colonizer through the Americans.[100] Described as the "oddest Western colonial adventure in Southeast Asia," the Americans declared war against the Spaniards and then subsequently purchased the Philippines from Spain – suiting better the Americans' Pacific policy as the Philippines would strengthen the United States' position in Southeast Asia.[101] The United States then had not only apprehensions of Japan seeking to expand its influence,[102] but congruently, colonizing the Philippines likewise catered to the United States economic interests.[103]

Colonial experience mostly defined the national borders, created modern political and administrative institutions, established some basic parameters of economic systems, and charted industrialization and modern internal development through the introduction of Western laws, urban

---

94 *Reid*, p. 120; *Tarling*, pp. 21-25; *Tilman*, p. 17.
95 *Reid*, p. 121; *Tarling*, p. 34.
96 *Reid*, pp. 123-124; *Tarling*, pp. 25-26.
97 *Cotterell*, pp. 239-268; *SarDesai*, pp. 87-132; *Tarling*, pp. 39-41.
98 *SarDesai*, p. 140. See also *Solidum*, p. 4.
99 *Ricklefs/Lockhart/Lau, et al.*, p. 167; *SarDesai*, pp. 133-139; *Tarling*, pp. 69-74. See for further information, *Ricklefs/Lockhart/Lau, et al.*, pp. 227-237.
100 *SarDesai*, p. 155.
101 *Cotterell*, p. 266.
102 *Cotterell*, p. 266.
103 *Ricklefs/Lockhart/Lau, et al.*, pp. 251-252; *SarDesai*, pp. 156-157.

planning, educational institutions, immigration policies, money markets, location of administrative centers, as well as transportation and communication lines.[104] In addition, the colonized states were fortified against neighbors thought to be hostile, were made part of an international network of posts subject to a single authority, and governed by regularly replaced administrators.[105]

This modernity notwithstanding, it consequently caused pervasive and inherent economic dislocation and distress and had the undesirable effect of actually lowering the economic well-being of people.[106] Traditional structure and values of rural society was undermined intentionally – ultimately disrupting its economy and way of life, resulting in changes in the social strata.[107] With the introduction of modern internal development and other forms of innovation, colonizers reinforced distinction between elites and masses, and social distances were prescribed, which defined and delineated social classes.[108]

Additionally, colonialism reinforced a different kind of cultural hybridity amongst their colonized states.[109] Among all the colonizers Southeast Asia had, the Portuguese, although the first to have colonized parts of the region, had little influence in the course of history in the new nations of Southeast Asia.[110] As Robert Tilman narrates, the French had much more impact on Vietnam, Kampuchea, and Laos; the British on Burma, Malaysia, and Singapore; the Spanish and Americans on the Philippines; and the Dutch, on Indonesia.[111] That said, it was the Philippines which had the most unique colonization experience among all Southeast Asian countries and consequently received the most impact of colonial contact and cultural penetration.[112] Having been colonized long before other countries in Southeast Asia were, colonial ways of doing things were more established.[113] The Spaniards were principally governed by considerations of religion with religious and civil-political authorities heavily intertwined, forcefully converting most Pilipinos to Catholicism notwithstanding even

104 *SarDesai*, pp. 141, 146; *Tilman*, p. 17.
105 *Reid*, p. 121.
106 *SarDesai*, p. 161.
107 *Reid*, pp. 130-132; *SarDesai*, p. 161.
108 *Tilman*, p. 17.
109 *Reid*, pp. 130-132.
110 *Tilman*, p. 17.
111 *Tilman*, p. 17.
112 *SarDesai*, pp. 63, 82.
113 *Ricklefs/Lockhart/Lau, et al.*, p. 193.

the strong Islamic resistance then in southern Philippines.[114] Then after being colonized by the Americans, the Philippines was immersed further to American policy and westernized education, literature, language, elite-led politics, and other aspects of culture.[115]

Through colonization, the majority of Asian countries were reduced from flourishing and autonomous communities to colonies, protectorates, or client states with western encroachment either land or by sea, regardless of how colonizers tried to rationalize their occupation and whether their colonial experience was either unabashedly abusive or benign and benevolent.[116] Correlatively, the different colonial legacies each country in the region experienced has, as one wrote, drawn up "curtains of ignorance and separation between the nations of Southeast Asia, cut off thitherto flourishing contacts among their peoples," and even "established new patterns of trade."[117] This later resulted in a variance of national experiences, diversity of institutions, and difference in strategic outlooks.[118] One could observe Southeast Asia less and less in terms of a *Schicksalgemeinschaft* – or a community with a shared destiny, with the progressive and aggressive Western intrusions in Southeast Asia.[119] Rather, one is exposed to a "startling paradox", wherein Western intrusion or colonization resulted in the region's high political fragmentation into self-contained political and economic domains catering to imperial interests.[120] Interaction amongst the countries, mostly through the "ebb and flow of migrants and traders" within the region seemingly ceased,[121] and whatever history of "Southeast Asia" developed during this period could understandably be entangled with the history of European colonial regime.[122] Thus, it was not surprising, as many historians suggested, the colonial period introduced far-reaching changes, consolidated and divided cultures and communities, and becomes a significant contributor and/or factor to how modern Southeast Asia was shaped and contoured as to how it is known presently, including

114 *Reid,* pp. 112-113; *Ricklefs/Lockhart/Lau, et al.,* pp. 194-195; *SarDesai,* pp. 70-73, 82.
115 *Ricklefs/Lockhart/Lau, et al.,* p. 227; *SarDesai,* pp. 158-165.
116 *Cotterell,* p. 239; *SarDesai,* p. 141.
117 *Severino,* ASEAN, p. 4.
118 *Severino,* ASEAN, p. 4.
119 *Benda,* p. 112.
120 *Acharya,* p. 1007; *Appadorai,* p. 277; *Benda,* p. 112.
121 *Appadorai,* p. 277; *Severino,* ASEAN, p. 4.
122 *Benda,* p. 112.

how states dealt with one another and forged socio-political and economic relationships.[123]

c. The Times of War

As narrated above, colonialism has brought a lot of changes in the Southeast Asian region, one of which is the sudden shift from being autonomous communities to being subservient states. Instead of having actions and resources catering to one's own interests, it catered to another. Economic dislocation, distress, and exploitation, as above mentioned, was not uncommon during the colonial era. Thus, it did not take long until small elite groups of people among the colonized groups sought to be taken out of traditional trappings, escape alien rule, and find independence through the participation in nationalist movements.[124]

Colonialism itself provided the means to the creation of a nationalist consciousness among elites in Southeast Asia.[125] Through the introduction of modern intellectualism, industrialization, and/or education, on one hand, the minds of the youth were opened to "political ideas of the West, including self-government and the fundamental freedoms of press, assembly, and speech" and equally brought knowledge of revolutions elsewhere in Western experience.[126] On the other hand, there came with a proliferation of imperial philosophies after empires were consolidated in the Southeast Asian region in some parts of the region.[127] At the same time, colonialism ironically had the effect of re-fueling a glorious historical past for most Southeast Asians. Due to Western efforts to undertake archaeological excavations, historical antiquities were unearthed, temples restored, and arts studied, that consequently ignited pride amongst nationalists about their magnificent history and hopes for a brighter future.[128]

---

123 *Benda*, p. 112; *Ricklefs/Lockhart/Lau, et al.*, p. 166; *SarDesai*, p. 141; *Tilman*, p. 16.

124 *SarDesai*, pp. 144-147.

125 *SarDesai*, pp. 141, 147.

126 *SarDesai*, p. 147.

127 Examples were the Dutch "Ethical Policy" and the French *mission civilisatrice*, which basically said that colonial rule should yield reciprocal benefits: colonial empires are more of a responsibility to give better government, education, and welfare and that it is important to stress the imperial participation of European-educated native elites.*Christie*, pp. 9-10.

128 *SarDesai*, p. 147.

Nationalist movements in the region could be described in phases. At the beginning, especially prior to 1914, a majority of the nationalist movements in Southeast Asia focused more on "self-strengthening" initiatives and endeavors rather than "anti-colonial."[129] The indigenous elite were familiar with the warnings of Social Darwinism: a civilization that fails to adapt to changing times would be susceptible to decay and failure.[130] Steering away from this majority was the Philippines, which was the first in Asia to successfully mature in terms of nationalism and carry out anti-colonial nationalist movements for independence albeit the same were earlier besieged with stumbling blocks.[131] As mentioned earlier, Pilipinos declared their independence from the Spaniards in 1898 but got cheated in the process when Americans "extended their assistance" to drive the Spaniards out.[132] Nationalist movements nonetheless continued under the American rule but the same was more toned down as Americans gave them more concessions to realize their self-government.[133]

Thereafter, there was an obvious change in tone in nationalist movements in the Southeast Asian region starting from the First World War. There was an upsurge of anti-colonial movements across the region and throughout Asia.[134] Underlying these movements were different competing ideologies such as nationalism, communism and Islam, which were arguably symptoms of the upheaval against the colonial agenda.[135] The myth of European imperial superiority and invulnerability was seemingly debunked during this time period.[136] At the same time, it did not help that in throwing support to the Allies, the United States chose to put an ideological sugarcoating over the aims of the Allies during the war.[137] If the Allies were fighting for the right to self-determination for all the peoples of Europe, it should not be surprising that the colonized states would demand for such right as well.[138]

Such circumstances affected the imperial systems in the region. Some countries such as Burma and the Philippines saw significant changes and

---

129 *Christie*, p. 10.
130 *Christie*, p. 10.
131 *Ricklefs/Lockhart/Lau, et al.*, pp. 197-198, 224-227; *SarDesai*, pp. 150-165.
132 *Ricklefs/Lockhart/Lau, et al.*, p. 227; *SarDesai*, pp. 155, 204.
133 *SarDesai*, p. 204.See generally*Ricklefs/Lockhart/Lau, et al.*, pp. 283-291.
134 *Christie*, p. 11.
135 *Christie*, p. 11.
136 *Beeson*, p. 8; *SarDesai*, pp. 204-205.
137 *Christie*, p. 11.
138 *Christie*, p. 11.

were allowed to some degree to have self-governments.[139] On the other hand, those colonies which did not have any significant political changes or any concrete self-government movements found themselves heavily influenced by revolutionary communist ideologies, which point to the direct relationship between capitalism and imperialism.[140] Communism flourished as a radical political agenda in the struggle for national liberation.[141] Nationalism prevailed in the region nonetheless as it engendered unity above everything else: a self-conscious, sustained effort to make a united identity.[142]

Any momentum gained by nationalist movements for self-government was later interrupted through the Japanese interregnum and Second World War. Japan while acting through the "Greater East Asia Prosperity Sphere" campaign had three goals in conquering the western colonies of Southeast Asia and making the latter alternative sources of supply during its war with China and eventual conflict with western powers: (1) "seizing the so-called Southern Resource Area, (2) securing a defense perimeter through the Pacific Islands through the eastern border and against India in the west, and (3) containing China".[143] Japan eventually allied itself with Germany and Italy in the Second World War, staging a theatre of war in the Southeast Asian region.[144] Starting its assault in 1941, the Japanese invasion of the Western colonies in Southeast Asia was efficacious, complete, and swift – conquering all either through diplomatic pressure or force by 1942.[145]

Notably, it was more or less during this time period when the term "Southeast Asia" came into prominence, through the identification of the region in political and military terms by United States President Franklin Roosevelt and British Prime Minister Winston Churchill through the establishment of the Supreme Allied Command in Southeast Asia ("SEAC") in August 1943.[146] Albeit the boundaries of SEAC were changed from time to time during the Second World War, it was concerned with discussions of geographical extent, command arrangements and relationships, and

139 *Christie*, p. 12.
140 *Christie*, p. 12.
141 *Christie*, p. 13.
142 *Christie*, p. 13.
143 *Cotterell*, p. 270; *Ricklefs/Lockhart/Lau, et al.*, p. 293.See also *Reid*, p. 323.
144 *Cotterell*, p. 272.
145 *Cotterell*, pp. 270-280; *Reid*, p. 324; *Ricklefs/Lockhart/Lau, et al.*, pp. 293-294.
146 *Solidum*, p. 5.

other related matters.[147] At the same time, perceptions of "Southeast Asia" heavily derived from the Japanese interregnum which changed colonial fortunes and partition brought by the Western powers.[148]

With the Japanese interregnum dismantling European and American colonial administrations, some indigenous political activists either found themselves aligning with the Japanese in creating an "Asia for Asians" and propagating the Greater East Asia Prosperity Sphere whilst some found themselves imprisoned or punished for continuing to support European and/or American endeavors.[149] The Japanese postured itself as the liberator of Southeast Asia and attempted to win over local supporters through deliberate, even haphazard, violent propaganda.[150] Despite the foregoing, the Japanese failed to win over Southeast Asian peoples.[151] Repression was an aspect of Japanese rule but at the end of the day, its severity was self-defeating and even counter-intuitive to the promise Japanese occupation brought.[152] Stating it otherwise, the Japanese did not practice what they preached: while condemning the violence and exploitation the Westerners did to the colonized, the Japanese had also no qualms in perpetuating the same.[153]

The foregoing notwithstanding, Japanese interregnum had an undeniable impact on the process of decolonization in Southeast Asia and the ushering of a so-called Southeast Asian renaissance.[154] With the ousting of European and American colonial authority, nationalist leaders had the opportunity to communicate and cooperate with rural communities and espouse ideas of an independent nation – something unspeakable, even seditious, under European or American colonial rule.[155] At the same time, student leaders, nationalists, activists, and politicians, who were previously

---

147 *Solidum*, pp. 5-6. See also *Beeson*, p. 18.

148 *Cotterell*, pp. 269-270, 280; *Solidum*, p. 6.

149 *Reid*, pp. 324, 326; *Ricklefs/Lockhart/Lau, et al.*, p. 294.

150 Japan humiliated publicly Westerners amongst local populations, allowed nationalist governments to be established in countries such as Indonesia, Myanmar, and the Philippines, while promoting local languages and indigenous cultural monuments through the censorship of European and/or American symbols of governance. *Christie*, p. 14; *Cotterell*, p. 280; *Ricklefs/Lockhart/Lau, et al.*, p. 295; *SarDesai*, p. 205; *Solidum*, p. 20.

151 *Cotterell*, p. 281.

152 *Cotterell*, p. 281; *Ricklefs/Lockhart/Lau, et al.*, p. 295.

153 See *Cotterell*, pp. 281-284; *Ricklefs/Lockhart/Lau, et al.*, pp. 295-300.

154 *Beeson*, p. 8; *SarDesai*, p. 204.

155 *Ricklefs/Lockhart/Lau, et al.*, p. 316.

censored, were now allowed to articulate their ideas.[156] In the meantime, any brutality the Japanese exhibited opened further the consciousness to rid the region of foreign overlords.[157]

Following the surrender of the Japanese in August 1945, key elements in shaping the post-colonial/post-war period were already identified.[158] Despite being keen of retaking their colonies back after the Japanese occupation, the Western colonizers not only lacked the needed resources but more importantly, were confronted with a differently charged spirit of nationalism and yearning for independence.[159] To the exception of the Philippines, which relatively had a smoother transition to independence, some Western colonizers like the British and Dutch had difficulties letting go and thus, negotiations and revolutions anew and all in efforts to gain independence occurred in other parts of Southeast Asia: from the First Indochina War (Viet Minh against the French), Indonesian revolution, Burmese threat of revolution, to conflicting movements in Laos and Cambodia.[160] Ultimately, the Philippines, Burma, Indonesia, and Malaya gained their independence in 1946, 1948, 1949, and 1957, respectively, while Singapore and Borneo territories were strategically attached to Malaya in the 1950's.[161]

Despite being conferred independence, dissension became apparent in some parts of the region amongst those where minority rights, views, "loyalist communities," and political structures designed to protect these interests tended to be forgotten.[162] In a rush for some colonial powers to appease increasing nationalist movements, those in the ethnic minorities or "loyalist communities" were positioned in a marginal position.[163] The same can be said with ideologically or religiously based movements in the region, especially Communism, which was already far-reaching and has noticeably spread its influence and impact in the Southeast Asian region.[164] Its influence remarkably eroded in some parts of Southeast Asia

---

156 See *Ricklefs/Lockhart/Lau, et al.*, pp. 300-316. See for how transition to independence movements were supported by the Japanese, *Reid*, pp. 327-331.

157 *Ricklefs/Lockhart/Lau, et al.*, p. 316. See also *Reid*, p. 326.

158 *Christie*, p. 16; *Ricklefs/Lockhart/Lau, et al.*, p. 317.

159 *Christie*, p. 16; *Cotterell*, pp. 287-291; *Ricklefs/Lockhart/Lau, et al.*, p. 317; *Tarling*, p. 120.

160 See *Christie*, p. 16; *Cotterell*, pp. 291-294; *Ricklefs/Lockhart/Lau, et al.*, p. 317.

161 See *Ricklefs/Lockhart/Lau, et al.*, pp. 321-345.

162 *Christie*, p. 19.

163 *Christie*, p. 19.

164 See in general*Ganesan*, pp. 212-213; *Pasadilla*, p. 2.

during the independence negotiations, "a key period when the nationalist organizations needed simultaneously to reassure the international community and the departing colonial powers that their governments would be 'responsible' and broad-based, and also to ensure firm control of the new state apparatuses that were being created."[165] Thus, it did not come as a surprise during this time period that Southeast Asian countries like Indonesia, Burma, Malaya, and the Philippines were confronting a rise of communist, Islamic, and ethnic minority insurgencies and coups.[166] It did not help either that during the same time frame, the Vietnamese nationalist and communist groups were about to overtake the French in the anti-colonial First Indochina War.[167]

During these hard times, it became apparent that while the process of decolonization in the region may have been aided unintentionally by the Japanese interregnum and how the Americans marketed the Allied forces' ideology during the war, these factors only formed parts of the way toward the creation of a coherent region.[168] As Beeson remarked, the region as a whole might have pierced the myth of European imperial superiority and foundations for an Asian renaissance period may have been laid down, but at the end of the day, the newly independent Southeast Asian countries were confronted with national consolidation issues, "let alone any broader process of regional coordination or institution building".[169] Admittedly, once the joys and excitement of newly-found independence settled in, the newly independent Southeast Asian countries were confronted with twin problems of nation building and economic development – herculean issues given that these countries did not have much economic resources left after a long period of colonization but moreover, there were common issues of internal dissent and heterogeneous societies amongst themselves, as well as colonial political models, which were not quite applicable anymore to the newly independent states' status and needs.[170] It did not help either that since the outbreak of the Second World War, the idea of a "Southeast Asia" region was made more visible, legitimated, and given a political connotation.[171] Understandably, the region then unwittingly or

165 *Christie*, p. 20.
166 *Christie*, pp. 1, 20; *Weatherbee*, International Relations, p. 63.
167 *Ganesan*, p. 213; *Weatherbee*, International Relations, pp. 64-65, 79.
168 *Beeson*, p. 8.
169 *Beeson*, p. 8.
170 *Beeson*, p. 8; *Tarling*, p. 92; *Tilman*, p. 19.
171 *Emmerson*, pp. 8-9.

unwillingly garners attention and needed to prove that they could stand independently of their former colonizers.

d. New challenges while paving avenues for regional cooperation

One of the thought-of solutions Southeast Asian countries made, together with other neighboring countries in Asia, which more or less were similarly situated and confronting similar issues and problems, was to make efforts to open communication amongst themselves and perhaps forge cooperation.[172] The first attempts at this possible Asian cooperation was seen through the Asian Relations Conference, led by India through its first Prime Minister Jawaharlal Nehru, in 1947 and 1949, respectively – the same period when not all Asian countries were not yet fully independent.[173] Unofficial in nature, two major purposes were highlighted: (1) to have a better understanding of Asia's problems and (2) efforts for cooperation.[174] Eight (8) issues were listed as part of the conference's agenda,[175] and within this context, there was a common sentiment amongst all participants against foreign dominance in Asia and the need for them to focus on self-determination and racial equality.[176] In connection thereto, the 1947 conference bore witness to the development of prescribing common rules for domestic affairs, especially those affecting countries' respect for the principle of equality amongst all citizens, whilst the 1949 conference bore witness to how the participating countries agreed to consult amongst themselves how to promote coordination and cooperation within the framework of the United Nations.[177]

During the 1947 conference, the establishment of an Asian Relations Organization was envisioned as a precursor to maintaining progress that has already been made, but the said organization, meant to be led by

172 *Acharya*, p. 34; *Appadorai*, pp. 275-276.

173 *Acharya*, Whose Ideas Matter?, p. 34.

174 *Appadorai*, p. 276.

175 These issues are the following: "national movements for freedom, racial problems, inter-Asian migration, transition from colonial to national economy, agricultural reconstruction and industrial development, labor problems and social services, cultural problems, and status of women and women's movements." See *Acharya*, Whose Ideas Matter?, p. 34; *Appadorai*, p. 207; *Appadorai*, The Asian Relations Conference in Perspective, p. 279; *McCallum*, p. 14; *Solidum*, p. 13.

176 *Acharya*, Whose Ideas Matter?, pp. 34-35.

177 *Acharya*, Whose Ideas Matter?, p. 34; *Solidum*, p. 14.

Nehru as President, unfortunately failed to properly take off.[178] Aside from conflicting political interests on the part of India back then,[179] competition between India and China for leadership became pronounced and this was to the dislike of many participants.[180] Moreover, the Asian Relations Conference to begin with was organized with pan-Asian sentiments, or the future establishment of a pan-Asian federation, which were weak and discredited by the willingness of leaders to only provide either political or moral support to those facing their own anti-colonial struggles.[181] Any aspiration of an Asian Unity during this time period seemed farfetched and did not reflect the *zeitgeist*.[182] Thus, it did not come as a surprise that the Asian Relations Conference, together with the so-called Asian Relations Organization failed to further develop.

This unfortunate circumstance notwithstanding, a seed was planted amongst Southeast Asian countries during this conference towards the benefits of regionalism. Burma's Aung San had the opinion previously that while India and China each should remain single entities, the Southeast Asian countries would benefit more if they form a sub-regional entity.[183] It became even more prevalent during the second Asian Relations Conference in 1949 that neither India nor China would support the individual nationalist interests of some participants (such as Burma), that debates and talks were held among Indonesia, Burma, Thailand, Philippines, and Malaya on creating a Southeast Asian Association that would first closely cooperate culturally and economically but could later be a more closely knit political cooperation.[184] This "Southeast Asian Association" did not however materialize after such talks during the Asian Relations Conference.

Not to be hampered by the failure of Asian Relations Conference to continue, the Philippines on 04 July 1949 attempted to create an organization for cooperation amongst states in Asia.[185] Called the "Asia-Pacific Union", it sought to secure the sovereignty of all countries in Asia while identifying

---

178 *Appadorai,* The Asian Relations Conference in Perspective, pp. 282-283.

179 *Appadorai,* The Asian Relations Conference in Perspective, pp. 283-284.

180 *Solidum,* p. 13.

181 *Acharya,* Whose Ideas Matter?, pp. 35-36; *Appadorai,* The Asian Relations Conference in Perspective, pp. 283-284. *See also Acharya,* Asia is Not One, p. 1006.

182 *Appadorai,* The Asian Relations Conference in Perspective, p. 283.

183 *Acharya,* Asia is Not One, p. 1008.

184 *Acharya,* Asia is Not One, p. 1008.

185 *Solidum,* p. 14.

Communism as a threat.[186] However, such organization failed to get the participation of most countries in the region because they neither wanted to be embroiled in the then brewing Cold War nor thought it was the right time for such an Asian pact.[187]

As attempts such as the Asian Relations Organization, negotiations for a Southeast Asian Association, and proposals for an Asia-Pacific Union unraveled, talks remained amongst South and Southeast Asian countries. Through a conference held in May 1950 at Baguio, Philippines, wherein the participants acknowledged the value of consulting one another to further the "interests of the people of the region and to ensure that in any consideration of the special problems of South and Southeast Asia, the point of view of the peoples of this area be prominently kept in mind."[188] Despite not having an organized group during this time, this meeting facilitated even further the "taking of a more or less common attitude on the part of the members of the region" in handling common issues such as colonialism, racial discrimination, and the like.[189]

In the meantime, the United States was strategically placing itself as a dominant and influential figure in Asian international relations.[190] After the Second World War, the United States and the Soviet Union rose as the two superpowers of the world.[191] A rivalry that eventually turned to conflict arose between Communism and the West in Europe ("Cold War"), which later spilled over globally in 1947, when the Soviet Union propagated that the world is divided into two irreconcilable communist and capitalist camps, whilst the United States identified Communism as a global threat.[192] East and Southeast Asia were eventually thrown into the Cold War stage through the triumph of communists against nationalists in the Chinese Civil War; the attack of communist North Korea against non-communist South Korea in 1950; the emergence of the Democratic Republic of Vietnam as a full-fledged communist state in 1950-51 and its continued full-military assaults against the French.[193]

Having scant interest in having a regional organization in Asia until the outbreak of the Korean War, the Americans were more interested in

186 *Solidum*, p. 14.
187 *Solidum*, p. 14.
188 *Appadorai*, The Bandung Conference, p. 208.
189 *Appadorai*, The Bandung Conference, p. 208.
190 See*Weatherbee*, International Relations, p. 63.
191 *Tarling*, p. 119.
192 *Christie*, p. 21; *Tarling*, pp. 119-120.
193 *Christie*, p. 21; *Tarling*, pp. 120-121.

collective defense or "mutual security."[194] Recognizing political developments favoring Communism in some parts of the region and the need to contain it, as well as the development problems these newly-independent states were encountering, the United States tactically offered political and economic aid in exchange for alliance in the Southeast Asian and overall Asia Pacific region. It branded itself to be the champion of anti-communist unity or leader of the "free world" and fought against any form of communist aggression.[195] While some states viewed these offers with disdain and/or animosity,[196] some were willing to hear what the United States had to say, albeit with reservations.[197] Those against the proposal of collective defense believe in particular that such kind of agreements encroaches against the concepts of non-intervention and non-alignment, which was a growing sentiment among the Asian countries during this time period.[198] At the same time, it increases the risk of involving the Asian countries into the power struggle between the world powers, especially since there is a general opinion to have an independent voice in world politics.[199]

These concerns being legitimate notwithstanding, American influence prevailed through the establishment in 1954 of the Southeast Asian Treaty Organization ("SEATO") wherein two Southeast Asian countries, Thailand and the Philippines, agreed to join together with great powers such as United States, Great Britain, Australia, New Zealand, and Pakistan, with the aim to fight communist aggression in the region through collective economic and military action.[200] Time-wise, the establishment of SEATO coincided with the role the United States inherited from the French in propping up non-communist South Vietnam after Vietnam's partition into communist North and non-communist South during the Geneva Conference.[201]

Although only Thailand and Philippines are the Southeast Asian countries who are part of the organization, SEATO could be arguably considered the first regional grouping in Southeast Asia, though great power-led, considering that the operative heart of the treaty creating SEATO lies in

194 *Acharya,* Whose Ideas Matter?, p. 42; *Brands,* pp. 250-270; *Dingman,* pp. 463-465.

195 *Brands,* p. 265; *Dingman,* pp. 458, 460-462, 467-479; *Ganesan,* pp. 212-213; *Weatherbee,* International Relations, pp. 63-34.

196 *See for example, Acharya,* p. 51; *Weatherbee,* International Relations, pp. 63-34.

197 *Dingman,* pp. 463-465.*See in general, Brands, pp. 250-270.*

198 *Acharya,* Whose Ideas Matter?, p. 54.

199 *Acharya,* Whose Ideas Matter?, p. 54.

200 *Dingman,* p. 474; *Weatherbee,* International Relations, p. 65.

201 *Christie,* p. 21.

the containment of communism in the Southeast Asia region.[202] SEATO, however, was different from the North American Treaty Organization ("NATO"), to which the former can easily be likened.[203] Unlike the NATO, there were neither military units assigned to the organization nor was there any unified military structure.[204] SEATO did not likewise call for collective defense, but rather consultation should there be a threat or attack.[205] If at all, SEATO was never meant to be a military alliance compared to NATO, but rather, it was a political tool to legitimize the containment strategy and interference maneuvers being then employed by the United States in the Southeast Asian region.[206]

The establishment of the SEATO did not settle well with the other Southeast Asian countries and their Third World contemporaries. SEATO was not considered by many as reflective of a Southeast Asian endeavor because it was made through initiatives of the United States to strengthen their alliance with other world powers and secure their defense in the Southeast Asian region.[207] For many, it was clearly "Cold War gerrymandering":[208] a way of creating new forms of spheres of influence as well as another manner of imposing dominance over weaker state-associates. Undeniably, there was a brewing power struggle in Asia and more likely than not, countries in it would be caught in the crossfire unwittingly and unwillingly.[209]

Given such strong resentment towards the influence being imposed by the United States, consultations and meetings were already being held among leaders of Southeast Asian countries such as Ceylon (now Sri Lanka), India, Pakistan, Burma, and Indonesia, focusing on how the "united voice of Asia could be heard in the councils of the world" during the same timeframe when negotiations and preparations were being made by the United States in the establishment of SEATO.[210] Having their first meeting

---

202 *Weatherbee,* International Relations, p. 65.
203 *Brands,* p. 269.
204 *Weatherbee,* International Relations, p. 65.
205 *Hemmer/Katzenstein,* p. 578; *Weatherbee,* International Relations, p. 65.
206 *Acharya,* Whose Ideas Matter?, pp. 42-43; *Ganesan,* p. 213; *Hemmer/Katzenstein,* p. 578; *Weatherbee,* International Relations, pp. 65-66.
207 *Reid,* p. 23.
208 *Acharya,* Whose Ideas Matter?, pp. 45-46; *Emmerson,* p. 9.
209 *See Acharya,* Constructing a Security Community, p. 51; *Acharya,* p. 20; *Weatherbee,* International Relations, p. 66.
210 *Acharya,* Whose Ideas Matter?, pp. 37-38; *Ang,* pp. 29-31; *Reid,* The Bandung Conference and Southeast Asian Regionalism, p. 23; *Weatherbee,* International Relations, p. 66.

in April 1954 in Colombo, these states were later dubbed the "Colombo Powers",[211] which argued for the importance of non-intervention in Asia.[212] The meeting in Colombo was initially for proposing regionalism to derail the further initiatives of the United States as well as the condemnation of any external interference in domestic affairs by either communist or anti-communist forces.[213] Indonesia, under the leadership of Prime Minister Sukarno, was keen in making this condemnation as Sukarno viewed US-intervention with disdain.[214] India's Nehru shared similar sentiments. Nehru believed that by building regional pacts in Asia, it shrinks the area of peace and increases the opportunity for world powers to intervene anew in internal affairs, which contradicts the general opinion of the newly-independent states.[215] Needless to state, Southeast Asian countries should have a "place in the negotiation table on issues of regional relevance" and not just be forced in choosing sides.[216]

In view of these purposes, together with having a more coherent regional position and promotion of mutual cooperation,[217] the Colombo Powers agreed in their December 1954 meeting in Bolor, Indonesia to organize a conference between Asian and African heads of government and/or foreign ministers to discuss these issues.[218] In April 1955, this Conference came into fruition when twenty-nine African and Asian heads (though predominantly Asian) of government and/or foreign ministers, including China, convened in Bandung, Indonesia.[219] Known as the "Bandung Conference", it became a hallmark event in the emergence of a stronger sen-

---

211 It was imperative to the interests of the United States for the Colombo Powers to acquiesce to the SEATO, believing that without them, there would be not much hold in Southeast Asia. Hence, the United States exerted much effort in convincing the latter to join. However, given the Colombo Power's strong opposition, the United States had to settle with the cooperation of both Thailand and the Philippines. *See Acharya,* Whose Ideas Matter?, pp. 50-60.

212 *Acharya,* Whose Ideas Matter?, p. 37.

213 *Abraham*, p. 197; *Weatherbee,* International Relations, p. 66.

214 *Weatherbee,* International Relations, p. 66.

215 *Acharya,* Whose Ideas Matter?, p. 46.

216 *Abraham,* p. 197; *Acharya,* Asia is Not One, p. 1007; *Weatherbee,* International Relations, p. 66.

217 *Appadorai,* The Bandung Conference, p. 235; *Weatherbee,* International Relations, p. 67.

218 *Acharya,* Whose Ideas Matter?, p. 38; *Appadorai,* The Bandung Conference, pp. 209-210.

219 *Ang,* p. 27; *Gupta*, p. 65.

timent towards an independent and neutral Third World as well as the establishment of a regional order in the Southeast Asian region.[220]

The Bandung Conference differed with the defunct Asian Relations Conference because it was interested more in maintaining the true sense of independence and autonomy. Moreover, as Burke remarked, the Bandung Conference was the first time that states of both Asia and Africa, most of which were newly independent, were able to come together and freely discuss common issues and attempt to formulate a unified approach vis-à-vis international relations.[221] Whilst some viewed the Bandung conference as a gathering with purely anti-Western undertones and rejection of anything Western leaders have contributed,[222] the conference was a forum for leaders of Asia and Africa to discuss and freely express themselves, without the imposition of any world power on issues transcending anti-imperialism such as human rights, the concept of freedom, national self-determination, and even peaceful relations notwithstanding differences.[223] Its contributions to regional order have been summarized in the conference's final communique, which sets forth the so-called Bandung principles, observance of which could lead to peaceful coexistence and friendly cooperation amongst one another.[224] Finding influence in the so-called Five Principles of Peaceful Cooperation,[225] these principles among others include "respect for sovereignty and territorial integrity of all countries," "abstention from intervention or interference in the internal affairs of another country,"

---

220 *Acharya/Tan*, p. 1; *Burke*, p. 948; *Gupta*, p. 65.

221 *Burke*, p. 948.

222 *Acharya/Tan*, p. 1; *Ang*, p. 29; *Burke*, p. 949.

223 *Appadorai*, The Bandung Conference, p. 212; *Burke*, pp. 950-961; *Weatherbee*, International Relations, p. 66.

224 *Acharya/Tan*, pp. 3-11; *Appadorai*, The Bandung Conference, p. 214; *Weatherbee*, International Relations, p. 67.

225 The „Five Principles of Peaceful Cooperation", also known as "Five Principles" or "PanchShila," finds it roots *per se* in the treaty between India and China in 29 April 1954, which called for "mutual respect for each other's territorial integrity and sovereignty, mutual non-aggression, mutual non-interference in each other's internal affairs, equality and mutual benefit, and peaceful existence." This was later on popularly invoked and/or adapted in the Geneva Convention on Indochina, Bandung Conference, and Moscow convocation of Communists in celebration of the 40th Anniversary of the Bolshevik Revolution. In general, these principles have been supported by communists and non-communists alike. It is only the Western and non-Western governments who dislike the principles in how it was written. *See Appadorai*, The Bandung Conference, p. 214; *Fifield*, pp. 504-505; *Richardson*, p. 5.

"settlement of all international disputes by peaceful means," and "promotion of mutual interests and cooperation."[226]

In relation to the foregoing, recognition of non-intrusive, informal, and consensus-based diplomacy has been given primordial consideration through the Bandung conference.[227] It was emphasized during the conference that no contentious issues would be discussed and in lieu of majority voting, consensus shall be done in decision-making.[228] Stating it otherwise: not one voice would dominate the discussions. There was more emphasis "on social trust rather than on the rule of law in negotiations."[229] As a participant once recollected, this process of consultation and consensus became imperative to the success of the Bandung conference, wherein parties were rooted in "relatively unstructured discussions, a high degree of informality, pragmatism, expediency, and a search for a practical minimal solution that all parties can live with."[230]

After the Bandung conference of 1955, there were expectations that another conference would be held the following year.[231] This did not seem to happen, and no similar conference followed suit (to the relief of some countries like the United States, which viewed the Bandung Conference with worry and caution).[232] There seemed to be irreconcilable differences between those in Southeast Asia and South Asia, as India then (a Bandung Conference co-convener and member of the Colombo Powers) was more concerned in promoting its own agenda, which is the strengthening of its relations with China.[233] It did not help likewise that it butted heads with other participants, when it tried to dominate discussions and impose on others its views.[234]

In light of this, it can be noted at this juncture that on one hand, attempts to regionalize and organize themselves become attractive at the notion of respecting autonomy, sovereignty, and upholding non-intervention. On the other hand, attempts ultimately fail or a proposal fails to launch at the outset when one or some try to dominate the agenda or

---

226 *Stubbs*, p. 457; *Weatherbee,* International Relations, p. 67.

227 *Acharya/Tan,* p. 10; *Appadorai,* The Bandung Conference, pp. 232-233; *Stubbs,* p. 458.

228 *Acharya/Tan,* p. 10.

229 *Stubbs,* p. 458.

230 *Abdulgani*, pp. 71-72; *Acharya/Tan,* p. 10; *Stubbs,* pp. 458-459.

231 *Abraham,* p. 211.

232 *Ang,* p. 39.

233 *Reid,* The Bandung Conference and Southeast Asian Regionalism, pp. 24-25.

234 *Reid,* The Bandung Conference and Southeast Asian Regionalism, p. 24.

impose its own interest upon the others (regardless of whether a world power or participating state in the conference).

Moreover, as some observed, neutralism seemed to lose its appeal and commitments under the Bandung Conference could no longer be observed due to nationalist or ideological considerations.[235] On one hand, China by the end of 1958, albeit an original participant during the first (and only) Bandung conference, was shifting its foreign policies while pursuing its own interests in the Southeast Asian region – even violating the principle of non-intervention – and gradually pulling away from its association from the Soviet Union, which was also pursuing new agenda.[236] On the other hand, India had to consequently face its own disputes with China and Pakistan.[237] Moreover, internal struggles were reaching new heights in countries like Vietnam, Laos, and Cambodia.[238]

Despite the discontinuance of the Bandung conference, its principles were integral to another regional movement in Southeast Asia. As some observers pointed out, the Bandung Conference eventually represented the first steps towards a non-alignment movement in the Southeast Asian region.[239]

In 1961, a conference was held in Belgrade wherein Southeast Asian countries Burma, Indonesia, and Cambodia were present together with other countries from Asia, Africa, the Middle East, and Europe.[240] During the same, the Non-Alignment Movement ("NAM") was established.[241] This was underpinned by many – somehow unsettling – events that occurred around the globe within six (6) years between the Belgrade Conference and the Bandung Conference, that Third World states, especially the

---

235 *Ang*, p. 39.

236 *Acharya*, Asia is Not One, p. 1009; *Ang*, p. 39; *Ganesan*, p. 213; *Jian*, pp. 89-99; *Zhang*, pp. 523-526.

237 *Abraham*, p. 212.

238 *Ang*, pp. 39-42. There was a growing resolution, as propounded by Vietnam's Ho Chi Minh, amongst these three (3) countries of helping one another politically and/or militarily because a success or failure of the other has direct impact on the other. Hence, in the revolutionary movements in each country, there was a trickle-down effect on the other's territory. *See in general* Acharya, Asia is Not One, p. 1008.

239 *Abraham*, p. 197.

240 *Abraham*, p. 197; *Weatherbee*, International Relations, p. 68.

241 *Abraham*, p. 197; *Weatherbee*, International Relations, p. 68.

newly-independent ones, could not help but be fearful for the fragility of their sovereignty.[242]

Acting with an anti-imperialism platform and adherence to the Five Principles of Peaceful Cooperation akin to the Bandung Conference,[243] the Non-Alignment Movement distinguishes itself from the Bandung Conference with its different intellectual content, set of participants, and the degree by which the great powers sought to interfere with its outcome.[244] NAM specifically zeroes in the importance of establishing security equidistance between the dangers of the Cold War and the need for collective action to avoid further world tension.[245] Conversely, the Bandung Conference was focused on post-colonial considerations affecting foreign policy issues.[246] In relation to this, the Bandung Conference underlines the moral violence being perpetrated by the continuation of discredited political systems and excluding Asian states in global decision-making, while NAM emphasizes the desire of Third World countries "to preserve a measure of independence for themselves" and the corresponding need to take an active role in the international order in pursuit of individual and collective interests.[247] The NAM distinguished itself from neutrality, which connoted a "passive and isolationalist policy of non-involvement in all conflicts."[248]

In the same year when the NAM was established, attempts at regionalism were being made specifically in Southeast Asia through the establishment in 1960 of the Association of Southeast Asia ("ASA").[249] Southeast Asia (perhaps reconsidering the ideas planted as early as the Asian Re-

---

242 *Gupta,* p. 65. As Gupta enumerated, there were the "Suez Canal crisis and the Soviet invasion of Hungary in 1965, the admission of 16 newly independent African countries to the United Nations in 1960, the escalation of the Cold War tensions following the downing of an American U2 spy plane over Soviet airspace in 1959, and growing U.S. involvement in places as diverse as Cuba, Vietnam, Congo, and Laos."

243 *See Fifield,* pp. 504-505; *Richardson,* p. 5.

244 *Abraham,* p. 197.

245 *Abraham,* p. 197; *Park,* p. 45; *Weatherbee,* International Relations, p. 68.

246 *Abraham,* p. 197.

247 *Abraham,* p. 211; *Gupta,* p. 67; *Park,* p. 45.

248 *Gupta,* p. 65. Interestingly, NAM made constant criticism of the West's cultural imperialism which resulted in the displeasure of countries such as the United States, which thought of NAM as a communist Trojan horse. This did not dissuaded the growth in membership however, though more of an "anti-bloc" rather than a formal institution. See further, *Park,* pp. 56-57; *Weatherbee,* International Relations, p. 68.

249 *Ganesan,* pp. 212-213.

lations Conferences) was taking the helm in promoting regionalism in Asia and ASA was arguably the first genuine Southeast Asian regional institution.[250] ASA, composed of Malaya (now Federation of Malaysia), Philippines, and Thailand, only lasted for two years, or until 1963 given the formation of the Federation of Malaysia, which included Sabah, a territory the Philippines had a claim to.[251] Further, ASA was composed without Indonesia, which was arguably then the strongest nation in Southeast Asia.[252] Indonesia then viewed ASA as a neocolonialist inspired organization and did not want to become involved in an organization whose policies were focused on the negative, given that it was "anti-this and anti-that."[253]

With the failure of ASA, Malaya, together with Indonesia and the Philippines, again attempted to form in July-August 1963 a regional organization called MAPHILINDO.[254] On paper, MAPHILINDO sought to construct a quasi-confederal framework for relations amongst the three countries in pursuit of uniting the Malay race or forming a "Greater Malay Federation."[255] Later on it was revealed that MAPHILINDO was politically motivated on the part of the Philippines and Indonesia to frustrate the establishment of the Federation of Malaysia, which, through former Indonesian Prime Minister Sukarno's strong influence was thought to be a continuation of British imperialism as Malaysia heavily favored their former colonizers.[256] Prime Minister Sukarno of Indonesia was a stark supporter of anti-imperialism and he condemned Malaysia's pro-British ways.[257] Thus, even before MAPHILINDO could be truly functional, the same was "stillborn" due to declaration of Malaysia in September 1963 and corresponding armed confrontation (*"konfrontasi"*) made by Indonesia, as led by then Prime Minister Sukarno, against Malaysia between 1964 and 1966.[258] It did not likewise help alleviate the brewing tension when Singa-

---

250 *Acharya,* Asia is Not One, p. 1009; *Ganesan,* pp. 212-213.
251 *Crozier*, p. 17; *Frost*, p. 4; *Ganesan,* p. 213; *Hensengerth*, pp. 7-8; *Takagi*, p. 268.
252 *Acharya,* Whose Ideas Matter?, p. 83.
253 *Crozier,* p. 17.
254 *Di Floristella*, pp. 56-57; *Ganesan,* p. 213; *Takagi,* p. 269; *Weatherbee,* International Relations, p. 71.
255 *Acharya,* Asia is Not One, p. 1009; *Crozier,* p. 17; *Takagi,* p. 269.
256 *Hensengerth,* p. 8; *Weatherbee,* International Relations, p. 73.
257 *Kivimäki*, p. 19.
258 *Acharya,* Asia is Not One, p. 1009; *Davidson/Kammen*, pp. 55-57; *Di Floristella,* pp. 56-57; *Frost,* p. 4; *Ganesan,* p. 213; *Takagi,* p. 269; *Weatherbee,* International Relations, p. 71.

pore in 1965 was separated from the Federation of Malaysia due to political and governmental differences,[259] and Malaysia took it against Brunei Darussalam when the latter refused to join the Malaysian federation while giving asylum to the former's dissidents.[260]

Notably, the collapse of ASA and the failure to launch MAPHILINDO was symptomatic of weak processes built not on convergence of interests, but of one trying to put its interest more than the other.[261] While this phenomenon may be explained by cultural undertones and differently formed perceptions, this could be equally observed in the beginning of regional discussions in Southeast Asia such as the Bandung Conference and NAM, wherein, amidst the free-flowing informal discussions that were able to dilute any attempt at dominance by any participant, one could observe how Sukarno-led Indonesia tried to dominate discussions through the imposition of its own agenda and ideals, and how a Nehru-led India thought itself and its ideas more superior than others while attempting to talk down those which did not conform to its ideas.[262] As experiences from these failures suggest, political and military interests should be taken out of the negotiation table during the formative years of learning cooperation; goodwill and trust are imperative; and Asian solutions for Asian problems should be applied in preserving peace.[263]

Moreover, the collapse of early attempts at regionalism placed a magnifying glass on the underlying strained bilateral relations amongst the Southeast Asian countries.[264] There was an obvious strain in the relationships between Malaysia and Indonesia due to the *konfrontasi,* although in the meantime, Prime Minister Sukarno has been ousted from his position and replaced by General Suharto, who negotiated the end of the *konfrontasi*;[265] Malaysia and the Philippines, due to territorial claims to Sabah; Indonesia and Singapore, due to the former's decision for terrorists to bomb the latter during the *konfrontasi* and the latter's decision to execute two Indonesian soldiers involved in the *konfrontasi* attacks; and between Malaysia and Singapore, due to the latter's separation from the former.[266]

---

259 *Cotterell,* p. 391; *Frost,* p. 4.

260 *Thambipillai,* p. 45.

261 *Di Floristella,* p. 57.

262 *Acharya,* Asia is Not One, p. 1007; *Reid,* The Bandung Conference and Southeast Asian Regionalism, pp. 24-25; *Solidum,* p. 20.

263 *Solidum,* p. 18.

264 *Ganesan,* p. 212.

265 *Davidson/Kammen,* pp. 57-28.

266 *Funston,* p. 208; *Ganesan,* p. 212; *Weatherbee,* International Relations, pp. 70-72.

Making things worse, as attempts to create regional movements and/or groupings started to unfold in Southeast Asia, together with establishing international relations amongst the countries in it and their neighboring countries, localized conflicts were already greatly exaggerated through the intervention of external agents brought by the bipolarizing conflict between the Soviet Union and the United States as well as the increasing influence of China in the region.[267] As the United States took over the French in 1954, the former intervened in the escalated conflict between North and South Vietnam in 1963, which sparked the Second Indochina War.[268] Rallying support from Southeast Asian countries such as Thailand and the Philippines, the United States launched an offensive against the communist Viet Cong.[269] Additionally, the United States, together with Thailand, launched a "secret war" in neutral Laos upon learning that Pathet Laos was a North Vietnam ally.[270] Cambodia, wanting then to maintain neutrality, ultimately aligned with the United States after the ousting of its leader, while indigenous communist groups called the Khmer Rouge tried on their own to cease power in the country.[271]

The above-mentioned circumstances were understandably alarming not only for the countries in Southeast Asian but also the entire Asia Pacific region and needed to be addressed.[272] In response, two developments in regional institution building could be cited: the Asia and Pacific Council ("ASPAC") founded in Seoul, Korea in 1966 and the Association of Southeast Asian Nations ("ASEAN") founded a year later in Bangkok, Thailand.[273] On one hand, ASPAC was designed to bring together most of the non-communist Western Pacific nations to deal with external threats and at the same time, provide a possible framework for cooperation.[274] Having Australia, Japan, Malaysia, Taiwan, New Zealand, Philippines, South Korea, South Vietnam, and Thailand as its members, ASPAC sought to present itself as an indigenous Asian group, which sought to complement, if not substitute, SEATO – providing an Asian voice in Asia back then.[275]

---

267 *Di Floristella*, p. 2; *Ganesan*, p. 212.
268 *Cotterell*, p. 390; *Weatherbee*, International Relations, pp. 68-70.
269 *Weatherbee*, International Relations, pp. 68-69.
270 *Weatherbee*, International Relations, p. 69.
271 *Becker*, pp. 117-118; *Weatherbee*, International Relations, p. 69.
272 *Severino*, p. 13; *Weatherbee*, International Relations, p. 72.
273 *Acharya*, Whose Ideas Matter?, pp. 81-82.
274 *Acharya*, Whose Ideas Matter?, p. 82; *Frost*, p. 3.
275 *Acharya*, Whose Ideas Matter?, p. 82.

On the other hand, the ASEAN was formed on 08 August 1967, in Bangkok, Thailand amongst Indonesia, Malaysia, Singapore, Thailand, and the Philippines, through the signing of the "Bangkok Declaration", which represented the convergence of interests in seeking progressive economic growth, social progress, and cultural development vis-à-vis the development of a regional identity.[276] The ASEAN, like ASPAC, presented itself as an indigenous Asian organization, initiated "within the community of nations of the area to help themselves."[277] Implicitly, the ASEAN had the function of fostering regional peace and security.[278] As former Indonesian Deputy Prime Minister Adam Malik noted, national and regional security loomed in the minds of the ASEAN founding fathers.[279] In particular, there was a need to address the intervention of superpowers in the Southeast Asian region that aggravated localized conflicts as well as the re-integration of Indonesia in the region after the ousting of its former dictator-Prime Minister Sukarno and cessation of *Konfrontasi*.[280] However, the Bangkok Declaration intentionally downplayed political and security matters to avoid it being viewed as a defense pact or military alliance, or a threat that favors one side over another, or an arena for the "quarrels of the strong."[281] In light of this, the ASEAN, together with ASPAC, brought in a new dawn in the Southeast Asian region and was not seen to serve any military function, but rather cater to a new concept of security that catered on coordinated and concerted political actions based on joint undertakings.[282] Furthermore, the ASEAN was viewed to serve to ease tensions amongst its member states, limit competition, and be able to produce tangible outcomes.[283] As early as the Bangkok Declaration, there was emphasis amongst the member states, like in the Bandung Conference, on consultation and consensus-based decision-making.[284]

Both ASPAC and ASEAN were then viewed as complementary forms of indigenous regionalism. As noted by former United States President

---

276 *Acharya,* Whose Ideas Matter?, p. 83; *Di Floristella,* pp. 1, 57; *Severino,* ASEAN, p. 1; *Weatherbee,* International Relations, p. 77.

277 *Acharya,* Whose Ideas Matter?, p. 83.

278 *Severino,* ASEAN, p. 1.

279 *Di Floristella,* p. 57.

280 *Severino,* ASEAN, p. 12; *Weatherbee,* International Relations, p. 77.

281 *Severino,* ASEAN, p. 11.

282 *Di Floristella,* pp. 1, 57; *Severino,* ASEAN, pp. 11-13.

283 *Di Floristella,* p. 57; *Severino,* ASEAN, p. 13.

284 *Acharya,* p. 10; *Di Floristella,* pp. 68-70; *Severino,* ASEAN Today and Tomorrow, p. 24; *Weatherbee,* International Relations, p. 99.

Richard Nixon, during this time period, there was a flourishing active regionalism and positioning of "influence of Asia's smaller states in the future political environment of the region."[285] There was a "developing coherence of Asian regional thinking" that considered "problems and loyalties in regional terms," and evolved "regional approaches to development needs and to the evolution of a new world order," having recognized that Asia could stand as a rightful counterbalance to the West and that ultimately, Asian solutions are needed for Asian problems through cooperation.[286]

This notwithstanding, the ASEAN outlives ASPAC as a regional institution, when the latter winded up operations in 1972.[287] As Acharya narrated, not only was ASPAC believed to be a Western front against China and communism but its legitimacy was questionable given the membership of the likes of South Vietnam, Australia, and New Zealand, which were admittedly of western influence.[288] ASPAC also had little chance of further expanding its membership, with other countries in the region believing it to be a sugarcoated regional security agreement, especially since all member states of ASPAC, except Malaysia, have military ties with the United States, and the latter was still active in its foreign policy in the Asia-Pacific region.[289]

The short lifespan of ASPAC did not mean however that the ASEAN had it easy. The ASEAN and its member states could not help but be confronted with criticism and cynicism within and outside the Southeast Asian region. To illustrate, some believed it to be illustrative of ASEAN lacking any concrete vision,[290] as it is a more ambitious organization by having no limits in setting goals for itself, compared to organizations of the same nature which preceded it in the region.[291] Likewise, the ASEAN gave inadvertedly the wrong signal of being non-inclusive to communist states because the founding member states were all non-communist,[292] despite the ASEAN promoted itself to be a voluntary association where all countries in the Southeast Asian region could be members to. Consequently, it could not be helped that when the ASEAN sent invitations to Burma

285 *Acharya,* Whose Ideas Matter?, p. 84.
286 *Nixon,* p. 131.
287 *Frost,* p. 3.
288 *Acharya,* Whose Ideas Matter?, pp. 84-85.
289 *Acharya,* Whose Ideas Matter?, p. 85; *Nixon,* p. 116.
290 *Hensengerth,* p. 8.
291 *Severino,* ASEAN, pp. 2-3.
292 *Hensengerth,* p. 8; *Severino,* ASEAN, p. 3.

and Cambodia, these two states declined as they wanted to preserve their non-aligned status.[293] It did not help that communist states such as China, North Vietnam, and the Soviet Union already condemned the ASEAN to be an extension of SEATO and "puppet of American imperialism."[294]

2. Historical Development of the ASEAN

The foregoing developments did not hamper the ASEAN from moving forward. The regional organization underwent an interesting historical development since its establishment in 1967, and with it multi-faceted changes were brought in the organization. This historical development could be better understood, as Cabellero-Anthony propounded, by dividing these phases loosely into three periods of (1) consolidation, (2) expansion, and (3) reconsolidation,[295] which would be elucidated below.

a. Consolidation Stage

The ASEAN's early consolidation period proved to be a rough start. Even if the ASEAN was a promising regional organization, it understandably needed to prove itself and put things in order by tackling the different internal and external issues it was facing. Being dubbed as the "Balkans of the East" in the early 1960's even if the same was not the intention of the founding member states,[296] the Southeast Asian region was in a tumultuous situation and many thought that the ASEAN perhaps would not survive its infancy.[297] Thus, it was in the course of things that each member state had a real stake with its membership and making the ASEAN work. To put things in perspective: Indonesia needs to redeem its reputation after the *Konfrontasi*; Malaysia needed to prove it was not a neo-colonial state; Singapore was the newest state after being expelled by Malaysia from the latter's federation; Philippines and Malaysia needed to work together despite their territorial disputes; and Thailand, after experi-

293 *Severino*, ASEAN, p. 3.
294 *Anwar*, p. 132; *Fifield*, p. 53.
295 *Caballero-Anthony*, p. 5.
296 *Caballero-Anthony*, p. 20; *Crozier*, p. 20.
297 *Lee*, p. ix.

encing disappointment with SEATO, had always wanted an environment where there is mutual support among neighboring countries.[298]

Three (3) things were first in order: (1) to prevent the Southeast Asian region from being embroiled further in the Cold War; (2) to manage the localized conflicts affecting the region (e.g. Indochina war situation); and (3) to establish the norms they need to adhere to vis-à-vis their inter-state and external relations. By this time, the Cold War was still ongoing and the Second Indochina War escalating. The solution was not however easily available because the Bangkok Declaration, which established ASEAN, did not include any specific reference as to how conflict management should be carried out.[299] The Bangkok Declaration only provided four (4) main points: (1) a stripped down institutional machinery wherein foreign ministers shall have annual meetings to be chaired by in rotation by the host country, with special meetings as may be required; (2) a standing committee consisting of ambassadors of the member states; (3) permanent committees for specific subjects; and (4) the establishment of national secretariats.[300]

Therefore, Malaysia was prompted in early 1968 to suggest the idea of neutralization for the ASEAN member states.[301] The initial idea was to have a collective declaration of neutrality that needs to be guaranteed by the world powers themselves and to have non-aggression treaties amongst each other.[302] Later changed to forming a "zone of peace, freedom, and neutrality," such was proposed to be implemented into two levels: first, ASEAN member states must espouse non-aggression principles amongst each other on the basis of mutual respect on sovereignty and territorial integrity, and to enact measures ensuring peace and security amongst themselves; and second, neutrality must be guaranteed by the external powers.[303]

In response, some member states articulated a more autonomous regional order during the Third ASEAN Ministerial Meeting in December 1969.[304] Three (3) options were raised: aligning with a foreign power, getting Southeast Asia to be declared a neutral zone, or coming up with

---

298 *Solidum*, pp. 22-23.
299 *Amer*, p. 1032.
300 *Crozier*, p. 19.
301 *Saravanamuttu*, p. 186.
302 *Saravanamuttu*, p. 186.
303 *Saravanamuttu*, p. 186.
304 *Saravanamuttu*, p. 186; *Tarling*, p. 159.

an indigenous form of stability, the last of which was favored.[305] Watering down further the original Malaysian proposal by disposing with foreign power guarantees, the Kuala Lumpur Declaration of 1971 which established Southeast Asia as a Zone of Peace, Freedom, and Neutrality ("ZOPFAN") or a zone "free from any form of interference of outside powers" was produced as a kind of *acquis associational* in a special meeting of the ASEAN foreign ministers in Kuala Lumpur, Malaysia in 27 November 1971.[306] ZOPFAN as the first regional political initiative of ASEAN,[307] it intended to define and guide ASEAN's relations with extra-regional states and was the first indication of the Association's ideas of what the code of conduct of states should be, within and outside the Association.[308] While being not exactly a declaration of neutrality but rather of an intent which does not impose legal obligations upon its signatories – allowing each ASEAN member state to freely construct its own meaning of the concept – ZOPFAN was fashioned to be a proactive regional strategy independent of the United States' security policy, one which was not threatening to the Indochinese states, and preventive of any further intrusion of great powers in the Southeast Asian region.[309] Indeed, ASEAN was threading on thin ice during this time with a menagerie of political and security uncertainties in the region: communists having consolidated their force in Indochina, lesser presence of the United States in the region, the brewing conflict between China and the United States, and call for collective security of the Soviet Union in the region, among others.[310]

ZOPFAN had its share of criticism, especially from Vietnam, which believed ZOPFAN to be supportive of American imperialism and out of touch from the real struggles of Southeast Asia.[311] It also received lukewarm response from even ASEAN member states such as Singapore, which preferred a balance of power in the region.[312] This notwithstanding, ZOPFAN remained in place.

---

305 *Tarling*, p. 159.
306 *Crozier*, p. 21; *Tarling*, p. 159.
307 *Weatherbee*, International Relations, p. 74.
308 *Caballero-Anthony*, p. 63.
309 *Weatherbee*, International Relations, p. 74.
310 *Caballero-Anthony*, p. 63.
311 *Weatherbee*, International Relations, p. 74.
312 *Saravanamuttu*, p. 188.

Meanwhile, communist victories in Cambodia, Laos, and Vietnam in April 1975 occurred.[313] This shifted the political problem in Southeast Asia to how structures can be devised that would accommodate both the non-communist and communist Indochina states.[314] Weatherbee narrates that ASEAN member states were particularly concerned with Vietnam and the latter's intentions in the region, given that it not only was becoming arrogant and triumphalist,[315] but there was also growing support that Vietnam and China were giving to communist insurgencies in different parts of the region.[316] What made matters more difficult for the ASEAN was that China and the Soviet Union were still heavily tied to the region despite the United States distancing itself. While China supported the Khmer Rouge in Cambodia, the Soviet Union, on the other hand, supported Laos and Vietnam.[317] This situation prompted ASEAN member states to privately discuss amongst themselves that perhaps, a US political role could prove useful as counterweight in the growing Sino-Soviet competition in the region.[318] Given the Philippines' existing bilateral alliance (maintaining military bases in the country) with the United States, the former was able to contribute to easing the situation by highlighting the "umbilical cord of the American security commitment to the region."[319] Moreover, the United States and China have just normalized their relations through the "Shanghai Communique" in 1972.[320] This led three ASEAN member states – Malaysia, Philippines, and Thailand – to reconsider their lack of relations with China, while Indonesia and Singapore remained cynical.[321] Consequently, open diplomatic relations were paved between China and these respective countries, their respective bilateral agreements each containing a "antihegemony clause" (a clause similarly found in the Shanghai

313 To illustrate, the Khmer Rouge forces successfully seized Phnom Penh after a five-year long civil war, communist forces seized the presidential palace in Saigon after defeating the United States in Vietnam, and communist victories in Laos soon followed. *Ciorciari*, pp. 13,56; *Weatherbee*, International Relations, p. 75.

314 *Weatherbee*, International Relations, p. 75.

315 *Lee*, p. x.

316 *Weatherbee*, International Relations, p. 75. See also *Ciorciari*, p. 57.

317 *Ciorciari*, pp. 58-60.

318 *Weatherbee*, International Relations, p. 75.

319 *Weatherbee*, International Relations, p. 75.

320 *Glaubitz*, p. 205; *Weatherbee*, International Relations, p. 75.

321 *Weatherbee*, International Relations, pp. 75-76.

communique), opposing any country or group of countries from establishing hegemony or any sphere of influence at any part of the region.[322]

Coincident with the rise of communist-led Indochina, Portuguese colonial rule ended in East Timor in 1975 and this prompted different indigenous political groups to race for power and occupation of said territory.[323] Soon after, the Revolutionary Front for an Independent East Timor ("FRETILIN") won and proclaimed the Democratic Republic of East Timor ("DRET").[324] Fretting the idea of a communist stronghold within reach of its territory (given that China and Hanoi ha championed the DRET), Indonesia took matters in its own hands and went for military invasion, annexing East Timor as one of its provinces[325] – an act which raised questions among other ASEAN member states as to what the true territorial ambitions of Indonesia were.[326]

The annexation of East Timor notwithstanding, it was the emergence of communist victories and total communist control in Indochina which was viewed as the bigger elephant in the room that ASEAN member states needed to address.[327] Without securing stronger regional cooperation, such elephant might thrust its tusks through regional security and safety.[328] Henceforth, in less than a year since the victories, or in February 1976, ASEAN member states conducted the ASEAN's first summit, wherein all founding member state leaders were present to, among others, strengthen political and security cooperation frameworks, establish a central secretariat (composed of a Secretary-General, three bureau directors, and support staff), and codify the norms that would dictate inter-state relations in the region.[329] There was likewise a paradigm shift to stronger economic cooperation and also, two political documents were produced in this first summit.[330]

---

322 *Glaubitz*, pp. 205, 212-213; *Weatherbee*, International Relations, p. 75. As a side note, China defines „hegemony" as any expansion of political and economic power and exercise of control. See *Glaubitz*, pp. 205-206.

323 *Weatherbee*, International Relations, p. 77.

324 *Weatherbee*, International Relations, p. 77.

325 *Cotterell*, pp. 343, 360.

326 *Weatherbee*, International Relations, p. 77.

327 *Narine*, p. 415.

328 *Tuan*, p. 64; *Weatherbee*, International Relations, p. 76.

329 *Crozier*, p. 22; *Severino*, ASEAN, pp. 6-7; *Weatherbee*, International Relations, p. 76.

330 *Crozier*, p. 21; *Tuan*, p. 64.

First, there was the Declaration of ASEAN Concord ("Bali Concord I"), which in cross-referencing the Bandung Principles and the United Nations Charter, laid down the ASEAN's objectives and principles to ensure political stability in the region.[331] Such Declaration enumerates various programs for action (ranging from political and economic, to strengthening of ASEAN machinery) in efforts to operationalize the general goals and vision embodied earlier in the Bangkok Declaration.[332] In terms of its political program, among others, the ASEAN member states called for the "strengthening of political solidarity by promoting the harmonization of views, coordinating positions and, where possible and desirable, taking common action."[333] Beginning with an informal meeting of foreign ministers, the ASEAN member states agreed to meet at least once a year to discuss imperative international issues affecting the region.[334] As for its economic program, ASEAN member states gave more focus in efforts to achieve economic cooperation in the region.[335]

Second, there was the Treaty of Amity and Cooperation ("TAC"). Being the first ASEAN treaty, the TAC codified the norms and dispute settlement mechanism that would define one member state's relationship with another.[336] In dealing with each other, the TAC provided the following five (5) points: (1) ASEAN member states "should be guided by mutual respect for the independence, sovereignty, equality, territorial integrity, and national identity of all nations;" (2) expressed "the expectation that all nations should have a right to conduct their national existence free from external interference, subversion or coercion; (3) asserted the principle that none of the signatories should interfere in the internal affairs of any of the others; (4) declared that peaceful means should be the appropriate method of resolving disputes between members and renounced the use of force; and, finally, (5) promised effective future co-operation among the signatories."[337]

The TAC was a fundamental development for the ASEAN as it was a "charter of security and political dialogue and cooperation that aimed to

---

331 Declaration of ASEAN Concord, Bali, Indonesia, 24 February 1976. [hereinafter "Bali Concord I"].

332 *Amer*, p. 1033.

333 Bali Concord I, A(1); *Weatherbee*, International Relations, p. 76.

334 *Weatherbee*, International Relations, p. 76.

335 *Crozier*, p. 21.

336 *Narine*, Forty Years of ASEAN, p. 415; *Tuan*, p. 64.

337 1976 Treaty of Amity and Cooperation in Southeast Asia, entered into force 24 February 1976. See also*Crozier, p. 22; Severino, ASEAN, p. 7.*

ensure stability in the Southeast Asia by cooperation" amongst the member states on the "basis of self-confidence, self-reliance, and mutual respect for one another."[338] The TAC highlights vis-à-vis conflict resolution three (3) factors such as non-interference, resolution of conflict through peaceful means, and overall cooperation.[339] Such helped to stabilize relations among the ASEAN member states and reduce any further possibility of violent conflict.[340] In what seemed to be a convergence of political outlook from the ASEAN member states, they would not allow disputes and/or conflicts to serve as stumbling blocks or erupt into more violent situations as what history taught them.[341] Congruently, member states endorsed familiar principles prevalent in the region as well as the importance of cooperation for economic development, peace, and stability, which evinced the member states' high understanding of how to properly handle conflict with each other and within the grouping.[342] And while the Declaration of ASEAN Concord could be thought as something mutually exclusive to ASEAN member states, the TAC became applicable to other parties in Southeast Asia which were not yet members of ASEAN.[343] It later became open to accession from non-Southeast Asian countries which wish to adhere to the norms enshrined in the TAC.[344]

In connection to the two documents produced during the ASEAN first summit, ASEAN member states seemed to have built more confidence, familiarity, and understanding of each one's position on problems and issues through informal and formal meetings amongst their representatives and heads of states, albeit the same was through a gradual process.[345] But then again, such gradual process could easily be attributed to the decision-making process the ASEAN has adopted for itself. In a nutshell, as the same would be further discussed in the next Chapter, the ASEAN adopts a decision-making process based on consultation and consensus rooted on tradition found in Indonesia, Malaysia, and the Philippines.[346] Later to be known as the "ASEAN Way", focus is given on principles

338 *Crozier*, p. 22.

339 *Amer*, p. 1034; *Tarling*, p. 159.

340 *Severino*, ASEAN, p. 16.

341 *Severino*, ASEAN, pp. 12-13.

342 *Amer*, p. 1035; *Tarling*, p. 159.

343 Treaty of Amity and Cooperation, art. 18.

344 First Protocol to the Treaty of Amity and Cooperation, art. 1; Second Protocol to the Treaty of Amity and Cooperation, art. 1. See also *Amer*, p. 1033.

345 *Amer*, p. 1036.

346 *Acharya*, Bandung Revisited, p. 10; *Amer*, p. 1036.

of informality and mutual respect, rather than reliance on formalistic or legalistic mechanisms.[347]

These developments at hand, the ASEAN made efforts to call for a friendly and harmonious relationship with Vietnam but to no avail.[348] Nonetheless, Vietnam's relationship with the ASEAN improved by its establishment of bilateral diplomatic relations with the member states and conducting a peace offensive.[349] But in a sudden change of course, and receiving renewed support from the Soviet Union, Vietnam deposed the Khmer Rouge regime and invaded Cambodia in December 1978.[350] Despite intra-ASEAN friction and needing to raise arms, the ASEAN had a coherent front against the invasion and gave full cooperation for the conflict's resolution.[351]

Meanwhile, Brunei Darussalam joined the ASEAN in January 1984 after finally gaining its sovereignty and being extended an open invitation to join ASEAN in the late 1970's and joining as an observer the 14th Foreign Ministers Meeting in Manila in July 1981.[352]

At this juncture, it becomes important to note that while the ASEAN is focused in resolving conflict in the region and maintaining regional security, the ASEAN also equally valued economic development;[353] thus, a majority of agreements that followed the TAC were all economically motivated, the treaty following the TAC being a Preferential Tariff Agreement.[354] Strong economic cooperation was pursued through the establishment of an ASEAN Free Trade Area ("AFTA") through a framework agreement in 1992. Market liberalization in different economic sectors through a framework agreement on services in 1995, a Dispute Settlement Mechanism vis-à-vis economic issues through a protocol in 1996, and an ASEAN Investment Area through another framework agreement in 1998 were established.[355] ASEAN and its member states in the meantime came up instead with Declarations as to other concerns, which did not impose any legal obligation upon its signatories. And it was notably only after the

---

347 *Acharya,* Bandung Revisited, p. 10.
348 *Weatherbee,* International Relations, p. 77.
349 *Weatherbee,* International Relations, p. 77.
350 *Narine,* Forty Years of ASEAN, p. 415.
351 *Narine,* Forty Years of ASEAN, pp. 415-417. See also *Weatherbee,* International Relations, pp. 80-83.
352 *Crozier,* p. 20; *Thambipillai,* pp. 44-45.
353 *Crozier,* p. 23.
354 *Severino,* ASEAN Today and Tomorrow, p. 25.
355 *Yoshimatsu,* p. 122.

establishment of the AFTA in 1992, when binding agreements came at a more increasing frequency.[356]

Based on the foregoing developments it would be easy to assume that the ASEAN only centered on economic issues. However, security concerns were equally addressed. In the mid-1990's, the ASEAN member states believed it was important to hold dialogues as a result of the changing political climate brought by the cessation of the Cold War, reforms being implemented in China, and the settlement of the conflict in Cambodia.[357] By this time, the Paris Conference in Cambodia was already held in 1989, with the Paris Peace Treaty ending the external dimension of the Third Indochina War in October 1991.[358] Although its intervention was only partial in the resolution of the Vietnam-Cambodia conflict, the ASEAN was arguably at a high point vis-à-vis its unity and international effectiveness, diplomatic maneuvering, and lobbying efforts.[359] This eventually led to at least two notable developments within the organization.

First, the ASEAN in January 1992 thought it was high time to formalized political-security matters,[360] and consequently intensify dialogues with external partners, by using the post-ministerial conferences, which initially was economically motivated.[361] This plan of action eventually led to the establishment of the ASEAN Regional Forum ("ARF") in 1994, which became the forum for discussion amongst interested parties in political and security matters affecting the Asia-Pacific region.[362] The establishment of the ARF was not without criticism as others saw it as a mere "talk shop".[363] The efficacy of the ARF in question notwithstanding, it provided a forum, albeit oft informally, for state representatives to talk over about their disagreements.[364]

Second, the office of the ASEAN Secretary-General was reorganized during the ASEAN Fourth Summit in 1992. While formerly catering simply to the Secretariat, the Secretary-General could now cater to the entire Association, even being able to recommend policies for the consideration

356 *Severino,* ASEAN Today and Tomorrow, p. 25.
357 *Severino,* ASEAN, p. 93.
358 *Narine,* Forty Years of ASEAN, p. 417.
359 *Chongkittavorn*, p. 40; *Narine,* Forty Years of ASEAN, p. 417.
360 *Caballero-Anthony*.
361 *Severino,* ASEAN, p. 93.
362 *Severino,* ASEAN, p. 93.
363 *Narine,* Forty Years of ASEAN, p. 418.
364 *Narine,* Forty Years of ASEAN, p. 418.

of the concerned ASEAN bodies.[365] Also, the ASEAN Secretariat was made properly professional through the initiation of an "open and competitive recruitment" and its set of functions and responsibilities was expanded to initiate, coordinate and implement ASEAN activities.[366]

b. Expansion Stage

It did not take long and the ASEAN went through an enlargement phase in the late 1990's through the membership of Vietnam in 1995, Laos and Myanmar in 1997, and Cambodia in 1999.[367] After years since its inception, the ASEAN faced a duplicity of membership from the original five to ten members.[368] Such expansion phase is said to be attributable to the gradual process of rapprochement between the ASEAN member states and Cambodia, Laos, Burma, and Vietnam, respectively.[369]

---

365 *Crozier*, p. 24.

366 *Crozier*, p. 24; *Solidum*, p. 30.

367 *Amer*, p. 1037; *Caballero-Anthony*, p. 5; *Tarling*, p. 161. See also *Weatherbee*, International Relations, pp. 93-96.

368 *Caballero-Anthony*, p. 5.

369 *Amer*, p. 1037. As Amer narrated herein, „xxx The gradual rapprochement with Laos and Vietnam went hand in hand with the regional initiatives to resolve the Cambodian conflict in the latter half of the 1980s, with the major breakthrough in improved relations following the formal resolution of the Cambodian conflict through the Paris Agreements on Cambodia of October 1991. The rapprochement between ASEAN and Vietnam was displayed by the establishment of diplomatic relations between Vietnam and Singapore and between Vietnam and Brunei Darussalam, respectively, thus bringing about normal relations between Vietnam and all ASEAN members. Vietnam acceded to the Bali Treaty in 1992, became an ASEAN Observer the same year and was granted full membership in ASEAN in 1995. In the case of Laos, accession to the Bali Treaty also took place in 1992 and the same year Laos became an ASEAN Observer. Finally, Laos was granted full membership in the association in 1997. Following the United Nations peacekeeping operation and the formation of a new coalition government after general elections in May 1993, Cambodia's relations with ASEAN were normalized and expanded. Cambodia acceded to the Bali Treaty in 1994 and became an ASEAN Observer in 1995. Finally, Burma has been brought closer to ASEAN through a process which has officially been termed 'constructive engagement' by ASEAN. Burma acceded to the Bali Treaty in 1995, became an ASEAN Observer in 1996 and was granted full membership in 1997. This overall process led to the expansion of membership in ASEAN from six to nine members between 1995 and 1997. Cambodia was supposed to have joined the organization in July 1997 alongside Laos and Myanmar but

In connection to this, Amer argued that ASEAN's success in being able to expand and have all Southeast Asian nations as members could be attributed to the existing conflict management mechanism the organization had in place.[370] This was seconded by others which said that the norms ASEAN and its member states live by, as codified in the TAC, prevailed in whatever role ASEAN and its member states played in the resolution of prevailing conflicts within the region and its neighboring non-ASEAN countries.[371] As experts such as Caballero-Anthony and Tarling among others observed, norms and mechanisms to manage regional order became more prevalent in the active role the ASEAN has played: not only were the norms kept within the ASEAN member states but there was an active socialization of those not within the organization so that they may likewise internalize the same norms in the conduct of their own inter-state relations.[372] This even underlined the ASEAN member states' decision to make it compulsory in 1987 for one to accede to the TAC as a condition precedent before being conferred ASEAN membership.[373] Using such norms and existing mechanisms of conflict management, ASEAN member states eventually were able to ease the animosity between them and the Indochina states and influence Myanmar to abandon their isolationist policy.[374]

c. Reconsolidation Stage

The next stage in the historical development of the ASEAN began with a hard challenge to the organization. The ASEAN and its member states were confronted with a debilitating financial crisis in July 1997.[375] The first symptoms started in Thailand, when foreign currency speculators attacked the Thai Baht and the Thai government's inability to protect

its membership was put on hold because of the internal political problems in the country, i.e. the fighting in July 1997 which led to the ousting of the then First Prime Minister Norodom Ranariddh by Second Prime Minister Hun Sen. Eventually, Cambodia was admitted as ASEAN'S 10th member through a decision taken at the sixth ASEAN summit in Hanoi on 16 December 1998."

370 *Amer*, p. 1037.

371 *Caballero-Anthony*, p. 5; *Tarling*, pp. 160-161.

372 *Caballero-Anthony*, p. 5.

373 *Severino*, ASEAN, pp. 94-95.

374 *Amer*, pp. 1037-1039.

375 *Narine*, Forty Years of ASEAN, p. 419.

it caused its value to decline.[376] Soon after, the crisis rapidly spread to other countries of supposedly "Asian economic miracle" – causing local currencies to devalue and economies to crash – and the ASEAN as an organization seemed unable to give a regional response.[377] When the crisis struck, the ASEAN was not in the right position to respond outright and cohesively – it admittedly lacked economic resources and sufficient institutional structures.[378] Instead of having a direct hand in resolving the financial issue, ASEAN financial ministers were prompted to put up appeals instead before the International Monetary Fund ("IMF") and larger economies like the United States, European Union, and Japan to help.[379] And though some were of the opinion that it was unreasonable to expect the ASEAN to directly deal with the damage caused by the financial crisis,[380] such still struck the ASEAN in three (3) points: (1) it undermined the confidence in whatever economic success the ASEAN has achieved; (2) the sort of inability to respond undermined claims of being a strong, united regional front; and (3) the crisis introduced problems that could not be resolved solely by the ASEAN way.[381] Worse, international media and observers faulted the ASEAN for its apparent lack of response to the haze that engulfed the region in the latter half of 1997 to 1998, the coup in Cambodia, the human rights complaints in Myanmar right after its admission in the Association, and the violence and human rights violations that occurred in East Timor after it voted for independence from Indonesia.[382] The goodwill the ASEAN has established thus far seemed to have dissipated, as it was seen only as a failure.[383]

In efforts to remedy the tainted reputation suffered by the ASEAN during the 1997 financial crisis, the organization thought it would be better to reevaluate its purpose, significance, and goals – thus entering its recon-

---

376 *Caballero-Anthony,* p. 204; *Narine,* Forty Years of ASEAN, p. 420.

377 *Caballero-Anthony,* p. 204; *Funston,* p. 206; *Rüland/Jetschke*, p. 398.

378 *Narine,* Forty Years of ASEAN, p. 420; *Narine*, p. 374.

379 *Caballero-Anthony,* p. 205; *Funston,* p. 213; *Narine,* Forty Years of ASEAN, p. 420.

380 *Narine,* ASEAN, p. 374.

381 *Narine,* Forty Years of ASEAN, p. 420.

382 *Caballero-Anthony,* pp. 208-209, 213-216; *Funston,* p. 206; *Narine,* Forty Years of ASEAN, p. 421. For more information about the human rights violations in Myanmar during this time period see *Emmerson*, pp. 71-74. For more information about the alleged inaction of ASEAN in addressing the East Timor crisis, see *Haacke*, pp. 65-71.

383 *Funston,* p. 206.

solidation phase.[384] One of the proposals forwarded during the immediately following ASEAN Ministers Meeting was for the ASEAN to adopt "flexible engagement" (deviating from the principle of non-intervention) to enable ASEAN to quickly avoid and/or address problems and issues with regional repercussions: this meant the "practice of ASEAN members discussing the domestic policies of other members when those policies had regional/cross-border implications."[385] Only Thailand and the Philippines supported this idea however as most were of the opinion that such open criticism could open up old wounds ASEAN sought to alleviate.[386] If one would recall, the ASEAN was built on conflicts and misunderstandings between the original member states. It was further founded on a mutual understanding that what happens inside one borders remains the concern of the affected member state alone. Thus, there is the risk that "flexible engagement" could disturb the peace the ASEAN has long worked for.

Compromising, all agreed on the use of "enhanced interaction", a process wherein individual member states could comment on domestic policies of another, should the same has regional repercussions, but would leave the ASEAN out of the equation.[387] Aside from adopting a variance of its principle of non-intervention, the ASEAN likewise adopted in the December 1997 meeting in Kuala Lumpur the so-called ASEAN Vision 2020, which called for partnership in dynamic development – the purpose of which was the encouragement of closer economic integration within the region," a community of caring societies, and a more outward-looking ASEAN.[388] Under said ASEAN Vision 2020, ASEAN member states would endeavor to intensify further economic cooperation and integration amongst each other.[389] Plans of action to put the ASEAN Vision 2020 into fruition, beginning with the Hanoi Plan of Action of 1998 were thereafter made.[390]

---

384 *Caballero-Anthony*, p. 6.

385 *Acharya*, Whose Ideas Matter?, p. 128; *Funston*, p. 206; *Narine*, Forty Years of ASEAN, p. 421.

386 *Acharya*, Whose Ideas Matter?, p. 132; *Funston*, p. 206; *Narine*, Forty Years of ASEAN, p. 421.

387 *Acharya*, Whose Ideas Matter?, p. 134; *Narine*, Forty Years of ASEAN, p. 421.

388 See *Crozier*, p. 24; *Narine*, Forty Years of ASEAN, p. 420.

389 ASEAN Vision 2020; See also *Crozier*, p. 24.

390 *Crozier*, p. 24.The Hanoi Plan Action sought to accelerate the full implementation of the AFTA, expansion of the ASEAN Investment Area, and liberalization of trade in services, among others. See *Narine*, Forty Years of ASEAN, p. 420.

Alongside these changes, the office of the ASEAN Secretariat was again revamped and was given new responsibilities.[391] Congruently, an ASEAN Surveillance Program ("ASP") was established in February 1998 (after being proposed during the ASEAN Foreign Ministers Meeting in November 1997), which would work hand-in-hand with the IMF and World Bank in monitoring economic fundamentals and serving as an early warning system for any economic problems.[392] The ASEAN also announced the creation of the ASEAN Action Plan on Social Safety Nets in October 1998, which had a corresponding task force "with the objective of developing and implementing an action plan to ameliorate the impact of the crisis."[393] In line with the creation of the said action plan, Thailand proposed the ASEAN Troika, which would be composed of past, present, and future ASEAN Standing Committee, to address regional issues and stability.[394] The ASEAN Troika would not be a decision-making body however, and at the same time is prohibited from undertaking tasks not assigned to it by the ASEAN or delving into internal matters of the ASEAN member states.[395]

The reconsolidation stage, from the late 1990's onwards, paved way as well to political and security developments in the ASEAN. In March 1997, the ASEAN established the Southeast Asian Nuclear Weapons Free Zone ("SEANWFZ") as an integral component of the ZOPFAN and contribution to the global nuclear anti-proliferation regime, which shows the ASEAN commitment to promote international peace and security.[396] Modeled after the 1963 Treaty of Tlatelolco declaring Latin America a nuclear-free zone and the 1985 Treaty of Rarotonga establishing the South Pacific Nuclear Free Zone,[397] signatories will not "develop, manufacture, or otherwise acquire, possess, or have control over nuclear weapons; station or transport nuclear weapons by any means; or test or use nuclear weapons in the region."[398] They shall also not be allowed to dump, discharge, or dispose radioactive material or waste anywhere in the area covered by the

---

391 *Narine,* Forty Years of ASEAN, p. 420.

392 *Acharya,* Whose Ideas Matter?, p. 134; *Narine,* Forty Years of ASEAN, p. 420.

393 ASEAN Action Plan on Social Safety Nets, § 3; *Narine,* Forty Years of ASEAN, p. 420.

394 *Narine,* Forty Years of ASEAN, p. 420.

395 *Haacke,* pp. 73-74; *Narine,* Forty Years of ASEAN, p. 420.

396 *Severino,* ASEAN, p. 14; *Solidum,* p. 90.

397 *Solidum,* p. 90; *Weatherbee,* International Relations, p. 86.

398 *Severino,* ASEAN, p. 14. Treaty on the Southeast Asia Nuclear Weapons Free Zone, art. 3(1).

Treaty.[399] Other states are likewise prohibited from doing the same and may only be allowed for matters of transport.[400]

In 11 September 2001, the entire world was caught in surprise by the terrorist attacks in the United States. The United States thereafter announced that the Southeast Asian region was the second front on the global war on terror.[401] Albeit ASEAN member states had varying degrees of enthusiasm in the United States-led war against terrorism, they all continued cooperation and coordination as regards regional counterterrorism measures, considering that terrorism problems in many Southeast Asian countries are localized and terrorist networks might be operating in the region (e.g. Abu Sayyaf Group in the Philippines, Jema'ah Islamiyah in Indonesia).[402] Recognizing that terrorist groups' organizational, recruitment, and financial scope is transnational, the ASEAN came up in the November 2001 ASEAN Summit with a Declaration on Joint Action to Counter Terrorism, wherein they expressed their joint commitment to combat terrorism, including initiating cooperative joint practical counterterrorism measures that are in line with a member state's specific circumstances.[403] It bears mentioning

---

399 Treaty on the Southeast Asia Nuclear Weapons Free Zone, art. 3(3).

400 *Severino,* ASEAN, p. 14. Treaty on the Southeast Asia Nuclear Weapons Free Zone, art. 3(2).

401 *Caballero-Anthony,* p. 216; *Weatherbee,* International Relations, p. 193.

402 *Caballero-Anthony,* p. 213; *Weatherbee,* Southeast Asia and ASEAN: Running in Place, pp. 192-193.

403 *Weatherbee,* International Relations, p. 195.These measures include the following (See ASEAN Declaration on Joint Action to Counter Terrorism; *Caballero-Anthony,* p. 217.):
"1. Review and strengthen our national mechanisms to combat terrorism;
"2. Call for the early signing/ratification of or accession to all relevant anti-terrorist conventions including the International Convention for the Suppression of the Financing of Terrorism;
"3. Deepen cooperation among our front-line law enforcement agencies in combatting terrorism and sharing "best practices";
"4. Study relevant international conventions on terrorism with the view to integrating them with ASEAN mechanisms on combating international terrorism;
"5. Enhance information/intelligence exchange to facilitate the flow of information, in particular, on terrorists and terrorist organisations, their movement and funding, and any other information needed to protect lives, property and the security of all modes of travel;
"6. Strengthen existing cooperation and coordination between the AMMTC and other relevant ASEAN bodies in countering, preventing and suppressing all forms of terrorists (sic) acts. Particular attention would be paid to finding ways to combat terrorist organisations, support infrastructure and funding and bringing the perpetrators to justice;

that while practically speaking, the counterterrorism measures laid down in said Declaration were not new, they were meant to increase the capacity of existing frameworks in combating transnational crime.[404]

In addition to the foregoing, the ASEAN member states under the ASEAN framework entered into an Agreement on Information Exchange and Establishment of Communication Procedures on 07 May 2002 to promote cooperation in combating transnational crime, including terrorism.[405] Participation and cooperation shall be done through the establishment of communication networks, logistical arrangements, combined training, and border controls, among others.[406] Malaysia, Indonesia, and the Philippines were the first signatories to the said agreement, to be followed by Cambodia, Brunei, and Thailand.[407]

Thereafter, the ASEAN and the United States issued a Joint Declaration for Cooperation to Combat International Terrorism on 01 August 2002, which committed the ASEAN member states and the United States to "improve intelligence gathering efforts, confidence-building measures, and enhance mutual cooperation."[408]

Counter-terrorism measures were also initiated under the auspices of the ASEAN-led ARF. Two workshops were held after the 11 September attacks: first, was the Malaysia-United States workshop in confidence-building measures on 24-25 March 2002 in Honolulu, while the other was a Thailand-Australia workshop on terrorism prevention on 17-19 April

---

"7. Develop regional capacity building programmes to enhance existing capabilities of ASEAN member countries to investigate, detect, monitor and report on terrorist acts;

"8. Discuss and explore practical ideas and initiatives to increase ASEAN's role in and involvement with the international community including extra-regional partners within existing frameworks such as the ASEAN + 3, the ASEAN Dialogue Partners and the ASEAN Regional Forum (ARF), to make the fight against terrorism a truly regional and global endeavor;

"9. Strengthen cooperation at bilateral, regional and international levels in combating terrorism in a comprehensive manner and affirm that at the international level the United Nations should play a major role in this regard."

404 *Weatherbee*, International Relations, p. 195.

405 Agreement on Information Exchange and Establishment of Communication Procedures, arts. 2 and 3; *Caballero-Anthony*, p. 217.

406 Agreement on Information Exchange and Establishment of Communication Procedures, arts. 4 and 5; *Caballero-Anthony*, p. 217.

407 *Caballero-Anthony*, p. 217; *Soesilowati*, p. 235.

408 *Caballero-Anthony*, p. 217.

2002.[409] Recommendations and findings from these workshops formed part of the ARF statement during its ninth meeting in July 2002.[410]

It should be noted at this point of discussion that in dealing with terrorism, the ASEAN grappled with challenges on existing regional mechanisms, to which threats of terrorism threw a new dimension to.[411] Even with a united regional front, efforts have been stalled and/or hampered by domestic politics and public sensitivities, especially in Muslim-majority countries such as Malaysia and Indonesia, or those with large Muslim-minorities such as the Philippines and Thailand.[412] This notwithstanding, the ASEAN equivocally rejected any identification of terrorism with religion and was clear in saying that "terrorist elements" refer to Islamic extremists.[413]

In connection to terrorism, one could also witness developments vis-à-vis transnational crime during the same time period. Following the hard times defined by the Cold War, the Indochina conflicts, East Timor human rights violations, and violence in Myanmar among others, an overall regime of inter-state peace and relative stability has settled in Southeast Asia, wherein security threats to Southeast Asian nations by virtue of policies and actions of other states have greatly diminished.[414] Yet, one could witness a changing face to security and stability unveil, brought by new forms of transnational problems that have regional consequences.[415] Undeniably, one of these transnational problems, together with terrorism, is transnational crime. In relation thereto, the United Nations Convention against Transnational Organized Crime ("TOC" or the "Palermo Convention") is the main international instrument as regards the fight against transnational crime.[416] Adopted in 2001 and entered into force in 2003, ASEAN member states are signatories to the TOC, with the aim of enhancing international cooperation against the expansion and strengthening of criminal syndicate networks around the globe.[417] That said, the ASEAN

---

409 *Caballero-Anthony*, p. 217.

410 *Caballero-Anthony*, p. 218; *Weatherbee*, International Relations, p. 195.

411 *Caballero-Anthony*, p. 218.

412 *Caballero-Anthony*, p. 218; *Soesilowati*, pp. 233-235; *Weatherbee*, International Relations, p. 194.

413 ASEAN Declaration on Joint Action to Counter Terrorism; *Soesilowati*, p. 234; *Weatherbee*, International Relations, p. 195.

414 *Severino*, ASEAN, p. 33.

415 *Severino*, ASEAN, p. 33.

416 *Weatherbee*, International Relations, p. 200.

417 *Weatherbee*, International Relations, p. 200.

had always articulated the problem of transnational crime in security terms and already had a declaratory anti-crime regime as early as 1976 with the Bali Concord I, when it called for the "intensification of cooperation among member states as well as with the relevant international bodies in the prevention and eradication of the abuse of narcotics and the illegal trafficking of drugs."[418] However, the first effort to establish a regional framework happened was the 1997 ASEAN Declaration on Transnational Crime, through the establishment of an ASEAN Ministers' Meeting on Transnational Crime ("AMMTC"), which shall coordinate activities, among others, between the ASEAN Senior Officials on Drug Matters ("ASOD") and the ASEAN Chiefs of Police Association ("ASEANAPOL"), and other officials in charge of functional areas such as customs, consular services, and immigration.[419]

The agreements and developments on counter-terrorism and against transnational crime aside, one of the most significant political and security developments during the reconsolidation stage of the ASEAN would probably be the Declaration of ASEAN Concord II in Bali in 2003, where ASEAN member states decided to establish a three-pillared ASEAN Community, the completion date of which is in 2015:[420]

> "An ASEAN Community shall be established comprising three pillars, namely political and security cooperation, economic cooperation, and socio-cultural cooperation that are closely intertwined and mutually reinforcing for the purpose of ensuring durable peace, stability and shared prosperity in the region".[421]

The ASEAN envisions further implementation of liberalization and cooperation measures and the enhancement of cooperation and integration in a wide array of areas:[422] the ASEAN Economic Community ("AEC") envisions an integrated single market and production base, building on the AFTA, AIA, and the ASEAN Framework Agreement on Services ("AFAS"); the ASEAN Security Community ("ASC"), on taking political and security cooperation to a higher plane – while still respecting the principle of non-intervention, more weight is given to security structures

---

418 Declaration of ASEAN Concord I, §C (4); *Emmers*, p. 15; *Weatherbee*, International Relations, p. 201.

419 *Severino*, ASEAN, pp. 33-34; *Weatherbee*, International Relations, p. 201.

420 *Crozier*, p. 25.

421 Declaration of ASEAN Concord II; *Crozier*, p. 25.

422 *Crozier*, p. 26.

such as the TAC and the ARF; the ASEAN Socio-Cultural Community ("ASCC"), in building a regional community furthering state building and development, enabling states to provide basic services to the poorest citizen.[423] To put things into fruition, the ASEAN member states adopted during the tenth ASEAN Summit in November 2004 the Vientiane Action Programme ("VAP"), which prescribes specific measures to operationalize the Declaration of Bali Concord II.[424]

Riding the momentum built by the Declaration of Bali Concord II and Vientiane Action Plan, Malaysia proposed in 2004 the need to instill changes to the institutional framework, working methods, and rules of the ASEAN to successfully establish an ASEAN community – thus, the need to draft a Charter.[425] At the 11th ASEAN Summit in Kuala Lumpur, Malaysia in 2005, the ASEAN issued a Declaration on the ASEAN Charter, and with it, constituted an Eminent Persons Group ("EPG"), which was composed of representatives from the different ASEAN member states, tasked of submitting recommendations and ideas for the Charter and encouraged to conduct a bottom-up approach of consulting with civil society groups, business sectors, and other parties that might have a stake on the new Charter.[426]

As per the Declaration, the ASEAN Charter was meant to be a constitutional document embodying the fundamentals, ideals, goals, and structure of ASEAN cooperation meant to meet the needs of the ASEAN Community and beyond, and at the same time, promising a "forward-looking, rules-based organization in a normative framework of democracy, transparency, and governance, while upholding the ASEAN way of consensus decision-making, respect for sovereignty and non-interference."[427] Based on this, one could predict a paradigm shift from informalistic to formalistic mechanisms in the organization. The EPG thereafter conducted various consultative meetings with different groups,[428] and made final recommendations

423 *Lim*, pp. 34-37; *Narine*, Forty Years of ASEAN, p. 422.

424 *Severino*, ASEAN, p. 37.

425 *Caballero-Anthony*, pp. 71-72.

426 *Caballero-Anthony*, The ASEAN Charter, p. 72.

427 *Narine*, Forty Years of ASEAN, p. 422; *Weatherbee*, International Relations, p. 105.

428 *Caballero-Anthony*, The ASEAN Charter, pp. 72-73. For purposes of clarity, Track II diplomacy or "backchannel diplomacy" is the practice of "non-governmental, informal and unofficial contacts and activities between private citizens or groups of individuals, sometimes called 'non-state actors'".

during the twelfth ASEAN Summit in the Philippines in January 2007,[429] among which included the establishment of a dispute settlement mechanism, the use of majority vote in concerns other than security and foreign policy, monitoring mechanisms to ensure compliance amongst member states, and imposition of sanctions, including expulsion or suspension of membership, in case of breach.[430] The EPG also called, alongside the existing norms and principles of the ASEAN, "the active strengthening of democratic values, good governance, rejection of unconstitutional and undemocratic changes of government, through the respect and institutionalization of the rule of law, including humanitarian law."[431]

In August 2007, the ASEAN celebrated its 40th founding Anniversary and by this time, it has been acknowledged as the engine of regionalism in Asia-Pacific with its multiple achievements and has gained a "paradigmatic status" in cooperation as "new regionalism."[432] Commemoration of the 40th Anniversary was planned for the 13th ASEAN Summit in Singapore on November 2007. A High Level Task Force in the meantime was already appointed to draft the ASEAN Charter, taking into consideration the reports given by the EPG, making sure to include practical and doable provisions.[433]

Prior to said 13th ASEAN Summit though, the ASEAN was caught by surprise with demonstrations in Myanmar in September 2007: week-long demonstrations by Buddhist monks in different parts of Myanmar were met with violence and severe repression by the military junta.[434] Such violence and corresponding human rights violation perpetrated by the military junta threatened to dampen any celebratory mood and there were calls for ASEAN to either disavow Myanmar or otherwise react to the situation.[435] Though not as quick as one could expect, the ASEAN then made a response condemning the violence committed and requested Myanmar's government to exercise restraint as well as seek political

429 *Caballero-Anthony,* The ASEAN Charter, p. 73.

430 *Caballero-Anthony,* The ASEAN Charter, p. 74; *Narine,* Forty Years of ASEAN, p. 422; *Weatherbee,* International Relations, p. 396.

431 *Caballero-Anthony,* The ASEAN Charter, p. 74.

432 *Rüland/Jetschke,* p. 398; *Weatherbee,* International Relations, p. 91.

433 *Caballero-Anthony,* The ASEAN Charter, p. 75.

434 *Caballero-Anthony,* The ASEAN Charter, p. 75; *Emmerson,* ASEAN's" Black Swans", pp. 71-72.

435 *Caballero-Anthony,* The ASEAN Charter, p. 75; *Emmerson,* ASEAN's" Black Swans", p. 72.

solutions to foster national unity.[436] And while one can naturally expect that the 13th ASEAN Summit would not push through, it still did and even with the participation of Myanmar.[437] The 40th founding anniversary was still commemorated and the ASEAN member states momentously accepted the ASEAN Charter during the said summit, becoming ASEAN law later in December 2008.[438]

Albeit one would expect that the EPG's recommendations vis-à-vis the ASEAN Charter would be accepted based on the idea of the supposed paradigm shift in the regional organization, the body of text constituting the Charter was a watered-down version of the initial inputs and recommendations given by the EPG. In other words, the 180-degree paradigm shift most were expecting with the ASEAN Charter did not happen. Nonetheless, the ASEAN Charter was arguably able to get pass the hurdle of being able to accommodate the least democratic countries in the Association.[439]

At the same time, the ASEAN Charter still was able to cater to the following purposes: "(1) formally accord ASEAN legal personality, (2) establish greater institutional accountability and compliance system, and (3) reinforce the perception of ASEAN as a serious regional player in the future of the Asia-Pacific region."[440] Stating it differently, the ASEAN by virtue of the Charter now has a juridical personality that, among others, enables it to enter into agreements on its own right; a culture of adherence to rule and serious compliance to obligations shall supplement the ASEAN way; the stakes facing ASEAN are high and hopefully through the Charter, ASEAN shall be able to reinforce its credibility considering the criticism it has faced previously.[441] Likewise, the ASEAN Charter introduced changes to the institutional structure of the Association through, among others, the introduction of an ASEAN Coordinating Council ("ACC") composed of ASEAN foreign ministers, ASEAN human rights body, single chairmanship for key high-level ASEAN bodies, and appointment of permanent representatives to ASEAN.[442]

---

436 *Emmerson*, ASEAN's" Black Swans", p. 72.
437 *Caballero-Anthony*, The ASEAN Charter, p. 75.
438 *Emmerson*, ASEAN's" Black Swans", pp. 70-71; *Weatherbee*, International Relations, p. 105.
439 *Weatherbee*, International Relations, p. 105.
440 *Caballero-Anthony*, The ASEAN Charter, p. 76.
441 *Caballero-Anthony*, The ASEAN Charter, pp. 76-82.
442 *Caballero-Anthony*, The ASEAN Charter, p. 76; *Weatherbee*, International Relations, p. 106.

The Charter is also mentioned to be the first step taken by the ASEAN by which human rights are codified within ASEAN operative rules.[443] In purview of Article 14 of the Charter, protection and promotion of human rights shall be a high priority among ASEAN member states and in connection therewith, an ASEAN human rights body shall be established.[444] Albeit the Charter was silent as to how the same would be operationalized,[445] the ASEAN established on 23 October 2008 the ASEAN Intergovernmental Commission on Human Rights ("AICHR") following such pronouncement in the Charter.[446] Its Terms of Reference ("TOR") mandated it to focus primarily in the promotion of human rights and act as an advisory body to the ASEAN Secretariat and member states.[447] Acting on its mandate, the AICHR drafted and proposed the ASEAN Human Rights Declaration ("AHRD"), which was unanimously adopted and affirmed by all ASEAN member states in the 18th of November 2012.[448] The said declaration explicitly adopts the civil and political rights as well as the economic and social rights enshrined in the Universal Declaration of Human Rights,[449] but at the same time, explicitly adds the right to "safe drinking water and sanitation",[450] "the right to a safe, clean and sustainable environment",[451] protection from discrimination in treatment for "people suffering from communicable diseases, including HIV/AIDS",[452] the right to development which enjoins ASEAN member states to enact projects "aimed at poverty alleviation, the creation of conditions including the protection and sustainability of the environment",[453] and the right to peace wherein every person have the right to enjoy peace "within an ASEAN framework of security, stability, neutrality, and freedom…".

In addition to the foregoing, the ASEAN also had good developments with regard fostering relations with its external partners. As early as 1972, the ASEAN has fostered a dialogue partnership with the European Econo-

443 *Tan*, p. 5.
444 ASEAN Charter, art. 14.
445 ASEAN Charter, art. 14.
446 *Tan*, p. 4.
447 *Kelsall*, p. 2.
448 ASEAN Phnom Penh Statement, 18 November 2012.
449 ASEAN Human Rights Declaration, arts. 10, 26.
450 ASEAN Human Rights Declaration, art. 28(e).
451 ASEAN Human Rights Declaration, art. 28(f).
452 ASEAN Human Rights Declaration, art. 28(g).
453 ASEAN Human Rights Declaration, arts. 35, 36.

mic Community.[454] This dialogue partnership paved way to a more formal relationship through the 1980 European Community-ASEAN Cooperation Agreement, which institutionalized the ASEAN-EU Ministerial Meetings ("AEMM"), which occurs once every two years.[455] Such was followed by the launching of the Asia-Europe Meetings ("ASEM"), which was launched in 1996 and conducted once every two years, alternating between Asia and Europe, with Asian and European ministers meeting each other in between summits.[456]

In addition to the European Union, by 1977, the ASEAN has already dialogue partnerships with the likes of Japan, Australia, New Zealand, and ASEAN foreign ministers regularly met with their counterparts from other countries, otherwise known as the ASEAN's "official dialogue partners" in Post-Ministerial Conferences ("PMC").[457] In such official dialogue setting, one member state shall act as a coordinator for a dialogue partner in a three-year rotation.[458] Over the years, these dialogue partnerships were translated into more formal partnerships as illustrated by Figure 1 below provides the formal dialogue partnerships forged and the respective dates of signing:

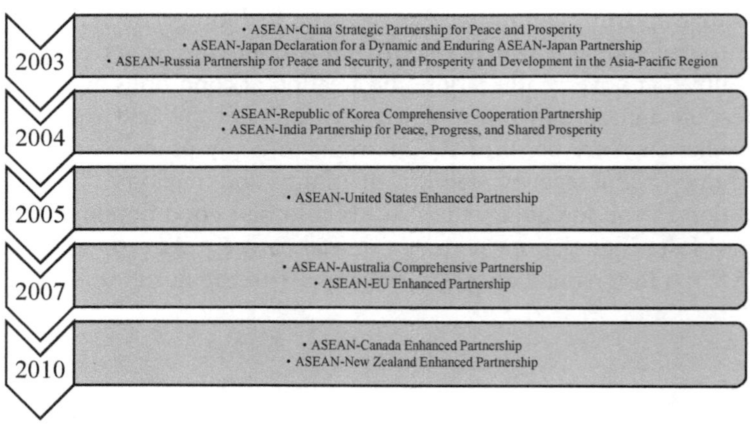

Figure 1: List of ASEAN Dialogue Partnerships

---

454 *Tiwari*, p. 31.
455 *Weatherbee*, International Relations, p. 113.
456 *Weatherbee*, International Relations, pp. 113-114.
457 *Weatherbee*, International Relations, p. 109.
458 *Weatherbee*, International Relations, p. 109.

Initially, PMC were conducted into two phases: the ASEAN member states shall meet with their dialogue partners as a group in a closed door meeting; thereafter, the ASEAN member states shall meet individually with each dialogue partner to discuss bilateral relationships.[459] The first phase later evolved to the establishment of the ASEAN Regional Forum, which serves as the forum for political and security discussions.[460]

In addition to the existing ARF, the ASEAN further established the so-called "ASEAN plus Three" in December 1997 with China, Japan, and the Republic of Korea. The Asian Financial Crisis gave valuable insight that Northeast and Southeast Asian countries were linked to one another.[461] Hence, ASEAN+3 has taken off with an ASEAN leadership and spawned later on offshoots such as the Chiang Mai Initiative.[462] The ASEAN+3 gatherings and/or meetings are of an informal nature, with mostly economic discussions, composed of 16 active forums (and a pending endorsement of four new ones) with no less than 48 mechanisms managing the activities and/or projects, and all geared into fostering areas of cooperation among the Northeast and Southeast Asian countries.[463]

Furthermore, the ASEAN realized the benefits it and India could gain by intensifying cooperation between each other. The same rings true with Australia and New Zealand. Hence, the ASEAN organized and established the East Asia Summit ("EAS"), with its first meeting in conjunction with the ASEAN Summit in 2005, consisting of ASEAN member states, China, Japan, Republic of Korea, India, Australia, and New Zealand.[464] The EAS was meant to be a forum for Asia-Pacific leaders to have dialogues about security and economic issues in which all participants have shared interests, which includes, but not limited to, energy, environment, natural disaster relief, terrorism, piracy, maritime security, and nonproliferation.[465] With the inclusion of the United States and Russia in the EAS, the participants came up during their sixth meeting in 2011 a "Declaration of East Asia Summit Principles of Mutually Beneficial Relations", adding to the norms of state conduct already existing in the region.[466]

---

459 *Weatherbee*, International Relations, p. 109.
460 *Weatherbee*, International Relations, p. 109.
461 *Lee*, p. xii; *Weatherbee*, International Relations, p. 111.
462 *Lee*, p. xii; *Severino*, ASEAN, p. 95.
463 *Severino*, ASEAN, p. 95; *Weatherbee*, International Relations, p. 111.
464 *Lee*, p. xii; *Weatherbee*, International Relations, p. 111.
465 *Weatherbee*, International Relations, p. 112.
466 *Weatherbee*, International Relations, p. 112.

Aside from continuously flourishing relationships with its external partners, the ASEAN saw the development of various sub-regional multilateral frameworks as well as membership of the individual member states in different transregional cooperative frameworks.[467] Although such subregional and transregional groupings were developed outside the formal ASEAN framework and not necessarily linked to the ASEAN in a dialogue format, these can be viewed as integral in enhancing and furthering capacities of the ASEAN Economic Community and reflective of national interests not easily apparent through an ASEAN membership.[468]

B. Present Institutional and Legal Framework

This next chapter of the study would try to make sense of ASEAN as an organization or regional institution. First, the reader would be walked through what the ASEAN is in general as a regional organization. This would include a discussion of the present organizational structure applicable to the ASEAN and its related organizational mechanisms. This necessarily would bring the reader to understand the norms the ASEAN lives by, including the decision-making processes and whatever conflict management mechanisms are in place should there be issues that arise amongst the member states or those that affect the ASEAN itself. Second, focus shall be given to the ASEAN institutional structure vis-à-vis regional security, specifically transnational crime, and efforts made in combating new forms of threats to regional security.

---

467 *Weatherbee,* International Relations, pp. 114, 120.Subregional groupings include, but are not limited to, the Indonesia-Malaysia-Singapore Growth Triangle ("IMS-GT"), Brunei-Indonesia-Malaysia-Philippines East ASEAN Growth Area ("BIMP-EAGA"), Cambodia-Laos-Myanmar-Vietnam ("CMLV") Cooperation Framework, etc. On the other hand, transregional groupings include, but are not limited to, Asian Cooperation Dialogue ("ACD"), Mekong-Ganga Cooperation ("MGC"), Indian Ocean Rim Association for Regional Cooperation ("IOR-ARC"), Southwest Pacific Dialogue, Coral Triangle Initiative ("CTI"), and Forum for East Asia and Latin America Cooperation ("FEALAC").

468 *Weatherbee,* International Relations, pp. 115, 120.

1. ASEAN as a Regional Organization

The ASEAN is an inter-governmental entity – a voluntary association among governments.[469] Decisions are made by governments and aside from discussions and debates amongst themselves, consultations are made with different lobby groups, non-governmental organizations, and civil society groups.[470] That said, the ASEAN as an inter-governmental association does not have a supranational government with authority superior to its member states and should not be viewed as an autonomous regional organization promoting and/or espousing supranational ideas unlike its other regional organization counterparts.[471] ASEAN member states instead cooperate on various issues whenever they could.[472]

Admittedly, the ASEAN as an international actor is a "soft" multilateral structure through which the collective policy will of member states are expressed in areas where there is consensus and act as a vehicle for the implementation of national functions.[473] The ASEAN takes in consideration that it is a "hodgepodge grouping" of states with disparate levels of political, historical, economic, and social development, from which sensibilities and centrifugal tendencies arise and remain.[474] As Muntarbhorn observed, regionalism is not being pursued as an end goal in itself but as a supplementary means to promote national development.[475] In other words, complementary national interests are sought to be harmonized by collective decision making seeking to maximize national interest through regional cooperation.[476] Thus, the ASEAN has not been historically fond of binding treaties for collective action, and there is absence of coercive instruments that make members comply with principles.[477] Regional cooperation's elaboration is by small, incremental steps, wherein member states work together on the basis of formal and informal structures as well as voluntary and informal arrangements which might eventually lead

469 *Severino,* ASEAN: What It Cannot Do, p. 3; *Weatherbee,* International Relations, p. 99.
470 *Severino,* ASEAN: What It Cannot Do, p. 3.
471 *Chesterman*, p. 200; *Crozier,* p. 19; *Severino,* ASEAN Today and Tomorrow, p. 13; *Severino,* ASEAN: What It Cannot Do, p. 4.
472 *Liu*, p. 19.
473 *Muntarbhorn*, p. 12; *Weatherbee,* International Relations, p. 91.
474 *Liu,* p. 19; *Severino,* ASEAN Today and Tomorrow, p. 15.
475 *Muntarbhorn*, p. 12.
476 *Weatherbee,* International Relations, p. 91.
477 *Di Floristella,* p. 32.

to more binding and institutionalized agreements.[478] In this respect, it is not surprising to find different forms of agreements in the purview of the ASEAN – principal agreements (treaties/arrangements/memoranda of understanding), declarations, ministerial statements, protocols, and secondary protocols – the majority of which are declarations or normative statements on common objectives without exactly imposing a legal obligation.[479] In relation to this, declarations and ministerial statements are both of a soft law nature, wherein they are concluded quickly without needing ratification.[480] While not formal and legalistic in nature, it shows an intent to form an agreement without needing to shoulder the reputational costs of any breach.[481]

Interestingly, such flexible institutional design of the ASEAN greatly reflects its historical circumstances marked by the need to consolidate the independence of post-colonial states.[482] And in light of this, the ASEAN mirrors to a degree, if not completely, neo-liberal institutionalism on how it structures social action: institutions could become effective guides to social action not only by making use of incentives and sanctions but also in terms of owning one's roles, rituals, duties, and obligations that do not necessarily follow a Western model.[483]

The general characteristics of the ASEAN as a regional organization are easily carried over to its external relations. As mentioned earlier in the Introduction, the ASEAN believes in "inclusiveness" and espouses political and economic openness to the rest of the world,[484] which necessitates openness to constructive relations with the rest of the world inclusiveness in its approach to regional endeavors should one want regional stability and security in Southeast Asia.[485] As Former ASEAN Secretary-General Rodolfo Severino once stated, "If ASEAN is anything, it is not inward-looking. It is outward-looking. It is open to trade, economic links, and security dialogues with other countries and groups of countries and with other international organizations."[486] The ASEAN was henceforth a pioneer in the system of dialogue partnerships, which would link it to its

478 *Crozier*, p. 20; *Weatherbee*, International Relations, p. 91.
479 *Cockerham*, p. 169.
480 *Cockerham*, p. 169.
481 *Cockerham*, p. 169.
482 *Di Floristella*, pp. 33-34.
483 *Di Floristella*, p. 34.
484 *Severino*, ASEAN: What It Cannot Do, p. 5.
485 *Severino*, ASEAN, pp. 13, 25; *Severino*, ASEAN: What It Cannot Do, p. 5.
486 *Severino*, ASEAN Today and Tomorrow, p. 226.

external partners for the mutual benefit of both.[487] Dialogues between the ASEAN and its external partners started with economic motives but later have evolved to include political and security dimensions, with such dialogues being held during the ASEAN Foreign Minister's Annual Post-Ministerial Conferences with dialogue partners.[488] Later on, the ASEAN Regional Forum ("ARF") was established in 1994, which became the sole forum for political and security issues in the Asia Pacific.[489] Led and established by the ASEAN, ASEAN member states, China, United States, India, Pakistan, North and South Korea, and other countries with interests in the security and other affairs of the Asia Pacific region are gathered in one framework.[490]

As regards regional security and peace, the ASEAN in a real sense has been a form of security community even before it has decided to establish the ASEAN Security Community pillar by virtue of the Declaration of Bali Concord II.[491] However, such security function must not be construed to be in a military sense or defense agreement.[492] Thus, the ASEAN does not have a common armed force to deploy in armed intervention in a member state or in a neighboring nation.[493] As Severino explains, that should there have been an incident when a member state sent an armed contingent in a trouble spot, like what the Philippines and Thailand did when East Timor was transitioning to independence, the said member states did the same on their own and outside the ambits of the ASEAN.[494] Instead, the ASEAN has taken the leading role in the creation and maintenance of regional peace and security through establishing networks for "peaceful contact and habits of cooperation", which have made recourse to inter-state armed conflict and/or violence unthinkable.[495] As di Floristella describes, the regional security framework followed by the ASEAN is more of a regional security partnership, "an arrangement created by a majority of states in

---

487 ASEAN's dialogue partners include Australia, Canada, China, the European Union, India, Japan, the Republic of Korea, New Zealand, Russia, and the United States.*Severino,* ASEAN: What It Cannot Do, p. 5; *Tiwari,* p. 31.

488 *Severino,* ASEAN, p. 25; *Tiwari,* p. 31.

489 *Severino,* ASEAN, p. 25; *Severino,* ASEAN: What It Cannot Do, pp. 5-6.

490 *Severino,* ASEAN: What It Cannot Do, p. 6.

491 *Severino,* ASEAN, p. 36.

492 *Di Floristella,* p. 1.

493 *Narine,* Forty Years of ASEAN, p. 414; *Severino,* ASEAN: What It Cannot Do, p. 4.

494 *Severino,* ASEAN: What It Cannot Do, p. 4.

495 *Di Floristella,* p. 1; *Severino,* ASEAN, p. 36.

the region and by extraregional powers, who act as partners in upholding plurality of means to manage regional security."[496] The partnership contemplated herein arises from the realization of ASEAN governments that it is preferable, if not practical, to construct a security system based on jointly managed mechanisms and programs, rather than one entirely founded on relative strength of a military alliance.[497]

At the same time, the ASEAN views regional security and stability more broadly, taking into account non-traditional security ("NTS") threats as well.[498] For purposes of the discussion, NTS threats are a relative new security concept that has been introduced to "capture the broadening and deepening of the security and threat agenda after the end of the Cold War."[499] It is security related to any form of threat perception, may it be ecological, terrorist, pandemic among others, falling short of the "traditional state versus state pattern."[500] Needless to mention, NTS redefines the security paradigm and necessitates non-military security approaches.[501]

Significant to the case of the ASEAN with respect non-traditional security however is that the state or military remains at the crux of security, notwithstanding the potential of NTS to shift the focus away from the state towards the individual members of society (that could possibly integrate non-military or civil-military solutions to non-traditional threats).[502] This can be further elaborated in another contribution but for purposes of this study, security in Southeast Asia encompasses both the traditional and non-traditional sense but despite this, the move towards the individual as a security reverent remains unpopular due to the existing state centrality in ASEAN affairs.[503]

---

496 *Di Floristella*, p. 38.

497 *Di Floristella*, p. 38.

498 *Di Floristella*, pp. 109-116; *Maier-Knapp*, p. 78.

499 *Maier-Knapp*, p. 78.

500 *Maier-Knapp*, p. 78.

501 *Maier-Knapp*, p. 78.

502 *Maier-Knapp*, p. 79.

503 *Maier-Knapp*, p. 79.As Evans explaines further:
"The resistance to connecting nontraditional security to human security is declining, though some remain worried that at least the narrow conception of human security is either inappropriate to Asia or will slow progress in getting state action in addressing the nontradi- tional security agenda. What is distinctive about many of the approaches to nontraditional security is (1) that they are ambiguous about whether the referent of security is the state or the individual and do not dwell on tensions between the two; and (2) that its advocates normally emphasize the state and state-centric means as the best ways of responding to

Given the foregoing, the ASEAN still meets criticism and often dismissed as a mere social club or talk shop.[504] Yet, the ASEAN normalized informal processes for regional issues to be resolved in non-violent ways, whilst providing a regional context within which peaceful negotiations could be conducted.[505] Occasionally, tensions occur among member states due to centrifugal tendencies brought by diversity of membership or otherwise some remaining degree of mutual suspicion, but at the same time, no conflict has erupted in Southeast Asia.[506] Based thereon, the ASEAN espouses regional security on the basis of mutual confidence, consensus, and balance of interests.[507]

2. The ASEAN Organizational Structure

The ASEAN Charter is a step towards institutionalization, albeit a codification of existing practices,[508] e.g. sectoral bodies working on their respective sectors (or compartments) and implementing what has been decided on the highest level (such as the ASEAN Summit). Through it, the organizational structure and applicable mechanisms of the ASEAN have been reorganized. The ASEAN Charter provides that the following are now the organs within the ASEAN, namely, the ASEAN Summit, the ASEAN Coordinating Council, the ASEAN Community Councils, the ASEAN Sectoral Minister Bodies, the ASEAN Secretary-General together with the ASEAN Secretariat, the Committee of Permanent Representatives to the ASEAN, ASEAN National Secretariats, the ASEAN Human Rights Body, and the ASEAN Foundation. Especially for the ASEAN Summit, ASEAN Community Councils, and ASEAN Sectoral Ministerial Bodies, the ASEAN organs constitute the institutionalized consultative mechanisms initially formulated in the Bangkok Declaration of 1967 and have been a prominent feature of the ASEAN process of forging regional ties and maintaining a pleasant regional environment.[509] Said mechanisms do

---

these threats, normally preferring to address these issues within their own states rather than on a regional basis. The threats may be new, but the instruments prescribed for dealing with them usually are not." See *Evans*, p. 277.

504 *Severino*, ASEAN Today and Tomorrow, p. 16.

505 *Severino*, ASEAN, p. 36.

506 *Severino*, ASEAN Today and Tomorrow, pp. 14-15.

507 *Severino*, ASEAN Today and Tomorrow, pp. 21-22.

508 *Cockerham*, pp. 180-184.

509 *Caballero-Anthony*, Regional Security in Southeast Asia, p. 57.

not only instill habits of dialogue and consultation, but more so, are meant to build trust and confidence among each other as well as deepen the socialization of ASEAN leaders and ministers, immersing them into the overall ASEAN mechanism of cooperation.[510]

For purposes of the present study, a description of each body hereunder is important due to how decision and policymaking is done in the ASEAN, which is basically top-down or bottom-top approach and at each level, discussions and implementation could be done at each level that can affect the turnout of policies the ASEAN comes out with.

a. ASEAN Summit

The ASEAN Summit is the supreme policy-making body of the ASEAN, where the highest level of decision making takes place and which is comprised of the Heads of State or Government of the member states.[511] It shall primarily "deliberate, provide policy guidance and take decisions on key issues pertaining to the realization of the objectives of ASEAN, important matters of interest to Member States and all issues referred to it by the ASEAN Coordinating Councils and ASEAN Sectoral Ministerial Bodies."[512] It could instruct relevant ministers to conduct meetings and address issues.[513] At the same time, the ASEAN Summit has authority to handle emergency situations affecting ASEAN and is primarily responsible for decision-making and settlement of disputes, as may be referred to it, in the ASEAN.[514]

b. ASEAN Coordinating Council

Next in line is the ASEAN Coordinating Council, which is comprised of the foreign ministers of the member states and shall meet at least twice

---

510 *Caballero-Anthony,* Regional Security in Southeast Asia, p. 57.

511 The ASEAN Charter presently provides that the ASEAN Summit should hold two (2) meetings annually, without prejudice to special and ad hoc meetings, when necessary. See ASEAN Charter, art. 7(1) and (2)(a); *Caballero-Anthony,* Regional Security in Southeast Asia, p. 55.

512 ASEAN Charter, art. 7(2)(b).

513 ASEAN Charter, art. 7(2)(c).

514 ASEAN Charter, art. 7(2)(d)(e) and arts. 20-28.

a year.[515] The ASEAN Coordinating Council shall among others, prepare the meetings of the ASEAN Summit, coordinate the implementation of the decisions and agreements of the ASEAN Summit with the relevant community councils, and make sure policy coherence, efficiency, and cooperation is enhanced.[516]

c. ASEAN Community Councils and ASEAN Sectoral Ministerial Bodies

Furthermore, there shall be three ASEAN Community Councils, each representing the different ASEAN Communities as established in the ASEAN Charter, namely, the ASEAN Political-Security Community Council, ASEAN Economic Community Council, and the ASEAN Security Community Council.[517] Under the purview of these ASEAN Community Councils shall be the relevant ASEAN Sectoral Ministerial Bodies.[518]

These ASEAN Community Councils are the relevant machineries to realize the objectives of their respective ASEAN Communities. In doing so, they shall ensure to implement the decisions of the ASEAN Summit, coordinate the different works of the sections working under them, and submit the necessary reports and recommendations.[519] They shall meet at least twice a year and shall be chaired by the appropriate minister from the member state holding the ASEAN chairmanship for the applicable year.[520]

On the other hand, the ASEAN Sectoral Ministerial Bodies shall primarily function in accordance with their respective given mandates, implement the agreements and decisions on the ASEAN Summit-level as may be applicable to their respective responsibilities, strengthen cooperation in their respective fields in support of ASEAN integration and community building, and submit the necessary reports and recommendations.[521] Figure 2 below shows the organizational structure of the ASEAN Sectoral Ministerial Bodies:

---

515 ASEAN Charter, art. 8(1).
516 ASEAN Charter, art. 8(2).
517 ASEAN Charter, art. 9(1).
518 ASEAN Charter, art. 9(2).
519 ASEAN Charter, art. 9(4).
520 ASEAN Charter, art. 9(5).
521 ASEAN Charter, art. 10(1).

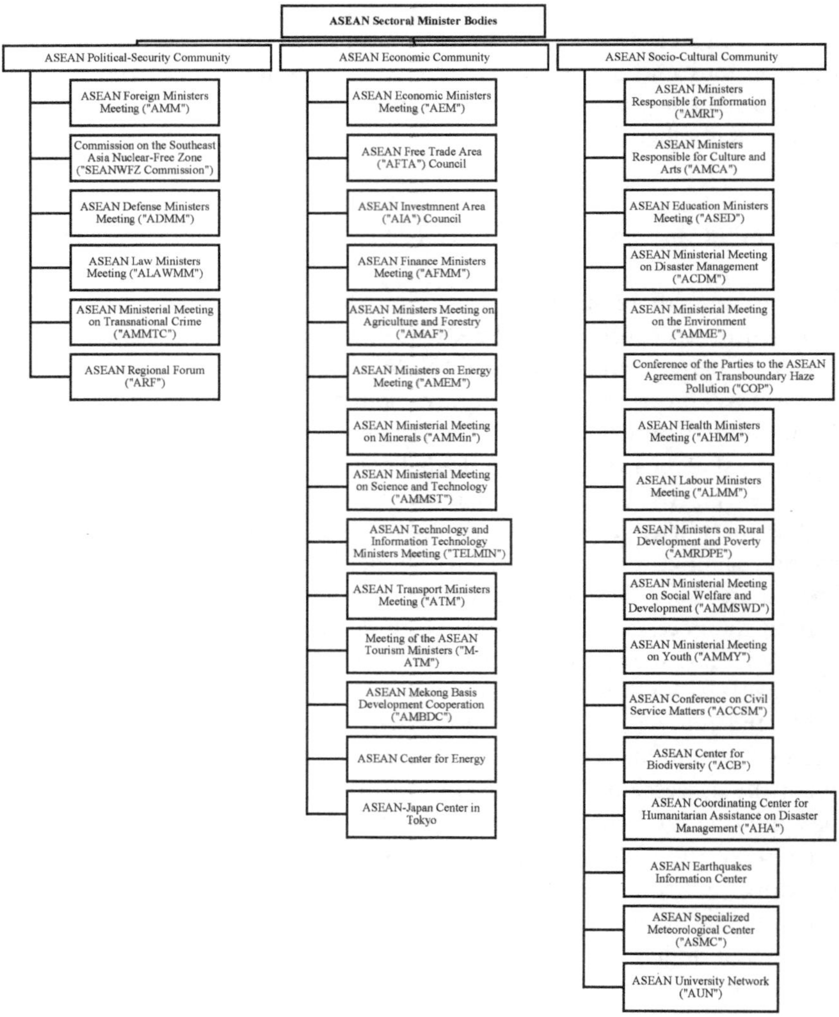

Figure 2: ASEAN Sectoral Minister Bodies

d. ASEAN Secretary-General and ASEAN Secretariat

The Secretary-General is appointed by the ASEAN Summit for a non-renewable term of five years, selected amongst nationals of the ASEAN member states based on "alphabetical rotation with due consideration to integrity, capability, and professional experience, and gender equality."[522] Aside from being the Chief Administrative Officer of ASEAN, Article 11(2) of the ASEAN Charter enumerates that the Secretary-General shall carry out duties and responsibilities as may be laid down in the ASEAN Charter and other relevant instruments; facilitate and monitor progress in the implementation of ASEAN agreements and decisions, and correspondingly submit relevant reports to the ASEAN Summit; participate in all meetings of the ASEAN Summit, ASEAN Coordinating Councils, ASEAN Community Councils, ASEAN Sectoral Minister Bodies, and other relevant ASEAN meetings; and basically be the spokesperson of ASEAN in dealing with external partners by expressing the views of ASEAN during meetings with the latter in accordance with guidelines given by the ASEAN Summit.[523] Moreover, the office of Secretary-General shall be assisted by four deputy Secretary-Generals and shall be of different nationalities from the Secretary-General and shall come from four of the ASEAN member states.[524]

In relation to this, the ASEAN Secretariat shall be composed of the Secretary-General and the staff as may be required. Aside from providing the duties of upholding integrity, efficiency, and competency, the ASEAN Charter unequivocally provides that the ASEAN Secretariat shall not seek or receive instructions from any government or external party to ASEAN and that at all times, it shall refrain from actions that may reflect on their position as ASEAN Secretariat officials responsible only to the ASEAN.[525]Accordingly, each member state undertakes to respect the exclusively ASEAN character of the Secretary-General and the staff, and not to seek to influence them in the discharge of their responsibilities.[526]

e. Committee of Permanent Representatives to the ASEAN

Every member state is mandated to appoint a permanent representative to the ASEAN with rank of Ambassador based in Jakarta, Indonesia, where the office of the ASEAN Secretariat is currently located.[527] Such

522 ASEAN Charter, art. 11(1).
523 ASEAN Charter, art. 11(2) and (3).
524 ASEAN Charter, art. 11(4) and (5).
525 ASEAN Charter, art. 11(8).
526 ASEAN Charter, art. 11(9).
527 ASEAN Charter, art. 12(1).

permanent representatives shall comprise a committee that would act as a support group to the ASEAN Community Councils and ASEAN Sectoral Ministerial Bodies, coordinate with the different ASEAN National Secretariats and ASEAN Sectoral Ministerial Bodies, liaise with the ASEAN Secretariat and Secretary-General, facilitate cooperation between ASEAN and external partners, and perform other functions as may be mandated from the committee.[528]

f. ASEAN National Secretariats

Each member state shall establish a National Secretariat which shall serve as a national focal point; be a repository of information on all ASEAN matters at the national level; coordinate the implementation of ASEAN decisions on a national level; coordinate and support the national preparations of ASEAN meetings; promote ASEAN identity and awareness at the national level; and contribute to community building.[529]

g. ASEAN Intergovernmental Commission on Human Rights ("AICHR")

One of the purposes and principles established by the ASEAN in its Charter is the promotion and protection of human rights. In light of this, the ASEAN has established an ASEAN Human Rights Body as one of the organs of the Association. However, the ASEAN Charter left the functionalities of this organ open-ended by leaving its mandate to the discretion of whatever terms of reference may be established by the ASEAN Foreign Ministers Meeting.[530] Subsequent to this pronouncement, the ASEAN established the AICHR on 23 October 2009.[531] The AICHR was instrumental in the drafting and preparation of the ASEAN Human Rights Declaration, which was unanimously adopted by the ASEAN member states in November 2012.[532]

---

528 ASEAN Charter, art. 12(2).

529 ASEAN Charter, art. 13.

530 ASEAN Charter, art. 14; *Caballero-Anthony*, The ASEAN Charter, p. 81.

531 *Chongkittavorn*, p. 41; *Tan*, p. 4.

532 ASEAN Phnom Penh Statement, 18 November 2012.

3. ASEAN Fundamental Principles, Norms, and Practices

The different principles, norms, and practices existing in the ASEAN can provide better understanding of how the regional organization functions and what fuels its decision and policymaking: basically its different principles, norms, and practices define and also explain the machinations existing within the ASEAN.

At the outset, these were inspired by those found in charters or agreements such as, but not perhaps limited to, the United Nations Charter, Bandung Declaration of 1955, Declaration of the ASA of 1961, and Manila Agreements of 1963 on the MAPHILINDO.[533] They later evolved as new issues or problems arose and ASEAN leaders were confronted with the opportunity to realign interests and give form to new ideas.[534] Many theories could be cited to explain these changes but as to the moral foundation of such evolution of norms, Solidum cites the shared cultural values among ASEAN member states:

> "Asians view the world holistically and not compartmentally. Such a view proceeds from the desire to be in harmony with nature. For example, needs are always part of the whole situation because needs are identifiable with the communal nature of Asians. Every one becomes part of a situation or need and this is why Asian thought and actions acquire a moral sense. Experts have found out that Asian thinking, unlike the West, does not proceed on a linear deductive line but by induction and intuition using symbols, riddles, and feeling. In this way, there is no fear of missing some objects on the way, which might not be along the linear deductive line. Asian thought consists of enveloping moves, only focusing on a specific center whenever this is sensed."[535]

That said, ASEAN principles and norms can be distinguished into either legal-rational or socio-cultural norms, wherein the former are the formal rationalistic principles of law while the latter are the basis for informal social controls and habits within ASEAN.[536] The following portion discusses each one.

---

533 *Solidum*, pp. 79, 80.
534 *Solidum*, pp. 79, 80.
535 *Solidum*, p. 79.
536 *Narine*, Forty Years of ASEAN, p. 413.

a. Constitutional Principles

A reading of the ASEAN Charter would show the different principles that govern the ASEAN and its member states. These principles are the following: (1) respect for independence, sovereignty, equality, territorial integrity, and national identity of all member states; (2) shared commitment and collective responsibility in enhancing regional peace, security, and prosperity; (3) renunciation of aggression and of the threat or use of force or other actions in any manner inconsistent with international law; (4) reliance on peaceful settlement of disputes; (5) non-interference in the internal affairs of ASEAN member states; (6) respect for the right of every member state to lead its national existence free from external interference, subversion and coercion; (7) enhanced consultations on matters seriously affecting the common interest of the ASEAN; (8) adherence to the rule of law, good governance, the principles of democracy and constitutional government; (9) respect for fundamental freedoms, the promotion and protection of human rights, and the promotion of social justice; (10) upholding the United Nations Charter and international law, including international humanitarian law, subscribed to by ASEAN member states; (11) abstention from participation in any policy or activity, including the use of its territory, pursued by any ASEAN member state or non-ASEAN state or any non-state actor, which threatens the sovereignty, territorial integrity or political and economic stability of ASEAN member states; (12) respect for the different cultures, languages, and religions of the peoples of the ASEAN, while emphasizing their common values in the spirit of unity in diversity; (13) the centrality of the ASEAN in external political, economic, social and cultural relations remaining actively engaged, outward-looking, inclusive, and non-discriminatory; and (14) adherence to multilateral trade rules and ASEAN rules-based regimes for effective implementation of economic commitments and progressive reduction towards elimination of all barriers to regional economic integration, in a market-driven economy.[537]

One can derive from the foregoing enumeration, among others, the different legal-rationalistic norms that define and guide ASEAN actions as well as govern the relationships between member states. To begin, the ASEAN recognizes through ZOPFAN the "right of every state, large or small, to lead its national existence free from outside interference in its internal affairs as this interference would adversely affect its freedom, independence, and integrity, and declared that the neutralization of South-

537 ASEAN Charter, art. 2.

east Asia is a desirable objective."[538] In relation thereto, the TAC laid down the following legal-rationalistic norms the ASEAN abides to: "(1) prohibition against the use of force and a commitment to pacific settlement of disputes, (2) regional autonomy, (3) doctrine of non-interference, and (4) no military pacts and a preference for bilateral defense cooperation."[539] Further, Article 11 of TAC enjoins member states to endeavor "to strengthen their respective national resilience in their political, economic, socio-cultural, as well as security fields in conformity with their respective aspirations, free from external interference as well as internal subversive activities in order to preserve national identities."[540]

The principle of non-interference is not unique to the ASEAN as it virtually exists in other regional organizations and said to underpin the entire inter-state system.[541] This notwithstanding, the ASEAN was able to make the said principle their own as follows:

At the outset, the use of the principle of non-intervention in the ASEAN was grounded on a background of the following facts: history of colonial intervention, the great military intervention during the Cold War, and "the emergence of post-colonial nation-states in Southeast Asia, whose interstate disputes were compounded by internal problems with no regard for territorial frontiers".[542] As such, the use of the principle was a response to the challenges and problems then faced by the ASEAN, the member states of which were relatively newly independent and have "weak" internal structures.[543] There was emphasis on building each member states' national or internal resiliency to promote regional security and collaboration instead of relying on the "military umbrella of any great power" – "if each member nation can accomplish an overall national development and overcome internal threats, regional resilience will automatically result much in the same way a chain derives its overall strength from the strength

538 ZOPFAN Declaration of 1971; *Ramcharan*, p. 65.

539 TAC, art. 2; *Goh*, p. 114; *Narine*, Forty Years of ASEAN, p. 413; *Ramcharan*, p. 65.

540 TAC, art. 11; *Ramcharan*, p. 65.

541 *Severino*, ASEAN Today and Tomorrow, pp. 60-61.Said principle originated from writings of eighteenth century European legal scholars. It was then popularized by Latin American states in the 19th and 20th centuries, when they invoked the same to rebuff recolonization and meddling by Europeans, and when they wanted the United States to accept said doctrine, respectively. Thereafter, said principle found itself in the Charter of the United Nations. See *Acharya*, Whose Ideas Matter?, pp. 32-33; *Solidum*, p. 79.

542 *Ramcharan*, p. 65.

543 *Acharya*, Constructing a Security Community, p. 57.

of its constituent parts."[544] Moving forward, the principle of non-intervention was contemplated by the ASEAN as a moral and strategic doctrine, to "protect the weak from the strong".[545]

The principle of non-intervention as applied in the ASEAN context must be understood to be more than a mere reiteration of the original European or Latin American concept.[546] It does not only contemplate one's right to self-determination or the prohibition of entering into great power-led military arrangement, but in operative terms, it likewise covers the following aspects: "(1) refraining from criticizing the actions of a member government towards its own people, including violation of human rights, and from making the domestic political system of states and the political styles of government as basis for deciding membership in the ASEAN; (2) criticizing the actions of states, which were deemed to have breached the non-interference principle; (3) denying recognition, sanctuary, or other forms of support to any rebel group seeking to destabilize or overthrow the government of a neighboring state; (4) providing political support and material assistance to member states in their campaign against subversive and destabilizing activities."[547] Stating it otherwise, the principle contemplates minding one's own domestic business and affairs, refraining from actions and decisions that have a domestic effect on the other fellow member state, and/or keeping to themselves any criticism or comment that they may have against the actions or decisions of the other state. Herein the non-confrontational aspect of the ASEAN is illustrated.

In connection to the abovementioned, a variation of the first mentioned aspect of non-intervention, i.e. "refraining from criticizing the actions of a member government towards its own people, including violation of human rights, and from making the domestic political system of states and the political styles of government as basis for deciding membership in ASEAN," was proposed historically at two instances in between the periods when the ASEAN was expanding its membership and the time it was reconsolidating itself after facing many challenges and problems in the Southeast Asian region.

The first time the proposal to change the principle of non-intervention was during the invasion of Cambodia when a Malaysian political leader criticized the norm of non-intervention as playing a role in the failure

544 *Acharya,* Constructing a Security Community, p. 57.
545 *Acharya,* Whose Ideas Matter?, p. 73.
546 *Acharya,* Whose Ideas Matter?, p. 38.
547 *Acharya,* Constructing a Security Community, p. 57.

of ASEAN to address then Cambodia's problem and suggested the use of "constructive intervention", which had similarities with the concepts of humanitarian assistance, collective intervention, and peace-building.[548] This suggestion however died its natural death when said political leader was removed from office.[549]

The second time was during the 1997 financial crisis. In a domestic problem that spilled over regionally, the then foreign minister of Thailand, Surin Pitsuwan, raised that the principle of non-intervention should be modified to allow the ASEAN to play a constructive role in managing domestic issues with regional consequences.[550] The concept of "flexible engagement" (deviating from the principle of non-intervention) was then proposed to enable the ASEAN to quickly avoid and/or address problems and issues with regional repercussions: this meant the "practice of ASEAN members discussing the domestic policies of other members when those policies had regional/cross-border implications."[551]

Only the Philippines supported this idea however.[552] Most were wary that such open criticism could open up old wounds ASEAN sought to alleviate.[553] Instead, as a compromise, the member states all agreed on the use of "enhanced interaction", a process wherein individual member states could comment on domestic policies of another, should these have regional repercussions, but would leave ASEAN out of the equation.[554] This same "enhanced interaction" was subsequently used in establishing the ASEAN Surveillance Process and ministerial troika, and eventually found itself in the ASEAN Charter.[555] Moreover, should there be instances when it would seem that the "flexible engagement" concept has been accepted, like for instance in how ASEAN member states dealt with the leaders of the military junta in Burma, recent institutional changes in the ASEAN, overall, are evolutionary rather than a break from established principles and norms, like as it how with the principle of non-intervention.[556]

---

548 *Acharya,* Whose Ideas Matter?, p. 126.

549 *Acharya,* Whose Ideas Matter?, p. 127.

550 *Acharya,* Whose Ideas Matter?, p. 127.

551 *Acharya,* Whose Ideas Matter?, p. 128; *Funston,* p. 206; *Narine,* Forty Years of ASEAN, p. 421.

552 *Acharya,* Whose Ideas Matter?, p. 132.

553 *Acharya,* Whose Ideas Matter?, p. 132; *Funston,* p. 206; *Narine,* Forty Years of ASEAN, p. 421.

554 *Acharya,* Whose Ideas Matter?, p. 134; *Narine,* Forty Years of ASEAN, p. 421.

555 ASEAN Charter, art. 2; *Narine,* Forty Years of ASEAN, p. 420.

556 *Acharya,* Whose Ideas Matter?, pp. 137-139, 149.

b. Normative Principles

Aside from the legal-rationalistic norms abovementioned, which mainly emphasizes the primacy of the principle of non-intervention in ASEAN dealings, the ASEAN Charter provides the different fundamental principles on which the ASEAN is grounded on. These more or less represent a set of values held in common by the member states, which they decide to be part and parcel of the governing principles of ASEAN. These include (1) adherence to the rule of law, good governance, the principles of democracy and constitutional government; (2) respect for fundamental freedoms, the promotion and protection of human rights, and the promotion of social justice; (3) upholding the United Nations Charter and international law, including international humanitarian law, subscribed to by ASEAN member states; and (4) upholding unity while still maintaining respect for cultural diversity.[557]

c. Decision-making norms: ASEAN Way

ASEAN socio-cultural norms are distinct to Southeast Asia and are designated as the "ASEAN Way".[558] The ASEAN Way constitutes working guidelines by which conflicts could be managed and also describe the means of carrying out actions, not specific ends, within the ASEAN.[559] The ASEAN Way includes the following principles: "principle of seeking agreement and harmony, the principle of sensitivity, politeness, non-confrontation and agreeability, the principle of quiet, private, and elitist diplomacy versus the public washing of dirty linen, and the principle of being non-Cartesian, non-legalistic."[560] If one would recall the principle of non-intervention, which can be best described as non-confrontational, then the ASEAN Way reinforces this characteristic through the aforementioned characterization of what it denotes.

In reaching common organizational positions, the processes of consultation and consensus building are used.[561] Based on Javanese tradition,

557 ASEAN Charter, art. 2.

558 *Narine*, Forty Years of ASEAN, p. 414.

559 *Goh*, p. 114.

560 *Acharya*, Whose Ideas Matter?, p. 94; *Goh*, p. 114.

561 *Acharya*, Constructing a Security Community, p. 65; *Narine*, Forty Years of ASEAN, p. 414.

consensus building has two (2) components: *muswarayah*(consultations) and *mufakat*(consensus).[562]As Emmerson explained:[563]

> "xxx The underlying approach to decision-making in ASEAN is the consensus approach, embodied in the Malay terms *musyawarah* and *mufakat*, which relies largely on patient consensus-building to arrive at informal understandings or loose agreements. As the former Prime Minister of Singapore, Lee Kuan Yew, has commented, 'We have made progress in an ASEAN manner, not through rules and regulations, but through *Musyawarah*and consensus.'
>
> "*Musyawarah*, the process of decision-making through discussion and consultation, and *mufakat*, the unanimous decision that is arrived at, are associated with the traditional approach to decision-making in the region and have played a role in village politics for centuries and, culturally, can be identified as part of the regional social system. The concept involves processes including intensive informal and discreet discussions behind the scenes to work out a general consensus which then acts as the starting point around which the unanimous decision is finally accepted in more formal meetings, rather than across-the-table negotiations involving bargaining and give-and-take that result in deals enforceable in a court of law. The 'ASEAN way' relies to a large extent on the personal approach in contrast to the Western way of dependence on structures and their functions. The way of making regional decisions dealing with co-operation among the member States adopted by ASEAN reflects its attitude of rejecting being a supra-national body like the European Communities.' xxx"[564]

In line with this, it is believed that while majority voting might put "a strain at the fabric" of the ASEAN,[565] decision-making through *muswarayah* and *mufukat* is based on the understanding that "a leader should not act arbitrarily or impose his will, but rather make gentle suggestions of the path a community must follow, being careful always to

---

562 *Acharya*, Constructing a Security Community, pp. 65-66.

563 *Davidson*, p. 167., *citing* Opening Address by H.E. Lee Kuan Yew, (then) Prime Minister of Singapore, in 15th ASEAN Ministerial Meeting and Post-Ministerial Meeting with the Dialogue Countries, Singapore, 14–18 June 1982, ASEAN Secretariat (1982).

564 See also *Di Floristella*, p. 24; *Narine*, The New ASEAN in Asia Pacific and Beyond, pp. 17-19.

565 *Severino*, ASEAN Today and Tomorrow, pp. 16-17.

consult all other participants fully and to take their views and feelings into consideration before delivering his synthesis conclusions."[566] Thus, during the *muswarayah* process, paramount consideration is given to inclusiveness, informality, and equality, while participants are allowed to air their differences without the threat of the majority imposing views on the minority, and consequently, no member state would feel its national interests are threatened by collective decisions and consequently avoid derailing cooperation in other areas.[567] Additionally, the psychological setting of the process is important not to be hostile, limiting discussions to non-contentious issues and the same being "not as opponents but between friends and brothers."[568]

Considering this, the idea of consensus is believed to be a pragmatic way in carrying out ASEAN affairs.[569] However, it must not be confused with unanimity, but rather, it is a commitment in finding ways to move forward by establishing matters which already have broad support.[570] In other words, one may not always be comfortable but as long as one's basic interests are not trampled on, one must go along.

A necessary consequence of this consensus building process is that ASEAN decision-making is often "at the pace of its slowest member", making sure that no one would be left behind.[571] At the same time, the ASEAN follows the "ASEAN minus X" principle, wherein member states are allowed to opt out of agreements with the option of joining at a later time to avoid slowing down institutional progress.[572] Herein, the quiet diplomacy, for which the ASEAN has later been additionally known for, applies: in the event that the member states cannot resolve contentious issues between themselves, they can compartmentalize them in the meantime so they could focus on other areas in their agenda.[573] And should ASEAN member states cannot agree on a common policy, they would go their separate ways while "couching their differences in language

566 *Acharya,* Constructing a Security Community, p. 66.

567 *Acharya,* Constructing a Security Community, p. 66; *Di Floristella,* pp. 54-55; *Narine,* Forty Years of ASEAN, p. 414; *Weatherbee,* International Relations, p. 99.

568 *Acharya,* Constructing a Security Community, p. 66.

569 *Acharya,* Constructing a Security Community, p. 66.

570 *Acharya,* Constructing a Security Community, p. 67.

571 *Weatherbee,* International Relations, p. 99.

572 *Narine,* Forty Years of ASEAN, p. 414.

573 *Narine, The New ASEAN in Asia Pacific and Beyond, p. 19.*

that obscures differences."[574] Understandably, some would criticize these circumstances as some lack of political will from ASEAN.[575] Nevertheless, it is a manner by which the ASEAN thought to avoid compromising political cohesion by conflicts over functional programs where competitive national interests might come into play.[576] As such, ASEAN Way may be described as a way to highlight existing least common denominators among member states and use the same in a manner most beneficial to the regional framework, while not letting other irreconcilable differences get in the way of progress.

C. Cross-border movement of evidence: ASEAN Mutual Legal Assistance in Criminal Matters

The following discussion centers on the applicable regime on mutual legal assistance in criminal matters by the ASEAN. It starts with its historical development, which includes an insight on how ASEAN deals with criminal matters, how it developed its policy on the same throughout the years and in response to circumstances, and how the regional organization fostered and/or promoted cooperation in criminal matters, in general. Through this exercise, one would get a sense of how the ASEAN positions itself and decides vis-à-vis legal cooperation, particularly mutual legal assistance in criminal matters. Afterwards, essential substantive and procedural provisions are discussed.

1. Historical Development of ASEAN Mutual Legal Assistance

The problem of transnational crime is severe and pervasive in the Southeast Asian region and consists of illicit drug trafficking, human trafficking, money laundering, transnational prostitution, piracy, arms smuggling, international economic crimes, cybercrime, and corruption.[577] It bears emphasis, for example, that drug trafficking is one of, if not the most, serious transnational criminal problems in the region, given that three ASEAN member states (e.g. Myanmar, Laos, and Thailand) are major producers

574 *Narine*, Forty Years of ASEAN, p. 414.
575 *Weatherbee*, International Relations, p. 99.
576 *Weatherbee*, International Relations, p. 99.
577 *Emmers*, Securitization of Transnational Crime, p. 6; *Sovannasam*, p. 77.

of narcotics and transit points for drugs sent to North America, Europe, and other parts of Asia.[578] At the same time, some of the largest and most dangerous criminal organizations operate in the region (e.g. Chinese triads, Japanese yakuza, Vietnamese gangs).[579]

As early as 1972 the ASEAN exerted efforts to combat transnational crime.[580] Beginning with drug abuse and illicit trafficking, the ASEAN established an ASEAN Expert Group Meeting on the Prevention and Control of Drug Abuse.[581] Immediately following said meeting was the establishment of the ASEAN Legal Experts on Narcotics in September 1973.[582] The Declaration of Bali Concord I was a further development in addressing the problem, when the same called for intensified cooperation among member states and relevant international bodies in the prevention and eradication of narcotics abuse and drug trafficking.[583] The same Declaration delved on the possibility of developing judicial cooperation, including an extradition treaty.[584] Following suit are the following ASEAN endeavors as summarized in Table 2 below:[585]

Date	Description
June 1976	Declaration of Principles to Combat Drug Abuse, signed by the ASEAN Foreign Ministers
1976	ASEAN Drug Experts held first meeting under the auspices of the ASEAN Permanent Committee on Socio-Cultural Activities
1998	Sixth ASEAN Summit and Hanoi Plan of Action called for operationalization of ASEAN Work Program to operationalize ASEAN Plan of Action on Drug Abuse Control by 2004

578 *Emmers*, Securitization of Transnational Crime, p. 6; *Kulsudjarit*, pp. 447-455.
579 *Emmers*, Securitization of Transnational Crime, p. 6.
580 *Sovannasam*, p. 78.
581 *Solidum*, p. 146.
582 *Solidum*, p. 146.
583 *Sovannasam*, p. 78.
584 *Sovannasam*, p. 78.
585 *Solidum*, pp. 146-147.

Date	Description
July 1998	Joint Declaration for a Drug-Free ASEAN by year 2020, embodying measures to reduce demand and supply, eradicate illicit drug production, processing, and trafficking in ASEAN, as well as encourage linkages among ASEAN Senior Officials on Drug Matters ("ASOD"), ASEANAPOL, and ASEAN Ministerial Meeting on Transnational Crime

Table 1: ASEAN initial efforts to combat drug abuse and illicit trafficking

These initial efforts notwithstanding, globalization, technological advancement, greater mobility of people and resources through national borders has enabled transnational crime to become more pervasive, diversified, and organized.[586] The region had to acknowledge and deal with many new forms of organized crimes that transcend national borders and political sovereignty such as terrorism, new types of drug abuse and trafficking, innovative forms of money laundering activities, arms smuggling, trafficking in women and children, and piracy.[587]

At the Fifth ASEAN Summit in December 1995 in Bangkok, ASEAN leaders called for enhanced "cooperative efforts against drug abuse and illicit trafficking with special emphasis being given to demand reduction programs and information exchange and dissemination, with the aim of creating a drug-free ASEAN."[588] ASEAN Foreign Ministers also recognized the need for closer cooperation and coordinated efforts on combating transnational crime. During the 29th ASEAN Ministerial Meeting in Jakarta in July 1996, they shared the view that the management of transnational issues, such as narcotics trafficking, economic crimes (including money laundering), environmental crimes, and illegal migration, is imperative so that they would not affect the long-term viability of ASEAN and its member states.[589] This shared point of view was carried on further during

586 ASEAN Plan of Action to Combat Transnational Crime; Joint Communiqué of the Second ASEAN Ministerial Meeting on Transnational Crime (AMMTC), Yangon, Myanmar, 23 June 1999; *Sovannasam*, pp. 77,78-79.

587 ASEAN Plan of Action to Combat Transnational Crime; *Sovannasam*, p. 77.

588 ASEAN Plan of Action to Combat Transnational Crime.

589 ASEAN Plan of Action to Combat Transnational Crime, p.3; *Emmers*, Securitization of Transnational Crime, p. 9; *Sovannasam*, p. 79.

the 30th and 31st ASEAN Ministerial Meetings in 1997 and 1998, respectively.[590]

Correspondingly, ASEAN leaders raised again its call to study the possibility of closer regional cooperation on criminal matters, including the possibility of having an extradition treaty, and resolved to take firmer and sterner measures to combat transnational crime such as drug trafficking and trafficking of persons, during the First Informal Summit in November 1996 and Second Informal Summit in December 1997, respectively.[591] Notably, it was during the same Second Informal Summit in December 1997 when the ASEAN Vision 2020 was adopted and likewise, ASEAN member states adopted an ASEAN Declaration on Transnational Crime, which though still includes illicit drug trade, expands the scope of definition of what constitutes transnational crime.[592] This could be considered as the first Asian regional framework in combating drug abuse and illegal trafficking, as well as other forms of transnational crimes. Through said Declaration, the ASEAN Ministers' Meeting on Transnational Crime ("AMMTC") was established.[593] The AMMTC shall convene once every two years, and together with its senior-officials counterpart, shall become regular ASEAN forums encompassing bodies such as the ASEAN Senior Officials on Drug Matters ("ASOD") and officials dealing with functional areas such as customs, consular matters, and immigration.[594] Notably, the ASOD is one of the oldest ASEAN platforms for regional cooperation dealing with regional problems, which focuses on "prevention and rehabilitation, education, public awareness, and law enforcement."[595]

There is also an association of police forces of the different ASEAN member states called the ASEANAPOL, with which the ASEAN authorities could coordinate with, although independent and outside the formal ASEAN framework. The ASEANAPOL serves a vital role as more or less a coordinating body that shares information, intelligence, databases, and otherwise cooperates at the operational level.[596] Furthermore, the Declaration on Transnational Crime introduced proposals that encourage member

---

590 *Emmers*, Securitization of Transnational Crime, p. 9.

591 ASEAN Plan of Action to Combat Transnational Crime; *Emmers*, Securitization of Transnational Crime, pp. 8-9; *Sovannasam*, p. 79.

592 *Solidum*, p. 147; *Sovannasam*, p. 79.

593 ASEAN Declaration on Transnational Crime, para. 2; *Severino*, ASEAN, p. 33.

594 *Emmers*, Securitization of Transnational Crime, p. 10; *Severino*, ASEAN, pp. 33-34; *Weatherbee*, International Relations, p. 201.

595 *Severino*, ASEAN, p. 34.

596 *Severino*, ASEAN, p. 34.

states "to exchange and disseminate information, to sign bilateral treaties and mutual assistance agreements, to assign police liaison officers to other Southeast Asian capitals and to explore ways of extending cooperation with the dialogue partners, the UN, and other organizations."[597]

As Emmers notes, the establishment of the AMMTC was integral in the securitization of transnational crime: transnational crime was a non-traditional threat to ASEAN member states and their respective societies.[598] Subscribing to the principle of comprehensive security, which goes beyond the requirements of traditional security (e.g. military) and takes into consideration NTS threats or aspects vital to regional and national resilience,[599] the ASEAN believes that transnational crime is a threat "to state security and regional stability, to sovereignty and rule of law, to social and moral fabrics of Southeast Asian countries, and economic development," which in general, has the potential of eroding the political, social, and economic well-being of the ASEAN.[600] Having said this, in view of the aims laid down in the abovementioned Declaration, the ASEAN did not waste time and thereafter entered into joint declarations and/or agreements with other countries in efforts to combat transnational crime. Table 2 below provides these declarations and/or agreements.[601] Significantly, terrorism was designated by the ASEAN ministers as early as 1997 as one of the crimes on which they would cooperate and further collaboration and cooperation in terms of counter-terrorism measures was witnessed after the 11 September 2001 attacks in the United States.[602] Discussion about fortifying counter-terrorism measures resulted eventually, among others, to the Convention on Counter-Terrorism in 2007.

---

597 *Emmers*, Securitization of Transnational Crime, p. 10.

598 *Emmers*, Securitization of Transnational Crime, p. 11.

599 If one backtracks to the chapter discussing the institutional framework and legal framework of the ASEAN, in particular the discussion on the position of the ASEAN as regards regional security, the ASEAN concept of "regional security" is not limited to the the concept of traditional security, which is state and military-centered kind of security (e.g. defense, etc.) but there is a slow but steady process of integrating NTS in the discussion. However, NTS remains to revolve around state actors and the concept of having the individual as a security reverent remains unpopular in the region.

600 *Emmers*, Securitization of Transnational Crime, p. 15; *Sovannasam*, p. 78.

601 *ASEAN Political-Security Department*, pp. 9-106.

602 *Severino*, ASEAN, p. 34; *Sovannasam*, p. 80.

Date	Name of Agreement and/or Declaration
Transnational Crime, in general	
25 March 1998	Manila Declaration on the Prevention and Control of Transnational Crime
23 June 1999	ASEAN Plan of Action to Combat Transnational Crime
02 October 2015	Kuala Lumpur Declaration in Combating Transnational Crime
20 September 2017	ASEAN Plan of Action to Combat Transnational Crime (2016-2025)
Counter-Terrorism	
5 November 2001	2001 ASEAN Declaration on Joint Action to Counter Terrorism
1 August 2002	ASEAN-US Joint Declaration for Cooperation to Combat International Terrorism
3 November 2002	Declaration on Terrorism by the 8th ASEAN Summit
4 November 2002	Joint Declaration of ASEAN and China on Cooperation in the Field of Non-Traditional Security Issues
27 January 2003	Joint Declaration for Cooperation to Combat International Terrorism, 14th ASEAN-EU Ministerial Meeting
8 October 2003	ASEAN-India Joint Declaration for Cooperation to Combat International Terrorism
10 January 2004	Memorandum of Understanding ("MOU") between the Governments of the Member Countries of the Association of Southeast Asian Nations and the People's Republic of China on Cooperation in the Field of Non-Traditional Issues
1 July 2004	ASEAN-Australia Joint Declaration for Cooperation to Combat International Terrorism
2 July 2004	ASEAN-Russian Federation Joint Declaration for Cooperation to Combat International Terrorism
30 November 2004	ASEAN-Japan Joint Declaration for Cooperation to Combat International Terrorism

Date	Name of Agreement and/or Declaration
27 July 2005	ASEAN-Republic of Korea Joint Declaration for Co-operation to Combat International Terrorism
29 July 2005	ASEAN-New Zealand Joint Declaration for Cooperation to Combat International Terrorism
29 July 2005	ASEAN-Pakistan Joint Declaration for Cooperation to Combat International Terrorism
28 July 2006	ASEAN-Canada Joint Declaration for Cooperation to Combat International Terrorism
13 January 2007	ASEAN Convention on Counter-Terrorism
30 June 2009	ASEAN Comprehensive Plan of Action on Counter Terrorism
Drugs	
25 July 1998	Joint Declaration on Drug-Free ASEAN
24-25 July 2000	Joint Statement by the 33rd ASEAN Ministerial Meeting
11-13 October 2000	Bangkok Political Declaration: In Pursuit of a Drug-Free ASEAN 2015
20 October 2005	ACCORD Plan of Action on Drug Free ASEAN
17 November 2009	ASEAN Work Plan on Combating Illicit Drug Production, Trafficking and Use (2009-2015)
Human Trafficking	
29 October 2004	Memorandum of Understanding on Cooperation against Trafficking in Persons in the Greater Mekong Subregion (COMMIT)
29 November 2004	ASEAN Declaration against Trafficking in Persons Particularly Women and Children
13 January 2007	ASEAN Declaration on the Protection and Promotion of the Rights of Migrant Workers
25 June 2007	ASEAN Practitioner Guidelines on an Effective Criminal Justice Response to Trafficking in Persons
2007	Guidelines for the Protection of the Rights of Trafficked Children in Southeast Asia
August 2010	ASEAN Handbook on International Legal Cooperation in Trafficking in Persons Cases

Date	Name of Agreement and/or Declaration
21 November 2015	ASEAN Plan of Action against Trafficking in Persons, especially Women and Children
21 November 2015	ASEAN Convention against Trafficking in Persons, Especially Women and Children
October 2016	Gender Sensitive Guidelines for Handling of Women Victims of Trafficking in Persons
Consular and Immigration	
25 July 2006	ASEAN Framework Agreement on Visa Exemption
29-30 July 2007	Guidelines for the Provision of Emergency Assistance by ASEAN Missions in Third Countries to Nationals of Member Countries in Crisis Situation

Table 2: ASEAN Documents, Declarations, and Agreements vis-a-vis Transnational Crime

In between the aforementioned agreements, declarations, and other documents, ASEAN member states under the ASEAN framework likewise entered into an Agreement on Information Exchange and Establishment of Communication Procedures on 07 May 2002 to promote cooperation in combating transnational crime, including terrorism.[603] Thus far, signatories to said Agreement are the Philippines, Indonesia, Malaysia, Thailand, Brunei, and Cambodia.[604]

As regards the 1999 Plan of Action to Combat Transnational Crime (adopted during the second AMMTC in June 1999), general and specific objectives in combating transnational crime were enumerated, including, but not limited to, different programmes of action that would expand regional norms related to combating transnational crime such as information exchange, legal matters, law enforcement matters, training, institutional capacity-building, and extra-regional cooperation.[605]

Furthermore, the same Plan of Action additionally defined and delineated the existing institutional framework in combating transnational crime

603 Agreement on Information Exchange and Establishment of Communication Procedures, arts. 2 and 3; *Caballero-Anthony*, Regional Security in Southeast Asia, p. 217; *Sovannasam*, p. 80.

604 *Soesilowati*, p. 235; *Sovannasam*, p. 80.

605 ASEAN Plan of Action to Combat Transnational Crime; *Emmers*, Securitization of Transnational Crime, p. 11; *Reeves*, p. 85.

in three (3) ways. First, the AMMTC has been designated as the highest policy-making body and main authority on ASEAN cooperation vis-à-vis transnational crime.[606] Composed of ministerial-level representatives of each ASEAN member state responsible for combating transnational crime, the AMMTC would supervise the activities of ASEANAPOL, ASOD, ASEAN Directors-General of Immigration Departments and Heads of Consular Affairs of the Ministries of Foreign Affairs ("DGICM"), and the ASEAN Directors-General of Customs ("ADGC"), and coordinate closely with the ASEAN Senior Law Officials' Meeting ("ASLOM") and the ASEAN Attorney Generals' Meeting.[607] Second, a Senior Officials Meeting on Transnational Crime ("SOMTEC") has been institutionalized to carry out and coordinate measures approved by the AMMTC and simultaneously build a work programme to implement the plan of action.[608] Third, an ASEAN Center for Combating Transnational Crime ("ACTC") has in principle been set up, which shall "implement the plan of action, propose regional strategies, collect data on legal matters and promote intelligence sharing among the members."[609]

Albeit the aforementioned is the primary institutional framework in combating transnational crime, there are a number of other ASEAN bodies which serve an ancillary function in combating transnational crime. As Un Sovannasam, a Senior Officer in the ASEAN Secretariat notes, these ASEAN bodies are the ASEAN Finance Ministers ("AFM"), the ASEAN Law Ministers Meeting ("ALMM"), and the ASEAN Committee on Disaster Management ("ACDM").[610] The AFM, though primarily responsible in enhancing cooperation in customs activities through the ASEAN Agreement on Customs, should also strengthen cooperation in combating trafficking of narcotics and psychotropic substances while at the same time facilitate joint efforts in anti-smuggling and customs control.[611] The ALMM, on the other hand, shall assist the ASLOM in ASEAN legal cooperation.[612] In the same vein, the ACDM is responsible for ASEAN cooperation in disaster management, whether said disaster is natural or man-made, with a

606 *Reeves*, p. 85; *Sovannasam*, pp. 81, 82.
607 See ASEAN Plan of Action to Combat Transnational Crime; *Emmers*, Securitization of Transnational Crime, p. 11; *Reeves*, p. 85; *Sovannasam*, p. 81.
608 *Emmers*, Securitization of Transnational Crime, p. 11; *Sovannasam*, p. 81.
609 *Emmers*, Securitization of Transnational Crime, p. 11.
610 *Sovannasam*, pp. 81-82.
611 *Sovannasam*, p. 81.
612 *Sovannasam*, p. 82.

view to manage adverse consequences to the social and economic development of ASEAN.[613]

The foregoing mechanisms and legal framework on transnational crime were formally placed under the auspices of the ASEAN Security Community by virtue of the Declaration of Bali Concord II in 2003. Compared to a tacit declaration in its 1967 Bangkok Declaration, the ASEAN this time explicitly declared and defined its efforts to pursue its political and security purposes through the establishment of the ASEAN Security Community.[614] In light of this, one of the objectives of the ASEAN Security Community is the full utilization of "the existing institutions and mechanisms within ASEAN with a view to strengthening national and regional capacities to counter terrorism, drug trafficking, trafficking in persons and other transnational crimes; and shall work to ensure that the Southeast Asian Region remains free of all weapons of mass destruction."[615]

To implement the ASEAN Security Community, together with the ASEAN Economic Community and ASEAN Socio-Cultural Community, the ASEAN came up with the Vientiane Action Programme("VAP") in November 2004 that provided measures that sought to put the Declaration of Bali Concord II into action.[616] In connection to said VAP, one of the programme areas and measures provided under the ASEAN Security Community is to undertake preparatory steps with a view of establishing an ASEAN Treaty on Mutual Legal Assistance on Criminal Matters.[617] A mutual legal assistance treaty would enable the ASEAN member states to request another to provide information and evidence for the purpose of an investigation or prosecution.[618] Simultaneously, the VAP enjoins the establishment of an ASEAN extradition treaty, which was already envisaged by the 1976 Declaration of ASEAN Concord.[619] Such an extradition treaty would allow ASEAN member states to request from another the arrest and/or surrender of an individual to face criminal proceedings and/or execution of sentence in the requesting state.[620] Said envisioned

---

613 *Sovannasam*, p. 82.
614 *Severino*, ASEAN, p. 36.
615 Declaration of Bali Concord II, §A(10).
616 *Severino*, ASEAN, p. 37.
617 Vientiane Action Programme, „Programme Areas and Measures", § 1.2.5.
618 *Secretariat*, p. 22.
619 Vientiane Action Programme, „Programme Areas and Measures", § 1.2.6.
620 *Secretariat*, p. 22; *Bassiouni*, p. 4; *Klip*, p. 456.

extradition treaty shall be drafted under the purview of the ASEAN Senior Law Officials Meeting ("ASLOM").[621]

An ASEAN extradition treaty has yet to be established among the ASEAN member states. At most, there was an endorsed 2019 Model ASEAN Extradition Treaty as well as certain provisions regarding extradition are provided in the 2007 ASEAN Convention on Counter-Terrorism.[622] Nonetheless, ASEAN member states have entered on 29 November 2004 into a "Treaty on Mutual Legal Assistance in Criminal Matters among Like-Minded ASEAN Member Countries" ("ASEAN MLAT").[623] This treaty is said to be predicated by the Jakarta bombings of the Marriot Hotel and Australian embassy in August and September 2004, respectively.[624] The treaty is thus believed to facilitate and enhance further efforts to combat transnational crime in the Southeast Asian region.[625] The ASEAN MLAT makes assistance obligatory as a matter of international law. Traditionally, international cooperation was done between member states through processes such as letters rogatory.[626] This means that previously, when assistance is sought through this traditional manner, the requested state is not obligated to accept the request or act pursuant thereto.[627] It is fully discretionary.

Furthermore, the ASEAN MLAT does not only provide a process by which member states can request and give assistance to one another in the collection of evidence and/or information for criminal investigations and criminal proceedings, but it likewise facilitates the ASEAN member states' obligations under different mutual legal assistance in criminal matters regimes that have been established through other international instruments such as the United Nations Convention on Transnational Organized Crime ("UNTOC"), United Nations Convention Against Corruption ("UNCAC"), and the UN Counter-Terrorism Conventions.[628]

The ASEAN MLAT is intended to operate in conjunction with existing mutual legal assistance mechanisms, both informal and formal.[629] Notably, international cooperation comes in various forms: informal and for-

621 Vientiane Action Programme, „Programme Areas and Measures", § 1.2.6.2.
622 ASEAN Convention on Counter-Terrorism, art. XIII.
623 *Severino*, ASEAN, p. 34.
624 *Soesilowati*, p. 235.
625 *Secretariat*, p. 26.
626 See *Zagaris*, p. 385.
627 *Bassiouni*, p. 8.
628 *Secretariat*, p. 26.
629 *Secretariat*, p. 27.

mal. Formal tools of cooperation include the aforementioned mutual legal assistance and extradition requests. Informal cooperation, on the other hand, refers to "exchange of information that occurs directly between law enforcement and regulatory agencies with their foreign counterparts."[630] Normally used prior to an investigation becoming official and/or prior to commencement of court proceedings, it is a "separate, less rule-bound international crime cooperation tool, which is available outside the formal mutual assistance regime" and the same enables law enforcement and regulatory agencies to "directly share information and intelligence with their foreign counterparts without any requirement to make a formal mutual assistance request."[631] Among the ASEAN member states, the ASEANAPOL provides an illustration for how this arrangement works.[632] Within the ASEAN framework itself, the Heads of Specialist Trafficking Units ("HSU") process vis-à-vis human trafficking is a relevant example on how informal cooperation works.[633] With regard to this, informal and formal tools of cooperation are not necessarily mutually exclusive from one another, but instead, are most of the time complementary.[634] Hence, the ASEAN MLAT does not detract from existing cooperative mechanisms and instead sought to enhance the existing working relationships amongst security and law enforcement agencies in the Southeast Asian region by providing another tool to combat transnational crime.[635]

Significantly, the ASEAN MLAT is cross-referenced in the 2007 ASEAN Convention on Counter-Terrorism,[636] and 2015 ASEAN Convention against Trafficking in Persons, Especially Women and Children,[637] respectively.

On late April 2019, the ASEAN MLAT has been elevated to an "ASEAN treaty" and made into a truly regional instrument like the TAC that allows non-ASEAN member states to accede and become contracting parties.

630 *Secretariat,* p. 22.
631 *Secretariat,* p. 22. See also *Bassiouni,* p. 19.
632 *Secretariat,* p. 22.
633 *Secretariat,* p. 22.
634 *Secretariat,* p. 23.
635 *Secretariat,* p. 27.
636 2007 ASEAN Convention on Counter-Terrorism, art. 12.
637 2015 ASEAN Convention against Trafficking in Persons, Especially Women and Children, art. 18.

2. Substantive Provisions: ASEAN MLAT

The ASEAN MLAT is composed of different provisions, differentiated between the substantive and the procedural, including but not limited to, the scope of application, and the different applicable principles, conditions, and exceptions, and the manner requests should be made and executed.

a. Applicability of Assistance

As regards the aspect of applicability of assistance, four (4) things can be mentioned. First, the ASEAN MLAT reflects a mechanism found in traditional mutual legal assistance wherein the requesting state sends a request to another state (requested state) for the latter to provide the needed legal assistance.[638] This connotes that any cross-border access or transfer of information and/or evidence is subject to the discretion of the requested state.

It must be understood at this juncture that the mutual legal assistance contemplated in the ASEAN MLAT is assistance in its traditional sense.[639] The ASEAN MLAT does not apply to the following: (1) arrest or detention of a person in view of extraditing that person; (2) enforcement in the requested member state of criminal judgments imposed in the requesting member state (except as to the extent sanctioned by the requesting member state's domestic laws); (3) transfer of persons in custody to serve sentences; and (4) transfer of criminal proceedings.[640] Moreover, nothing in said ASEAN MLAT "entitles a state-party to undertake in the territory of another party the exercise of jurisdiction and/or perform functions reserved exclusively for the authorities of that other party by its domestic laws."[641] Hence, exercise of extraterritorial jurisdiction is not conferred. One would need the consent of the other member state beforehand. Interestingly, while this kind of provision could probably be found in other mutual legal assistance arrangements, this provision evinces arguably the ASEAN principle of respect for the other's sovereignty and territorial integrity.

---

638 See in general *Heard/Mansell*, p. 354.

639 *Secretariat*, p. 36.

640 2004 ASEAN Mutual Legal Assistance Treaty, art. 2, § 1.

641 2004 ASEAN Mutual Legal Assistance Treaty, art. 2, § 2.

Second, the ASEAN MLAT applies to all "criminal matters", namely investigations, prosecutions, and resulting proceedings,[642] and obligates state parties to "render to one another the widest possible measure of mutual legal assistance" in accordance with the provisions of the treaty and subject to the respective domestic laws applicable.[643] One may construe this as state parties having comparatively lesser discretion to refuse assistance.[644] It is only when there are legal provisions or provisions in the ASEAN MLAT or other treaty provision precluding assistance, then the requested member state may refuse assistance.[645] The ASEAN MLAT allows a requested member state the discretion to deny a request for assistance should there be non-compliance to any material terms of the ASEAN MLAT or other relevant arrangements.[646] Such discretionary ground being found in other MLA agreements, Bassiouni once interpreted this kind of provision as serving the dual purpose of reminding the requesting state to conform to treaty provisions and specifically granting the requested state the power to insist that a defective request be corrected or to deny the request altogether.[647]

Third, the ASEAN MLAT applies solely to the provision of mutual assistance among the state parties. The provisions contained therein do not create a right on the part of any private person "to obtain, suppress, exclude any evidence or to impede the execution of a request for assistance."[648]

Fourth, the territorial application of the ASEAN MLAT was intended to cover the ASEAN member states. By virtue however of being a true regional instrument like the TAC, the ASEAN MLAT is open to signature by other states, which are not ASEAN member states. At the date of this writing, there has been no other contracting party to the ASEAN MLAT other than the ASEAN member states, although according to an official in the ASEAN, there were states that manifested intent of being a signatory.[649]

---

642 2004 ASEAN Mutual Legal Assistance Treaty, art. 1, § 1.

643 2004 ASEAN Mutual Legal Assistance Treaty, art. 1, § 1.

644 See *Bassiouni*, p. 388.

645 See *Bassiouni*, Multilateral and Bilateral Enforcement Mechanisms, p. 388.

646 2004 ASEAN Mutual Legal Assistance Treaty, art. 3, § 2.

647 *Bassiouni*, Multilateral and Bilateral Enforcement Mechanisms, p. 390.

648 2004 ASEAN Mutual Legal Assistance Treaty, art. 1, § 3.

649 Email correspondence with Sendy Hermawati (ASEAN Secretariat) dated 15 May 2019.

b. Types of Mutual Legal Assistance

As to what types of mutual legal assistance could be provided, the ASEAN MLAT enables the following types of assistance: "(1) taking of evidence or obtaining voluntary statements from persons; (2) making arrangements for persons to give evidence or to assist in criminal investigations; (3) effective service of judicial documents; (4) executing searches and seizures; (5) examining objects and sites; (6) providing original or certified copies of relevant documents, records, etc.; (7) identifying or tracing property derived from the commission of the offense and instrumentalities of the crime; (8) the restraining of dealings in property or the freezing of property derived from crime that may be recovered, forfeited, or confiscated; (9) the recovery, forfeiture, or confiscation of property derived from the commission of the offense; and (10) locating and identifying witnesses and suspects."[650] This list is not however mutually exclusive as the ASEAN MLAT provides a catch-all provision, in which it shall likewise cover "the provision of such other assistance as may be agreed and which is consistent with the objects of this treaty and the laws of the requested member state."[651] In other words, should any other form of mutual legal assistance be required, it could be granted depending on what the state parties may agree upon and whether the same is allowable by the domestic laws of the requested member state.

c. Compatibility with Other Arrangements

As initially noted above, the ASEAN MLAT recognizes that obligations for mutual legal assistance among the state parties can be found in other instruments. Hence, the ASEAN MLAT does not detract state parties from "providing assistance to each other pursuant to other treaties, arrangements, or the provisions of their national laws."[652]

To the same degree, the ASEAN itself acknowledges the existence of both informal and formal forms of cooperation in combating transnational crime. On one end, there could be other existing extradition and/or mutual legal assistance treaties ASEAN member states may have with each other. As it stands, no ASEAN extradition treaty exists. What is currently

650 2004 ASEAN Mutual Legal Assistance Treaty, art. 1, § 2; *Secretariat, pp. 36-37.*
651 2004 ASEAN Mutual Legal Assistance Treaty, art. 1, § 2(k); *Secretariat, p. 37.*
652 2004 ASEAN Mutual Legal Assistance Treaty, art. 23.

existing is only a ASEAN Model Extradition Treaty. On another end, informal cooperation exists amongst law enforcement and administrative agencies. Albeit independent of ASEAN as an organization, the ASEAN acknowledges the existence of the ASEANAPOL, which enables networking and information-sharing among the different Chiefs of Police of each ASEAN member state.

d. Principles, Conditions, and Exceptions Applicable

A reading of mutual legal assistance treaties would reveal that a state party needs to satisfy certain principles and conditions as well as avoid any provided exceptions before mutual legal assistance requests can generally succeed.[653] These principles, conditions, and exceptions are generally said to be a reflection of state practices that have developed over time in response to concerns of protecting interests of both requesting and requested states, as well as human rights issues vis-à-vis the criminal justice process.[654] The ASEAN Secretariat had the occasion to enumerate the major principles, conditions, and exceptions as applicable to mutual legal assistance treaties as follows: (1) sufficiency of evidence, (2) dual criminality, (3) double jeopardy, (4) reciprocity, (5) speciality or use limitation, (6) human rights considerations, (7) rights of the accused or person charged of a criminal offense, (8) consideration of likely severity of punishment, (9) political offenses, (10) military offenses, (11) national and political interests, and (12) bank secrecy and financial offenses.[655] The following is a discussion of these different principles, conditions, and exceptions, which can be found as "limitations on assistance" in the ASEAN MLAT.[656]

i. Sufficiency of Evidence

The requirement of sufficiency of evidence is normally found in extradition regimes, especially in common law countries, wherein upon submission of an extradition request, the authority or tribunal for extradition

653 *Secretariat,* p. 44.
654 *Secretariat,* p. 44.
655 *Secretariat,* pp. 44-50; *Bassiouni,* Modalities of International Cooperation, pp. 5, 8-9; *Boister,* pp. 203-206, 218-219, 221, 226.
656 ASEAN MLAT, art. 3.

determines if there is sufficiency of admissible evidence to justify extradition.[657] In these cases however, full disclosure of evidence is not required, and there is typically a variation from one extradition regime to another as to the gamut of evidence needed to be presented.[658] After determining that there is legal basis to seek legal assistance, the requesting member state must then provide information to support its request and such information shall depend on the jurisdiction and nature of assistance sought.[659] Such sufficiency of evidence requirement has been imported in some mutual legal assistance treaties and normally, the information provided is directly proportional to the intrusiveness of the assistance sought: the more intrusive assistance is requested, the more supporting information the requesting state should provide.[660]

Applying this to the ASEAN MLAT, a sufficiency of evidence test can be found vis-à-vis execution of search and seizures: the requested member state shall execute a request for the search, seizure, and delivery of documents, records, or items "if there reasonable grounds for believing that the documents, records, or items are relevant to a criminal matter in the requesting state."[661] A similar import can be found in providing assistance in forfeiture proceedings, when the requesting member state must provide all information which the requested member state considers necessary in executing the forfeiture order.[662] Further, the requesting member state is obligated to furnish the requested member state, in addition to the mutual legal assistance request, the supporting original signed order or a duly authenticated copy thereof.[663]

ii. Dual Criminality

Akin to extradition, mutual legal assistance usually requires dual or double criminality and the test is whether the conduct subject of the mutual legal assistance request be considered as a criminal offense in both the requesting and requested state, and not whether the conduct is punishable

657 *Boister*, p. 221.
658 *Boister*, p. 221.
659 See 2004 ASEAN Mutual Legal Assistance Treaty, art. 6: *Secretariat*, p. 44.
660 *Secretariat*, p. 44.
661 2004 ASEAN Mutual Legal Assistance Treaty, art. 18: *Secretariat*, p. 44.
662 2004 ASEAN Mutual Legal Assistance Treaty, art. 22, § 1.
663 2004 ASEAN Mutual Legal Assistance Treaty, art. 22, § 2.

as exactly the same offense in the states involved.[664] Practically speaking, this principle intends to ensure that states would only provide assistance to one another vis-à-vis conduct that they themselves consider "criminal".[665]

As a general rule, the absence of dual criminality is a mandatory ground to refuse assistance. The ASEAN MLAT provides that the requested member state shall refuse assistance if in its opinion "the request relates to the investigation, prosecution or punishment of a person in respect of an act or omission" that, if it had occurred in the requested member state, "would not have constituted an offense against the laws of the requested member state."[666] This is regardless of the type of assistance being requested as the ASEAN MLAT provision does not provide any qualification. The provision admits of an exception however: the requested member state "may provide assistance in the absence of dual criminality if permitted by its domestic laws.[667]

iii. Double Jeopardy

Double jeopardy (*ne bis in idem*) is part of international law, including international human rights law, wherein „no one shall be liable to be tried or punished again for an offense for which he has already been convicted or acquitted in accordance with the law and penal procedure of each State. "[668] It is correspondingly a condition in different mutual legal assistance instruments, albeit mentioned or defined in various manners.[669]

Double jeopardy is provided in the ASEAN MLAT as a mandatory ground for refusal. A requested state shall deny assistance when the request relates to an investigation, prosecution, or punishment of a person for an offense where the person either "has been convicted, acquitted, or pardoned by a competent court or other authority in the requesting or requested member state" or "has undergone the punishment provided by law of that requesting or requested member state, in respect of that

664 2004 ASEAN Mutual Legal Assistance Treaty, art. 3, § 1(e); *Secretariat*, pp. 44-45; *Bassiouni*, Modalities of International Cooperation, pp. 5, 9.

665 *Secretariat*, p. 44.

666 2004 ASEAN Mutual Legal Assistance Treaty, art.3, § 1(e).

667 2004 ASEAN Mutual Legal Assistance Treaty, art.3, § 1(e); *Secretariat*, p. 44.

668 International Covenant on Civil and Political Rights, art. 14, § 7.

669 *Secretariat*, p. 44.

offense or of another offense constitute by the same act or omission as the first-mentioned offense."[670]

In respect to this one could initially observe the existing transnational element of the prohibition against double jeopardy, albeit the transnational element is limited to the requested and requesting states. There is a consideration of whether the person-in-interest has been convicted, acquitted, or pardoned in either the requesting or requested state, or whether said person has undergone the punishment already in either of the states involved in the MLA request. The applicable provision is however silent on whether it shall extend to convictions, acquittals, or pardons, or undergoing punishment for the same offense or set of facts in another ASEAN member state or third party state.

It must be further mentioned that the ASEAN MLAT provision mirrors more or less the double jeopardy prohibition contained in the ASEAN Human Rights Declaration regarding double jeopardy, to wit, "no person shall be liable to be tried or punished for an offense he or she has already been finally convicted or acquitted in accordance with the law and penal procedure of each ASEAN member state".[671] Notably, the double jeopardy prohibition in the ASEAN Human Rights Declaration is subjected to the domestic law and penal procedure of the ASEAN member state and does not necessarily embody the same kind of transnational element the ASEAN MLAT provides.

iv. Substantive Considerations of Human Rights

Treaties on international cooperation normally enshrine human rights considerations and instill measures to protect individuals subject to mutual legal assistance requests.[672] Rights that may be relevant in the context of mutual legal assistance requests include, but not limited to, the right to life; the right to liberty and security of a person; the right to property; right not to be subjected to torture or cruel, inhumane, and degrading punishment; right to equality before the law; right to a fair and public hearing, legal representation, interpretation/translation; and the right not to be held guilty of retrospectively operative offenses or penalties.[673]

---

670 2004 ASEAN Mutual Legal Assistance Treaty, art.3, § 1(d).

671 ASEAN Human Rights Declaration, art. 20(c).

672 *Secretariat*, p. 47; *Boister*, p. 206.

673 *Secretariat*, p. 47.

Applying this to the ASEAN regional level, its own ASEAN Human Rights Declaration completely adopts the rights provided for in the Universal Declaration of Human Rights.[674] Another instrument in the regional level that illustrates how the ASEAN as a regional organization considers and values human rights are those in relation to human trafficking, i.e. ASEAN Declaration against Trafficking in Persons, especially Women and Children, the ASEAN Declaration against Transnational Crime, as well as the ASEAN Vision 2020. The trust of these instruments do not only focus on the prosecution of human trafficking and/or transnational crime, but also on the protection of victims.

The consideration of human rights that shall be tackled in this section involves the use of human rights as an exemption or condition prior to granting and/or executing a request. A reading of the ASEAN MLAT and overall framework would show that this discussion is evident in two points: first, the specific grounds for refusal based on human rights, and second, the consideration of severity of punishment in the equation.

1. Human Rights as a Ground to Refuse a MLA Request

Human rights considerations are present in three (3) points vis-a-vis the grounds to refuse a MLA request in the ASEAN MLAT. At the outset, there is the mandatory ground for refusal by reason of double jeopardy, as mentioned above. Second, the ASEAN MLAT includes a non-discrimination clause wherein a requested member state shall refuse a request should there be "substantial grounds for believing that the request was made for the purpose of investigating, prosecuting, punishing or otherwise causing prejudice to a person on account of the person's race, religion, sex, ethnic origin, nationality or political opinions."[675] And third, in assisting the attendance of a person in the requesting member state, the requested member state shall "invite the person to give or provide evidence or assistance in relation to a criminal matter in the requesting member state" if "satisfactory arrangements for that person's safety will be made by the requesting member state."[676]

674 ASEAN Human Rights Declaration, art. 10.
675 2004 ASEAN Mutual Legal Assistance Treaty, art. 3, § 1(c).
676 2004 ASEAN Mutual Legal Assistance Treaty, art. 14.

2. Limited Applicable Human Rights Obligations vis-à-vis Ground for refusal; Severity of Punishment Issue

Other than the three mentioned above, no other human rights obligation is provided as a ground to refuse a MLA request. To illustrate, another aspect important to the discussion of human rights considerations in the ASEAN MLAT is on severity of punishment, or the proscription of death penalty, torture, or severe, inhumane, and degrading punishment and/or treatment. In light of this, one could note that whilst the issue of severity of punishment has been a strong consideration in extradition cases,[677] there is an ongoing trend wherein requested state parties in mutual legal assistance requests, on human rights considerations, increasingly ask assurances from the requesting state parties that "the evidence requested through mutual legal assistance will not lead to death penalty, or the imposition of cruel, inhumane, or degrading punishment, or torture of a person."[678] The ASEAN MLAT however is bereft of such provisions, despite the explicit prohibition on torture, cruel, and inhumane treatment and/or punishment being included in the ASEAN's own human rights instrument.[679]

A possible explanation for this is the long-standing ASEAN norm on the principle of non-interference, which basically entails deference given by one member state to another member state and the former refrains from commenting, questioning, or otherwise interfering in the domestic affairs or policies of the latter. To recall, such principle likewise encompasses that member states shall refrain "from criticizing the actions of a member government towards its own people, including violation of human rights, and from making the domestic political system of states and the political styles of government as basis for deciding membership in ASEAN."[680] If one would walk back to the time when Myanmar was admitted as a member to the ASEAN amidst issues of political instability and human rights violations, the ASEAN was of the position that these matters were domestic in nature to which it or its member states cannot intervene.[681] Whilst enhanced interaction is now allowed among ASEAN member states, wherein one member state can inquire or comment about

677 *Boister*, p. 227.
678 *Secretariat*, p. 48.
679 ASEAN Human Rights Declaration, art. 14.
680 *Acharya*, Constructing a Security Community, p. 57.
681 *Flers*, p. 5.

domestic affairs of the other should the same have regional repercussions and as long as the same is done outside the ASEAN framework,[682] the principle of non-interference still generally holds. Following this raison d'être, then issues on severity of punishment or any alleged violation of the prohibition against torture, or cruel, inhumane, degrading punishment or treatment would be a hands-off concern for the ASEAN and its member states as to one another.

At the same time, while the prohibition on death penalty, torture and inhumane, degrading punishment exists in other international instruments, ASEAN member states have different interpretations and beliefs regarding said issue. In fact, there would be states such as Singapore and Malaysia, the constitutions of which allow the imposition of the death penalty for severe offenses. Thus, it becomes reasonable then that no such principle on considerations of severity of punishment be found in a treaty on mutual legal assistance such as the ASEAN MLAT. This is of course without prejudice to whatever may be agreed upon between the requesting state and requested state, subject to their respective domestic laws. If one would recall, the ASEAN MLAT provides for this allowance.

v. Reciprocity

International cooperation, such as mutual legal assistance, relies on goodwill and reciprocity of states. The ASEAN MLAT reinforces the importance of reciprocity in its provisions. Firstly, it provides that subject to their respective domestic laws, the state parties shall "reciprocate any assistance granted in respect of an equivalent offense irrespective of the applicable penalty."[683] Further, the ASEAN MLAT provides reciprocity as a discretionary ground for refusal wherein a requested member state may refuse a request, should the requesting member state fail "to undertake that it will be able to comply with a future request of a similar nature by the requested member state for assistance in a criminal matter."[684]

---

682 *Acharya*, Whose Ideas Matter?, p. 134; *Narine*, Forty Years of ASEAN, p. 421.
683 2004 ASEAN Mutual Legal Assistance Treaty, art.3, § 10.
684 2004 ASEAN Mutual Legal Assistance Treaty, art.3, § 1(g).

vi. Speciality or use limitation

Application of the doctrine of speciality or use limitation to requests for the provisions of documents and other forms of evidence means that the same „can only be legally used for the request for which they are handed over."[685] In the context of the ASEAN MLAT, a requesting member state shall not, without the consent of the requested member state and subject to terms and conditions as the requested member state may determine, „use or disclose or transfer information or evidence" provided by the requested member state for purposes other than those provided in the legal assistance request.[686]

In the event the charge subject of the information or evidence requested is amended, the ASEAN MLAT allows the same information or evidence to be used, provided that the following requisites are met: (1) there is consent of the requested member state; (2) the offense, as charged, is an offense in respect of which mutual legal assistance can be provided under the ASEAN MLAT; (3) and the offense, as charged is made out by the facts on which the request has been made.[687] With regard to this, in submitting mutual legal assistance requests, the requesting member state is obliged to make an undertaking that the information and/or evidence requested "will not be used for a matter other than the criminal matter in respect of which the request was made and the requested member state has not consented to waive such undertaking" and failure to do such undertaking allows the requested member state to refuse the request.[688]

vii. Special Offenses and National Interest Cases

Some states deny cooperation because it might prejudice their national interests in general, which might include certain types of offenses, security, economic interest, public interest, public order, foreign affairs, or prejudice to a present investigation.[689] The ASEAN MLAT includes provisions of a similar import as shown in the following three (3) instances.

---

685 *Boister*, p. 204.
686 2004 ASEAN Mutual Legal Assistance Treaty, art.3, § 8(1).
687 2004 ASEAN Mutual Legal Assistance Treaty, art.3, § 8(2).
688 2004 ASEAN Mutual Legal Assistance Treaty, art.3, § 1(h).
689 *Secretariat*, p. 49.

Firstly, it is a mandatory ground to refuse a request based on national interests should either (1)"the provision of the assistance would affect the sovereignty, security, public order, public interest or essential interests of the requested member state;" (2)"the provision of the assistance could prejudice a criminal matter in the requested member state;" or (3)"the provision of the assistance would require steps to be taken that would be contrary to the laws of the requested member state."[690] In relation to this, the requested member state may also refuse a request when "the provision of the assistance would, or would be likely to prejudice the safety of any person, whether that person is within or outside the territory of the requested member state; or the provision of the assistance would impose an excessive burden on the resources of the requested member state."[691]

Secondly, national interests also come into play when a requested member state is sanctioned by the ASEAN MLAT to postpone execution "if its immediate execution would interfere with any ongoing criminal matters in the requested member state."[692] It is worth noting that in cases wherein postponement of execution is necessitated by any ongoing criminal matter in the requested member state, or when in general, the requested member state is inclined to refuse a request, it should take into consideration whether assistance could still be provided under certain terms and conditions.[693] Provided further, that should the assistance then be provided under certain terms and conditions, the requesting member state undertakes to comply with the same.[694] In any case, the requested member state should, at any time it refuses or postpones execution of a mutual legal assistance request, promptly inform the requesting member state of the grounds for refusal or postponement.[695]

Thirdly, some states are sanctioned to deny mutual legal assistance on the basis that the offense subject of the request is of a special offense such as it being either a political or military offense. Traditionally, assistance shall be declined on the basis that the subject offense is of a political nature.[696] This is grounded on historical tolerance of armed struggle against anti-democratic, authoritarian regimes.[697] Like in extradition

690 2004 ASEAN Mutual Legal Assistance Treaty, art. 3, § 1(f), (j), (k).
691 2004 ASEAN Mutual Legal Assistance Treaty, art. 3, § 2.
692 2004 ASEAN Mutual Legal Assistance Treaty, art. 3, § 6.
693 2004 ASEAN Mutual Legal Assistance Treaty, art.3, § 7.
694 2004 ASEAN Mutual Legal Assistance Treaty, art.3, § 8.
695 2004 ASEAN Mutual Legal Assistance Treaty, art.3, § 9.
696 *Secretariat,* p. 49.
697 *Secretariat,* p. 49.

regimes, there is steady pressure to remove the political offenses exception in mutual legal assistance regimes.[698] This notwithstanding, the ASEAN MLAT retains political offenses as a mandatory ground to refuse mutual legal assistance requests.[699] However, the ASEAN MLAT narrows the political offense exception by not including the following as political offenses: (1) offenses against the "life or person of a Head of State or a member of the immediate family of the Head of State;" and (2) offenses against the "life or person of a Head of a central Government, of a minister of a central Government."[700]

In connection thereto, requests cannot be made for military offenses that are not considered crimes under general criminal law.[701] The ASEAN MLAT allows this a mandatory ground for refusal.

It is a different story altogether with regard fiscal offenses. Previously, states are allowed to decline assistance requests on the ground of bank secrecy and that the information is subject to regulations involving fiscal offenses.[702] Nowadays however, there has been a paradigm shift wherein the aforementioned reasons are no longer legitimate to decline assistance requests.[703] The same applies to the ASEAN MLAT wherein it provides that assistance shall not be declined by reason of secrecy of banks and similar financial institutions or that the subject offense is also considered fiscal matters.[704]

3. Procedural Provisions: ASEAN MLAT

a. Designation of Central Authorities

Mutual legal assistance in the ASEAN is highly centralized. The ASEAN MLAT uses a vertical form of cooperation through the designation of central authorities in facilitating mutual legal assistance among the member states. The relevant provision mandates state parties to designate a central authority to make and receive requests pursuant to such treaty.[705] Desig-

698 *Boister,* p. 205.
699 2004 ASEAN Mutual Legal Assistance Treaty, art. 3, § 1(a).
700 2004 ASEAN Mutual Legal Assistance Treaty, art. 3, § 3.
701 2004 ASEAN Mutual Legal Assistance Treaty, art. 3, § 1(b); *Boister,* p. 205.
702 *Secretariat,* p. 50.
703 *Secretariat,* p. 50.
704 2004 ASEAN Mutual Legal Assistance Treaty, art. 3, § 5.
705 2004 ASEAN Mutual Legal Assistance Treaty, art. 4, § 1.

nated at the time of deposit of the instrument for ratification, approval, or accession, said central authorities shall communicate directly with one another, but may, if they choose, communicate through diplomatic channels vis-à-vis requests for mutual legal assistance.[706]

b. Preparation of Requests under the ASEAN MLAT

i. Requirements for Requests

Requests under the ASEAN MLAT shall be made in writing, or "where possible, by any means capable of producing a written record under conditions allowing the requested member state to establish authenticity. In urgent situations and where permitted by the law of the requested member state, requests may be made orally, but in such cases the requests shall be confirmed in writing within five (5) days."[707]

The designated central authority shall be primarily responsible in the transmission of requests and any communication in relation thereto; however, "in urgent situations and where permitted by the law of the requested member state, requests and any communication related thereto may be transmitted through the International Criminal Police Organization (INTERPOL) or the Southeast Asian Police Organization (ASEANAPOL)."[708]

In light of this, the ASEAN Secretariat underlines the important role of the prosecuting authority in initiating a request for mutual legal assistance via the central authority.[709] The prosecutor, together with the investigator, would know the case best, including a "clear understanding of what evidence is already available and what evidence is required to support the case."[710] Furthermore, the prosecutor knows the timelines, key dates, and what may be needed in court.[711] Thus it would be imperative for the prosecutor or key investigator to coordinate with the central authority about these issues.[712]

The ASEAN Secretariat likewise stresses the importance of communication which is key to effective handling of requests between all those

706 2004 ASEAN Mutual Legal Assistance Treaty, art. 4, §§ 2-4.
707 2004 ASEAN Mutual Legal Assistance Treaty, art.5, § 1.
708 2004 ASEAN Mutual Legal Assistance Treaty, art.5, § 1.
709 *Secretariat,* p. 51.
710 *Secretariat,* p. 51.
711 *Secretariat,* p. 51.
712 *Secretariat,* p. 51.

involved – the central authority, prosecutors and investigators in both the requested and requesting member states.[713] Open and proper channels of communication is encouraged as every liaison between the requesting and requested member states, according to the ASEAN Secretariat, will help "avoid misunderstandings and secure agreement on how to best achieve the outcomes for which the assistance is sought."[714] Early open communication may also be mutually advantageous to both requesting and requested member states before a formal request is made.[715] Member states are then encouraged to make use of the online directory of the UNODC on Competent National Authorities Directory ("CNAD") which does not only provide updated contact information on competent national authorities in most states of the world, but also a means of communication and information on legal requirements for cooperation.[716] Needless to state, by making this toolkit available to the ASEAN member states – that is not exactly produced under the ASEAN framework – central authorities can assess the needed information to prepare and send an MLA request.

As to the formal requirements of a request, the request shall be made in English, including supporting documents and communication pursuant thereto, and, "if necessary, accompanied by a translation into the language of the requested member state or another language acceptable to the requested member state."[717] The request shall contain information needed to execute the request, including, "(1) the name of the requesting office and the competent authority conducting the investigation or criminal proceedings to which the request relates; (2) the purpose of the request and the nature of the assistance sought; (3) a description of the nature of the criminal matter and its current status, and a statement setting out a summary of the relevant facts and laws; (4) a description of the offense to which the request relates, including its maximum penalty; (5) a description of the facts alleged to constitute the offense and a statement or text of the relevant laws; (6) a description of the essential acts or omissions or matters alleged or sought to be ascertained; (7) a description of the evidence, information or other assistance sought; (8) the reasons for and details of any particular procedure or requirement that the requesting member state wishes to be followed; (9) specification of any time limit within which

713 *Secretariat*, p. 51.
714 *Secretariat*, p. 51.
715 *Secretariat*, p. 51.
716 *Secretariat*, p. 52.
717 2004 ASEAN Mutual Legal Assistance Treaty, art.6, § 3.

compliance with the request is desired; (10) any special requirements for confidentiality and the reasons for it; and (11) such other information or undertakings as may be required under the domestic laws of the requested member state or which is otherwise necessary for the proper execution of the request."[718]

It may also include the following information, as may be necessary to the request: "(1) the identity, nationality and location of the person or persons who are the subject of the investigation or criminal proceedings; (2) the identity and location of any person from whom evidence is sought; (3) the identity and location of a person to be served, that person's relationship to the criminal proceedings and the manner in which service is to be made; (4) information on the identity and whereabouts of a person to be located; (5) a description of the manner in which any testimony or statement is to be taken and recorded; (6) a list of questions to be asked of a witness; (7) a description of the documents, records or items of evidence to be produced as well as a description of the appropriate person to be asked to produce them and, to the extent not otherwise provided for, the form in which they should be reproduced and authenticated; (8) a statement as to whether sworn or affirmed evidence or statements are required; (9) a description of the property, asset or article to which the request relates, including its identity and location; and (10) any court order relating to the assistance requested and a statement relating to the finality of that order."[719]

As to what specific requirements one would need to comply with in a request for mutual legal assistance, the ASEAN MLAT provides legroom for a requested member state to ask the requesting member state for additional information to enable the former to execute or effectuate a request. Hence, the requesting member state shall furnish the additional information as may be necessary to effectuate the request or undertake the necessary steps in relation thereto.[720]

ii. Person or Authority Initiating the Request

In relation to the foregoing requirements, there is no mention in the ASEAN MLAT as to whose instance would a MLA request be issued. Giv-

718 2004 ASEAN Mutual Legal Assistance Treaty, art.6, § 1.
719 2004 ASEAN Mutual Legal Assistance Treaty, art.6, § 2.
720 2004 ASEAN Mutual Legal Assistance Treaty, art.6, § 4.

en that mutual legal assistance is mainly a government to government endeavor, and that it would be the central authorities which would transmit or receive the respective MLA requests, then MLA requests shall implicitly be made at the instance of governments or the prosecution.

As to whether a private individual or a suspect or accused person can request that a MLA request be issued on the former's behalf, *prima facie* the ASEAN MLAT has been silent on the same. However, a careful reading of its provisions, in particular to Article 1(3), wherein it says that the provisions contained in the ASEAN MLAT does not create a right on the part of any private person "to obtain, suppress, exclude any evidence or to impede the execution a request for assistance," would lead one to conclude that the participation of private parties is excluded in the MLA process. Taking this and the guidelines from the ASEAN Secretariat directed towards prosecutors and investigators on preparation of requests into account, there is reason to believe that the ASEAN MLAT is centered towards the investigative and/or prosecutorial side of criminal proceedings that is state or government-centered while it is unsettled whether a private individual or suspect or accused can benefit from the same kind of instrument.

c. Execution of Requests

i. Applicable Law on Execution

In the execution of requests, "requests for assistance shall be carried out promptly, in the manner provided for by the laws and practices of the requested party."[721] Based on this provision, there is the idea that the ASEAN framework follows the principle of *locus regit actum* in general. The subject provision then continues by stating that this is without prejudice however to implementing assistance in the manner requested by the requesting member state but the same is subject to the domestic laws of the requested member state.[722] In other words, the requested member state could accommodate the requests of the requesting member state as regards the manner of executing the request but in case of conflict, the domestic law or *lex loci* would prevail. It is unclear however to which degree must it be "subject to the domestic laws of the requested state" as the ASEAN

721 2004 ASEAN Mutual Legal Assistance Treaty, art.7, § 1; See for discussion on *forum regitactum*and *legit regitactum*, *Vermeulen/De Bondt/Van Damme*, p. 105.

722 2004 ASEAN Mutual Legal Assistance Treaty, art.7, § 1.

MLAT does not explain any further. Thus, this would be discretionary on the part of the requested member state.

Taking this into account, the requested member state shall "make all necessary arrangements for the representation of the requesting member state in the requested member state in any criminal proceedings arising out of a request for assistance and shall otherwise represent the interests of the requesting member state," should there be a request to do so by the requesting member state and the same is allowed by the requested member state's domestic laws.[723]

ii. Applicable Procedural Rights

1. Importance of Defense Rights

The following discussion takes into account the human rights that play a role in the procedural aspect of ASEAN mutual legal assistance among its member states. Whilst human rights play a considerable part in the substantive provisions of mutual legal assistance, human rights is equally considered in the procedural aspect as follows:

Considering that the ASEAN and its member states made a commitment to follow international covenants and agreements on human rights for example, as a bare minimum, the International Covenant on Civil and Political Rights ("ICCPR") provides the right to be informed at the time of an arrest of the reason of the arrest and any charges against the person arrested.[724] Further, it provides that the accused has "the right to be presumed innocent until proven guilty in accordance with law; the right to be informed promptly of the nature and cause of the charges against him, in a language in which he/she understands; right to have adequate time and facilities to prepare a defense and communicate with a lawyer of his/her choosing; the right not to be compelled to testify against himself/herself or to confess guilt."[725]

This set of procedural rights however are not reflected completely or provided in the ASEAN Human Rights Declaration, which is the soft law on human rights governing the ASEAN member states. Said human rights instrument vis-à-vis rights of the accused only provides protection

723 2004 ASEAN Mutual Legal Assistance Treaty, art.7, § 2.

724 International Covenant on Civil and Political Rights, art. 9(2).

725 International Covenant on Civil and Political Rights, arts. 9, 14.

against "arbitrary arrest, search, detention, abduction, or any other form of deprivation of liberty",[726] the right to be presumed innocent until proven guilty, as well as the protection against *ex post facto* laws and the enactment of bills of attainder, among others.[727] The ASEAN instrument on human rights is wanting of any provision regarding an accused's right to be informed, right against self-incrimination, right to have adequate time and facilities to prepare for one's defense, or right to counsel, which can be found in other human rights instruments.

2. Human Rights Considerations in Procedures Provided

Despite such want of quintessential defense rights in the ASEAN Human Rights Declaration, the ASEAN MLAT takes into consideration rights of the accused or any person charged of an offense in its provisions. This is despite the fact that the ASEAN Human Rights Declaration was formed at a later date than the ASEAN MLAT. On one hand, in obtaining testimony or sworn statements, "the parties to the relevant criminal proceedings in the requesting member state or their legal representatives may, subject to the domestic laws of the requested member state, appear and question the person giving that evidence."[728] In relation to this, the person (who may be any person who would give testimony or sworn statement as the ASEAN MLAT does not qualify) may refuse to give a sworn testimony or produce evidence where "(a) the law of the requested member state permits or requires that person to decline to do so in similar circumstances in proceedings originating in the requested member state; or (b) the law of the requesting member state permits or requires that person to decline to do so in similar circumstances in proceedings originating in the requesting member state."[729] The ASEAN MLAT further provides that "if the person claims that there is a right to decline to give sworn or affirmed testimony or produce documents, records or other evidence" under the law of the requesting member state, "the requesting member state shall, if so requested, provide a certificate to the requested member state as to the existence or otherwise of that right."[730] In other words, it is incumbent upon the

726 ASEAN Human Rights Declaration, art.12.
727 ASEAN Human Rights Declaration, art. 20.
728 2004 ASEAN Mutual Legal Assistance Treaty, art. 11.
729 2004 ASEAN Mutual Legal Assistance Treaty, art. 12, § 1.
730 2004 ASEAN Mutual Legal Assistance Treaty, art. 12, § 2.

person giving testimony or evidence to evince the existence of his/her right to testimony, which may arise from different possible reasons such as the right against self-incrimination, privilege communication, or other grounds sanctioned by the law of either requesting or requested member state.

On the other hand, in transferring persons in custody, the requesting member state ought to fulfill certain obligations for the protection of the subject person's human rights. These obligations are four-fold. First, the requesting member state is required to make an undertaking prior to approval of its request "(a) to bear and be responsible for all the expenses of the transfer of custody; (b) to keep the person under lawful custody throughout the transfer of his custody; and (c) to return him into the custody of the requested member state immediately upon his attendance before the competent authority or court in the requesting member state is dispensed with."[731]

Second, "the period during which such person was under the custody of the requesting member state shall count towards the period of his imprisonment or detention in the requested member state."[732] Thus, the duration of the person's stay in the requesting member state shall be credited to said person's benefit and time of imprisonment served.

Third, safe conduct provisions have been provided in the ASEAN MLAT. When a transfer of person in custody is made to assist in proceedings in the requesting member state, such person "(a) shall not be detained, prosecuted, punished or subjected to any other restriction of personal liberty in the requesting member state in respect of any acts or omissions or convictions for any offense against the law of the requesting member state that is alleged to have been committed, or that was committed, before the person's departure from the requested member state;" "(b) shall not, without that person's consent, be required to give evidence in any criminal matter in the requesting member state other than the criminal matter to which the request relates;" or "(c) shall not be subjected to any civil suit in respect of any act or omission of the person that is alleged to have occurred, or that had occurred, before the person's departure from the requested member state."[733] The same shall cease to apply "if that person, being free and able to leave, has not left the requesting member state within a period of 15 consecutive days after that person has been

731 2004 ASEAN Mutual Legal Assistance Treaty, art. 15, § 6.
732 2004 ASEAN Mutual Legal Assistance Treaty, art. 15, § 5.
733 2004 ASEAN Mutual Legal Assistance Treaty, art. 16, § 1.

officially told or notified that his presence is no longer required or, having left, has voluntarily returned."[734]

Fourth, such person giving testimony or appearing before the competent authority of the requesting member state "shall not be subject to prosecution based on such testimony except that that person shall be subject to the laws of the requesting member state in relation to contempt of court and perjury."[735] And in the event such person does not consent for its custody to be transferred or to attend in the requesting member state, such shall not be subjected to any penalty or liability or otherwise prejudiced in law notwithstanding anything to the contrary in the request.[736]

3. Defendant's Participation in the Execution of a MLA Request

In respect to any remedy that an affected person may pursue should the abovementioned rights, or any other right, be violated, the ASEAN MLAT states that it does not create a right on the part of any private person "to obtain, suppress, exclude any evidence or to impede the execution a request for assistance." One can thus not only conclude that the participation of private parties is excluded in the MLA process, but also any remedial right is not to be based on the ASEAN instrument for any remedy an affected person may pursue.

iii. Time Element on Execution

There are no time constraints or limits provided in the ASEAN MLAT by which a receiving state ought to comply with in the execution of a request. What the applicable provision only provides, is that requests for assistance shall be "carried out promptly in the manner provided for by the laws and practice of the requested member state."[737] Additionally, the requesting member state shall "respond as soon as possible to reasonable inquiries by the requested member state concerning progress toward execution of the request."[738] At most, the urgency of any request shall be

734 2004 ASEAN Mutual Legal Assistance Treaty, art. 16, § 2.
735 2004 ASEAN Mutual Legal Assistance Treaty, art. 16, § 3.
736 2004 ASEAN Mutual Legal Assistance Treaty, art. 16, § 4.
737 2004 ASEAN Mutual Legal Assistance Treaty, art. 7, § 1.
738 2004 ASEAN Mutual Legal Assistance Treaty, art. 7, § 3.

relayed through the communication between the requesting authority, prosecutor, or investigator involved. As previously mentioned, open and preliminary communication and coordination is encouraged between the involved parties to facilitate any MLA request.

iv. Authentication of Documents

As mentioned earlier, requests for MLA shall be in writing or by any other means capable of producing a written record for purposes of ascertaining authenticity. In relation to this, authentication of documents is not required to effectuate requests but this is without prejudice to parties requesting each other to authenticate any documents or material that may be transmitted to the other party.[739] It shall be considered authenticated for purposes of the ASEAN MLAT should "(1) it purports to be signed or certified by a judge, magistrate, or officer in or of the Party transmitting the document duly authorized by the law of that Party; and (2) either (a) it is verified by the oath or affirmation of a witness, or of an officer of the government of that party; or (b) it purports to be sealed with an official or public seal of that party or of a Minister of State, or of a department or officer of the government, of that party."[740] Moreover, subject to the domestic laws of the parties concerned, the ASEAN MLAT allows digital and electronic signatures as long as it is in accordance with the laws of the party concerned, and any such signature shall be considered legally binding.[741] Correspondingly, any digitally or electronically signed document shall be considered a legally binding document.[742] The aforementioned shall not however prevent the "proof of any matter or admission of any evidence in accordance with the law of the requesting member state."[743]

v. Importance of Confidentiality

The requesting member state has the responsibility of confidentiality under the ASEAN MLAT. It shall "take all appropriate measures to keep

---

739 2004 ASEAN Mutual Legal Assistance Treaty, art.24, § 1.
740 2004 ASEAN Mutual Legal Assistance Treaty, art.24, § 2.
741 2004 ASEAN Mutual Legal Assistance Treaty, art.24, § 4(b).
742 2004 ASEAN Mutual Legal Assistance Treaty, art.24, § 4(a).
743 2004 ASEAN Mutual Legal Assistance Treaty, art.24, § 3.

confidential the request for assistance, its contents and its supporting documents, the fact of granting of such assistance and any action taken pursuant to the request. If the request cannot be executed without breaching confidentiality requirements, the requested member state shall so inform the requesting member state, which shall then determine whether the request should nevertheless be executed."[744] Pursuant thereto, the requesting member state shall make arrangements "(1) to keep confidential information and evidence provided by the requested member state, except to the extent that the evidence and information is needed for the purposes described in the request; and (2) to ensure that the information and evidence is protected against loss and unauthorized access, use, modification, disclosure or other misuse."[745]

vi. Return of Documents

Regardless of the type of assistance requested, the requesting member state is obliged upon the conclusion of the criminal matter in respect of which the request for assistance was made to "return to the requested member state any documents, records or items provided to the requesting member state" pursuant to the request.[746] This is without prejudice however to returning temporarily to the requested member state, upon request, "any documents, records or items provided to the requesting member state pursuant to a request" under the ASEAN MLAT if the same are needed for a criminal matter in the requested member state.[747]

vii. Specific Procedures per Type of Assistance Rendered

The abovementioned general provisions regarding execution of requests notwithstanding, the ASEAN MLAT made specific provisions as to how each particular type of mutual legal assistance shall be executed by a requested state. Specifically, the ASEAN MLAT provides specific and/or additional requirements as regards taking of evidence and obtaining voluntary statements (Articles 10 to 12); making arrangements for persons to

---

744 2004 ASEAN Mutual Legal Assistance Treaty, art.9, § 1.
745 2004 ASEAN Mutual Legal Assistance Treaty, art.9, § 2.
746 2004 ASEAN Mutual Legal Assistance Treaty, art.19, § 1.
747 2004 ASEAN Mutual Legal Assistance Treaty, art.19, § 2.

give evidence or to assist in criminal matters (Articles 14 to 17); effective service of judicial documents (Article 21); searches and seizures (Article 18); providing original or certified copies of relevant documents, records, and items of evidence (Article 13); assistance in forfeiture proceedings (Article 22); and location and identification of persons (Article 20).

In connection to these specific provisions, the ASEAN MLAT would provide grounds for a person, for example, to refuse giving voluntary statements or assisting in criminal matters.[748]

Furthermore, it can be noted that the ASEAN MLAT does not provide a provision as to how a request shall be executed by the requested member state should it fall under the catch-all provision that allows mutual legal assistance requests not otherwise specifically stated therein. At most, following the wording of said applicable catch-all provision, the same shall be executed in accordance with the domestic law of the requested member state and whatever has been agreed upon by the parties.

II. Implementation in the member state level: Philippines

The following portions of the study is a discussion as to how the ASEAN MLAT is being implemented in the member states which are signatories to the same. In particular, attention shall be given to the Philippines and Malaysia, which are two of the founding member states of the ASEAN. One would be walked through any historical development of mutual legal assistance in criminal matters in said countries, the available legal framework vis-à-vis mutual legal assistance, including conditions and exceptions being followed, and how the same applies in practice.

A. Historical Development of Mutual Legal Assistance in Criminal Matters in the Philippines

1. Bilateral, Regional, and Multilateral MLA Treaties

The Philippines has presently a total of nine (9) bilateral mutual legal assistance in criminal matters treaties with the following countries: Australia, China, Hong Kong, South Korea, Russia, Spain, Switzerland, the United

748 2004 ASEAN Mutual Legal Assistance Treaty, art.12, § 1.

Kingdom, and the United States.[749] It is likewise a signatory to the ASEAN Mutual Legal Assistance Treaty, the United Nations Convention on Transnational Organized Crime ("UNTOC" or "Palermo Convention"), and the United Nations Convention against Corruption ("UNCAC"), the latter two including mutual legal assistance provisions.[750] More recently, the Philippines acceded to the Budapest Convention on Cybercrime which provides for international cooperation between contracting states with respect to cybercrime.

2. Domestic Instruments on Mutual Legal Assistance

Under the Philippine legal framework, formal forms of international cooperation in criminal matters can be done through either traditional letters or commission rogatory, transfer of sentenced persons, extradition, or mutual legal assistance. However, it is only as regards letters rogatory and extradition, for which the Philippines has dedicated domestic legislation. The Philippines does not have a specific domestic legislation on mutual legal assistance.

For letters rogatory, the Philippine Rules on Civil Procedure provides the following procedure:

> "Sec. 11. Persons before whom depositions may be taken in foreign countries.
>
> "In a foreign state or country, depositions may be taken (a) on notice before a secretary of embassy or legation, consul general, consul, vice-consul, or consular agent of the Republic of the Philippines; (b) before such person or officer as may be appointed by commission or under letters rogatory; or (c) the person referred to in section 14 hereof.
>
> "Sec. 12. Commission or letters rogatory.
>
> "A commission or letters rogatory shall be issued only when necessary or convenient, on application and notice, and on such terms and with such direction as are just and appropriate. Officers may be designated in notices or commissions either by name or descriptive title and

---

749 *Secretariat,* p. 36; *Department of Foreign Affairs,* p. 1; *Malaya/Monedero-Arnesto,* pp. 2, 9; *Soriano,* p. 136; *Quintana,* p. 141.

750 *United Nations,* p. 1; *United Nations Office on Drugs and Crime,* p. 1..

letters rogatory may be addressed to the appropriate judicial authority in the foreign country."[751]

Extradition is governed by Presidential Decree No. 1069, otherwise entitled as "Prescribing the Procedure for the Extradition of Persons Who Have Committed Crimes in a Foreign Country," or Philippine Extradition Law for brevity. As for the other international cooperation mechanisms for criminal matters, the Philippines does not have specific legislation on both mutual legal assistance and transfer of sentenced persons.[752] The legal framework for these two is normally provided by treaty.

In respect of mutual legal assistance, the Philippines, together with Cambodia,[753] does not have specific domestic legislation handling specifically mutual legal assistance in criminal matters among the ASEAN member states.[754] Instead, minute domestic law provisions on mutual legal assistance in criminal matters can be found in Philippine law for specific classes of offenses such as on anti-money laundering under the Philippine Anti Money Laundering Act, where the Philippines or another foreign state can make a request for assistance in the investigation or prosecution of a money laundering offense,[755] as well as cybercrime offenses mentioned in the Philippine Cybercrime Prevention Act, wherein permission to use international cooperation such as mutual legal assistance is provided, which allows cross-border exchange and transborder access to online evidence vis-à-vis cybercrime cases.[756] International cooperation mechanisms such as mutual legal assistance have likewise been referred to in the recent Rules on Cybercrime Warrants, which became effective on 15 August 2018.[757]

---

751 Philippine Rules of Civil Procedure, Rule 23, §§ 11, 12.

752 As regards the lack of domestic law for transfer of sentenced persons see *Malaya/Monedero-Arnesto/Paras*, p. 7.

753 In the future, mutual legal assistance and extradition will be governed by Title IV of the New Code of Criminal Procedure. See *Ku*, p. 48.

754 *Secretariat*, p. 36.

755 Republic Act No. 9160, as amended by Republic Act No. 9194, § 13.

756 Republic Act No. 10175, Philippine Cybercrime Prevention Act of 2012.

757 At this juncture it is significant to mention that albeit A.M. 17-11-13-SC or the Rules on Cybercrime Warrants, which covers warrants to be issued for the production, preservation, disclosure, interception, search and seizure, destruction, etc. of online evidence vis-à-vis cybercrime cases, acknowledges the use of mutual legal assistance vis-à-vis cross-border and transnational access to online evidence, the same Rule also allows the issuance of domestic warrants/orders to service providers as long as these providers offer their services within the territory of the Philippines. Thus, it is inconsequential whether a service provider

This notwithstanding, the Philippines still has an applicable framework through the different bilateral and multilateral treaties it entered into concerning mutual legal assistance in criminal matters. These treaties and international agreements as per the doctrine of international law applied by the Philippines would be the basis in law themselves for Philippine authorities to send and receive mutual legal assistance requests, to wit:

The Philippine Supreme Court held that under the 1987 Philippine Constitution, international law can become part of the sphere of domestic law either by transformation or by incorporation: the transformation method requires "that an international law principle be transformed into domestic law through a constitutional mechanism, such as local legislation", whilst the incorporation method "applies when by mere constitutional declaration, international law is deemed to have the force of domestic law."[758] Applying the foregoing, the Philippines follows pursuant to Article 2, Section 2 of the 1987 Philippine Constitution the doctrine of incorporation in respect of generally accepted principles of international law and customary international law.[759] General accepted principles of international law in this regard includes "norms of general or customary international law which are binding on all states."[760] To illustrate, the Philippine Supreme Court in the case of *Kuroda v. Jalandoni* held that although the Philippines was not yet then a signatory to the Hague and Geneva Conventions, war crimes are punishable in the Philippines because international jurisprudence is automatically incorporated in Philippine law.[761] Same underlying considerations were used in the cases of *Lo Ching v. Archbishop of Manila* and *Borovsky v. Commissioner of Immigration*, when the Supreme Court held that the prolonged detention of a stateless alien pending deportation as illegal, citing the Universal Declaration of Human Rights which is incorporated in Philippine law.[762]

---

or tech company is located outside of the Philippines, a cybercrime warrant can be issued against it by a Philippine judicial authority as long as it offers service within Philippine territorial jurisdiction. No mutual legal assistance request is necessitated by these circumstances and the traditional government-to-government cooperation usually does not apply.

758 Pharmaceutical and Health Care Association of the Philippines v. Duque, G.R. No. 173034, 09 October 2007.

759 1987 Philippine Constitution, art. 2, § 2.

760 Pharmaceutical and Health Care Association of the Philippines v. Duque, G.R. No. 173034, 09 October 2007.

761 Kuroda v. Jalandoni, 83 Phil. 171, 178 (1949).

762 Lo Ching v. Archbishop of Manila, 81 Phil. 101; Borovsky of Immigration, G.R. No. L-4362 (1951)

Conversely, the doctrine of transformation applies to treaties or international agreements wherein they become part of the law of the land pursuant to Article 7, Section 21 of the 1987 Philippine Constitution, which provides, that "no treaty or international agreement shall be valid and effective unless concurred in by at least two-thirds of all the members of the Senate." In other words, as long as treaties or international agreements follow the prescribed constitutional mechanism – ratified or concurred in by at least two-thirds of all members of the Philippine Senate – it is transformed into domestic law that can be applied locally in the Philippines.[763]

In view of the foregoing, there is still an existing domestic legal framework applicable albeit limited as treaties normally do not provide the minute details of execution. Treaties on mutual legal assistance in criminal matters, which have correspondingly been ratified by the Philippine Senate, have been considered as self-executory and the same have been enforced.[764] In particular, the ASEAN MLAT has been ratified through Resolution No. 126, entitled "Resolution Concurring in the Ratification of the ASEAN Treaty on Mutual Legal Assistance in Criminal Matters" dated 06 October 2008.[765] The ASEAN MLAT is hence considered domestic law in light of Philippine Constitutional Law and can be used as a framework in catering to requests made and/or received for mutual legal assistance in criminal matters from other ASEAN member states.

Nonetheless, a domestic law tackling international cooperation in criminal matters such as mutual legal assistance would be ideal to have because as would be illustrated further on, the ASEAN MLAT in itself as a legal basis is incomplete with certain details being left to the discretion and/or national laws of the member states to be implemented. It can provide the skeletal structure of how MLA can be requested and executed between ASEAN member states but the other provisions for it to be efficacious are left to be desired.

---

763 Pharmaceutical and Health Care Association of the Philippines v. Duque, G.R. No. 173034, 09 October 2007.

764 *Gana Jr*, p. 56.

765 Philippine Senate Resolution No. 126, dated 06 October 2008.

B. Substantive Provisions: Mutual Legal Assistance in Criminal Matters

1. Applicability of Assistance

Mutual legal assistance as it applies in the Philippines denotes a request-based system wherein requests are sent to and from the Philippines in relation to the cross-border exchange and transfer of information and/or evidence in criminal matters. The scope of application of the ASEAN MLAT applies in all criminal matters in the Philippines, excluding the arrest and surrender of a person in view of extradition, enforcement of sentences, transfer of persons in custody to serve sentences, and transfer of criminal proceedings.[766] Foreign Affairs Undersecretary Malaya et al. clarify that mutual legal assistance must relate to criminal cases only and not to purely administrative proceedings or civil actions, unless the civil action is closely linked or related to the criminal proceeding.[767] To illustrate, albeit the ASEAN MLAT is not the applicable MLA treaty herein, the Philippines sent a mutual legal assistance request to the United States of America in order to recover proceeds of corruption of two former generals of the Armed Forces of the Philippines pursuant to a civil case for forfeiture and not a criminal proceeding.[768] For the request to proceed, a clear nexus must be established between the civil action wherein legal assistance is sought vis-à-vis the criminal case for graft and corruption filed against the public officials.[769]

One of the ways to establish and prove this nexus is when the civil liability arises from the criminal liability itself. According to Article 100 of the Philippine Revised Penal Code, anyone who is held criminally liable is also civilly liable. The general rule is when a criminal action is instituted in the Philippines, the civil action for the recovery of civil liability arising from the offense charged is deemed instituted with the criminal action (Rules of Criminal Procedure, Rule 111, Section 1). The exception to the rule under the Rules of Criminal Procedure would be when either the right to institute the civil action is waived, or when the right to institute it separately is reserved, or the civil action has been instituted prior to the criminal action. Using this legal basis, the Philippines could support any outgoing mutual legal assistance request it issues should there be questions

766 See ASEAN Mutual Legal Assistance Treaty, arts. 1 and 2.
767 *Malaya/Monedero-Arnesto,* p. 8.
768 *Malaya/Monedero-Arnesto,* p. 8.
769 *Malaya/Monedero-Arnesto,* p. 8.

around a civil action or administrative proceeding in connection to a criminal case. The same can be true for the Philippines as a receiving or executing state, should these procedures apply in the requesting state.

In relation to this, the Philippines has domestic legislation mentioning mutual legal assistance and international cooperation in general for specific crimes involving money laundering and cybercrimes as defined and enumerated in the Anti-Money Laundering Act and Cybercrime Act of the Philippines, respectively.

Anent the level of assistance that state parties ought to provide vis-à-vis mutual legal assistance, there is the obligation to "render to one another the widest possible measure of mutual legal assistance" in accordance with the provisions of the treaty and subject to the respective domestic laws applicable under the ASEAN MLAT.[770] Due to being self-executory, this should be applicable in the Philippine setting. And as confirmed in interviews with officers in charge of MLA, this is indeed applied in the Philippine setting and the Philippines may render assistance to requesting states based on treaty or comity and reciprocity, albeit there is absence of a domestic statute on mutual legal assistance.[771]

To further elucidate, the Philippines adheres to the general principles of international law as a matter of state policy and endeavors to comply with its international obligations in good faith. As its Supreme Court explained in *Government of the United States of America v. Purganan*, though involving extradition, but still resonating state policy as regards entering into cooperation and treaty agreements:

> "Fourth, our executive branch of government voluntarily entered into the Extradition Treaty, and our legislative branch ratified it. Hence, the Treaty carries the presumption that its implementation will serve the national interest.
>
> "Fulfilling our obligations under the Extradition Treaty promotes comity with the requesting state. On the other hand, failure to fulfill our obligations thereunder paints a bad image of our country before the world community. Such failure would discourage other states from entering into treaties with us, particularly an extradition treaty that hinges on reciprocity.

---

770 2004 ASEAN Mutual Legal Assistance Treaty, art. 1, para.1.

771 See also *Soriano*, p. 136.

> "Verily, we are bound by *pacta sunt servanda* to comply in good faith with our obligations under the Treaty. This principle requires that we deliver the accused to the requesting country if the conditions precedent to extradition, as set forth in the Treaty, are satisfied. In other words, [t]he demanding government, when it has done all that the treaty and the law require it to do, is entitled to the delivery of the accused on the issue of the proper warrant, and the other government is under obligation to make the surrender. Accordingly, the Philippines must be ready and in a position to deliver the accused, should it be found proper."[772]

2. Types of Assistance Rendered

The ASEAN MLAT lists ten types of assistance that can be rendered between and among ASEAN member states, including, but not limited to, the taking of evidence or obtaining voluntary statements from persons, making arrangements for transfers of persons to give statements or assist in criminal matters, effecting service of judicial documents, identifying or tracing the location of persons, etc.[773]

As explained above, this list applies equally to the Philippine setting and thus, said types of assistance should be rendered by the Philippines. Nonetheless, it must be mentioned that in the event that a type of assistance is not specifically provided for in the ASEAN MLAT, the Philippines in practice, according to the official in charge in the Department of Justice, generally still provides the assistance requested for, as long as the same is agreed upon by the parties and the same does not conflict with Philippine domestic law.[774] In an interview with the relevant officials handling mutual legal assistance in the Philippines, they would normally advise the requesting member state of the applicable Philippine law and procedure to the assistance request on whether the same is feasible or not.[775] There is an open communication line between authorities in ASEAN and preliminary consultation exists that helps facilitate effectuating MLA requests.

---

772 Government of the United States of America v. Purganan, G.R. No. 148571, 24 September 2002.

773 ASEAN Mutual Legal Assistance Treaty, art. 1, § 2.

774 Interview with Department of Justice Senior State Council Meredith Alvor.

775 Interview with Department of Justice Senior State Council Meredith Alvor.

In line with this, the Philippines may provide types of assistance not specifically enumerated in the ASEAN MLAT but nonetheless falling under its catch-all provision. To illustrate, the Philippine government may provide assistance with regard the interception of communication and communication data as Philippine domestic law sanctions this. Although the relevant provision of the 1987 Philippine Constitution mentions that the privacy of communication and correspondence shall remain inviolable, it nonetheless allows intrusion should there be a lawful order of the court, or when public safety or order requires, as may be otherwise determined by law.[776] As to which laws these could be, one could look into either of the following: Republic Act No. 4200 or the "Act to Prohibit and Penalized Wire Tapping and Other Related Violations of Private Communication and Other Purposes" (hereinafter "Anti-Wiretapping Law"), Republic Act No. 9372 or the Human Security Act of 2007 (under Sections 7-15 for interception of communication in terrorism cases) as amended by Republic Act No. 11479 or the Philippine Anti-Terrorism Act of 2020 (under Sections 16 to 24), the Philippine Cybercrime Act of 2012 vis-à-vis online data.[777] Procedurally, one could look into the Philippine Rules on Criminal Procedure and the Rule on Cybercrime Warrants, on general application for coercive orders and cybercrime warrants, respectively.

Going specifically to online evidence in terms of international cooperation, the implementing rules and regulations of the Philippine Cybercrime Act provides that the Philippine Department of Justice shall cooperate and render assistance to other contracting parties, as well as request assistance from foreign states, for purposes of detection, investigation, and

776 1987 Philippine Constitution, art. 3, § 3.

777 On one hand, wiretapping or interception of communication and/or communication data without consent under the Anti-Wiretapping Law is illegal. It is likewise illegal to keep and/or disclose records of the same. It would not be unlawful however for any law enforcement officer to do either acts with a lawfully obtained order in cases involving terrorism and the "crimes of treason, espionage, provoking war and disloyalty in case of war, piracy, mutiny in the high seas, rebellion, conspiracy and proposal to commit rebellion, inciting to rebellion, sedition, conspiracy to commit sedition, inciting to sedition, kidnapping as defined by the Revised Penal Code, and violations of Commonwealth Act No. 616, punishing espionage and other offenses against national security" (Anti-Wiretapping Law, § 3; Human Security Act of 2007, §§ 7-15 vis-à-vis Anti-Terrorism Act, §§ 16-24). On the other hand, the Philippine Cybercrime Act equivocally provides in Section 22 that general international cooperation agreements that may come into application vis-à-vis online evidence and cybercrime cases shall be given full force and effect.

prosecution of offenses related to the pertinent law, such as illegal access, illegal interception, data interference, system interference, misuse of devices, computer-related offenses, cyber-squatting, cybersex, online child pornography, etc., and in the collection of evidence in electronic form in relation thereto.[778] In this respect, the principles of all existing cooperation laws such as Presidential Degree No. 1069 (Extradition Law), and existing extradition and mutual legal assistance treaties, shall apply.[779]

As to what the specific types of assistance the Implementing Rules and Regulations provide, the Philippines can, namely, (1) provide assistance in the real-time collection of traffic and/or content data with specified communications in the country transmitted by means of a computer system with respect to offenses defined under the Philippine Cybercrime Prevention Act; (2) allow another state to access publicly available stored computer data located in the country or elsewhere; (3) allow another state to access or receive, through a computer system located in the country, stored computer data located in another country, if the other state obtained the lawful and voluntary consent of the person who has the lawful authority to disclose the data to said other state through that computer system; (4) receive a request of another state for it to order or obtain the expeditious preservation of data stored by means of a computer system located within the country, and (5) accommodate request from another state to search, access, seize, secure or disclose stored data by means of a computer system located within the country, including data which has been preserved under the immediately preceding type of assistance.[780]

It bears to stress that as per the enumeration by the Implementing Rules and Regulations of the types of assistance available vis-à-vis online data and/or communication, it is only with the two last enumerated types of assistance that the rules specifically mention the requirement of a formal request for mutual legal assistance be made for the search or similar access, seizure or similar securing, or disclosure of the stored computer data. Given such, it becomes questionable therefore whether a formal request for mutual legal assistance is required for the other enumerated types of assistance. It remains however in practice that formal requests for assistance

778 Implementing Rules and Regulations to the Philippine Cybercrime Prevention Act, §§ 4, 25.

779 Implementing Rules and Regulations to the Philippine Cybercrime Prevention Law, § 25.

780 Implementing Rules and Regulations to the Philippine Cybercrime Prevention Law, § 25.

are required for any form of assistance, especially if the same shall be used in evidence and prosecutorial purposes, and not merely investigative.

Based on the foregoing, the Philippines presents an interesting case of having the legal framework to render assistance falling under the catch-all provision of its self-executory legal basis (the ASEAN MLAT) and yet it does not have a general domestic law on international cooperation which its fellow ASEAN member states have. A perusal of the different substantial law and procedural rules reveals this situation, which allows the Philippines then to render the widest possible measure of assistance it could provide.

What makes matters more interesting is that the types of assistance mentioned in the Philippine Cybercrime Act under the provisions on international cooperation mirrors to some degree, *mutatis mutandis*, the types of assistance basically provided by the ASEAN MLAT, despite the fact that the Cybercrime Act was not intended, as its title suggests, to be the implementing law of the ASEAN MLAT. This observed similarity as regards types of assistance can equally be said with another law, the Anti-Money Laundering Act, wherein requests for mutual assistance can be made by the Philippines vis-à-vis money laundering offenses in (1) the identifying, freezing, restraining, and seizing of assets alleged to be proceeds of any unlawful activity; (2) obtaining information related to any covered transaction, money laundering offense, or any matter directly or indirectly related thereto; (3) subject to the laws of the requested state, search and seize documents, materials, or objects; and (4) apply for a forfeiture order of any monetary instrument or property.[781] On the other hand, requests from a foreign state may be received as regards the following: (1) identifying, freezing, restraining, and seizing of assets; (2) giving information as regards matters needed by the foreign state vis-à-vis the Anti-Money Laundering Act; and (3) applying for a forfeiture order.[782]

The foregoing contemplated types of assistance under the Anti-Money Laundering Act are covered by the types of mutual legal assistance that can be rendered under the ASEAN MLAT, specifically those involving the identification, tracking, restriction, and/or recovery and forfeiture of properties involved in or derived from a commission of a crime. There seems to be an overlap that might lead later on to confusion, despite the disclosure from authorities that there would be no issue arising from overlaps and both the Anti-Money Laundering Act and the ASEAN MLAT

781 Republic Act No. 9160 (as amended), § 13(c).
782 Republic Act No. 9160 (as amended), § 13(b).

shall be cited as legal bases in support for the request. All legal bases that may be thought to be applicable shall be cited in the respective MLA requests. In such a case, it could either be construed as a complete disclosure of applicable legal grounds for a certain request, or a shotgun approach wherein the priority is more on breadth, quantity, or spread (to increase chances of getting the legal basis right) rather than prioritizing quality and accuracy.

Given these issues, Philippine authorities are willing and able to advise on the applicable law and procedure as well as whether a particular request is feasible or not. The open consultation and preliminary communication between parties help overcome the stumbling block posed by any lack of specific domestic legislation, or the lack of standardization in the legal framework that would spell out what is required and can be given.

3. Compatibility with other Agreements

Regarding how the ASEAN MLAT fits within the international cooperation commitments of the Philippines, the Philippines practices both informal and formal cooperation with its fellow ASEAN member states. On one hand, the Philippines is a signatory to treaties such as the United Nations Convention Against Transnational Organized Crime ("UNTOC") and United Nations Convention on Corruption ("UNCOC"), both of which provide for mutual legal assistance provisions, and to which the other ASEAN member states are also signatories.

The Philippines is also, within the ASEAN framework, as aforementioned, a part of the Agreement on Information Exchange and Establishment of Communication Procedures of 07 May 2002 to promote cooperation in combating transnational crime, including terrorism, through the establishment of communication networks, logistical arrangements, combined training, and border controls, among others.[783] The Philippines is a signatory together with Malaysia, Indonesia, Cambodia, Brunei, and Thailand.[784]

---

783 Agreement on Information Exchange and Establishment of Communication Procedures, arts. 4 and 5; *Caballero-Anthony*, Regional Security in Southeast Asia, p. 217. Municipal law as referred to herein is another nomenclature for domestic law. These terms are used interchangeably in the Philippine legal framework.

784 *Caballero-Anthony*, Regional Security in Southeast Asia, p. 217; *Soesilowati*, p. 235.

Interviews with Philippine officials highlight existing agreements or arrangements between law enforcement authorities or regulatory bodies that facilitate cooperation with each other. For example, the Philippine National Police ("PNP") has existing agreements with other police agencies of other ASEAN member states to cooperate and help each other in terms of law enforcement activities such as, but not limited to, joint police exercises, border controls, training camps, information exchange, or just undertakings that each is willing to extend assistance – either formally or informally – should it be requested or needed by the other party.[785] These agreements are normally facilitated through the ASEANAPOL network.

The Philippines, according to an interview with a PNP official, still treats these types of agreements (even if the subject matter involves informal means of cooperation) as formal agreements because before the PNP can acquiesce to these, they need to get approval like any other executive agreement and/or treaty.[786] Before any agreement can be concluded, officials of the PNP, which is under the Department of Interior and Local Government ("DILG"), consult with the Department of Foreign Affairs ("DFA") which would be the authority to give the green light to any agreement as per Executive Order No. 459 providing for the guidelines in the negotiation of international agreements and its ratification.

Further, cooperation is also done in other law enforcement authorities and administrative agencies such as the Philippine Central Bank.[787] Mostly concerned with money laundering incidents or cases, the Central Bank communicates directly with other regulatory authorities on money laundering and other financial crimes.[788] Thus, while not equivocally elucidated in the interviews, cooperation and coordination with their respective counterparts form part and parcel of their everyday functioning. This highlights the important role this cooperation plays in the entire criminal justice architecture because if one would recall, informal cooperation refers to "exchange of information that occurs directly between law enforcement and regulatory agencies with their foreign counterparts."[789] This is normally used prior to an investigation becoming official and/or prior to commencement of court proceedings, and law enforcement and regulatory agencies are enabled to "directly share information and intelligence with

---

785 Interview with Philippine National Police Officer Joie Quieta.
786 Interview with Philippine National Police Officer Joie Quieta.
787 Interview with Atty. Arnold Frane.
788 Interview with Atty. Arnold Frane.
789 *Secretariat*, p. 22.

their foreign counterparts without any requirement to make a formal mutual assistance request."[790]

4. Principles, Conditions, and Exceptions

Undersecretary Malaya and others mention in their publication that the passage of a domestic law would be useful in providing standardized guidelines for the issuance and execution of MLA requests, negotiation of MLA agreements, and bases for the grant or refusal of requests.[791] While this has yet to happen, there is a need to find other sources to determine principles, conditions, and exceptions the Philippines apply to mutual legal assistance, which are illustrated as the mandatory or discretionary grounds used by the Philippines in refusing a MLA request. One can refer to the ASEAN MLAT due to its self-executory nature as a legal basis for mutual legal assistance between ASEAN member states (or any other state party that may later on accede to the treaty). One can also look unto other existing law and jurisprudence that discusses international cooperation in criminal matters as well as the investigative measures that fall within the ambits of a mutual legal assistance request. In light of this, laws and procedure as provided by the Philippine Constitution, Rules of Criminal Procedure, Anti-Wiretapping Act, Anti-Money Laundering Act, and Philippine Cybercrime Prevention Act among others are taken into account. Although navigating through different laws, jurisprudence, and other legal materials may seem to be a herculean task to be able to pinpoint what is applicable, it is mentioned that in practice, they work to approve all requests received and normally, requests received and sent among ASEAN member-countries are executed.[792] In other words, the end in sight is generally to make things work. To avoid denial of requests, open communication channels are maintained and preliminary consultations and communication are often done between authorities and they advise one another as to the correct content or procedure to be followed.

790 *Secretariat*, p. 22. See also *Bassiouni*, Modalities of International Cooperation, p. 19.
791 *Malaya/Monedero-Arnesto/Paras*, p. 16.
792 Interview with Department of Justice Senior State Council Meredith Alvor.

a. Sufficiency of Evidence Requirement

On the basis of the ASEAN MLAT, there is a tacit sufficiency of evidence requirement written in between its provisions: the more coercive an investigative measure is, e.g. search and seizures, the more evidence or information the requesting state must provide prior to the approval of a MLA request.

Given that this is self-executory in the Philippine setting this should be then applied. However, the ASEAN MLAT does not answer for how this would be operationalized. In this case, one then must look into the relevant and related laws as to how sufficiency of evidence applies and use the same vis-à-vis Philippine framework on mutual legal assistance.

In light of this, one can look then into existing Philippine framework on extradition, given that it is connected to mutual legal assistance as an international cooperation mechanism. There historically exists a sufficiency of evidence requirement in the granting of requests for extradition. Under the relevant provision of Presidential Decree No. 1069, for example, the court may deny a request should there be a lack of a *prima facie* case against the subject person to be extradited.[793] Significantly, international cooperation experts state that a sufficiency of evidence requirement is carried over to mutual legal assistance requests especially those entailing coercive measures as they generally require a lawful court order to be executed lawfully, although a bit more relaxed compared to extradition cases, particularly for measurers involving production of documents or taking of statements of witnesses.[794]

Anent what constitutes this sufficiency of evidence requirement, one can look first into what the Philippine Constitution provides. First, in terms of the people's rights to be secure in their persons, houses, papers, and effects against unreasonable searches and seizures, the Philippine Constitution provides under Article III or the Bill of Rights:

> "SECTION 2. The right of the people to be secure in their persons, houses, papers, and effects against unreasonable searches and seizures of whatever nature and for any purpose shall be inviolable, and no search warrant or warrant of arrest shall issue except upon probable cause to be determined personally by the judge after examination under oath or affirmation of the complainant and the witnesses he

793 Presidential Decree No. 1069, § 10.
794 *Malaya/Monedero-Arnesto/Paras*, p. 13.

may produce, and particularly describing the place to be searched and the persons or things to be seized."[795]

The Philippine Supreme Court in a plethora of cases has explained the abovementioned constitutional provision. For example, in *People of the Philippines v. Cogaed*, the Court held as follows:

> "This provision requires that the court examine with care and diligence whether searches and seizures are 'reasonable.' As a general rule, searches conducted with a warrant that meets all the requirements of this provision are reasonable. This warrant requires the existence of probable cause that can only be determined by a judge. The existence of probable cause must be established by the judge after asking searching questions and answers. Probable cause at this stage can only exist if there is an offense alleged to be committed. Also, the warrant frames the searches done by the law enforcers. There must be a particular description of the place and the things to be searched."[796]

In other words, the probable cause requirement needs to be satisfied should a mutual legal assistance request entail coercive measures.

As to what constitutes probable cause in Philippine Constitutional and Criminal Law, it is more than bare suspicion but less than what is needed to secure conviction in a criminal case ("guilt beyond reasonable ground"):[797] the Philippine Supreme Court defines "probable cause" as "a reasonable ground of suspicion supported by circumstances sufficiently strong in themselves to warrant a cautious man to believe that the person accused is guilty of the offense with which he is charged" and "that the objects sought in connection with the offense are in the place sought to be searched."[798] Stating it differently, it is the "existence of such facts and circumstances that can lead a reasonably discreet and prudent man to believe that an offense has been committed, and that the items, articles or

795 1987 Philippine Constitution, art. III, § 2.

796 People of the Philippines v. Cogaed, G.R. No. 200334, 30 July 2014.

797 Clay and Feather International v. Lichaytoo, G.R. No. 193105, 30 May 2011; Hon Ne Chan v. Honda Motor Co., G.R. No. 172775, 19 December 2007; Sarigumba v. Sandiganbayan, G.R. Nos. 154239-41, 16 February 2005; Microsoft Corporation and Lotus Development Corporation v. Maxicorp, Inc., G.R. No. 140946, 13 September 2004, 438 SCRA 224, 225; Okabe v. Gutierrez, G.R. No. 150185, 27 May 2004.

798 People of the Philippines v. Cogaed, G.R. No. 200334, 30 July 2014; Kho v. Hon. Lanzanas, G.R. No. 150877, 4 May 2006; People v. Aruta, 351 Phil. 868, 880 (1998).

objects sought in connection with said offense or subject to seizure and destruction by law are in the place to be searched."[799] As the Philippine Supreme Court elucidated in *Clay and Feather International v. Lichaytoo:*

> "xxx In determining probable cause, the average person weighs facts and circumstances without resorting to the calibrations of the rules of evidence of which he has no technical knowledge. He relies on common sense. A finding of probable cause needs only to rest on evidence showing that, more likely than not, a crime has been committed and that it was committed by the accused. Probable cause demands more than bare suspicion, but it requires less than evidence that would justify a conviction.

> "A finding of probable cause does not require an inquiry as to whether there is sufficient evidence to secure a conviction. It is enough that the act or omission complained of constitutes the offense charged. The term does not mean 'actual and positive cause' nor does it import absolute certainty. It is merely based on opinion and reasonable belief. A trial is intended precisely for the reception of prosecution evidence in support of the charge. The court is tasked to determine guilt beyond reasonable doubt based on the evidence presented by the parties at a trial on the merits."[800]

The foregoing is carried over to the Philippine Rules of Criminal Procedure, wherein the following requisites must be satisfied before a search warrant can be properly issued: "(1) it must be issued upon probable cause; (2) the probable cause must be determined by the judge himself and not by the applicant or any other person; (3) in the determination of probable cause, the judge must examine, under oath or affirmation, the complainant and such witnesses as the latter may produce; and (4) the warrant issued must particularly describe the place to be searched and persons or things to be seized."[801] Notably, the oath required must refer to "the truth of the facts within the personal knowledge of the petitioner or his witnesses, because the purpose thereof is to convince the commit-

---

799 People of the Philippines v. Mariacos, G.R. No. 188611, 16 June 2010; Hon Ne Chan v. Honda Motor Co., G.R. No. 172775, 19 December 2007.

800 Clay and Feather International v. Lichaytoo, G.R. No. 193105, 30 May 2011.

801 Philippine Rules of Criminal Procedure, Rule 126, § 4; Hon Ne Chan v. Honda Motor Co., G.R. No. 172775, 19 December 2007; Republic v. Sandiganbayan, G.R. Nos. 112708-09, 29 March 1996.

ting magistrate, not the individual making the affidavit and seeking the issuance of the warrant, of the existence of probable cause."[802]

Taking into account the foregoing into a mutual legal assistance framework, it becomes paramount then that the requesting member state provides Philippine authorities sufficient information to allow the latter to apply accordingly for a warrant before the Philippine courts and be able to consequently execute a request for search and seizure. Anything less provided by the requesting member state, or in other words, information and/or evidence not sufficient to satisfy the *onus probandi* of probable cause might result to the denial of the issuance of a warrant.

Moreover, authorities from both the requesting member state and the Philippines are mandated to particularly indicate or describe the location of the place to be searched and/or items, documents, and records to be seized to enable law enforcement officers serving the warrant to "(1) readily identify the properties to be seized and thus prevent them from seizing the wrong items;" and (2) leave said officers "with no discretion regarding the articles to be seized and thus prevent unreasonable searches and seizures."[803] The Philippine Constitution seeks to protect against "search warrants of broad or general characterization or sweeping descriptions, which will authorize police officers to undertake a fishing expedition to seize and confiscate any and all kinds of evidence or articles relating to an offense."[804] The avoidance of fishing expeditions applies across the board and thus equally applies to mutual legal assistance in criminal matters: evidentiary requirements ought to be likewise met in such circumstances.[805] This notwithstanding, authorities are not required to describe everything in "precise and minute detail as to leave no room for doubt on the part of the searching authorities", especially those which by their nature needed to be described in general as otherwise, no warrant shall issue due to lack of technical description.[806] Concomitantly, one of the tests jurisprudence provides as regards particularity of description is "when the things

---

802 Hon Ne Chan v. Honda Motor Co., G.R. No. 172775, 19 December 2007; Prudente v. Dayrit, G.R. No. 82870, 14 December 1989.

803 Hon Ne Chan v. Honda Motor Co., G.R. No. 172775, 19 December 2007; People v. Tee, G.R. Nos. 140546-47, 20 January 2003.

804 People v. Tee, G.R. Nos. 140546-47, 20 January 2003.

805 *Malaya/Monedero-Arnesto/Paras*, p. 16.

806 Hon Ne Chan v. Honda Motor Co., G.R. No. 172775, 19 December 2007; People v. Tee, G.R. Nos. 140546-47, 20 January 2003.

described are limited to those which bear direct relation to the offense for which the warrant is being issued."[807]

In connection to these requirements, if one would recall, there is a paramount consideration to privacy and privacy of communication under Philippine Constitutional Law. As mentioned earlier, the privacy of communication and correspondence shall remain generally inviolable except upon lawful order of the court, or when public safety or order requires as may be otherwise determined by law.[808] The lawful order or warrant for such interception of communication and/or communication data, including online data, is pursuant to the Anti-Wiretapping Law, Cybercrime Prevention Act, or more recently, the Philippine Anti-Terrorism Act respectively, which more or less follow the same requirements laid down in the Rules on Criminal Procedure.[809]

The Philippine Cybercrime Prevention Act provides further parameters and/or requirements with respect to online data, communication, and correspondence. To begin with, a service provider must keep, retain, and preserve the integrity of traffic data and subscriber information for a minimum period of six (6) months from date of transaction.[810] Content data shall likewise be preserved for six (6) months from date of receipt of any order from law enforcement authorities requiring its preservation.[811] A one-time extension of six (6) months is allowed and the implementing rules and regulations provide that once the preserved, transmitted, or stored data is used as evidence in a case, the mere act of furnishing the service provider with a copy of the transmittal document to the Office of Prosecutor constitutes already notification to preserve the computer data until the final termination of the case and/or as ordered by the relevant court, as the case may be.[812]

Law enforcement authorities are allowed to collect or record by technical or electronic means computer data upon valid issuance of the applica-

---

807 Hon Ne Chan v. Honda Motor Co., G.R. No. 172775, 19 December 2007.

808 1987 Philippine Constitution, art. 3, § 3.

809 *See* Anti-Wiretapping Law, § 3; Philippine Cybercrime Prevention Act, § 12; Anti-Terrorism Act, §§ 16-24; Implementing Rules and Regulations of the Philippine Cybercrime Prevention Act, § 13.

810 Implementing Rules and Regulations of the Philippine Cybercrime Prevention Act, § 12(1).

811 Implementing Rules and Regulations of the Philippine Cybercrime Prevention Act, § 12(1).

812 Implementing Rules and Regulations of the Philippine Cybercrime Prevention Act, § 12(1).

ble court warrant. The applicable Rule is A.M 17-11-03-SC or the Rule on Cybercrime Warrants. The said Rule was approved by the Philippine Supreme Court and became effective on 15 August 2018. The Philippine Supreme Court approved said Rule to allow law enforcement officers to apply for the issuance of said warrants for either the "preservation, disclosure, interception, search, seizure, and/or examination, custody, and destruction of computer data" in relation to the country's Cybercrime Prevention Act (Section 1.2). The warrants that could be issued under said Rule involves Philippine law enforcement authorities as well as service providers and tech companies wherein the former can order the latter with the appropriate warrant to preserve, disclose, intercept, search, seize, and/or examine, take into custody, or destroy computer data. This is irrespective of where the service provider or tech company is located as long as it is offering its services within the territory of the Philippines (Section 1.4[q]).

A reading of the Rule on Cybercrime Warrants would show common requirements as to what an application for a warrant to either disclose, intercept, or search, seize, and examine data should contain, and only indicating therein whether the warrant is to disclose, intercept, or search, seize, and examine: (1) the probable offense involved; (2) relevance and necessity of the computer data or subscriber's information sought to be disclosed for the purpose of the investigation; (3) names of the individuals or entities whose computer data or subscriber's information are sought to be disclosed/intercepted/examined/searched and seized, including the names of the individuals or entities who have control, possession or access thereto, if available; (4) particular description of the computer data or subscriber's information sought to be disclosed; (5) place where the disclosure of computer data or subscriber's information is to be enforced, if available; (6) manner or method by which the disclosure of the computer data or subscriber's information is to be carried out, if available; and (7) other relevant information that will persuade the court that there is a probable cause to issue the appropriate warrant (Section 4.3). Based on these requirements, the Rules entertain the idea that the place where the disclosure, interception, or search, seizure, and examination of data shall be enforced is unknown, which is otherwise unfathomable in normal coercive measures such as search and seizure as earlier noted above.

Aside from coercive measures involving communication and communication data, the sufficiency of evidence requirement is equally relevant to requests in relation to examination of bank accounts as well as locating, seizing, restraining, or forfeiture of assets and/or other properties.[813] These matters are covered in a mutual legal assistance request. Regarding the applicable Philippine laws, one can look mainly into the Anti-Money Laundering Act (as amended), Human Security Act of 2007, Terrorism Financing Prevention and Suppression Act of 2012, and the Anti-Terrorism Act of 2020 which enable not only the examination of bank accounts, monetary instruments, and properties involved in money laundering and unlawful activities such as terrorism and financing of terrorism, but also the freezing and sequestration of the relevant monetary instruments and properties.[814]

The Anti-Money Laundering Act (as amended) is the applicable Philippine law that penalizes money laundering and the first domestic statute that provides for mutual legal assistance to be requested and rendered by the Philippines.[815] In relation thereto, the Anti-Money Laundering Council, which is the Philippine administrative body primarily in charge of handling money laundering affairs and cases,[816] as well as acts and omissions connected to financing of terrorism as defined by law,[817] has the authority to "inquire into or examine any particular deposit or investment with any banking institution or non-bank financial institution upon any order of a competent court when it has been established that there is probable cause that the deposits or investments" are related to an unlawful activity or money laundering case as defined in the law.[818] Said court order is however not required in predicate offenses such as kidnapping, a narcotics offense, hijacking, destructive arson, murder, terrorism and conspiracy to commit terrorism. Nevertheless, the Anti-Money Laundering Council ought to act under the requirement of probable cause.[819]

The same Anti-Money Laundering Council is authorized to apply or file a petition *ex parte* with the Philippines' Court of Appeals for any freezing

---

813 See ASEAN MLAT, art. 1, § 2(g)-(i).

814 Anti-Money Laundering Act (as amended), §§ 10, 11, 12; Anti-Terrorism Act, §§ 35, 36; Terrorism Financing Prevention and Suppression Act, §§ 10-12.

815 Anti-Money Laundering Act (as amended), §§ 4, 13.

816 Anti-Money Laundering Act (as amended), § 7.

817 Anti-Terrorism Act, §§ 35, 36.

818 Anti-Money Laundering Act (as amended), § 11

819 Anti-Money Laundering Act (as amended), §§ 11; 3(11). Unlawful activities include, but is not limited to, crimes such as kidnapping for ransom, violations of the Philippines' Comprehensive Dangerous Drugs Act, violations of the Anti-Graft and Corrupt Practices Act, plunder, terrorism and conspiracy to commit terrorism, terrorism financing, illegal gambling, piracy, qualified theft, smuggling, swindling, violations of Electronic Commerce Act, hijacking, etc.

of any monetary instrument or property alleged to be laundered, proceeds from, or instrumentalities used in or intended for use in any unlawful activity and said Court of Appeals shall issue the corresponding freezing order should probable cause exist as regards the same monetary instrument or property.[820] Furthermore, the Anti-Money Laundering Council can file an *ex parte* verified petition for forfeiture proceedings against any monetary instrument or property, upon its determination that probable cause exists that any monetary instrument or property is in any way related to an unlawful activity or money laundering offense as defined in the Act.[821] In relation to said petition, the appropriate court could issue provisional asset protection order when there is probable cause to believe that said order should be issued.[822]

Taking this into account, it bears mentioning that these forfeiture proceedings are not necessarily criminal in nature which as mentioned in the earlier sections is imperative for mutual legal assistance in criminal matters to apply. This notwithstanding, the nexus can be established between the forfeiture proceedings and the criminal case of anti-money laundering, which would make any request for assistance pertaining to the same within the penumbra of the ASEAN MLAT. Additionally, forfeiture proceedings is contemplated specifically in the list of the types of assistance that can be rendered and requested between the ASEAN member states.

Having said that, one can moreover note that it is imperative to satisfy the probable cause requirement before action can be taken by the Anti-Money Laundering Council, and of course the Department of Justice, as the central authority for mutual legal assistance requests. In this respect, it is understandable that in submitting requests by foreign states, the Anti-Money Laundering Act requires that they contain the information as detailed below, and that they are able to satisfy the probable cause requirement, at the least, in the process:

> "Section 13. Mutual Assistance among States.
>
> "xxx
>
> "(e) Requirements for Requests for Mutual Assistance from Foreign States. A request for mutual assistance from a foreign State must (1) confirm that an investigation or prosecution is being conducted

820 Anti-Money Laundering Act (as amended), §§ 7(6), 10; Anti-Terrorism Act, §§ 35, 36.

821 Anti-Money Laundering Act (as amended), § 12.

822 A.M. No. 05-11-04-SC, § 11.

> in respect of a money launderer named therein or that he has been convicted of any money laundering offense; (2) state the grounds on which any person is being investigated or prosecuted for money laundering or the details of his conviction; (3) give sufficient particulars as to the identity of said person; (4) give particulars sufficient to identify any covered institution believed to have any information, document, material or object which may be of assistance to the investigation or prosecution; (5) ask from the covered institution concerned any information, document, material or object which may be of assistance to the investigation or prosecution; (6) specify the manner in which and to whom said information, document, material or object obtained pursuant to said request, is to be produced; (7) give all the particulars necessary for the issuance by the court in the requested State of the writs, orders or processes needed by the requesting State; and (8) contain such other information as may assist in the execution of the request."[823]

Taking these into account, said requirement needs to be satisfied whenever a request for assistance entails coercive measures, regardless of what is sought is a general search and seizure procedure, an interception or intrusion of privacy of communication and correspondence, including online data, or an examination of bank deposits and other monetary instrument, including its freezing or forfeiture. In case of non-coercive measures, the requirement for establishing probable cause is in general not so stringent.

b. Dual Criminality

Dual criminality is provided as a mandatory ground for refusal in the ASEAN MLAT. In practice however, as shown in available reports, the Philippines does not decline requests for mutual legal assistance, regardless of being based on treaty or not, on the ground of dual criminality.[824] This is notably allowed by the ASEAN MLAT and such fact has been confirmed in an interview with the person-in-charge of mutual legal assistance requests within the Department of Justice. The same is likewise provided in the implementing rules and regulations of the Cybercrime Prevention

---

823 Anti-Money Laundering Act (as amended), § 13(e).
824 *Soriano*, p. 138.

Act, wherein dual criminality has been categorically excluded as a valid ground to refuse any request for assistance by a requesting state.[825]

As to the reason why the Philippines shall still proceed in executing a request for mutual legal assistance despite the non-existence of the dual criminality requirement as provided for in the ASEAN MLAT, Philippine jurisprudence may shed light as to why. It acknowledges the country's interest in suppressing crime:

> "The Philippines also has a national interest to help in suppressing crimes and one way to do it is to facilitate the extradition of persons covered by treaties duly entered [into] by our government. More and more, crimes are becoming the concern of one world. Laws involving crimes and crime prevention are undergoing universalization. One manifest purpose of this trend towards globalization is to deny easy refuge to a criminal whose activities threaten the peace and progress of civilized countries. It is to the great interest of the Philippines to be part of this irreversible movement in light of its vulnerability to crimes, especially transnational crimes."[826]

The Philippines gives merit in being able to afford assistance to other states through the different tools of international cooperation, in order to likewise suppress crime in its own country:

> "Indeed, in this era of globalization, easier and faster international travel, and an expanding ring of international crimes and criminals, we cannot afford to be an isolationist state. We need to cooperate with other states in order to improve our chances of suppressing crime in our own country."[827]

Moreover, the Philippines values, as a state policy, comity with other states and failure to comply with treaty obligations vis-à-vis international cooperation such as extradition and/or mutual legal assistance is thought to bring a risk of dissuading other states to enter into other treaties with it, especially those involving international cooperation which is founded on

825 Implementing Rules and Regulations to the Cybercrime Prevention Act, § 25(d).

826 Secretary of Justice v. Lantion, G.R. No. 139465, 17 October 2000; Government of the United States of America v. Purgunan, G.R. No. 148571, 24 September 2002.

827 Government of the United States of America v. Purgunan, G.R. No. 148571, 24 September 2002.

reciprocity.[828] Therefore, it becomes understandable why the Philippines overlooks the requirement of double criminality to facilitate requests for mutual legal assistance.

c. Double Jeopardy

Double jeopardy is a mandatory ground for refusal under the ASEAN MLAT. To recall, a requested state shall deny assistance when the request relates to an investigation, prosecution, or punishment of a person for an offense where the person either "has been convicted, acquitted, or pardoned by a competent court or other authority in the requesting or requested member state" or "has undergone the punishment provided by law of that requesting or requested member state, in respect of that offense or of another offense constitute by the same act or omission as the first-mentioned offense."[829] Due to the self-executory nature of the ASEAN MLAT vis-à-vis mutual legal assistance the Philippines renders and requests with fellow ASEAN member states, this ought to be applicable in the Philippine setting. Thus, when the MLA request received relates to an offense wherein the subject person has been convicted, acquitted, or pardoned, or otherwise has undergone the punishment provided for, in the requesting state, then the Philippines should deny the said request. The Philippines should likewise expect a denial of a request it sends if the same circumstances exist in the requested state.

In light of the treaty provision, the concept of transnational or international double jeopardy in the Philippines has yet to be decided in jurisprudence. There has been no test case thus far when the Philippine Supreme Court upheld the prohibition on double jeopardy on the basis that the subject person has been convicted, acquitted, or pardoned, or otherwise undergone the punishment provided by the law of another state. This is especially the case with respect to mutual legal assistance matters.

In respect of this, it becomes imperative to understand then what the prohibition against double jeopardy means within the Philippine context and how it would apply in terms of requesting and receiving MLA requests. This does not include all branches and applications of the prohibi-

---

828 Government of the United States of America v. Purgunan, G.R. No. 148571, 24 September 2002.

829 2004 ASEAN Mutual Legal Assistance Treaty, art.3, § 1(d).

tion but mostly centers on what would be important in a mutual legal assistance framework.

At the outset, it can be said that the prohibition against double jeopardy as provided in the Philippine Constitution is constructed in general terms. Under Article III of the Bill of Rights in the 1987 Philippine Constitution, Section 21 provides that "no person shall be put twice in jeopardy of punishment for the same offense."[830] And should the offense be punishable by both a law and an ordinance, a conviction for either shall constitute a bar to another prosecution on the same act.[831]

Under Philippine law, double jeopardy arises when the following requisites are present: "(1) a first jeopardy attached prior to the second; (2) the first jeopardy has been validly terminated; and (3) a second jeopardy is for the same offense as in the first."[832] First jeopardy attaches when the following exist: "(1) a valid complaint or information; (2) a court of competent jurisdiction; (3) the defendant had pleaded to the charge; and (4) the defendant was acquitted, or convicted or the case against him was dismissed or otherwise terminated without his express consent."[833]

Philippine jurisprudence admits of exceptions as to when double jeopardy could still attach even if the dismissal of the case was due to the motion of the accused: "(1) where the dismissal is based on a demurrer to evidence filed by the accused after the prosecution has rested, which has the effect of a judgment on the merits and operates as an acquittal; (2) where the dismissal is made, also on motion of the accused, because of the denial of his right to a speedy trial which is in effect a failure to prosecute."[834] In these instances, the accused cannot invoke the right against double jeopardy should it be apparent that "the trial court acted with grave abuse of discretion amounting to lack or excess of jurisdiction, such as where the prosecution was not allowed the opportunity to make

830 1987 Philippine Constitution, art. 3, § 21.

831 1987 Philippine Constitution, art. 3, § 21.Given the above-quoted constitutional provision, Philippine law contemplates two (2) kinds of double jeopardy: (1) that no person shall be put twice in jeopardy for the same offense; and (2) if an act is punished by a law and an ordinance, conviction or acquittal under either shall constitute a bar to another prosecution for the same act. See 1987 Philippine Constitution, art. 3, § 21; Rules of Criminal Procedure, Rule 117, § 7.

832 Cerezo v. People of the Philippines, G.R. No. 185230, 01 June 2011; Rules of Criminal Procedure, Rule 117, § 7.

833 Bangayan v. Bangayan, G.R. Nos. 172777 and 172792, 19 October 2011.

834 Bangayan v. Bangayan, G.R. Nos. 172777 and 172792, 19 October 2011; Paulin v. Gimenez, G.R. No. 103323, 21 January 1993, 217 SCRA 386, 389.

its case against the accused or where the trial was a sham."[835] To illustrate, double jeopardy does not exist, according to Philippine jurisprudence, "(1) where the trial court prematurely terminated the presentation of the prosecution's evidence and forthwith dismissed the information for insufficiency of evidence; and (2) where the case was dismissed at a time when the case was not ready for trial and adjudication."[836]

Furthermore, double jeopardy shall not attach and the conviction of the accused shall not be a bar to another prosecution for an offense which necessarily includes the offense charged in the former complaint or information under any of the following instances: "(1) the graver offense developed due to supervening facts arising from the same act or omission constituting the former charge; (2) the facts constituting the graver charge became known or were discovered only after a plea was entered in the former complaint or information; or (3) the plea of guilty to the lesser offense was made without the consent of the prosecutor and of the offended party except as provided in section 1(f) of Rule 116."[837] In any of these foregoing cases, the applicable provision further provides that, "where the accused satisfies or serves in whole or in part the judgment, he shall be credited with the same in the event of conviction for the graver offense."[838]

Considering the abovementioned, together with the Philippine policy cooperating in good faith and in suppressing crime, one is confronted with two different interests. On one hand, there is the general prohibition against double jeopardy, which if one follows the spirit of the constitutional prohibition itself, can lead to a conclusion that the prohibition should be upheld as regards potentially transnational crimes (and concurrent jurisdictions between countries). This would be consistent with the treaty provision. On the other hand, there is the value of being cooperative in suppressing crime altogether. The Philippines in practice generally grants all mutual legal assistance requests it receives and the commitment to suppress crime could be an explanation for this.

As to how this should be applied then, the first interest outweighs the other especially if the conviction, acquittal, pardon, or service of punishment occurred in either the requesting state or the Philippines as a requested state. This is in accordance with the mandatory ground for refusal laid

---

835 Bangayan v. Bangayan, G.R. Nos. 172777 and 172792, 19 October 2011.

836 Bangayan v. Bangayan, G.R. Nos. 172777 and 172792, 19 October 2011; Paulin v. Gimenez, G.R. No. 103323, 21 January 1993, 217 SCRA 386, 389.

837 Rules of Criminal Procedure, Rule 117, § 7.

838 Rules of Criminal Procedure, Rule 117, § 7.

down in the ASEAN MLAT. It is different however should the conviction, acquittal, pardon, or service of punishment occurred in a third state – or fellow ASEAN member state – for the same offense or facts constituting the offense, because the ASEAN MLAT is limited to what is between the requesting and requested state. The question then is not easily answerable given the weighing of values involved.

Further, the position of the Philippines as requesting or requested state ought to be taken into account. If the Philippines is a requesting state, then Philippine courts would need to consider the constitutional prohibition because the evidence procured would be used within Philippine jurisdiction. Thus, domestic law and principles ought to be taken into account. If the conviction, acquittal, pardon, or service of punishment occurred elsewhere, even if it is a third state or other ASEAN member state, then such circumstance could be material in determining double jeopardy. If the Philippines however is a requested state, it is unsettled whether it can apply its own constitutional values to deny a request because it potentially violates the constitutional prohibition against double jeopardy, despite this being technically allowed in the ASEAN MLAT (although limited between the requested and requesting states). Having mentioned these potential issues or hurdles, authorities have yet to encounter this exact kind of scenario in practice. What is normally done in general is to use the open communication channels and preliminary consultation to ease out any concerns or issues that may potentially arise vis-à-vis a MLA request. Given the lack of domestic legislation or specific jurisprudence or guidelines however, these deliberations or decisions would remain ad hoc and highly dependent on what has been resolved between the requesting state or requested state.

d. Substantive Considerations of Human Rights

At this juncture, human rights considerations on a substantive level shall be looked into in respect to mutual legal assistance in the Philippines. This involves two points. First, there are human rights considerations used as grounds to refuse MLA request. As the discussion below would show, one would look deeply into Philippine law and jurisprudence to understand what human rights obligations could play a role in the refusal or execution of a MLA request. Second, there is a discussion of how limited the applicable human rights considerations are vis-à-vis grounds to refuse a request. This includes a discussion of the severity of punishment and the position of the Philippines on the proscription of torture and cruel, inhumane, and degrading punishment and treatment and how the Philippines' position matters in terms of handling MLA requests.

i. Human Rights Considerations as Grounds to Refuse

Considering that there is no readily made available domestic instrument spelling out the human rights to be taken into account vis-à-vis mutual legal assistance on a substantive level, other than those provided by the treaties and international agreements the Philippines enters into, consultation with authorities was imperative to know how practice goes. In interviews with Philippine authorities involved in mutual legal assistance requests, they mentioned that general human rights considerations come into play in mutual legal assistance, in the same way as it applies in cases of extradition. As to what these human rights are with regard to mutual legal assistance, or how any mechanism regarding the same would work, it is imperative to examine the different legal instruments, including jurisprudence.

First, there ought to be discussion of the role human rights play as grounds to refuse execution of a MLA request. In the publication of Malaya et al. (authorities in mutual legal assistance), human rights considerations comprise one of the grounds cited to refuse a MLA request in general, together with national or public interest, severity of punishment, bank secrecy, political offenses, double jeopardy (albeit this also could fall within the penumbra of human rights considerations), the rights of suspects charged with criminal offenses may be prejudiced, and specific types of assistance involving seizing and freezing of assets.[839] In light of this, a reading of the ASEAN MLAT would reveal that a request shall be denied if it violates the prohibition against double jeopardy (as discussed earlier), or is issued on reasons of discrimination, or in the transfer of persons to give evidence and/or information, the safety of said person ought to be ensured prior to the request being granted.

Alongside these grounds for refusal provided by the ASEAN MLAT itself, certain human rights aspects also ought to be taken into account by authorities vis-à-vis the practice of mutual legal assistance. At the outset, it can be said that the Philippines is replete with details and parameters in its law and jurisprudence as regards the importance of human rights

---

839 *Malaya/Monedero-Arnesto/Paras*, p. 15.

and defense rights in criminal matters, including those with earmarks of a criminal process, i.e. extradition and mutual legal assistance. Any violation generally results to grave consequences such as inadmissibility of evidence or the dismissal of the criminal case altogether. The right against double jeopardy is one of these human rights considerations, which has been tackled earlier. Generally, there would be negative consequences should the prohibition against double jeopardy be violated, although admittedly case law is left to be desired as regards any issue of double jeopardy vis-à-vis mutual legal assistance.

Additionally, there is the right to privacy, or the right to be let alone, which was institutionalized in the 1987 Philippine Constitution "as a facet of the right protected by the guarantee against unreasonable searches and seizures."[840] In Philippine law and jurisprudence, the right to privacy exists independently from one's right to liberty and in itself is deserving of constitutional protection. In relation to this, Philippine legal doctrine adheres to the so-called "zones of privacy":

> "Zones of privacy are recognized and protected in our laws. Within these zones, any form of intrusion is impermissible unless excused by law and in accordance with customary legal process. The meticulous regard we accord to these zones arises not only from our conviction that the right to privacy is a 'constitutional right' and 'the right most valued by civilized men,' but also from our adherence to the Universal Declaration of Human Rights which mandates that, 'no one shall be subjected to arbitrary interference with his privacy' and 'everyone has the right to the protection of the law against such interference or attacks."[841]

The aforementioned "zones of privacy" is created by the constitutionally conferred rights against "unreasonable searches and seizures of whatever nature and for any purpose" and the right to privacy of communication and correspondence.[842] In an earlier discussion on the existence of a probable cause requirement in the Philippines, it was already mentioned that there could only be a lawful search and seizure of one's person, property,

840 Disini v. Secretary of Justice, G.R. No. 203335, 18 February 2014, citing Pollo v. Constantino-David, G.R. No. 181881, 18 October 2011, 659 SCRA 189, 204-205.

841 Disini v. Secretary of Justice, G.R. No. 203335, 18 February 2014; See also In the Matter of the Petititon for the Issuance of Writ of Habeas Corpus of Sabio v. Senator Gordon, 535 Phil. 687, 714-715 (2006).

842 1987 Philippine Constitution, art. 3, §§ 2, 3.

house, and effects, and/or lawful interception of one's communication and correspondence, including online data or evidence (via the relevant domestic law) through a lawful order issued by the court. Stating it differently, Philippine law and jurisprudence, although admitting of some exceptions, generally requires a lawful arrest warrant before a person could be lawfully arrested and a lawful search warrant before police officers can effectuate any kind of search and seizure, including online evidence or data. Philippine law and jurisprudence further provides for stringent requirements that ought to be followed. In light of this, the Philippines adheres to the so-called exclusionary rule. No less than its Constitution provides the same:

> "Section 3.

xxx

> "(2) Any evidence obtained in violation of this or the preceding section shall be inadmissible for any purpose in any proceeding."[843]

Such exclusionary rule prevents the state from profiteering from its agents' stark violations of constitutionally enshrined rights.[844] As the former Supreme Court Justice Claudio Teehankee explained in his separate opinion in Nolasco v. Paño:

> "This constitutional mandate expressly adopting the exclusionary rule has proved by historical experience to be the only practical means of enforcing the constitutional injunction against unreasonable searches and seizures by outlawing all evidence illegally seized and thereby removing the incentive on the part of state and police officers to disregard such basic rights. What the plain language of the Constitution mandates is beyond the power of the courts to change or modify."[845]

The exclusionary rule extends to the application of the "fruit of the poisonous tree" doctrine in Philippine jurisdiction. Originating from United States jurisprudence, the same doctrine likewise finds application under Philippine law and jurisprudence:

---

843 1987 Philippine Constitution, art. 3, § 3(2).

844 Esquillo v. People of the Philippines, G.R. No. 182010, 25 August 2010 (J. Bersamin, dissenting), citing Walder v. US, 347 US 62, 64-65 (1954).

845 Nolasco v. Paño, G.R. No. L-69803, 08 October 1985 (J. Teehankee, separate). See also People of the Philippines v. Cogaed, G.R. No. 200334, 30 July 2014.

> "We have not only constitutionalized the Miranda warnings in our jurisdiction. We have also adopted the libertarian exclusionary rule known as the 'fruit of the poisonous tree,' a phrase minted by Mr. Justice Felix Frankfurter in the celebrated case of Nardone v. United States. According to this rule, once the primary source (the 'tree') is shown to have been unlawfully obtained, any secondary or derivative evidence (the ' fruit') derived from it is also inadmissible. Stated otherwise, illegally seized evidence is obtained as a direct result of the illegal act, whereas the 'fruit of the poisonous tree' is the indirect result of the same illegal act. The 'fruit of the poisonous tree' is at least once removed from the illegally seized evidence, but it is equally inadmissible. The rule is based on the principle that evidence illegally obtained by the State should not be used to gain other evidence because the originally illegally obtained evidence taints all evidence subsequently obtained. We applied this exclusionary rule in the recent case of People vs. Salanga, et al., a ponencia of Mr. Justice Regalado. Salanga was the appellant in the rape and killing of a 15-year old barrio lass. He was, however, illegally arrested. Soldiers took him into custody. They gave him a body search which yielded a lady's underwear. The underwear was later identified as that of the victim. We acquitted Salanga. Among other reasons, we ruled that 'the underwear allegedly taken from the appellant is inadmissible in evidence, being a so-called 'fruit of the poisonous tree.'"[846]

The right against unreasonable searches and seizures and the protection of privacy of communications and correspondence find application in mutual legal assistance requests not only because a MLA request could pertain to search and seizures, but also because MLA requests involve the taking of evidence and/or voluntary statements, or forfeiture proceedings. In these instances, for the search, seizure, or forfeiture (including procedures such as freezing, etc.) to be lawful, valid warrants and/or court orders are necessitated and would depend on the information provided in a request. Otherwise, the consequent arrest, search, seizure, freezing, or any other coercive measure shall be deemed illegal and any evidence obtained in relation to this are considered inadmissible as evidence. Therefore, for example, MLA requests that are more of fishing expeditions or formulated capriciously must be denied by Philippine authorities in respect of one's constitutional rights as abovestated. The same holds true even more when

846 People of the Philippines v. Alicando, G.R. No. 117487, 12 December 1995.

the Philippines is the requesting state in a mutual legal assistance request. For evidence or information obtained through mutual legal assistance to be deemed admissible, the same must be in accordance with the requirements laid down by Philippine law and jurisprudence. Hence, it is incumbent upon Philippine authorities, especially when it is at the requesting end, to specify the procedure and requirements to be followed, should it seek to use any evidence or information obtained in court proceedings at home.

Alongside the right against unreasonable search and seizures and protection of one's privacy of correspondence and communications, the Philippine Constitution provides for one's right to due process. Under Article III, Section 1, no one shall be deprived of life, liberty, or property without due process of law. The right contemplated herein heavily follows the United States doctrine on due process, which contemplates both substantive and procedural components: substantive due process "requires the intrinsic validity of the law in interfering with the rights of the person to his life, liberty, or property," while procedural due process "consists of the two basic rights of notice and hearing, as well as the guarantee of being heard by an impartial and competent tribunal."[847] In other words, the former is concerned about what ought to be done and the latter, how it ought to be done.

Applying the right to substantive due process to mutual legal assistance requests, there is no specific judicial pronouncement and/or elucidation on its applicability in a MLA framework. Nevertheless, a look into substantive due process issues would lead one to infer that a MLA request and/or the criminal matter indicated therein must not be vague nor incomplete. The Philippine Supreme Court is remindful with regard to this, reminding in many cases that "due process requires that the terms of a penal statue must be sufficiently explicit to inform those who are subject to it what conduct on their part will render them liable to its penalties."[848] In the cases of People of the Philippines v. Dela Piedra and Romualdez v. Sandiganbayan, the Court held that "a criminal statute that fails to give a person of common intelligence fair notice that his contemplated conduct is forbidden by the statute or is so indefinite that it encourages arbitrary or erratic arrests and convictions is void for vagueness. The constitutional vice in a vague or indefinite statute is the injustice to the accused in placing him on trial for

847 Secretary of Justice v. Lantion, G.R. No. 139465, 18 January 2000.
848 Romualdez v. Sandiganbayan, G.R. No. 152259, 29 July 2004.

an offense, the nature of which he is given no fair warning."[849] Commonly known as the void-for-vagueness doctrine, which again is influenced by United States doctrine and commonly applied to free speech cases, it could be applied to a certain degree on criminal cases and the Supreme Court had the occasion to provide a test for the same:

> "A statute establishing a criminal offense must define the offense with sufficient definiteness that persons of ordinary intelligence can understand what conduct is prohibited by the statute. It can only be invoked against that species of legislation that is utterly vague on its face, i.e., that which cannot be clarified either by a saving clause or by construction.
>
> "A statute or act may be said to be vague when it lacks comprehensible standards that men of common intelligence must necessarily guess at its meaning and differ in its application. In such instance, the statute is repugnant to the Constitution in two (2) respects - it violates due process for failure to accord persons, especially the parties targeted by it, fair notice of what conduct to avoid; and, it leaves law enforcers unbridled discretion in carrying out its provisions and becomes an arbitrary flexing of the Government muscle. But the doctrine does not apply as against legislations that are merely couched in imprecise language but which nonetheless specify a standard though defectively phrased; or to those that are apparently ambiguous yet fairly applicable to certain types of activities. The first may be 'saved' by proper construction, while no challenge may be mounted as against the second whenever directed against such activities. With more reason, the doctrine cannot be invoked where the assailed statute is clear and free from ambiguity, as in this case.
>
> "The test in determining whether a criminal statute is void for uncertainty is whether the language conveys a sufficiently definite warning as to the proscribed conduct when measured by common understanding and practice. xxx"[850]

The Court clarified however that "the 'vagueness' doctrine merely requires a reasonable degree of certainty for the statute to be upheld - not absolute

---

849 People v. dela Piedra, G.R. No. 121777, 24 January 2001, 350 SCRA 163; Romualdez v. Sandiganbayan, G.R. No. 152259, 29 July 2004 (J. Tinga, separate opinion).

850 Romualdez v. Sandiganbayan, G.R. No. 152259, 29 July 2004.

precision or mathematical exactitude."[851] "Flexibility, rather than meticulous specificity," according to the Court, "is permissible as long as the metes and bounds of the statute are clearly delineated."[852] An act will not be held invalid or void "merely because it might have been more explicit in its wordings or detailed in its provisions, especially where, because of the nature of the act, it would be impossible to provide all the details in advance as in all other statutes."[853]

In light of these pronouncements, should the mutual legal assistance request be incomplete or vague as to what criminal matter is involved, or the request is not specific as to what criminal matter it covers or the purpose the assistance requested for relates to, or the request seems rather a shotgun approach or fishing expedition, then substantive due process issues shall arise. Should the Philippines be at the receiving end of such a request, then it would be constitutionally enjoined to deny said requests, or ask the requesting state to be more definite in what is indicated in the subject request.

In sum, the foregoing should be taken substantively into consideration alongside what has been specifically provided in the ASEAN MLAT in the requesting and receiving of MLA requests.

ii. Limited Applicable Human Rights Obligations vis-à-vis Grounds to Refuse; Severity of Punishment Issue

Additionally, one cannot help but take a look into what Philippine law and jurisprudence provides regarding torture, violence, and intimidation, and/or cruel, inhumane, degrading treatment. While mutual legal assistance is unlike extradition wherein arrest and surrender of a person involved, information and/or evidence gathered through a mutual legal assistance request can equally lead to the success of a criminal investigation and/or prosecution and eventual risk of losing one's liberty. Thus, the discussion on punishment is only imperative.

On one hand, the Philippine Constitution provides the proscription of torture, violence, intimidation, etc. during the custodial investigation of a

---

851 Romualdez v. Sandiganbayan, G.R. No. 152259, 29 July 2004.

852 Estrada v. Sandiganbayan, 421 Phil. 290, 430, 19 November 2001; Romualdez v. Sandiganbayan, G.R. No. 152259, 29 July 2004.

853 Estrada v. Sandiganbayan, 421 Phil. 290, 430, 19 November 2001; Romualdez v. Sandiganbayan, G.R. No. 152259, 29 July 2004.

suspect, wherein "no torture, force, violence, threat, intimidation, or any other means which vitiate the free will shall be used against him."[854] Moreover, "secret detention places, solitary, incommunicado, or other similar forms of detention are prohibited."[855] And should any confession or admission be obtained through the foregoing means, the same is considered inadmissible as evidence.[856] Applying the same to mutual legal assistance, the Philippines, either as a requested or requesting state, should ensure that its authorities do not engage in any form of torture, violence, intimidation or any other means that vitiate the free will of an individual while effectuating a mutual legal assistance request. Should authorities need to take someone in their custody for purposes of mutual legal assistance, they should ensure the well-being of this person and at all times, respect the person's human rights.

On the other hand, there is also a constitutional proscription on torture and/or cruel, inhumane, or degrading treatment as a form of punishment:

> "Section 19. (1) Excessive fines shall not be imposed, nor cruel, degrading or inhuman punishment inflicted. Neither shall death penalty be imposed, unless, for compelling reasons involving heinous crimes, the Congress hereafter provides for it. Any death penalty already imposed shall be reduced to *reclusion perpetua*.
> "(2) The employment of physical, psychological, or degrading punishment against any prisoner or detainee or the use of substandard or inadequate penal facilities under subhuman conditions shall be dealt with by law."[857]

One can note two things from the above-quoted constitutional provision. First, the Philippine Constitution does not necessarily proscribe the imposition of the death penalty. Nonetheless, it limits its imposition to those considered as "heinous crimes" and compelling reasons as may be provided in law by the Philippine Congress.[858] Furthermore, the Philippine Constitution does not automatically equate the "employment of physical, psychological, or degrading punishment against any prisoner or detainee or the use of substandard or inadequate penal facilities under subhuman

854 1987 Philippine Constitution, art. 3, § 12.
855 1987 Philippine Constitution, art. 3, § 12(2).
856 1987 Philippine Constitution, art. 3, § 12(3).
857 1987 Philippine Constitution, art. 3, § 19.
858 See People v. Echegaray, G.R. No. 117472, 25 June 1996.

conditions" to torture and/or cruel, inhumane, degrading punishment.[859] Instead, it gives the discretion to Philippine legislature to deal with the same.[860]

All things considered, given the foregoing different human rights espoused in the Philippines, one must take into account that the ASEAN MLAT would allow for a limited number of grounds based on human rights, on the basis of which a requested state can deny a request. With such given circumstances, one cannot help but ask whether the Philippines can still invoke "general human rights considerations" as a ground to refuse a request when it is a requested state and the MLA request involves a matter that violates, threatens to violate, or is inconsistent with the Philippines' human rights obligations as enshrined in its Constitution, laws, and other treaty obligations.

There are two possible arising scenarios. On one hand, if the ASEAN MLAT is followed to the letter as the legal basis, then the Philippines cannot invoke "general human rights considerations" as a ground for refusal because it is not truly provided for, except in very particularly enumerated instances. Furthermore, the Philippines as illustrated in extradition cases follows in general a hands-off approach. In deciding on an extradition matter, which more or less is carved from the same cloth as mutual legal assistance,[861] the Supreme Court acknowledged five (5) postulates of extradition which includes the grant of due process rights to the accused by the requesting state as follows:

> "Second, an extradition treaty presupposes that both parties thereto have examined, and that both accept and trust, each other[']s legal system and judicial process. More pointedly, our duly authorized representatives signature on an extradition treaty signifies our confidence in the capacity and the willingness of the other state to protect the basic rights of the person sought to be extradited. That signature signifies our full faith that the accused will be given, upon extradition to the requesting state, all relevant and basic rights in the criminal proceedings that will take place therein; otherwise, the treaty would

---

859 1987 Philippine Constitution, art. 3, § 19(2).

860 People v. Echegaray, G.R. No. 117472, 25 June 1996.

861 Government of the United States of America v. Purgunan, G.R. No. 148571, 24 September 2002.

> not have been signed, or would have been directly attacked for its unconstitutionality."[862]

It seems that there is a tacit acceptance that the Philippines would not probe or interfere with how the requesting member state's legal system and judicial process works. Instead, it works on mutual trust and confidence that the requesting member state shall do what is right in the protection of the rights of the accused. Arguably, this can be translated to mutual legal assistance requests, which although of a lesser degree than extradition, also involves criminal matters.

At the same time, Philippine courts are enjoined to more or less follow the rule of non-inquiry as follows:

> "The Court realizes that extradition is basically an executive, not a judicial, responsibility arising from the presidential power to conduct foreign relations. In its barest concept, it partakes of the nature of police assistance amongst states, which is not normally a judicial prerogative. Hence, any intrusion by the courts into the exercise of this power should be characterized by caution, so that the vital international and bilateral interests of our country will not be unreasonably impeded or compromised. In short, while this Court is ever protective of the sporting idea of fair play, it also recognizes the limits of its own prerogatives and the need to fulfill international obligations."[863]

The Supreme Court further clarifies:

> "On the other hand, courts merely perform oversight functions and exercise review authority to prevent or excise grave abuse and tyranny. They should not allow contortions, delays and over-due process every little step of the way, lest these summary extradition proceedings become not only inutile but also sources of international embarrassment due to our inability to comply in good faith with a treaty partners simple request to return a fugitive. Worse, our country should not be converted into a dubious haven where fugitives and escapees can unreasonably delay, mummify, mock, frustrate, checkmate and defeat the quest for bilateral justice and international cooperation."[864]

---

862 Government of the United States of America v. Purgunan, G.R. No. 148571, 24 September 2002.

863 Government of the United States of America v. Purgunan, G.R. No. 148571, 24 September 2002.

864 Government of the United States of America v. Purgunan, G.R. No. 148571, 24 September 2002.

Thus, the Philippine courts generally maintain a hands-off position and only an oversight function through judicial review to avoid grave abuse of discretion and possible tyranny with respect to the use of international cooperation instruments.

On the other hand, the Philippines can alternatively apply "national interest" as a ground to refuse a MLA request. Albeit catch-all and subjective in nature, national and public interest is involved vis-à-vis human rights obligations because no less than the Philippine Constitution provides that adherence to human rights is part of the Philippines' state principles and policies. This would also be more consistent with the Supreme Court's recent decision to tackle the propriety of an investigative measure (deposition through written interrogatories) vis-à-vis a granted mutual legal assistance request and the question of whether one's right to confrontation of witnesses in a criminal case is infringed by virtue thereof. In the case of *People of the Philippines v. Sergio*,[865] the Court, while not delving into the validity of the execution of the mutual legal assistance, painstakingly looked into the merits of the case and the requested investigative measure to settle issues involving rights. Although the rights discussed are more on procedural rights, a reading of the case reveals the importance given by the Supreme Court on the tenets of due process, orderly administration of justice, and fair play. Thus, a hands-off policy may be the general rule in terms of international cooperation but the Supreme Court shall not quickly turn a blind eye on human rights issues if called for by the circumstances.

Given these two possible routes, Philippine authorities have yet to deny requests for mutual legal assistance on the ground of the possible conflict with its human rights obligations, such as its constitutional prohibition on the use of torture, cruel, inhumane, and/or degrading punishment, or the imposition of the death penalty. Because as intimated during interviews, no request has been denied on this ground yet.[866] The Philippines seemingly gives paramount consideration to fulfilling its treaty obligations and the absence of this condition might be reason enough for the Philippines to not use the same. But then again, it would be a case-to-case basis. Authorities interviewed mention the need for balancing of values – on whether again the member state shall give more importance to fulfilling treaty obligations blindly or provide resistance when human rights considerations are involved. Should there be any consolation to this purportedly

865 People of the Philippines v. Sergio, G.R. No. 240053, 09 October 2019.
866 Interview with Department of Justice Senior State Council Meredith Alvor.

stumbling block in upholding human right considerations, Philippine authorities are always in constant communication and consultation with its counterparts from other ASEAN member-countries.[867] Thus, they advise and assist one another as to avoid fielding in requests that contain grounds for refusal, such as those involving human rights violations. Nevertheless, open lines of communication and consultation may be insufficient solutions to address issues involving human rights. In view of this, a possible threshold would be those constitutionally provided or those rights in accordance with customary law obligations. These could be positioned as non-negotiables, regardless of whether the evidence and/or information obtained is to be used elsewhere.

e. Reciprocity

The ASEAN MLAT, as applied as a framework in the Philippines, provides reciprocity as a discretionary ground for refusal of a request for mutual legal assistance in criminal matters. This is in a way resonated in the Anti-Money Laundering Law wherein it is provided that the principles of mutuality and reciprocity shall be at all times recognized in affording mutual legal assistance.[868] Taking it more generally, the Philippines values as mentioned above as a state policy, comity with other states and failure to comply with treaty obligations vis-à-vis international cooperation such as extradition and/or mutual legal assistance is thought to bring a risk of dissuading other states to enter into other treaties with it, especially those involving international cooperation which is founded on reciprocity.[869] Thus it is not surprising that in practice, reciprocity is paramount in the handling of mutual legal assistance requests especially in the ASEAN.[870] Thus far, according to authorities, no ASEAN country has risked being denied a request for violation of reciprocity and comity because they know the repercussions of reneging on their treaty and international obligations.[871]

867 Interview with Department of Justice Senior State Council Meredith Alvor.

868 Anti-Money Laundering Act (as amended), § 13(a).

869 Government of the United States of America v. Purgunan, G.R. No. 148571, 24 September 2002.

870 Interview with Department of Justice Senior State Council Meredith Alvor.

871 Interview with Department of Justice Senior State Council Meredith Alvor.

f. Speciality or Use Limitation

The ASEAN MLAT allows a requesting member state to refuse a request on the ground that the other party fails to undertake that it shall not use the item requested for a matter other than the criminal matter indicated in its request and that the requested member state has not waive such undertaking. In the examination of Philippine domestic law mentioning mutual legal assistance or international cooperation in general, the speciality and use limitation cannot be found in the relevant provisions of the Anti-Money Laundering Act but can otherwise be found in the implementing rules and regulations of the Cybercrime Prevention Act, wherein the requesting state is required to use the requested information subject to the conditions specified in the grant.[872] Such speciality and use limitation is understandable in cybercrime instances wherein data protection is given primordial consideration in the law. Also, in a report by Philippine authorities, it was mentioned that such use limitation would apply in practice, and actually a standard provision in MLA arrangements of the Philippines with other countries.[873]

Given these circumstances, there is admittedly on its face a gap as to how this omission could be explained. A closer inspection would however reveal that the speciality or use limitation should apply, especially in instances wherein coercive measures are required in a MLA request. If one would recall, the Philippines has stringent requirements before a lawful search and seizure, arrest, or any other coercive measure can be done. One of this is the probable cause requirement before a lawful court order can be issued authorizing such coercive measure needed. Non-compliance with this in addition to other requirements would engage the so-called exclusionary rule and fruit of the poisonous tree doctrine, which would be deemed as evidence obtained in violation of rights and the law as inadmissible. In light of the same, it was also mentioned earlier that fishing expeditions and shotgun approaches in terms of searches and seizures as well as other coercive measures is frowned upon by Philippine law and jurisprudence. Philippine jurisprudence elucidated this clearly.

Thus, there ought to be particularity in the item to be seized, place to be searched, person to be arrested, etc. It follows that particularity is necessarily stated in the purpose of said coercive measure. This means that

872 Implementing Rules and Regulations to the Cybercrime Prevention Act, § 25(e).

873 *Quintana*, p. 142; *Soriano*, p. 138.

a court order that authorizes a coercive measure for a particular case and/or object cannot be used to do the same coercive measure for the same object but for a different case. This is regardless whether the applicant of the court order suddenly had the epiphany or realization that said evidence to be obtained is useful elsewhere. Otherwise this would violate one's rights as provided in no less than the Philippine Constitution. Based on this rudimentary requirements that exist in Philippine law, the speciality and use limitation should then apply to mutual legal assistance requests especially to those obtained through coercive measures because to use evidence obtained through a coercive measure other than the purpose for which it was requested would violate one's right against unreasonable searches and seizures. To avoid any infringement of rights, one should apply anew for a coercive measure to be done (if needed) to obtain evidence or information for another criminal matter not covered by the original MLA request.

g. Special Offenses and National Interest Cases

In the Philippine setting, national and public interest considerations are grounds to refuse assistance in the Anti-Money Laundering Act. A request may be refused if it is in violation of the Philippine Constitution or domestic law, or affects public order or national interest, unless the request is covered by a treaty to which the Philippines and the requesting state are parties to.[874] The Philippines may therefore still effectuate a mutual legal assistance request if this has been granted through an applicable treaty or international agreement.

The same ground for refusal can be found in the implementing rules and regulations of the Cybercrime Prevention Act wherein a request may be refused if the government considers the request to be prejudicial to its sovereignty, security, public order, or other national interest.

The ASEAN MLAT allows likewise a requested state to deny a request for assistance should the offense involved be considered a political offense. Under the Philippine setting, while the same is not provided as a ground for refusal in the Anti-Money Laundering Act, it can be found in the implementing rules and regulations of the Cybercrime Prevention Act.[875]

---

874 Republic Act No. 9160 (as amended), § 13(d).

875 Implementing Rules and Regulations to the Cybercrime Prevention Act, § 25(3)(i).

Bank secrecy is not an exception to mutual legal assistance requests under the ASEAN MLAT. In the Philippine setting however, there was cited difficulty in executing requests involving coercive measures as regards examination of bank deposits.[876] While the same is allowed under the Anti-Money Laundering Law under certain conditions,[877]the Philippines still has strict bank secrecy laws especially with respect to foreign bank deposits.[878] At most, only the law against terrorism financing clearly allows examination of foreign bank accounts.[879] Still, there is no definite judicial determination whether the mutual legal assistance treaties, since they were entered into by the Philippines on a later date, repeal the applicable bank secrecy law.[880] What the Department of Justice then does to comply – even substantially – with requests is to proceed with filing its application to the appropriate courts and let the latter decide on whether to approve it or not.[881]

C. Procedural Provisions on Mutual Legal Assistance

1. Designation of Central Authority

The Department of Justice serves as the central authority for all mutual legal assistance requests. In pursuant to this, requests are directly made by or transmitted from the Department of Justice, which is the Central Authority for all mutual legal assistance requests, unless the subject treaty expressly states that the requests shall be transmitted through diplomatic channels.[882] Formerly, it was the International Affairs Division ("IAD") of the Department of Justice which assists in the processing and implementation of such requests.[883] This division was however recently abolished and it is now the Office of the Chief State Counsel ("OCSC"), likewise of the Department of Justice, which assists the Justice Secretary in handling mutual legal assistance requests, together with requests for extradition.[884]

876 *Quintana*, p. 146.
877 Republic Act No. 9160 (as amended), § 11.
878 *Gana Jr*, p. 57.
879 The Terrorism Financing Prevention and Suppression Act of 2012, § 10.
880 *Gana Jr*, p. 57.
881 *Gana Jr*, p. 57.
882 *Quintana*, p. 142.
883 *Gana Jr*, p. 50.
884 *Quintana*, p. 142.

Despite the lead role being played by the Department of Justice in MLA matters, the Department of Foreign Affairs still has a hand in implementing and/or executing MLA agreements or international cooperation, in general. As mentioned above this mandate comes from Executive Order No. 459 issued then by former President Fidel Ramos, which essentially provides authority to the Department of Foreign Affairs as the point person as regards negotiations and ratification of international agreements. More importantly, it is grounded on the quintessential function of the Foreign Affairs department to oversee diplomatic relations between countries. This rings true even with the existing ASEAN MLAT between ASEAN member states. While the Department of Justice acts mainly on legal matters, requirements, etc., the Department of Foreign Affairs ensures smooth sailing relationships between member states. To illustrate, the Philippine government in April 2015 famously invoked the ASEAN MLAT in trying to stop the execution of Mary Jane Veloso, who was convicted for drug trafficking in Indonesia.[885] The Department of Justice sent a MLA request to Indonesia, alleging therein that Mary Jane Veloso is the private complainant in the criminal case for illegal recruitment in the Philippines against her recruiter, who allegedly conned Veloso into smuggling kilos of illegal drugs to Indonesia. Should the illegal recruiter of Veloso be convicted in the case, it would prove that Veloso was a victim of human trafficking and not a drug trafficker. In the case herein, the DFA plays an imperative role in brokering negotiations to have the MLA request effectuated despite Veloso being in death row already.[886]

2. Preparation of Requests

a. Requirements for Requests

Given that there is no general statute on mutual legal assistance in criminal matters in the Philippines, or any jurisprudence defining and delineating what should be stated in mutual legal assistance requests and as to what types of assistance can be requested by the Philippines, one can conclude that on paper, what the Philippines only has so far are the provisions

---

885 *Esmaquel*, p. 1.

886 See *Department of Foreign Affairs*, p. 1; *Human Rights in ASEAN*, p. 1; *Department of Foreign Affairs*, DFA statement on the stay of execution of Mary Jane Veloso, p. 1.

of the ASEAN MLAT on preparation of requests vis-à-vis requests that it can issue or execute from its fellow ASEAN member states.

According to Undersecretary Malaya et al., a request issued by or received for mutual legal assistance from the Philippines should have, as a minimum, the following information: "(1) the name of the requesting office and the competent authority conducting the investigation or criminal proceedings to which the request relates; (2) the purpose of the request; (3) the basis of the request; (4) the nature of the assistance sought; (5) a description of the criminal matter and its current status; (6) a statement setting out a summary of the relevant facts and laws; (7) a description of the offense to which the request relates to, including the corresponding maximum penalty therefor; (8) a description of the facts alleged to constitute the offense and a statement or text of the relevant laws of the requesting state; (9) a description of the essential acts or omissions or matters alleged or sought to be alleged; (10) a description of the information or other assistance sought; (11) the reasons for and the details of any particular procedure or requirement that the requesting State wishes to be observed; (12) a specification of any time limit within which compliance with the request is desired; (13) any special requirements for confidentiality and the reasons therefor; (14) such other information or undertaking as may be required under the domestic law of the requested state or which is otherwise necessary for the proper execution of the request."[887]

While the foregoing may be the general information that ought to be provided in a request, specificities could be found in the specific domestic laws tackling or mentioning mutual legal assistance, such as what is provided in the Anti-Money Laundering Act as regards money laundering offenses (as well as terrorism or terrorism financing cases) when either the Philippines is the requesting or requested state,[888] and in the Implementing Rules and Regulations of the Philippine Cybercrime Act as regards cybercrimes.[889]

The specificities provided by existing laws on mutual legal requests involving money laundering and cybercrime offenses notwithstanding, the general lack of concrete and easily identifiable requirements on how requests for assistance may be prepared by and for the Philippines would have its advantages and disadvantages. On one hand, Philippine officials

887 *Malaya/Monedero-Arnesto/Paras*, p. 14.
888 Republic Act No. 9160 (as amended), § 13(c) and (e).
889 Implementing Rules and Regulations to the Cybercrime Prevention Act, § 25(d).

during the Sixth Good Governance Seminar for Southeast Asian Countries reported that having no domestic law on mutual legal assistance serves as a problem even if the Philippines allow the framework provided in treaties to be self-executory.[890] Effectuating requests is made cautiously given the absence of definitive jurisprudence and generally, authorities need to second guess on what is and what is not allowed.[891] Consequently, it is rather indistinct as to what other information the Philippines would need from the requesting member state to make things work. At most, what Philippine authorities could rely on are the domestic provisions per type of assistance requested. Should the request for assistance need to go through the courts, what the authorities could only do is rely on the court's discretion, whether it shall grant the application or not. As the Philippine representative noted, the ability to render the widest range of assistance to non-treaty partners is heavily hampered.[892]

On the other hand, the lack of specificities on what a request must contain, etc., could also be advantageous because it gives the Philippine central authority elbow room on whether to grant a request or not. Not much formality is required as long as the minimum required information is provided and the substantial requirements are complied with, to the exception of money laundering and cybercrime offenses wherein certain specificities should be met. Moreover, the practice of open communication and preliminary consultation in ASEAN helps alleviate the issues of having no specific domestic legislation. As mentioned by Philippine authorities in interviews, ASEAN authorities are able to consult one another as to how to proceed with a certain request and this helps overcome any problem or issue that may hinder the preparation and execution of a request. And while no clear written law is provided for, though desirable, it does not prevent authorities from keeping abreast of each member state's laws and regulations.

b. Person or Authority Initiating the Request

Based on this, all requests sent and received shall be coursed through the Department of Justice as central authority. These requests are coursed likewise through diplomatic channels, or in the Philippines' case, the De-

890 *Quintana*, p. 146; *Soriano*, p. 140.
891 *Gana Jr*, p. 57.
892 *Quintana*, p. 146.

partment of Foreign Affairs. In relation to this, there is no clearly defined and delineated law that allows a private individual – may it be a private offended party, accused, or suspected person – to initiate or request for a mutual legal assistance request to be issued on its behalf. There is also no test case or jurisprudence yet discussing this matter.[893] Whilst a litigant or party in a criminal case can ask for such a relief in court through filing the necessary motion under Rule 15 of the Philippine Revised Rules of Court, there is no adequately defined legal basis under the same rules that allows a mutual legal assistance request to be issued. At most, the Revised Rules of Court provides for issuance of letters rogatory (Rule 23, Sections 11 and 12) and/or the use of modes of discovery, i.e depositions, interrogatories, request for admission, production of documents or evidence, and physical or mental examination of persons, as provided under Rules 23 to 29 of the Revised Rules of Court.

3. Execution of Requests

The ASEAN MLAT procedural provisions vis-à-vis execution of requests shall be equally applicable in the Philippine setting as domestic law. That said, no specific provisions have been provided as to how requests for mutual legal assistance vis-à-vis money laundering cases be handled and effectuated. And aside from the ASEAN MLAT itself and other MLA treaties the Philippines is a party to, there is no statutory provisions in handling mutual legal assistance requests in general.

a. Applicable Law on Execution

Following the mandate of the ASEAN MLAT, the Philippines executes requests for mutual legal assistance subject to its domestic law. Philippine authorities have confirmed this approach during interviews. Nonetheless, requesting states can inform about how they would like their requests to be carried out and the Philippine authorities shall as much as possible, and as long as the same does not prohibit domestic law, concede to such requests. Issues, i.e. meeting the requirements for search and seizure actions, would normally arise, according to Philippine authorities, when

893 According to interviews as well, there has been no instance yet when a private individual asked for a MLA request to be issued on his or her behalf.

the requests need to be coursed through the courts because of compliance with evidentiary requirements, etc.

b. Applicable Procedural Rights

i. Importance of Defense Rights; Human Rights Considerations in MLA and Criminal Processes in General

Consideration of defense rights is apparent in the Philippine criminal justice system. It is not only ingrained in the Philippine Constitution but one also ought to take safeguards into account across the many stages of a criminal matter. The same rings true in the execution of a MLA request. While there is no specific pronouncement domestically as to what applies to mutual legal assistance aside from what is provided in the ASEAN MLAT itself (see Part I, C, 3(b)for a complete discussion), e.g. safe conduct or safe harbor provisions, consent to be transferred, etc., a study of the pertinent Philippine laws, rules, and jurisprudence on criminal procedure can be used what these rights are.

ii. Human Rights Considerations in MLA and Criminal Processes in General

First, procedural due process considerations should be applied. This is the second facet of one's right to due process under Philippine jurisdiction. The first one – substantive due process – was discussed earlier in the discussion of human rights considerations in the substantive provisions of MLA. While again there is no specific judicial pronouncement vis-à-vis mutual legal assistance, the case of Secretary of Justice v. Lantion, which relates to extradition, can be illustrative of the importance of procedural due process in MLA proceedings.

The Supreme Court said in the case at bar that procedural due process is indispensable, even in extradition proceedings notwithstanding the lack of mention in the law and in the treaty applicable.[894] It is satisfied when the following are present: "(1) a court or tribunal clothed with judicial power to hear and determine the matter before it; (2) jurisdiction lawfully acquired by the court over the person of the defendant or over the

894 Secretary of Justice v. Lantion, G.R. No. 139465, 18 January 2000.

property subject of the proceedings; (3) the defendant must be given an opportunity to be heard, and (4) judgment must be rendered upon lawful hearing."[895]

And such procedural due process can only be foregone in three (3) instances: (1) in a proceeding where there is an urgent need for immediate action, "like the summary abatement of a nuisance per se, the preventive suspension of a public servant facing administrative charges, the padlocking of filthy restaurants or theaters showing obscene movies or like establishments which are immediate threats to public health and decency, and the cancellation of a passport of a person sought for criminal prosecution;" (2) where there is "tentativeness of administrative action, that is, where the respondent is not precluded from enjoying the right to notice and hearing at a later time without prejudice to the person affected, such as the summary distraint and levy of a delinquent taxpayer, and the replacement of a temporary appointee;" (3) "where the twin rights have been previously offered but the right to exercise them had not been claimed."[896] It is only when these exceptions are availing that procedural due process can be foregone. In light of this, the Supreme Court had once explained that extradition is not a criminal proceeding:

> "Even if the potential extraditee is a criminal, an extradition proceeding is not by its nature criminal, for it is not punishment for a crime, even though such punishment may follow extradition. It is *sui generis*, tracing its existence wholly to treaty obligations between different nations. It is not a trial to determine the guilt or innocence of the potential extraditee. Nor is it a full-blown civil action, but one that is merely administrative in character. Its object is to prevent the escape of a person accused or convicted of a crime and to secure his return to the state from which he fled, for the purpose of trial or punishment.
>
> "But while extradition is not a criminal proceeding, it is characterized by the following: (a) it entails a deprivation of liberty on the part of the potential extraditee and (b) the means employed to attain the purpose of extradition is also 'the machinery of criminal law.' This is shown by Section 6 of P.D. No. 1069 (The Philippine Extradition Law) which mandates the "immediate arrest and temporary detention of the accused" if such "will best serve the interest of justice." We further note that Section 20 allows the requesting state 'in case of urgency' to

895 People of the Philippines v. Buemio, G.R. Nos. 114011-22, 16 December 1996.
896 Secretary of Justice v. Lantion, G.R. No. 139465, 18 January 2000.

> ask for the 'provisional arrest of the accused, pending receipt of the request for extradition;' and that release from provisional arrest "shall not prejudice re-arrest and extradition of the accused if a request for extradition is received subsequently."[897]

Albeit not technically a criminal proceeding and ostensibly administrative in nature, the Supreme Court recognizes that an extradition proceeding bears the "earmarks of a criminal process": "A potential extraditee may be subjected to arrest, to a prolonged restraint of liberty, and forced to transfer to the demanding state following the proceedings. 'Temporary detention' may be a necessary step in the process of extradition, but the length of time of the detention should be reasonable."[898]

The principles of extradition are arguably applicable, more or less, in mutual legal assistance requests because the latter also involves international cooperation and the criminal process.[899] It is most of the time treaty-based, but sometimes also reciprocity-based, cooperation to which the Philippines adheres to the international law principle of *pacta sunt servanda* and comity.[900] Mutual legal assistance, like extradition, is an administrative proceeding with earmarks of a criminal process, wherein certain rights available during criminal proceedings may be engaged in the effectuating or rendering of a mutual legal assistance request especially in requests involving taking of evidence and/or voluntary statements, searches and seizures, making arrangements to appear in requesting state, transfer of persons in custody, and the like. Therefore, it is only sensible that due process should also be considered in effectuating and making mutual legal assistance requests in the same manner it does to extradition proceedings. It follows that in processing and effectuating mutual legal assistance requests, regardless on whether the instrument enabling the same is silent on due process, it is incumbent upon Philippine authorities to uphold due process both as a requesting and requested state, and should it come to a situation it is endangered to be violated or already entrenched upon,

---

897 Government of Hong Kong Special Administrative Region v. Olalia, G.R. No. 153675, 19 April 2007.

898 Government of Hong Kong Special Administrative Region v. Olalia, G.R. No. 153675, 19 April 2007.

899 See Government of the United States of America v. Purgunan, G.R. No. 148571, 24 September 2002.

900 See Government of the United States of America v. Purgunan, G.R. No. 148571, 24 September 2002.

then Philippine law and jurisprudence dictates that Philippine authorities should uphold human rights.

Second, there is one's right to remain silent, wherein the use as evidence of confessions and admissions of the accused as against himself is prohibited if the same does not comply with the requirements provided by law and jurisprudence.[901] At the outset, the right to remain silent, or otherwise called the right against self-incrimination, applies to all proceedings, whether civil, criminal, and administrative.[902] No one shall be compelled to be a witness against himself.[903] Philippine law has strict requirements regarding this, and in turn, provides for when confessions and admissions could be considered admissible. Under the Constitution and existing law and jurisprudence, "a confession to be admissible must satisfy the following requirements: (1) it must be voluntary; (2) it must be made with the assistance of competent and independent counsel; (3) it must be express; and (4) it must be in writing."[904]

While waiving this right is acceptable, the waiver to be valid must "however, be voluntary, knowing and intelligent, and must be made in the presence and with the assistance of counsel."[905] Absence of a valid waiver and/or requirements of a valid confession results to any admission or confession being held as inadmissible as evidence.[906] The same is another application of the exclusionary rule or "fruit of the poisonous tree" rule in Philippine law and jurisprudence. As the Court once said, "Even if the confession contains a grain of truth, if it was made without the assistance of counsel, it becomes inadmissible in evidence, regardless of the absence of coercion or even if it had been voluntarily given."[907]

Significantly however, the right to remain silent or the right against self-incrimination "extends only to testimonial compulsion and not when the body of the accused is proposed to be examined."[908] In fact, "an accused may validly be compelled to be photographed or measured, or his garments or shoes removed or replaced, or to move his body to enable the foregoing things to be done, without running afoul of the proscription

---

901 Ho Wai Pang v. People of the Philippines, G.R. No. 176229, 19 October 2011.
902 Philippine Constitution, art. 3, § 17; Bermudez v. Castillo, 64 Phil 483 (1937).
903 Philippine Constitution, art. 3, § 17.
904 People of the Philippines v. Tan, G.R. No. 117321, 11 February 1998.
905 People of the Philippines v. Tan, G.R. No. 117321, 11 February 1998.
906 People of the Philippines v. Tan, G.R. No. 117321, 11 February 1998.
907 People of the Philippines v. Tan, G.R. No. 117321, 11 February 1998.
908 People of the Philippines v. Piedad, G.R. No. 131923, 05 December 2002.

against testimonial compulsion."[909] These situations only entail mechanical acts, when an accused or person "was made to undergo which was not meant to unearth undisclosed facts but to ascertain physical attributes determinable by simple observation."[910] Hence, the right to counsel, or even the right against self-incrimination, does not operate when an accused, or any person in general, is subjected to examinations such as DNA tests, taking of urine samples for drug tests, paraffin tests, or even the use of marked money in the person's apprehension.[911]

Such "mechanical acts" do not cover signatures, providing a handwriting sample, or writing in general, however, as the same involves "something more than moving the body, or the hands, or the fingers" and "requires the application of intelligence and attention".[912] In some cases, the Supreme Court has even been considered that providing a signature is as a declaration against interest or tacit admission of the crime charged, and thus if done without the assistance of counsel, is deemed to violate the right against self-incrimination.[913] And as such, are deemed inadmissible in evidence.[914]

That said, the tier of protection given by the right against self-incrimination works differently when one is an accused called as a prosecution witness and when one is only an ordinary witness: "whereas an ordinary witness may be compelled to take the witness stand and claim the privilege as each question requiring an incriminating answer is shot at him, and accused may altogether refuse to take the witness stand and refuse to answer any and all questions."[915] As the Court acknowledges that the accused is admittedly called to the witness stand by the prosecution for the purpose of incriminating him and the rule intends to avoid and prohibit such procedure to compel a person "to furnish the missing evidence necessary for

---

909 People of the Philippines v. Paynor, G.R. No. 116222, 9 September 1996; Gutang v. People of the Philippines, G.R. No. 135406, 11 July 2000.

910 Gutang v. People of the Philippines, G.R. No. 135406, 11 July 2000.

911 See People of the Philippines v. Gamboa, G.R. No. 91374, 25 February 1991; Gutang v. People of the Philippines, G.R. No. 135406, 11 July 2000; People of the Philippines v. Piedad, G.R. No. 131923, 05 December 2002.

912 Beltran v. Samson, G.R. No. 32025, 23 September 1929.

913 People of the Philippines v. Bandin, G.R. No. 104494, 10 September 1993.

914 People of the Philippines v. Bandin, G.R. No. 104494, 10 September 1993.

915 Chavez v. Court of Appeals, G.R. No. L-29169, 19 August 1968.

his conviction."[916] Accordingly, this rule may apply even to a co-defendant in a joint trial.[917]

As to how these rights apply to mutual legal assistance requests, there could be requests that involve getting a person to give statements or evidence that tend to incriminate said person. It is likewise possible that this person is actually a person-in-interest, suspect, or accused person, who instead of being extradited first, his/her statement or testimony is taken. In this case, the person can raise his right against self-incrimination. However, said person is not allowed not to appear altogether or refuse to take part, but only to refuse to answer each incriminating question shot at him. Alternatively, the same person may also be subjected to physical tests that require mechanical acts, e.g. provide urine or blood samples, etc., then at this instance, no right against self-incrimination or right to counsel attaches. Said person could be placed under any physical and/or medical examination. It would be a different story under Philippine law and jurisprudence, however, should the person be asked to write or sign something, to be used as a specimen later on for a criminal matter in the requesting state. In such case, the Philippine authorities must make sure that the rights against self-incrimination shall be respected.

Third, the Philippine Constitution confers rights to an accused in a criminal case. An accused is entitled to the right to be presumed innocent until proven guilty, right to be heard and produce evidence by accused or his counsel, right to be informed, right to speedy, impartial, and public trial, and the right to confront evidence and/or witnesses.[918] In terms of mutual legal assistance, the right to counsel and the right to be informed can come into play.

Anent the right to counsel, the Supreme Court acknowledges that the right to be heard will be incomplete without the right to counsel:

> "The right to be heard would be of little avail if it does not include the right to be heard by counsel. Even the most intelligent or educated man may have no skill in the science of the law, particularly in the rules of procedure, and, without counsel, he may be convicted not because he is guilty but because he does not know how to establish his innocence. And this can happen more easily to persons who are ignorant or uneducated. It is for this reason that the right to be assisted

---

916 Chavez v. Court of Appeals, G.R. No. L-29169, 19 August 1968.
917 Chavez v. Court of Appeals, G.R. No. L-29169, 19 August 1968.
918 1987 Philippine Constitution, art. 3, § 14.

> by counsel is deemed so important that it has become a constitutional right and it is so implemented that under our rules of procedure it is not enough for the Court to apprise an accused of his right to have an attorney, it is not enough to ask him whether he desires the aid of an attorney, but it is essential that the court should assign one de officio if he so desires and he is poor grant him a reasonable time to procure an attorney of his own."[919]

Accordingly, the right to counsel is guaranteed "to minimize the imbalance in the adversarial system where the accused is pitted against the awesome prosecutor machinery of the State."[920] It proceeds from one's right to due process, which is more than a "mere formality that can be dispensed with or performed perfunctorily."[921] As regards this, a court judge is duty-bound by the rules of procedure and by jurisprudence to do the following should the accused be unaided by counsel during the court proceedings: "(1) it must inform the defendant that it is his right to have attorney before being arraigned; (2) after giving him such information the court must ask him if he desires the aid of an attorney; (3) if he desires and is unable to employ attorney, the court must assign attorney de officio to defend him; and (4) if the accused desires to procure an attorney of his own the court must grant him a reasonable time therefor."[922]

In light of having one's right to counsel during criminal proceedings, the Supreme Court has clarified that primordial consideration of a suspect or accused person's preference for counsel applies more aptly and specifically to a person under investigation.[923] And even if said right of preference extends to a criminal case, the Supreme Court held that "such preferential discretion cannot partake of a discretion so absolute and arbitrary as would make the choice of counsel refer exclusively to the predilection of the accused."[924]

---

919 People of the Philippines v. Holgado, G.R. No. L-2809, 22 March 1950.

920 Inacay v. People of the Philippines, G.R. 223506, 28 November 2016.

921 Inacay v. People of the Philippines, G.R. 223506, 28 November 2016.

922 People of the Philippines v. Holgado, G.R. No. L-2809, 22 March 1950.

923 1987 Philippine Constitution, art. 3, § 14(2); Amion v. Chiongson, AM No. RTJ-97-1371, 22 January 1999.

924 Amion v. Chiongson, AM No. RTJ-97-1371, 22 January 1999. As held in People v. Barasina:
"Withal, the word preferably under Section 12(1), Article 3 of the 1987 Constitution does not convey the message that the choice of a lawyer by a person under investigation is exclusive as to preclude other equally competent and independent attorneys from handling his defense. If the rule were otherwise,

Applying the principle above to criminal proceedings in court, the Supreme Court held it "may likewise say that the accused's discretion in a criminal prosecution with respect to his choice of counsel is not so much as to grant him a plenary prerogative which would preclude other equally competent and independent counsels from representing him. Otherwise, the pace of a criminal prosecution will be entirely dictated by the accused to the detriment of the eventual resolution of the case."[925] Stating it otherwise, the right to counsel in criminal proceedings cannot be interpreted to mean that an accused can hijack proceedings.

On the other hand, there is the right of an accused to be informed of the nature and cause of the accusations against him.[926] The objectives of this right are three-fold: "(1) to furnish the accused with such a description of the charge against him as will enable him to make the defense; (2) to avail himself of his conviction or acquittal for protection against further prosecution for the same cause; (3) to inform the court of the facts alleged, so that it may decide whether they are sufficient in law to support a conviction if one should be had."[927] Public policy prohibits waiver of said right, and thus, "the complaint or information filed against the accused be complete to meet its objectives," meaning, "an indictment must fully state the elements of the specific offense alleged to have been committed."[928]

In implementing the right, the Rules of Criminal Procedure specifically require that "the acts or omissions complained of as constituting the offense, including the qualifying and aggravating circumstances, must be stated in ordinary and concise language, not necessarily in the language used in the statute, but in terms sufficient to enable a person of common understanding to know what offense is being charged and the attendant qualifying and aggravating circumstances present, so that the accused can properly defend himself and the court can pronounce judgment."[929] In

---

then, the tempo of a custodial investigation, will be solely in the hands of the accused who can impede, nay, obstruct the progress of the interrogation by simply selecting a lawyer, who for one reason or another, is not available to protect his interest. This absurd scenario could not have been contemplated by the framers of the charter." People of the Philippines v. Barasina, G.R. No. 109993, 21January 1994, as cited in Amion v. Chiongson, AM No. RTJ-97-1371, 22 January 1999.

925 Amion v. Chiongson, AM No. RTJ-97-1371, 22 January 1999.

926 1987 Philippine Constitution, art. 3, § 14(1); Go v. BangkoSentral ng Pilipinas, G.R. No. 178429, 23 October 2009.

927 People of the Philippines v. Flores, G. R. No. 128823-24, 27 December 2002.

928 People of the Philippines v. Flores, G. R. No. 128823-24, 27 December 2002.

929 Go v. BangkoSentral ng Pilipinas, G.R. No. 178429, 23 October 2009.

connection thereto, law and jurisprudence allows quashal of a complaint or information should it fail to allege the facts constituting the offense and even provided a test to appreciate a motion to quash due to insufficiency of facts.[930]

In addition to allowing an accused to file a motion to quash, the right to be informed means that a person cannot be convicted, even if the crime was duly proven, unless the same is included or necessarily included in the complaint or information.[931]

Taking these rights of the accused together, the Supreme Court had explained that albeit certain rights should only come into play during the trial stage, they have been equally conferred in administrative proceedings, which have a criminal or penal nature.[932] Thus, the right to counsel, together with the right to due process and the right against self-incrimination have been extended to apply to administrative proceedings of criminal nature.[933] One of these proceedings concerns the evaluation stage of extradition proceedings, which according to the Supreme Court, are akin to a preliminary investigation.[934] As explained earlier, extradition proceedings have earmarks of a criminal process and one's liberty might consequently be at stake. Thus, the Supreme Court found it fitting to allow a person to exercise the aforementioned constitutional rights during such proceedings. And as mutual legal assistance proceedings are on the same plane as extradition in being an administrative proceeding with criminal nature – or as stated earlier, having the "earmarks of a criminal process" – the conferred rights should equally apply as well in such circumstances.

---

930 According to the cases of People of the Philippines v. Romualdez, G.R. No. 166510, 23 July 2008, and Go v. BangkoSentral ng Pilipinas, G.R. No. 178429, 23 October 2009:
"The determinative test in appreciating a motion to quash xxx is the sufficiency of the averments in the information, that is, whether the facts alleged, if hypothetically admitted, would establish the essential elements of the offense as defined by law without considering matters aliunde. As Section 6, Rule 110 of the Rules of Criminal Procedure requires, the information only needs to state the ultimate facts; the evidentiary and other details can be provided during the trial.
"To restate the rule, an Information only needs to state the ultimate facts constituting the offense, not the finer details of why and how the illegal acts alleged amounted to undue injury or damage matters that are appropriate for the trial."

931 People of the Philippines v. Flores, G. R. No. 128823-24, 27 December 2002.

932 See Secretary of Justice v. Lantion, G.R. No. 139465, 18 January 2000.

933 Secretary of Justice v. Lantion, G.R. No. 139465, 18 January 2000.

934 Secretary of Justice v. Lantion, G.R. No. 139465, 18 January 2000.

As regards the right to be informed and the right to be informed of the nature and cause of the accusation, the Supreme Court qualifies vis-à-vis the evaluation stage of an extradition proceeding, which is akin to what can occur in mutual legal assistance requests:

> "In the case at bar, the papers requested by private respondent pertain to official government action from the U. S. Government. No official action from our country has yet been taken. Moreover, the papers have some relation to matters of foreign relations with the U. S. Government. Consequently, if a third party invokes this constitutional provision, stating that the extradition papers are matters of public concern since they may result in the extradition of a Filipino, we are afraid that the balance must be tilted, at such particular time, in favor of the interests necessary for the proper functioning of the government. During the evaluation procedure, no official governmental action of our own government has as yet been done; hence the invocation of the right is premature. Later, and in contrast, records of the extradition hearing would already fall under matters of public concern, because our government by then shall have already made an official decision to grant the extradition request. The extradition of a fellow Filipino would be forthcoming."[935]

In other words, the right to be informed only becomes applicable after the evaluation stage of an extradition request, or when the government has made a decision as to how to proceed. Prior to such decision, the right to be informed does not exist and the confidentiality of some documents and communication ought to be respected. This can be equally applied to mutual legal assistance requests, wherein confidential and diplomatic information may also be exchanged between the Philippines and the requesting state during the evaluation stages. It is only after the Philippines has decided to effectuate the request may a person invoke the right to be informed should said person be affected by the mutual legal assistance request.

Taking the different rights mentioned, it can be settled that mutual legal assistance has earmarks of a criminal process. It is also a tool for criminal law enforcement and subsequently, prosecution. Like extradition, mutual legal assistance requires speed and efficiency but following what the Supreme Court held in the Secretary of Justice v. Lantion case, the Philippine Constitution recognizes values more than speed and efficiency

---

935 Secretary of Justice v. Lantion, G.R. No. 139465, 18 January 2000.

and while government action can be applauded, it should not be detrimental to the values of a vulnerable citizenry, which is protected by rights such as due process and other rights of an accused.[936] Therefore, even if mutual legal assistance requests are administrative in nature too, it does not excuse itself from respecting rights, even if the same is not equivocally provided for in law or jurisprudence. Besides, the Philippines as a state policy applies the rules of fair play in the absence of a law or principle of law.[937] In terms of the ASEAN MLAT, an application of the basic twin due process rights of notice and hearing or the basic rights of someone subjected to either investigation or prosecution will not go against it.[938]

In addition to the foregoing, it might be worthwhile to discuss herein the constitutional rights during custodial investigation, which is "any questioning initiated by law enforcement officers after a person has been taken into custody or otherwise deprived of his freedom of action in any significant way."[939] Admittedly, arrest and detention normally apply in extradition or transfer of sentenced persons. Furthermore, the ASEAN MLAT is equivocal in establishing safe conduct (or safe harbor) provisions, which disallows in general detention or any other form of restriction of liberty, prosecution, etc. for any crime committed prior to the transfer, or otherwise to be held criminally liable for any statement made unless for perjury or contempt in court. Nonetheless, rights of custodial investigation can still apply because there are investigative measures through mutual legal assistance, e.g. taking of evidence and/or information, voluntary statements, etc., that can trigger these rights depending on the questioning involved or the direction authorities are taking towards the interviewee. As relevant jurisprudence provides, the test herein to determine whether rights should apply is "when a person is taken into custody and is singled out as a suspect in the commission of the crime under investigation and the police officers begin to ask questions on the suspect's participation therein and which tend to elicit an admission."[940] Thus, if at any part of the giving of information or testimony this test is satisfied, then the safe conduct provisions should be engaged, wherein the requested state's

---

936 See Secretary of Justice v. Lantion, G.R. No. 139465, 18 January 2000; Association of Small Landowners in the Philippines, Inc. v. Secretary of Agrarian Reform, G.R. Nos. 78742, 79310, 79744, 79777, 14 July 1989; Stanley v. Illinois, 404 US 645, 656 (1972).

937 See Secretary of Justice v. Lantion, G.R. No. 139465, 18 January 2000.

938 See Secretary of Justice v. Lantion, G.R. No. 139465, 18 January 2000.

939 Sebastian v. Garchitorena, G.R. No. 114028, 18 October 2000.

940 People of the Philippines v. Pavillare, G.R. No. 129970, 05 April 2000.

attention is called on the matter, find for judicial relief, and/or the rights conferred by the Constitution apply.

Should the nature of the taking of evidence indeed evolve to one of "custodial investigation" and questioning proceeds, Article 3, Section 12 of the Constitution provides that "any person under investigation for the commission of an offense shall have the right to remain silent and to have competent and independent counsel preferably of his own choice. If the person cannot afford the services of counsel, he must be provided with one. These rights cannot be waived except in writing and in the presence of counsel." Notably, this constitutional provision follows the rationale as enshrined in the 1966 American case of Miranda v. Arizona, which applies the Fifth Amendment in the United States Constitution to custodial investigations.[941]

Incommunicado interrogation of individuals in police-dominated atmosphere, while not physical intimidation, is equally destructive of human dignity, and current practice is at odds with principle that individual may not be compelled to incriminate himself.[942] The rights engaged during custodial investigation by virtue of the Miranda case are meant "to prohibit incommunicado interrogation of individuals in a police-dominated atmosphere, resulting in self-incriminating statements without full warnings of constitutional rights."[943]

As regards these rights, firstly, a person has the right to be informed of one's right to remain silent and to counsel: the Constitution herein contemplates the right to be informed of one's right to remain silent and to counsel as "to contemplate the transmission of a meaningful information rather than just a ceremonial and perfunctory recitation of an abstract

---

941 Miranda v. Arizona, 384 U.S. 436, 467-468 (1966).According to Miranda:
"Today, then, there can be no doubt that the Fifth Amendment privilege is available outside of criminal court proceedings, and serves to protect persons in all settings in which their freedom of action is curtailed in any significant way from being compelled to incriminate themselves. We have concluded that, without proper safeguards, the process of in-custody interrogation of persons suspected or accused of crime contains inherently compelling pressures which work to undermine the individual's will to resist and to compel him to speak where he would not otherwise do so freely. In order to combat these pressures and to permit a full opportunity to exercise the privilege against self-incrimination, the accused must be adequately and effectively apprised of his rights, and the exercise of those rights must be fully honored."

942 See Miranda v. Arizona, 384 U.S. 436 (1966).

943 People of the Philippines v. Canton, G.R. No. 148825, 27 December 2002.

constitutional principle."[944] The said right under custodial investigation to be informed "implies a correlative obligation on the part of the police investigator to explain, and contemplates an effective communication that results in understanding what is conveyed."[945] Anything short of this is said to be a denial of the right, and since the right entails comprehension, "the degree of explanation required will necessary vary, depending upon the education, intelligence and other relevant personal circumstances of the person under investigation. Suffice it to say that a simpler and more lucid explanation is needed where the subject is unlettered."[946] Thus, when a person is already being treated as a "suspect", authorities ought to inform the subject person immediately. Otherwise there is already a violation of one's rights.

Secondly, there is the right to remain silent as already discussed above. Thirdly, the right to counsel is also available during custodial investigations and herein the suspect has the right to a competent and independent counsel, who is preferably his/her own choice. As clarified above, the consideration of the suspect's preference is given more during custodial investigations rather than during trial and it is important that this preference is not used as a tool to hijack proceedings.

iii. Defendant's Participation in the Refusal or Execution of a MLA Request

Given the foregoing plethora of rights that can be engaged in the execution of MLA requests in the Philippines, it becomes interesting to know where a suspect or accused person, or otherwise interested person, stands in terms of finding relief vis-à-vis the sending or executing of a MLA request. On the basis of the ASEAN MLAT, it states that the "provisions of this Treaty shall not create any right on the part of any private person to obtain, suppress or exclude any evidence or to impede the execution of any request for assistance" (Article 1, 1[3]). This provision could then be interpreted to either mean that a private person, may it be a suspect,

944 People of the Philippines v. Nicandro, G.R. No. L-59378, 11 February 1986; People of the Philippines v. Pinlac, G.R. Nos. 74123-24, 26 September 1988; See also People of the Philippines v. Tan, G.R. No. 117321, 11 February 1998: People of the Philippines v. de la Cruz, G.R. No. 118866-68, 17 September 1997.

945 People of the Philippines v. Nicandro, G.R. No. L-59378, 11 February 1986; People of the Philippines v. Pinlac, G.R. Nos. 74123-24, 26 September 1988.

946 People of the Philippines v. Nicandro, G.R. No. L-59378, 11 February 1986.

accused, or third person, to request that a MLA request be issued on its behalf to secure evidence, or said person cannot ask for the exclusion or suppression of any evidence, or impede the execution of a MLA request, obtained through the provisions of the ASEAN MLAT should there have been misfeasance or non-feasance. In other words, a private person – with no qualification on whether he/she is a suspect or accused person – has no business in MLA requests.

Notwithstanding the apparent exclusion of a private person who might be affected by a MLA request or the execution thereof, an affected person – like in extradition cases – still has the right of action to question the granting of the MLA request or any investigative measure executed by virtue of a MLA request under Philippine jurisdiction. The Philippine Judiciary is imbued under Article VIII, Section 1 of the Philippine Constitution with judicial power, which includes the power to determine whether or not there has been grave abuse of discretion amounting to lack or excess of jurisdiction on the part of any branch or instrumentality of the government. Known as expanded power of judicial review or certiorari jurisdiction, such power allows the Supreme Court or the lower courts (if delegated by the Supreme Court through the Rules of Court) to test the validity of executive and legislative acts for their conformity with law and the Constitution.[947] In such cases, the courts have no power to substitute its judgment for that of the concerned government authority, e.g executive or Department of Justice vis-à-vis mutual legal assistance, but it can nonetheless look into the question of whether there has been "improvident exercise" or abuse of such power that gives rise to justiciable controversy:[948] whether there has been lack or excess of jurisdiction or grave abuse of discretion amounting to lack or excess of jurisdiction. Petitions invoking the power of judicial review are normally anchored on Rule 65, Section 1 of the Rules of Civil Procedure through a special civil action for certiorari.[949]

---

947 Congressman Garcia v. Executive Secretary, G.R. 157584, 02 April 2009.

948 Congressman Garcia v. Executive Secretary, G.R. 157584, 02 April 2009; Integrated Bar of the Philippines v. Zamora, G.R. No. 141284, August 15, 2000, 338 SCRA 81, citing Tañada v. Cuenco, 103 Phil. 1051 and Baker v. Carr, 369 U.S. 186.

949 Rule 65, Section 1 of the Revised Rules of Civil Procedure provides: "Section 1. *Petition for certiorari.* - When any tribunal, board or officer exercising judicial or quasi-judicial functions has acted without or in excess of its or his jurisdiction, or with grave abuse of discretion amounting to lack or excess of its or his jurisdiction, and there is no appeal, or any plain, speedy, and adequate remedy

The Philippine Supreme Court defines grave abuse of discretion as "to mean the capricious or whimsical exercise of judgment that is so patent and gross as to amount to an evasion of positive duty or a virtual refusal to perform a duty enjoined by law, or to act at all in contemplation of law, as where the power is exercised in an arbitrary and despotic manner by reason of passion or hostility."[950] It is also present when an act is either "(1) done contrary to the Constitution, the law, or jurisprudence, or (2) executed whimsically, capriciously, or arbitrarily out of malice, ill will, or personal bias."[951]

Therefore, the affected person or petitioner has the right of action to resort to the courts should he/she believe that the MLA request has either been issued by the Philippine authorities or granted (or executed) by the Philippine authorities with grave abuse of discretion as above stated. Examples that could be used herein is the gross violation of the rights abovementioned, or patent disregard for the same, or any action or decision that illustrates the aforementioned.

It is a different question altogether whether a person affected by an MLA request due to any violation of the rights abovestated, can receive the relief. It has yet to be fully tested with Philippine courts in terms of whether a MLA request can be withdrawn or the execution thereof can be suspended or stopped as a form of relief to an affected indivdual.[952] At most, one could look into the decision of the Philippine Supreme Court in *People of the Philippines v. Sergio* involving the case of Mary Jane Veloso, which as mentioned earlier is one of the more popular and well-known Philippine cases involving the use of the ASEAN MLAT. Interestingly, a reading of the case would show not only the novelty and complexity surrounding mutual legal assistance and the rights it could affect in criminal

---

in the ordinary course of law, a person aggrieved thereby may file a verified petition in the proper court, alleging the facts with certainty and praying that judgment be rendered annulling or modifying the proceedings of such tribunal, board or officer, and granting such incidental reliefs as law and justice may require." See further Arceta v. Mangrobang, G.R. No. 152895, 15 June 2004.

950 Congressman Garcia v. Executive Secretary, G.R. 157584, 02 April 2009. See also Chua v. People of the Philippnes, G.R. No. 195248, 22 November 2017, citing Yu v. Judge Reyes-Carpio, 667 Phil. 474 (2011).

951 Commissioner of Internal Revenue v. Court of Tax Appeals, G.R. No. 203403, 14 November 2018, citing Air Transportation Office v. CA, et al., 737 Phil. 61, 84 (2014).

952 *Malaya/Monedero-Arnesto/Paras*, p. 16.

proceedings, but there is also the confirmation that relief can be granted depending on the circumstances.

The facts of the case are as follows. The Philippine government was able to request the Indonesian government to stay the execution of Mary Jane Veloso pending the criminal case for illegal recruitment she filed against her alleged illegal recruiter in the Philippines.[953] Herein the Philippine government was able to request that Veloso's deposition be taken while she was being held in prison in Indonesia, which was intended to be used as evidence in the illegal recruitment case. Indonesia granted the request but imposed the following conditions relative to the taking of Mary Jane Veloso's testimony: (1) she will remain in detention; (2) no cameras shall be allowed; (3) the lawyers of the parties shall not be present; and (4) the questions to be propounded shall be in writing.[954] Thereafter a motion for leave was filed with the court *a quo* to proceed with the deposition through written interrogatories.[955] The taking of the deposition proceeded despite the accused's contention that the actual presence of the witness is required in the illegal recruitment case filed against them as otherwise, their right of confrontation shall be violated.[956] This prompted the accused to question the trial court's ruling. Needless to state, whatever resolution the Supreme Court adopted on said matter, including the admissibility of the deposition as evidence in the illegal recruitment case, can send a butterfly effect as to how one views mutual legal assistance requests and the use of evidence pursuant thereto, including the general protection of human rights and interests of individuals that might be affected by the investigative measures involved.[957]

In its Decision, one can note how the Supreme Court gave more weight into the issue of rights at hand rather than solely focusing on procedure. At the outset, there was no need to dwell on the propriety of the mutual legal assistance request and its subsequent grant. There was focus instead on the investigative measure to be carried out. The Supreme Court upheld the taking of deposition through written interrogatories as well as ruled that the accused's right to confrontation would not be violated by virtue thereof. The Court held that the extraordinary circumstances surrounding Mary Jane Veloso were compelling reasons enough to allow the deposition

---

953 *Malaya/Monedero-Arnesto/Paras*, p. 16.
954 People of the Philippines v. Sergio, G.R. No. 240053, 09 October 2019.
955 People of the Philippines v. Sergio, G.R. No. 240053, 09 October 2019.
956 *Malaya/Monedero-Arnesto/Paras*, p. 16.
957 *Malaya/Monedero-Arnesto/Paras*, p. 16.

and its use as evidence against the accused. The Court upheld the principle that rules shall be "liberally construed to promote their objective of securing a just, speedy, and inexpensive disposition of every action and proceeding."[958] Stating differently, procedural rules are meant to facilitate an orderly administration of justice and should not be strictly applied causing injury to a substantive right of a party to a case.[959] Citing the relevant provisions of the ASEAN MLAT and the conditions imposed by the Indonesian authorities for the reprieve given to Mary Jane Veloso, the Supreme Court noted that the Rules of Criminal Procedure are bereft of any provision as to how a deposition of a prosecution witness, who is both convicted of a grave offense by final judgment and imprisoned in a foreign jurisdiction, may be taken to perpetuate the testimony of such witness. In particular, nothing in the Rules provide for a situation when a witness is unable to testify in open court because he is imprisoned in another country.

Depositions are however recognized under the Rules of Civil Procedure and in a plethora of cases, the Court has allowed the Rules of Civil Procedure to be applied suppletorily in criminal proceedings under compelling reasons. It is on this score that the Supreme Court found no reason to depart from its practice of liberally construing procedural rules for the orderly administration of substantial justice. Any strict application of the rules would defeat the very purpose of the grant of reprieve by the Indonesian authorities to Veloso and also, as the Supreme Court held, would not be in congruence with the purpose of the ASEAN MLAT to render mutual legal assistance in criminal matters.[960]

Discussing further, the Supreme Court upheld the right to due process of both Mary Jane Veloso and the state to prove her innocence before the Indonesian authorities, present the case against the accused, as well as comply with the conditions set for the grant of reprieve by the Indonesian

---

958 People of the Philippines v. Sergio, G.R. No. 240053, 09 October 2019.

959 The Court was quick to remind though that procedural rules are not to be belittled or dismissed simply because their non-observance may have prejudiced a party's substantive rights. Thus, the bare invocation of "the interest of substantial justice" is not a magic phrase that will automatically oblige the Supreme Court to suspend procedural rules. Like all rules, they are required to be followed except only for the most pervasive of reasons when they may be relaxed to relieve the litigant of an injustice not commensurate with the degree of his thoughtlessness in not complying with the procedure prescribed. People of the Philippines v. Sergio, G.R. No. 240053, 09 October 2019.

960 People of the Philippines v. Sergio, G.R. No. 240053, 09 October 2019.

government, respectively.[961] According to its Decision, "the benchmark of the right to due process in criminal justice is to ensure that all the parties have their day in court. It is in accord with the duty of the government to follow a fair process of decision-making when it acts to deprive a person of his liberty. But just as an accused is accorded this constitutional protection, so is the state entitled to due process in criminal prosecutions. It must likewise be given an equal chance to present its evidence in support of a charge."[962] Thus, the Supreme Court held that the trial court acted correctly within its jurisdiction to grant the taking of deposition by written interrogatories:

"The grant of the written interrogatories by the Indonesian Government perceives the State's opportunity to present all its desired witnesses in the prosecution of its cases against Cristina and Julius. It is afforded fair opportunity to present witnesses and evidence it deem vital to ensure that the injury sustained by the People in the commission of the criminal acts will be well compensated and, most of all, that justice be achieved. Hence, the right of the State to prosecute and prove its case have been fully upheld and protected.

Further, the right of the State to prove the criminal liability of Cristina and Julius should not be derailed and prevented by the stringent application of the procedural rules. Otherwise, it will constitute a violation of the basic constitutional rights of the State and of Mary Jane to due process which this Court cannot disregard.

The fundamental rights of both the accused and the State must be equally upheld and protected so that justice can prevail in the truest sense of the word. To do justice to accused and injustice to the State is no justice at all. Justice must be dispensed to all the parties alike."[963]

As regards the accused's constitutional right to confront a witness, the Court considered meticulously the merits of the case and held that there would be no infringement under the circumstances. Considering the two-fold purpose of the right,[964] the Court held that whilst it is true that the

---

961 The Supreme Court referred likewise to Secretary of Justice v. Lantion to remind about the importance of due process, the elasticity in its interpretation, and its dynamic and resilient character that allows it to meet every modern problem whilst accommodating progress and improvement. People of the Philippines v. Sergio, G.R. No. 240053, 09 October 2019.

962 People of the Philippines v. Sergio, G.R. No. 240053, 09 October 2019.

963 People of the Philippines v. Sergio, G.R. No. 240053, 09 October 2019.

964 The two-fold purpose is as follows: (1) primarily to afford the accused an opportunity to test the testimony of the witness by cross-examination; and (2)

accused would not be able to confront Mary Jane Veloso face-to-face under the present circumstances, the terms and conditions laid down by the trial court are enough to ensure ample opportunity to cross examine by way of written interrogatories: (1) the accused through counsel are required to file the necessary comment and may raise objections to the proposed questions in the written interrogatories submitted by the prosecution; (2) the trial judge shall promptly rule on the objections and only the final questions would be asked during the taking of deposition in Indonesia; (3) the answers shall be written verbatim and a transcribed copy shall be given to the counsel of the accused who in turn shall submit their proposed cross interrogatory questions to the prosecution; (4) should there be objections from the prosecution to the questions, the trial judge shall promptly rule on the same and the final cross interrogatory questions shall then be conducted; and (5) the witness' answers shall be taken in verbatim and a transcribed copy thereof shall be given to the prosecution.[965]

The second purpose of the right – to allow the judge to observe the deportment of the witness – has likewise been upheld because under the same terms and conditions, the trial court judge shall be present during the conduct of written interrogatories. This will give the "ample opportunity to observe and to examine the demeanor of the witness closely."[966] Moreover, the trial court judge can still carefully perceive the reaction and deportment of the witness as she answers each question propounded to her both by the prosecution and the defense, albeit the deposition is in writing.[967]

Considering the tenor of the Philippine Supreme Court's decision, one can note that while it is still left unclear whether an affected person may question the validity of the MLA request itself and/or the grant thereof, he/she is not precluded from questioning the resulting investigative measure from such a request, the implementation of said measure, as well as the admissibility of any evidence obtained therefrom. Furthermore, the Supreme Court could grant the needed relief and provide the needed redress for any violation of rights as long as circumstances may warrant it. As *People of the Philippines v. Sergio* illustrated, the Court shall not avoid the

---

secondarily, to allow the judge to observe the deportment of the witness. See People of the Philippines v. Nicolas, G.R. No. 135877, 22 August 2002, as cited in People of the Philippines v. Sergio, G.R. No. 240053, 09 October 2019.

965 People of the Philippines v. Sergio, G.R. No. 240053, 09 October 2019.

966 People of the Philippines v. Sergio, G.R. No. 240053, 09 October 2019.

967 People of the Philippines v. Sergio, G.R. No. 240053, 09 October 2019.

question on whether a constitutional right is infringed. This is especially the case when the Philippines is the requesting state, the criminal proceedings are situated in the Philippines, and the evidence obtained through MLA is used in Philippine courts. As the present case and a cantina of other Philippine cases illustrate, there would always be paramount consideration of due process, orderly administration of substantive justice, and fair play. Thus, the merits of each case shall be weighed and any question of (possible) infringement shall be addressed accordingly. Furthermore, if one would recall the discussion on substantive rights, the Philippines follows the exclusionary rule and fruit of poisonous tree doctrine. Hence, going through the merits is a necessary step. If there is a court finding that one's right has been violated in obtaining evidence, said investigative measure is held as void or invalid, and any resulting evidence is inadmissible in court. This means that in the Philippine context, one can assail the evidence itself should there be questions on the admissibility of any evidence obtained through MLA.

c. Applicable Time Element on Execution

Given the lack of specific domestic legislation on facilitating and making of mutual legal assistance requests, there is no legislated time limit within which the Philippines as a requested state should execute a request. Despite this, it was mentioned earlier that in the minimum requirements a MLA request should generally have, regardless of whether the Philippines is a requesting or requested state, any time limit within which compliance with the request is desired should be specified. In respect thereto, the Philippines as a requested state or the foreign state (or in terms of the ASEAN MLAT, the ASEAN member state) would be advised accordingly as to the time element involved in the investigative measure being requested.

Taking this into account, the Philippines is more or less aware of the importance of time elements in executing requests. In fact, the Department of Justice uses the following procedure in practice vis-à-vis requests for assistance: (1) requests for mutual legal assistance are transmitted directly in general between the central authorities of the two states; (2) for requests made based on treaty, the Department of Justice shall evaluate the request; (3) after evaluation, the Department of Justice shall transmit the request to the competent authority: for example, the Anti-Money Laundering Council ("AMLC") for money laundering cases and the Office of the Ombudsman for corruption cases; (4) for requests made on the basis of reciprocity (which happens when the request is not based on treaty), then the Department of Foreign Affairs will have the opportunity to review the same; (5) the appropriate applications shall be filed in appropriate Regional Trial Courts for requests involving coercive measures such as search and seizure, forfeiture, etc.; and then (6) documents or evidence taken in relation to the request shall be transmitted through the fastest possible means.[968]

Having said that, interviews with Philippine authorities made it clear that there is normally no problem executing a request quickly should the request be in order and requirements are fulfilled, especially if the request does not require any coercive order or court warrant before it can be implemented.[969] As mentioned, delay normally arises when the authorities would need to go through the court process.[970] Should the information, document, or evidence requested need not go through the court, conformity with other additional formalities is not necessary. The Philippines is under the obligation to execute as fast as possible the request and give the same without any issue .[971] Moreover, there is, as mentioned earlier, an existing practice among ASEAN member states of an open line of communications. There is always an open line of communication and preliminary consultation with one another to ensure that requests for assistance are effectuated, and if possible, effectuated promptly as divulged through the interview with Philippine authorities. The Philippines as either requested or requesting state may consult preliminarily with its counterpart to ensure that the request for assistance is in order and should there be any problems, determine what could be done to still allow the request to be implemented. Open line of communication and preliminary consultation also takes the form of sending to each other draft and/or unofficial copies of the request so that the receiving party can deliberate and act on said request quicker.

968 *Quintana*, p. 142

969 Interviews with Department of Justice Senior State Council Meredith Alvor, Atty. Arnold Frane, Ms. Joie Quieta.

970 Interview with Department of Justice Senior State Council Meredith Alvor.

971 Interview with Department of Justice Senior State Council Meredith Alvor.

d. Authentication of Documents

As one would recall, the ASEAN MLAT does not require further authentication to effectuate requests, or as regards evidence that may be transmitted to the requesting party, but this is without prejudice to any request from a party to the other to authenticate any documents or material that may be transmitted to the other party, even though the same is not required to effectuate any request for assistance made. The ASEAN MLAT likewise provides certain conditions, when these materials are deemed authenticated.

In light of this, the Philippines Rules of Court were originally bereft of provisions tackling specifically evidence obtained through mutual legal assistance. There were no rules regarding authentication or the need for further proof. Instead, what was provided are the basic rules on authentication that might need to be accounted for when presenting evidence obtained through mutual legal assistance. With the new amendments to the Rules of Evidence made by the Philippine Supreme Court through A.M. No. 19-08-15-SC (2019 Proposed Amendments to the Revised Rules of Evidence), which became effective last 01 May 2020, further proof and/or authentication of evidence obtained through mutual legal assistance is arguably unnecessary.

At the outset, the Philippine Revised Rules of Court distinguishes between public and private documents and the nature of such documentary evidence to be presented determines which rules shall apply.[972] On one hand, public documents are self-authenticating and admissible as evidence without need for further proof.[973] These documents are either "(a) the written official acts, or records of the official acts of the sovereign authority, official bodies and tribunals, and public officers, whether of the Philippines, or of a foreign country; (b) documents acknowledge before a notary public except last wills and testaments; (c) documents that are considered public documents under treaties and conventions which are in force between the Philippines and the country of source; and (d) public records, kept in the Philippines, of private documents required by

972 Asian Terminals v. Philam Life Insurance, G.R. Nos. 181163, 181262, 181319, 24 July 2013; Salas v. Sta. Mesa Market Corporation, G.R. No. 157766, 12 July 2007.

973 Philippine Revised Rules of Court, Rule 132, §§ 23, 24, 25, 27 and 30 (as amended).

law to be entered therein."[974] Documentary evidence and/or information obtained through a mutual legal assistance framework falls under this classification, especially when one looks into the conditions of when a document is authenticated under the ASEAN MLAT and/or the information transmitted is an official act of a government body as abovestated.

Accordingly, the Philippine Rules of Court provide that "documents consisting of entries in public records made in the performance of a duty by a public officer are *prima facie* evidence of the facts therein stated."[975] The Rules of Court further provide that "all other public documents are evidence, even against a third person, of the fact which gave rise to their execution and of the date of the latter."[976] Furthermore, should the public document refer to "the written official acts, or records of the official acts of the sovereign authority, official bodies and tribunals, and public officers, whether of the Philippines, or of a foreign country" – when admissible for any purpose – "may be evidenced by an official publication thereof or by a copy attested by the officer having the legal custody of the record, or by his deputy, and accompanied, if the record is not kept in the Philippines, with a certificate that such officer has the custody."[977]

Further, in cases where the office in which the record is kept is in a foreign country, two scenarios are possible. First, if the foreign country involved is a contracting party to a treaty or convention to which the Philippines is also a party, or considered a public document under such treaty or convention, "the certificate or its equivalent shall be in the form prescribed by such treaty or convention subject to reciprocity granted to public documents originating from the Philippines."[978] Second, for documents originating from a foreign country which is not a contracting party to a treaty or convention referred to in the next preceding sentence, "the certificate may be made by a secretary of the embassy or legation, consul general, consul, vice consul, or consular agent or by any officer in the foreign service of the Philippines stationed in the foreign country in which the record is kept, and authenticated by the seal of his office."[979]In relation to these, "a document that is accompanied by a certificate or its equivalent may be presented in evidence without further proof, the

974 Philippine Revised Rules of Court, Rule 132, § 19 (as amended).
975 Philippine Revised Rules of Court, Rule 132, § 23.
976 Philippine Revised Rules of Court, Rule 132, § 23.
977 Phillipine Revised Rules of Court, Rule 132, § 24 (as amended).
978 Phillipine Revised Rules of Court, Rule 132, § 24 (as amended).
979 Phillipine Revised Rules of Court, Rule 132, § 24 (as amended).

certificate or its equivalent being *prima facie* evidence of the due execution and genuineness of the document involved. The certificate shall not be required when a treaty or convention between a foreign country and the Philippines has abolished the requirement, or has exempted the document itself from this formality."[980]

Applying these new amended rules to evidence obtained through mutual legal assistance, especially as regards "public documents", Philippine authorities do not need to present further proof and/or authenticate these kinds of evidence when being presented in court, as long as certain conditions are met. It can likewise be gainsaid that any exchange of evidence and/or information through mutual legal assistance when the Philippines is a requesting party is streamlined as the Philippines is relieved of any obligation to ask the requested party to undertake additional steps vis-à-vis authentication for purposes of presenting evidence in court.

As regards instances when the Philippines is the requested party and attestation is required, the Rules provide likewise how this attestation should be made, the relevant Rules provide that it should state "in substance, that the copy is a correct copy of the original, or a specific part thereof, as the case may be."[981] Moreover, "the attestation must be under the official seal of the attesting officer, if there be any, or if he be the clerk of a court having a seal, under the seal of such court."[982] One must further take note that "any public record, an official copy of which is admissible in evidence, must not be removed from the office in which it is kept, except upon order of a court where the inspection of the record is essential to the just determination of a pending case."[983] Further, should the public document refers to "public record of a private document", it may be proved "by the original record, or by a copy thereof, attested by the legal custodian of the record, with an appropriate certificate that such officer has the custody."[984]

In relation to this, there could be instances in a mutual legal assistance framework when private documents, as defined under the Philippine Rules of Evidence are adduced, e.g. a person whose testimony or evidence is taken presents or submits evidence not considered "public". For this, authentication of private documents have a different set of rules, to which authorities must adhere to should these be presented later in court. A doc-

980 Phillipine Revised Rules of Court, Rule 132, § 24 (as amended).
981 Philippine Revised Rules of Court, Rule 132, § 25.
982 Philippine Revised Rules of Court, Rule 132, § 25.
983 Philippine Revised Rules of Court, Rule 132, § 26.
984 Philippine Revised Rules of Court, Rule 132, § 27.

ument is considered private within the ambits of Philippine law as "any other writing, deed or instrument executed by a private person without the intervention of a notary or other person legally authorized by which some disposition or agreement is proved or set forth."[985] Notably, "before any private document offered as authentic is received in evidence, its due execution and authenticity must be proved either: (a) by anyone who saw the document executed or written; (b) by evidence of the genuineness of the signature or handwriting of the maker; or (c) by other evidence showing its due execution and authenticity."[986] Any other private document need only be identified as that which it is claimed to be.[987] During authentication in court, as Philippine jurisprudence provides, "a witness positively testifies that a document presented as evidence is genuine and has been duly executed or that the document is neither spurious nor counterfeit nor executed by mistake or under duress."[988]

As to how authenticity and genuineness of handwriting can be proven, "the handwriting of a person may be proved by any witness who believes it to be the handwriting of such person because he has seen the person write, or has seen writing purporting to be his upon which the witness has acted or been charged, and has thus acquired knowledge of the handwriting of such person."[989] Moreover, "evidence respecting the handwriting may also be given by a comparison, made by the witness or the court, with writings admitted or treated as genuine by the party against whom the evidence is offered, or proved to be genuine to the satisfaction of the judge."[990]

In relation to this, the authentication of a private document before the Philippine courts is only excused in four instances. As jurisprudence summarizes, authentication is not required either: (1) "when the document is an ancient one," or "a private document is more than thirty years old, is produced from the custody in which it would naturally be found if genuine, and is unblemished by any alterations or circumstances of suspicion;" (2) "when the genuineness and authenticity of the actionable document have not been specifically denied under oath by the adverse party;

985 Asian Terminals v. Philam Life Insurance, G.R. Nos. 181163, 181262, 181319, 24 July 2013; Philippine Revised Rules of Court, Rule 131, § 21.
986 Philippine Revised Rules of Court, Rule 132, § 20 (as amended).
987 Philippine Revised Rules of Court, Rule 132, § 20 (as amended).
988 Salas v. Sta. Mesa Market Corporation, G.R. No. 157766, 12 July 2007.
989 Philippine Revised Rules of Court, Rule 132, § 22.
990 Philippine Revised Rules of Court, Rule 132, § 22.

(3) when the genuineness and authenticity of the document have been admitted; or (4) when the document is not being offered as genuine."[991]

In line with the foregoing, the Philippine Rules on Electronic Evidence as well as E-Commerce Act would gain significance vis-à-vis digital authentication. As per the Rules on Electronic Evidence, electronic signatures or digital signatures are deemed admissible in evidence "as the functional equivalent of the signature of a person on a written document" as long as they properly authenticated in accordance with the rules.[992]

In addition to the foregoing discussion, there would be naturally some instances wherein the authentication of a documentary evidence is required for courts outside of the Philippines. Accordingly, the authentication of documents in this instance is done through the Department of Foreign Affairs, specifically under its Office of Consular Services, in the context of the 1963 Vienna Convention on Consular Services.

e. Importance of Confidentiality

Lack of domestic legislation notwithstanding, confidentiality is of primordial consideration at all times in handling requests for mutual legal assistance. The need for confidentiality is even required to be disclosed as minimum information in MLA requests. Irregardless of any request or mention of the need for confidentiality, the Department of Justice exerts its best efforts to keep the same confidential, including its contents and the actions taken regarding it.[993] In cases where confidentiality has been breached, the requesting member state shall be duly informed of the same to determine if it still wants to pursue the request.[994] This notwithstanding, should the request require filing of an application before the appropriate courts, the request and information provided therein shall, in accordance with Philippine law, be considered public record.[995]

---

991 Salas v. Sta. Mesa Market Corporation, G.R. No. 157766, 12 July 2007.

992 Philippine Rules on Electronic Evidence, Rule 6, §§ 1, 2; see also E-Commerce Act, §§ 7, 8.

993 *Soriano*, p. 138.

994 *Soriano*, p. 138.

995 *Soriano*, p. 138.

f. Return of Evidence

Like the issue on applicability of the speciality and use limitation on MLA requests, there is an apparent gap in the law regarding the obligation to return evidence. While the self-executory ASEAN MLAT would provide the obligation to return evidence to the requested member state upon cessation of proceedings or finishing of the criminal matter subject of the MLA request, there is no other law which would mention the obligation to return evidence to the Philippines. It would seem however that the obligation to return evidence to Philippine authorities can be implied, aside from referencing solely to the ASEAN MLAT.

By backtracking again to how coercive measures could be lawfully done in the Philippines, one could notice the requirement of making the appropriate return on the warrant after said warrant has been executed. In executing validly issued search warrants, for example, the officer tasked to do the search and seizure must "deliver the property seized to the judge who issued the warrant, together with a true inventory thereof duly verified under oath."[996] The rules further provide that the issuing judge shall ascertain if the return has been made "ten (10) days after issuance of the search warrant," and "if none, shall summon the person to whom the warrant was issued and require him to explain why no return was made."[997] If the return has been made, the judge shall ascertain whether a receipt for the property seized (Section 11 of the Rules) has been "complied with and shall require that the property seized be delivered to him."[998] In the same vein, any return on the search warrant "shall be filed and kept by the custodian of the log book on search warrants who shall enter therein the date of the return, the result, and other actions of the judge."[999]

Further, the applicant-law enforcement officer is obliged to give to the custody of the Regional Trial Court which issued authorization within 48 hours since the authorization's expiration all made recordings, etc. in relation to said authorization.[1000] The same kind of return is mandated

---

996 Philippine Rules of Criminal Procedure, Rule 126, § 12(a).
997 Philippine Rules of Criminal Procedure, Rule 126, § 12(b).
998 Philippine Rules of Criminal Procedure, Rule 126, § 12(b).
999 Philippine Rules of Criminal Procedure, Rule 126, § 12(c).
1000 Authorization shall not exceed sixty days from the date of issuance of the order, unless extended or renewed by the Court upon being satisfied that such extension or renewal is in the public interest. Additionally, Republic Act No. 4200, Anti-Wiretapping Law, § 3 provides: "All recordings made under court authorization shall, within forty-eight hours after the expiration of the period

vis-à-vis online data under the Cybercrime Prevention Act and Rules on Cybercrime Warrants, wherein there are rules on depositing to the custody of the relevant Regional Trial Court and certification of the relevant law enforcement authorities as to what was collected or intercepted.[1001] This includes a certification that no duplicates of the whole or the part thereof have been made, or if made, have been accordingly submitted to the court.[1002] Simultaneously, there is also the duty for service providers and law enforcement authorities to destroy computer data completely and immediately after the expiration of the relevant periods provided by law, as the case may be.[1003] And regardless of whether the interception and/or intrusion involves traditional wiretapping or computer data, the exclusionary rule equally applies, wherein any evidence gathered without a valid warrant or beyond the authority conferred by the warrant shall be inadmissible as evidence before any court or tribunal.[1004]

Given these requirements, and lack of amendment thereof as regards international cooperation matters such as mutual legal assistance, it would be proper to require the return of evidence after a particular criminal matter subject of a MLA request has been finished and the evidence, object and/or information requested is no longer required for that particular criminal matter. This would allow executing authorities in the Philippines to comply with their positive duty as provided by law.

---

fixed in the order, be deposited with the court in a sealed envelope or sealed package, and shall be accompanied by an affidavit of the peace officer granted such authority stating the number of recordings made, the dates and times covered by each recording, the number of tapes, discs, or records included in the deposit, and certifying that no duplicates or copies of the whole or any part thereof have been made, or if made, that all such duplicates or copies are included in the envelope or package deposited with the court. The envelope or package so deposited shall not be opened, or the recordings replayed, or used in evidence, or their contents revealed, except upon order of the court, which shall not be granted except upon motion, with due notice and opportunity to be heard to the person or persons whose conversation or communications have been recorded." Similar import can be found nowadays in the Anti-Terrorism Act of 2020.

1001 Implementing Rules and Regulations of the Philippine Cybercrime Prevention Act, § 16; Rules on Cybercrime Warrants, §§ 4.5, 5.5, 6.6, 6.8, 7.1 (submission to custody of court).

1002 Anti-Wiretapping Law, § 3.

1003 Implementing Rules and Regulations of the Philippine Cybercrime Prevention Act, §§ 16, 17; Rules on Cybercrime Warrants, § 8.2.

1004 Implementing Rules and Regulations of the Philippine Cybercrime Prevention Act, § 18.

g. Specific Procedures per Type of Assistance

It has been stressed before that a domestic statute on mutual legal assistance, or even something that would define and delineate how requests for mutual legal assistance shall be dealt with – or at least, consolidate existing principles, conditions, exceptions, as well as procedure and other requirements – is left to be desired. This in turn creates the need to consolidate what can be found in existing law, rules of court procedure, and other rules and regulations to discern the different procedures as to how specific types of mutual legal assistance is being executed or effectuated in the Philippine setting. This includes whatever intricacies each investigative measure has.

To illustrate these complexities and the problems that could arise due to lack of any straightforward standardization, one can look into the commonly requested investigative measure via mutual legal assistance: taking of evidence and/or voluntary statements. As discussed below, the Philippines presents itself as a unique case because despite the usual notion that taking of evidence and/or voluntary statements is a straightforward process, different nuances or issues arise from how the laws and procedures that could apply are scattered across different planes, making it complex to assuredly determine the direction one must take. Stating it differently, the Philippines within its own domestic context present the problem of lack of harmonization and standardization necessary to an effective machinery of international cooperation such as mutual legal assistance.

With respect to any request for mutual legal assistance in the taking of evidence and/or voluntary statements, the Department of Justice shall evaluate and should find the same meritorious, endorses the request to the National Bureau of Investigation and/or National Prosecution Service to process and effectuate the same.[1005] The said units may then proceed to issue the necessary subpoena, which is "a process directed to a person requiring him to attend and to testify at the hearing or the trial of an action, or at any investigation conducted by competent authority, or for the taking of his deposition" and/or "may also require him to bring with him any books, documents, or other things under his control."[1006] Under Philippine remedial law, the first refers to a *subpoena ad testificandum*

1005 See Executive Order No. 292 (Administrative Code of the Philippines), Title III, §§ 1, 3-4, 11-13; *Soriano*, p. 131.

1006 Act Establishing a Bureau of Investigation (Republic Act No. 157), § 5; Prosecutor Service Act of 2010, § 9; Philippine Rules of Court, Rule 21, § 1.

whilst the latter refers to a *subpoena duces tecum*, and when issued together, is referred to as *subpoena ad testificandum et duces tecum*.[1007]

With respect to this, should said *subpoena duces tecum* be "unreasonable and oppressive, or the relevancy of the books, documents or things does not appear, or if the person in whose behalf the subpoena is issued fails to advance the reasonable cost of production thereof," or "that the witness is not bound thereby," the issuing authority may quash the issued subpoena "upon motion promptly made and, in any event, at or before the time specified therein."[1008] This necessarily means that any request for mutual legal assistance should sufficiently provide the required information to justify the attendance of a person to either give testimony or produce documents and other pieces of evidence, or both. Otherwise, there is the risk of having a motion filed to quash any subpoena issued with respect to any mutual legal assistance request.

The relevant rules of procedure likewise provide for how said subpoena should be sent to the relevant person, who either needs to provide testimony or produce documents or evidence, or both.[1009]

In addition, if one looks further into the Rules of Court, taking of evidence and/or voluntary statements from a person through the use of discovery and deposition mechanisms is also sanctioned in the Philippines.[1010] While the use of modes of discovery is equally sanctioned for criminal cases in the Philippines,[1011] there is no clear cut definition and delineation of its usage in mutual legal assistance proceedings. Going back to *People of the Philippines v. Sergio* and how the Supreme Court decided to accommodate the deposition of Mary Jane Veloso through written interrogatories whilst being imprisoned in Indonesia, it would seem that deposition was allowed due to the special circumstances of this case. Here-

1007 Remedial Law refers to the Rules of Court or Procedural Law in the Philippines. Philippine Rules of Court, Rule 21, § 1.

1008 Philippine Rules of Court, Rule 21, § 4.

1009 Accordingly, summons shall be served, whenever practicable, by handling a copy thereof personally to the person involved, or when it cannot be done due to justifiable causes, "(a) by leaving copies of the summons at the defendant's residence with some person of suitable age and discretion then residing therein, or (b) by leaving the copies at defendant's office or regular place of business with some competent person in charge thereof." Service should be made to allow the person against whom the subpoena is issued should be given reasonable time to prepare and travel to the place of attendance. *See* Philippine Rules of Court, Rule 14, §§ 6-7, Rule 21, § 6.

1010 Philippine Rules of Court, Rules 21, 23, 24-25.

1011 See Rules of Criminal Procedure, Rule 114, § 10.

in, the rules were liberally applied because the rules of criminal procedure were bereft of any provision applicable to the condition of Mary Jane Veloso who while being an indispensable witness to an illegal recruitment case in the Philippines, was also convicted of a grave offense, currently incarcerated in a foreign country, and in death row. Further, any strict application according to the Supreme Court will not be in congruence with purpose of the ASEAN MLAT, "which is enforced precisely to be applied in circumstances like in the case of Mary Jane."[1012] The ASEAN MLAT, according to the Court, recognizes the significance of cooperation and coordination among the states to prevent, investigate and prosecute criminal offenses especially if perpetuated not only in a single state just like in the case of drug and human trafficking, and illegal recruitment, the very charges that were filed against the accused Sergio et al.

Albeit there is comfort in knowing that no less than the Supreme Court recognizes modes of discovery as consistent with the aim and purpose of mutual legal assistance, one cannot simply rely on the Court's pronouncement herein to conclude with certainty that modes of discovery such as depositions through written interrogatories vis-à-vis mutual legal assistance are sanctioned. If the case did not involve the special circumstances surrounding Mary Jane Veloso, then the Court would have definitely decided differently. If there is anything else one can learn from *Sergio*, it would be to ensure that Philippine law and procedure is standardized to avoid further confusion or the need to resort to liberal construction of procedural rules in the first place. This is the first order of business. But while one waits for this momentous occasion to come, if one follows the analogy given in *Sergio* as well as by Undersecretary Malaya et al. between mutual legal assistance and "depositions pending action" under Rule 23 of the Rules of Court, wherein they mention how mutual legal assistance does not require an ongoing criminal case to be effectuated (currently being in the investigative stage suffices),[1013] then there would be reasonable ground to argue that the usage of modes of discovery is sanctioned. Further, if one acts on the premise of reciprocity and the rationale of mutual legal assistance being a more efficient and modern way of facilitating judicial cooperation, then discovery procedures should be deemed allowed as a procedure to effectuate mutual legal assistance requests. That said, the relevant provisions provide that depositions or recourse to discovery pro-

---

1012 People of the Philippines v. Sergio, G.R. No. 240053, 09 October 2019.

1013 *Malaya/Monedero-Arnesto/Paras*, p. 7.

cedures are available pending court action, before action, and pending appeal.[1014] And in case one is similarly situated as Mary Jane Veloso, then deposition through written interrogatories is allowed to perpetuate testimony.

It becomes more complex when one considers the different rules in the taking of evidence and/or voluntary statements as regards persons who are currently in custody or imprisoned in the Philippines. As per the applicable rules, "when application for a subpoena to a prisoner is made, the judge or officer shall examine and study carefully such application to determine whether the same is made for a valid purpose."[1015] Further, the rules provide that "no prisoner sentenced to death, reclusion perpetua or life imprisonment and who is confined in any penal institution shall be brought outside the said penal institution for appearance or attendance in any court unless authorized by the Supreme Court."[1016] In the same vein, depositions made on persons who are currently imprisoned shall only be made through leave of court on such terms as the court prescribes.[1017] In other words, should the mutual legal assistance request refer to taking of voluntary statements of persons currently imprisoned, there is no other recourse but to go to court about it.

Another nuance about the taking of evidence and/or voluntary statements involves the production and inspection of documents or other pieces of evidence as well as the physical and mental examination of persons. On one hand, there is the production and inspection of documents, etc., wherein the court in which an action is pending may "(a) order any party to produce and permit the inspection and copying or photographing, by or on behalf of the moving party, of any designated documents, papers, books, accounts, letters, photographs, objects or tangible things, not privileged, which constitute or contain evidence material to any matter involved in the action and which are in his possession, custody or control, or (b) order any party to permit entry upon designated land or other property in his possession or control for the purpose of inspecting, measuring, surveying, or photographing the property or any designated relevant object or operation thereon," upon motion for good cause of a party.[1018]

1014 Philippine Rules of Court, Rules 23, 24, 25.
1015 Philippine Rules of Court, Rule 14, § 2.
1016 Philippine Rules of Court, Rule 14, § 2.
1017 Philippine Rules of Court, Rule 23, § 1.
1018 Philippine Rules of Court, Rule 27, § 1.

On the other hand, as regards the physical and/or mental examination of persons, it is allowed in actions where the physical and/or mental condition of a person is in question.[1019] The court in which the action is pending may in its discretion order a person to submit to a physical or mental examination by a physician.[1020] In line with this, there shall be a waiver of privilege, meaning, "the party examined waives any privilege he may have in that action or any other involving the same controversy, regarding the testimony of every other person who has examined or may thereafter examine him in respect of the same mental or physical examination."[1021]

According to the ASEAN MLAT, which is the Philippine legal basis, a person, who is required to give a sworn statement or testimony, or produce documents, records, or other forms of evidence pursuant to a request for assistance, may decline to do so on two accounts: "(1) the law of the requested member state permits or requires that person to decline to do so in similar circumstances in proceedings originating in the requested member state; or (2) the law of the requesting member state permits or requires that person to decline to do so in similar circumstances in proceedings originating in the requesting member state."[1022] Should the person decline on the second given ground, "the requesting member state shall, if so requested, provide a certificate to the requested member state as to the existence or otherwise of that right."[1023]

Considering these, there are arguably unsettled issues that need to be straightened out as soon as possible. Agreeing with the statement of Undersecretary Malaya et al. above, there is the need for domestic legislation on mutual legal assistance to provide the parameters, baselines, and guidelines de rigeur. In other words, there is a want of harmonization and/or standardization in the domestic legal system itself.

As regards other types of assistance not specifically listed in the ASEAN MLAT, the lack of any singular instrument that would define, delineate, and explain the different forms of assistance the Philippines is problematic in effectively sending and receiving mutual legal assistance requests, as arguably, a requesting state should either second-guess or outright be abreast of the different laws which could be applicable when sending a request to the Philippines. It can particularly be difficult if the requesting state

1019 Philippine Rules of Court, Rule 28, § 1.
1020 Philippine Rules of Court, Rule 28, § 1.
1021 Philippine Rules of Court, Rule 28, § 4.
1022 2004 ASEAN Mutual Legal Assistance Treaty, art.12, § 1.
1023 2004 ASEAN Mutual Legal Assistance Treaty, art.12, § 2.

would be unfamiliar with the legal system applicable to the Philippines. In practice, the hurdles could be however surpassed through constant communication and consultation with other central authorities. As per interviews with authorities involved in mutual legal assistance requests, they advised one another on the applicable law and procedure, or whether the said requested assistance can be effectuated or not.

III. Implementation in the member state level: Malaysia

The next portion discusses mutual legal assistance in Malaysia, the other member-state which the present study looks into as regards mutual legal assistance within the ASEAN. Interestingly, and as mentioned as early as the introduction of the present study, Malaysia, together with the Philippines, is one of the founding member states of the ASEAN. Furthermore, Malaysia was the member state that proposed and helped in drafting the present provisions of the ASEAN MLAT according to the treaty's explanatory note. In the next following sections and pages, one would be walked through to how mutual legal assistance developed historically in Malaysia, what the present legal framework is vis-à-vis substantive and procedural provisions of mutual legal assistance, including a discussion of how the said provisions are applied in practice, as well as issues and problems that may be highlighted or pointed out.

A. Historical Development of Mutual Legal Assistance

1. Bilateral, Regional, and Multilateral Mutual Legal Assistance Treaties

Malaysia has entered into different bilateral and multilateral treaties. It is a signatory to the ASEAN MLAT, and five (5) bilateral mutual legal assistance treaties, namely with Australia, Hong Kong, United States of America, United Kingdom, and India.[1024] Additionally, Malaysia is a signatory to treaties containing provisions on mutual legal assistance, such as the UNCAC and UNTOC.[1025]

1024 *Kamal*, p. 87.
1025 See *Kamal*, p. 87.

2. Domestic Legislation on Mutual Legal Assistance

Aside from entering into bilateral, regional, and multilateral treaties, Malaysia has various domestic instruments on international cooperation. As regards mutual legal assistance, such is provided for in the following: Dangerous Drugs Act 1988 (with regard forfeiture of property), Order 66 of the Rules of the High Court 1980, and the Mutual Assistance in Criminal Matters Act 2002 ("MACMA"), which is supplemented by the Mutual Assistance in Criminal Matters Regulations 2003.[1026]

MACMA entered into force in 01 May 2003 and is mainly the Malaysian law that governs mutual legal assistance in criminal matters between Malaysia and other countries, including other matters in relation therewith. It applies to requests made both pursuant to a MLAT and those made on a non-treaty basis. Needless to state, its provisions are controlling with respect to mutual legal assistance in criminal matters in Malaysia.

As to how the MACMA relates to the ASEAN MLAT, Malaysia ought to enact domestic laws such as the MACMA, which in turn is imperative to effectuate treaties, such as those relating to mutual legal assistance, locally.

To understand the context, Malaysia historically followed the practice of British courts with respect to international law: doctrine of transformation vis-à-vis treaties or international agreements while doctrine of incorporation vis-à-vis customary international law.[1027] Presently, Malaysia is one of the states, in respect of which its Constitution does not provide anything as to the status of international law vis-à-vis its domestic law.[1028] This notwithstanding, Malaysia follows the doctrine of transformation with regard treaties and international agreements.[1029]

In view thereof, one can find provisions in the Constitution nonetheless that speak of the treaty-making capacity in Malaysia.[1030] On one hand, the Federal Constitution of Malaysia, in Article 74(1), provides that the "Parliament may make laws with respect to the matters enumerated in the 'Federal List' or the 'Concurrent List'."[1031] Accordingly, such "Federal List" includes, in the Ninth Schedule, "External Affairs", which enumerates among others "treaties, agreements, conventions with other countries

---

1026 Explanatory note to the ASEAN Model Treaty for Mutual Legal Assistance in Criminal Matters, p. 2; *Kamal*, p. 83.

1027 *Hamid/Sein*, pp. 196, 197.

1028 *Dewanto*, p. 5; *Hamid/Sein*, p. 198.

1029 *Hamid/Sein*, p. 200.

1030 *Hamid/Sein*, p. 198.

1031 Federal Constitution of Malaysia, art. 74(1); *Hamid/Sein*, p. 198.

and all matters which bring the Federation into relations with other countries" and "implementation of treaties, agreements, and conventions with other countries."[1032] It can be concluded thereon that the Federal Parliament has the exclusive power to implement international treaties and make them operative domestically.[1033]

On the other hand, Article 39 of the same Federal Constitution vests executive authority to the "constitutional Monarch and Head of State Yang di-PertuanAgong and exercisable by him or by the Cabinet or any Minister authorized by the Cabinet."[1034] Such authority extends, as Article 80(1) of the Federal Constitution provides, to all matters with regard to which the Parliament may legislate laws.[1035] Therefore, the executive authority of the Federation – vis-a-vis the Federal List that enumerates among others treaties and international agreements – extends to the making and conclusion of treaties, agreements, and conventions with other countries.[1036]

Such has been reaffirmed in the case of *The Government of the State of Kelantan v. the Government of the Federation of Malaya and Tunku Abdul Rahman Putra Al-Haj*, wherein Kelantan assailed the constitutionality of Malaysia Agreement, an international treaty among the United Kingdom, Malaysia, and Singapore.[1037] The Kelantan government was of the position that the consent of the individual federal states is required before international arrangements for Malaysia can be lawfully implemented.[1038] In sustaining the validity of the Malaysia Agreement, the High Court stated that there is nothing in the Constitution requiring consultation with any State Government or the Ruler of any State, before an international agreement can be implemented.[1039] Based on the foregoing, it can be then concluded that the Federal Government has the treaty-making power in Malaysia while the Parliament has the power to legislate to give treaties legal effect domestically, especially for those treaties that affect rights of private persons or involves changes in domestic laws.[1040]

1032 *Hamid/Sein*, p. 198.
1033 *Hamid/Sein*, p. 198.
1034 Federal Constitution of Malaysia, art. 39; *Hamid/Sein*, p. 198.
1035 Federal Constitution of Malaysia, art. 80(1); *Hamid/Sein*, p. 199.
1036 *Hamid/Sein*, p. 199.
1037 [1963] MLJ 355 (Federation of Malaya High Court); *Hamid/Sein*, p. 199.
1038 *Hamid/Sein*, p. 199.
1039 The Government of the State of Kelantan v. the Government of the Federation of Malaya and Tunku Abdul Rahman Putra Al-Haj, [1963] MLJ 355 (Federation of Malaya High Court); *Hamid/Sein*, p. 199.
1040 *Hamid/Sein*, pp. 199-200.

In view of the foregoing provisions, the MACMA is the domestic legal basis for for mutual legal assistance in Malaysia and is necessary to implement and/or operationalize the ASEAN MLAT and other mutual legal assistance treaties Malaysia is a signatory of or to otherwise give legal effect to the same locally. Consequently, the MACMA provisions apply whenever Malaysia sends or receives requests for mutual legal assistance in criminal matters.

B. Substantive Provisions: Mutual Legal Assistance in Criminal Matters

1. Applicability of Assistance

MACMA illustrates a request-based system on mutual legal assistance in Malaysia wherein requests are sent to and from Malaysia for the cross-border exchange and transfer of information and/or evidence in criminal matters. The law provides that assistance shall be provided in criminal matters. "Criminal matters" is not necessarily defined but is mentioned that it is "in respect of a serious offense or foreign serious offense, as the case may be, and enumerates the following to included hereto: (1) a criminal investigation, (2) criminal proceedings, or (3) ancillary criminal matter.[1041] MACMA further defines ancillary criminal matters as those involving either "the restraining of dealing with, or the seizure, forfeiture, or confiscation of, property in connection with a serious offense or a foreign serious offense, as the case may be" or "the obtaining, enforcement or satisfaction of a forfeiture order or a foreign forfeiture order, as the case may be."[1042]

Not all criminal offenses are subject to mutual legal assistance but are only limited to those which are "serious offenses" or "foreign serious offenses", which MACMA defines as either (1) "an offense defined under the Anti-Money Laundering Act 2001", (2) "an offense against the laws of Malaysia where (i) the maximum penalty for the offense is death or (ii) the minimum term of imprisonment is not less than one year", or (3) any attempt, abetment or conspiracy to commit any of the preceding two offenses.[1043] On the other hand, foreign serious offenses are either offenses (1) "against the law of a prescribed foreign State stated in a certificate pur-

1041 MACMA, § 1.
1042 MACMA, § 1.
1043 MACMA, § 1.

porting to be issued by or on behalf of the government of that prescribed foreign State", or (2) "that consists of or includes activity which, if it had occurred in Malaysia, would have constituted a serious offense."[1044]

Assistance may be given by Malaysia to both treaty and non-treaty based requests.[1045] MACMA provides for "prescribed foreign states", which are foreign states with existing treaties or agreements with Malaysia. Those without existing agreements are not considered as such. In connection to this, to be formally a "prescribed foreign state", the Minister in charge of legal affairs declares by order that there is any treaty or other agreement between Malaysia and that foreign state under which the latter has agreed to provide mutual legal assistance to the former;[1046] and any such order may provide limitations, restrictions, exceptions, modifications, adaptations, conditions, or qualifications.[1047] It is also subject to revocation or amendment by subsequent order by the Minister.[1048] Notably, any order declaring a foreign state as a prescribed foreign state shall not only be conclusive evidence that the arrangement indicated therein is in compliance with the provisions of MACMA, but that MACMA also applies in the case of said foreign state and that the validity of the order shall not be questioned in any legal proceedings.[1049]

On the other hand, before a non-prescribed foreign state – or a foreign state without any treaty or agreement with Malaysia vis-à-vis mutual legal assistance – is afforded assistance, the Minister in charge of legal affairs, upon recommendation of the Attorney General, gives a special direction in writing that MACMA shall apply in relation to the requested mutual legal assistance "subject to any restriction, limitation, exception, modification, adaptation, condition, or qualification contained in the direction."[1050]

2. Types of Assistance Rendered

MACMA enables Malaysia to provide and obtain international assistance in criminal matters, to the exclusion of extradition, arrest, or detention with a view to extradite, of any person, which is covered by other laws,

1044 MACMA, § 1.
1045 MACMA, §§ 16, 17.
1046 MACMA, § 17(1).
1047 MACMA, § 17(2).
1048 MACMA, § 17(4).
1049 MACMA, § 17(3).
1050 MACMA, § 18.

in the following forms: "(1) providing and obtaining evidence or things; (2) the making of arrangements for persons to give evidence, or to assist in criminal investigations; (3) the recovery, forfeiture, or confiscation of property in respect of a serious offense or a foreign serious offense; (4) the restraining of dealings in property, or the freezing of property, that may be recovered in respect of a serious offense or foreign serious offense; (5) the execution of requests for search and seizure; (6) the location and identification of witnesses and suspects; (7) the service of processes; (8) the identification or tracing of proceeds of crime and property and instrumentalities derived from or used in the commission of a serious offense or foreign serious offense; (8) the recovery of pecuniary penalties in respect of a serious offense or foreign serious offense; and (9) the examination of things and premises."[1051]

MACMA also contains a catch-all provision wherein nothing in said MACMA prevents the provision or obtaining of international assistance to or from any foreign state other than those above enumerated.[1052] As to how this provision applies in practice, in an interview with officials from the Transnational Crime Unit of the Prosecution Division in the Attorney General's Chambers, which acts as the central authority for both extradition and mutual legal assistance requests in Malaysia, requesting states normally do a preliminary consultation to ask whether a particular type of assistance is allowed and thereafter the said Transnational Crime Unit shall assist and check the applicable domestic laws and accordingly advise.

Interestingly, a reading of the list of types of assistance that could be rendered under the MACMA would reveal that interception of communication and online evidence is not explicitly provided for. In consultation with Malaysian officials, it was mentioned that these forms of assistance normally is done through the informal channels.[1053]Wiretapping by public officials is only sanctioned for offenses committed in Malaysia and has not been expanded to cover aspects of international cooperation.[1054] At the same time, should interception of communication and/or correspondence as well as online evidence is requested from Malaysia and allowed, it does

1051 MACMA, §§ 3, 5.
1052 MACMA, § 4(2).
1053 Interview with prosecutors from the Office of the Attorney-General.
1054 Interview with prosecutors from the Office of the Attorney-General.

not cover content of said communication/correspondence but only the fact that it occurred.[1055]

3. Compatibility with Other Agreements

MACMA explicitly provides that it does not prevent the provision or obtaining of international assistance in criminal matters to and from the International Criminal Police Organization ("INTERPOL") or any other international organization.[1056] At the same time, MACMA does not prevent, although it has become the primary legal basis for mutual legal assistance requests, the rendering and receiving of mutual legal assistance as may be provided in other earlier written laws, such as those provided under Order 66 of the Rules of the High Court 1980, Part VII of the Dangerous Drugs Act 1988 on Forfeiture of Property, and Sections 50 and 52 of the Extradition Act 1992.[1057]

In the same vein as rendering and receiving assistance from INTERPOL and other international organizations, assistance upon an informal request or other form of arrangement is not provided for in the MACMA.[1058] In light of this, Malaysian officials do not shy away from acknowledging and promoting how informal assistance is an invaluable tool in international cooperation in combating crime.[1059] At the preliminary stages of investigation, when coercive measures are not yet required, some "informal assistance" may suffice to provide useful information.[1060] This "informal assistance" is understood to be assistance through channels outside of the formal mutual legal assistance regime, often through direct communications between counterparts or police sharing intelligence or data, which is legally available through domestic databases.[1061] Admittedly, its strength relies on networking and exchange of information.[1062]

1055 Interview with prosecutors from the Office of the Attorney-General.

1056 MACMA, § 4(1).

1057 MACMA, § 4(3); Dato' Mohamed Hashim Shamsuddin v. Attorney General, Hong Kong [1986] 2 MLJ 112; Lorrain Esme Osman v Attorney General of Malaysia [1986] 2 MLJ 288; *Office of the Attorney General.*

1058 MACMA, § 4(2); *Kamal*, p. 92.

1059 *Kamal*, p. 92; *Sidek*, p. 122.

1060 *Kamal*, p. 92.

1061 *Kamal*, p. 92.

1062 *Sidek*, p. 122.

To illustrate, the Malaysian Anti-Corruption Commission ("MACC") may request their counterparts abroad to provide intelligence or information and similarly may provide assistance to their counterparts.[1063] It has thus far relied on informal assistance provided by Komisi Pemberantasan Korupsi (Corruption Eradicating Corruption or "KPK") in Indonesia, Corrupt Practices Investigation Bureau ("CPIB") in Singapore, and the Independent Commission against Corruption ("ICAC") in Hong Kong in its detection and investigation of certain individuals.[1064] The same informal assistance occurs between different Malaysian agencies, such as the Central Bank, and their foreign counterparts.

Having said this, the most common example of informal assistance arguably occurs in police-to-police cooperation in Malaysia. In an interview with the Royal Malaysian Police's point person for mutual legal assistance and extradition requests, police-to-police cooperation is recognized as vital with respect to investigation and information gathering. Malaysian Police maintains a network with other police authorities around the world and in the ASEAN, and the ASEANAPOL (albeit an independent body from the ASEAN) serves as an indispensable conduit. The same officer clarifies that more often than not, whatever information gathered during this said police-to-police cooperation serves as stirring information that leads to more formal requests for cooperation. He stressed that whatever is gathered during police-to-police cooperation is not used as evidence before the courts. What is used as evidence are those gathered through the prosecutorial stage and/or the government-to-government cooperation which happens through mutual legal assistance.

4. Principles, Conditions, and Exemptions

The MACMA provides categorically the mandatory and discretionary grounds for refusal, which are more or less the principles, conditions, and exceptions Malaysia applies to mutual legal assistance in criminal matters.[1065] In practice, officials of the Attorney General's Chambers intimated that they work to approve all requests received and normally, requests received and sent among ASEAN member-countries are executed. To avoid denial of requests, open communication channels are maintained and

1063 *Kamal*, p. 92; *Sidek*, p. 122.
1064 *Sidek*, p. 122.
1065 MACMA, § 20(1)(3); *Kamal*, pp. 85-86.

preliminary consultations and communication are often done between authorities and they advise one another as to the correct content or procedure to be followed.

a. Sufficiency of Evidence

On the basis of the MACMA, there is a tacit sufficiency of evidence requirement written in between its provisions: the more coercive an investigative measure is, e.g. search and seizures, the more evidence or information the requesting state must provide prior to the approval of a MLA request. At the outset, a reading of the provisions of MACMA would reveal that before any assistance can be given by Malaysia to a foreign state, it must be satisfied that the information or evidence requested is relevant to the criminal matter subject of the mutual legal assistance request.[1066] Moreover, there are types of assistance requests which have a sufficiency of evidence requirement before assistance can be rendered by the government of Malaysia, in particular, are the requests for taking of evidence for criminal proceedings, production orders for criminal matters, including requests for search and seizure, requests for attendance of persons in prescribed foreign state, and locating and/or identifying persons.[1067] For instance, in effectuating requests for search and seizures against a person, a court order is firstly required and prior to an issuance of the same, the court needs to be satisfied that "there are reasonable grounds for suspecting that a person specified in the request has committed or has benefited from a foreign serious offense".[1068] Likewise, in locating and/or identifying persons, the Attorney General may grant the request if he is satisfied, among others, that there are reasonable grounds to believe that the person being sought to be located and/or identified is or might be concerned in, or could give or provide evidence or assistance relevant to, the criminal matter, and that the person is in Malaysia.[1069]

In connection to this, the applicable Malaysian law provides a consequent ground for refusal when the sufficiency of evidence requirement is not satisfied. One of the mandatory grounds for refusal provided for is insufficiency of importance – when the thing requested for is of insufficient

1066 See for example MACMA, § 35(1), (2).
1067 MACMA, §§ 22, 23-26, 27, 34, 35-36, 39.
1068 MACMA, § 36(2).
1069 MACMA, § 39(2).

importance to the investigation or could be reasonably obtained by other means.[1070] Discerning importance necessarily entails the weighing of the evidence and/or information the prescribed foreign state provided with the resources required to fulfill said request. In this regard, the process of open communication and preliminary consultations in practice plays a significant role to avoid incidents of denial resulting from insufficiency of importance.

b. Dual Criminality

Dual criminality exists as a requirement in MACMA as it is a mandatory ground for refusal under Section 20(1)(f). A request may be denied should it relate to an "investigation, prosecution, or punishment of a person in respect of an act or omission that, if it had occurred in Malaysia, would not have constituted an offense against the laws of Malaysia."[1071] Based on this provision, what matters is not the nomenclature of the criminal offense but the act or omission constituting this criminal offense. Thus, following the provision, should the act or omission the MLA request relates to is not punishable in Malaysia, then Malaysia can deny the request.

While being a strict requirement, in practice, there is no automatic denial of requests based on this ground. The central authorities of Malaysia and the other relevant state advise one another as to what law could apply by looking into particulars.[1072] This pertains to cases wherein the case is punishable as a crime in Malaysian domestic law but the requested state does not seem to have the same kind of law, and vice versa.

c. Double Jeopardy

Double jeopardy is provided as a mandatory ground for refusal under Section 20(1)(e) MACMA when Malaysia is the requested state. A request shall be denied should it pertain to the investigation, prosecution, or punishment of a person for an offense in case where either (1) the person has been convicted, acquitted, or pardoned by a competent court or other

1070 MACMA, § 20(1)(h).
1071 MACMA, § 20(1)(f).
1072 Interview with prosecutors from the Office of the Attorney-General.

authority in the prescribed foreign state; or (2) has undergone the punishment provided by the law of that prescribed foreign state.

Two things can be mentioned at the outset with this provision. First, it can be gainsaid based on said provision that the MACMA adopts to a certain extent a transnational element in the application of double jeopardy as a mandatory ground for refusal because Malaysia shall consider if a conviction, acquittal, pardon, or service of punishment has already occurred in another state – herein, the requesting "prescribed foreign state." One should note however that herein only the requesting state is involved. There is no involvement of any other state, wherein conviction, acquittal, pardon, or service of punishment may have occurred. Second, one can note with this provision that the conviction, acquittal, pardon, or service of punishment pertains to the prescribed foreign state (requesting state herein) and not Malaysia. Stating it otherwise, if the conviction, acquittal, pardon, or service of punishment occurred in Malaysia, then strictly following the MACMA provision, the double jeopardy as mandatory ground for refusal shall not apply.

Notwithstanding the foregoing observations, it remains questionable if this strict application should be the case, given that there is a prohibition against double jeopardy in Malaysia itself. To begin with, the protection against double jeopardy is provided in the Federal Constitution of Malaysia, wherein "a person who has been acquitted or convicted of an offence shall not be tried again for the same offence except where the conviction or acquittal has been quashed and a retrial ordered by a court superior to that by which he was acquitted or convicted."[1073] The said protection is likewise provided for in Article 302 of the Malaysian Criminal Procedure

1073 Federal Constitution of Malaysia, art.7(2).

Code.[1074] The same article in the Malaysian Criminal Procedure Code further provides illustrative examples of how the provisions apply.[1075]

It must be understood however that in Malaysian domestic law, the protection against double jeopardy, or otherwise known as the protection against repeated trials, is not absolute and admits of many exceptions. Thus, some have commented that the protection in actuality has slim prac-

---

1074 Criminal Procedure Code, art. 302 provides:
"Person once convicted or acquitted not to be tried again for same offence
302. (1) A person who has been tried by a Court of competent jurisdiction for an offence and convicted or acquitted of that offence shall, while the conviction or acquittal remains in force, not be liable to be tried again for the same offence nor on the same facts for any other offence for which a different charge from the one made against him might have been made under section 166 or for which he might have been convicted under section 167.
(2) A person acquitted or convicted of any offence may be afterwards tried for any distinct offence for which a separate charge might have been made against him on the former trial under subsection 165(1).
(3) A person convicted of any offence constituted by any act causing consequences which, together with that act, constituted a different offence from that of which he was convicted, may be afterwards tried for that last-mentioned offence, if the consequences had not happened or were not known to the Court to have happened at the time when he was convicted.
(4) A person acquitted or convicted of any offence constituted by any acts may, notwithstanding the acquittal or conviction, be subsequently charged with and tried for any other offence constituted by the same acts which he may have committed, if the Court by which he was first tried was not competent to try the offence with which he is subsequently charged.
(5) The dismissal of a complaint, or the discharge of the accused, is not an acquittal for the purposes of this section."

1075 (a) A is tried upon a charge of theft as a servant and acquitted. He cannot afterwards, while the acquittal remains in force, be charged upon the same facts with theft as a servant, or with theft simply, or with criminal breach of trust.
(b) A is tried upon a charge of murder and acquitted. There is no charge of robbery but it appears from the facts that A committed robbery at the time when the murder was committed; he may afterwards be charged with and tried for robbery.
(c) A is tried for causing grievous hurt and convicted. The person injured afterwards dies. A may be tried again for culpable homicide.
(d) A is tried and convicted of the culpable homicide of B. A may not afterwards be tried on the same facts for the murder of B.
(e) A is charged and convicted of voluntarily causing hurt to B. A may not afterwards be tried for voluntarily causing grievous hurt to B on the same facts unless the case comes within subsection (3) of this section.

tical significance.[1076]The following are the four (4) main circumstances wherein the rule on double jeopardy is not deemed violated and retrial is not sanctioned:

First, when proceedings have been discharged. Discharge of proceedings can result from different reasons, but does not automatically result to double jeopardy being consequently engaged.[1077] Normally, discharge of proceedings shall result to acquittal of the accused should it become expressed or apparent that the prosecution is not interested in pursuing the case any further, or that there shall be failure to prosecute the case for good reasons, or it is unlikely that the case can be prosecuted expeditiously in the short future.[1078]

Second, double jeopardy does not apply whenever the superior courts order the quashing of previous proceedings and a retrial. The constitutional provision explicitly provides this, and has been reaffirmed in a number of cases.[1079] Retrial, as contemplated here, means that everything should start anew, and all pieces of evidence "should be therefore tendered afresh and decided upon accordingly by a new trial judge."[1080] One must take note however, that in exercising the power to order a retrial, the said power is discretionary and there is no yard stick as to when it should or should not be ordered.[1081] At most, the appellate court must be guided by what is in the interest of justice and whether the "preponderance of justice is against or in favor of a retrial."[1082]

Third, double jeopardy does not also apply when a person is charged with a different offense on the basis of the same set of facts in a subsequent trial, if the accused could not have been charged with or convicted of that different offence in the court which convicted him first.[1083] "Different offense" is contemplated to mean that the previous offense for which the

---

1076 *Harding*, p. 224.

1077 *Fook/Mansoor/Hassan*, pp. 41-59.

1078 Public Prosecutor v. Lau Ngiik Yin, [2007] MLJU 668 at [4]; *Fook/Mansoor/Hassan*, p. 49.

1079 Federal Constitution of Malaysia, art.7(2); Sau Soo Kim v. Public Prosecutor [1975] 2 MLJ 134; Fan Yew Teng v. Public Prosecutor, [1975] 2 MLJ 235.

1080 *Fook/Mansoor/Hassan*, p. 653.

1081 *Fook/Mansoor/Hassan*, pp. 653, 655-656.

1082 *Fook/Mansoor/Hassan*, pp. 654, 656.

1083 *Faruqi*; *Harding*, p. 224.

accused has been tried and the subsequent offense must not have the same essential ingredients.[1084]

Fourth, double jeopardy does not apply when retrial is due to technical errors. After being detained in West Malaysia for an alleged violation of a law only applicable in Sarawak, a writ of habeas corpus was issued to order the release of Datuk James Wong Kim Min.[1085] However, this did not constitute a bar to any subsequent detention resulting in the application of the correct law.[1086]

At the same time, double jeopardy does not attach during appeals, preventive detention, different proceedings, as well as civil proceedings (civil liability arising from criminal liability) under Malaysian law. When either a prosecutor in a criminal case appeals the acquittal of the accused,[1087] or when the suspect/accused was only preventively detained under the now repealed Internal Security Act or other law allowing preventive detention,[1088] or when a non-criminal action or civil action arises against the accused to whom a criminal penalty has already been imposed or criminal action has been initiated,[1089] the same does not constitute double jeopardy.

Taking all intricacies and provisions into account, in a mutual legal assistance context, two conclusions can be derived. On one hand, when Malaysia is the requesting state, the prohibition against double jeopardy as explained above should be taken into account. Whatever MLA request Malaysian authorities would send would naturally involve investigative measures, evidence, and other information that shall be used in Malaysian courts. These Malaysian courts would naturally uphold Malaysian law, including constitutional prohibitions such as that against double jeopardy. Thus, the parameters as stated above would be material in a Malaysian context.

On the other hand, Malaysia shall not consider it indeed as a mandatory ground for refusal should the conviction, acquittal, pardon, or service of punishment occurred in Malaysia or a third state other than the requesting state. A reading of the MACMA provision would point to this direction.

1084 Jamali bin Adnan v. Public Prosecutor [1986] 1 MLJ 162; [1985] CLJ (Rep) 167; Public Prosecutor v. Teh Cheng Poh, [1978] 1 MLJ 68; See also Federal Constitution of Malaysia, art.7(2); Interpretation Act 1967, § 59; Criminal Procedure Code, § 302.

1085 Re: Datuk James Wong Kim Min [1976] MLJ 245; *Faruqi*.

1086 *Faruqi*.

1087 Criminal Procedure Code, §§ 306, 307.

1088 *Harding*, pp. 172-178; *Harding*, Law and Goverment, pp. 215-223.

1089 Federal Constitution of Malaysia, art. 7(2); *Faruqi*.

Thus, Malaysia would not concern itself whether the mutual legal assistance request involves something to which a person has already been convicted, acquitted, pardoned, or has undergone punishment already in its own domestic shores. Instead, with the prohibition against double jeopardy as mandatory ground for refusal, Malaysia as requested state exercises an oversight function to pinpoint to the requesting state that the request violates the prohibition against double jeopardy because within the requesting state, the subject person has already been either convicted, acquitted, pardoned, or underwent the punishment already. Stating it differently, Malaysia as a requested state is imbued with a function to prevent the requesting state from violating the prohibition. Given as such, the open communication and preliminary consultation occurring between ASEAN member state authorities play a key role. Notwithstanding the lack of consideration of any conviction, acquittal, etc. in Malaysia as a mandatory ground to refuse a MLA request, this is without prejudice to Malaysia to mention this to the requesting state, especially for matters which might involve extraterritorial jurisdiction or transnational crimes. The same applies for matters that might raise a red flag for a possible violation of the prohibition on the part of the requesting state as per convictions, acquittals, etc. in its own domestic level or third state.

d. Substantive Considerations of Human Rights

At this point of the discussion, it is imperative to look at how human rights are considered on a substantive level vis-à-vis Malaysia and mutual legal assistance. For purposes of the discussion two points shall be addressed. First, how human rights play a role in the context of grounds to refuse a mutual legal assistance request. Second, how does the general proscription on torture, cruel, inhumane, and degrading treatment and punishment come into play in dealing with mutual legal assistance requests. Third, whether Malaysia can raise its human rights obligations to deny a request.

i. Applicable Human Rights Obligations vis-à-vis Mutual Legal Assistance

As to the first question, one can look into the MACMA to get what specifically applies or not in a mutual legal assistance context. One of these is double jeopardy being a ground to mandatorily refuse a request for legal assistance, as stated above. Moreover, MACMA includes a non-discrimination provision wherein requests shall be denied if it is a violation of non-discrimination rights of a person.[1090] Interestingly, this reflects the fundamental right to equality as enshrined in Article 8 (specifically the second clause) of the Malaysian Federal Constitution. Further, the Attorney General may refuse requests for legal assistance if the same would, or likely, impair the safety of a person, whether the person is within or outside Malaysia.[1091] Other than the foregoing grounds, the MACMA does not provide for any other ground for refusal based on human rights considerations or obligations Malaysia may have.

ii. Limited Applicable Human Rights Obligations vis-à-vis Grounds to Refuse; Severity of Punishment Issue

Having mentioned the foregoing human rights being considered in a mutual legal assistance context in Malaysia, another question that would be interesting to raise at this juncture is as regards how the likely severity of punishment, including torture, death penalty, and cruel, inhumane, and degrading punishment come into play with respect to mutual legal assistance requests from and to Malaysia. As mentioned earlier, considerations of severity of punishment, torture, or death penalty have been factored in some mutual legal assistance agreements.

There is a general international proscription against the imposition of the death penalty or those considered as cruel, inhumane, and degrading treatment and/or punishment.[1092] On one hand, imposition of the death penalty is limited to the "most serious crimes" as per the relevant provision of the International Covenant on Political and Civil Rights, and is further subjected to safeguard provisions enacted through the United Nations Economic and Social Council.[1093] On the other hand, whipping or flogging has been held to be forms of cruel, inhumane, and degrading punishment.[1094] Several reports and statements from different human rights bodies condemn the use of the same as a form of punishment.[1095]

1090 MACMA, § 20(1)(d).

1091 MACMA, § 20(3)(b).

1092 See in general *Bentele*, pp. 297-303.

1093 International Covenant on Civil and Political Rights, art. 6(2); Economic and Social Council Resolution 1984/50.

1094 *International Bar Association*, p. 3.

1095 See *Bahrampour*, p. 1065; *Nowak*, pp. 6-8.

This notwithstanding, the death penalty and whipping presently remains as sanctioned forms of punishment in Malaysia.

In understanding why said forms of penalties are sanctioned in Malaysia, one must understand that Malaysian criminal law puts a strong emphasis on both crime control and public protection.[1096] Deviant behavior would attract punishment and Malaysian criminal law allows the imposition of the following forms of punishment: imprisonment, combination of imprisonment and fine, fine, whipping, and death, the imposition of which depends on public interest, circumstances of the offense, accompanying mitigating and aggravating factors, and antecedents of the offender.[1097] In light of this, capital punishment is not *per se* unconstitutional and the Malaysian Parliament is sanctioned by no less than the Malaysian Federal Constitution itself to impose said capital punishment.[1098] Malaysian criminal law does not find anything unusual in making the death penalty for certain offenses as mandatory, as perhaps its efficiency as a deterrence may be, to an extent, diminished if it was otherwise.[1099] A sentence of death in Malaysian criminal law is viewed to not only signify the gravity of the offense and stress the public disapproval, but also to serve as a warning to others, punish the offender, and protect the public.[1100] In fact, the Malaysian Supreme Court emphasizes that courts, in the imposition of the death penalty – dependent on circumstances of the case such as gravity of the offense, accused's previous offenses, public interest in crimes of such nature, and a sufficient factor of deterrence for others – should take great responsibility and there must be great courage in the imposition of said penalty.[1101] In this respect, the Malaysian Supreme Court has been remindful that when the circumstances of the case warrant death, the court should not hesitate from its duty to impose such sentence.[1102] Henceforth, the Supreme Court has once changed a penalty of imprisonment and fine to a punishment of death for the trafficking of 550 grams of heroin, on the ground that the penalty of life imprisonment and whipping was deemed

1096 See Sinnathurai Subramaniam v. Public Prosecutor, [2011] 5 CLJ 56, CA; *Fook/Mansoor/Hassan*, p. 427.

1097 *Fook/Mansoor/Hassan*, pp. 427, 487-491.

1098 Malaysian Federal Constitution, art.5(1); *Fook/Mansoor/Hassan*, p. 428.

1099 See Public Prosecutor v. Lau KeeHoo, [1983] 1 MLJ 157, FC; *Fook/Mansoor/Hassan*, p. 428.

1100 See Chang Liang Sang &Ors v. Public Prosecutor, [1982] 2 MLJ 231, FC; *Fook/Mansoor/Hassan*, pp. 427-428.

1101 *Fook/Mansoor/Hassan*, pp. 491-492.

1102 *Fook/Mansoor/Hassan*, pp. 491-492.

inadequate vis-à-vis the circumstances of the offense and that the accused was a repeat offender:

> "[T]he learned judge had the percipience to see the special malignancy of the offense and the antecedents of the offender but not the courage to reflect it in the sentence. We are of the view that he was clearly in error which entitles this court to interfere."[1103]

Another controversial type of imposable punishment in Malaysia is whipping, as it is prescribed by legislation and the courts are given the discretion on whether to impose the same.[1104] In relation to this, one can note the different applicable and existing principles vis-à-vis the imposition of whipping as a punishment. Firstly, the Malaysian Criminal Procedure limits the number of imposable strokes, which cannot be carried out in installments, to not more than 24 strokes and 10 strokes, in the case of an adult or youthful offender, respectively.[1105] In line with this, the relevant Malaysian law provides that the age of the youthful offender is determined from the date of the commission of the offense.[1106] At the same time, Malaysia's Subordinate Courts Act of 1948 restricts the competence of a First Class Magistrate to a sentence of only 12 strokes.[1107]

Malaysian criminal law allows a single trial for two or more distinct offenses. In the event that a person has been convicted for these two or more distinct offenses, any two or more is punishable by whipping, the combined sentences of whipping shall still not exceed the maximum threshold of 24 strokes for adults and 10 strokes for youthful offenders.[1108] This same threshold applies even if the offenses for which the accused was convicted of calls for mandatory whipping.[1109]

The aforementioned maximum threshold applies only when there is a single trial. In the event that one is convicted of an offense wherein the imposable penalty is whipping, then he/she is convicted for another

1103 Loc Hock Seng v. Anor and Public Prosecutor, [1980] 2 MLJ 13, FC; *Fook/Mansoor/Hassan,* pp. 491-492.

1104 *Fook/Mansoor/Hassan,* p. 506.

1105 Malaysian Criminal Procedure Code, §§ 288(1), 289; LiawKwaiWah v. Public Prosecutor, [1987] 2 MLJ 69, 71, SC; *Fook/Mansoor/Hassan,* p. 506.

1106 Malaysian Child Act of 2001, § 16; Ong Lai Kim v. Public Prosecutor, [1991] 3 MLJ 111, 115; *Fook/Mansoor/Hassan,* p. 506.

1107 Malaysian Subordinate Court Act of 1948, § 87(1)(c).

1108 Malaysian Criminal Procedure Code, § 288(5); Tuan Mat bin Tuan Lonik v. Public Prosecutor; *Fook/Mansoor/Hassan,* p. 506.

1109 Public Prosecutor v. Tan SweeHoon, [1993] 3 SLR 758, 762; *Fook/Mansoor/Hassan,* p. 506.

offense, but in another trial albeit the trial was held in the same day, wherein the imposable penalty is again whipping, the maximum threshold would not apply and said convicted person can be whipped as many times as the judgments from each trial court indicated.[1110] This notwithstanding, sentences of whipping could be aggregated but are not allowed to run concurrently.[1111]

Not all can be subjected to whipping under Malaysian criminal law. Females, males sentenced to death, and males whom the court considers more than 50 years of age are exempted from the sentence of whipping, except those males who have been sentenced under particular provisions of the Penal Code.[1112]

Additionally, the penalty of whipping under Malaysian criminal law is imposable to make the criminals feel the taste of the violence which they have inflicted on their victims.[1113] Arguably this is due to the overarching themes of public interest (it is believed in Malaysian criminal law that society through the courts must show its abhorrence of certain crimes which is translated to the different sentences courts pass), retribution, deterrence, and reformation that apply as Malaysia's principles on sentencing.[1114] As such, whipping, should it be imposed, ought to be effective.[1115] The law recognizes though that there would be incidents that the prisoner shall be unfit to undergo whipping or it is stopped on medical advice before it is carried out. In such circumstances, a report shall be made to the court, which then shall have the discretion to either remit the sentence or sentence the prisoner to a term of imprisonment of not more than 24 months in lieu of the foregone or suspended whipping.[1116]

Taking the foregoing into account, one can get the sense of a strong criminal sentencing culture from Malaysia, which includes the imposition of both capital punishment and judicial corporeal punishment, the quantum of which depends on the circumstances of each case brought before the court. In this respect, said strong criminal sentencing culture can pro-

---

1110 Chai Ah Kau v. Public Prosecutor, [1974] MLJ 2 191, 192, [1972-1974] SLR 609; *Fook/Mansoor/Hassan*, p. 507.

1111 Public Prosecutor v. Chan Chuan and Amor, [1991] 2 MLJ 538, 540; *Fook/Mansoor/Hassan*, p. 508.

1112 *Fook/Mansoor/Hassan*, p. 508.

1113 *Fook/Mansoor/Hassan*, p. 509.

1114 *Fook/Mansoor/Hassan*, pp. 401-407.

1115 See Jaa'far&Ors v. Public Prosecutor, [1961] MLJ 186; *Fook/Mansoor/Hassan*, p. 509.

1116 Malaysian Criminal Procedure Code, § 291; *Fook/Mansoor/Hassan*, p. 509.

vide a basis as to why no such condition of looking into the likely severity of the punishment can be found in the applicable law on mutual legal assistance in Malaysia. Aside from the fact that Malaysia itself imposes the controversial death penalty and whipping, it is also a reflection of reigning Malaysian criminal law principles and guidelines Malaysia lives by.

Based on the foregoing, the imposition of death penalty and whipping as punishment in Malaysia has not been an issue in mutual legal assistance requests with other ASEAN member states in practice. As per clarification with the officials of its central authority and point person for mutual legal assistance requests in the Royal Malaysian Police, problems regarding Malaysia's imposition of death penalty or whipping as punishment only arise with non-ASEAN countries (e.g. Australia), which do not impose the death penalty or whipping as punishment, or otherwise proscribes the imposition of such. In such cases, Malaysia is made to undertake that should a person be found guilty in the prosecution of the criminal matter to which a request for mutual legal assistance has been made, Malaysia shall not impose the death penalty or whipping as a form of punishment.

All things considered, one cannot help but ask whether Malaysia can invoke "general human rights considerations" as a ground to refuse a request when it is a requested state and the MLA request involves a matter that violates, threatens to violate, or is inconsistent with the Malaysia's human rights obligations as enshrined in its Constitution, laws, and other treaty obligations. In light of this, if one strictly adheres to what the relevant law provides, the answer would be in the negative. The law only provides a limited number of grounds to refuse a request based on human rights (as stated earlier). There is nothing that allows Malaysian authorities to refuse requests on other human rights considerations. This means that under the law, Malaysia is proscribed from raising any possible violation or actual violation of human rights obligations as a ground to refuse a mutual legal assistance request. Significantly, if one backtracks to the use of the prohibition against double jeopardy as a ground to refuse wherein there has been either a conviction, acquittal, pardon, or service of punishment already for the same offense or facts constituting the offense, the said ground only takes into account the requesting state. As discussed above, any similar incident in Malaysia is not taken into account. It is then safe to surmise that Malaysia adopts more or less a rule of non-inquiry and does not factor in its own domestic obligations or prohibitions in the equation of whether to approve or not a mutual legal assistance request.

Alternatively, if any conflict would arise between a MLA request and Malaysia's standing human rights obligations, Malaysia could possibly raise essential public interest as a ground to refuse, to wit, "the provision of the assistance would affect the sovereignty, security, public order or other essential public interest of Malaysia." Essential public interest could involve a gamut of things affecting the state and thus, can be raised should there be an ensuing conflict from a received MLA request.

Having mentioned this, Malaysia in practice has yet to encounter this kind of issue, regardless of it being with its fellow ASEAN member states or other states sending mutual legal assistance requests. Herein the open communication and preliminary consultation again plays a crucial role between requesting and requested states to discuss any possible stumbling blocks and/or hurdles as regards a MLA request and the best possible route to overcome these issues. Nevertheless, preliminary consultation may prove insufficient to address human rights issues. Thus, a possible solution would be to place a threshold wherein human rights obligations constitutionally provided or those rights in accordance with customary law obligations are considered non-negotiables.

e. Reciprocity

The requesting state is required to undertake reciprocity under the MACMA.[1117] Malaysia shall refuse a request should the appropriate authoritiy of the prescribed foreign state, in respect of the request, failed to comply with the terms of any treaty or other agreement between Malaysia and that prescribed foreign state.[1118] Further, the Attorney General will refuse a request should the requesting state fail to undertake that it will, subject to its laws, assist Malaysia in any future request for mutual legal assistance, if that requesting state is not a party to a treaty with Malaysia.[1119] This rarely happens however in practice. Reciprocity is practiced by Malaysia and so far, no problems have been encountered vis-à-vis mutual legal assistance with other ASEAN member states as from experience, ASEAN member states extend to one another the widest possible measure of assistance needed and work with each other in efforts to effectuate requests.

1117 MACMA, § 20(3)(d).
1118 MACMA, § 20(1)(a).
1119 *Kamal*, p. 84.

f. Speciality or use limitation

The government of Malaysia shall refuse a request for assistance should the requesting state fail to undertake that the thing requested will not be used for a matter other than the criminal matter in respect of which the request was made.[1120] Such mandatory ground for refusal shall not be applied should the lack of undertaking be made with the consent of the Attorney General.[1121] Officials from the Attorney General's Chambers, admitted that there are certain circumstances wherein it is discovered that a piece of information, document, or evidence can be likewise used for another criminal matter not covered by the original request. The requesting state cannot just use the said piece of information, document, or evidence already possessed. The requesting state, even if it is Malaysia, should go through the said process of sending a request anew for the subject information, document, or evidence be used for the other criminal matter.

g. Special Offenses and National Interest Cases

National or public interest is sanctioned as a mandatory ground for refusal. The Attorney General shall refuse requests for assistance should the same impair the sovereignty, security, public order, or other essential public interest of Malaysia.[1122] Requests shall also be refused should the assistance require acts that are contrary to any Malaysian written law.[1123] As clarified by officials from the Attorney General's Chambers on what applies in practice, Malaysian domestic law shall always prevail in assessing requests, should there be discrepancies between the applicable laws.

The aspect of national and public interest branches out to other mandatory grounds for refusal in the MACMA, such as "insufficient gravity" and "insufficient importance to the investigation." With respect to insufficient gravity, requests shall be denied should "the facts constituting the offense to which the request relates do not indicate an offense of sufficient gravity."[1124] And likewise, requests shall be denied should "the thing requested for is of insufficient importance to the investigation or could reasonably

1120 MACMA, § 20(1)(j).
1121 MACMA, § 20(2).
1122 MACMA, § 20(1)(i).
1123 MACMA, § 20(1)(m).
1124 MACMA, § 20(1)(g).

be obtained by other means."[1125] While the same on its face may seem like stumbling blocks in making requests, officials have clarified in interviews that in practice, the Attorney General could advise beforehand during preliminary consultations that the criminal matter subject of the request is of insufficient gravity and suggest to the requesting state to look for another applicable law, which could be used and of which imposes a higher penalty than the criminal case which was originally intended. In such a situation, the person subject of the criminal matter being investigated or prosecuted shall be charged differently or with a higher penalty vis-à-vis its equivalent in Malaysia. At the same time, the mandatory ground for refusal "insufficient importance", as explained by the Royal Malaysian Police officer in charge of mutual legal assistance requests, was placed as a safeguard against fishing expeditions, which is not the goal of mutual legal assistance requests. Nonetheless, open communications still remain to make requests possible. What the requesting state could do is to file the request again and supplant further information that would justify its request.

It is also a matter of national and public interest when the request involves a pending criminal matter and/or investigation in Malaysia or when the same contradicts domestic law.[1126] As explained during the relevant interviews, Malaysian proceedings (i.e. investigation, prosecution) shall take precedence. Following the so-called sub judice rule, any request in relation to any pending matter shall only be entertained once proceedings in Malaysia are finished. Should information be shared while criminal matters are pending, at most it shall be through informal assistance and whatever information is shared shall only be used for personal consumption and not as evidence before the courts.

Additionally, it is also an aspect of denying requests on the ground of national and public interest wherein the Attorney General has the discretion to deny the request if in the opinion of the Attorney General, the provision being requested for shall impose an excessive burden on the resources of Malaysia.[1127] The MACMA however further provides that in the event that the costs and expenses in relation to the assistance requested or being effectuated is of extraordinary or substantial nature, the Attorney General shall communicate with the appropriate authority of the request-

1125 MACMA, § 20(1)(h).
1126 MACMA, § 20(1)(l)(m).
1127 MACMA, § 20(3)(c).

ing member state on the conditions the assistance shall be effectuated or under which the Attorney General shall cease to give effect to it.[1128]

Aside from national and public interest, the Attorney General shall deny requests for assistance should the same involve offenses which are political or military in nature.[1129] MACMA however limits the political offense exception to not include the following offenses as "political": (1) offenses against the life or person of a Head of State or a member of his/her immediate family; (2) offenses against the life or person of a Head of Government or a member of his/her immediate family; (3) any offense established under any multilateral treaty or agreement to which Malaysia and the requesting member state are signatories of and which is correspondingly declared as non-political offense for purposes of mutual legal assistance; (4) any other offense declared by the Minister in charge of legal affairs by order published in the Gazette; and (5) any attempt, abetment, or conspiracy to commit the immediately preceding stated offenses.[1130] MACMA further provides that the Attorney General may restrict the application of the foregoing provisions to a "request from a prescribed foreign state that has made similar provisions in its laws."[1131]

In relation to political offenses, Malaysia has already experienced in practice being denied a request because the criminal matter subject of the request is "political" in nature. Malaysian authorities did not elaborate further on the facts of the case but nonetheless disclosed that they needed to ask for reconsideration and provide more information that what they are interested in is the criminal matter only and not at any political nature of the same.

Bank secrecy and/or fiscal offenses are not grounds for refusal in the MACMA. Stating it otherwise, no request shall be denied by Malaysia due to this reason. Requests for assistance in relation to bank accounts, fiscal offenses, etc., shall be accordingly effectuated in relation to existing Malaysian laws such as those on money laundering, terrorism financing, etc. More often than not, the Attorney General shall already advise the Central Bank and the relevant bank subject of the request should the former already receive a preliminary copy of the request from any ASEAN member state.

1128 MACMA, § 20(4).
1129 MACMA, § 20(1)(b)(c).
1130 MACMA, § 21(1).
1131 MACMA, § 21(2).

C. Procedural Provisions: Mutual Legal Assistance

1. Designation of Central Authority

MACMA designates the office of the Attorney General of Malaysia as the central authority for mutual legal assistance who is authorized to make or receive formal requests to and from other states, which shall be coursed through diplomatic channels.[1132] In the interview with officials from the Attorney General's Chambers, it was clarified that the Transnational Crime Unit of the Prosecution Division is responsible for incoming and outgoing mutual legal assistance (together with extradition) requests, in addition to negotiating and drafting mutual legal assistance and extradition treaties. These tasks used to belong to the General Chamber's International Affairs Division but to streamline processes, these are assigned presently to the Prosecution Division.

Given that the Attorney General is responsible for incoming and outgoing mutual legal assistance requests, during the interview it was likewise mentioned that said central authority closely works with other agencies such as, but not limited to, the Royal Malaysian Police, Interpol, Securities Commission, Malaysian Anti-Corruption Commission, Malaysian Maritime Enforcement Agency, and Central Bank to effectuate the requests received and sent. This gives them first-hand knowledge of issues and matters arising from international cooperation requests such as mutual legal assistance.

It must be noted further that while the Attorney General only concerns itself with formal requests, the officials interviewed mentioned that informal requests to the Malaysian Central Bank likewise go through their office as mandated by law.

In relation to being the designated central authority for mutual legal assistance requests, the Attorney General is mandated to keep and maintain a Register, which shall contain information pertaining to requests for assistance under MACMA, including the following 15 pieces of information: (1) requests made by Malaysia to a foreign state under MACMA; (2) the results of requests made by Malaysia to a foreign state under MACMA; (3) details of the things seized pursuant to a request made by Malaysia to a foreign state under MACMA and the return of such things to the appropriate authority of the foreign state, where applicable; (4) details of the prisoners or persons under detention transported to Malaysia pursuant

1132 MACMA, §§ 7, 19; *Kamal*, p. 83.

to a request made by Malaysia to a foreign state under MACMA; (5) details of the assets traced, restrained, and recovered pursuant to a request made by Malaysia to a foreign state under MACMA to enforce a forfeiture order; (6) details of the persons located pursuant to a request made by Malaysia to a foreign state under MACMA; (7) details of the processes served in a foreign state pursuant to a request made by Malaysia to a foreign state under MACMA; (8) requests received by Malaysia from a prescribed foreign state under MACMA; (9) results of requests received by Malaysia from a prescribed foreign state under MACMA; (10) details of the things seized pursuant to a request received by Malaysia from a prescribed foreign state under MACMA, the return of such things to the appropriate authority of Malaysia, where applicable, and the return of such things to the rightful owner, where applicable; (11) details of the persons who have travelled to and the prisoners and persons under detention who have been transported to a prescribed foreign state pursuant to a request received by Malaysia from a prescribed foreign state under MACMA; (12) details of the assets traced, restrained, and recovered pursuant to a request received by Malaysia from a prescribed foreign state under MACMA and their disposal; (13) details of the persons located pursuant to a request received by Malaysia from a prescribed foreign state under the Act; (14) details of the processes served in Malaysia pursuant to a request received by Malaysia from a prescribed foreign state under MACMA; and (15) such other information as the Attorney General considers appropriate.[1133]

2. Preparation of Requests

a. Requirements for Requests

Every received request shall "(1) specify the purpose of the request and the nature of the assistance being sought;" and (2) "identify the person or authority that initiated the request." It shall likewise be accompanied by the following: (1) "a certificate from the appropriate authority of that prescribed foreign state that the request is made in respect of a criminal matter" within the meaning of MACMA; (2) "a description of the nature of the criminal matter and a statement setting out a summary of the relevant facts and laws;" (3) where the request refers to either (a) "the location of a person who is suspected to be involved in or to have benefited from

1133 Mutual Assistance in Criminal Matters Regulations, § 35.

the commission of a foreign serious offense;" or (b) "the tracing of property that is suspected to be connected with a foreign serious offense", "the name, identity, nationality, location or description of that person, or the location and description of the property, if known, and a statement setting forth the basis for suspecting the matter;" (4) "a description of the offense to which the criminal matter relates, including its maximum penalty;" (5) "details of the procedure which that prescribed foreign state wishes Malaysia to follow in giving effect to the request, including details of the manner and form in which any information or thing is to be supplied to that prescribed foreign state pursuant to the request;" (6) "where the request is for assistance relating to an ancillary criminal matter and judicial proceedings to obtain a foreign forfeiture order have not been instituted in that prescribed foreign state, a statement indicating when the judicial proceedings are likely to be instituted;" (7) "a statement setting out the wishes of that prescribed foreign State concerning the confidentiality of the request and the reason for those wishes;" (8) "details of the period within which that prescribed foreign state wishes the request to be met;" (9) "if the request involves a person travelling from Malaysia to that prescribed foreign state, details of allowances to which the person will be entitled, and of the arrangements for security and accommodation for the person while he is in that prescribed foreign state pursuant to the request;" (10) "any other information required to be included with the request under any treaty or other agreement between Malaysia and that prescribed foreign state, if any;" and (11) "any other information that may assist in giving effect to the request" or which is required under the provisions of MACMA or any regulation in connection thereto.[1134]

Insufficiency in information or general failure to comply with the foregoing shall not be a ground for refusing assistance.[1135]

As reported during the 2012 seminar on cooperation, the Office of the Attorney General has encountered challenges when dealing with preparing outgoing requests for mutual legal assistance. The problems cited were, namely, (1) the failure of some states to identify or designate a responsible central authority to facilitate the implementation of mutual legal assistance requests; (2) unavailability of practical guides regarding domestic mutual legal assistance legal frameworks and guidelines; (3) delay in effectuating mutual legal assistance requests; (4) states not regularly reviewing treaties and laws to keep abreast on best practices as to international mu-

1134 MACMA, § 19(3)(c).
1135 MACMA, § 19(4).

tual legal assistance; (5) lack of training of personnel involved in mutual legal assistance; (6) the complexity of MLA; (7) states who refuse extraditing their own nationals and decide to prosecute the latter themselves get involved in complex requests for mutual legal assistance; (8) some states are not in a position to maintain confidentiality; (9) requests are executed not in accordance with procedures specified in the request.[1136] With respect to other ASEAN member states, on the other hand, Malaysian officials, through interviews, have clarified that even if there may seem to be stumbling blocks vis-à-vis mutual legal requests, there is nothing considerable that has prevented Malaysia and/or the other ASEAN member states to render and request mutual legal assistance among each other. The open consultation and communications definitely help the process as the respective authorities could guide each other accordingly as to the substantial and procedural requirements needed to be satisfied before a request can be executed. Moreover, the sending of draft copies or advance copies to one another helps ease the downtime needed to process requests and each country could then advise one another outright should a red flag regarding grounds for refusal arise. In the same vein, Malaysian officials point to numerous trainings and seminars available to ASEAN member state authorities on international and regional cooperation, and specifically mutual legal assistance, which help them identify rooms for improvement, and adopt best practices.

Given the foregoing circumstances, the MACMA and its regulations provide a concrete guide on how requests should be prepared and what requirements ought to be met. Aside from the general requirements stated above, the MACMA and regulations provide for specific requirements for the preparation of certain specific types of assistance, especially those which the Attorney General should comply with should Malaysia be the requesting state. These specific types of assistance include the request for taking of evidence;[1137] attendance of persons in Malaysia;[1138] enforcement

1136 *Kamal*, p. 92.

1137 MACMA, § 8; See also Mutual Assistance in Criminal Matters Regulations, § 6(a).

1138 MACMA, §§ 9, 10, 11, 12. See also Mutual Assistance in Criminal Matters Regulations, § 7(1).

of forfeiture orders;[1139] assistance in locating or identifying persons;[1140] and assistance in service of processes.[1141]

b. Person or Authority Initiating the Request

Regardless of whether Malaysia makes or receives the requests, all requests shall be made by or through the office of the Attorney General and any request shall be made through diplomatic channels.[1142] Thus, requests shall be made at the instance of the Attorney General.

In relation to this, the law is silent as to any participation from a private individual or suspect or accused person to ask that a MLA request be issued on their behalf by the Attorney General. As the current provisions of the Malaysian law is drafted, it is more centered on the use of the MLA instrument for prosecution and investigation.

3. Execution of Requests

a. Applicable Law on Execution

Requests made to Malaysia shall be subject to the domestic law. However, this does not preclude the application of a procedure which the requesting state wishes Malaysia to follow in executing a request. Under § 4 of the Mutual Assistance Criminal Matters Regulations [hereinafter "MACMA Regulations"] 2003, which supplants the provisions of MACMA, a requesting state requesting assistance in a criminal matter may provide details of a procedure it wishes Malaysia to follow in effectuating the former's request.[1143] The same shall then be applied by Malaysia insofar it does not conflict or violate any of its domestic legislation or the provisions of the MACMA Regulations, and in such case "the relevant provisions of the Criminal Procedure Code shall apply with the necessary modifications."[1144] This resonates what an interviewee has mentioned about mutual

1139 MACMA, § 13. See also Mutual Assistance in Criminal Matters Regulations, § 9.
1140 MACMA, § 14.
1141 MACMA, § 15.
1142 MACMA, § 17.
1143 Mutual Assistance in Criminal Matters Regulations, § 4(2).
1144 Mutual Assistance in Criminal Matters Regulations, § 4(2).

legal assistance requests being "robotic" in nature.[1145] The requesting state must provide point-by-point the procedure to be followed by the requested state in executing the request. Otherwise, the requested state shall follow its own laws.

b. Applicable Procedural Rights

Considerations have been given to human rights and rights of the accused or persons charged of an offense in the procedure involved in executing requests for mutual legal assistance in Malaysia. This is in the context of the pertinent constitutional and statutory laws applicable together with criminal procedural rules, as well as the MACMA which provides the procedure to be followed in executing investigatory measures.

i. Importance of Defense Rights; Human Rights Considerations in MLA and Criminal Processes in General

At the outset, in its rudimentary level the Malaysian Federal Constitution, as supplemented by the relevant provision of the Criminal Procedure Code, grants an accused the basic right to be informed as soon as may be of the grounds of his/her arrest and the right to be allowed to consult and be defended by a legal practitioner of his choice.[1146] In relation to the right to be informed, it is a condition precedent to a lawful arrest that the party arrested as soon as may be, should know on what charge or on suspicion of what crime he/she is arrested, or at least the facts which are said to constitute a crime on his/her part, albeit "as soon as may be" depends on the facts of the case.[1147] In relation to this, the cause for one's arrest must be equivocally provided. Thus, in one occasion the Court held that the cause written in a detention order cannot be written in an alternative form as the same violates the constitutional right of an accused to be informed of the reason for his arrest.[1148] Said condition is applicable across

1145 Interview with ASP Loh from Royal Malaysian Police.

1146 Malaysian Federal Constitution, art.5(3); Malaysian Criminal Procedure Code, § 28A; *Fook/Mansoor/Hassan*, pp. 78-79; *Harding*, Law and Goverment, p. 213.

1147 R v. Lemsatef [1977] 2 All ER 835; Abdul Rahman v. Tan Jo Koh [1968] 1 MLJ 25, FC; *Fook/Mansoor/Hassan*, p. 79.

1148 Lee Gee Lam v. Timbalan Menteri Hal Ehwal Dalam Negeri, Malaysia and Anor [1993] 3 MLJ 265.

the board, even to arrests done by virtue of the now repealed Emergency Ordinance 1969 and other still applicable preventive detention laws.[1149]

Other than the right to be informed, the accused has a constitutional right to counsel, which applies to different stages in the criminal process: consultation in the police station and representation in court.[1150] This right to legal representation naturally covers remand proceedings (wherein police authorities would need to either reinvestigate or continue investigations)[1151] and is also applicable to non-criminal proceedings.[1152] In connection thereto, the police must inform the arrested person before any questioning can commence, that the latter may communicate or attempt to communicate with a friend or relative to inform of his whereabouts; and/or communicate or attempt to communicate and consult with a legal practitioner of his choice.[1153]

This constitutional conferment notwithstanding, Harding commented that this conferred right is actually lamentable in practice.[1154] While the constitutional right is not qualified to be afforded "as soon as may be", the Federal Court of Malaysia has earlier declared that the right to counsel should be balanced with the duty of the police to gather evidence and even if the former is engaged immediately upon arrest, it cannot be exercised if it shall impede police investigation or the administration of justice.[1155] Thus, in certain cases, denial of outright access to counsel during police investigation for a period of ten and six days respectively, was held justifiable as an example of the "public interest" exemption provided in the Constitution.[1156] As Harding commented, these cases almost rendered unenforceable in practice, especially since habeas corpus is not an available remedy herein, given that an arrest remains lawful notwithstanding the denial of the right to counsel.[1157] That said, the right must be granted within a reasonable period of time and the *onus probandi* is with the police authorities to prove that the right shall impede police investigations and/or

1149 *Fook/Mansoor/Hassan*, pp. 78-79; *Harding*, Law and Goverment, p. 213.
1150 *Harding*, Law and Goverment.
1151 *Fook/Mansoor/Hassan*, pp. 86-89; *Harding*, Law and Goverment, p. 214.
1152 *Fook/Mansoor/Hassan*, pp. 84-85.
1153 Malaysian Criminal Procedure Code, § 28A; *Fook/Mansoor/Hassan*, p. 82.
1154 *Harding*, Law and Goverment, p. 213.
1155 *Harding*, Law and Goverment, p. 213.
1156 Ooi Ah Phua v. Officer-in-Charge of Criminal Investigations, Kedah/Perlis [1975] 2 MLJ 198; Hashim Bin Saud v. Yahaya Bin Hashim [1977] 2 MLJ 116; *Harding*, Law and Goverment, p. 213.
1157 *Harding*, Law and Goverment, p. 214.

administration of justice.[1158] Police authorities cannot deny or obstruct the exercise of the right on frivolous or arbitrary grounds, and should the right be exercised by the accused, it must be held outside the hearing of the police authorities, though within their sight.[1159]

With respect to trial proceedings, one can note that the right to counsel would have two components, namely, the reasonable opportunity to obtain the service of counsel, and said counsel is his particular choice.[1160] Such components to the right to counsel during trial notwithstanding, one must understand however, that the constitutional right does not preempt trial proceedings just because the accused has not secured services of a counsel of his own choice.[1161] As a former Chief Justice explained, what the right means is that the accused is entitled to be represented by counsel of his choice if the latter is willing and able to represent him.[1162] The Court had occasion to discuss further this right in *Mohamed bin Abdullah v. Public Prosecutor.* In said case, the accused sought to appeal his conviction on the ground that at the date of hearing his criminal case, the Sessions Court judge proceeded with trial even if the counsel of the accused had an urgent matter to attend to and was not present during said hearing.[1163] And when the accused was about to present his defense, his second counsel appeared and asked him to exercise his right to remain silent. Accused was thereafter adjudged guilty. It was held that there had been no miscarriage of justice; said right does not confer a right to counsel in every case, and that it does not mean that an accused person cannot be tried unless he is represented by counsel.[1164] Taking these things into consideration, Harding explains that the right to counsel is a good example of a constitutional right that gives way to demands of public interest and convenience.[1165]

1158 Ramli Bin Salleh v. Yahaya Bin Hashim [1973] 1 MLJ 54; *Harding,* Law and Goverment, p. 214.

1159 Ramli Bin Salleh v. Yahaya Bin Hashim [1973] 1 MLJ 54; *Harding,* Law and Goverment, p. 214.

1160 *Fook/Mansoor/Hassan,* pp. 86, 88.

1161 *Fook/Mansoor/Hassan,* p. 88; *Harding,* Law and Goverment, p. 214.

1162 PalaniappaChettiar v. ArunasalamChettiar, FM Civil Appeal No. 34 of 1958, [1961] MLJ xxxii; Bakar bin Ahmad v. Public Prosecutor [1968] 4 MC 294; *Fook/Mansoor/Hassan,* p. 88.

1163 *Fook/Mansoor/Hassan,* p. 88.

1164 *Fook/Mansoor/Hassan,* p. 88.

1165 *Harding,* Law and Goverment, p. 214.

ii. Human Rights Considerations in MLA and Criminal Processes in General

In light of the foregoing rudimentary rights applicable to an accused or person suspected of an offense or crime, applications of these rights are arguably in place in rendering and requesting mutual legal assistance in criminal matters. In taking evidence in Malaysia to be used for criminal proceedings in the requesting state, the person who is subject of the criminal proceedings in the requesting state and/or his legal representative is authorized to be present in the proceedings related to the taking of evidence in Malaysia.[1166] Further, the person subject of the criminal proceedings in the requesting state is considered by Malaysian law as competent but not compellable as a witness.[1167]At the same time, no person who is required to give evidence for the purpose of any criminal proceeding in the requesting state can be compelled to answer any question that said person could not be compelled to answer in the proceedings in the requesting state. Stating it differently, a mutual legal assistance request in taking evidence in Malaysia for purposes of a criminal proceeding in the requesting state cannot be used as a tool to circumvent one's right to remain silent during proceedings in the requesting state.

Rights of the accused are also taken into consideration with respect to requests for attendance in the requesting state of a person in Malaysia. In complying with such request, the person whose attendance is requested, cannot either: (1) be detained, prosecuted or punished for any offence against the law of the requesting state that is alleged to have been committed, or that was committed, before the person's departure from Malaysia; (2) be subjected to any civil suit in respect of any act or omission of the person that is alleged to have occurred, or that had occurred, before the person's departure from Malaysia; or (3) be required to give evidence or assistance in relation to any criminal matter in the requesting State other than the criminal matter to which the request relates.[1168] The latter can only be done should the person have left the requesting state or the person has had the opportunity of leaving the requesting state and has remained in the requesting state otherwise than for the purpose of giving

1166 MACMA, § 22(3).
1167 MACMA, § 22(7).
1168 MACMA, § 27(3)(a).

evidence or assistance in relation to the criminal matter to which the request relates.[1169]

Furthermore, any evidence to be given by said person, whose attendance was requested in the requesting state, will be inadmissible or otherwise disqualified from use in the prosecution of the person for an offense against the law of the requesting state, other than the offense of perjury or contempt of court with respect of the giving of evidence.[1170] In connection thereto, a person whose attendance has been requested in the requesting state, cannot be held liable should it refuse or fail to attend, as requested.[1171] A similar provision can be found in assistance in service of process, when the attendance of a person is required by virtue of said process from the requesting state.[1172]

The same consideration of accused's rights can be said with regard requests for executions of foreign forfeiture orders. Malaysian law requires registration of said foreign forfeiture orders.[1173] In view thereof, before the High Court registers the same, it assures that the person affected by the order, if not present during the proceedings in the requesting state, has still been notified accordingly.[1174]

Another instance refers to requests for production orders in criminal matters. It imports similar provisions as to one's right not to be compelled to produce or make available anything that it cannot be compelled to produce or make available in the requesting state's criminal proceedings; as well as the right to remain silent and the right of the person, who is subject of criminal proceedings in the requesting state, or his/her legal representation to be present in local proceedings in Malaysia in view of the assistance request made.[1175] This notwithstanding, it seems that the right against self-incrimination is not applicable in cases where a person is not excused from producing or making available a thing subject of a production order. This logic is based on the grounds that "the production or making available of the thing might tend to incriminate the person or make the person liable to a penalty" or the "production or making available of the thing would be in breach of an obligation, whether imposed by

1169 MACMA, § 27(3)(a).
1170 MACMA, § 27(3)(b).
1171 MACMA, § 27(4).
1172 MACMA, § 41.
1173 MACMA, § 32(1).
1174 MACMA, § 32(2).
1175 MACMA, § 23.

law or otherwise, of the person not to disclose the existence of the contents of the thing."[1176]

Reading the same would give the idea that the person subject of the production order then must comply notwithstanding threat or risk of being held criminally, civilly, or administratively liable. However, further reading of the provisions would reveal that no such threat of liability exists as following provisions in the law provide immunity from civil and criminal action to the person complying with the production order and the same was done in good faith.[1177] Criminal liability shall only exist, as per provisions on production order, should there be non-compliance without reasonable excuse with the production order, or whether in purported compliance with the order, the person either fails to indicate to the authorized officer any false or misleading information the former knows of, or provide the correct information the person is in possession of, or can reasonably acquire.[1178]

iii. Defendant's Participation in the Refusal or Execution of a MLA Request

Given the foregoing rights integrated and applicable in a mutual legal assistance framework, a question arises whether an affected person, may it be the accused or suspected person himself (or someone collaterally affected by the mutual legal assistance request or the execution thereof) can find relief in the Malaysian courts through judicial review vis-à-vis a mutual legal assistance request and/or its execution. At the outset, the MACMA is bereft of any provision providing for judicial relief.[1179] Thus, there is initial uncertainty as regards what procedures one individual may undertake should one be affected by a mutual legal assistance request or the execution thereof.

1176 MACMA, § 24.

1177 MACMA, § 25.

1178 MACMA, § 26.

1179 This is in stark contrast to the Malaysian Extradition Act 1992, which provides for remedies such as *habeas corpus* and judicial review under Sections 31 and 32, respectively, for persons who may be affected by an extradition order. See for a case illustrating judicial relief vis-à-vis extradition, as well as explaining the availability of appeal from the High Court to the Court of Appeal, Public Prosecutor v. Ottavio Quattrocchi, 30 April 2003, [2003] 2 CLJ 613.

Nonetheless, a reading of the Malaysian Rules of Court 2012 would show that judicial relief is still available through the use of Order 53 or judicial review. Judicial review is available against any government order and includes the power of the High Court(s) "to issue to any person or authority directions, orders or writs, including writs of the nature of habeas corpus, mandamus, prohibition, quo warranto and certiorari, or any others, for the enforcement of the rights conferred by Part II of the Constitution,[1180] or any of them, or for any purpose" as provided in the first paragraph of the Schedule to the Courts of Judicature Act 1964.[1181] Hence, any person adversely affected by any mutual legal assistance order and/or the execution thereof vis-à-vis fundamental liberties, may apply accordingly for judicial review.[1182]

It is a different question however on whether such relief shall be granted. As of the time of this writing, there has been no test case or jurisprudence tackling mutual legal assistance and/or the execution thereof as it affects an individual, accused, or suspected person. At most, there has only been case law vis-à-vis extradition and judicial review provided for in the applicable law. Thus, it is yet to be seen which direction courts would take should relief be sought vis-à-vis mutual legal assistance. Furthermore, there has been a standing debate on the applicability of one's right to access to justice or ask for judicial relief when none is provided for in the law. Albeit judicial review is an option for aggrieved parties when fundamental liberties are at stake, judicial determination on this issue prior to the Rules of Court 2012 has not been the same especially when it involves a law which does not provide any remedy. Whilst the Court of Appeal in two popular incidents cited the constitutionality of one's right to access to justice or ask for judicial relief,[1183] which allows relief to be granted by the courts, the Malaysian Federal Court overruled the Court of Appeal and held that the constitutional right is not absolute and judicial review

1180 Part II of the Constitution constitutes the fundamental liberties, i.e. the right to life and liberty, no slavery, prohibition against ex post facto laws and double jeopardy, equality, prohibition of banishment and freedom of movement, freedom of speech, assembly, and association, freedom of religion, rights in respect of education, and rights to property.

1181 Malaysian Rules of Court 2012, Order 53, para. 1.

1182 Malaysian Rules of Court 2012, Order 53, para. 2.

1183 KekatongSdnBhd v. DanahartaUrusSdnBhd, [2003] 3 MLJ 1; Sugumar Balakrishnan v. PengarahImigresenNegeri Sabah, [1998] 3 MLJ 289.

cannot be overstretched when the statute does not provide for any judicial remedy.[1184]

Taking this into account, it becomes likewise interesting to note that aside from questioning the MLA request and/or its execution, an affected person is not prejudiced to question the admissibility of evidence obtained through MLA. The amendments to the Evidence Act of 1950 provide that no further proof is required as regards evidence obtained through MLA as long as certain conditions are satisfied. Nevertheless, there may be instances in the execution of investigative measures vis-à-vis a MLA request wherein the subsequent reception of evidence offends against public policy (or public interest) or a particular rule of law, e.g. evidence of matters which are privileged against disclosure.[1185] In this case, it is incumbent upon the court to decide on the admissibility of evidence under Section 136 of the Evidence Act.

c. Applicable Time Element on Execution

The MACMA or its Regulations does not provide for time periods by which requests must be acted on by Malaysia as a requested state. While the law and regulations painstakingly specifies the applicable procedure per type of assistance, there is no mention of any time limit that Malaysian authorities ought to abide with. In relation to this, the interview conducted of the Malaysian authorities in the Office of the Attorney General showed that lack of time limits notwithstanding, there would be no issue on executing requests for assistance quickly should the requirements be complied with and that the assistance requested does not require a court order to be given by Malaysia. Reverting to the information ought to be provided in a request as a minimum, the request could indicate the time element involved within which the request should be effectuated or executed. According to the authorities interviewed, the problem normally arises as regards time whenever an application before the court is needed to be made and on average, it could take as much as one (1) year before any coercive order will be issued.

As to how expedite the execution of requests, the Malaysian authorities divulged that there is open communication and preliminary consultation

1184 Danaharta Urus SdnBhd v. KekatongSdnBhd, [2004] 2 MLJ at 257; Pihak-BerkuasaNegeri Sabah v. Sugumar Balakrishnan, [2002] 3 MLJ 72.

1185 Suruhanjaya Sekuriti v. Datuk Ishak Ismail [2016] 3 CLJ 19 FC.

among the ASEAN member states vis-à-vis mutual legal assistance. Authorities of each member states can consult with one another regarding their respective requests to make sure that requirements are being complied with, and should there be some issue or for example, a ground for refusal exists, then they could easily discuss how to go about the problem to be still able to effectuate a request. Moreover, it has been an ASEAN practice for requesting states to send draft and/or unofficial copies of requests to allow processing to start, or be able to know if anything should be changed in a request.

d. Authentication of Documents

Subject to the MACMA provisions on requests for forfeiture orders (§ 13), proof of orders of prescribed foreign state (§ 33), and evidence in relation to proceedings and orders in prescribed foreign state (§ 34), and any law relating to admissibility of evidence, the MACMA provides under Section 42 that any document obtained, provided, or produced pursuant to a request made under this Act and that is duly authenticated is admissible in evidence without further proof in any criminal proceedings.[1186] The same Section 42 continues by stating that a document is considered duly authenticated if (1) it purports to be signed or certified by a judge, magistrate, or officer in or of the prescribed foreign state, and (2) either it is (a) verified by the oath or affirmation of a witness, or of an officer of the government of that prescribed foreign state, or (b) it purports to be sealed with an official or public seal of the prescribed foreign state or of a minister of the state, or of a department or officer of the government, of that prescribed foreign state.[1187] In line of these provisions, the MACMA then enjoins all Malaysian courts to take judicial notice of the official or public seal previously referred to.[1188] One must understand in relation to these provisions that the same does not prevent the proof of any matter or admission to evidence of any document in accordance with other provisions of the MACMA or any other Malaysian law.[1189]

Alongside Section 42, the same MACMA in Section 8(1) and (2) provides *inter alia*, that in situations wherein Malaysia is the requesting state,

1186 MACMA, § 42(1).
1187 MACMA, § 42(2).
1188 MACMA, § 42(3).
1189 MACMA, § 42(4).

the Attorney General may "request for evidence or thing in a foreign state to be taken and sent to him if he satisfied that there are reasonable grounds for believing that such evidence or thing are relevant to a criminal proceeding or criminal matter in Malaysia." Additionally, Section 8(3) provides that any evidence or thing received pursuant to a MLA request maybe admitted subject to the provisions of the Malaysian Evidence Act and Criminal Procedure Code. In light of this, the Malaysian Evidence Act of 1950 (as amended in 2012) includes Chapter VA containing sections 90D, 90E, and 90F, which all generally relate to the admissibility of evidence obtained through mutual legal assistance in Malaysian courts.[1190] According to the amendments, any evidence procedure through mutual legal assistance shall be admitted as evidence without further proof, provided certain minimum requirements are met.

Interestingly, the insertions to the Evidence Act was prompted by a case wherein the Federal Court ruled that the evidence obtained through a MLA request was not admissible in evidence, which in turn resulted in the acquittal of an accused. In Public Prosecutor v. Tan Sir Eric Chia Eng Hock, evidence taken in Hong Kong was obtained by Malaysia through mutual legal assistance. Accused was charged for criminal breach of trust for allegedly authorizing payments to another company, purportedly for the technical assistance to be provided by the latter. However, said technical assistance turned out to be free of charge and the authorized payments were traced later in the foreign accounts of the relatives of the accused. The pieces of evidence obtained through mutual legal assistance was then used in the criminal proceedings against the accused.[1191] Subsequently, the Sessions Court acquitted the accused by stating that the prosecution failed to prove a *prima facie* case as well as the pieces of evidence obtained through mutual legal assistance were inadmissible due to authentication issues.[1192]

1190 *bin Musa/bin Jaafar*, pp. 104-106.

1191 Tan Sri Eric Chia Eng Hock v. PP [2007] 1 CLJ 565.

1192 The Sessions Court cited non-compliance with Section 33 of the Evidence Act, which provides, among others, that evidence given by a witness in a judicial proceeding, or before any person authorized by law to take it, is relevant for the purpose of proving in a subsequent judicial proceeding, or in a later stage of the same judicial proceeding, the truth of the facts which it states, when the witness is dead or cannot be found or is incapable of giving evidence, or is kept out of the way by the adverse party, or if his presence cannot be obtained without an amount of delay or expense which under the circumstances of the

When judgment was rendered in the trial court, there was yet no amendment to the Evidence Act tackling evidence obtained through MLA and the applicable provisions were only found in the MACMA vis-à-vis taking evidence by Malaysia through the Attorney General, i.e admitted subject to provisions of the Evidence Act and Criminal Procedure Code.[1193] This was eventually appealed by the prosecution and in both instances before the High Court and Court of Appeal, the trial court's decision was overturned with the finding that the Hong Kong evidence was admissible.[1194] The High Court was of the position, as affirmed later on by the Court of Appeal, that the MACMA is actually a special piece of legislation to facilitate mutual legal assistance and should not be hampered by the provisions of the Evidence Act notwithstanding the mention of the said law in Section 8(3). Subjecting the operationalization of the MACMA to the technical requirements of the Evidence Act, according to the High Court, renders nugatory or redundant the intention of a speedy and convenient method of cross-border exchange of evidence. Notably, this position from the High Court – and later by the Court of Appeal – is reflected in Section 42 of the MACMA, although not discussed in the case at bar. Despite however the position of the High Court and the Court of Appeal, their decisions were overturned upon appeal to the highest court of the land (Federal Court) by the accused; ergo, the evidence obtained through mutual legal assistance was inadmissible as evidence due to lack of authentication.[1195]

Thus, the decision in the Eric Chia case prompted the eventual amendment of the Evidence Act 1950. This amendment notwithstanding, authorities remain wary how the new provisions are to be tested in courts: it is plausible according to them that new technical legal challenges would arise in future cases where the prosecution would wish to offer foreign evidence obtained through MLA, which may touch on areas not covered by the present amendments to the Evidence Act.[1196]

---

case the court considers unreasonable.Tan Sri Eric Chia Eng Hock v. PP [2007] 1 CLJ 565; *bin Musa/bin Jaafar*, p. 103.

1193 Tan Sri Eric Chia Eng Hock v. PP [2007] 1 CLJ 565; *bin Musa/bin Jaafar*, p. 103.

1194 Tan Sri Eric Chia Eng Hock v. PP [2007] 1 CLJ 565; *bin Musa/bin Jaafar*, p. 103.

1195 See for facts of the case, Tan Sri Eric Chia Eng Hock v. PP [2007] 1 CLJ 565; *bin Musa/bin Jaafar*, p. 104.

1196 Tan Sri Eric Chia Eng Hock v. PP [2007] 1 CLJ 565; *bin Musa/bin Jaafar*, p. 106.

e. Importance of Confidentiality

A reading of the relevant law would reveal that confidentiality is not a mandatory duty of Malaysia as a requested state. In the provisions regarding requests made to Malaysia through the Attorney-General, the requesting state must explicitly make a statement setting out its wishes concerning the confidentiality of the request and the reason for the wishes.[1197] That said, one can surmise upon interviewing Malaysian officials regarding mutual legal assistance, they uphold the confidentiality of the requests they make and receive and are not in liberty to disclose full details on these requests. If they provide illustrations or examples of requests they have handled, they provide only general information.

f. Return of Evidence

It is a mandatory ground for refusal should a requesting state fail to undertake the return of the evidence requested to the Attorney General upon the latter's request after the completion of the criminal matter in respect of which the request was made.[1198] Thus, the requested evidence and/or information cannot be withhold by the requesting state irrespective of whether the requested evidence could be used for another matter. As discussed earlier, there is an applicable speciality and use limitation to evidence and/or information requested. It is limited to the criminal matter specified in the request. Instead of withholding or postponing the evidence and/or information requested, the proper recourse of the requesting state would be to return upon request of the Attorney General and completion of the criminal matter subject of the original request, and in the meanwhile or thereafter, give a request anew. While the same would seem tedious and tend to prolong proceedings even further, in practice, the requesting state could already furnish Malaysian authorities draft and/or advance copies of its new requests so that the latter could outright take cognizance thereof. Sending of draft and/or advance copies, as earlier discussed, is a prevalent practice among ASEAN member-countries with regard mutual legal assistance requests to expedite processing of requests, as disclosed by Malaysian authorities.

1197 MACMA, § 19(3)(vii).
1198 MACMA, § 20(1)(k).

g. Specific Procedures per Type of Assistance

MACMA additionally provides the different procedural provisions as to how certain types of assistance shall be carried out. This includes the taking of evidence for criminal proceedings (§ 22); production order for criminal matters (§ 23); attendance of person in requesting member state (§§ 27 to 30); enforcement of foreign forfeiture orders (§§ 31 to 34); searches and seizures (§§ 35 to 38); assistance in locating and identifying persons (§ 39); and assistance in service of processes (§ 40).

With specific provisions on specific types of assistance, Malaysia as a requesting state or another ASEAN member state sending a MLA request to Malaysia shall be accordingly apprised of the specific requirements that needs to be met before a request could be allowed or executed. There is no additional step needed to look into other statutes, regulations, or texts as the MACMA and its corresponding Regulation provides for the same.

This includes the applicable rights that need to be taken into account. To illustrate, MACMA considers the person vis-à-vis requests for taking of evidence or voluntary statements, who is subject of the criminal proceedings in the prescribed criminal state, as competent, yet not compellable, to give evidence.[1199] His/her right against self-incrimination shall be respected at all costs and any statement/testimony he/she shall give shall not be used against him for purposes of any judicial proceeding, disciplinary proceeding, or other proceedings in Malaysia, except in a prosecution for perjury, contempt of court in respect of that evidence, or using the evidence to impeach the credibility of the person who gave said evidence in any judicial proceedings for the purposes under the Evidence Act 1950.[1200]

Another example is the request of attendance of a person in a foreign country. In addition to obtaining consent from the subject person, the appropriate authority of the requesting foreign state must give the adequate undertakings in relation to its request before said request can be effectuated (MACMA, § 27[2][c][d], § 27[3]): (1) that the person shall not (a) be detained, prosecuted or punished for any offense against the law of the prescribed foreign State that is alleged to have been committed, or that was committed, before the person's departure from Malaysia; (b) be subjected to any civil suit in respect of any act or omission of the person that is alleged to have occurred, or that had occurred, before the person's departure from Malaysia; or (c) be required to give evidence or assistance

1199 MACMA, § 22(7).
1200 MACMA, § 22(8), (10) and (11).

in relation to any criminal matter in the prescribed foreign State other than the criminal matter to which the request relates, unless the person has left the prescribed foreign state or the person has had the opportunity of leaving the prescribed foreign state and has remained in the prescribed foreign State otherwise than for the purpose of giving evidence or assistance in relation to the criminal matter to which the request relates; (2) that any evidence given by the person in the criminal proceedings to which the request relates, if any, will be inadmissible or otherwise disqualified from use in the prosecution of the person for an offense against the law of the prescribed foreign state, other than for the offense of perjury or contempt of court in relation to the giving of that evidence; (3) that the person will be returned to Malaysia in accordance with arrangements agreed to by the Attorney General; and (4) such other matters as the Attorney General thinks appropriate.

Under the law, the person whose attendance is requested in the prescribed foreign state shall not be subjected to penalty or liability by sole reason of its refusal or failure to consent to attend as requested.[1201]

Having said the foregoing, there could be issues arising from the lack of provisions in the law as regards those other types of assistance not specifically mentioned in the MACMA. In response, the interviewed authorities from the Attorney General said that preliminary consultation is available to advise on the applicable provisions and requirements per type of assistance.

IV. Comparing the Philippines and Malaysia with the Regional Framework

The following portion of the study endeavors to compare the ASEAN regional framework with the member state frameworks of the Philippines and Malaysia. Through the exercise of comparing and contrasting the regional and member state frameworks, one can determine not only whether and to what extent the international requirements have been implemented in the national legal systems, but also the existing gaps, problems and issues that ought to be addressed in the mutual legal assistance regime within the ASEAN. To do so, this chapter shall be divided into three (3) main points as done above – a discussion of the historical development of mutual legal assistance, the important substantive provisions, and the

1201 MACMA, § 27(4).

procedural provisions applicable to the ASEAN MLAT and member state frameworks.

A. Need for Implementing Legislation and Harmonization of Legal Framework

At the outset, the historical development of a mutual legal assistance instrument and legislation on the regional sphere would show that on a regional level, the acknowledgment to foster and strengthen cooperation among the different ASEAN member states has been there from the beginning, when the ASEAN was formed by the original five member states. This is in line with the acknowledgment that transnational crime, including terrorism, is not only a national concern and also has regional security implications. This further reinforces the idea that regional security and safety has always been a primordial consideration for the ASEAN albeit in the formative years of the Association, there were formal arrangements only as regards economic policies while those involving socio-political and/or regional security matters remained mainly informalistic despite the numerous declarations, meetings, and arrangements the ASEAN and its member states entered into vis-à-vis transnational crime (starting with drugs). There were only more formal arrangements among member states when the ASEAN took on the challenge to form the ASEAN Communities and lumping altogether within the ASEAN Security Community matters, arrangements, and agreements concerning transnational crime, terrorism, and other matters involving regional security and safety. Included herein is the inclusion of more sectoral bodies with ancillary – but not less significant – roles and functions to combat transnational crime and terrorism in the region. It must be noted though that whilst more sectoral bodies have been involved, with the ASOMTC mainly taking the helm in implementing policies vis-à-vis transnational crime, these sectoral bodies in light of the ASEAN's intergovernmental and now pillarized organization are generally compartmentalized and mainly worked on their respective sectors and function areas independently. Coordination among sectoral bodies can be illustrated mostly as one goes one step up the hierarchy in the ASEAN organizational structure, e.g ASEAN Community Councils, Coordinating Council, ASEAN Summit.

The discussion on international cooperation among ASEAN member states has not been foreign to the regional organization. In fact, discussions began about an extradition treaty as early as the inception of the ASEAN but heretofore, there is no ASEAN Extradition Treaty to discuss. The ASEAN member states are still at the negotiation table on this matter, albeit the same has been taking a lot of time. So far, what they have come up with is only an ASEAN Model Extradition Treaty that is neither binding nor executory among the member states. It is a different story however with regard the ASEAN Mutual Legal Assistance Treaty, which entered into force in 2004. As discussed earlier, this enables member states to give the widest possible measure of assistance in criminal matters. And with making it a regional instrument, this widest possible of assistance is now not limited among the ASEAN member states but is also open to other non-ASEAN state parties.

On a member state level, the Philippines and Malaysia have existing bilateral and multilateral agreements as regards international cooperation and mutual legal assistance in particular. Nonetheless, Malaysia is the only one between the two which has a domestic legislation specifically tackling mutual legal assistance in criminal matters. Together with Cambodia among the ASEAN member states (although Cambodia is in the process of making the necessary changes), the Philippines does not have any specific legislation other than having mini-MLA provisions found in its Anti-Money Laundering Act and Cybercrime Prevention Act, for example. In relation to this, Malaysia needs domestic legislation to give domestic effect to treaties and arrangements it enters into. As its case law explains, while the head of state has the treaty making power to enter into international agreements, etc., domestic legislation is required on the other hand to give these international agreements and treaties domestic effect. Thus, in Malaysia's case in respect of mutual legal assistance has the Mutual Assistance in Criminal Matters Act ("MACMA").

As regards the Philippines, it follows the doctrine of transformation in international law as regards treaties and international agreements. As long as the constitutional requirements are followed, i.e. ratified by the required percentage in the Senate, treaties and international agreements entered into by the Philippines could be considered self-executory. With respect to mutual legal assistance between the Philippines and the other ASEAN member states, the ASEAN MLAT became the legal basis for the same absent any other specific domestic legislation on mutual legal assistance.

This self-executory mechanism notwithstanding, a look into the Philippine situation would show that a domestic law specifically consolidating matters about international cooperation, or specifically mutual legal assistance in criminal matters, as well as providing the needed standardization, definition, and delineation of procedural guidelines is strongly needed.

As will be further elaborated below, the Philippines suffers from a lack of harmonization and standardization vis-à-vis international cooperation. Although authorities such as those in the member state's Department of Justice or Department of Foreign Affairs could fill in the gaps vis-à-vis implementation and execution or describe a general way of practice, the fact that the different legal, jurisprudential, and procedural bases are not streamlined causes different nuances, gray areas, issues, etc. that ought to be addressed in the soonest possible time. Furthermore, given that the Philippines has now nine (9) mutual legal assistance treaties with different countries in addition to the ASEAN MLAT which applies among the ten ASEAN member states, this means that the Philippines could be confronted with nine plus nine different ways of handling mutual legal assistance. Hence, it is most likely that the central authorities and/or administrative agencies handling MLA are immersed in an ad hoc kind of practice per type of scenario, honed only through time by practice and experience, but without a formative and reliable legal framework available. This triggers a ripple effect, wherein questions on admissibility, reliefs available to affected persons, etc. inevitably arise but yet remain undetermined and unsolved. Further, there is also no baseline approach in negotiating MLA agreements with other possible countries, which is different from how streamlined and detailed the Malaysian law is. And indeed, no less than Philippine authorities themselves admit this problem. This problem remains true despite the existence of open communication channels and preliminary consultation between authorities because while open communication is a welcomed development among practitioners, it does not erase the other pervasive problems caused by the absence of a domestic legislation.

It bears mentioning herein that while specific domestic legislation is imperative, it is equally important that such domestic legislation is harmonized with the rest of the applicable domestic legal framework to be efficacious when operationalized and applied. The applicable domestic legislation must be consistent with the other laws and rules of court or criminal procedure. Stating it differently, statutes and rules touching on mutual legal assistance or international cooperation in general must be *in pari materia*, i.e. wherein they can be construed seamlessly (as one law) with reference to each other. Otherwise, stumbling blocks could arise that render the purpose of mutual legal assistance nugatory. This was shown in the case of Malaysia, which, despite having a specific domestic legislation on mutual legal assistance, was confronted in the criminal case against Eric Chia (Perwaja case) with the issue of authentication of evidence obtained through mutual legal assistance in its use in Malaysian courts. To recall, the Evidence Act and Criminal Procedure Code were mentioned in the MACMA although the provision likewise mentions that evidence obtained through MLA requires no further proof as to the facts stated therein. Nonetheless, the lack of the appropriate provision then in the Evidence Act tackling evidence obtained through MLA prompted the Federal Court to rule in favor of the accused as regards lack of authentication of evidence. Malaysia has subsequently made the necessary amendments albeit still unsure if the same would suffice in future cases touching on technical issues not tackled by the amendments. Henceforth, it is important for the member states to ensure that their respective domestic frameworks are sufficient and consistent to ensure mutual legal assistance would work efficaciously.

B. Substantive Provisions

1. Applicability of Assistance

The ASEAN mutual legal assistance mechanism reflects that of a traditional one, wherein it is request-based: one state sending another a request to another state for the cross-border exchange and/or transfer of information and/or evidence in criminal matters. This traditional sense also connotes the existence of discretion on the part of the requested state to decide whether to execute or comply with the MLA request. Despite the existence of discretion, the ASEAN MLAT and respective local legislations limit the grounds to refuse a request. Further, the member states are enjoined to give the widest possible amount of assistance vis-à-vis a received request. In practice, officials both from the Philippines and Malaysia intimated the endeavor to make mutual legal assistance between the ASEAN member states smooth sailing.

The obligation to render assistance for the ASEAN, the Philippines, and Malaysia, at the outset does not differ. It applies to criminal matters but would not apply to the extradition, arrest, detention in view of arrest, transfer of proceedings, satisfaction of judgment. While these compose the genus of international cooperation, they are not contemplated in the ASEAN MLAT, the MACMA, and the Philippine implementation of the ASEAN MLAT. In other words, should these be requested, the requesting member state ought to look somewhere else for legal basis.

Criminal matters is not defined across all levels (especially the Philippines given that it would follow what the ASEAN MLAT provides) but rather, what generally constitutes criminal matters is enumerated, i.e criminal investigations, prosecutions, and resulting proceedings. Malaysia refers to the resulting proceedings in its domestic law as "ancillary criminal matters" which involves, for example, forfeiture proceedings and the like as a result of criminal liability. Philippine authorities further elucidate that while mutual legal assistance pertains solely to criminal matters, there are instances wherein it is allowed for administrative proceedings or civil actions arising from the criminal action (civil liability arising from criminal liability). The nexus however needs to be established.

It is interesting that in the obligation to assist, both the Philippines and Malaysia would render treaty-based and non-treaty based mutual legal assistance in criminal matters, with the latter mostly relying on reciprocity. Malaysia takes it a step further in this aspect through specificities in its domestic legislation as to how a request proceeds should the requesting member state be a preferred foreign state – which is requesting based on an existing treaty – and one which is not a preferred foreign state. Notably, in the regional and member state levels, no distinctions or delineations are provided as regards whether the subject of the mutual legal assistance is a natural or legal person. Without such clear exception, it can be assumed that it is applicable to both.

Despite the seeming willingness and cooperative attitude both the Philippines and Malaysia show vis-à-vis the implementation of the ASEAN MLAT and facilitating international cooperation, MACMA provides a limitation to the obligation to render assistance: the criminal offense must be either a "serious offense" or "serious foreign offense", which means it must be punishable for at least one (1) year, which is a limitation not present in the ASEAN MLA instrument. Tacitly, the Philippines places the same limitation when it requires as a general rule in the requests it issues and receives information about the criminal matter in relation to the MLA request, including information on the possible punishment and/or sanctions. Considering these limitations resonate with one another, the ASEAN MLAT provides as a ground to refuse a request should it cause undue burden to the requested state and/or the same relates to national interests, which includes the mobilization of resources most of the time.

2. Types of Mutual Legal Assistance

Anent the types of assistance that could be rendered, the ASEAN MLAT provides a list of 11 types of assistance, with the last provision being a catch-all provision, wherein parties may render assistance not specifically enumerated as long as the parties agreed on the same and the same is not in violation of the requested state's domestic law. Notably, the ASEAN MLAT does not mention assistance in the form of covert operations, interception of communications and correspondence, or the collection and interception of online data, which might be imperative or necessitated by the times when technology is so advanced.

The want of any mention of these types of assistance can be seen as well in the Malaysian legislation. When asked about interception of communications and online data however, Malaysian authorities mentioned it is normally done through informal forms of cooperation, or when the interception of communications is done, it does not involve content data and would relate to crimes committed in Malaysia.

As regards the Philippines, on the other hand, it is admittedly difficult to determine the exact types of assistance it can render given the lack of specific legislation other than the ASEAN MLAT spelling these out. The ASEAN MLAT can provide on a minimum an idea as to what the types of assistance can be given, and generally, authorities would grant a MLA request as long as the parties agree and the request does not contravene domestic law. That being said, it becomes apparent upon execution of certain types of assistance, as discussed above that a specific domestic legislation or guidelines *de rigeur* is strongly left to be desired because of nuances scattered across the entire domestic framework and the general vagueness and uncertainty as to how issues are to be addressed in law and procedure. This can potentially lead to problems with investigative measures involving getting to court, e.g. transfer of persons in custody to take evidence or give information, etc.

Hurdles and issues notwithstanding on specific types of assistance the ASEAN MLAT enumerated, a reading of the Philippine domestic legal framework would interestingly reveal that the Philippines despite the lack of domestic legislation could effectuate investigative measures not otherwise specifically provided for in the ASEAN MLAT – or in other words, those that might fall under the catch-all provision. This includes interception of communication data, online evidence, etc. which as mentioned, is not provided for in the Malaysian legislation. Additionally, the international cooperation provisions, requirements, and parameters in the

Philippine Cybercrime Act mirror the types of assistance or cooperation mechanism found in the ASEAN MLAT. This therefore reveals that while there is a want of domestic legislation, the Philippines might be slowly getting to the point of standardizing its international cooperation mechanism.

Having mentioned the foregoing, interviews with Philippine officials and Malaysian officials alike reveal the importance and benefits of preliminary consultation and open communication between ASEAN member states as regards mutual legal assistance, and they openly assist each other as to what type of assistance is feasible or not, including the concomitant legal basis for the same. The Philippines for one, as mentioned by its authorities, would effectuate almost 100% of the time MLA requests it receives. The open communication channels also account for how Philippines despite a lack of domestic law is still able to render assistance. This similarity in expression from authorities reveal the willingness to provide the widest possible measure of assistance to one another, as well as the adoption of the same language among practitioners that notwithstanding issues and problems that may arise, they are willing to cooperate with one another to make the system work.

3. Compatibility with other Arrangements

Both the regional and member state level recognize and accept that giving and effectuating MLA requests is compatible with other existing arrangements and treaties, including informal forms of cooperation. Informal channels of cooperation mostly happen between law enforcement agencies and administrative agencies handling criminal matters. Thus, in the ASEAN context, mutual legal assistance does not preclude assistance that can be obtained through the use of INTERPOL, ASEANPOL, or otherwise police-to-police cooperation between member states.

As regards the Philippines and Malaysia, both are engaged actively in this kind of cooperation amongst their respective law enforcement authorities and regulatory bodies. The Philippines for example, if one would look into the Implementing Rules and Regulations of its Cybercrime Prevention Act as discussed in the types of assistance involved vis-à-vis online data, delineates when formal requests are needed. Formal requests are needed for those that will be used as evidence in court. One does not need to go through the process of formal cooperation if the data or information for investigative purposes only. And as explained by some

Malaysian authorities, informal forms of cooperation are normally resorted to during investigations and before any formal prosecution or criminal case is filed. It is also resorted to if a formal government-to-government arrangement is not yet necessary in the process or the piece of evidence or information does not require going through the court. Stating it differently, whatever is obtained through an informal cooperation does not result to this information and/or evidence being used in criminal proceedings but could otherwise help in building a case against a suspect and/or accused person. Informal forms of cooperation are thus actually encouraged to some extent.

In line with this, a Philippine official mentioned that in the case of the Philippines, should there be arrangements or agreements made by its law enforcement agencies with other law enforcement agencies of other countries, like other ASEAN member states, they would still consider these as "formal arrangements" needing consultation with the Department of Justice and Department of Foreign Affairs to make sure these agreements are in order. This could include joint capacity building, joint exercises, as well as informal channels of cooperation. In other words, any commitment for informal cooperation between each other is formalized in writing.

4. Principles, Conditions, and Exceptions

Comparing the regional framework and respective member state frameworks with one another reveals interesting insights as regards the different principles, conditions, and exceptions applicable in mutual legal assistance. These principles, conditions, and exceptions can be divided into seven, to wit: (1) sufficiency of evidence requirement, (2) dual criminality, (3) double jeopardy, (4) substantive consideration of human rights, (5) reciprocity, (6) speciality or use limitation, and (7) special offenses.

First, a look at the regional instrument shows that a sufficiency of evidence requirement exists in a manner wherein the more intrusive a requested measure is, the more information should be provided by the requesting member state. This applies equally to Malaysia wherein the sufficiency of evidence requirement can be observed in certain types of assistance it can render to a requesting state, in particular those which involve coercive measures such as production orders, searches and seizures, and even the location and identification of persons. The same would be granted if there are "reasonable grounds to believe" that the particular subject of the coercive measure is connected to the criminal matter and/or located in Malaysia. Additionally, there are consequences under Malaysian law when the sufficiency of evidence requirement is not met. Under the MACMA, a request received by Malaysia can be denied if there is "insufficient information," which, if one steps back to statements from Malaysian authorities, relates to the avoidance of the use of MLA as part of fishing expeditions.

It is interesting to note that the Philippines would arguably have the most well-defined and delineated sufficiency of evidence requirement as its law and jurisprudence would provide. It involves the establishment of probable cause, which does not exist as a standard in Malaysia, before a warrant may be issued for any coercive measure, may it be searches and seizures, interception of communications and correspondence such as wire-tapping, and/or interception and collection of online data and evidence. Accordingly, probable cause is defined to be more than reasonable suspicion but less than reasonable doubt and entails the existence of such facts and circumstances that would lead a reasonable man to believe that a crime has been committed and that the objects to be seized, place to be searched, or person to be arrested is connected to the crime. This consequently means that should requests involving coercive measures be made to the Philippines, the requesting member state ought to provide sufficient information and evidence to support its request to enable Philippine authorities to convince the court upon application for any coercive measure to grant its application and lawfully proceed with the applied coercive measure. Admittedly though, the evidentiary requirement with respect to MLA requests is less stringent compared to extradition requests.

Second, as regards the dual criminality requirement, the said requirement exists at the regional and member state level. Dual criminality simply means that the act(s) and/or omission(s) mentioned in the MLA request ought to be punishable in both the requested and requesting states. As per the ASEAN MLAT, dual criminality is a mandatory ground to refuse a request regardless of type of assistance covered by the MLA request. A similar application can be found in MACMA.

Being a mandatory ground for refusal in the ASEAN MLAT and MACMA of Malaysia, the dual criminality requirement does not noticeably exist in the Philippine Cybercrime Prevention Act while the same exists as a mandatory ground for refusal under the Anti-Money Laundering Act. The Cybercrime Prevention Act is a later legislative enactment and more or less what reflects in practice in the Philippines. In practice and more or less as a policy, the Philippines would not deny a MLA request even if the dual criminality requirement is not satisfied. It can be thus said that although dual criminality is a mandatory ground for refusal with regard the ASEAN MLAT framework, it is generally treated otherwise on the Philippine domestic level. Malaysian authorities, on the other hand, mention that in instances wherein the subject act or omission included in the MLA request, they try to make it work with their counterparts in suggesting what could otherwise fall under a punishable criminal offense in Malaysia so that the MLA request can be effectuated. Taking this into account, dual criminality is one of the important principles at the crux of mutual legal assistance and must be given utmost consideration and discussion. Nonetheless, as the member state examples show, there is either an easing of the requirement or it is not treated as a stumbling block in the execution of an offense. The propensity even, as shown by the Philippines, is to disregard its significance in the execution of requests.

Third, the double jeopardy prohibition in the regional and member state level of ASEAN can be different from one another to a certain extent. In the ASEAN MLAT, there is the prohibition of double jeopardy and it is a mandatory ground to refuse a request should it exist, wherein a requested state shall deny assistance when the request relates to an investigation, prosecution, or punishment of a person for an offense where the person either has been convicted, acquitted, or pardoned by a competent court or other authority in the requesting or requested member state; or has undergone the punishment provided by law of that requesting or requested member state, in respect of that offense or of another offense constitute by the same act or omission as the first-mentioned offense. The same has arguably a transnational element (although limited between the requesting and requested states) in application and is reasonably consistent with the provisions provided in the ASEAN Human Rights Declaration regarding double jeopardy, to wit, "no person shall be liable to be tried or punished for an offense he or she has already been finally convicted or acquitted in accordance with the law and penal procedure of each ASEAN member state." In relation to this, at least three (3) observations can be said:

One: the double jeopardy prohibition in the ASEAN Human Rights Declaration is subjected to the domestic law and penal procedure of the respective ASEAN member states. Relying on each member state's domestic law and penal procedure just means that there is no ASEAN-wide applicable standard or accepted definition on when double jeopardy shall be engaged. The lack of any ASEAN adjudicatory body regarding human rights makes it improbable that an ASEAN-accepted definition and/or standard would take shape anytime soon. Thus, any development of the prohibition (or principle) in a regional sense would be heavily be reliant or take shape on a domestic level.

Two: one can add to this the general lack of harmonization in the first place among ASEAN member states of their respective laws. A look into Malaysia and the Philippines alone show that while on its face, they espouse similar values as to how they treat the prohibition on double jeopardy (the prohibition being encapsulated in their respective constitutions), there had been criticism for example on Malaysia that the prohibition can be lamentable in practice most of the time given the many exceptions to the prohibition. There are also differences as to how the first jeopardy could attach and other idiosyncrasies of each member state. In fact, it must be pointed out that there is no well-defined and delineated framework of double jeopardy vis-à-vis mutual legal assistance for both countries, albeit they entertain double jeopardy as a mandatory ground to refuse a MLA request in the ASEAN MLAT context. Furthermore, even if it is the most ideal and in accordance with spirit of the prohibition to be applied transnationally, it has yet to be seen on whether the respective constitutional prohibitions of Malaysia and the Philippines would be expanded on a transnational application through case law or statute, especially in cases wherein transnational crimes are involved and/or there could be a possible exercise of either universal or extraterritorial jurisdiction.

Three: the prohibition on double jeopardy as contemplated in the ASEAN MLAT, although it lends a transnational character to the prohibition against double jeopardy as it considers both the requesting and requested states, it does not look beyond these two parties. There is no mention as to what would then happen if for the offense subject of the offense occurred, the accused or person involved has been convicted, acquitted, or pardoned in a third state, which is not necessarily an ASEAN member state. This situation can likewise contemplate instances wherein the accused or person involved has satisfied the judgment or undergone the punishment for the same contemplated offense or crime.

In the same vein, the Malaysian law suffers from the same handicap wherein in the usage of the prohibition against double jeopardy as a ground to refuse a request, the law only considers a conviction, acquittal, pardon, or service of punishment in the requesting state. Any similar incident in Malaysia is not taken into account in the relevant provision.

Two conclusions can be derived and it also depends whether the state involved is the requested or requesting state. First, when either the Philippines and Malaysia are the requesting states, the evidence or information requested through the MLA request would naturally be used within their respective domestic courts, which concomitantly should apply domestic laws and principles. Thus, it is without question that the prohibition against double jeopardy as applied domestically ought to be applied. It is prudent to take into account any conviction, acquittal, pardon, or service of punishment that has occurred elsewhere, regardless of the requested state or third state.

Second, the conclusion is altered when the subject state is the requested state and with different possible outcomes for both the Philippines and Malaysia. Based on the skeletal reading of the pertinent ASEAN MLAT provision, *verba legis*, the answer would be for the Philippines to proceed with the request notwithstanding a circumstance wherein the conviction, acquittal, pardon, or service of punishment occurred in a third state, because the provision in the treaty only considers the requested or requesting state. Following strictly the MACMA provision, on the other hand, would limit Malaysia to deny a request only when the conviction, acquittal, pardon, or service of punishment occurred in the requesting state. Malaysia would not concern itself if the circumstances occurred on its own domestic soil.

Conversely, the spirit of the prohibition in its transnational sense should result to a denial of the request, or at the least make the requested state wary of granting the request, in both cases wherein the circumstances occurred in Malaysia or in a third state. Considering the foregoing, the fact that this has not been encountered in practice, as well as the fact of the need to balance interests on a case-to-case basis, the solution would probably lie in the preliminary consultation and open communication between authorities in the ASEAN. For posterity sake, the officials of the requested and requesting state could likewise call the attention or coordinate with the appropriate officials of the third state or other ASEAN member state, wherein the person involved has been convicted, acquitted, or pardoned, or otherwise underwent the punishment for the questioned offense or crime. For Malaysia specifically, if the request triggers the prohibition as provided in Malaysian law, then it should call the requesting state's attention. The ASEAN MLAT allows the same anyway, wherein should there be questions or inquiries about a particular request, the requested and requesting states may consult each other.

Fourth, general human rights considerations as substantive provisions in mutual legal assistance in criminal matters in the ASEAN regime were also examined. On a regional level, one of the more recent developments within ASEAN is the ASEAN Declaration of Human Rights, which basically mirrors the UN Declaration of Human Rights but adding other rights not included in the latter. With the said ASEAN Human Rights Declaration, one could note that there is no enforcement mechanism or corresponding ASEAN Human Rights Court established to adjudicate rights and redress violations of said instrument. Interestingly, the ASEAN Declaration of Human Rights was made through the work of the ASEAN Intergovernmental Commission on Human Rights. The establishment of any regional court or adjudicatory body would not fall under their mandate but instead fall another ASEAN body, i.e. ASEAN Law Ministers Meeting. Lack of enforcement mechanism notwithstanding, there are certain human rights that are included in said Declaration that may be relevant in the context of mutual legal assistance and criminal matters in general.

Looking then at the specific ASEAN MLAT instrument, considerations of certain rights come into play with respect to the substantive provisions of valid and mandatory grounds for refusal. There is, at the outset, the mandatory ground for refusal by reason of double jeopardy in the ASEAN mutual legal assistance regime. A request can be denied also when it was issued on discrimination grounds. Further, one can look into the human right safeguard in assisting the attendance of a person in the requesting member state, wherein the requested member state shall "invite the person to give or provide evidence or assistance in relation to a criminal matter in the requesting member state" if "satisfactory arrangements for that person's safety will be made by the requesting member state." In other words, satisfactory arrangements for the person's safety is a condition precedent before transfer of persons to give and/or provide evidence or assistance is allowed.

These considerations are equally available in the Philippines and Malaysia. With regard the Philippines, it follows what the ASEAN MLAT provides, but a step further is necessary to capture the requirements ought to be followed in the Philippines in light of human rights not only due to the lack of a domestic legislation specifically addressing these issues, but likewise the non-mention of further details or applicable rights in the ASEAN MLAT. To state the least, the ASEAN MLAT as a legal basis can only provide so little information as to what Philippine authorities ought to consider. For other details or general human rights to be considered, other relevant Philippine law and jurisprudence ought to be perused, which is different if one considers the MACMA as mostly a one-stop shop in knowing how MLA works in Malaysia. Thus, it should not be surprising that in the discussion of the Philippine and Malaysian frameworks, the discussion of the Philippine framework is apparently more exhaustive because there is no law or jurisprudence that settles the matter. Any apparent disjunct or "incomparability" is thus explained by the need to fill in missing links and probe different sources to find answers.

In connection to this, a study of relevant Philippine law and jurisprudence reveals the importance of respecting one's constitutional right to privacy in correspondence and communication, the right against unreasonable searches and seizures, and one's right to substantive due process. Violation of these rights has repercussions not only on the validity of a mutual legal assistance request (i.e. right to privacy and against unreasonable searches and seizures demands that a MLA request shall not be made on a shotgun approach or fishing expedition) but also on the admissibility of evidence (considering that the Philippines follow the exclusionary rule and fruits of the poisonous tree doctrine). Moreover, substantive due process under Philippine law requires that the MLA request is complete and not vague. Otherwise, not only is one's right to be informed violated and one's right to substantive due process infringed, but the intrinsic validity of the MLA request likewise becomes questionable.

In addition to the aforementioned grounds for refusal on the basis of human rights, one can also look into how the issue of severity of punishment or the imposition of torture, cruel, inhumane, or degrading punishment is factored in the MLA framework. While being given a strong consideration in extradition cases, this has not been done within the context of ASEAN mutual legal assistance, despite the explicit prohibition on torture, cruel, and inhumane treatment and/or punishment being included in the ASEAN's own human rights instrument. A possible explanation of this is the ASEAN principle of non-interference, wherein member states shall refrain "from criticizing the actions of a member government towards its own people, including violation of human rights, and from making the domestic political system of states and the political styles of government as basis for deciding membership in ASEAN." This is also reminiscent of ASEAN's argumentation regarding Myanmar's membership in the organization despite its political instability and human rights violations. The ASEAN posited that these matters are domestic in nature and outside the concerns of the organization or its member states pursuant to the principle of non-intervention. Naturally, issues of severity of punishment or prohibition against torture and cruel, inhumane, degrading punishment or treatment fall within the ambits of human rights violations. Thus, it can be arguably be excluded from being a concern of fellow member states or the ASEAN as an organization.

Even if enhanced interaction now more or less exists in different planes of ASEAN policies, wherein one member state can inquire or comment about domestic affairs of the other should the same have regional repercussions and as long as the same is done outside the ASEAN framework, it would be a stretch to implore "enhanced interaction" in these circumstances as there is a weak nexus, if any such connection exists, between imposition of punishment within a state's domestic jurisdiction and regional repercussions. Imposition of punishment is ingrained in a state's culture as illustrated in Malaysia that it can be arguably considered an internal affair to the exclusion of any possible interference from others. The principle of non-interference still generally holds and arguably explains the absence of said principle involving the consideration of severity of punishment.

Accordingly, Malaysia allows the imposition of the death penalty and whipping as forms of punishment to the extent that its Supreme Court had the occasion to even reprimand judges who hesitated to impose the same even if taking account of the circumstances should warrant the imposition of the death penalty. As regards whipping, the Federal Constitution and Malaysian Criminal Law imposes parameters for its imposition. To that extent, conditions are improved. Interestingly, Malaysia would actually have the experience of being either denied extradition or mutual legal assistance requests, or being required to make undertakings they would not subject the accused to the death penalty by some countries outside ASEAN, which prohibit the imposition of the death penalty and with which Malaysia has existing treaties or agreements.

On the other hand, the Philippines constitutionally prohibits torture and the imposition of severe, inhumane, and degrading punishment, and does not necessarily constitutionally prohibit the imposition of the death penalty but limits its imposition to heinous crimes as may be defined by the legislature. The death penalty is currently suspended. However, it remains to be seen whether the Philippines would take the extra step of denying requests it receives if the same involves a violation on the imposition of the death penalty and severe, inhumane, and degrading punishment. One would be inclined to answer in the negative. Judging from state policy elucidated in Philippine jurisprudence, the Philippine judiciary would not only adopt a general hands-off policy in these matters but moreover, the Philippine authorities rather work on a mutual trust that the requesting state knows what it is doing.

In relation to the foregoing substantive considerations of human rights in the MLA framework, it becomes imperative to inquire whether member states could invoke other general human rights considerations in order to deny a MLA request, i.e. domestic human rights principles, values, prohibitions, and international human rights obligations, which may conflict with a request received. If one follows the strict letter of the ASEAN MLAT and the MACMA, the answer is in the negative. No ground for refusal is provided wherein a requested state can deny a request if the same conflicts with an existing human rights obligation. This is further supported by existing rule of non-inquiry the Philippines follows as regards international cooperation requests. There is a good faith compliance that the requesting state adheres to the law or human rights obligations. The same can be derived from Malaysia as well, by excluding any circumstance occurring in Malaysia vis-à-vis double jeopardy when it is the requested state.

Alternatively, should the member state be placed in a position of strong urgency to uphold its human rights obligations over a MLA request received, especially with those constitutionally provided or falling under customary international law obligations, then it could resort to the use of the "national interest" ground for refusal, because arguably they cannot go against constitutional principles and standards or those considered customary law. Having mentioned this, both Malaysia and the Philippines have yet to encounter this in practice. At most, the member states would openly communicate and consult with one another about any issue that would arise in respect of any human rights issues or problems that may arise due to a MLA request. This open communication avoids admittedly the issue and not directly addresses it, however.

The fifth principle or condition that can be mentioned is reciprocity. On both a regional and member state level, this exists. A request may be denied if there is no undertaking for reciprocity in the ASEAN MLAT and the same applies to the Philippines and Malaysia. From the perspective of authorities from both Malaysia and the Philippines, there has been no problem rendering and requesting assistance with other ASEAN member states on the basis of reciprocity. There seems to be a tacit understanding that ASEAN member states shall be willing, ready, and able to provide the required assistance in criminal matters.

The sixth principle or condition is the speciality and use limitation which also exists on both the regional and member state level. The ASEAN MLAT and Malaysian legislation clearly provides this, while this is seen in practice in the Philippines. Any evidence or information may not be used for any other criminal matter other than that subject of the MLA request, regardless of the realization that it can be used elsewhere. What must be done is to write or make a request anew, both in Malaysia and the Philippines. Advance notice can be given however, given the open channels of communication between ASEAN member states' authorities. In relation to this, should one be interested to what is the basis of such speciality and use limitation being used in practice in the Philippines, this is based on the stringent requirements provided by no less than its Constitution on the use of coercive measures. The same applies when one applies for the appropriate warrant in Malaysia. There is a particularity requirement on what needs to be seized, which to be searched, etc., that it arguably applies to MLA requests involving the same kind of coercive measures. Further, there is a general requirement to make a return on the information and/or evidence seized, as well as details as to how a certain warrant or order was served, or the date subsequently destroyed. To illustrate, the Philippine Cybercrime Act or Anti-Wiretapping Act requires the destruction of any recording made after usage as evidence and/or lapse of a certain period of time.

Lastly, special offenses and national interest are often identified as exceptions to mutual legal assistance. These play a substantive part in the granting and executing of MLA requests. While political offenses and military offenses exceptions have been limited in the ASEAN MLAT as exceptions to mutual legal assistance, fiscal offenses may no longer be used as an excuse to deny a MLA request. Further, there are a lot of political reasons a state may use in denying a MLA request. These include instances when there is a pending criminal matter or investigation in the requested state or when the national interest of the requested state shall be affected. As to what these national interests can be, a state can define unilaterally what falls under national interest. Having said this, there seems to be no semblance of this being invoked often by ASEAN member states on the basis of what has been mentioned in interviews about granting almost 100% of the time all requests received from each other. Also, there exists an open communication and preliminary consultation, even to the extent of sending draft or advance copies of requests to each other, to ensure that the same are in order and feasible to be executed without encountering any grounds for refusal or any violation of the requested state's domestic law.

C. Procedural Provisions

The following discussion focuses on salient procedural aspects of mutual legal assistance: (1) the designation of central authorities which highlights vertical cooperation in the ASEAN framework; (2) preparation of requests; and (3) execution of requests.

1. Usage of Vertical Cooperation in Mutual Legal Assistance: Central Authorities

In respect of the designation of central authorities, the ASEAN and its member states all espouse a vertical type of cooperation as regards mutual legal assistance, wherein requests for international cooperation go through a single focal point or central authority, which shall be then in charge of sending and receiving requests for mutual legal assistance in criminal matters. This is vertical in nature because it follows a top-down or bottom-top approach in facilitating requests. For the Philippines, this shall be the Department of Justice through its Office of the General Counsel. For Malaysia, this shall be the Attorney General's Chambers through the Prosecution's Office, in particular, the Transnational Crimes Division. These authorities then coordinate with the respective agencies to effectuate any request and basically would be on top of any matter in relation to the MLA request received or sent. Notably, informal forms of cooperation generally do not course through these central authorities but it could still happen. For Malaysia, informal requests to the Central Bank are mandated by law to still be coursed through the central authority, for example.

It must be noted that despite the designation of the respective Department of Justice or Attorney General's Chambers as the central authorities for the Philippines and Malaysia, their respective Foreign Affairs Department still plays a role in the negotiation, implementation, and execution of mutual legal assistance requests. This is sanctioned by the ASEAN MLAT itself in allowing member states to require coursing MLA requests through diplomatic channels.

2. Preparation of Requests

As regards preparation of requests, said preparation on both the regional and member state level have minimum general requirements – for example, having the request written in English and in a form capable of producing written records for purposes of establishing authenticity – additional information can and must be provided dependent on the type of assistance requested. This can be connected to the sufficiency of evidence requirement generally existing in mutual legal assistance wherein more information ought to be provided the more intrusive the measure requested is. Malaysia, in relation to this, would provide in its law how Malaysia should make their own requests, as well as how requests made to

Malaysia should be. On the other hand, despite the lack of specific domestic legislation, requirements for request can be found in the micro-MLA provisions in some Philippine laws. Likewise, minimum information to be indicated in a request in general was provided by Philippine authorities, although this is without prejudice for requesting additional information that may be necessitated to execute a request.

In relation to this, the open communication between authorities and any preliminary consultation that occurs between them makes the ASEAN MLA system work and facilitates better preparation of requests and if needed, there would be proper guidance as to what may be wanting, questionable, or problematic in a request received. This follows the recommendations of the ASEAN Secretariat. The ASEAN Secretariat recommends the availability of open and effective channels of communication between authorities and even mentioned that most of the time it would be mutually beneficial to both parties to have liaison and communication prior to sending out any request to ensure the effectiveness of execution and at the same time, to communicate any issues and intricacies relating to the assistance being sought. The ASEAN Secretariat even encourages the use of the CNAD built through the efforts of the UNODC which contains updated contact information of the different national authorities from most states in the world, provides means of communication, and provides the different requirements to satisfy when sending a request to another state. With respect to this, the entire ASEAN framework, including the member states, have a useful toolkit in their possession, albeit not necessarily constructed under the auspices of the ASEAN framework but nevertheless readily made available by an international office such as the UNODC to cater to the needs of the ASEAN member states.

As to whose instance a MLA request shall be made, it is both apparent in the regional and member state level that it shall be prepared and issued by the respective central authorities, like the Attorney General of Malaysia. In connection to this, the ASEAN Secretariat mentioned the role of the prosecutor and/or investigator to coordinate and communicate with the respective central authority in sending out a request because said prosecutor/investigator would have the best knowledge of the case details as well as the information that needs to be obtained. There is no mention in both a regional and member state level whether a private individual, suspect, or accused person, have any right for a MLA request to be issued on its behalf. It is uncertain whether any participation is allowed. If one looks into the provisions of the ASEAN MLAT, whilst it is silent in general on who may initiate a MLA request, it equivocally provides that a private person cannot derive any right from the instrument to obtain, secure, or exclude any evidence. The MACMA also does not provide the option. As regards the Philippines, it is not so clear cut absent any specific domestic legislation. At most, one could try to file the necessary motion (for relief) in court but the Rules of Court and Criminal Procedure are bereft of any further specific provision tackling MLA. At most, one has only the discussion of the rules on discoveries and depositions. One can thus interpret this in general as excluding private parties, including suspected or accused persons, from initiating a MLA request. The MLA process remains a government-to-government endeavor or prosecutorial instrument to the exclusion of defense.

3. Execution of Requests

a. Applicable Law

The applicable law in the regional and member state level do not conflict one another as regards the execution of requests. At both levels, the general rule is the application of the *locus regit actum* principle wherein generally, what would be applicable shall be the law of the requested state. This is without prejudice to the requesting state requesting that its own law and procedure be followed in the execution of a request, as long as the requested state acquiesces and the same is not in violation of the latter's domestic law. In other words, *lex loci* is prioritized over *lex fori.* To further understand, one interviewee explained that the requesting state should clearly provide and define how it would want its MLA request to be executed and normally the requested state shall execute the same "robotically" or on a non-discretionary manner. Absent any specific instructions, the requested state shall execute in accordance with its laws. Thus, it would be imperative that a requesting state lay down with particularity how they would want their respective MLA request to proceed should it be executed.

Although the same has been stressed many times already, the open communication and preliminary consultation among ASEAN authorities help overall in the effectuating of MLA requests in the region. As one interviewee in the Philippines commented, there are less requests denied execution because authorities find a way to overcome any ground for refusal that could have existed vis-à-vis a request. Authorities work together and cooperate with one another to make sure MLA is well facilitated.

Given that one another is technically just a phone call away, any problems and issues are better ironed out should there be any.

b. Applicable Procedural Rights

Reverting to the ASEAN Human Rights Declaration, there are some rights of an accused encapsulated in the International Covenant on Political and Civil Rights which are considerably absent. Said ASEAN Declaration vis-à-vis rights of the accused only provides at most protection against "arbitrary arrest, search, detention, abduction, or any other form of deprivation of liberty", the right to be presumed innocent until proven guilty, as well as the protection against *ex post facto* laws and the enactment of bills of attainder, among others. The ASEAN instrument on human rights is bereft of any provision regarding an accused's right to be informed, right against self-incrimination, right to have adequate time and facilities to prepare for one's defense, or right to counsel. In other words, the quintessential procedural rights are not found in the ASEAN instrument.

On the contrary, these rights are constitutionally conferred in the Philippines and Malaysia. The Philippines also has a specific constitutional provision on one's right during custodial investigation (patterned from the US' Miranda doctrine) and as regards the rights of the accused, this has been jurisprudentially held to be applicable to extradition proceedings and arguably, to mutual legal assistance ones too, because while these proceedings are administrative in nature, they bear earmarks of the criminal process which may prejudice rights. Notably, the constitutional right to be informed is only engaged with extradition and MLA proceedings after the evaluation stage. Malaysia equally confers these rights.

How Malaysia and the Philippines take into account human rights in general and the rights of the accused resonates with the safeguards found mainly in the execution of requests for mutual legal assistance in the ASEAN MLAT. Herein are considerations of one's right to be informed, to counsel or legal representative, to confront witnesses, and against self-incrimination, the latter also being present in safe conduct provisions vis-à-vis transferring of persons in custody. Further safeguards include crediting the person's length of stay in the other member state to the time served for the said person's punishment. It can be stated then that the ASEAN MLAT provides the procedural rights that needed to be respected and upheld, which the ASEAN Human Rights Declaration – a later instrument – otherwise does not.

In light of the foregoing, there is the question on whether a private individual affected by a MLA request and/or the execution thereof can find relief on a domestic level. Both Malaysia and the Philippines provide for judicial review, wherein an affected individual can file the necessary application (under Order 53 of the Malaysian Rules of Court) or petition (under Rule 65 of the Philippine Rules of Court). It is a different question altogether whether judicial relief can be actually obtained. To illustrate, under Rule 65 of the Philippine Rules of Court a petitioner must be able to establish that the MLA request and/or the execution thereof was made with excess or lack of jurisdiction, or grave abuse of discretion amounting to lack of discretion. In other words, an error of jurisdiction must be established. Following however how the Philippine Supreme Court decided in *People of the Philippines v. Sergio*, it can be gainsaid that under Philippine jurisdiction, while it is still left unclear whether the Supreme Court shall touch on the validity of a mutual legal assistance request or the propriety of the request and/or any following procedure at the instance of an affected individual, the Supreme Court shall not hesitate to rule on the investigative measure arising from said mutual legal assistance request, its implementation, and any right that is adversely affected by it, especially if the criminal proceedings are held in Philippine jurisdiction. Although the Supreme Court upheld the deposition through written interrogatories and held that the accused's right to confrontation of witnesses was not violated, nothing in the Decision precludes the Supreme Court from granting redress or relief should circumstances warrant in the future.

Having mentioned these, there is further remedy available to an individual to question the admissibility of evidence in both the Philippines and Malaysia. The Philippines follow the so-called exclusionary rule that demands exclusion of an investigative measure and any evidence obtained through it (fruit of poisonous tree doctrine) if there has been a violation of human rights. While there is no exact 1:1 correspondence with Malaysia on such doctrine, Malaysia also has its share of exclusionary rules and courts are given the mandate to rule on the admissibility of evidence should the same be obtained against public policy or interest, or generally affects the notion of fairness of proceedings.

c. Applicable Time Limits

There are no time limits involved in the execution of requests in both the regional and member state level aside from what is provided in the

ASEAN MLAT that the requesting state should execute requests "promptly", there is a conscious effort to be informed among Philippine and Malaysian authorities whether there is a time element involved in the execution of a request. This applies whether they are in the issuing or receiving end of a request. A look into the information required to be contained in a request, both the Philippines and Malaysia provide therein that it should be mentioned when the request is expected to be executed and/or effectuated. The initial and preliminary consultation among member states help ease the problems encountered in relation to any delay in execution. During this initial and preliminary consultation, member states can also send each other draft and advance copies of their requests so that the requested member state can already work on the same. Based on interviews, this only happens vis-à-vis MLA requests among ASEAN countries. Additionally, promptness of execution is highly affected when the request involves coercive measures and application before the courts. Once submitted before the courts, there is little the authorities may do in influencing how fast applications would be processed. In other words, it is within the control of their respective courts as to how expedient a court order or grant of application shall be issued. Otherwise, execution of requests would be relatively fast, as described by Philippine authorities above. Moreover, should the request be faster through informal channels and the object or evidence requested is not necessitated to be presented before the courts, this method is encouraged.

d. Authentication of Documents

Whilst the ASEAN MLAT mentions that objects, evidence, or information received through MLA do not need further authentication, it is without prejudice to any request for authentication. There are provisions in the ASEAN MLAT that states what is considered to be authenticated for purposes of treaty. In the Philippines, the new amendments to the Rules of Evidence dispense the requirement of authentication for "public documents" issued in relation to a treaty or convention to which the Philippines and the source foreign country are parties to. Considering that evidence transferred through mutual legal assistance are considered "public documents" in accordance with the Philippine Rules of Evidence, then the process is now streamlined for authorities to use this evidence in courts. Further authentication would however be taken into account in relation to "private documents" such as evidence brought forward by witnesses/persons offering testimony through MLA and not necessarily already in the possession of a requested state. In this case, Philippine law provides the requirements.

In Malaysia, the MACMA provides evidence obtained through MLA requires no further proof provided certain requirements are met and the same being subjected to the Evidence Act and Criminal Procedure Code. Later on, provisions were inserted in the Evidence Act in 2012 to reflect these rules.

Although the abovementioned provisions and/or rules seem clear-cut, direct to the point, and would facilitate the importance of mutual legal assistance, this was not necessarily the case for Malaysia in one landmark case, which resulted in the acquittal of the accused. To wit, the insertions made to the Evidence Act was prompted by the problem encountered by Malaysian authorities in the usage of evidence obtained through mutual legal assistance. Said evidence was used in a criminal case before the Malaysian courts. The accused insisted that while the MACMA provides that no further proof is required, it has to be subjected still to the rules of authentication provided in the Evidence Act and/or Criminal Procedure Code. The Sessions Court (court *a quo*) sided with the accused and ruled for an acquittal. The High Court and Court of Appeal held in favor of the prosecution, stating among others, that the MACMA was a special kind of legislation that subjecting it to the requirements of the Evidence Act is counter-intutive and renders the purpose of mutual legal assistance nugatory. The Federal Court however sustained the ruling of the Sessions Court and upheld the acquittal. Thus, the Evidence Act was amended to harmonize the applicable domestic laws and hopefully avoid the same problem encountered in the case.

It can be likewise mentioned that the abovementioned case highlights the need to harmonize laws with one another because despite having clear-cut provisions in one, if the necessary amendments and rules are not made in another, then stumbling blocks or problems might ensue. This can be made worse if one does not have the specific domestic legislation to begin with. Any issue is only alleviated in the case of the Philippines due to the recent amendments to its rules of evidence, which no less than its own Supreme Court authored, to avoid possible issues vis-à-vis documents and/or evidence obtained in relation to a treaty or convention.

e. Confidentiality

Confidentiality is important in requests for MLA. The ASEAN member states have the positive duty to maintain it in the receipt and execution of requests. As regards Philippine practice, the authorities make sure that confidentiality is maintained all throughout the proceedings and would promptly involve the requesting member state should the same be compromised or otherwise endangered to be violated. This is regardless of whether the request indicates the need for confidentiality. However, should the MLA request involved be coursed through the courts due to any coercive measure to be executed, the same forms part of public record and on this degree, not covered by confidentiality. The Malaysian legislation, on the other hand, does not explicitly mention the positive duty of confidentiality but in practice seems to be highly maintained.

f. Return of Documents

Return of documents is also a procedural provision one needs to consider in terms of MLA. This can be connected to the speciality and use limitation most of the time. Once the requesting state is finished with the criminal matter subject of the MLA request and the requested state asks for the return of the object, document, or other evidence requested, the requesting state is duty-bound to return the same notwithstanding any further use it may realize for the said object, document, or evidence for any other criminal matter. This is clear in the regional instrument and the domestic law of Malaysia on MLA. Regardless of any further use of the object, evidence, or information being held on to pursuant to a MLA request, the requesting state needs to make a request anew to be able to properly use the evidence for any other purpose. There is admittedly a gap in the law vis-à-vis the Philippines but looking into the applicable law and procedure on coercive measures and the need to make the appropriate return and/or report to the courts after being granted the appropriate warrant for the execution of a coercive measure, and surrendering whatever was seized or collected during said execution, then the return of evidence would be important.

g. Specific Procedures

And last but not the least, the ASEAN MLAT and MACMA would provide specific procedures for the specific types of assistance. These include the safeguards authorities need to comply with. Countries with no specific MLA legislation like the Philippines admittedly lack this and one would need to look into different and scattered laws that could be made applicable. Thus, for the Philippines, one can look into procedures that may be found in its Rules of Court, etc. for what may be made applicable to a particular type of request. To illustrate, one could look into the procedure vis-à-vis the taking of evidence and/or voluntary statements which branch out to different possible issues and problems. The lack of streamlining and harmonization in Philippine law leads to gray areas and unsettled issues that need to be straightened out as soon as possible. There is the need for domestic legislation on mutual legal assistance to provide the parameters, baselines, and guidelines de rigeur. In other words, there is a want of harmonization and/or standardization in the domestic legal system itself.

In addition to this, one can note that the ASEAN MLAT and MACMA, while providing specific provisions, do not necessarily go with the times in terms of assistance that may be provided involving technology or online evidence. It does not provide explicitly for the interception of communications and online data, which, in Malaysia, generally occurs through informal modes of cooperation, and if ever allowed, involves offenses punishable in Malaysia and does not concern with content data. Philippine legislation, although not specifically centered on MLA, covers cooperation clearly in these areas. Additionally, it must be mentioned that even if the ASEAN MLAT would contain these types of assistance then in the catch-all provision, it would have been a good value-added if provisions have been provided for types of assistance that go ahead with technological, and general, global advances. Thus, as mentioned, the Philippines presents an odd but effective case of not having the domestic statutes covering specifically mutual legal assistance but it later turns out that it has the framework to support investigative measures not mentioned specifically in the ASEAN MLAT.

Part 2: The European Union

The present study shall now focus on another regional organization: the European Union. Following the same exercise made with the ASEAN, the following part shall be divided into different sections.

First, the present study shall explore the historical development of the European Union which shall begin from the early modern ages in Europe, including discussion on the times of war, to the historical development of the European Union itself as a regional organization. Such historical development shall focus on three stages such as what was done with the ASEAN, namely, the consolidation stage, the expansion stage, and the reconsolidation stage. Akin to the objective for the study of the historical development of the ASEAN starting from the historical development of the southeast Asian region, the earlier historical development of Europe cannot be completely ignored considering that the European Union came into being exactly because of the historical development in the region. This notwithstanding, this first portion of this section does not intend to bombard with every minute detail about European history but what would only be mentioned are those which have a nexus to understand the present day affairs of the European Union, its member states, decision and policymaking processes, and how it administers and conducts its external relations and cooperation mechanisms with other states.

Second, the present institutional and legal framework of the European Union shall be discussed, including the salient features of the regional organization, its organizational structure, and its fundamental principles, norms, and practices. As with the ASEAN part of the study, the fundamental principles, norms, and practices shall include the constitutional, normative, and decision-making principles.

Third, discussion shall focus on the cross-border movement of evidence. This portion of the study shall include the historical development of mutual legal assistance and the present EIO instrument in the regional level as well as the substantive and procedural provisions.

After centering on the regional level, it shall be followed by discussion of the respective member state level frameworks of the United Kingdom and Germany. The discussion of these respective member states shall follow the same exercise as what was done in the examination of the regional level framework.

Thereafter, the frameworks of the regional level and member state level shall be compared and contrasted with each other.

I. Regional Framework

A. Historical Development

1. Early Modern Ages

a. Europe in the Early Ages

An integral part of understanding the historical development of the European Union is understanding the historical development of Europe in general. Borrowing what has been previously mentioned in the review of the historical development of Southeast Asia and the ASEAN, understanding European history is not for the purpose of setting a barometer for the region's or the EU's future development but a review of the region's history could "illuminate the present," making clear internal dynamics within the region, and in relation to the subsequent establishment of the EU, understand how its development and decisions arguably emerge "from unique historical circumstances and will likely evolve in its own particular way."[1202]

At the outset, European civilization was a product of many things and built mainly on three (3) elements, namely, the culture from the classical antiquities of Ancient Greece and Ancient Rome, influence from Christianity, and the culture from German warriors who invaded the Roman Empire.[1203] The interaction between these three elements and its corresponding effects, which mainly occurred during the early medieval period of 300-1050, can be thought of as one of the most formative periods of European historical development.[1204]

First, civilization developed with influence from the cultures of the ancient antiquities such as the periods of Ancient Greece and Ancient Rome domination.[1205] This period has admittedly influenced greatly how

1202 See *Acharya*, Ideas, Identity and Institution-Building, p. 327; *Benda*, p. 111; *Evans*, p. 303; *Osborne*, p. 17.
1203 *Hirst*, p. 11.
1204 *Rollason*, p. 3.
1205 See *Stråth/Wagner*, p. 40.

Europe presently is. Ancient Greece was not only integral in the proliferation of various philosophical approaches and way of thinking but was also integral in the establishment of many colonies across the region.[1206] Thereafter, the rise of the Roman Empire from a city-state to an overarching empire which redefined or otherwise established the notions of imperial rule.[1207] The Roman political dominance had broad consequences for those conquered which was not only limited to political unification and/or subjugation, but also social, economic, religious, linguistic, and cultural change.[1208] These changes became generally universal throughout Europe; nonetheless, the exact cultural responses would still differ in its details, with some retaining at least parts of their own culture, religion, and languages.[1209] Understandably, any cultural change was not single-directional and one-dimensional in its process.[1210] Any cultural integration was a complex process that resulted from complex interactions between the Roman state and its representatives and the indigenous communities, the latter not being homogenous to begin with.[1211] Nevertheless, the his-

---

1206 *Hirst,* p. 11. Interestingly, Ancient Greece was able to establish colonies in what is now Turkey, North Africa, Spain, southern France, and southern Italy. It was in Italy where Ancient Greece and Ancient Rome intersected, with the latter learning from the Ancient Greece many things and even improved on the same.

1207 See *Cooper*, pp. 158-160.

1208 *Roselaar*, p. 1. See for illustration *Lulić*, pp. 25-34.

1209 *Roselaar,* pp. 1,7.

1210 See *Lulić,* p. 21.

1211 *Roselaar,* pp. 1, 11.Roselaar herein explains:
"Protoracist views about the inferiority of 'barbarian' peoples helped to justify war, subjugation, mass murder, enslavement, and exploitation on an unprecedented scale across vast territories. Although it cannot be denied that living standards on average grew and that many people profited from their incorporation in the Roman state, the violence of the conquest must not be forgotten. After the conquest, rather than striving for integration and connectedness as aims in themselves, the main goal of the Romans was to gather material wealth from the conquered territories. 'The Roman Empire was not run on altruistic lines; it developed mechanisms for the exploitation of land and people.' Although there were undoubtedly benefits to being part of the Roman state, the Romans were mostly concerned with effectively exploiting the economic and manpower resources of their subjects – at Melos, for example, or in the trade between Italy and the transalpine regions, Romans were at the head of the economic chain. Locals benefited from these economic activities but they were not in control of them. 'Romanization' therefore was a result of elite negotiation and native agency, but this agency was only available to those who survived the conquest and remained loyal to Rome, especially the elites.

torical experience was ingrained in those whom the Romans ruled, which influenced their actions as will be shown later on.

Second, Christianity and the Christian Church played a centuries-long influential and important role in European history and the development of European civilization. Christianity first developed in the Middle East and spread further into the East as well as the Roman Empire, in particular the Roman North Africa.[1212] Christianity transformed thereafter into a world religion and would spread throughout the entire Roman empire.[1213] By the fourth century it was transformed in a state religion in what is now Algeria.[1214] The entirety of Europe was eventually Christianized during the middle Ages and Ethiopia remained Christian.[1215]

Other than Christianity and the classical antiquities, historian Hirst argues that a third element in the development of European civilization were the Germanic warriors who invaded the Roman Empire in western Europe.[1216] They were said to have lived on the northern borders and in the 400s they flooded in the territories of the Roman Empire in the west.[1217] By 476 AD they had destroyed the empire in the west and it was in Britain, France, Spain, and Italy that the mixture of European civilization took shape through the rise of different small kingdoms.[1218]

The three elements formed the foundation on which European civilization was built. For purposes of understanding European historical development vis-à-vis the subject matter at hand (development of international cooperation and/or mutual legal assistance), there is no need to delve into microscopic details of history. Needless to state, the interaction of these three elements brought about not only entanglement of church and state, which led to a distinguishable congruence and assimilation of the structures, policies, and nature of one another, but also the consolidation and creation of nation-states, administrative units, and/or new territories.[1219] Thus, one can note a common denominator existing across Europe in socio-political culture.

---

xxx" See also for illustration, *Gregoratti*, pp. 239-249; *Le Quéré*, pp. 224-236; *Scopacasa*, pp. 41-42.

1212 *Rublack*, p. 577.

1213 *Hirst*, p. 22.

1214 *Rublack*, p. 577.

1215 *Rublack*, p. 577.

1216 *Hirst*, p. 23.

1217 *Hirst*, p. 23.

1218 *Collins*, pp. 173-429; *Hirst*, p. 23; *Rollason*, p. 3.

1219 *Collins*, pp. 62-63; *Hirst*, p. 25; *Rollason*, pp. 236, 279.

The influence of Christianity in Europe is widespread but not necessarily linear as illustrated by the different cultural changes for different countries and peoples.[1220] Internally, there was the difference spurring from within Christianity itself and the consequences thereof, for example, through the division of Eastern Orthodoxy from Roman Catholicism in the eleventh century, with the former settling in the Balkans, Russia, and Greek archipelago.[1221]

On an external level, one would likely be persecuted and expelled elsewhere if one was not part of the Catholic majority clique. The European Jews were a great example, being the ones closest to home.[1222] The same kind of antagonism equally applied to Muslims, Hindus, and even other forms of Christianity.[1223] Such continued in this period with Latin Christianity's encounter with Mediterranean Islam, which traditionally were already part of the European social landscape: they constituted the ruling

---

1220 See *Collins S.J*, p. 545. See for illustration on assimilation of Christianity in socio-political environment especially in Northern Europe, *Wickham*, pp. 80-98.

1221 This was through the division of Eastern Orthodoxy from Roman Catholicism in the eleventh century, with the former settling in the Balkans, Russia, and Greek archipelago. *Rublack*, p. 577.At one point in time, when Byzantine fell, papal legates were reaching out to other Christians to accept papal jurisdiction and recognition in some form in exchange of political protection which Byzantine could no longer then afford. The papacy also reached out to make amends with the Greek church (which had Constantinople as its institutional center) – the both branches of Christianity considered themselves in schism since the 12th century, but was ultimately rejected by the latter even if initially reconciliation seemed promising. See *Collins S.J*, p. 553. There was also the existence of other religions in the region. See *Rublack*, p. 577.

1222 Jews were expelled from England and from France in 1290 and 1394 respectively, and their largest concentration was in the Latin West spanning from Spain and the Rhineland to the Italian peninsula.Jews were expelled from England and from France in 1290 and 1394 respectively, and their largest concentration was in the Latin West spanning from Spain and the Rhineland to the Italian peninsula. The year 1391 is often taken as a turning point in the relationship between Christians and Jews in the Iberian Peninsula, wherein there was a shift from a previously peaceful coexistence between Christians and non-Christians to a popular and legal hostility of an increasingly inward-focused Spanish Christian society that resulted eventually to the numerous riots and anti-Jewish persecutions that occurred. The entanglement between church and state played a role with the Crown then entrusting to the Spanish Inquisition and Church in general the eradication of the Jewish religion and culture. Additionally, while the study of Hebrew was acknowledged to be important, it was often met with opposition and persecution.*Collins S.J*, p. 552.

1223 See *Terpstra*, p. 606.

class in Ottoman southeast and central Europe, while in Polish-Lithuanian Commonwealth were a substantial, enfranchised community with full religious and civil rights, and in western Europe, they comprised small but relevant communities in key trade, scholarly, slave, and diplomatic centers.[1224]

As Muslim existence in Europe has long been established, encounters with them by the Christian Church can be described as similarly complex as the one with Jews and wherein contact was normally on three (3) points: military (through eastward incursion of crusaders and westward movement of the Ottoman Turks into the Balkans), social (through the remnant Muslim peoples in the Iberian Peninsula), and commercial (through transactions with the southern and eastern rim of the Mediterranean).[1225] Notably, the military success of the Ottoman Turks had political, social, religious repercussions: by establishing a strong foothold in the Balkans by the end of the 14th century, for example, occupying the city of Constantinople, and playing a third-party role in European power politics by the middle of the 16th century.[1226] The occupation of Constantinople brought much worry as it symbolized the fall of the Roman Empire and the loss of an ancient center of Christianity.[1227]

The encounters as described above, both with other religions and other forms of Christianity, as well as different cultures and belief systems fundamentally affected European social and political order: the antagonistical patterns that befittedly describe how European Catholic responded to these differences resulted in forced conversions and purgations, numerous religious wars, merging of religion and nationalism, and forced refugees as a mass European phenomenon.[1228] Hundreds of thousands of people suffered forced migration and exile by reason of religious creed, and are often made worse by economic, political, and racial factors.[1229]

In addition to the changes on social and cultural order brought by Christianity and the Church in Europe, the rise of legitimizing bodies such as parliaments and councils gains more significance as one notes the birth of the modern state, which happened shortly before or during the time when the European elites and nobles started to gain significance in

---

1224 *Krstić*, p. 688.
1225 *Collins S.J*, pp. 552-553.
1226 *Collins S.J*, p. 553.
1227 *Collins S.J*, p. 553.
1228 *Terpstra*, p. 606.
1229 *Terpstra*, p. 606.

European society. The "modern state" was born in Western Europe in the fourteenth century as a natural child of war and taxation.[1230] A public finance system was developed to sustain the costs of war then coincided with the appearance of consolidated territories.[1231] This formed the origins of the unitary, "modern" state, which, while the term "modern" is not absolute, it often either denotes a democratic, liberal state, or connote the effectiveness of the institutional organization to "govern centrally and mobilize human and material resources."[1232]

As the foundations for the modern state were laid down, one could witness anew the political tension between the authority being exerted by monarchs and the other members of society such as the nobles and the ordinary people. During this time period, there was an effort to exercise absolute monarchism.[1233] This did not go uncontested although opposition was not always successful.[1234] Nevertheless, one could see political and legal discussions as well increased understanding in some parts of European society on what is "public good" and the direction it should take.[1235]

Moreover, one could witness papal legates reaching out to other Christian sectors within Europe. This transformed the medieval church immensely from a monolith to a "confederation of tribes and cultures that appropriated in a variety of ways the Christian faith" by the end of the 16th century.[1236] Linked with the evolution of the nation state, states started to coalesce towards princely courts and conflict over a prince's role in church affairs entered a new stage.[1237] Due to many factors, princely courts

1230 *Zmora*, p. 8.

1231 There was an endemic and incessant war between the monarchs of England and France. To able to sustain the costs of this war, which later spilled over to other parts of Europe such as the Iberian Peninsula, taxes were needed to be imposed on the constituents as current revenues were insufficient. There was lesser reliance on the existing "classical" feudal orders, which proved inadequate to meet the new circumstances. Instead, one can see how demands of monarchs impinge on the lives of those to whom the former could claim supreme jurisdiction. *Zmora*, p. 11.

1232 *Zmora*, pp. 11-12.

1233 There was an attempt for state monopoly on coercion and taxation: in France for example, lords and other nobles were prohibited from the use of physical force and a state monopoly was imposed on the levy of taxes and other duties.*Zmora*, pp. 37-38.

1234 *Zmora*, pp. 39-54.

1235 *Wickham*, p. 243.

1236 *Collins S.J*, p. 556.

1237 See *Collins S.J*, p. 556.

subsequently gained the upperhand in increasing its role in church affairs, including having a say on ecclesiastical finances and appointment of local officials, and eventually, the Church was nationalized in many European states such as France, Germany, Spain, England, etc.[1238]

One of the factors for the nationalization of the church in England and Germany was the growing Protestant Reformation, which challenged the church's existing structures and policies, pushed for reform, and consequently was able to garner support from many.[1239] Subsequently, Protestantism as both a religious and reform movement was not confined as a mere European story but had spread its influence to other parts of the world, and able to support various geographies of adherence, alliances between church and state, patterns of adherence, inter-faith relations, among others.[1240]

b. Building Empires and Colonies: East-West Relationship

Together with the early foundations of the European socio-political-cultural order that more or less still exists until today, one can also note the heavy influence the Roman Empire had on European structure as it has provided posterity with "rich and eclectic legacy" – from architecture to engineering, to the government structure and welfare – which merited emulation and admiration throughout the years.[1241] The Roman Empire expressed itself as an universal empire not sharing space with other political entities and only saw those outside its borders as barbarians.[1242]

The Romans also were said to have influenced the hegemonic rhetoric later espoused by European colonizers.[1243] While not being the first imperialists of the Western World, the Romans nevertheless were the first to "adopt a sophisticated language that justified interventionalist expansionism under a veneer of altruism and even humanitarism," even if their true intentions were far from being altruistic or benevolent.[1244] They were also seen to be fond of informal imperialism wherein instead of preferring

---

1238 *Collins S.J*, p. 556.
1239 *Collins S.J*, pp. 556-557, 558-566. See also *Rublack*, pp. 573-576.
1240 *Rublack*, pp. 576-577.
1241 *Parchami*, p. 105.
1242 *Cooper*, pp. 158-159.
1243 *Cooper*, p. 158; *Parchami*, p. 105.
1244 *Parchami*, pp. 105, 106-113.

direct rule and territorial annexation, they used existing sociopolitical structures to control and exploit.[1245]

In line with this, the period between approximately 1450-1500 and 1800 has been referred to as the early modern epoch of European history and there was a growing relationship of Europe to the world during this period through different voyages of exploration and the beginnings of the so-called "global age" especially with regard commerce.[1246] This period marked also the beginning of the colonization and/or spread of imperialism by the European states in Asian and African countries, wherein more or less the Roman influence was visible in this exercise.[1247] These explorations and subsequent colonizations ended up in many parts of the world, including Africa and Asia, where the Westerners were particularly lured by trade, economic gain, or generally establishing a power stronghold.[1248]

During this time period, Europe was coincidentally broken down into nation-states, which dealt with the limits of state expansion, lack of resources, and a high demand for security and domination over each other, driving them to seek power and wealth overseas.[1249] There was thus motivation to explore and/or colonize through trade competition, great

---

1245 *Parchami*, p. 105. See also *Cooper*, pp. 158-160.

1246 *Fernández-Armesto*, pp. 184-191; *Scott*, pp. 1, 3.

1247 *Cotterell*, p. 239; *Tilman*, p. 17. See for example *Cooper*, pp. 159, 163-168.

1248 Exploration around the globe started as early as the 15th century, the Spanish and Portuguese were the first European states at the onset of the 16th century that began to colonize other countries. It showed that the Spanish and Portuguese conquests could be seen as defining spaces of empire, although they were not necessarily extensions of national power but signaled the beginnings of early western European empires. Forging overseas territories (or empires) after a period of conflict and dealing with domestic upheaval, Spain and Portugal expanded westwards and eastwards from the Iberian Peninsula and through circumnavigational endeavors of various kinds literally around the globe, such as the voyages of Vasco de Gama and Ferdinand Magellan. It was the Portuguese who first colonized parts of North Africa in 1415 and later ended up as also the first colonizers of some parts of India and the Southeast Asian region, when they captured Mallorca in 1511. The former was followed by the Dutch and the Spaniards which later on superseded the Portuguese as strong European powers in the region. The Spaniards began to colonize the Philippines in 1559. The Dutch followed in around 1606-1609 through the Dutch East India Company or the so-called VOC. See *Cotterell*, pp. 240-268; *Ricklefs/Lockhart/Lau, et al.*, pp. 165-166; *Solidum*, p. 4. See also for territories explored and later occupied *Christie*, p. 6; *Cotterell*, pp. 240-268; *Fernández-Armesto*, pp. 184-190; *SarDesai*, pp. 140-141; *Tarling*, pp. 22, 40-41.

1249 *Fernández-Armesto*, pp. 177-178; *Healy/Dal Lago*, p. 4; *Sèbe*, p. 125; *Tarling*, p. 22.

wealth accumulation, cultural expression, or the need to secure and extend political power.[1250]

The age of absolutism coincided with colonization and exploration in the 17th century, specifically during 1650 to 1720.[1251] While the first signs of absolutism occurred in the 13th to 14th century through efforts to have state monopoly on coercion and taxation, absolutism came into full throttle later on when rulers of continental Europe extended their powers.[1252] Although some western sovereigns had representative bodies such as parliaments, councils, etc., sovereigns of France, Prussia, Russia, Austria, and Sweden, in particular, became absolute rulers who are above challenge from within the state itself.[1253] Asserting a supreme right to maintain order, proclaim laws and levy taxes through a centralized and efficient bureaucracy, absolutism during this era was a response or effort to reassert public order and coercive state authority after several years of war that badly disrupted trade and agricultural production, which contributed to social and political chaos.[1254] Further, the age of absolutism coincided with the concept of "balance of power" gradually taking hold among the many European courts, wherein great powers should be in equilibrium and one power should not be allowed to become too powerful.[1255]

Consequently, the creation of the modern state came into fruition during the said age of absolutism. Through extending their respective authorities and expanding dynastic territories, state bureaucracies were developed and long standing armies were established.[1256] Thus, even if one can say that the foundations for the modern state were laid down during the 13th or 14th century when the long-lasting and pervasive wars started between European nations, the birth of the modern state became clearer in the 18th century.

At the beginning of the 19th century, the British, French, and Americans landed in Southeast Asian shores and colonized most of the territories.[1257] Also, Europe witnessed the rise of the first French empire or as others posit, the first modern empire, which studies would show was a blend of

---

1250 *Christie*, pp. 3-8; *Fernández-Armesto*, pp. 173-179.
1251 *Merriman*, p. 274.
1252 *Merriman*, p. 274.
1253 *Merriman*, p. 274.
1254 *Merriman*, pp. 275, 277.
1255 *Merriman*, p. 316.
1256 *Merriman*, p. 323.
1257 *Reid*, A History of Southeast Asia, pp. 123-124; *Tarling*, pp. 25-26.

old and new imperial regimes.[1258] Whilst the Napoleonic empire made different socio-political contributions across Europe, for purposes of this study, it is significant to note that a self-conscious discussion during the 1815 Congress of Vienna about a post-Napoleonic future after the end of this empire's reign.[1259] With the said Congress still hinging on the aftermath of the Napoleonic empire, it claimed to have restored legitimate sovereigns, reduced the number of small states, and allowed France to remain a large one, while concurrently making declarations about state morality.[1260] It was not clear however with this 1815 Congress on whether the new Europe would be a Europe of nations through the participation of British, Germanic, Russian, and Austrian-Hungarian empires.[1261] It was clear though that there was by post-Vienna Congress a rise in industry, and subsequently, wealth and power, though asymmetrically distributed.[1262]

Interestingly, with the industrial progress being experienced by Europe during these years, the marriage between throne and altar came to an abrupt end when Europe was convulsed by revolution in 1830 to 1931 and at a bigger scale never seen before in European history.[1263] In the meantime, the idea of a European-wide consensus was later reinforced in the Conferences in Berlin and Brussels in 1884 and 1890, respectively, which set out rules of the expansion of overseas empires and definitions of boundaries.[1264] By this time, there was acknowledgment that empire-making and eventually, world domination, was part of 19th century European history.[1265]

Exploration and colonization in Africa started in around 1879 through King Leopold II of Belgium acting as a private citizen and organizing the Congo Company to explore Central Africa.[1266] Soon after, other European countries followed by conquering and competing for other parts of the African continent.[1267] Subsequently, the European powers and America divided the entire Pacific region in their quest for economic advantage

---

1258 *Cooper*, p. 168.
1259 *Cooper*, p. 171; *Merriman*, pp. 587, 589-592.
1260 *Cooper*, p. 171; *Merriman*, pp. 592-595.
1261 *Cooper*, p. 171.
1262 *Merriman*, pp. 844-857; *Stråth/Wagner*, p. 7.
1263 *Aston*, p. 331.
1264 *Cooper*, p. 171.
1265 *Cooper*, p. 171; *Stråth/Wagner*, p. 7.
1266 *Merriman*, p. 959.
1267 *Merriman*, pp. 959-977.

and political power.[1268] By 1913 or shortly before the First World War began, one could see that in Southeast Asia alone, the French colonized Indochina; the British, the Malay states and Brunei; and the Dutch, Indonesia.[1269] Japan was the only country in Asia which maintained real independence, because even if Thailand escaped imperialism and remained independent, it was at the cost of losing some of its territories to the British and French.[1270] By this same time period, the Americans colonized the Philippines after the latter declared in 1868 independence from the Spaniards (which colonized the former for 333 years).[1271]

The relationship of Europe during this colonial experience with its colonies became intrinsic to the former's identity during this period.[1272] Moreover, the European colonizers could be described as producers of norms and changes in the countries they have colonized, which is a trait carried on until the present with the European Union, as will be discussed in the next chapters. In relation to this, there was internally in Europe during this time period a continuous evolution of patterns of thought and there were coinciding movements in Europe that reflected human progress such as the granting of more democratic rights, etc.[1273] Noticeably however was that such ideas of human progress, etc. did not necessarily translate to what the actual circumstances were.[1274] As Deutsch illustrated, there are two kinds of European reality: there was unprecedented colonial expansion in other parts of the world such as Asia and Africa while democratic rights are being granted to male citizens in most European countries.[1275] And while the promotion of industrial-wage-labor-based economies was flourishing, one can equally witness the use of chattel slavery, forced labor, or indentured-labor-based ones somewhere else.[1276] In this respect, any true sense or idea of human progress or democratization that occurred post-colonialization should not be attributed to the

---

1268 *Merriman*, pp. 977-984.

1269 *Cotterell*, pp. 239-268; *SarDesai*, pp. 87-132; *Tarling*, pp. 39-41. See also *SarDesai*, p. 140.

1270 *Merriman*, p. 577; *Solidum*, p. 4. See for further information, *Ricklefs/Lockhart/Lau, et al.*, p. 167; *SarDesai*, pp. 133-139; *Tarling*, pp. 69-74.

1271 *Ricklefs/Lockhart/Lau, et al.*, pp. 227-237.

1272 *Kennedy*, p. 20.

1273 *Healy/Dal Lago*, p. 3. For further illustrations see *King*, pp. 3-26; *Robertson*, pp. 141-165.

1274 *Deutsch*, p. 36; *Scott*, p. 3.

1275 *Deutsch*, p. 36.

1276 *Deutsch*, p. 36; *Pacquette*, pp. 296-300.

European colonizers themselves, even if sometimes it was a legacy attributed to them, but instead through human progress and democratization on the part of the colonized occurring as reflex to the colonizers' stimuli of aggression and inhumane treatment.[1277]

This duality of reality has been created in the first place between the European world and its colonies from how the European colonizers viewed their colonized states. This same point of view quite explains equally the notion of European leadership in the success of its explorations and colonizations in general. It was not uncommon for European colonizers to imbibe the idea of how the countries they colonized, especially Africa, constituted the barbarian "other" and not part of the "modern World" – even to the point that one European explorer in 1830 even said how Africa lied on the threshold of world history but was not part of it.[1278] Indeed, the sense of European superiority – the sense that its societies were in some way ahead of all others – was strong and widespread – even if in hindsight, there is not much difference between social and economic life in Europe and other parts of the world, particularly Asia.[1279] Significantly, the practices and norms of the European Union with respect to its external actions is highly indicative of this belief, as will be further discussed in the next following chapters, when it flexes its normative powers towards others, by projecting its values and beliefs – even to the point of unsolicited intervention.[1280]

As to why this paradigm was necessary, it was seemingly to legitimize or rationalize their actions: it was "predominantly self-congratulatory" and made Europeans feel good and had little to do with the colonized countries themselves.[1281] This notably resonates what the Romans used before to justify interventionalist expansionism, with the sugar coating of altruism and humanitarianism.[1282] Thus, with such a mentality, colonial enthusiasts in Europe took upon themselves to embark on their colonial

1277 See *Deutsch*, p. 36.

1278 *Bose*, p. 47.

1279 *Stråth/Wagner*, pp. 4-5, 6.

1280 One need not look further than the example given in the introduction as to how the EU after the Cold War has started projecting its values and beliefs to the ASEAN and ASEAN member states by introducing discussion on human rights and democratization together with aids and economic assistance, which the ASEAN believed to be undue intervention.

1281 *Deutsch*, p. 35.

1282 See *Deutsch*, pp. 36, 37.

project because they purported the idea that they needed to civilize or enlighten those which allegedly needed it.[1283]

This idea more or less influenced how colonization brought new definitions and demarcations. In Asia, one could witness changes to existing national borders, the creation of modern political and administrative institutions, establishment of some basic parameters of economic systems, as well as industrialization and modern internal development through the introduction of Western laws, urban planning, educational institutions, immigration policies, money markets, location of administrative centers, as well as transportation and communication lines.[1284] In addition, the colonized states were fortified against neighbors thought to be hostile, were made part of an international network of posts subject to a single authority, and governed by regularly replaced administrators.[1285] This could have possibly mirrored the development in Europe of the "modern state", through the growth in authority of the central governments, which was evident through its growing agencies and responsibilities, higher fiscal income, and much enlarged armed forces.[1286]

While these observations might be equally applicable to the African colonized states, accounts of violence were more known. Despite the image of bringing enlightenment and civilization, what was initially seen from European colonizers were instead violence and abuses. Colonizers were said to not restrain from violent means should it be deemed necessary to curtail activities in view of the values it wanted to espouse.[1287] Moreover, slavery continued to be a practice in African colonies and later on, colonizers had no qualms to forcefully recruit people to send off during the First World War under the notion of empire as a legitimate polity in which all members, including the colonized, had a stake.[1288]

Indeed, terror and violence tactics regardless of whether in Asia or Africa – mass slaughters, collective punishments, etc. – were defining char-

1283 *Parchami,* p. 105. See also for explanation of "civilizing mission", *Merriman,* pp. 995-996.

1284 See *Deutsch,* p. 37.

1285 See *SarDesai,* pp. 141, 146; *Tilman,* p. 17.

1286 See *Reid,* A History of Southeast Asia, p. 121.

1287 *Scott,* p. 3. There were accounts of the South African War, King Leopold's Congo policies, German atrocities in South-West Africa, and persistence of large-scale African resistance to repressive forms of colonial rule and instances of "ferocious economic exploitation" that had ran counter claims on the purpose and benefits of the colonial project. See also *Deutsch,* p. 38.

1288 *Cooper,* p. 185; *Deutsch,* p. 38.

acteristics of colonization and imperialism to maintain control.[1289] This "terrify-and-move-on" aspect of colonial rule nonetheless reflected weaknesses of routinized administration and policing employed by European colonizers and the need to keep administrative costs low at all times.[1290] At the end, notions of "modernity" and "European civilization were like a contagious disease to the African people and the consequent de-tribalization in Africa haunted European imagination, so much so that colonizers revisited their policies."[1291] The result was to perhaps adopt a strategy of "indirect rule" – especially for those under the British administration (something the British learned from the Romans) – which still encourage economic development (for government revenue tax purposes and benefits of European companies) but to maintain African political institutions, customs and traditions, and even restore the same if needed in areas destroyed by European rule.[1292]

This notwithstanding, and regardless of whether being in Asia or Africa, the colonial experience and the changes it brought consequently caused economic dislocation and distress and had the undesirable effect of actually lowering the economic well-being of people.[1293] Traditional structure and values of rural society was undermined intentionally – ultimately disrupting its economy and way of life, resulting in changes in the social strata.[1294] With the introduction of modern internal development and other forms of innovation, most colonizers reinforced distinction between elites and masses, and social distances were prescribed, which defined and delineated social classes.[1295] In Africa, for example, social research showed relentless poverty and insecurity in African cities, with evidence of joblessness, low skill levels among workers and presence of "large floating populations" in cities.[1296] In addition, colonization brought the non-development of a common language and past, which, if combined with insecurities of an urban life, prompted people to maintain rural ties instead.[1297] Any quest to fit African urbanization and industrialization into any universal model was strong but there were too many countertenden-

---

1289 *Cooper*, p. 157.
1290 *Cooper*, p. 157.
1291 *Deutsch*, p. 38.
1292 *Deutsch*, p. 39.
1293 See *Parchami*, p. 105.
1294 *SarDesai*, p. 161.
1295 *Reid*, A History of Southeast Asia, pp. 130-132; *SarDesai*, p. 161.
1296 *Cooper*, p. 39.
1297 *Cooper*, p. 39.

cies and complexities that resulted from colonization that complicates the situation.[1298]

Furthermore, the colonial experience more or less threatened the moral well-being of societies and traditions, especially since in most accounts, colonialism reinforced a different kind of cultural hybridity as well as heterogeneity amongst their colonized states.[1299] As Tilman narrates for Southeast Asia, for example, that while the Portuguese did not exert too much influence on their colonies, the French had much more impact on Vietnam, Kampuchea, and Laos; the British on Burma, Malaysia, and Singapore; the Spanish and Americans on the Philippines; and the Dutch, on Indonesia.[1300] Some colonizers were principally governed by considerations of religion with religious and civil-political authorities heavily intertwined, forcefully converting their colonies to religion such as Catholicism.[1301] As Collins described, "ecclesiastical efforts progressed hand in hand with the globalization of European political and economic power," even pointing out to the initial motivation of Christopher Columbus to outflank the Muslims by circumnavigating the globe while at the same time regaining Jerusalem for Christendom.[1302]

1298 *Cooper*, p. 39.

1299 *Pacquette*, p. 280; *Tilman*, p. 17.

1300 *Deutsch*, p. 39; *Reid*, A History of Southeast Asia, pp. 130-132.

1301 *Tilman*, p. 17.

1302 *Collins S.J*, pp. 553-554. Ecclesiastical efforts were also used by the Portuguese when they started colonizing in the eastern hemisphere, as they acted under the imprimatur of the Pope to "christianize the heathens of the world, and when they conducted a comprehensive inquisition in Goa, India in the beginning of 1560 to assure the Church that converts were not reverting to their previous religions. *Reid*, A History of Southeast Asia, pp. 112-113; *Ricklefs/Lockhart/Lau, et al.*, pp. 194-195; *SarDesai*, pp. 70-73, 82. The Spaniards were no different when they were given the imprimatur to conquer Africa in efforts to stage a war against Islam therein. The Spaniards were equally guilty of forcefully converting their colonial subjects to Christianity, like what they did when they colonized the Philippines in the 16th century. And aside from converting, colonizers like the Portuguese in the name of Christianity intervened on the laws of the colonized in efforts to make them better Christian subjects. On the other hand, in the African continent, European ideals and systems were brought in but the European colonizers like the British and French were mainly motivated by their profitable presence out of slave trade, for example, as well as their own scientific curiosity, economic interests, and existing geopolitical rivalries with one another. See *Reid*, A History of Southeast Asia, pp. 112-113; *Ricklefs/Lockhart/Lau/Reyes/Aung-Thwin*, pp. 194-195; *SarDesai*, pp. 70-73, 82

At this juncture imperial expansion or colonial experience was not the only theme in Europe's agenda. In between, ideas for an integrated Europe have been articulated before the arrival of the 20th century, which includes the establishment of an European Parliament by English Quaker, William Penn, after the state mosaic in 1693.[1303] However, strong sentiments of nationalism and great power politics overtook these propositions.[1304] Nationalism and great power politics notwithstanding, one could witness a continuous push and pull movement between integration and disintegration among the nation-states and within the international order.[1305] Two areas with such kind of movement is on economic integration and the transnational dimension in the work of legal scholars: the Anglo-French treaty of 1860, for example, inaugurated a period of commercial treaty-making so extensive, while on the other hand, there is a vast recognition that the power to create law was not exclusive to the states but also among a commonality of vital interests among a plurality of subjects and the consciousness of such commonality.[1306]

Moreover, the calls for the establishment of a European federation was prominent during the 19th century, with some pointing out that it was for a practical value of helping shape public opinion.[1307] In the late 19th century, an English historian, Sir John Robert Seeley, even considered the prospect of a United States of Europe, following the footsteps of the United States of America.[1308] Despite forwarding the prediction that Russia and the United States of America would overtake Europe in the future, the vision of empires and nationalistic interests nonetheless prevailed.[1309]

c. The Times of War

The campaign for European unity and/or integration was not over just yet as the following circumstances would show:

When the First World War began, the myth of European imperial superiority and invulnerability was seemingly debunked.[1310] Included herewith

1303 *Healy/Dal Lago*, p. 5.
1304 *Craig/de Búrca*, p. 4.
1305 *Stirk*, p. 12.
1306 *Stirk*, p. 13.
1307 *Stirk*, p. 17.
1308 *Stirk*, p. 17.
1309 *Stirk*, p. 17.
1310 *Stirk*, p. 17.

was the crumbling down of the purported reputation of natural sovereignty of European culture, its economic rationality, or political mastery.[1311] At the same time, it did not help that in throwing support to the Allies, the United States chose to put an ideological sugarcoating over the aims of the Allies during the war.[1312] If the Allies were fighting for the right to self-determination for all the peoples of Europe, it should not be surprising that the colonized states would demand for such right as well.[1313] Moreover, the disastrous effects to Africa brought by the First World War became known: there was not only the forced recruitment of African soldiers, as mentioned earlier, to die in the trenches of Flanders but there was also the incompetent and brutal conduct of war in East Africa that allegedly resulted in the death and serious injury of a quarter of a million African civilians.[1314] This resulted in Europe not only being confronted with the problems of the war but also problems in their colonized states.[1315]

Not long after, the Japanese interregnum and Second World War happened. Acting through the "Greater East Asia Prosperity Sphere" campaign, Japan conquered the Western colonies in Asia, particularly the southeast portion, as an alternative source of supply to sustain itself during its war against China and eventual conflict with Western powers.[1316] Japan eventually allied itself with Germany and Italy in the Second World War, and brought the war to the Southeast Asian region.[1317] This consequently caused problems with Europe, or the allies in general despite for example the establishment of America and Britain of the Supreme Allied Command in Southeast Asia ("SEAC") in August 1943.[1318] With the Japanese interregnum dismantling European and American colonial administrations, allied supporters in the colonized countries found themselves imprisoned or punished for continuing to support European and/or American endeavors.[1319]

1311 *Beeson*, p. 8; *SarDesai*, pp. 204-205.
1312 *Deutsch*, p. 39.
1313 *Christie*, p. 11.
1314 *Christie*, p. 11.
1315 *Deutsch*, p. 39.
1316 *Christie*, p. 11. See also *Cotterell*, p. 270; *Ricklefs/Lockhart/Lau, et al.*, p. 293.
1317 *Reid*, A History of Southeast Asia, p. 323.
1318 See *Cotterell*, pp. 270-280; *Reid*, A History of Southeast Asia, p. 324; *Ricklefs/Lockhart/Lau, et al.*, pp. 293-294.
1319 *Solidum*, p. 5.

The Japanese interregnum had an undeniable impact to the process of decolonization in Asia.[1320] To illustrate, there was the opportunity to communicate and cooperate with rural communities and espouse ideas of an independent nation – something unspeakable, even seditious, under European or American colonial rule.[1321] In the meantime, any brutality the Japanese exhibited opened further the consciousness to rid the region of foreign overlords:[1322] foreign lords did not bring anything but harm and danger. To the same degree, African colonies were demystified of the European superiority both in political and military power as well as in culture to the point that the former did not want anything to do anymore with their European colonizers, urging them in the long run to be emboldened to stand ground against colonialism.[1323]

Both the First and Second World Wars brought with them devastating effects and ruined sites – both figuratively and literally – at its helm that needed to be reconstructed addressed, among others, by new communities or ideologies.[1324] On the external aspect, Western colonizers wanted to take back the colonies and territories taken from them during the Second World War but they did not only lack the needed resources to do so but after the war, there was also a differently charged spirit of nationalism and opposition to colonial rule that prevented re-colonization.[1325] There was shaking of European self-confidence and for both Africans and Asians, there was the experience of contingency of imperial rule.[1326]

Despite this, some Western colonizers like the French, British, and Dutch had difficulties letting go and thus, negotiations and revolutions anew and all in efforts to gain independence occurred.[1327] Stating it dif-

---

1320 *Reid,* A History of Southeast Asia, pp. 324, 326; *Ricklefs/Lockhart/Lau, et al.*, p. 294.

1321 *Beeson,* p. 8; *SarDesai,* p. 204. There were also student leaders, nationalists, activists, and politicians who were able to voice out their ideas, which would have not been plausible under colonial rule. See for how transition to independence movements were supported by the Japanese, *Ricklefs/Lockhart/Lau, et al.*, pp. 300-316.

1322 *Reid,* A History of Southeast Asia, pp. 327-331. See also *Ricklefs/Lockhart/Lau, et al.*, p. 316.

1323 See *Deutsch,* p. 39.

1324 *Ioannou-Naoum-Wokoun/Ruelling*, p. 100; *Reid,* A History of Southeast Asia, p. 326.

1325 *Couperus/Kaal*, p. 1.

1326 *Cooper,* p. 187.

1327 See *Christie,* p. 16; *Cotterell,* pp. 287-291; *Ricklefs/Lockhart/Lau, et al.*, p. 317; *Tarling,* p. 120.

ferently, the colonized were willing to take up arms just to remove themselves from the clutches of their European colonizers and gain their autonomy without further foreign intervention. Asian countries subsequently gained their independence in from 1946 to 1957.[1328] Moreover, Asian colonies were organizing themselves to better deal with continuous problems brought by colonization.[1329]

As regards African colonized states, there were equally various social and political movements – even stages of civil unrest and war – while asking for equivalence one after another, as well as the general desire for cultural and political autonomy "conjugated with the quest for material improvement."[1330] One can cite incidents such as the Algerian War and the politics of decolonization in sub-Saharan Africa as examples.[1331] At first, colonizers such as the British and French tried to spin colonial rule out with a development idea for the region but colonial rule eventually fizzled out as there was revolutionary confrontation and the escalation of demands that "threatened to turn the rhetoric of imperial legitimacy into assertion of equivalent rights, voice, and standard of living."[1332] At the end of the day, especially in the context of a postwar decade, the costs of maintaining an empire and instilling development and social democracy were high.[1333] Eventually colonial rule in Africa also fell, with its interventionist movement collapsing first.[1334]

Within Europe on the other hand, there was as regards the build-up of society a transition from a society of communities to that of individuals, which is often referred to as a paradigm shift from a community-based society to an individual-based society.[1335] Within Europe, the notion of community permeated plans of rebuilding wherein the premise was that community is the social glue through which people tried to come to terms with the devastation brought by war, "where they tried to heal their wounds or urge for the redemption of past injustices." Accordingly, the many panaceas for the moral degeneration of humankind, which included

1328 See *Christie*, p. 16; *Cotterell*, pp. 291-294; *Ricklefs/Lockhart/Lau, et al.*, p. 317.
1329 See *Acharya*, Whose Ideas Matter?, p. 34; *Cooper*, p. 188.
1330 *Cooper*, p. 38.
1331 *Cooper*, p. 38.
1332 *Cooper*, p. 187.
1333 *Cooper*, p. 188.
1334 *Cooper*, p. 188.
1335 *Ricklefs/Lockhart/Lau, et al.*, pp. 321-345.

mass atrocities, etc., rested on a myriad of notions of what community is.[1336]

Aside from the foregoing, one could witness a gradual process in the late 1940s of the division of Europe into two spheres – the western was linked to the United States while the eastern was linked to the Soviet Union.[1337] If one may recall, this splitting into two world powers was already predicted by John Seeley when he proposed the concept of the United States of Europe.[1338] The Soviet Union, through its leader Josef Stalin, wanted to ascertain territorial security against future attacks, especially from Germany.[1339] He thought that the best way to achieve the same is to have buffer states in Eastern Europe and a disabled Germany.[1340] Poland was the most important buffer state of them all, given that it was through said country that Germany was able to conquer the Soviet Union in 1941.[1341] Through Poland and other buffer states, the Soviet Union would be able to build a sphere of influence.[1342] Likewise, Stalin thought of disabling Germany through various reparation payments in addition to economic and military restrictions that would impede German recovery for at least ten to fifteen years.[1343]

The United States was no different in pursuing goals in Europe as the war ended in 1945. It wanted to consolidate peace and prosperity in a new European-American relationship, which in turn would increase America's global influence, both economically and otherwise.[1344] This is very compatible with American foreign policy, which has always been to "maintain an external environment conducive to the survival and prosperity of the nation's domestic institutions."[1345] The methods employed in pursuit of the same has been notably varied and diversified. As Gaddis described, "methods employed in this search for security have varied considerably over the years: utopian efforts to reform the entire structure of international relations have coexisted with cold-blooded attempts to wield power within that system; military establishments have been both massive and

---

1336 *Scott*, p. 3.
1337 *Couperus/Kaal*, p. 1; *Ioannou-Naoum-Wokoun/Ruelling*, p. 100.
1338 *Stirk*, p. 17.
1339 *Messenger*, p. 36.
1340 *Messenger*, p. 37.
1341 *Messenger*, p. 37.
1342 *Messenger*, p. 37.
1343 *Messenger*, p. 37.
1344 *Messenger*, p. 37.
1345 *Messenger*, p. 37.

minute; interventionism has alternated with isolationism; multilateralism with rigid economic nationalism."[1346]

The differing views as above stated were highlighted during the tripartite agreements reached in 1945 in Yalta and Potsdam, respectively.[1347] In Yalta, Stalin wanted Soviet Union-friendly governments to be established in Poland and other Eastern European states.[1348] In other words, he wanted to build spheres of influence, which for all intents and purposes is a form of integration. The United States and Britain did not have qualms about the Soviet Union gaining influence in Eastern Europe and they even suggested that the communist party Lublin Poles in Poland could help in such endeavor.[1349] And although US President Roosevelt was in favor of Soviet-friendly Poland with some form of Soviet influence, its government should not merely be a Soviet puppet but still be able to maintain a level of independence in domestic policy.[1350] For example, there ought to be elections to give a chance to non-communist parties in Poland to go against Lublin Poles for government positions.[1351] Basically, Roosevelt wanted the Soviet Union to be discreet in establishing control over other countries, inasmuch as under the façade of democratic procedures.[1352] Additionally, Roosevelt wanted Stalin to abandon further attempts to spread communism outside the Soviet Union.[1353]

The Yalta conference resulted in the Declaration on Liberated Europe, which laid down how freed states from German control would go back to normal political lives and included a statement about how free elections were imperative.[1354] It is to be understood that even if the Declaration refers to "Europe", it actually refers only to Poland and the eastern European states.[1355] With respect to occupied Germany, there has been agreement in the same conference that the Allied Control Commission would be created as a form of cooperation among America, Britain, France, and the Soviet Union in running of the country.[1356] Last but not the least,

1346 *Gaddis*, p. 386.
1347 *Gaddis*, p. 387.
1348 *Messenger*, p. 37.
1349 *Messenger*, p. 37.
1350 *Messenger*, p. 37.
1351 *Messenger*, p. 37.
1352 *Messenger*, p. 37.
1353 *Gaddis, p. 388.*
1354 *Gaddis*, p. 388.
1355 *Messenger*, p. 38.
1356 *Messenger*, p. 38.

there was likewise agreement on key Soviet demands on its right to reparations.[1357]

In spite of the abovementioned agreement, cooperation did not wholly work due to the differing interpretations of the above involved countries.[1358] Differences in interpretation prompted the United States thereafter to look at Soviet Union's actions as litmus tests on the latter's true intentions, on whether cooperation is compatible with American national security goals.[1359] It became apparent soon after that the Soviet Union equated security with an insatiable craving for control over territory and states, which would ultimately undermine cooperation.[1360] And rightly so: Stalin never gave any indication the Soviet Union would make good the conditions agreed upon during the Yalta Conference.[1361] And when then US Secretary of State James Brynes was chastened for recognizing both Bulgarian and Romanian communist governments, it became apparent that the United States thought that the Soviet Union was failing the litmus tests miserably.[1362]

The events that followed illustrate the importance of trust among states for integration to be successful and effective. At this point in time, Germany was admittedly at the heart of changing threat perceptions of American policy-makers.[1363] Even if the Potsdam conference resulted in an agreement that the four powers have autonomy of decision in their respective spheres of influence, the seeds of distrust could not anymore be disregarded.[1364] Such distrust grew further in 1946, when George Kennan sent a "Long Telegram" from Moscow to the State Department in Washington, stating therein that the insecurity of Soviet leaders, together with the ideologies of Communism, sets the Soviet Union on an expansionist course.[1365] These worries were arguably valid as there was not only an

---

1357 *Messenger,* p. 38.

1358 *Messenger,* p. 38. For example, Stalin got the idea that he could make Poland a satellite state but the Americans however expected an election to be held immediately. When' the Truman administration succeeded Roosevelt's in the US, it accepted the foreign policy of allowing the Soviet Union to establish influence in Eastern Europe and that elections in Poland would not likely ensue.

1359 *Messenger,* p. 38.

1360 *Messenger,* p. 38.

1361 See *Messenger,* p. 38.

1362 *Gaddis,* p. 388.

1363 *Messenger,* p. 38.

1364 *Messenger,* p. 39.

1365 *Messenger,* p. 39.

employ of a "crude combination of internal subversion and external pressure" that allowed the Soviet Union to control countries such as Poland, Bulgaria, Romania, East Germany, Turkey, Iran, and Manchuria between 1944 and 1946, but there was also, among other things, the revival of an international communist movement, which showed clear prospects of unlimited international expansion.[1366] Truman's suspicious and worries were further fueled when he brought in Winston Churchill at Westminster College in Missouri, and the latter gave his famous speech about the Soviet Union placing an "iron curtain" all over Eastern Europe.[1367] This meant that the West had to act quickly to prevent the Soviets from expanding their influence further.[1368]

The tone of American policy further changed when Britain found itself in economic crisis and pleaded the United States to fill in the responsibility of supporting Turkey and Greece.[1369] There came a clearer realization for the United States: to be able to have a congenial international environment, Europe should not fall in the hands of a single, hostile state and it was imperative to ensure a balance of powers within the region.[1370] In agreeing to fill in Britain's shoes, America showed that it felt obligated to defend democracy wherever it was threatened by Soviet and Communist expansion.[1371] This eventually became known as the Truman doctrine and the prevailing theme of the Cold War.[1372] Subsequently, the aid given by the US to Turkey and Greece represented the containment policy in action: this was the first situation in which special appropriations were necessary to carry out the United States' program.[1373]

It has to be clarified however that despite such strong words from Truman, the United States never meant to equate the totalitarianism being seen from the Soviets as that of Nazi Germany prior to and during the Second World War, especially as evinced by its actions and participation in the recent Second World War.[1374] Despite the ideological differences, the United States has expected cooperation from the Soviet Union in re-

---

1366 *Gaddis*, pp. 388-389; *Messenger*, p. 39.
1367 *Gaddis*, p. 388.
1368 *Messenger*, p. 39.
1369 *Messenger*, p. 39.
1370 *Gaddis*, p. 389; *Messenger*, p. 39.
1371 *Gaddis*, p. 386.
1372 *Gaddis*, p. 386; *Messenger*, p. 39. See also *Ioannou-Naoum-Wokoun/Ruelling*, p. 100.
1373 *Messenger*, p. 39.
1374 *Gaddis*, p. 389; *Messenger*, p. 39.

constructing a peaceful postwar world.[1375] The United States however felt that the direction Stalin was bringing the Soviet Union into was making cooperation impossible and incompatible with the US foreign policy of ensuring balance of power in Europe.[1376]

In the meantime, Germany remained at the epicenter of policies of reconstruction and revitalization, especially with respect to the Western allies, and dealing with the said country after the war was an influential factor in the Cold War and European integration.[1377] Disagreements over Germany's reconstruction coincided with the Cold War and by then, the Americans argued that Germany needed to be restored quickly even if the same means losing Soviet cooperation.[1378] Plans were then made to combine the British and American zones to improve economic development in Germany, to which the French were initially aloof.[1379] Thereafter, the United States launched the Marshall Plan in June 1947 to revitalize Europe, including Germany, economically.[1380] European countries, including the Soviet Union, should work together to plan economic reconstruction, with the promise of American financial aid if such plan emerged.[1381] The Marshall Plan had many objectives in mind, including but not limited to, revitalization of the Western European economy, the diffusion of nationalism, including revitalization of German nationalism, and the need to contain possible Soviet expansion in Western Europe.[1382] Notably, the need to revitalize German nationalism was grounded on the idea that German resources were important in strengthening Western Europe.[1383] On this note, the French naturally was opposed to the thought that Germany was integral in taking Western Europe out of economic despair.[1384] Instead, French wanted to be ahead of Germany in certain industries, including steel, which was opposite to what the Marshall Plan was proposing: less about competition more on coordinating together each one's recovery measures – the initiatory steps toward integration and cooperation.[1385]

1375 *Gaddis*, p. 387.
1376 See *Gaddis*, p. 387.
1377 *Messenger*, p. 40.
1378 *Messenger*, p. 40.
1379 *Messenger*, p. 41.
1380 *Patrick*, p. 238.
1381 *Messenger*, pp. 42, 51.
1382 *Messenger*, p. 42.
1383 *Messenger*, p. 42.
1384 *Messenger*, p. 42.
1385 *Messenger*, p. 42.

It would seem that the Marshall Plan was fueling the flames at this point since the idea of unity within Europe had already shot into popularity after 1945, when various movements aimed at European integration were formed one after the other across Europe: various political families across Europe started forming organizations aimed at a federalist Europe.[1386] After the Second World War, many realized that cooperation created on a loose governmental basis, which is similar to the League of Nations and which operated in between the two world wars, could not provide a sufficient guarantee and safeguard for peaceful coexistence and development across and within the European states.[1387] Moreover, the Second World War has evinced that a state would not mind breaking existing cooperation with other countries and even starting a war should the same further its interests.[1388] Additionally, most in the western part of Europe realized after splitting up in the Second World War that Europe could become relevant again politically and economically, after suffering severe damage and loss, through integration.[1389]

In light of these realizations, regional economic cooperation seemed the viable option to boost many European countries with fragmented national markets, and also for recovering and bolstering the position occupied in the world economy.[1390] Admittedly however, these sentiments were still very much overshadowed by doubts and fears as regards integration, prompting most to prefer intergovernmental cooperation, in line with existing traditional policy-making of nation-states.[1391] Thus, when Western European officials met up in July 1947 vis-à-vis the framework laid down by the Marshall Plan on integration, they came up instead with an organization of intergovernmental nature through the establishment of the Committee on European Economic Cooperation, which later became the Organization for European Economic Cooperation ("OEEC").[1392] Although the aim of the Committee was to promote European trade, foster economic development and stability, distribute and coordinate the distribution of the aid received through the Marshall Plan,[1393] it was not what the Americans asked for because there was neither the establishment of

---

1386 *Messenger*, p. 42.
1387 *Horváth*, p. 26.
1388 *Horváth*, p. 25.
1389 *Horváth*, pp. 25-26.
1390 *Horváth*, p. 26. See also *Ioannou-Naoum-Wokoun/Ruelling*, p. 100.
1391 *Horváth*, p. 26.
1392 *Horváth*, p. 26. See also *Ioannou-Naoum-Wokoun/Ruelling*, p. 100.
1393 *Messenger*, p. 42.

strong, central institutions, nor the real sense of integrated, transnational planning for recovery.[1394]

At this point, one can already see visible traces of how the Cold War was related to the process of European integration by the manner the Soviet Union reacted to the various stages of the said process.[1395] As mentioned earlier, the Marshall Plan was meant to be inclusive of all European countries, including the Soviet Union. To the surprise of other participants, representatives of the Soviet Union were present during the July 1947 meeting and as Messenger explained, there are good reasons for their attendance: the fact that the Cold War has not completely set in, which makes reconciliation still possible albeit the chances are slim, and that the Soviet Union would benefit themselves should they take part of the American monies for their own rehabilitation.[1396]

The attendance was however short-lived with the seemingly self-reinforcing reaction by the Soviet Union to walk out of the July 1947 meeting in response to intelligence reports that the Marshall Plan was meant to "close ranks" among the United States and its western allies to ultimately break Europe into two blocs.[1397] Such closing of ranks by the Americans and western allies prompted further the Soviet Union to secure its own sphere in the east: a similar conference of primarily Eastern European communist parties was held. An organization called Cominform was formed in October 1947, and the same symbolized the Soviet Union's acknowledgment that Europe was divided into two irreconcilable camps.[1398] Cominform's leader, Andrei Zhdanov, mirrored Truman's speech, suggesting a high level of distrust, suspicion, and ideological conflict between the superpowers.[1399] As if to mirror the US containment policy, the Soviet Union employed a policy of "retrenchment" by expelling non-communist parties from government and purging political leaders who did not follow Stalin's lead.[1400] Such retrenchment policy led Western statesmen to consequently fear that the same was only the beginning of the Soviets' efforts to increase their influence, especially considering the spread of communist parties in

1394 *Horváth*, p. 28.
1395 *Ioannou-Naoum-Wokoun/Ruelling*, pp. 100-101; *Messenger*, p. 50.
1396 *Messenger*, p. 51.
1397 *Messenger*, p. 52.
1398 *Gaddis*, pp. 387-389.
1399 *Messenger*, p. 39.
1400 *Messenger*, p. 40.

central and western Europe and the support the Soviets give those who initiated coups in some areas of Europe.[1401]

Meanwhile, the intergovernmental nature of cooperation discussed by the western allies continued on when, Churchill presided over in May 1948 the Hague Congress. This was attended by European federalists, former political representatives, and current government officials, which resulted in the creation and establishment of the Council of Europe on 05 May 1949.[1402] Composed of Belgium, Denmark, France, Ireland, Italy, Luxembourg, the Netherlands, Norway, Sweden, and the United Kingdom, the Council of Europe was fueled by Churchil's idea of a "United States of Europe" but did not represent a block aiming at integration, but rather a "regional international organization in its traditional sense."[1403]

Interestingly, even if Britain was the one who took the reins in leading the establishment of the Council of Europe, it did not exactly meet expectations in promoting integration based on the American point of view. Americans assumed that they could find a stark supporter with the British as the leader in promoting the idea that economic recovery and national security was more attainable through a supranational framework that integrated Europe, including Germany.[1404] The Marshall Plan as can be seen above was actually premised on this idea.[1405] However, Britain was adamant in leading or even participating in such Western European integrative exercise.[1406] With its colonial and commonwealth interests still at play, it was not buying the idea of far-reaching plans for European integration and did not intend to join the organization aimed at integration in which national sovereignty was restricted through the operation of supranational institutions.[1407] Britain even asked the United States a special status within the Marshall aid scheme that would connote its alignment more with the United States than with other European states: different from countries like Belgium, Netherlands, and Luxembourg, which eagerly pushed the establishment of an organization in pursuit of economic cooperation.[1408] Also referred to as the Benelux countries, these three countries previously established the Benelux Customs Union by entering

1401 *Messenger,* p. 40.
1402 *Messenger,* p. 43.
1403 *Horváth,* pp. 26-27; *Messenger,* p. 43.
1404 *Horváth,* p. 26.
1405 *Messenger,* p. 43.
1406 See *Cini*, p. 20.
1407 *Cini,* p. 20; *Ioannou-Naoum-Wokoun/Ruelling,* pp. 102, 104.
1408 *Craig/de Búrca*, p. 3; *Horváth,* p. 27.

the relevant treaty in September 1944 and effectuating the same in January 1948.[1409]

While the foregoing incidents were going on, the Soviet Union later on supported the coup staged by Czech communists in February 1948 against their coalition partners and was viewed by Stalin as a continuation of its retrenchment policy, clearing up any commixtion occurring in their camps and not necessarily an attack against the West.[1410] While this evinces that Soviet expansion may not necessarily be military in nature, the Americans took upon themselves to recast their containment policy in more military terms, and that it was imperative to strengthen Western Europe politically and economically to prevent what happened in Czechoslovakia again and prevent further Soviet Union expansion.[1411] However, the United States experienced a stumbling block in its endeavor with Britain's reluctance to join the former's envisioned Western European integrative exercise, which was thought to be imperative to the success of the Marshall plan.[1412]

Additionally, it was becoming high time to address the white elephant in the room: the issue of Germany. The four occupying powers had their differences as to how they wanted to deal with their former enemy: France and the Soviet Union thought of Germany as still an ultimate threat though they differed as regards Germany's reconstitution as a single country – France strongly opposed the idea while the same was alright with the Soviets as long as Germany was Soviet-friendly and severely weakened economically and militarily.[1413] On the other hand, the Americans were keen on the idea that German resources and industry was vital in the economic growth of Western Europe.[1414]

US policy vis-à-vis European integration took a new turn in around October 1949, wherein its approach "would be built on a Franco-German rapprochement and would have British and American support in the form of military guarantees, economic collaboration and other measures that stopped short of merging sovereignties."[1415] The conflict between France and Germany needed to be resolved quickly anyway as a condition

1409 *Horváth*, p. 27.
1410 *Horváth*, p. 27.
1411 *Messenger*, p. 40.
1412 See *Messenger*, p. 40.
1413 *Cini*, p. 20. See also *Messenger*, p. 52.
1414 *Messenger*, p. 41.
1415 See *Messenger*, p. 40.

precedent for a successful European Union.[1416] Having historical rivalries between the two, specifically with regard the Rheinland and Ruhr coal and steel, had been one of the sources of conflict in modern Europe.[1417] Thereafter, the French might have made things worse when after the First World War, it insisted on ruinous reparations that factored in making the Second World War happen.[1418] The French initially pursued a hard line approach against the Germans and they harbored a lingering fear of a recovering Germany that raises more issues as to how the latter's power could be controlled.[1419] Needless to state, the French were at rock bottom after the Second World War, and seeing the Germans recovering made them worry that such recovery would outstrip their own.[1420]

By the end of 1947, there was a change in mood and tone: the Four-Power cooperation on Germany had already formally broken down with the collapse of the foreign ministers meeting in December 1947 and the departure of the Soviet Union from the Allied Control Commission in March 1948.[1421] This time, the French were willing to merge its zone with those of Britain and the United States to reconstruct West Germany.[1422] While the same could easily be thought of as an abandonment of France's position towards Germany, it was not. Rather, by participating in integration and cooperative institutions promoted by the United States, the French would not only benefit from financial aid to bolster its recovery but also, they would have a say in Germany's recovery, its overriding goal since the beginning.[1423]

The Cold War factored in as well. Seeing that containment of both Germany and the Soviet Union ("double containment") was more practical, the French were more amenable to the idea of building Europe by adding West Germany to Western Europe, rather than causing more division within Western Europe and aggravating the Cold War situation.[1424] Also taken into consideration was the need by the French to access the Ruhr coal line and agreement to steel production, which was integral

1416 *Cini*, p. 20.
1417 *Horváth*, pp. 27-28.
1418 *Best*, p. 336. See also *Best*, p. 336.
1419 *Horváth*, p. 28.
1420 *Best*, p. 336; *Horváth*, p. 28.
1421 *Best*, p. 337.
1422 *Messenger*, pp. 41,44.
1423 *Messenger*, p. 44.
1424 *Messenger*, p. 44.

into their recovery and further benefit.[1425] This time however, the French seemingly learned from their mistake post-First World War and did not intend to destroy German production, although reparations ought to have been made, but rather integrate the productive forces of Germany into the new international order.[1426] Stating it simply, joining forces with the Americans and joining the integration bandwagon allowed France to have their cake and eat it too.

The first steps were taken in June 1948, when the United States, Britain, and France gave the green light for a constitutional convention that would establish the Federal Republic of Germany (West Germany), with which they established a currency – the Deutsche Mark – in their unified zones, and permitted its use in West Berlin, which although divided among the Western powers, was located within the Soviet zone of eastern Germany.[1427] Seemingly in retaliation, the Soviets introduced an East German Mark and blocked all road and rail access to East Berlin.[1428] Such so-called Berlin Blockade was the first overt conflict of the Cold War and led the Americans to airlift supplies to West Berlin.[1429] Meanwhile, West Germany continued to move into statehood with the new Federal Republic coming into being in May 1949, which prompted the Soviet Union to establish the German Democratic Republic (East Germany) the following October.[1430]

At this juncture, one could observe that aside from overt and covert interventions made by the West in response to threat perceptions, it likewise strengthened democratic and capitalist institutions, starting with German revitalization.[1431] The integration of Western Europe, politically and economically, became imperative to the process, wherein there was American support for a variety of initiatives over the next few years.[1432] One could then say that this reinforces the idea once more of how the Cold War was instrumental in a number of ways in pushing Western Europe towards supranationalism.[1433]

It must not be forgotten that while both political and economic integration became important in Europe at this moment in time, it was a

1425 *Ioannou-Naoum-Wokoun/Ruelling*, p. 101; *Messenger*, p. 44.
1426 *Best*, p. 337.
1427 *Best*, p. 337.
1428 *Messenger*, p. 41.
1429 *Messenger*, p. 41.
1430 *Messenger*, p. 41.
1431 *Best*, p. 337.
1432 *Messenger*, p. 42.
1433 *Messenger*, p. 42.

different story altogether in the beginning when European integration was equated only with political integration. This standpoint significantly changed after the establishment of the Council of Europe.[1434] It was equally important that in promoting the same, modest proposals ought to be made to be acceptable and appealing to more countries to be able to put such plans into fruition.[1435]

One should likewise note that this process of integration was not mutually exclusive within Western Europe. Central and Eastern Europe states were also embarking on a similar process: starting with the Cominform in 1947, they later formed in 1949 the Council for Mutual Economic Assistance ("COMECON").[1436] The COMECON was Moscow's further response to the Marshall Plan: its purpose was to coordinate central plans and trade relations among the Soviet bloc states.[1437] Though not a *par excellance* example of supranational integration,[1438] such formation of a political and economic cluster by eastern Europe fueled integration ambitions of western Europe, which admittedly pursued a different course altogether.[1439]

Other than the political and the economic, there was also the building of military and defense strategy in Western Europe during this time. Notwithstanding the offer of the United States to maintain military presence in Germany, the existence of the Berlin blockade gave the possibility of armed conflict.[1440] Hence, it was imperative to strengthen the security and defense system for Western Europe as a whole.[1441]

In light of this, most states were reluctant to allow German rearmament and instead wanted full commitment of the United States military to the defense of Western Europe should war erupt.[1442] This prompted the United States to propose, and later establish, the North Atlantic Treaty Organization ("NATO") in 1949 which provided political, military, and defense security against the growing Soviet threat.[1443] NATO was meant to be a political and military organization – a military alliance – that ensures

---

1434 *Messenger,* p. 42.
1435 *Best,* p. 337; *Horváth,* p. 31.
1436 *Craig/de Búrca,* EU Law (6th edition), p. 3.
1437 *Anderson*, p. 257; *Horváth,* p. 29.
1438 *Anderson,* p. 257.
1439 *Anderson,* p. 257.
1440 *Horváth,* pp. 29-30.
1441 *Messenger,* p. 46.
1442 *Messenger,* p. 46.
1443 *Messenger,* p. 46.

overall European security.[1444] Notably, the presence of the United States meant a guarantee in military terms to western European states. But at the same time, western European states yearned for an economic-centered integration that could hopefully not only negate the communist threat, but also make the western part of Europe independent of American influence.[1445] In other words, the ideal situation would be to achieve their ambitions without American intervention.

On 09 May 1950 Robert Schuman (the then French minister for foreign affairs) and Jean Monnet (the then head of the planning department of the French government) forwarded a proposal which will be better known as the "Schuman Plan", which would eventually lay down the foundation for European integration.[1446] The Schuman plan focused on building on the idea of European unity while working on a German-French axis.[1447] Working on a step-by-step basis, Schuman and Monet employed the classic carrot on a stick approach and focused on a crucial area: central control of coal and steel industries in Europe would make preparations for war impossible.[1448] Creating a common market for German coal and French iron ore, which would then offer a number of economic advantages, would also make preparations for war by either France or Germany impossible.[1449] Said proposal was timely considering that the coal and steel industries are the foundation on which other industries, including armaments, were grounded on, but likewise, the shortages experienced in both industries by the forties and fifties.[1450]

In line with this, the plan was to put the German coal and French iron industries under a single central authority in a system open to other countries as well.[1451] It was a marriage between the French's goal to control Germany's recovery and the desire of the United States to foster European

1444 *Horváth*, p. 30.
1445 *Horváth*, p. 30.
1446 *Horváth*, p. 30. Even if named the "Schuman Plan", the mastermind and the international coordinator behind the creation of a common coal and steel market for France and Germany was actually Jean Monnet. He was neither a politician nor did he have political connections required to put the ideas into fruition. It was through Schumann's intervention that made the plans possible. See *Ioannou-Naoum-Wokoun/Ruelling*, p. 101.
1447 *Horváth*, p. 31.
1448 *Hartley*, p. 9; *Horváth*, p. 31.
1449 *Craig/de Búrca*, EU Law (6th edition), p. 3; *Horváth*, p. 31. See also *Craig/de Búrca*, EU Law (6th edition), p. 3; *Hartley*, p. 9; *Horváth*, p. 31.
1450 *Hartley*, p. 9.
1451 *Hartley*, pp. 9-10; *Horváth*, p. 31; *Klimek*, p. 12.

integration, using supranational management of the Ruhr's coal and steel industries as a model.[1452] Despite undergoing opposition from many, the carrot and stick approach worked and said proposal was accepted warmly by both Germany and France, together with the Benelux countries and Italy.[1453]

On the other hand, Britain and the Soviet Union was not buying into the idea. Britain was still adamant and unwilling in joining once again such far-reaching plans for European integration and was more comfortable in an intergovernmental setting, shying away from supranational organizations.[1454] As regards the Soviet Union, they had the growing perception that European integration as proposed by the Americans and its western allies was just a ploy to perpetuate any existing division caused by the Cold War and make permanent the division of Germany.[1455] This prompted Stalin to act and propose a new German peace treaty to replace the Occupation Statute in efforts to end Germany's division and thwart any further integration of West Germany in the Atlantic system.[1456] The Soviet Union also saw the integration of Germany's coal and steel industries as a blatant deprivation of any say in the management of these resources, which was askew from the idea of a neutral, unified, and demilitarized Germany as previously agreed upon.[1457]

d. New challenges while paving avenues toward regional integration

On 18 April 1951, Germany, Belgium, Italy, Netherlands, Luxembourg, and France, signed the treaty establishing the European Coal and Steel Community ("ECSC"), which entered into force on 25 July 1952.[1458] At the heart of the institutional system of the ECSC is the idea of a "high authority", consisting of independent civil servants as members nominated by their respective governments, and acting as the main executive institution with decision-making power.[1459] There was at the same time

---

1452 *Craig/de Búrca*, EU Law (6th edition), p. 3; *Horváth*, p. 31.
1453 *Messenger*, p. 45.
1454 *Horváth*, p. 31; *Parsons*, pp. 119-122.
1455 *Messenger*, p. 52.
1456 *Messenger*, p. 52.
1457 *Messenger*, p. 52.
1458 *Horváth*, p. 31.
1459 *Craig/de Búrca*, EU Law (6th edition), p. 3; *Hartley*, p. 9; *Horváth*, p. 32; *Ioannou-Naoum-Wokoun/Ruelling*, p. 101.

the Council composed of competent ministers of the member states to counterbalance the supranational orientation.[1460] The Council of Ministers in turn supervised the High Authority and fulfilled a consultative role and legislative function.[1461] Pursuant to the ECSC treaty further, the Assembly was established, consisting of delegates from member state parliaments and which had a consultative function, as well as a Court of Justice of the ECSC that provided a forum for legal disputes.[1462] Jean Monnet was the first president of the High Authority.[1463]

Not long after the Schuman Plan and the establishment of the ECSC, there were new pressures leading to more opportunities to be explored. On 25 June 1950, the Korean War imploded.[1464] The communists of northern Korea, who have been clandestinely assisted by covert Soviet forces, invaded the American-backed south of the country.[1465] Americans rallied its allies to halt the communists' advancement in a war that would last three years.[1466] It was apparent that the Soviet Union was then taking a more proactive role, including towards German policy as evinced by its many proposals and initiatives.[1467] The pressure for German rearmament built up due to the increasing Soviet Union threat (which was turning global) and great want for military forces on the ground in Europe.[1468]

During this time, diverging views arose among interested countries. On one hand, the Americans considered increasing military strength in West Germany, to the point of insisting to fit Germany into an integrated command structure of the NATO and lifting economic conditions limiting Germany's defense contribution.[1469] Needless to admit, the German rearmament has become the price for America's support and protection of Europe.[1470] To this end, the United States gave a "virtual ultimatum" in September 1950 to reconsider this proposition.[1471] On the other hand,

1460 *Best,* p. 337; *Craig/de Búrca,* EU Law (6th edition), p. 3; *Horváth,* p. 32.
1461 *Horváth,* p. 32.
1462 *Craig/de Búrca,* EU Law (6th edition), p. 3; *Horváth,* p. 32.
1463 *Craig/de Búrca,* EU Law (6th edition), p. 3; *Horváth,* p. 32.
1464 *Horváth,* p. 32.
1465 *Service,* p. 2.
1466 *Service,* p. 2.
1467 *Messenger,* p. 52.
1468 *Messenger,* p. 47.
1469 *Best,* p. 338.See also *Best,* p. 338; *Messenger,* p. 47; *Parsons,* p. 122; *Horváth,* p. 27.
1470 *Craig/de Búrca,* EU Law (6th edition), p. 4.
1471 *Best,* p. 338.

France and other earlier western European allies were not so eager to support such measure due to lack of fail-safety guarantees.[1472]

Given these concerns, promoters of federalism believed that political integration or European integration is the most plausible solution, or a good counter-proposal to what the US wants.[1473] This came through the idea of the European Defense Community ("EDC"), which sought to form a European defense force to be overseen by a common political and military authority.[1474] The EDC was to the German army as what the ECSC was to Ruhr – neutralize the potential threat posed by German strength by incorporating into a united European system.[1475]

Despite finding itself in a treaty to which some countries acceded to, the EDC eventually collapsed in August 1954 and promoters gave up on pursuing further.[1476] Countries like France, one of the promoters of a European army, were suddenly not so keen to lose control over its military, which it saw as integral in maintaining national sovereignty.[1477] It did not help that the British refused to join and French forces were being overwhelmed in the armed conflict in Indochina.[1478]

This being said, the rejection of a European Defense Community pulled back as well from its tracks the proposal to establish a European Political Community ("EPC").[1479] The EPC was meant to set the required European foreign policy, as well as establish a federal, parliamentary-style form of European integration, consisting of a two-level parliament with real legislative power and an Executive Council, which will act as the government of the EPC.[1480] Unfortunately for the proponents of a defense and military union however, the conditions were not compatible with the general *zeitgeist* and thus, plans for the same had to be canned in the meantime.[1481] It did not help as well that during the same time period, it was becoming

1472 *Messenger*, p. 47.
1473 *Best*, p. 338; *Horváth*, p. 27.
1474 *Best*, p. 338; *Craig/de Búrca*, EU Law (6th edition), p. 4.
1475 *Best*, p. 338; *Horváth*, p. 32; *Messenger*, p. 48. See also *Best*, p. 338.
1476 *Messenger*, p. 48. See further *Best*, p. 338; *Horváth*, p. 32; *Ludlow*, p. 17.
1477 *Ioannou-Naoum-Wokoun/Ruelling*, p. 102; *Parsons*, pp. 124-125.
1478 *Craig/de Búrca*, EU Law (6th edition), p. 4; *Horváth*, p. 32; *Ioannou-Naoum-Wokoun/Ruelling*, p. 102.
1479 *Parsons*, p. 123.
1480 *Craig/de Búrca*, EU Law (6th edition), p. 4; *Horváth*, pp. 32-33.
1481 *Craig/de Búrca*, EU Law (6th edition), p. 4; *Ioannou-Naoum-Wokoun/Ruelling*, p. 102.

clearer that the ECSC was not functioning well as hoped for by its promoters.[1482]

While the negotiations for the EDC was ongoing, the Soviet Union sent a note on March 1952 asking for immediate talks aimed at a neutral and unified Germany, an end to occupation within one year, and a ban on German participation in alliances against the big four allied countries during the war.[1483] There had been mixed interpretations on why the Soviets sent this "bombshell" note but regardless of what intent the Soviets had, their proposal was dismissed immediately by the United States and its western allies even when the Soviets came up with a second proposal asking for an all-German election to be held.[1484] The United States government instead insisted on the finalizing of the EDC and German treaty negotiations and it later became apparent to both western and Soviet policy makers that the resolution of integration, especially as regards Germany, became key to the "construction of the Cold War settlement in Europe".[1485]

Movements toward European integration were not dampened or halted notwithstanding the rejection of both the EDC and EPC.[1486] The canning of such ambitious projects led proponents of integration to give priority to the economic and political policy, while still considering the ideas discussed during the drafting of the EPC.[1487] And indeed, such was the case in the historical development of European integration.

On 01 and 02 June 1955, an ECSC meeting was held in Messina through the initiative of the Benelux states to talk about deepening and expanding economic integration, with institutional issues of possible cooperation in the area of atomic energy and a common market in general.[1488] Previously, the Netherlands proposed during the drafting of the EPC the idea of establishing a common market but most found the same too avant-garde considering that most had a protectionist economic culture.[1489] To give the idea a chance, an agreement to pursue a common market through a customs union and later through the so-called Spaak report (the committee tasked post-Messina conference to come up with a plan was headed by Paul-Henri Spaak) was reached. A proposal to have "an institutional-

1482 *Craig/de Búrca*, EU Law (6th edition), p. 4.
1483 *Messenger*, p. 53.
1484 *Messenger*, p. 53.
1485 *Messenger*, p. 53.
1486 *Best*, p. 338.
1487 *Craig/de Búrca*, EU Law (6th edition), p. 4.
1488 *Craig/de Búrca*, EU Law (6th edition), p. 4.
1489 *Craig/de Búrca*, EU Law (6th edition), p. 4; *Horváth*, p. 33.

ized community structure for the would-be organization of integration in which issues pertaining to general politics and the operation of the common market were to be handled separately was tabled as well."[1490]

Whilst that proposal would remain within the penumbra of the member states, a body with authority and central responsibility shall take up the function of ensuring the operation of the common market.[1491] Significantly, the Spaak committee report avoided talking about a supranational organization given the initial sour response to the EDC and the growing dissatisfaction with the High Authority of the ECSC.[1492] Said approach proved successful for the Spaak committee because its proposal was acceptable to all six ECSC member states and on 25 March 1957, all six members of the ECSC signed the treaties establishing the European Economic Community ("EEC") and the European Atomic Energy Community ("Euratom"), otherwise known as the Treaties of Rome, which became effective on 01 January 1958.[1493] The United Kingdom was, notably, once again invited to join said endeavor but the invitation was denied.[1494] The United Kingdom was more interested in free trade cooperation only and thus proceeded with forming the European Free Trade Association ("EFTA") composed mainly of countries not part of the EEC and Euratom.[1495]

While the institutional framework for the EEC and Euratom was based on the ECSC institutional framework, there was an apparent paradigm shift as regards decision-making.[1496] At the outset, the substantive scope seemed bigger with the same, especially concerning the EEC.[1497] While the ECSC is concerned more with creating a single market for the coal and steel industries, the EEC aims for an economic community.[1498] This aim would be reached through the following measures such as eliminating custom duties and quantitative restrictions, and of all other measures having equivalent effect; establishing a customs union – wherein trade among countries in a certain area shall be liberalized while common custom tariffs shall be imposed to those outside said area; allowing free movement of not only goods and services, but also labor and capital within the

1490 *Craig/de Búrca*, EU Law (6th edition), p. 4.
1491 *Horváth*, p. 33.
1492 *Horváth*, p. 33.
1493 *Horváth*, p. 33; *Klimek*, pp. 11-12.
1494 *Hartley*, pp. 11-12; *Horváth*, pp. 33-34; *Woods/Watson*, pp. 3-4.
1495 *Horváth*, p. 34; *Ioannou-Naoum-Wokoun/Ruelling*, p. 104.
1496 *Horváth*, p. 34.
1497 *Horváth*, p. 34; *Woods/Watson*, p. 4.
1498 *Woods/Watson*, p. 4.

Community; establishing a common policy in the areas of agriculture, transport, and competition; as well as having legal integration.[1499] The aforementioned measures in turn explains the centrality to the Community of the so-called "four freedoms", which are often regarded as the core of its economic constitution: free movement of goods, workers, capital, and establishment and the provision of services.[1500] The idea is, for example, to allow an individual to seek a job in another member state that has a high demand for workers, and consequently enriching the value of labor resource within the community.[1501]

The provisions of the EEC might have been primarily economic-centered but its aims were not exclusively so.[1502] Member states were "fueled with ideals" as well as economic practicalities, as stated in the preamble of the Treaty of Rome establishing the EEC, the EEC is seen to lay down the "foundations of an even closer union among the peoples of Europe" and the decision to pool each other's resources is to strengthen peace and unity.[1503]

The institutional framework of both the EEC and Euratom can be described to have more intergovernmental characteristics than supranational,[1504] which was crucial to the success of the Rome Treaties because if one would look into the reason why the EPC failed, it was primarily due its parliamentary orientation, to which member states of the ECSC were against even up to the negotiations of the Rome treaty.[1505]

While having more intergovernmental characteristics, a salient feature of the EEC and Euratom was the sharing of legislative and executive functions among institutions. This is characterized as the so-called "institutional balance" (as opposed to the strict notion of separation of powers): the need to ensure decision-making is made to serve the public good rather than individual interests and the same would only be achieved should the form of public ordering take into consideration equally the different interests of different sections of society.[1506] Institutional balance however is not self-executing; it presumes by its nature of normative and political judg-

1499 Treaty establishing the European Economic Community, art. 3; *Woods/Watson*, p. 4.
1500 *Horváth*, p. 35.
1501 *Craig/de Búrca*, EU Law (6th edition), p. 5.
1502 *Craig/de Búrca*, EU Law (6th edition), p. 5.
1503 *Woods/Watson*, p. 4.
1504 *Woods/Watson*, p. 4.
1505 *Hartley*, pp. 12-13; *Horváth*, p. 34.
1506 *Craig/de Búrca*, EU Law (6th edition), p. 5.

ment as to which institutions should be able to partake of legislative and executive power and what would be the ideal balance between them.[1507]

The first fifteen years of the EEC could be described by rapid internal integration: the removal of customs and other qualitative restrictions among the member states was accomplished two years earlier than the planned date in 1970 and common tariffs were introduced.[1508] In 1962, a decision has been made on working on a common agricultural policy, given that the establishment of a customs union and introduction of a common market only benefited the industrial markets.[1509] Said decision eventually led to unification within the Community in terms of agricultural protectionism.[1510] This milestone was important as it confirms the ability of the member states to cooperate with one another in areas where "considerable reallocation of revenues" was involved from one member state to another.[1511] It provided valuable insight as to what makes member states agree to a certain decision and policymaking.

In between 1958 to 1973 there was exponential growth in trading relations among the member states as a result of trade liberalization and customs union and consequently, integration led to economic boom.[1512] These positive results motivated the member states to pursue a monetary union as early as 1969 and 1970.[1513]At the beginning of the 1960s, the supranational community format has been undeniably consolidated as the "core architecture of post-war Europe."[1514] Details as to how to put this plan into fruition however had yet to be discussed.[1515] Moreover, establishing a free movement of labor and capital was easier said than

1507 *Craig/de Búrca*, p. 43.

1508 *Best*, p. 339.

1509 *Horváth*, p. 36.

1510 *Horváth*, p. 36.

1511 *Horváth*, p. 36.

1512 The period could be characterized with vast "technological development, radical modernization of the structure of the economy, dynamic expression of consumption," and remarkable increases in Gross Domestic Product ("GDP") by five percent (5%) each year. Among other things, on 14 December 1960, the OEEC was reorganized to become the Organization of Economic Cooperation and Development ("OECD"), a cooperation organization for industrialized countries. *Horváth*, p. 36.

1513 *Horváth*, p. 28.

1514 *Horváth*, p. 36.

1515 *Parsons*, p. 116.

done, although a customs union has been fairly easy to implement and all the conditions necessary for a common market has been provided.[1516]

These issues notwithstanding, the main confirmation of the success of the EEC is arguably the re-evaluation of the British political attitude towards the community. While being previously lukewarm and apprehensive, the British expressed twice – the first being in July 1961 and the second being in 1967 – their interest to join the community after seeing the advantages reaped so far by the EEC member states.[1517] This was unfortunately seen by French President De Gaulle as a threat and as such, vetoed the application on both occasions.[1518] De Gaulle's actions were arguably expected to a certain degree at the moment given that the British acknowledged how much the French were basking in the privileged role given to it by the EEC – as long as the British stayed outside.[1519] The British so far had kept abreast of European trade through the EFTA but De Gaulle likewise rejected participation in the same in order to safeguard his interests in France.[1520] These dynamics resulted unfortunately to creating complications in both the external relations and internal functioning of the communities.[1521] It is imperative to mention that during the same time period, there was an apparent tension between an intergovernmental view of the Community, as espoused by De Gaulle, and a supranational one, which was espoused by then Commission President Walter Hallstein.[1522]

These circumstances elucidate the complications of international cooperation. Despite being in a mainly intergovernmental cooperation mechanism, member states would still want to pursue their own national interests even at the expense of true integration. Although a number of states decided to form a regional organization, relations between one another are influenced by the respective idiosyncrasies of each one, which then gives an understanding of the steps needed to be taken. Herein one finds De Gaulle who was a mercantilist that prioritized exports over imports to be able to strengthen state power, and he previously wanted then for Germans, who eventually made concessions with the former, to absorb French surpluses even if American and British prices were obviously more

---

1516 *Horváth*, p. 37.
1517 *Horváth*, p. 37.
1518 *Griffiths*, p. 170.
1519 *Craig/de Búrca*, EU Law (6th edition), p. 6; *Horváth*, p. 37; *Vanke*, pp. 151-153.
1520 *Ioannou-Naoum-Wokoun/Ruelling*, p. 105; *Vanke*, p. 145.
1521 *Ioannou-Naoum-Wokoun/Ruelling*, p. 106; *Vanke*, p. 145.
1522 *Horváth*, p. 37.

competitive.[1523] More or less, De Gaulle was rubbing his fellow member states in the EEC the wrong way. The brewing tension coming out from this became apparent in 1965 due to transitional provisions of the treaty calling a shift from unanimous voting to qualified majority, and De Gaulle objected to the Commission's idea that more revenues would be raised through external tariffs and agricultural levies, rather than national contributions.[1524] And after it was obvious that neither De Gaulle would win the argument nor a compromise would be met, De Gaulle personally brought upon the communities a serious crisis in 1965 when he boycotted participation for half a year as part of his "empty chair policy", just because he was not in agreement with the proposals made for financing agricultural policy.[1525]

Solution was met only through the so-called Luxembourg compromise, which is basically an agreement to disagree: "even in cases governed by majority decision-making, discussion should continue until unanimity was reached whenever important national interests were at stake" but at the same time, the Council should in such circumstances endeavor within reasonable time to reach solutions that can be adopted by all.[1526] Thereafter, it would seemed that the French view has prevailed and whenever a member state would raise its national interest during discussions on a matter, the same was treated as a veto, which the other member states would respect.[1527] Qualified majority voting was the exception and not the general rule.[1528] Although De Gaulle defended the same to be in favor of member states, in reality it has just slowed down immensely the decision-making process of the communities.[1529]

In 1965, the member states of the Communities entered into the Merger Treaty, which would unite the three integration communities – ECSC, the EEC, and the Euratom – by July 1967.[1530] The Court of Justice, Assembly, Council, and the Commission, were all reorganized to serve all

1523 *Craig/de Búrca*, EU Law (6th edition), p. 6; *Craig*, p. 43.

1524 *Ioannou-Naoum-Wokoun/Ruelling*, p. 106; *Vanke*, pp. 146-147.

1525 *Craig/de Búrca*, EU Law (6th edition), p. 6; *Ioannou-Naoum-Wokoun/Ruelling*, p. 106. See for further explanation *Craig/de Búrca*, EU Law (6th edition), p. 6; *Horváth*, p. 37.

1526 *Ioannou-Naoum-Wokoun/Ruelling*, p. 106; *Vanke*, pp. 153-155.

1527 *Craig/de Búrca*, EU Law (6th edition), p. 6; *Craig*, p. 44; *Horváth*, p. 37; *Ioannou-Naoum-Wokoun/Ruelling*, p. 106.

1528 *Craig*, p. 44.

1529 *Craig*, p. 44.

1530 *Horváth*, p. 37; *Ioannou-Naoum-Wokoun/Ruelling*, p. 106.

institutions.[1531] The High Authority of the ECSC was merged with the Commission.[1532] While the name "European Communities" have been used for a long time, the Communities still retained their independent international legal statuses and only their institutions became common institutions via the Merger Treaty.[1533] Furthermore, in clarifying the competences of the three Communities since the Merger Treaty, the EEC Treaty must be applied generally in areas not specifically regulated by the ECSC and Euratom treaty.[1534]

De Gaulle resigned in April 1969 and it made possible the prospect of progress on the political front of integration considering that the pending issues left by France's empty chair policy could now be tackled.[1535] Three (3) new economic and monetary targets were placed on the agenda,[1536] while the obstacle to British entry was removed.[1537] In June 1970 accession talks began with the United Kingdom as well as Denmark, Ireland, and Norway, and following a ratification procedure, these countries, except for Norway, became members of the European Communities on 01 January 1973.[1538]

Meanwhile, there was a move for enhanced participation from the member states and intergovernmentalism. In 1970, the Davignon Report recommended the holding of quarterly meetings of the foreign ministers from the different member states, which eventually became an inter-governmental forum for cooperation in foreign policy.[1539] This became eventually known in 1973 as European Political Cooperation that enabled the EEC to be represented as one voice in other international organizations in which member states participated, but also enhanced intergovernmentalism in the Community.[1540]

At this point, the Cold War was definitely still ongoing despite the waxing and waning of the tensions between the United States and the Soviet Union.[1541] The EC did not seek to stand in for its member states

1531 *Craig/de Búrca,* EU Law (6th edition), p. 6; *Horváth,* p. 38.
1532 *Horváth,* p. 38.
1533 *Horváth,* p. 38.
1534 *Horváth,* p. 38.
1535 *Horváth,* p. 38.
1536 *Ioannou-Naoum-Wokoun/Ruelling,* p. 107.
1537 *Griffiths,* p. 169.
1538 *Griffiths,* p. 169. See further *Horváth,* p. 39; *Woods/Watson,* p. 4.
1539 *Michalski,* pp. 285-287.
1540 *Craig/de Búrca,* EU Law (6th edition), p. 7.
1541 See *Craig/de Búrca,* EU Law (6th edition), p. 7.

with regard to establishing ties with the Soviet Union or its satellites, especially given the open hostile non-recognition given to it by its Eastern European counterpart, the COMECON.[1542] Given the same, there was not much meddling involved when West Germany's foreign policy towards the Soviet Union and its eastern bloc satellites took a major turn in 1970.[1543] Prompted by complex security interests and domestic policies, West Germany's *Ostpolitik* sought to forge regional unity that could withstand the power struggle between superpowers and to promote unification by drawing East Germany into a deeper relationship.[1544]

Meanwhile, it has become undeniable that the European Communities have gained quite the increasing significance in the world economy in the 1970's due to its enlargement and this did not quite sit well with the Americans, who previously were supportive of the restoration and development of Europe.[1545] The Americans now see the European Communities more as a threat and direct competitor, which, while having protectionist aspirations, were able to present themselves in a common trade policy and was able to establish good relations with the Socialist countries and developing countries.[1546]

The increasing economic significance was nonetheless confronted with threats and challenges. Despite the economic potential harnessed by the enlargement of the European Communities, its early years could not be exactly counted as a complete success. The world oil shock caused by the Arab-Israeli War of 1973 (and which only ended in 1982 and 1983) and the breakdown of the Bretton Woods system in 1971 (which ought to have stabilized the international monetary system after World War 2) placed significant challenges to establishing a common market and furthering integration among the member states as they were individually constrained to initiate protectionist measures in light of financial difficulties being faced.[1547] It made the realization of the Economic and Monetary Union difficult.[1548] In addition to this, British membership proved difficult given that it always argued for lesser British contributions to the budget over a long period. The British were always net budget contributors due to

1542 *Anderson*, p. 258.
1543 *Anderson*, p. 258.
1544 *Anderson*, p. 258.
1545 *Anderson*, p. 258.
1546 *Horváth*, p. 39.
1547 *Anderson*, pp. 260-261.
1548 *Ioannou-Naoum-Wokoun/Ruelling*, p. 107.

increasing costs related to agricultural policy and the United Kingdom being an importer of agricultural products.[1549]

The foregoing notwithstanding, there has been greater mutual dependence among the member states in terms of micro- and macro-economic policy.[1550] By the mid-seventies, the member states had more or less common commercial policies and uniform trade policies as regards third countries.[1551] The most notable achievement by this period is the establishment of the European Monetary System ("EMS"), as a response to the difficulties confronting the EMU, which did not only create financial stability and but was also a major step toward the establishment of an economic union through connecting European currencies to the European Currency Unit ("ECU"), the latter of which represented the average value of all currencies that ensured stable exchange rates.[1552]

There was also in mid-1974 the approval of the plan to introduce a notification and consultation procedure covering economic cooperation and trading agreements with state-trading (i.e. COMECON) and oil-producing countries.[1553] The purpose of said plan was to regulate uncontrolled, competitive bidding among EC members for contracts with partners in these regions, with the Commission having primary responsibility for oversight and implementation.[1554]

Additionally, on an institutional perspective, by 1974 onwards, it became a regular occurrence for member states to consult one another through their respective heads of state.[1555] These regularized meetings, which were called otherwise the European Council, paved way for efficiency in decision-making in Europe and key decisions were made with regard to strategic issues, compromises, and guidelines.[1556] However, one must not mistake the European Council as a separate institution altogether, nor was it intended as part of the framework envisioned by the treaties; instead, it played the role of being a top-level forum that has become decisive on steps taken for further integration.[1557] Decisions made in the European Council found themselves as a framework within which binding

1549 *Horváth*, p. 39.
1550 *Horváth*, p. 40.
1551 *Horváth*, p. 40.
1552 *Horváth*, p. 40. See also *Ioannou-Naoum-Wokoun/Ruelling*, p. 107.
1553 *Anderson*, p. 261.
1554 *Anderson*, p. 261.
1555 *Heisenberg*, p. 236.
1556 *Craig/de Búrca*, EU Law (6th edition), p. 7; *Horváth*, p. 40.
1557 *Craig/de Búrca*, EU Law (6th edition), p. 7; *Horváth*, p. 40.

Community initiatives were being pursued, although said decisions are not formally binding at the outset.[1558]

In light of this, some might view the regularization of European Council meetings as a weakening of the supranational elements of the Community.[1559] Together with the previous Luxembourg compromise a few years back, these movements had more earmarks of intergovernmental rather than a supranational nature.[1560] Having said that, there were still developments within the Communities geared towards enhanced supranationalism: on one hand, there was an agreement in 1976 on direct elections to the Assembly, the first being held in 1979, which provided the EEC with a direct electoral mandate it previously lacked; on the other hand, there were developments regarding resources and budget, wherein in 1969 an agreement was reached for the Community to fund itself more from its own resources and less from national contributions, resulting into greater financial independence and strengthened role of the Parliament in budgetary concerns.[1561]

The mixed institutional developments within the Community (towards intergovernmental on one hand, supranational on the other) aside, one can observe a significant development vis-à-vis integration in the 1980's with further enlargement of the European Communities. Greece, which entered into an Association Agreement with the EEC as early as 1962, was finally allowed to join the European Communities in 1981 following an arduous democratization and modernization period that began in 1974 when the military junta fell from power.[1562] Longer periods of transition were observed for Spain and Portugal after they became independent from military regimes.[1563] Interestingly, this easily demonstrates how any integration that began with western Europe initially did not have in mind the integration of all non-communist states.[1564] Any division caused by the Cold War did not automatically result to intending all of western Europe to be integrated and form parts of the supranational project.[1565] It was only

1558 *Craig/de Búrca*, EU Law (6th edition), p. 7; *Horváth*, p. 40.
1559 *Craig/de Búrca*, EU Law (6th edition), p. 7.
1560 *Craig/de Búrca*, EU Law (6th edition), p. 7.
1561 *Craig/de Búrca*, EU Law (6th edition), p. 7.
1562 *Craig/de Búrca*, EU Law (6th edition), p. 7. See also *Michalski*, p. 288.
1563 *Woods/Watson*, p. 4. See for more details *Horváth*, p. 41.
1564 *Messenger*, p. 53.
1565 *Messenger*, p. 53.

in 1986 when the Iberian countries eventually became members, bringing the total membership to 12 countries.[1566]

In line with this, the non-inclusion in the initial stages of the integration project of some states becomes understandable later due to certain issues and problems that arose out of the southern enlargement.[1567] First, these three countries, albeit not necessarily communists, all just came from right-wing dictatorships and commonly had frozen economic, social, and democratic development.[1568] Second, the long period of time of economic difficulties and backwardness prompted a dilemma for new political regimes, which knew that democracy depended on economic and social modernization in order to garner support from the public and their national elite.[1569] Discussing the issue on social and economic cohesion became all the more relevant at this moment in time given that the Communities were no longer homogenous in composition, but instead were composed of member-countries of varying potential and development.[1570]

As mentioned earlier, the outbreak of the oil crisis caused member states to initiate protectionist measures, which subsequently and expectedly ran counter to what has been envisioned and established already in the Communities.[1571] Taking away these protectionist and restrictive measures was imperative should a common market be brought into front and it became later apparent that the only solution after the taxing oil crisis was deregulation.[1572] It was easier thought than done however as taking away the national-like administrative regulations proved challenging should unanimous voting remain.[1573] Hence, it became important to revisit how decision-making must be done in the Communities, which would only be possible to amend by amending the Rome Treaty itself.[1574]

Coincidentally, the time was ripe to discuss said amendments as national and community interests were at a point that member states were more inclined to sacrifice a bit of their national sovereignty for the sake of escaping the crisis together and creating further impetus for integration.[1575]

1566 *Michalski*, p. 289.
1567 *Horváth*, p. 41; *Woods/Watson*, p. 4.
1568 *Horváth*, p. 41.
1569 *Michalski*, p. 287.
1570 *Michalski*, p. 288.
1571 *Horváth*, p. 41.
1572 *Horváth*, p. 41.
1573 *Horváth*, p. 41.
1574 *Horváth*, p. 41.
1575 *Horváth*, pp. 41-42.

By this time period, or specifically the 1980's, the EC was experiencing stagflation: unacceptable high employment, sluggish growth bordering on recession, and high inflation.[1576] Making the markets more flexible and creating a real common market became an urgent issue.[1577] This was indispensable for Western Europe, which was then significantly lagging behind the United States and Japan in terms of technological and structural development.[1578] Whatever peak it gained previously has now turned into a downward slope.

To address these problems, the Single European Act ("SEA") amending the Treaty of Rome was adopted.[1579] Signed on 18 February 1986 and entered into force on 01 January 1987, the said Act provides that a single market shall be constituted by 31 December 1992.[1580] It was consequently imperative for intensive community legislation and legal harmonization among member states to happen in the following years.[1581]

Through the Single European Act, changes in the institutional framework of the Communities were introduced.[1582] For instance, the European Parliament was granted more influence, the Commission's competence was widened, and the voting system in the Council was changed to increase the significance of qualified majority voting.[1583] Prior to the SEA, the Commission proposes legislative action while the Council disposes.[1584] With the advent of the SEA, this previous reality has changed.[1585] There is now the "cooperation procedure" wherein input from the three players – Parliament, Commission, and Council, is necessitated in certain circumstances of the legislative process, and the Commission should not take lightly the views of the European Parliament, when applicable.[1586] It could be thus gainsaid that the Parliament has been given real power in the

---

1576 *Horváth*, p. 42.
1577 *Ludlow*, p. 218.
1578 *Horváth*, p. 42.
1579 *Horváth*, p. 42.
1580 *Horváth*, p. 42.
1581 *Horváth*, p. 42; *Woods/Watson*, p. 6.
1582 *Horváth*, pp. 42-43.
1583 *Horváth*, p. 43.
1584 *Craig/de Búrca*, EU Law (6th edition), pp. 8-9; *Horváth*, p. 43; *Ludlow*, From Deadlock to Dynamism, p. 227.
1585 *Craig/de Búrca*, EU Law (6th edition), p. 8.
1586 *Craig*, p. 56.

legislative process through the SEA.[1587] The SEA also established the Court of First Instance ("CFI") which shall assist the Court of Justice.[1588]

Moreover, there have been institutional changes vis-à-vis the EPC and formal acknowledgment of the European Council for the first time.[1589] This development is significant because the European Council has been playing a greater role in shaping EU policy. It has the central role in shaping and pacing EU policy, establishing the parameters, and even action points, within which other institutions would operate, and provided a forum at the highest political level for discussion and resolution of tensions and issues among member states.[1590] It was also at the crux of treaty reform as initiatives for intergovernmental conferences came from the European Council and being able to touch base with different issues and concerns affecting the Union and its member states, the European Council was able to come up with constitutional initiatives or policy strategies that affect how the Union would eventually operate.[1591]

Aside from the foregoing, the impact of the cooperation procedure was further enhanced by the substantial changes the SEA made, such as the formation of a single market.[1592] This single market programme eventually caught the attention of both internal and external players.[1593] The relaunch of the mid-1980s influenced the decision of Austria, Finland, and Sweden to seek membership in the EC, albeit during this time period they avowed neutrality in the East-West conflict.[1594]

Likewise, the said relaunch coincided with the sharp changes happening vis-à-vis the Cold War between the Soviet Union and the United States. Mikhael Gorbachev, as the then General Secretary of the Soviet Union, sought a partnership for peace in March 1985 with President Reagan of the United States.[1595] Reagan, who entered into office in 1981, was shocked to realize that the United States actually did not have anything to adequately protect itself should there be a nuclear attack.[1596] Albeit he adopted a

1587 *Craig/de Búrca,* EU Law (6th edition), p. 8; *Craig,* p. 56; *Ludlow,* From Deadlock to Dynamism, p. 227.

1588 *Craig,* p. 56.

1589 *Craig/de Búrca,* EU Law (6th edition), p. 8.

1590 *Craig/de Búrca,* EU Law (6th edition), p. 8; *Craig,* p. 55.

1591 *Craig,* p. 55.

1592 *Craig,* p. 55.

1593 *Craig/de Búrca,* EU Law (6th edition), p. 9.

1594 *Ludlow,* From Deadlock to Dynamism, pp. 228-229.

1595 *Service,* p. 3.

1596 *Service,* pp. 3, 16.

more proactive position, as compared to his predecessors' reactive and imperialist line of policy, he later would initiate an end to the arms race – by calling a reduction of stocks of atomic and nuclear weapons held by both superpowers – and this appeal was seemingly echoed likewise by Gorbachev.[1597] Closer ties between the Soviet Union and western Europe was also seen from the mid-to-late 1980's, which was also made possible through Gorbachev's leadership.[1598] There was an open acknowledgment of the economic and political power center emerging in western Europe and this prompted the Soviet Union's diplomatic campaign.[1599]

This occurred when the future of Europe seemingly was open-ended and the Soviet Union took the opportunity to convince the European community on issues like conventional disarmament, stationing of short-range missiles, etc., which echoed part and parcel the meeting of the minds between Gorbachev and Reagan to direct their respective administrations to cooperate in reducing the number of nuclear missiles held on land, sea, and air.[1600] If one would take a few steps back, this was not the case earlier between the US and Soviet Union, which previously held hard lines against each other. Contrary to the European Political Cooperation that was more amiable towards the Soviet Union, the American government maintained a hard-line stance against the Soviet Union.[1601] It was even commonplace for western European politicians and leaders to work with the Americans to end hostilities with the Soviet Union.[1602]

Given these developments one could be still rightfully wary that the Soviet Union's campaign was only pure talk, but one could later on be convinced as Gorbachev's repeated reference to a "common European home" went hand in hand with practical attempts to reorient perceptions in the continent, which consequently opened doors to a normalization process in Europe and the eventual reunification that transcended the Cold War divide.[1603] At the same time, rapprochement grew to the surprise of many and the Soviet Union dismantled its totalitarian politics and communist ideology as well as permitted measures for political and economic reform.[1604] Against all expectations, in 1987-1990 alone, there were

1597 *Service*, pp. 3, 5, 14-15.
1598 *Anderson*, p. 263.
1599 *Anderson*, p. 263.
1600 *Service*, p. 3.
1601 *Anderson*, pp. 263-264.
1602 *Service*, p. 5.
1603 *Anderson*, p. 264.
1604 *Service*, p. 3.

agreements between the superpowers on intermediate range and strategic nuclear weapons, on Afghanistan, on conventional forces, and on German reunification.[1605] Anticommunist revolutions were also happening in Eastern Europe in 1989.[1606] On a global scale, politics was never going to be the same again and then US President Bush felt it safe to declare the close to the Cold War.[1607] These circumstances naturally elicited various reactions from western Europe: some were enthusiastic, some were suspicious, while some were worried that Germany would forsake western Europe for a chance at eventual reunification.[1608]

2. European Union's Historical Development

a. Consolidation Stage

A reading of the historical development of European integration shows undeniably the intention to form a union as early as the Treaties of Rome.[1609] However, there was difficulty to fulfill the same because it did not coincide with the sign of the times.[1610] It was only after the changes in the overall landscape in the 1980's that the movement towards a closer European Union grew and the momentum gained further ground with the Single European Act in 1986.[1611]

In the meantime, one could witness the unveiling of German unification during the same time period. This coincided with the discussions and further deliberations on the draft treaty submitted by the Luxembourg presidency of the European Council, which resulted in the Maastricht Treaty coming into being in December 1991.[1612] The Maastricht Treaty came in the advent of the Yugoslav crisis, with trouble brewing within the Soviet Union and the Balkan republics.[1613] The Community then not only offered to serve as broker in the situation but it likewise engaged

1605 *Service*, p. 3.
1606 *Service*, p. 3.
1607 *Service*, p. 3.
1608 *Anderson*, p. 264.
1609 *Ludlow*, From Deadlock to Dynamism, p. 229.
1610 *Woods/Watson*, p. 4.
1611 *Horváth*, p. 43.
1612 *Craig/de Búrca*, EU Law (Fourth Edition), p. 14; *Woods/Watson*, p. 7.
1613 *Anderson*, p. 267.

its Conference on Security and Cooperation in Europe crisis consultation mechanism established earlier.[1614]

The Maastricht Treaty was subsequently agreed upon and the same introduced two parts: one part introduced amendments to the EEC Treaty and renamed it to "European Community (EC)" which was more reflective of the treaty's wider purpose; while the other part stood as a separate treaty, later to be known as the Treaty on European Union ("TEU"), establishing the European Union ("EU").[1615] The same laid down a number of general principles and specifically provided for (1) cooperation in view of joint action in terms of foreign and security policy ("FSP"), and (2) cooperation in view of justice and home affairs ("JHA").[1616] These two eventually became known as the second and third pillars of the European Union while the EC, Euratom, and the ECSC (until its expiration in 2002) constituted the first pillar, otherwise referred to as a whole as "European Communities".[1617] As Craig and de Búrca explained, the structure of the European Union was visualized in the Maastricht treaty as a temple wherein its objectives constituted as a roof while the pillars supported the same.[1618] Furthermore, one can take sight of changes to the applicable decision-making procedures among the different institutions. The Maastricht Treaty introduced the co-decision procedure, wherein both the Council and EP should first approve before a measure is adopted, ensuring that differing interests are taken into consideration.[1619]

With respect to the second and third pillars of the EU, they were intended to be intergovernmental in nature, compared to the supranational nature of the first pillar.[1620] Member states were looking for some established mechanism through which they could cooperate in the areas of foreign and security policies and justice and home affairs as there existed a strong sentiment that setting up *ad hoc* meetings for such matters was cumbersome and time-consuming, and the transaction costs involved were high.[1621] Nonetheless, the member states were not too keen on putting these matters under the same kind of supranational arrangement as the European Communities in the first pillar as the former involved naturally

---

1614 *Anderson*, p. 267.
1615 *Craig/de Búrca*, EU Law (Fourth Edition), p. 15. See also *Woods/Watson*, p. 7.
1616 *Craig/de Búrca*, EU Law (Fourth Edition), p. 15.
1617 *Craig*, p. 60; *Woods/Watson*, p. 7. See also *Woods/Watson*, p. 7.
1618 *Craig/de Búrca*, EU Law (Fourth Edition), p. 15.
1619 *Woods/Watson*, pp. 68, 70.
1620 *Craig*, p. 56.
1621 *Craig*; *Woods/Watson*, p. 9.

important and sensitive matters of policy touching on national sovereignty itself.[1622] Hence, it was decided to have the three-pillar structure that allows a more intergovernmental structure, wherein the primary power still dwells in the member states' respective hands.[1623] One must be careful at this point, however, of exaggerating the intergovernmental nature of the second and third pillars because even if the primary power belongs to the European Council, which represents the member states in this case, the importance of the Commission should not be discounted.[1624]

The Maastricht Treaty eventually entered into force on 01 November 1993, but not without the criticisms and heavy analysis given that it introduced extreme changes that aimed to expand and strengthen the previous institutional machinery.[1625] For instance, the pursuit of a full economic and monetary union by 1999 touched a lot of nerves in the process, proof of which is that on one hand, both Britain and Denmark were incessant in negotiating provisions that allowed them to opt out of this provision, while Germany encountered opposition in its own constitutional court because of its decision to enter into the single currency.[1626]

On 01 January 1995, the European Union gained new member states through the accession of Austria, Finland, and Sweden.[1627] As one may recall, these three countries earlier expressed interest in becoming members when the Single European Act came into view. Norway was supposedly part of this group of countries but for the second time in just twenty years, accession was denied through the results of a national referendum.[1628]

In relation to the further enlargement of the EU membership, an Agreement on the European Economic Area ("EEA") between the EC and EFTA was made four years prior, or in 1991, that provided for free movement provisions similar to the EC Treaty, similar competition policy and rules, and close cooperation in a range of other policy fields.[1629] Coming into force in 1994, the Agreement for a while was held incompatible with the EC treaty but after some revisions and amendments, including the establishment of an EFTA Court, which is independent and separate from

---

1622 *Craig*, p. 60; *Craig/de Búrca*, EU Law (Fourth Edition), p. 15.
1623 *Craig/de Búrca*, EU Law (Fourth Edition), p. 15; *Craig*, p. 60.
1624 *Craig/de Búrca*, EU Law (Fourth Edition), p. 15; *Craig*, p. 60.
1625 *Craig/de Búrca*, EU Law (Fourth Edition), p. 15.
1626 *Craig/de Búrca*, EU Law (Fourth Edition), p. 18; *Woods/Watson*, p. 7.
1627 *Craig/de Búrca*, EU Law (Fourth Edition), p. 17.
1628 *Woods/Watson*, p. 4.
1629 *Craig/de Búrca*, EU Law (Fourth Edition), p. 17.

the Court of Justice of the European Union ("CJEU"), its compatibility with the EC treaty was later upheld.[1630]

On 02 October 1997 the Treaty of Amsterdam (ToA) was signed as a product of regular intergovernmental conferences ("IGC") with its intended entry into force on 01 May 1999.[1631] It was declared to be more about "consolidation rather than extension of Community powers."[1632] The ToA was able to expand the competence of the EU through strengthening the EC pillar by streamlining decision-making processes and allocating new competencies, such as adding the principle of openness to Article 1 of the TEU, so that decisions are to be taken "as openly as possible" and as closely as possible to the citizens.[1633] The Amsterdam treaty likewise transferred provisions governing third-country nationals from the JHA to the then EC, and the Schengen Agreement, which although outside the EC/EU Framework, governs nonetheless internal borders among EU member states, was incorporated into the then EC treaty.[1634] Additional provisions were incorporated, including those on unemployment, and the previously annexed protocol on social policy, has found itself in the treaty's main text.[1635]

Given the foregoing, one can notice a shift of emphasis to build the image of the EU and assert its normative framework: what began as purely and mainly economic now involves more political ideas founded on fundamental rights and principles.[1636] Article 6 of the TEU was amended to mention that the Union is founded on human rights, democracy, and the rule of the law.[1637] Not only that, but respect for the same was made as condition *sine qua non* for any application for membership in the EU.[1638] One can place attention of the same degree on the emphasis to promote and instill equality and prohibit discrimination, to the point that the Council is authorized to take appropriate action to combat discrimination

1630 *Craig/de Búrca,* EU Law (Fourth Edition), p. 20.
1631 *Craig/de Búrca,* EU Law (Fourth Edition), p. 20.
1632 *Woods/Watson,* p. 9.
1633 *Woods/Watson,* p. 9.
1634 *Craig/de Búrca,* EU Law (Fourth Edition), p. 20; *Woods/Watson,* p. 10.
1635 *Craig/de Búrca,* EU Law (Fourth Edition), pp. 20, 22; *Woods/Watson,* p. 10.
1636 *Woods/Watson,* p. 10.
1637 *Craig/de Búrca,* EU Law (Fourth Edition), p. 20; *Woods/Watson,* p. 10.
1638 *Craig/de Búrca,* EU Law (Fourth Edition), p. 20.

on the basis of sex, racial or ethnic origin, religion or belief, disability, age or sexual orientation.[1639]

The Amsterdam Treaty additionally allowed "closer cooperation" between the member states.[1640] Viewed as an example of the principle of flexibility, this allows "different conceptions of the European ideal and different degrees of commitment to exist within the European framework."[1641] The ToA allowed member states to cooperate on areas within the general scope of the treaties although the same might not yet be subject to Union legislation.[1642] To some degree this gives the advantage of being open to compromise within the Union but then again, one could not really tell where the line is between being only within the sphere of the Union and the areas permitting close cooperation.[1643]

Overall, the Amsterdam Treaty has made a general impact in two respects: first, it eroded the demarcation and delineation between the three pillars which have been crafted four years earlier – this was seen in the transferring of provisions, i.e. on asylum and immigration, from the JHA to the EC pillar for example; second, there was the constitutionalization and legitimization of mechanisms for allowing different degrees of integration and/or cooperation among different groups of states.[1644] Differentiated integration, as demonstrated by the different provisions introduced by the Amsterdam Treaty has become at this juncture neither "an aberration within the EC and EU legal order nor as a temporary solution or means of gradually easing member states into a uniform system."[1645]

b. Expansion Stage

Throughout the history of the European Commission thus far, it has existed without any IGC from 1957 to 1985 but one could observe a continuous process of amendment since the advent of the SEA.[1646] This was the case even more after the Amsterdam Treaty entered into force.

1639 Treaty on the Functioning of the European Union ("TFEU"), arts. 18, 19; *Craig/de Búrca*, EU Law (Fourth Edition), p. 20.

1640 *Woods/Watson*, p. 11.

1641 *Woods/Watson*, p. 11.

1642 *Woods/Watson*, p. 11.

1643 *Woods/Watson*, p. 11.

1644 *Woods/Watson*, p. 11.

1645 *Craig/de Búrca*, EU Law (Fourth Edition), p. 21.

1646 *Craig/de Búrca*, EU Law (Fourth Edition), p. 25.

Should the Amsterdam Treaty's success be measured as to how it was able to address institutional issues concerning the eventual enlargement of the European Union within its provisions, then it would have failed to score high marks. This in turn is problematic because enlargement was already a decided vector in the development of the EU even before the process of coming up with the Amsterdam Treaty began.[1647] Thus, two months after the ToA was signed new treaty negotiations came forth when the European Council at the Cologne Summit of 1999 called for another intergovernmental conference to address unresolved issues such as the size and composition of the Commission, weighing of votes within the Council, the extension of the qualified majority voting ("QMV"), the legitimacy of the Union and how broad the scope of its power and authority is.[1648]

The scope of the contemplated treaty remained however narrow until the 2000 Feira European Council, wherein it was decided to include "enhanced cooperation" as a theme.[1649] Notably, such was already contemplated within the Amsterdam Treaty but this time around, there was a change in nomenclature from "closer" cooperation to "enhanced", wherein member states which are interested to forge cooperation with one another can use the existing mechanisms and procedures available as long as they are consistent with the spirit and letter of the existing treaties.[1650] Taking the same into consideration, the contemplated Treaty of Nice basically aimed to deal with the leftovers the ToA was not able to discuss.[1651]

The Nice Treaty was concluded in December 2000 after an otherwise "notoriously fractious and badly run" European Summit.[1652] It consisted of two parts wherein one part concerned substantial amendments to the EU and EC treaties while the other consisted of transitory and final provisions; four protocols on enlargement, Statue of the Court of Justice, financial consequences of the expiration of the ECSC treaty, and on Article 67 EC Treaty vis-à-vis free movement of persons; twenty-four declarations, including declarations on Enlargement and Future of the Union.[1653]

Ratification of the Nice Treaty was not easy as member states sought approval within their own legal orders.[1654] It was also a stumbling block

---

1647 *Craig/de Búrca,* EU Law (Fourth Edition), p. 25.
1648 *Craig/de Búrca,* EU Law (Fourth Edition), p. 25; *Woods/Watson,* p. 11.
1649 *Craig/de Búrca,* EU Law (Fourth Edition), p. 25; *Woods/Watson,* p. 11.
1650 *Woods/Watson,* p. 11.
1651 *Craig/de Búrca,* EU Law (Fourth Edition), p. 29.
1652 *Woods/Watson,* p. 11.
1653 *Craig/de Búrca,* EU Law (Fourth Edition), p. 26.
1654 *Craig/de Búrca,* EU Law (Fourth Edition), p. 26.

that the Irish voted "no" to it given that the Nice Treaty was supposedly an imperative precursor to further EU expansion.[1655] It was only through a second round of referendum in October 2002 that the Irish gave their thumbs up, while Ireland, on the other hand, lodged its ratification instrument on 18 December 2002.[1656] The Treaty of Nice came into force on 01 February 2003, as stated in the treaty.

As a precursor to enlargement of the EU and providing a roadmap as to how this enlargement could proceed, some heads of state and/or government expressed their intention to enter into accession negotiations with the most advanced candidates before the end of 2002 as well as allowing the latter's citizens to take part in the European Parliament elections in June 2004.[1657] Other than having this enlargement in mind, the Nice Treaty also concerned itself with other amendments, including the provision dealing with the suspension of a member state found to be in serious and persistent breach of the principles of respect for democracy, human rights, and the rule of law.[1658] Now, the concerned provision – Article 7 – provides for a more detailed provision before a negative determination could be made, such as an opportunity to be heard and for an independent report to be made, and also the possibility of acting where there is a clear risk of breach.[1659] There was also agreement on the institutional questions relevant to enlargement: setting the weighing of votes in the Council, distribution of seats in the European Parliament, and composition of the Commission.[1660]

In the meantime, the Cologne Council launched also an initiative of major constitutional significance, wherein a body would be constituted from national parliamentarians, European parliamentarians, and national government representatives to draft a Charter of Fundamental Rights.[1661] Said body eventually turned into a "Convention" that began work in 2000 and was able to come up with a "Charter" by the end of the year.[1662] In light of this, one could notice that the process of drafting the Charter was made in an unusually open and public way, with regular posting and sharing of documents, materials, and drafts in the dedicated website,

1655 *Woods/Watson*, p. 12.
1656 *Woods/Watson*, p. 12.
1657 *Woods/Watson*, p. 4.
1658 *Horváth*, p. 59.
1659 *Craig/de Búrca*, EU Law (Fourth Edition), p. 27.
1660 *Craig/de Búrca*, EU Law (Fourth Edition), p. 27.
1661 *Craig/de Búrca*, EU Law (Fourth Edition), p. 27.
1662 *Craig/de Búrca*, EU Law (Fourth Edition), p. 26.

and meetings were made openly.[1663] While it was solemnly proclaimed by the Commission, Parliament, and Council and politically approved by the member states at the December 2000 Nice Council, there were still questions as to its status and possible integration into the Treaties that were scheduled to be discussed instead in the 2004 intergovernmental conference.[1664]

With the aforementioned still very much on the table, the 11 September 2001 terrorist attacks in the United States shook the world and it was interesting to see how Europe reacted to the same. On one hand, one could see the outright sympathy given to the victims of the attacks and the initial outright support given for America's efforts to bring the perpetrators to justice, which subsequently led to a "level of transnational concord" unprecedented in history wherein European governments and the European Union were more than willing to adapt counterterrorism measures and create new ones in response to terrorism as an increasing security threat.[1665] This eventually led to a revamp of policy areas including, but not limited to, foreign and security policy, law enforcement, judicial affairs, migration, international trade, and even finance and democratization.[1666]

On the other hand, it became sooner or later undeniable that at the onset of the 9/11 attacks in the United States Europe had been providing said perpetrators a basis for these attacks.[1667] The realization did not take long that Europe too was a primary target of terrorism and such was not prompted by the September 2001 or the other attacks in Europe thereafter, but rather, by the growing number of marginalized and radicalized Muslim communities in European societies and the early warning signs such as the 1994-1995 attacks by Algerian Islamists in France or the thwarted attack on the Christmas market in Strasbourg, France on New Year's Day in 2000.[1668] With this in mind, Europe became a stronger partner in the global battle against the threat posed by transnational terrorism using the means available through the European Union and its member states.[1669]

1663 *Craig/de Búrca*, EU Law (Fourth Edition), p. 26.
1664 *Craig/de Búrca*, EU Law (Fourth Edition), p. 26.
1665 *Craig/de Búrca*, EU Law (Fourth Edition), p. 26; *Woods/Watson*, p. 11.
1666 *Eder/Senn*, p. 13.
1667 *Eder/Senn*, p. 13.
1668 *Eder/Senn*, p. 13.
1669 *Eder/Senn*, pp. 13-14.

The Nice roadmap was confirmed during the Laeken summit in December 2001.[1670] At the same time, 10 candidate countries were named to have a good chance of early entry: Cyprus, Czech Republic, Estonia, Hungary, Latvia, Lithuania, Malta, Poland, Slovakia, and Slovenia.[1671] Furthermore, the resulting Laeken Declaration confirmed by the next round of treaty negotiations the issues laid down in the Declaration on the Future of Europe, which was attached to the Treaty of Nice: "the delimitation of powers between the EU and the member states, the simplification of powers, and the role of the national parliaments in the EU," as well as the much-needed discussion as to the future of the EU.[1672] Through growing consensus from major institutional players, the aforementioned was thought to be reconciled with two other issues: content of the reform agenda and the reform process.[1673] With respect to the overall content of the reform agenda, it was realized that some issues that were not discussed in the Nice Treaty touched on the imperative need to re-evaluate and re-think the substantive and institutional rudiments of the EU.[1674] On the other hand, there was clamor that the reform process should at least be legitimated by a broader "constituency" than hitherto given the broad range of issues being tackled.[1675]

The Laeken Declaration then became the catalyst for a Convention in June 2003 which paved way to the draft Treaty establishing a Constitution for Europe ("the Constitution") and submitted for the consideration of the European Council in July.[1676] It consisted of four parts, discussing the (1) basic objectives and values of the EU, fundamental rights, competencies, forms of law-making, institutional division of power, etc.; (2) charter of rights; (3) policies and functions of the EU; and (4) general and final provisions.[1677] Included herein was the merger of the three pillars, creation of a single legal framework, and affording the European Union legal personality.[1678] The Constitution Treaty simplified decision making, including the streamlining of applicable procedures and defining matters

---

1670 *Eder/Senn*, p. 14.

1671 *Horváth*, p. 59.

1672 *Horváth*, p. 59.

1673 See *Craig*, p. 73; *Horváth*, p. 61; *Woods/Watson*, p. 12.

1674 *Craig/de Búrca*, EU Law (Fourth Edition), p. 31; *Craig*, p. 73; *Woods/Watson*, p. 12.

1675 *Craig/de Búrca*, EU Law (Fourth Edition), p. 27.

1676 *Craig/de Búrca*, EU Law (Fourth Edition), p. 27.

1677 *Craig/de Búrca*, EU Law (Fourth Edition), p. 33; *Craig*, p. 73.

1678 *Craig/de Búrca*, EU Law (Fourth Edition), p. 33.

for which unanimous voting is not required, and at the same time, defined what the competencies of the EU are and what were those that exclusively belonged to the member states.[1679] On this point, some were adamant about the inclusion of part III on the policies and functions of the EU as the same did not only put too much on the plate but it also endangered losing the complex bargains done over the years among the member states to the point that it might necessitate amendment of existing treaties to make them consistent with one another and the Constitution Treaty.[1680] Despite these issues and concerns, the Constitution Treaty was still signed on 29 October 2004 and was essentially a Convention on the future of Europe.[1681]

Uncertainty ensued because although it was ratified by 13 member states, France and the Netherlands disapproved.[1682] Such rejection by the French and Dutch raises the question on political legitimacy. One would realize that this was not an isolated incident considering that prior to this, there have been rejections made: the Danish rejection of the Maastricht Treaty in June 1992 is one, and the repeated closely contested referenda on treaty reform.[1683] There was restive public opinion about the scope and pace of European integration and unfamiliarity with the workings and accountability of EU institutions.[1684] Some political leaders point out that there was the fear of the people, for example in the Netherlands, that with the Constitution Treaty, their children would be less well-off than themselves.[1685] The French and Dutch public pointed out to the lingering problems and issues surrounding the different European countries and that the European Union was accountable as to what has it done for its citizens, how was EU membership beneficial to the daily lives of its citizens, and why the Constitution Treaty did not include provisions addressing these concerns.[1686] There was a general sense of mistrust and suspicion as regards what benefits and solutions the EU has delivered, which consequently prompted others to be conservative instead: as Frans Timmermans worded it, "if you believe things can only get worse, you try to hold on

---

1679 *Horváth*, p. 65.
1680 *Horváth*, p. 65.
1681 *Craig/de Búrca*, EU Law (Fourth Edition), p. 33.
1682 *Horváth*, pp. 66-67; *Woods/Watson*, pp. 12-13.
1683 *Horváth*, p. 67; *Woods/Watson*, p. 13.
1684 *Dinan*, p. 1.
1685 *Dinan*, p. 1.
1686 *Timmermans*, p. 106.

to what you have."[1687] It did not help likewise that national governments worsened the situation by always pointing the finger to EU decisions.[1688] These realizations and stumbling block on further integration definitely dealt a blow to the European Union which suddenly felt befuddled as to what next steps to take.[1689]

In light of this, many suggestions were brought to the table. The Netherlands, for example, suggested going back to the Nice Treaty, which obviously had shortcomings that ought to be rectified, while using elements found in the Constitution Treaty.[1690] It was important however that in doing so, it would be acceptable to all member states.[1691]

In the intervening time, the Nice Treaty as earlier mentioned was instrumental in accelerating the pace of accession negotiations in 2001 and 2002, resulting in negotiations with the earlier mentioned ten candidate countries to be concluded during the Copenhagen summit on 13 December 2002.[1692] The relevant Accession Treaty was signed in April 2003 and thereafter, ratification procedures were held in each candidate country.[1693] The resulting accession on 01 May 2004 of Czech Republic, Estonia, Cyprus, Latvia, Lithuania, Hungary, Malta, Poland, Slovenia, and Slovakia resulted in the biggest enlargement of the EU and at the same time, marked a significant event in its historical development.[1694] The entry of the aforementioned Eastern European countries in the EU meant the reunification of Europe, bringing an end to the division caused after the Second World War.[1695] As Horváth remarked, this event has symbolized that the "Iron Curtain" has finally fallen for good.[1696] And indeed, not so long after this accession, negotiations were concluded with Bulgaria and Romania during the summit in December 2004 and they acceded in 2007, while negotiations were then still ongoing with Croatia and Turkey.[1697]

1687 *Horváth*, p. 69.
1688 *Timmermans*, pp. 106, 107.
1689 *Dinan*, p. 1.
1690 *Horváth*, pp. 67, 68; *Woods/Watson*, p. 13.
1691 *Timmermans*, p. 107.
1692 *Timmermans*, p. 107.
1693 *Horváth*, p. 59; *Michalski*, pp. 292-293.
1694 *Horváth*, p. 59.
1695 *Craig/de Búrca*, EU Law (6th edition), p. 19; *Michalski*, p. 292.
1696 *Horváth*, p. 60.
1697 *Horváth*, p. 60.

Coinciding with the entry of new countries in May 2004, the European Union launched the European Neighborhood Policy ("ENP").[1698] Initially, countries outside the EU and found in the east, except for Russia, were not a priority in the EU agenda but due to the 2004 expansion, the EU found itself closer to them.[1699] There was then the need to ensure stability in the wider neighborhood because otherwise, any instability might risk itself of spilling over to the EU's borders.[1700] As Smith noted, the extension of EU borders became the most important of all foreign policy implications of enlargement during this time as it created new demarcating lines between insiders and outsiders, which in turn could create concerns and problems to those involved.[1701] Such issues led to the establishment of the ENP.[1702] And while the ENP was instituted for the benefit of the EU and stalling off any possible risk of instability brought upon by its enlargement, the rhetoric that could be found in the ENP is that the EU seeks to be a "force for good" in its dealings with neighboring countries.[1703] The European Security Strategy of 2003 had previously declared that building security in the neighborhood was one of the strategic objectives of the EU, which includes fostering well governed countries east of the European Union and on the borders of the Mediterranean, and furthering "a world seen as offering justice and opportunity for everyone" and in fulfilling the same, the EU endeavors to work proactively.[1704]

The ENP stretches over a large geographical area and covers a diversity of countries, including those, as aforementioned, in the east of the European Union and those bordering in the Mediterranean.[1705] It must be noted that prior to the ENP framework, there has been prior attempts to establish something similar: they either entailed discussions or meetings at high levels on political issues without necessarily establishing decision making frameworks, or avenues wherein bilateralism, multilateralism or moves towards regionalism were being promoted.[1706] Alternatively, the ENP framework distinguishes by not having regular scheduled meetings of all neighbors at any level but rather, a preference for bilateralism,

---

1698 *Craig/de Búrca*, EU Law (6th edition), p. 19; *Horváth*, p. 60; *Michalski*, p. 294.
1699 *Barbé/Johansson-Nogués*, p. 81; *Smith*, pp. 757, 758.
1700 *Smith*, p. 758.
1701 *Smith*, p. 758.
1702 *Smith*, p. 758.
1703 *Smith*, p. 758.
1704 *Barbé/Johansson-Nogués*, p. 81.
1705 *Barbé/Johansson-Nogués*, p. 81; *Smith*, p. 759.
1706 See *Smith*, p. 759.

wherein emphasis is given to fostering bilateral relations between the EU and individual countries to be able to influence, more or less, the latter's internal and external policies.[1707] In connection to this, the EU steers away from the use of sanctions to get what it wants but in its place, the EU seeks to be more "benevolent" by means of using incentives through the ENP to promote "stability, security and well-being for all" and to foster cooperation in areas of mutual consent and interest."[1708]

With the ENP as an instrument, the EU is not only able to have a proactive role in ensuring security and stability within its borders and those of its neighbors but it has also been able to promote the norms and values it espouses through the same.[1709] A reading of the action plans within the ENP would show the emphasis of the EU towards the promotion and use of human rights and democratic principles amongst its neighbors.[1710] Not only that but EU neighbors are expected to conform not only to EU values but likewise EU standards and laws in social and economic areas, to be able to build a good neighborhood relationship.[1711] While governing to the EU by approximating its standards and values is understandable to ensure growth and economic development,[1712] these provisions within the ENP undeniably likewise show how the ENP is being used by the EU to play its normative role with its global partners and neighbors.[1713]

By 2007, the new financial instrument for the ENP came into force and there was a noticeable increase in money allocated over previous EU aid programmes to countries covered by the same.[1714] The policy thus appears remarkably balanced in its attention to interest and values, soft in respect of the absence of elements of coercion and rather generous in its offer of material assistance.

c. Reconsolidation Stage

As the enlargement of the EU was ongoing, there was the going concern of how the EU was trying to bring its act together after the Constitution

1707 *Smith*, pp. 761-762.
1708 *Smith*, p. 762.
1709 *Barbé/Johansson-Nogués*, p. 81.
1710 *Smith*, p. 765.
1711 *Smith*, p. 765.
1712 *Smith*, p. 763.
1713 *Smith*, p. 763.
1714 *Manners*, pp. 45, 46.

Treaty. The European Council in 2005 thought it best to encourage the member states to reflect and engage their citizens into debate as regards the EU.[1715] Due to the failure of the Constitution Treaty, the EU then needed to function on the basis of the Rome Treaty, as amended by other treaties including the Nice Treaty.[1716] However, this was believed to be insufficient to guarantee the efficacy of the Union with a membership of around 25-27 member states.[1717]

In the first half of 2007, the German presidency of the European Council sought agreement on a so-called Reform Treaty, which shall primarily concern itself in amending both the TEU and EC Treaty, with the former retaining its name while the latter would be known as the Treaty on the Functioning of the EU ("TFEU").[1718] Coincidingly, the Union would embody a single personality and for purposes of consistency, the word "Community" shall be replaced by "Union".[1719] There was also a conscious effort to be careful with terminology, which obviously includes excising the mention of constitutional terms in the new treaty.[1720] This coincides with the issue that misunderstandings arose from the words and symbols used in the Constitution Treaty, which were normally reserved to the national level.[1721] Though drafters of the Constitution Treaty thought that usage of familiar terms would allow the people to understand the same better, this move backfired as people thought that the European level would then take over the national level – and this of course did not quell the fears already being harbored by many.[1722] Also, the usage of "Constitution Treaty" was itself a misnomer considering it was not a constitution.[1723] As a stark opponent of said treaty said, the problem was that in explaining the Constitution Treaty one must start by saying it is not a Constitution, and with this, the entire story surrounding it starts with a lie.[1724]

1715 *Barbé/Johansson-Nogués*, p. 81.
1716 *Craig/de Búrca*, EU Law (6th edition), p. 19.
1717 *Craig/de Búrca*, EU Law (6th edition), p. 19.
1718 *Horváth*, p. 61.
1719 *Craig/de Búrca*, EU Law (6th edition), p. 20; *Woods/Watson*, p. 14.
1720 *Craig/de Búrca*, EU Law (6th edition), p. 20. See for details *Craig/de Búrca*, EU Law (6th edition), p. 20.
1721 *Craig*, p. 75.
1722 *Timmermans*, p. 107.
1723 *Timmermans*, pp. 107-108.
1724 *Timmermans*, p. 108.

It must be mentioned that the year 2007 coincided with the 50th Anniversary of the European Union and to commemorate the same, its representatives signed the Berlin Declaration which includes the values, goals, and further aspirations for the European Union.[1725] With the agreement to come up with a Reform Treaty, including the formation of an IGC to work towards the same, there were rapid developments towards the same when the second half of 2007 came.[1726] The speed by which those involved worked was to some degree influenced by the Portuguese presidency of the European Council during this time, which wanted the new treaty to be attributed to it.[1727] Thus, the new Reform Treaty, which was now known as the Lisbon Treaty, came in fast and was signed and agreed upon in a special summit in Lisbon on 13 December 2007 and entered into force in 01 December 2009.[1728]

The Lisbon Treaty did not reach the finish line without obstacles, however. The Lisbon Treaty ought to be ratified by the member states and Ireland needed two referenda before it was able to ratify.[1729] On the other hand, the Czech president was initially unwilling to sign and only reluctantly did so when the constitutional challenge to the Lisbon Treaty was rejected by the Czech Constitutional Court and when other member states agreed to the inclusion of a protocol relating to the Czech Republic and Charter of Rights.[1730]

There was very much a hot debate regarding the Lisbon Treaty, especially given that it is heavily influenced by the Constitution that was previously voted "no" for by France and the Netherlands.[1731] To appease all parties, the treaty did not only need to be distinguishable from the Constitutional Treaty but also, it has to retain the proposed reforms in said Constitutional Treaty for the betterment of the Union.[1732] Moreover, concerns post-TEU period mainly involved the issue on how to make the EU function more efficacious, especially with respect to treaty-making.[1733]

More or less, the Lisbon Treaty was able to tackle these issues. At the outset, the Lisbon Treaty was able to fortify the co-decision procedure now

---

1725 *Timmermans*, p. 108.
1726 *Woods/Watson*, p. 14.
1727 *Craig/de Búrca*, EU Law (6th edition), p. 20.
1728 *Craig/de Búrca*, EU Law (6th edition), p. 20.
1729 *Craig/de Búrca*, EU Law (6th edition), p. 20; *Woods/Watson*, p. 14.
1730 *Craig/de Búrca*, EU Law (6th edition), p. 20.
1731 *Craig/de Búrca*, EU Law (6th edition), p. 20.
1732 *Woods/Watson*, p. 14.
1733 *Woods/Watson*, p. 14.

applicable in the primary, or ordinary, legislative process.[1734] Although the Commission retains its right of legislative initiative, it is now on an increasingly equal footing with both the EP and Council in the legislative areas in more policy areas.[1735] As Craig noted, this is a welcomed development as not only the Union's interest is represented in legislation through the Commission, but also the interests of the electorate and the member states themselves, through the EP and Council, respectively, which results to a framework of deliberative dialogue among the main Union institutions.[1736]

The Lisbon Treaty also tackled other themes, including those which give value to human beings as more than economic actors, but more so, as political and social beings.[1737] To illustrate, there was a change in status of the Charter of Fundamental Rights in light of the Lisbon Treaty: introduced during the Treaty of Nice but without any legal effect, the Lisbon Treaty now recognized the rights set forth therein and conferred the same legal value as any other treaty.[1738] Aside from this, the Lisbon Treaty introduced changes to freedom and security through its criminal law provisions.[1739] Another issue relates to democracy: changes were introduced vis-à-vis the role of national parliaments in EU processes through the emphasis of the principal of conferral and in the attempt to delimit EU competence more cautiously.[1740] There is also the applicability of the principle of subsidiarity that imposes the obligation to consult widely before proposing legislative acts, including the transmittal of legislative proposals to national parliaments coincidingly with the Union institutions.[1741] Some provisions regarding this are predicated on the idea that the power of the EU actually emanates from the member states and thus, provisions on member states opting out of the EU find themselves in the same line.[1742] Lastly, institutional innovations were introduced as regards giving the EU an external profile to the world, such as the new High Representative of the Union on Foreign Affairs and the legal personality of the EU.[1743]

1734 *Woods/Watson*, p. 15.
1735 *Craig*, p. 74.
1736 *Craig*, p. 74.
1737 *Craig*, p. 74.
1738 Lisbon Treaty, art. 6(1); *Woods/Watson*, p. 15.
1739 *Woods/Watson*, p. 148.
1740 *Woods/Watson*, p. 15.
1741 *Craig*, pp. 75-77.
1742 *Craig*, pp. 75-77; *Woods/Watson*, p. 15.
1743 *Woods/Watson*, p. 15.

In addition to the aforementioned, the Lisbon Treaty was like the Constitution Treaty inasmuch as it disposes of the pillar structure albeit there remains a demarcation between the first and third pillars and the CFSP.[1744] The first and third pillars now form a single treaty through the EC treaty and the new Treaty on the Functioning of the European Union ("TFEU"), while the CFSP remains with the TEU.[1745] In other words, while the JHA is within the penumbra of greater Union institutions as a part of the Area of Freedom, Security and Justice, CFSP remains intergovernmental in nature.[1746] Further, any reference to the "Community" are now references to the "Union" and unlike before, the EU through the Lisbon treaty has obtained legal personality.[1747]

The successful conclusion of the Lisbon Treaty corresponded with the time when the world economic crisis, which started with the collapse of the United States housing market in 2007, found its way in EU shores.[1748] If one may recall, one of things the Maastricht Treaty introduced was the establishment of a monetary and economic union, which connoted the use of a single currency to be overseen by the European Central Bank.[1749] The idea was that, with controlling national fiscal and budgetary policy, it ensures that member states would not spend more than they earn.[1750] Otherwise, the strength and stability of the Euro would be undermined.[1751]

Albeit the foregoing seems nice on paper, the financial crisis exposed inherent structural and policy flaws. It did not only show European central bankers and financial ministers how opaque EU banking supervision was,[1752] but more importantly, how two parts of the Maastricht settlement were out of sync and that apparently, EU control over national budgetary policy was relatively weak and unable to exert control over national economic policy.[1753]

The financial crisis in the EU happened on two fronts: banking crisis among member states and a sovereign debt crisis.[1754] As regards the bank-

1744 *Woods/Watson*, p. 15.
1745 *Woods/Watson*, p. 15.
1746 *Woods/Watson*, p. 15.
1747 *Woods/Watson*, p. 15.
1748 *Craig/de Búrca*, EU Law (6th edition), p. 22.
1749 *Craig/de Búrca*, EU Law (6th edition), p. 23; *Heisenberg*, p. 249.
1750 *Craig/de Búrca*, EU Law (6th edition), pp. 22-23.
1751 *Craig/de Búrca*, EU Law (6th edition), p. 23.
1752 *Craig/de Búrca*, EU Law (6th edition), p. 23.
1753 *Heisenberg*, p. 249.
1754 *Craig/de Búrca*, EU Law (6th edition), p. 23.

ing crisis, there was a snowball effect that occurred with regard financial institutions. It was difficult for the European Central Bank to discover how seriously affected major banks in member states were, given the different domestic institutions in the member states handling banking capitalization reporting and regulation.[1755] In respect of financial markets, the uncertainty resulted in reluctance to lending, even to the point that the banking sector was at a standstill because of lack of information on either the fundamental capitalization of banks or their involvement in then exotic securities and/or investments in the US or Spanish real estate.[1756] This eventually resulted in not only having the European Central Bank ("ECB") as the lender of last resort and instituting stability mechanisms to safeguard financial stability, but also institutional reforms that gave more authority to the ECB in EU banking supervision.[1757]

The banking crisis was only the tip of the iceberg. Before the 2007-2009 crisis, member states in the Eurozone were able to borrow at German interest rates, on the assumption that risk of being at default was negligible.[1758] It turns out however that the risk of sovereign default was high, especially for most southern states, which in turn prompted the EU to force austerity measures as suspensive condition for aid.[1759] The most acute problem came from Greece, whose credit rating to repay was downgraded to "junk status" after it requested a €45 Million loan from the IMF and EU.[1760] The concern over the budgetary health of other countries came into front.[1761] Interest rates pushed up and successively, there was downward pressure to the euro.[1762] The latter was only alleviated when other member states stepped in to provide financial assistance to Greece and the other states heavily affected.[1763] The financial assistance notably was under strict conditionality and fellow member states, especially Germany, did not mince their words against Greece as to how it ran its budgetary policy.[1764]

1755 *Heisenberg*, p. 249.
1756 *Heisenberg*, p. 249.
1757 *Heisenberg*, p. 249.
1758 *Heisenberg*, p. 249.
1759 *Heisenberg*, p. 250.
1760 *Heisenberg*, p. 250.
1761 *Craig/de Búrca*, EU Law (6th edition), p. 23; *Heisenberg*, p. 250.
1762 *Craig/de Búrca*, EU Law (6th edition), p. 23.
1763 *Craig/de Búrca*, EU Law (6th edition), p. 23; *Heisenberg*, p. 250.
1764 *Craig/de Búrca*, EU Law (6th edition), p. 23.

The economic and financial crisis had profound effects on the EU and contributed admittedly to the further evolution of the same.[1765] Emulating the famous adage of never allowing a serious crisis to go to waste, the EU endeavored on different institutional developments that would hopefully strengthen EU fiscal policy oversight and make it more effective.[1766]

In 2013, Croatia became a member likewise.[1767]

Prompted by a public vote through referendum in June 2016, the United Kingdom was the first EU member state to engage Article 50 TEU and exit the European Union.[1768] It formally left the EU on 31 January 2020 but negotiations are still needed during the transition period that would end in December 2020. By virtue of the so-called Trade and Cooperation Agreement, the EU and the UK entered into a form of partnership effective on 01 January 2021.

B. Present Institutional and Legal Framework

The next portion of the discussion focuses on the present institutional and legal framework of the European Union as a regional organization. This is mainly done in three (3) parts: (1) the EU as a Regional Organization; (2) its organizational structure; and (3) the different principles, norms, and practices of the EU.

1. European Union as a Regional Organization

The European Union is described as both an alliance and a legal person. As an alliance, the EU was not only founded on two treaties, namely the Treaty on European Union ("TEU") and Treaty on the Functioning of the European Union ("TFEU"), but the alliance character is also eminent from one its applicable principles, the principal of conferral of competencies, wherein whatever is not conferred to the Union shall remain within the competencies of the member states.[1769] The classic international law adage is also mentioned in the Treaties, wherein there is respect for the equal-

1765 *Heisenberg*, p. 250.
1766 *Craig/de Búrca*, EU Law (6th edition), p. 23.
1767 *Heisenberg*, pp. 251-252.
1768 *Gordon*, p. 21; *van Wijk*, p. 155.
1769 Treaty on European Union, art. 4(1); *Woods/Watson*, p. 4.

ity of state, their national identities, and their essential state functions, including ensuring territorial integrity, maintaining law and order, and safeguarding national security.[1770] It bears mentioning as well that in many accounts, the roles of member states are stronger, particularly the increased role of the European Council, which, although is an organ of the Union, still remains in many respects a conference of the governments of the member states, and given much authority to decide on important Union matters.[1771]

It is unequivocal too, that the Union is a legal person vis-à-vis its internal and external structure. On one hand, the Lisbon Treaty has explicitly referred to it as a single entity and refuses to acknowledge it having different regimes of different entities.[1772] This is further expressed by the fact that the European Union itself has organs and institutions that could act on its own.[1773] This is one of its distinguishing, if not most known characteristic: the European Union as a supranational organization has significant powers and authority itself that can be exercised independently and distinctly from its member states.[1774] It is a force of its own, existing more than member states acting together.[1775] The scope and level of power and authority given to its institutions is one of the defining features of the European Union, ensuring the Union's objectives are carried out efficaciously.[1776] The Union's objectives and the manner these objectives are being carried out by the institutions affect the EU as a whole with respect to its nature, and likewise influence the scope and content of EU law.[1777] In this respect, the EU as a supranational organization can pass legislation, in many instances wherein unanimity among member states cannot be reached, and said legislation is binding on the member states and must thereafter be applied by their respective courts and law enforcement agencies.[1778] Additionally, its judicial organ – the CJEU – can adjudicate cases originating from the member-countries, and even the member states are

1770 *Curtin/Dekker*, p. 164.
1771 *Curtin/Dekker*, p. 164.
1772 *Curtin/Dekker*, p. 164.
1773 *Curtin/Dekker*, p. 164.
1774 *Curtin/Dekker*, p. 165.
1775 *Hartley*, p. 1.
1776 *Hartley*, p. 1.
1777 *Woods/Watson*, p. 23.
1778 *Woods/Watson*, p. 23.

subject to the said court's compulsory jurisdiction in cases concerning the Treaties and/or Community legislation.[1779]

A word of caution must be forwarded in relation to the foregoing however. Inasmuch as the Union and its institutions can act on its own and on behalf of its member states as a supranational organization, this power is not all encompassing and without bounds. It may only act in the policy fields which the member states have conferred to it.[1780] No less than the TEU and TFEU themselves provide for these different competencies, which is mainly categorized into the following: exclusive competence, shared competence, and the competence to support, coordinate or supplement actions of the member states.[1781]

Exclusive competence, as the description suggests, means that it is only the EU which can act on these acts, which are the following: "(1) customs union; (2) the establishing of the competition rules necessary for the functioning of the internal market; (3) monetary policy for the member states whose currency is the euro; (4) conservation of marine biological resources under the common fisheries policy; (5) common commercial policy; (6) concluding international agreements."[1782] With respect to international agreements, the same is a matter of conditional exclusivity because as Article 3(2) of the TFEU provides, it could only be done when either (1) the conclusion is provided in a legislative act of the Union, or (2) when the same is necessary to enable the EU to exercise its internal competence, or (3) insofar as their conclusion may affect common rules or alter their scope.[1783] Accordingly, Article 3(2) should be read together with Article 216 of the same TFEU because as some explain, Article 216 explains whether the EU has competence to enter into international agreements, Article 3(2) then explains whether the same is exclusive or otherwise.[1784] Article 216 of the TFEU reads as follows:

> "1. The Union may conclude an agreement with one or more third countries or international organisations where the Treaties so provide or where the conclusion of an agreement is necessary in order to achieve, within the framework of the Union's policies, one of the objectives referred to in the Treaties, or is provided for in a legally

1779 *Hartley*, p. 1.
1780 Treaty on European Union, arts.5 and 13(1); *Hartley*, p. 1.
1781 Treaty on Functioning of the European Union, arts. 2-6; *Woods/Watson*, p. 50.
1782 Treaty on Functioning of the European Union, arts. 2, 3; *Woods/Watson*, p. 57.
1783 Treaty on Functioning of the European Union, art. 3(2).
1784 *Woods/Watson*, p. 57.

binding Union act or is likely to affect common rules or alter their scope.

"2. Agreements concluded by the Union are binding upon the institutions of the Union and on its Member States."[1785]

While admittedly the evolution of this given exclusive (but conditional) competence has been complex, the reality based on the foregoing is that it would be rare, if ever, that the EU lacks power to conclude an international agreement.[1786] Referring back to Article 3(2), should a legislative act provide for the conclusion of an international agreement, then the Union has exclusive external competence. This consequently preempts member states on acting independently or on their own, or even legislating or adopting any legally binding act.[1787] Secondly, as long as the EU has internal competence and conclusion of the international agreement shall be necessary to effectuate said competence, then the EU again has exclusive external competence, regardless of whether the same is exclusive or shared.[1788] And lastly, in being able to conclude international agreements that may affect common rules or alter their scope, this drives home the point that as long as the EU has exercised a power internally, it can then very well do so exercise external competence over said matter.[1789]

Other than the aforementioned exclusive competencies of the EU, there are the shared competencies, which in actuality are the general residual category.[1790] Article 2(2) of the TFEU explains the workings of this competence best as follows:

"2. When the Treaties confer on the Union a competence shared with the Member States in a specific area, the Union and the Member States may legislate and adopt legally binding acts in that area. The Member States shall exercise their competence to the extent that the Union has not exercised its competence. The Member States shall exercise their

1785 Treaty on Functioning of the European Union, art. 216.

1786 *Craig/de Búrca,* EU Law (6th edition), p. 79.

1787 See Treaty on Functioning of the European Union, art. 3(2); *Craig/de Búrca,* EU Law (6th edition), p. 79.

1788 See Treaty on Functioning of the European Union, art. 3(2); *Craig/de Búrca,* EU Law (6th edition), p. 79.

1789 See Treaty on Functioning of the European Union, art. 3(2); *Craig/de Búrca,* EU Law (6th edition), p. 79.

1790 *Craig/de Búrca,* EU Law (6th edition), p. 79.

competence again to the extent that the Union has decided to cease exercising its competence."[1791]

Article 4 of the TFEU correspondingly defines and enumerates the different areas where competence is shared, namely, (1) internal market; (2) social policy, limited to the aspects defined in the TFEU; (3) economic, social and territorial cohesion; (3) agriculture and fisheries, excluding the conservation of marine biological resources: (4) environment; (5) consumer protection; (6) transport; (7) trans-European networks; (8) energy; (9) area of freedom, security and justice; (10) common safety concerns in public health matters, limited to the aspects defined in the TFEU; (11) research, technological development and space; and (12) development cooperation and humanitarian aid.[1792]

As Article 2(2) provides, there is a preemption element with respect to shared competence as "member states shall exercise competence to the extent that the Union has not exercised its competence" and/or "to the extent that the Union has decided to cease exercising its competence." While these instances can diminish the amount of shared power over time, not all is lost for the member states because at the outset, one must look first in the detailed provisions that delineate what the EU can do in the diverse areas where power is shared, to be able to have a good gauge on limitation on Union competence.[1793] Secondly, preemption occurs to the extent the EU exercised its competence, meaning, there are various ways the Union could exercise its power without stopping member states from exercising their own competence outright.[1794] And even the possibility is still there that the EU shall exercise competence concerning an entire area, the Protocol on Shared Competence itself nonetheless provides to make things clearer that "the scope of exercise of competence only covers those elements governed by the Union act in question and does not cover the entire area."[1795] Thirdly, competence could always revert to the member states should the EU cease to exercise competence in the area

1791 Treaty on Functioning of the European Union, art. 2(2); *Craig/de Búrca*, EU Law (6th edition), p. 83.

1792 Treaty on Functioning of the European Union, art. 4.

1793 *Woods/Watson*, p. 57.

1794 *Craig/de Búrca*, EU Law (6th edition), p. 84.

1795 Protocol on Shared Competence, art. 2(2); *Craig/de Búrca*, EU Law (6th edition), pp. 84-85.

subject to shared competence.[1796] Lastly, member states are not preempted from pursuing on their own areas of shared competence should the EU exercise competence on the areas of research, technological development and space, as well as development cooperation and humanitarian aid.[1797]

Another area of competence when the EU as a regional organization could act on is the supporting, coordinating, or supplementing member state action, without necessarily superseding the latter's competence in these areas, and without entailing harmonization of member state laws.[1798] These areas include the (1) protection and improvement of human health; (2) health; (3) industry; (4) culture; (5) tourism; (6) education, vocational training, youth, and sports; (7) civil protection; and (8) administrative cooperation.[1799] In the exercise of this competence, the EU shall endeavor to complement national legislation on the foregoing topics and member states are still obliged to coordinate and/or liaise their national policies on said matters to the Commission.[1800] There could be coordination by the Commission thereafter on what could be the best practices, periodic monitoring, and evaluation, and even could still intervene through the use persuasive soft law such as formation of guidelines and the like, as well as incentive measures.[1801]

The demarcations between exclusive, shared, and supporting competence could be understood despite the stumbling blocks that may exist among each one.[1802] But in addition to these three (3) major competences enumerated in the Treaties, the latter creates a different type of competence altogether with regard economic, employment, and social policy, wherein member states are obliged to "coordinate their economic and employment policies within the arrangements determined by the Treaty, which the Union shall have competence to provide."[1803] The same applies to employment policies and social policies.[1804] As to why a different com-

1796 Treaty on Functioning of the European Union, art. 2(2); *Craig/de Búrca,* EU Law (6th edition), p. 85.

1797 Treaty on Functioning of the European Union, art. 2(2); *Craig/de Búrca,* EU Law (6th edition), p. 85.

1798 Treaty on Functioning of the European Union, art. 2(5).

1799 Treaty on Functioning of the European Union, art. 6.

1800 *Craig/de Búrca,* EU Law (6th edition), p. 85.

1801 *Craig/de Búrca,* EU Law (6th edition), pp. 86-87.

1802 *Craig/de Búrca,* EU Law (6th edition), p. 87.

1803 Treaty on Functioning of the European Union, arts. 2(4), 5; *Craig/de Búrca,* EU Law (6th edition), p. 88.

1804 Treaty on Functioning of the European Union, art. 5.

petence is needed for these areas, the reason is mainly political: on one hand, there would definitely be opposition should it be a shared competence given that there is always the possibility of preemption should the EU act within this area; on the other hand, just to coordinate, support, and supplant would just be too weak.[1805] Separating another category does not erase the difficulties encountered as above stated, particularly with regard social policy: there are certain aspects of social policy that belong within shared competence and within the category of supporting, coordinating, and supplementing action, but it is not clear cut theretofore which ones belong to each.[1806]

On this point, one might ask within which competence does common foreign and security policy, including defense, belong to. This has not been clearly mentioned as what is only provided for is that the Union shall accordingly have the competence with the provisions of the Treaty on European Union, to define and implement the common foreign and security policy, including the progressive framing of a common defense policy.[1807] With that being said, CFSP remains to be intergovernmental rather than supranational.[1808] In this area, the European Council and the Council dominate decision-making and legal instruments normally applicable to other Union objectives are distinct from those applicable to CFSP.[1809]

Given the foregoing different competencies the EU possesses as a regional and supranational organization, it is naturally important to know that the same are exercised through the different types of EU instruments. Article 288 of the TFEU is the foundational provision:

> "To exercise the Union's competences, the institutions shall adopt regulations, directives, decisions, recommendations and opinions.
> "A regulation shall have general application. It shall be binding in its entirety and directly applicable in all Member States.
> "A directive shall be binding, as to the result to be achieved, upon each Member State to which it is addressed, but shall leave to the national authorities the choice of form and methods.

1805 *Craig/de Búrca*, EU Law (6th edition), p. 88.
1806 *Craig/de Búrca*, EU Law (6th edition), p. 89.
1807 Treaty on Functioning of the European Union, art.2(4).
1808 *Craig/de Búrca*, EU Law (6th edition), p. 89.
1809 *Craig/de Búrca*, EU Law (6th edition), p. 90; *Cremona*.

> "A decision shall be binding in its entirety. A decision which specifies those to whom it is addressed shall be binding only on them.
> "Recommendations and opinions shall have no binding force."[1810]

Craig and de Búrca mention that there are five (5) points that ought to be taken into account in relation to the foregoing: (1) there is no formal hierarchy between these provisions; (2) these can take the form of legislative acts, delegated, or implementing acts, and the same shall determine on what place in the hierarchy of norms they would belong; (3) the Treaties may specify what instrument to be used but will often not do so; (4) there is an obligation to give reasons for legal acts, which may include proposals, initiatives, recommendations, requests, or opinions required by the Treaties; and (5) there are also specific rules to be followed in the making of the legal acts mentioned above.[1811]

Regulations, being binding in its entirety and directly applicable to the member states, they can be thought of as akin to national legislation.[1812] By stating that regulations are directly applicable, this could either mean that individuals have rights they could enforce through national courts, or that the regulations are already deemed part of the national legal system and member states do not need anything more to do to transform the same or adopt the same into their national legal systems.[1813] Nonetheless, member states may still need to modify their laws to further comply with the regulation, or make things consistent within their national legal orders, or provide legal measures to ensure full implementation and effect of the regulation.[1814]

Directives differ on two (2) points from regulations, as described above: they do not necessarily address all member states and they are only binding insofar as the end is concerned, while giving some elbow room to member states as to form and method.[1815] They are particularly useful when the aim is "to harmonize the laws within a certain area" or "introduce complex legislative change".[1816]

1810 Treaty on Functioning of the European Union, art. 288.

1811 Treaty on Functioning of the European Union, arts. 296, 297; *Craig/de Búrca,* EU Law (6th edition), p. 90.

1812 Treaty on Functioning of the European Union, art. 288; *Craig/de Búrca,* EU Law (6th edition), p. 106.

1813 Variola v. AmministrazionedelleFinanze, Case 34/73, [1973] ECR 981; *Craig/de Búrca,* EU Law (6th edition), p. 107.

1814 *Craig/de Búrca,* EU Law (6th edition), p. 107.

1815 *Craig/de Búrca,* EU Law (6th edition), p. 107.

1816 *Craig/de Búrca,* EU Law (6th edition), p. 108.

Decisions are similar to directives to a certain degree. They do not also necessarily bind all member states: a decision which specifies to whom it is addressed is binding only to them.[1817] As such, directives could either be in a general nature or individualized.[1818]

In light of the ongoing discussion, one could have an idea that there would be no room for informal law or soft law in the EU legal order because it is a supranational organization,. This is not true because the applicability of both formal and informal law is existing in any legal order, the EU included.[1819] Recommendations and opinions, together with the open method of coordination as a form of EU initiative and policy guidelines the Commission may issue in relation to state aids, illustrate this best.[1820] And although they are not necessarily binding in force, as indicated in Article 288 TFEU, recommendations and opinions may be referenced by member states before the CJEU concerning their interpretation and/or validity.[1821]

With much of the nature of the EU as a supranational entity being exhaustively touched upon, including the different ways it acts and/or enacts its objectives and policies, one can already get the idea that the EU is an international legal person. Indeed, many already harbored this presumption since the days of the European Community, the predecessor of the EU.[1822] This notwithstanding, the Lisbon Treaty still has belabored and spelled out clearly for everyone that the European Union has international legal personality.[1823] It is beyond doubt that said provision was not necessary for the EU to externally act from the time of its establishment, the EU nonetheless finally codified what have been a general and consistent practice.[1824] Said provision has now further legitimized the independence of the EU's actions, when it acts on its own right and not merely acting as a representative of a collective of member states, which is more important than the scope of its powers.[1825]

1817 Treaty on Functioning of the European Union, art. 288; *Craig/de Búrca,* EU Law (6th edition), p. 108.
1818 *Craig/de Búrca,* EU Law (6th edition), p. 108.
1819 *Craig/de Búrca,* EU Law (6th edition), p. 109.
1820 *Craig/de Búrca,* EU Law (6th edition), p. 109.
1821 Grimaldi v. Fonds des Maladies Professionelles, Case C-322/88, [1989] ECR 4407; *Craig/de Búrca,* EU Law (6th edition), p. 109.
1822 *Craig/de Búrca,* EU Law (6th edition), p. 109.
1823 Treaty on European Union, art. 4(1).
1824 *Curtin/Dekker,* p. 167.
1825 See *Curtin/Dekker,* p. 167.

In relation to this, one of the Union's actions revolves around its external relations and concluding agreements and arrangements with other countries and organizations. In this respect, the EU has the exclusive competence to enter into international agreements as long as conditions laid down by the Treaties are met.[1826] EU external action is comprised of four fields, namely, (1) a common commercial policy ("CCP"); (2) association, partnership, cooperation, and neighborhood policy; (3) development, technical cooperation and humanitarian aid; and (4) the external dimension of internal policies.[1827]

In relation to this, the EU can conclude agreements with one or more states, including international organizations agreements establishing an association involving reciprocal rights and obligations, common action, and special procedure.[1828] While what should be involved in an institution is not provided for, this has not stopped the EU from entering into a lot of association agreements with different countries as well as similar agreements with less intensive forms of integration or a narrower range of fields.[1829] Moreover, the EU has been greatly engaged with agreements involving development policy, or economic, technical, and financial cooperation, as a way of furthering its objective of developing and consolidating democracy and the rule of law, and the general objectives of human rights and fundamental freedoms.[1830]

At this juncture, one can observe that this external action is highly illustrative of what has been earlier mentioned in the EU's 1997 publication, "Agenda 2000: For a Stronger and Wider Europe".[1831] Reverting to the same, the European Commission proposed a range of ambitious, global roles for the European Union, which included the importance of the EU increasing its influence globally, while promoting values such as peace and security, democracy and human rights, and providing aid to less privileged countries, defend its social model, establish its presence on the world markets, prevent major damage to the environment, and ensure sustainable growth.[1832] As worded by the Agenda 2000 itself: "collective action by the European Union is an ever increasing necessity if these interests are to be

---

1826 See Treaty on Functioning of the European Union, arts. 3, 21.
1827 *Cremona*, p. 219.
1828 Treaty on Functioning of the European Union, art. 217.
1829 *Craig/de Búrca*, EU Law (6th edition), p. 335.
1830 *Craig/de Búrca*, EU Law (6th edition), p. 340.
1831 *Craig/de Búrca*, EU Law (6th edition), p. 341.
1832 *Bretherton/Vogler*, p. 15. See also *Bretherton/Vogler*, p. 15.

defended, if full advantage is to be taken of the benefits of globalization and if the constraints it imposes are to be faced successfully."[1833]

This vision-mission statement more or less found itself in the provisions of the Lisbon Treaty, wherein the European Union "shall uphold and promote its values and interests and contribute to the protection of its citizens. It shall contribute to peace, security, the sustainable development of the Earth, solidarity and mutual respect among peoples, free and fair trade, eradication of poverty and the protection of human rights, in particular the rights of the child, as well as to the strict observance and the development of international law, including respect for the principles of the United Nations Charter."[1834] The EU is expected as an international actor to be guided "by the principles which have inspired its own creation, development and enlargement, and which it seeks to advance in the wider world: democracy, the rule of law, the universality and indivisibility of human rights and fundamental freedoms, respect for human dignity, the principles of equality and solidarity, and respect for the principles of the United Nations Charter and international law."[1835]

Considering the foregoing, one could then easily gain the idea that as an external actor, the European Union does not only intend to be influential, but also more or less wishes to influence and/or transform the global world to imbibe and internalize the former's own values and norms, which it thinks are important and fundamental.[1836] Stating it otherwise, the EU sets itself apart as a normative power in global politics – sometimes even referred to by other authors as a "civilian power".[1837] A case in point is the numerous developmental programs it endeavors on. Another example is much closer to home: the European Neighborhood Policy, wherein the EU and its neighbor-partners agree on action plans grounded on incentives, which more or less caters to the EU standards and values within the socio-, economic, and political planes.[1838] Not all analysts however buy into the idea of the EU as solely a normative power. They believe that the EU does not act so benignly all the time but also as a "soft imperialism power": the emphasis on democratization projects, strategies for "new abroad" are seen as examples of the EU's hegemonic

1833 *Manners*, p. 46.
1834 Reform Treaty 2007, arts. 3-5; *Bretherton/Vogler*, p. 15.
1835 Reform Treaty 2007, art. 10; *Manners*, p. 47.
1836 See *Manners*, p. 48.
1837 *Bono*, p. 23; *Manners*, pp. 45, 46.
1838 *Bono*, p. 23; *Manners*, pp. 45, 46.

power driven by both normative and strategic interests such as the need for stability.[1839] The same examples cited earlier equally apply: a look into the historical development of the ENP, for example, was initiated at the first place to secure the EU's borders, believing that what happens with its neighbors might spill over to its affairs. The provisions of the ENP were fashioned more or less to cater to EU's stability and not only to influence the Union's neighbors to internalize EU values and policies.

As regards regional peace and security, the EU's historical development shows that the European integration project has been since its inception a security project, with its key output being a powerful security community.[1840] In light of this, the EU slowly eased out from its emphasis on "foreign policy" (diplomatic correspondence) towards "security policy", which focuses on mechanisms for ensuring security both among its member states and between them and the wider world, and influences thereafter the "fluctuating balance between the EU's position as consumer and producer of security."[1841] With regard the security and defense policy, the EU handles the same uniquely given that the EU commits itself in its external action to "effective multilateralism" and prevention rather than preemption as a means of conflict management.[1842] With respect to this commitment, not only has the EU deepened and broadened the reach of its foreign and security policy, but it likewise adheres to a more comprehensive concept of security.[1843] In relation to this comprehensive concept of security, the EU is equally devoted to it vis-à-vis the area of "freedom, security, and justice, which was created in the Treaty of Amsterdam.[1844] Thus, the EU has enacted a substantial number of measures in connection therewith, including, if not particularly, on police and judicial cooperation in criminal matters, which is all what was left of the Justice and Home Affairs after asylum, immigration, and civil matters were transferred to the EC after the Amsterdam Treaty.[1845]

1839 *Smith*, pp. 763-767.
1840 *Bono*, p. 24.
1841 *Smith*, p. 38.
1842 *Smith*, p. 39.
1843 *Smith*, p. 39.
1844 *Smith*, pp. 40-43.
1845 *Douglas-Scott*, p. 220.

2. EU Organizational Structure

Taking the foregoing discussion on the Union's distinguishing characteristics as a regional organization, external actor, and position on overall regional security in mind, it would be now interesting to know how the same is interplayed among the different components and institutions of the Union. The following discussion shall be a walkthrough of the Union's organization structure or the different EU institutions as mentioned in the Treaties. Focus however shall be given, for purposes of the present study, to the institutions which play a role in the general decision and policymaking in the EU.

In relation to this, there are underlying points ought to be discussed *en passant* at the outset in considering the institutions and how they work.[1846] First, there is the so-called institutional balance that ensures that within the institutions there are checks and balances.[1847] However, one should not be quick to associate the notion of institutional balance to the traditional notion of governmental functions of legislative, executive, and judicial powers. Instead of the traditional notion of separation of powers amongst national governments, the institutional balance contemplated within the Union is that of ensuring that an institutional actor from becoming too powerful.[1848] Secondly, one must understand the dynamism involved as regards how these institutions exercise their powers: it is not static but it undergoes an evolution in accordance with how the Union itself further develops and what people expect of its effectiveness, accountability, and responsibility.[1849] Lastly, although to some degree this has been reduced or eliminated by virtue of the Lisbon Treaty, the powers of the institutions depend on the different areas of competence and the same illustrates how different competencies interplay and interrelate with one another.[1850]

1846 See *Douglas-Scott*, p. 220.
1847 *Woods/Watson*, p. 23.
1848 *Woods/Watson*, p. 23.
1849 *Woods/Watson*, p. 23.
1850 *Woods/Watson*, p. 23.

a. Commission

When one speaks of the term "Commission" within the European Union, it could refer to either the College of Commissioners or the permanent Brussels bureaucracy which staff the Commission services.[1851]

The presidency of the Commission has a huge significance given that it places first among equals in the Commission and its authority has been increased over time.[1852] As to how the Commission President is elected, the Lisbon Treaty provides that it shall be indirectly elected by the European Council: the European Council acting by qualified majority and after appropriate consultation, shall forward a candidate to the European Parliament, which in turn shall elect on the candidate by a majority of its members.[1853] Should the candidate not receive majority support, the Council shall then forward a new candidate within one month's time, and the same procedure shall be followed.[1854] This naturally means that the candidate ought to have the support from the majority grouping in the Parliament.[1855]

The election procedure aside, the President takes the wheel with regard the workings of the Commission. It influences overall Commission policy, in negotiating with the Council and Parliament, and lays down the guidelines on how the Commission works, including deciding on its internal organization and the appointment of the Vice-Presidents of the Commission, the latter heading project teams with other Commissioners.[1856] Necessarily included in the President's powers and responsibilities is the power to allocate the different responsibilities of the Commissioner to the different Commissioners, including the power to reshuffle portfolios.[1857]

Together with the President, the Commission is also composed of the College of Commissioners, which after 2014 and by virtue of the Lisbon Treaty, shall be composed of members, including the President and High Representative for Foreign Affairs, who correspond to 2/3 of the member states, unless the European Council – acting unanimously – decides to

1851 *Woods/Watson*, p. 24.
1852 *Craig/de Búrca*, EU Law (6th edition), p. 31; *Woods/Watson*, pp. 37-38.
1853 Treaty on the European Union, art. 14(1).
1854 Treaty on the European Union, art. 14(1).
1855 *Craig/de Búrca*, EU Law (6th edition), p. 31.
1856 Treaty on the European Union, art. 17(6); *Craig/de Búrca*, EU Law (6th edition), p. 31.
1857 *Craig/de Búrca*, EU Law (6th edition), p. 32.

alter this number.[1858] It is imperative that member states are treated on a strictly equal footing vis-à-vis determination of the sequence of, and time spent by, their nationals as members in the Commission.[1859]

In line with this, the member states make suggestions as to who they want for Commissioners and by common agreement by the European Council and the President, shall submit a list for consideration of the European Parliament.[1860] The Parliament shall then give a vote of approval, on the basis of which the Council shall appoint formally the Commissioners.[1861] The appointed Commissioners shall have a term of five (5) years, subject to renewal.[1862] It must be mentioned additionally that Commissioners ought to be appointed based on their general competence and that their independence is beyond question.[1863] They ought to be independent in the fulfillment of their duties and responsibilities, and should not be influenced in their actions by any government or any other body, including the member states from which they were elected from.[1864] They shall meet collectively in the College of Commissioners that shall in turn operate under the President's guidance and take decisions by majority vote.[1865]

Another thing that ought to be mentioned regarding the Commission's structure is the applicable bureaucracy therein. Directorates-General ("DG") oversee major internal areas over which the Commission is responsible for.[1866] Accordingly, the Commission bureaucracy is composed of four (4) layers: there is the Commissioner who would have the portfolio for a particular area; the Director-General, who is the head bureaucrat of a particular DG and answerable to the Commissioner; Deputy Director General; Directors, who would formally head the different directorates under the DG; and the different heads of division or unit.[1867] Given the said layers, decisions and draft legislative proposals normally follow a

1858 *Craig/de Búrca*, EU Law (6th edition), p. 32.
1859 *Craig/de Búrca*, EU Law (6th edition), p. 32.
1860 Treaty on the European Union, art. 17(5).
1861 Treaty on the European Union, art. 17(5).
1862 Treaty on the European Union, art. 17(3).
1863 *Craig/de Búrca*, EU Law (6th edition), p. 32.
1864 Treaty on the European Union, art. 17(3).
1865 Treaty on the Functioning of the European Union, art. 250.
1866 *Craig/de Búrca*, EU Law (6th edition), p. 33.
1867 *Craig/de Búrca*, EU Law (6th edition), p. 34.

down-top approach – emanating from the lower part of the hierarchy, upwards towards the College of Commissioners.[1868]

The structure and bureaucracy notwithstanding, the Commission has a gamut of powers within the construct of the European Union, as set out in Article 17 of the TEU:

> "Article 17
> "1. The Commission shall promote the general interest of the Union and take appropriate initiatives to that end. It shall ensure the application of the Treaties, and of measures adopted by the institutions pursuant to them. It shall oversee the application of Union law under the control of the CJEU. It shall execute the budget and manage programmes. It shall exercise coordinating, executive and management functions, as laid down in the Treaties. With the exception of the common foreign and security policy, and other cases provided for in the Treaties, it shall ensure the Union's external representation. It shall initiate the Union's annual and multiannual programming with a view to achieving interinstitutional agreements.
> "2. Union legislative acts may only be adopted on the basis of a Commission proposal, except where the Treaties provide otherwise. Other acts shall be adopted on the basis of a Commission proposal where the Treaties so provide."[1869]

In light of the number of tasks listed above, the Commission is said to be entrusted with task of being an initiator, watchdog, and executive.[1870] The Commission's role as an initiator comes with respect to the legislative process, wherein it has the right of legislative initiative, which coincides with the Commission's role of being the EU's motor for integration.[1871] It may formulate proposals in any matter that maybe provided for by the TFEU, including those where the power is specifically granted or where general power is provided for.[1872] In light of this, the Council ought to make important decisions on the basis of the Commission's proposals and the power of the Parliament to request proposals from the Commission.[1873] This is without prejudice to the Council, on the other hand,

---

1868 *Craig/de Búrca*, EU Law (6th edition), p. 35.
1869 Treaty on European Union, art. 17.
1870 *Craig/de Búrca*, EU Law (6th edition), p. 35.
1871 Treaty on the European Union, art. 17(2), *Woods/Watson*, p. 38.
1872 Treaty on the Functioning of the European Union, art. 352, *Alesina/Perotti*, p. 29; *Craig/de Búrca*, EU Law (6th edition), p. 36; *Woods/Watson*, p. 38.
1873 *Woods/Watson*, p. 38.

requesting the Commission to conduct studies in relation to a matter the former deems important.[1874] Closely related to this is its development of an overall legislative plan for any single year.[1875] This sets the tone of what could be the priorities of the EU during any given year, which is consistent to what has been set in Article 17(1) TEU on the Commission initiating an annual or multi-annual programme that would ensure inter-institutional agreement within the EU. The Commission likewise affects the legislative process through its development of general policy strategies.[1876] Examples of this include the White Paper developed in furtherance of the Single European Act.[1877] Additionally, the Commission more or less exercises legislative power in its power to enact EU norms in certain areas without necessitating the involvement of other institutions, as well as the delegated power to the Commission to enact regulations within particular areas.[1878]

As regards the Commission's role of the watchdog, this more or less entails its role to ensure compliance with the Treaties vis-à-vis the Commission's judicial powers.[1879] At the outset, member states are expected to cooperate with the Union in carrying out tasks laid down in the Treaties under the principle of sincere cooperation:

> "xxx The Member States shall take any appropriate measure, general or particular, to ensure fulfilment of the obligations arising out of the Treaties or resulting from the acts of the institutions of the Union.
> "The Member States shall facilitate the achievement of the Union's tasks and refrain from any measure which could jeopardize the attainment of the Union's objectives."[1880]

The Commission is responsible to seek out and bring to an end any infringement being committed by any member state. In line with this, it can proceed in two (2) ways. On one hand, the Commission can initiate actions against member states when they are in breach of EU law before the CJEU.[1881] On the other hand, the Commission itself in certain areas could act as an investigator and initial judge of a treaty violation whether

---

1874 *Woods/Watson*, p. 38.
1875 *Woods/Watson*, p. 38.
1876 *Craig/de Búrca*, EU Law (6th edition), p. 36.
1877 *Craig/de Búrca*, EU Law (6th edition), p. 36.
1878 *Craig/de Búrca*, EU Law (6th edition), p. 36.
1879 *Craig/de Búrca*, EU Law (6th edition), p. 37.
1880 Treaty on European Union, art. 4(3).
1881 Treaty on the Functioning of the European Union, art. 258.

the same is committed by a member state or private firm.[1882] Two of these areas concern competition and state aid.[1883] By affording the Commission adjudicatory power, it can effectuate better the development of EU policy, although it ought to be remembered that the Commission's decision is subject to review by the General Court.[1884] In connection to this, there is an administrative element to the Commission's powers: the Commission shall manage programmes, including policies, which would naturally entail working using national agencies.[1885] The Commission shall have general oversight over these matters to ensure that the rules are properly applied within the member states.[1886]

As regards the Commission's executive role, the Commission is the executive of the Union.[1887] Once a policy decision has been made by the Council, it is incumbent upon the Commission to proceed with the detailed implementation of said policy, including further legislation, should the same be required.[1888] Additionally, the Commission has its own power of decision wherein regulations needed to be enacted entail decisions of an executive nature.[1889] The Commission also exercises an executive function with respect to finance and external relations: it has significant powers over expenditure and structural policy, and maintains extensive diplomatic missions abroad, respectively.[1890]

b. European Parliament

The European Parliament is an institution which underwent gradual transformation: from a relatively powerless Assembly under the 1959 ECSC Treaty to the considerable strengthened institution as defined in the Lisbon Treaty.[1891] Notably, it was not envisioned as a democratic body at the onset of the Rome Treaty but instead, it was constituted of members who

1882 *Alesina/Perotti*, p. 30; *Woods/Watson*, p. 39.
1883 *Craig/de Búrca*, EU Law (6th edition), p. 38.
1884 *Craig/de Búrca*, EU Law (6th edition), p. 38.
1885 Treaty on the European Union, art. 17(1).
1886 *Craig/de Búrca*, EU Law (6th edition), p. 38.
1887 *Craig/de Búrca*, EU Law (6th edition), p. 37.
1888 *Woods/Watson*, p. 39.
1889 *Alesina/Perotti*, pp. 29-30; *Woods/Watson*, p. 39.
1890 *Woods/Watson*, p. 40.
1891 *Craig/de Búrca*, EU Law (6th edition), pp. 37-38.

needed to be members of their own national parliaments.[1892] With the introduction of direct elections by the Lisbon treaty, there was increased democracy, competition, and expertise because members are now responsible to the electorate and not necessarily intertwined with duality of mandates in the national and European levels.[1893] This in turn creates a direct link between national electorates and Union political institutions.[1894]

As it presently stands, the European Parliament seats in Strasbourg, but there is a secretariat based in Luxembourg and some sessions and committee meetings are held in Brussels, to facilitate contact with the Commission and Council.[1895] The members of Parliament, just like the Commission, have a term of five (5) years,[1896] and the Parliament shall be composed as follows:

> "The European Parliament shall be composed of representatives of the Union's citizens. They shall not exceed seven hundred and fifty in number, plus the President. Representation of citizens shall be degressively proportional, with a minimum threshold of six members per Member State. No Member State shall be allocated more than ninety-six seats.
> "The European Council shall adopt by unanimity, on the initiative of the European Parliament and with its consent, a decision establishing the composition of the European Parliament, respecting the principles referred to in the first subparagraph."[1897]

Given the aforementioned, the European Parliament is entrusted with, jointly with the Council, legislative and budgetary functions.[1898] Under the legislative role the Parliament presently plays, it has a right of co-decision with the Council on certain matters.[1899] Referred to as the "ordinary legislative procedure", the Parliament is effectively an equal partner in the legislative process to the extent that it would have significant veto power in matters subject to the procedure.[1900] Further, the Parliament more or

1892 *Craig/de Búrca,* EU Law (6th edition), p. 50.
1893 *Woods/Watson,* p. 24.
1894 *Woods/Watson,* pp. 24-25.
1895 *Woods/Watson,* p. 25.
1896 Treaty on European Union, art. 14(3).
1897 Treaty on European Union, art. 14(2); *Craig/de Búrca,* EU Law (6th edition), p. 51.
1898 Treaty on European Union, art. 14(1).
1899 *Craig/de Búrca,* EU Law (6th edition), p. 51.
1900 *Woods/Watson,* p. 28.

less has the power of initiative, wherein it has the power to request the Commission, acting by a majority of its members, to submit any appropriate proposal on which it considers a Union act is necessitated for purposes of implementing the treaty.[1901] One must understand nonetheless at this instance that the operative word in this case is "request": the Parliament may only request from the Commission the policy initiative but not initiate any policy on its own.[1902]

At this juncture, it is best to discuss the role the European Parliament plays in terms of treaty negotiations, albeit the same is not strictly legislative in nature. The Commission is duty-bound to transmit regularly to the Parliament relevant documents and reports on the progress of trade negotiations, and at the same time, trade agreements require the Parliament's assent before they could be ratified.[1903] This has happened in some occasions wherein upon voting on a proposal by the Commission, it was turned down by the Parliament.[1904] There are however instances wherein the European Parliament has expressed concerns over existing international agreements and would desire that said agreements be suspended or terminated. In such instances, the TFEU is bereft of any provision granting formal powers to the Parliament to do so.[1905] This notwithstanding, the Parliament came up with a Resolution on October 2013 wherein it states that even if it does not have formal powers under the TFEU regarding suspension or termination of international agreements, it nonetheless expects the Commission to act appropriately should the Parliament withdraw its support for a particular agreement, and that on whether the Parliament shall support future agreements, it shall take into account the responses of both the Commission and Council in relation to the agreements the Parliament has withdrawn support from.[1906] Indeed, the EP has not shied away from its frequent use of legislation to defend its role in the legislative process.[1907] And after much hesitation, the CJEU held that the Parliament could be a plaintiff in annulment proceedings, where its prerogatives have been violated.[1908] This later became integrated in treaty amendments and

1901 Treaty on Functioning of European Union, art. 225; *Craig/de Búrca*, EU Law (6th edition), p. 54; *Woods/Watson*, p. 28.
1902 *Woods/Watson*, p. 28.
1903 Treaty on Functioning of European Union, art. 218; *Woods/Watson*, p. 28.
1904 See *Woods/Watson*, p. 28.
1905 *Woods/Watson*, p. 28.
1906 *Woods/Watson*, p. 29.
1907 *Woods/Watson*, p. 29.
1908 *Craig/de Búrca*, EU Law (6th edition), p. 54.

the Parliament, together with the Commission, Council, and any member state, has equal and full legal standing to bring annulment proceedings.[1909]

The Parliament also possesses dismissal and appointment power. The accountability of the Commission to the Parliament has gradually increased.[1910] The EP has the power to censure the Commission, the same is carried out through a vote of two-thirds majority of the votes cast, which should represent the majority of the Parliament.[1911] Notably however, that while the Parliament can exercise censure, the Commission exercises holdover of its position until such time their replacements are appointed.[1912] Further, there is no restriction as to the reappointment of the same censured Commission by the member states.[1913]

In connection to this, the European Parliament likewise has the power to appoint. This is necessarily connected to its supervisory power.[1914] The Parliament in its supervisory role exercises direct political control over the Commission.[1915] At the outset, the EP elects the President of the Commission, subject to the list of candidates the Council may submit for the former's consideration, in addition to approving the appointment of the Commissioners and the Commission as a whole.[1916] Furthermore, the EP monitors the Commission's activities and exercises direct political control over it through the asking of questions – to which the Commission ought to reply in writing or orally – and establishment of committees of inquiry.[1917] The Commission ought to also come up with a general report for the Parliament's perusal and in practice, the Parliament is consulted often by the former during pre-legislative phases.[1918] The Council is equally subject to the supervisory authority of the Parliament, although the latter does not exercise direct control of its actions: activities of the Council are reported three times a year and the President of the Council must address the Parliament at the beginning of every year, which is followed by a

1909 Treaty on Functioning of European Union, art. 263; *Craig/de Búrca,* EU Law (6th edition), p. 54.
1910 *Craig/de Búrca,* EU Law (6th edition), p. 54.
1911 Treaty on Functioning of European Union, art. 234; *Craig/de Búrca,* EU Law (6th edition), p. 54.
1912 *Woods/Watson,* p. 29.
1913 *Woods/Watson,* p. 29.
1914 *Woods/Watson,* p. 29.
1915 *Craig/de Búrca,* EU Law (6th edition), p. 54; *Woods/Watson,* p. 29.
1916 Treaty on European Union, art. 14(1); *Woods/Watson,* p. 29.
1917 *Craig/de Búrca,* EU Law (6th edition), p. 54; *Woods/Watson,* p. 29.
1918 *Craig/de Búrca,* EU Law (6th edition), p. 55; *Woods/Watson,* p. 29.

general debate.[1919] In addition to this, the Council President must present a report to the Parliament at the conclusion of every European Council meeting.[1920]

Complimentary to the supervisory role the Parliament plays is its task to establish the office of the Ombudsman under the Maastricht Treaty.[1921] Appointed for the duration of the EP and dismissible by the Court of Justice of the European Union ("CJEU") (on request by the Parliament) on instances of serious misconduct or non-fulfillment of the conditions of the office, the Ombudsman is tasked to receive complaints from Union citizens or resident third-country nationals or legal persons, concerning instances of "maladministration in the activities of Union institutions, agencies, bodies, and offices" and to "conduct inquiries for which he finds grounds, either on his own initiative, or on the basis of complaints submitted to him direct or through a member of the European Parliament."[1922] On account of this, the concerned EU institution must supply the requested information and give access to the imperative files, unless the ground of secrecy is applicable.[1923]

In addition to the foregoing, the Parliament shall exercise functions of political control and consultation as laid down in the Treaties.[1924] The Council of Ministers is required to consult the Parliament on legislation in relation to particular areas.[1925] It must be said however that while the Council ought to consult and take into account what the Parliament opines, it is of no obligation to follow the latter.[1926] That said, it remains an essential procedural requirement.[1927] Failure to oblige, or passing regulations without receiving the Parliament's opinion first, has promoted the Court to annul the said regulations for failure to satisfy the requirement.[1928] Nonetheless, should the opinion be required in urgency and the Council had made the best efforts to secure it, but still failed to meet the

---

1919 *Woods/Watson*, p. 29.
1920 *Woods/Watson*, p. 29.
1921 *Woods/Watson*, p. 29.
1922 Treaty on Functioning of European Union, art. 228(1); *Craig/de Búrca*, EU Law (6th edition), p. 55.
1923 *Craig/de Búrca*, EU Law (6th edition), p. 55.
1924 Treaty on European Union, art. 14(1).
1925 *Craig/de Búrca*, EU Law (6th edition), p. 55.
1926 *Woods/Watson*, p. 27.
1927 *Woods/Watson*, p. 27.
1928 Roquette Freres v. Council (case 138/79); Maizena GmbH v. Council (case C-21/94); *Woods/Watson*, p. 27.

deadline, the Court has upheld the regulation for the apparent failure of the Parliament in its duty to cooperate.[1929]

c. European Council

Formally established as a Union institution by the Lisbon Treaty,[1930] the European Council shall bring together Heads of State or of Government of the member states, the President of the Council, and the President of the Commission.[1931] Meeting at least twice a year, they shall be assisted by the Lisbon Treaty-created Representative for the Union for Foreign Affairs.[1932]

As to how the European Council plays a role in the European Union, it is not meant to exercise legislative function, yet it is the most influential body: it is here that all the major policy guidelines are set and that all decisions on the big issues are taken.[1933] It shall provide the Union with the necessary impetus for development and defining the general political directions and priorities thereof.[1934] In doing so, it acts by consensus.[1935]

d. Council

The Council shall consist of one representative from each member state, who needed to be at the ministerial level and able to commit the government of that member state.[1936] While there are recurring concerns on how members of the Council tend to look out for the interests of their own member state rather than what is best for the Union, ministers appointed to the Council are normally appointed as ministers in their respective member states for purposes of fulfilling their Union function.[1937]

Something distinguishable about the Council as a Union institution is that it is composed of different configurations, no less than the Lisbon

1929 Parliament v. Council (case C-65/93); *Woods/Watson*, p. 27.
1930 Treaty on European Union, art. 13(1).
1931 *Woods/Watson*, p. 27.
1932 *Woods/Watson*, p. 30. See also Treaty on Functioning of European Union, arts. 235-236.
1933 *Woods/Watson*, pp. 30-31.
1934 Treaty on European Union, art. 15(1).
1935 Treaty on European Union, art. 15(4).
1936 Treaty on European Union, art. 16(2).
1937 *Alesina/Perotti*, p. 29.

Treaty acknowledges.[1938] Its composition varies depending on the topic to be discussed.[1939] As a safety mechanism to ensure coordination and coherence, there is not only a General Affairs Council which coordinates all the work of the different configurations, but the European Council has been given to the power to determine the various configurations of the Council of Ministers.[1940] In connection to this, the Council Presidency comes into play: while the High Representative of the Union for Foreign Affairs presides over the Foreign Affairs Council, the European Council decides by qualified majority on the list of other Council formations and the Presidency of these formations.[1941] The Presidency of the formations, except the Foreign Affairs Council, must be made in accordance with the principle of equal rotation.[1942]

Given the abovementioned, the Lisbon Treaty provides that the work of the Council is prepared by the Committee on Permanent Representatives, which shall in turn effectuate the tasks given by the Council.[1943] Having its origins since the Rome Treaty, said Committee is composed of senior officials and operate on two (2) levels: one level is composed of permanent representatives in an ambassadorial rank and deal with more contentious issues such as economic and financial affairs as well as external relations; and the other, composed of permanent representatives responsible for issues such as environment, social affairs, the internal market, and transport.[1944] Working on two (2) levels, the Committee does not make substantive decisions on its own right but nonetheless plays an imperative role in decision-making in the EU as it considers the draft legislative proposals from the Commission and help set the agenda for Council meetings.[1945]

1938 Treaty on European Union, art. 16(6), (9); Treaty on Functioning of European Union, art. 236; *Woods/Watson*, p. 31.

1939 *Woods/Watson*, p. 31.

1940 Treaty on European Union, art. 16(6); Treaty on Functioning of European Union, art. 236; *Woods/Watson*, p. 31.

1941 Treaty on European Union, art. 16(6); Treaty on Functioning of European Union, art. 236; *Craig/de Búrca*, EU Law (6th edition), p. 41.

1942 Treaty on European Union, art. 16(6); Treaty on Functioning of European Union, art. 236; *Craig/de Búrca*, EU Law (6th edition), p. 41.

1943 Treaty on European Union, art. 16(7); Treaty on Functioning of European Union, art. 240(1).

1944 *Craig/de Búrca*, EU Law (6th edition), p. 41.

1945 *Craig/de Búrca*, EU Law (6th edition), p. 43; *Craig*, p. 45.

Alongside the Committee of Permanent Representatives, the Council also has a General Secretariat which provides general administrative support to it.[1946]

The composition and appointment of the Council aside, it plays a crucial role as both executive authority, which it has in large part delegated to the Commission, and legislative authority.[1947] It has to vote approval of almost all Commission proposals before the same can be law.[1948] As to whether vote shall be by unanimity, qualified majority, or simple majority depends on the applicable treaty provision.[1949] Moreover, the Council is empowered to take a proactive role by requesting the Commission through a simple majority request to undertake any studies the Council deems important to attain desirable objectives.[1950] At the same time, the Council can delegate the Commission power to pass further regulation within a particular area.[1951] The Council also plays a role in budgetary issues, on which many initiatives would depend.[1952] Additionally, the Council is responsible for concluding agreements on behalf of the Union with third states or international organizations.[1953]

The Council, in addition to the foregoing, also plays a significant role in the Common Foreign and Security Policy ("CFSP") by taking the necessary decisions for defining and implementing the CFSP in the light of guidelines that may have been established by the European Council.[1954] Closely related to this, the Council is also involved with the Area of Freedom, Security, and Justice.[1955]

e. Court of Justice of the European Union

The Court of Justice of the European Union shall include the Court of Justice, the General Court, and specialized courts.[1956]

1946 *Craig/de Búrca*, EU Law (6th edition), p. 43; *Craig*, p. 45.
1947 *Craig/de Búrca*, EU Law (6th edition), p. 43.
1948 Treaty on European Union, art. 16(3).
1949 Treaty on European Union, art. 16(3).
1950 Treaty on Functioning of the European Union, art. 241.
1951 Treaty on Functioning of the European Union, art. 290.
1952 *Alesina/Perotti*, p. 29.
1953 *Craig/de Búrca*, EU Law (6th edition), p. 44.
1954 *Craig/de Búrca*, EU Law (6th edition), p. 44.
1955 *Craig/de Búrca*, EU Law (6th edition), pp. 44-45.
1956 Treaty on European Union, art. 19(1).

With respect to the Court of Justice, there shall be one judge per member state and they shall be appointed by common accord of the governments of the member states, after consultation with a designated panel that looks into the suitability of the person to perform duties as a CJEU judge.[1957] Accordingly, those chosen must have independence and possess the qualifications making them eligible to be appointed to the highest judicial offices in their respective member states.[1958] The term of office shall be six (6) years, without prejudice to reappointment.[1959] Appointments are made in a staggered manner so that there will be reappointments made every three years.[1960] The Court elects among its own judges the President and Vice President, and likewise appoints its Registrar.[1961]

The CJEU is assisted by Advocates General, who are appointed in the same manner as CJEU judges, and their duty is to make in open court, reasoned submissions on cases.[1962]

In view of the foregoing, the CJEU can sit as a full court – Grand Chamber – composed of 15 judges, or in Chambers, in accordance with the rules set out by Statute.[1963] It sits as a full court in instances where the matter is of exceptionally important, or when the subject matter warrants, such as when it involves the removal of the Ombudsman or Commissioner.[1964] The Grand Chamber likewise applies when the member state or an institution that is a party to the proceedings so requests, and in complex and important cases.[1965]

Other than the Court of Justice, there is the General Court which is accorded the responsibility within the sphere of its jurisdiction to ensure the law is observed in the interpretation and application of the Treaty.[1966] It shall be comprised of at least one judge per member state, compared to the CJEU.[1967] There are no separate Advocates General in the General

---

1957 Treaty on Functioning of the European Union, arts. 253, 255.

1958 Treaty on European Union, art. 19(2); Treaty on Functioning of the European Union, art. 253.

1959 *Craig/de Búrca*, EU Law (6th edition), p. 45.

1960 Treaty on Functioning of the European Union, art. 253.

1961 Treaty on Functioning of the European Union, arts. 252, 253; *Craig/de Búrca*, EU Law (6th edition), p. 58.

1962 Treaty on Functioning of the European Union, art. 254; *Craig/de Búrca*, EU Law (6th edition), p. 58.

1963 *Craig/de Búrca*, EU Law (6th edition), p. 58.

1964 *Craig/de Búrca*, EU Law (6th edition), p. 58.

1965 *Craig/de Búrca*, EU Law (6th edition), p. 58.

1966 Treaty on European Union, art. 19(1).

1967 Treaty on European Union, art. 19(2).

Court but a judge can be requested to provide assistance as the same.[1968] Similar with the qualifications of being a judge in the Court of Justice, one should be independent without doubt and possess the ability required for appointment to high judicial office.[1969] They shall be appointed by common accord of the member states for a renewable term of six (6) years, upon consultation with the judicial panel that advises on judicial appointments.[1970] The General Court shall have its own Registrar and a President, whom shall be appointed among the judges.[1971] It can sit in chambers of three or five judges, or sometimes by a single judge, without prejudice to sitting as a Grand Chamber or full court when the case's complexity or independence demands it.[1972]

Any decision of the General Court is appealable to the Court of Justice within two (2) months from date of notification of said decision.[1973] This appeal shall be however limited to questions of law, which may cover "grounds of lack of competence of the General Court, a breach of procedure before it which adversely affects the interests of the appellant as well as the infringement of Union law by the General Court."[1974]

Aside from the Court of Justice and General Court, there are also the specialized courts meant to ease the caseload of the two previously mentioned.[1975] Accordingly, the European Parliament and the Council through ordinary legislative procedure establish these specialized courts attached to the General Court to hear at first instance certain classes of actions in certain areas.[1976]

Given the foregoing, the CJEU plays an imperative role among the EU institutions because it ensures that in the interpretation and implementation of the Treaties the law is always observed.[1977] In relation to this, the CJEU was instrumental in fashioning principles of the EU legal order, such as, but not limited to, direct effect, supremacy, and state liability in

---

1968 *Craig/de Búrca*, EU Law (6th edition), p. 58.
1969 Treaty on Functioning of European Union, art. 254.
1970 Treaty on Functioning of European Union, art. 255.
1971 Treaty on Functioning of European Union, art. 254.
1972 Protocol (No. 3) on the Statute of the European Court of Justice, art. 50.
1973 Protocol (No. 3) on the Statute of the European Court of Justice, art. 56.
1974 Protocol (No. 3) on the Statute of the European Court of Justice, art. 58.
1975 *Craig/de Búrca*, EU Law (6th edition), p. 59.
1976 Treaty of Functioning of the European Union, art. 257.
1977 Treaty on the European Union, art. 19(1); *Craig/de Búrca*, EU Law (6th edition), p. 60.

damages, which consequently defined the very nature of the EU.[1978] Craig and Búrca elucidate:

> "These principles have defined the very nature of the EU, constitutionalizing it and distinguishing it from other international treaties. They were especially significant in the years of so-called institutional malaise or stagnation. The Court rendered the Treaty and EC legislation effective when the provisions had not been implemented as required by the political institutions and the Member States. This was exemplified by the Court's role in the creation of the single market, requiring removal of national trade barriers, when progress towards completing the single market through legislative harmonization was hindered by institutional inaction."[1979]

With the foregoing in mind, the Court's role is rather dynamic than static, and not consistently an "activist" court at all times or in all policy areas: it may intervene in one aspect but lay low on another aspect.[1980] In connection to this, the Court normally engages into a purposive or tautological approach in its jurisprudence, meaning, it shall examine the whole context wherein a particular provision is located and gives the interpretation that shall most likely further the purpose sought to be achieved by the provision, which not be sometimes the literal interpretation of the subject Treaty or legislation.[1981]

3. EU Fundamental Principles, Norms, and Practices

As one knows the organizational structure of the Union, one would inevitably be interested on how Union works – whether there are principles, norms, or practices that the EU abide with and need to take into account of in its decision-making and actions in general. Indeed there are and these are clearly etched in the Treaties and reflected in the different legal and non-legal instruments.

1978 *Alesina/Perotti*, p. 30.
1979 *Craig/de Búrca*, EU Law (6th edition), p. 63.
1980 *Craig/de Búrca*, EU Law (6th edition), p. 63.
1981 *Craig/de Búrca*, EU Law (6th edition), p. 63.

a. Constitutional Principles

The constitutional principles of the EU provide the grounds for Union-level legitimacy and govern the relationship between the supranational and national levels.[1982] It must be mentioned that although the Treaties steered away from being referred to as a "Constitution", the EU member states in fact have broaden the scope of international agreements with the same by giving the Treaties the same function as a constitution by providing a primary body of law that "incorporates constitutional principles" and underpins the existence and mechanism of the Union.[1983]

First, there is the principle of conferral, which has been mentioned *en passant* with respect competencies of the Union. This means, the EU may only act on matters or policy fields which the member states have conferred upon it.[1984] Member states, hence, remain as "masters of the Treaties" and whatever they do not confer to the Union, remains to be their exclusive competence.[1985] In relation to this principle, there has been growing concerns on the expanding competence of the Union or the so-called "mission creep", wherein the Union has been accumulating more and more powers at the expense of member states.[1986] Jurisprudence has not overlooked these concerns, one of which is the landmark decision by the German Federal Constitutional Court ("FCC") in Brunner v. European Union Treaty on the issue of ratification by the German Parliament of the Maastricht Treaty. Whilst affirming the authority of the German Parliament to ratify the Maastricht Treaty, the Court was not afraid to issue a warning that because the EU was conferred limited powers and it does not have authority to expand its powers on its own, any claim of further powers and authority is dependent on the modification or amendment of the Treaty and the affirmative decisions of the national parliaments.[1987]

The second and third constitutional principles that could be found in the Treaties are the principles of subsidiarity and proportionality. While some member states' constitutional courts acted to preempt any further "mission creep" by the European Union, the apprehensions and worries persisted. In response, the principles of subsidiarity and proportionality

1982 *Craig/de Búrca*, EU Law (6th edition), p. 64. See for details on constitutionalization of Union law, *Stavrou*, pp. 1-9.

1983 *Von Bogdandy*, pp. 96-97. See *Stavrou*.

1984 Treaty on European Union, art. 1; *Von Bogdandy*, pp. 96-97.

1985 *Woods/Watson*, p. 50.

1986 *Woods/Watson*, p. 51.

1987 Brunner v. European Union Treaty, [1994] 1 CMLR 57; *Woods/Watson*, p. 51.

exist to provide a stop-lock gate to any further expansion of powers of the Union beyond what has been provided for.[1988] On one hand, the principle of subsidiarity decides, "where there are multiple layers of government, at which level policy decisions will be made."[1989] Accordingly, Article 10(3) TEU provides that decisions should be taken as close as possible to the citizen, mirroring the preamble of the TEU.[1990] Hence, while it might be discerned that the EU has competence to act, it is a different question altogether on whether said competence should be exercised or not.[1991] It must be qualified however, that the same pertains only to those matters outside the exclusive competence of the Union. As the relevant paragraph of Article 5(3) TEU provides:

> "Under the principle of subsidiarity, in areas which do not fall within its exclusive competence, the Union shall act only if and insofar as the objectives of the proposed action cannot be sufficiently achieved by the Member States, either at central level or at regional and local level, but can rather, by reason of the scale or effects of the proposed action, be better achieved at Union level."[1992]

The foregoing paragraph connotes (1) that no EU action ought to be taken unless said action cannot be sufficiently achieved by the member states; and (2) that EU action should be taken if it would better achieve the end result desired by reason of the proposed scale and effect of the proposed action.[1993] To discern, the subsidiary test could be applied, wherein one asks: (1) whether the issue has transnational effects, which cannot be satisfactorily regulated by the member states; (2) actions by member states alone would conflict with the requirements of the treaty, such as internal market provisions; and (3) action at Union level would clearly benefit by reason of its scale and effects.[1994] In connection to this, the Protocol on the Principles of Subsidiarity and Proportionality provide how the same shall be further implemented:

> "Draft legislative acts shall be justified with regard to the principles of subsidiarity and proportionality. Any draft legislative act should

1988 *Woods/Watson*, p. 51.
1989 *Woods/Watson*, p. 59.
1990 Treaty on European Union, art. 10(3).
1991 *Woods/Watson*, p. 59.
1992 Treaty on European Union, art. 5(3).
1993 *Woods/Watson*, p. 59.
1994 *Woods/Watson*, p. 59.

contain a detailed statement making it possible to appraise compliance with the principles of subsidiarity and proportionality. This statement should contain some assessment of the proposal's financial impact and, in the case of a directive, of its implications for the rules to be put in place by Member States, including, where necessary, the regional legislation. The reasons for concluding that a Union objective can be better achieved at Union level shall be substantiated by qualitative and, wherever possible, quantitative indicators. Draft legislative acts shall take account of the need for any burden, whether financial or administrative, falling upon the Union, national governments, regional or local authorities, economic operators and citizens, to be minimized and commensurate with the objective to be achieved."[1995]

Additionally, the national parliaments are given a role to play should they believe that the principle of subsidiarity has not been complied with. The relevant article provides:

"Any national Parliament or any chamber of a national Parliament may, within eight weeks from the date of transmission of a draft legislative act, in the official languages of the Union, send to the Presidents of the European Parliament, the Council and the Commission a reasoned opinion stating why it considers that the draft in question does not comply with the principle of subsidiarity. It will be for each national Parliament or each chamber of a national Parliament to consult, where appropriate, regional parliaments with legislative powers.

"If the draft legislative act originates from a group of Member States, the President of the Council shall forward the opinion to the governments of those Member States.

"If the draft legislative act originates from the Court of Justice, the European Central Bank or the European Investment Bank, the President of the Council shall forward the opinion to the institution or body concerned."[1996]

Going hand in hand with the principle of subsidiarity is the principle of proportionality. This principle states that the "content and form Union action shall not exceed what is necessary to achieve the objectives of the

1995 Protocol (No. 2) on the Application of the Principle of Subsidiarity and Proportionality, art. 5.

1996 Protocol (No. 2) on the Application of the Principle of Subsidiarity and Proportionality, art. 6.

Treaties."[1997] Applied in the context of administrative law, the principle requires that "the means used to achieve a given end must be no more than which is appropriate and necessary to achieve that end."[1998] Stating it more bluntly, action should not be an overkill and the means employed ought to be reasonable, taking into account likewise of other possible alternative actions.[1999]

The fourth constitutional principle that could be mentioned is the principle of institutional balance, or sometimes referred to as the division of powers among the different EU institutions. If one would recall the immediately preceding discussion on the different EU institutions, one would observe that each institution has its own duties and responsibilities independent of the other, and underlying these functions is the principle of institutional balance, which is not completely the same with the traditional notion of separation of powers amongst national governments. This institutional balance needs to be respected by the institutions as the same also governs their relationships with one another.[2000] In respect to this, institutions ought to act within bounds but it does not necessarily follow that there is a balanced distribution of weight among the different institutions' powers.[2001] Instead, it means that the Treaties provide the institutional structure every institution ought to follow and that they are not allowed to overstretch their powers to the detriment of the others.[2002] In other words, it ensures that no single institution becomes too powerful.[2003]

In light of the foregoing, the principle of institutional balance becomes imperative in the decision-making process and governing intra-institution practice. On one hand, the legal basis on which a particular decision of a particular institution normally needs to be scrutinized to determine whether the particular institution has acted within its prerogative. Moreover, one keeps in mind that the powers of the institutions depend on the different areas of competence and the same provides how different competencies should interplay and interrelate with one another.[2004] Said legal basis is a manifestation of the principle of institutional balance and should one have acted without legal basis, then the Court would not

---

1997 Treaty on European Union, art. 5(4).
1998 *Woods/Watson*, p. 60.
1999 See *Woods/Watson*, p. 159.
2000 *Woods/Watson*, p. 159.
2001 *Jacqué*, p. 383.
2002 *Jacqué*, p. 383.
2003 *Jacqué*, p. 384.
2004 *Jacqué*, p. 384; *Woods/Watson*, p. 23.

hesitate to sustain an action for annulment.[2005] As the Court of Justice once did, in sustaining the Parliament's action for annulment to preserve its prerogative:

> "Those prerogatives are one of the elements of the institutional balance created by the Treaties. The Treaties set up a system for distributing powers among the different Community institutions, assigning to each institution its own role in the institutional structure of the Community and the accomplishment of the tasks entrusted to the Community. Observance of the institutional balance means that each of the institutions must exercise its powers with due regard for the powers of the other institutions. It also requires that it should be possible to penalize any breach of that rule which may occur."[2006]

As Jacqué noted, the Court interpreted the principle in a dynamic way, wherein, while the principle only states that institutions should act within their boundaries, the Court now allows redress for any violation of the same.[2007]

In addition, the principle of institutional balance becomes important in terms of intra-institution practice. It was used by the Commission in blocking actions of the Parliament.[2008] The Parliament, on the other hand, has historically been codifying its vision as regards the role it ought to play, or already playing in the legislative process that the Commission and Council ought to respect, which the latter – also on the basis of institutional balance – object to.[2009] The use of the principle to embolden opposition notwithstanding, the principle also paved way to inter-institutional agreements between the Council, Commission, and the Parliament: said agreements act like a "constitutional glue through which the institutions could resolve high-level issues, provide guiding principles, or lay the groundwork for concrete legislative action.[2010] Sanctioned by the treaties, Article 295 TFEU enjoins the Parliament, Council, and Commission to consult each other and by common agreement make arrangements for cooperation, which in turn, may arise to inter-institutional agreements.[2011]

2005 *Woods/Watson*, p. 24.

2006 Case 70/88, Parliament v. Council, [1990] ECR I-2041, §§ 21–22, as cited in *Jacqué*, p. 386.

2007 *Jacqué*, p. 386.

2008 *Jacqué*, p. 386.

2009 *Jacqué*, p. 386.

2010 See *Craig/de Búrca*, EU Law (6th edition), p. 54; *Jacqué*, p. 386.

2011 Treaty on Functioning of the European Union, art. 295.

It can be said that the principle applies herein because each institution needs to acknowledge the role the other plays in the legislative and overall decision-making process, and thus, instead of butting heads with one another, find ways to cooperate and coordinate more efficiently with one another.

Lastly, there is the constitutional principle of delegated sovereignty. When a member state decides to join the European Union, it gives up its sovereignty but not its entirety given that as mentioned above, whatever competence was not conferred to the Union, remains exclusively to the member states. Moreover, a member state can opt out of the Union subject to the applicable provisions of the Treaties. Article 50 TEU provides:

> "1. Any Member State may decide to withdraw from the Union in accordance with its own constitutional requirements.
> "2. A Member State which decides to withdraw shall notify the European Council of its intention. In the light of the guidelines provided by the European Council, the Union shall negotiate and conclude an agreement with that State, setting out the arrangements for its withdrawal, taking account of the framework for its future relationship with the Union. That agreement shall be negotiated in accordance with Article 218(3) of the Treaty on the Functioning of the European Union. It shall be concluded on behalf of the Union by the Council, acting by a qualified majority, after obtaining the consent of the European Parliament.
> "3. The Treaties shall cease to apply to the State in question from the date of entry into force of the withdrawal agreement or, failing that, two years after the notification referred to in paragraph 2, unless the European Council, in agreement with the Member State concerned, unanimously decides to extend this period.
> "4. For the purposes of paragraphs 2 and 3, the member of the European Council or of the Council representing the withdrawing Member State shall not participate in the discussions of the European Council or Council or in decisions concerning it.
> "A qualified majority shall be defined in accordance with Article 238(3)(b) of the Treaty on the Functioning of the European Union."[2012]

The decision of withdrawal does not solely rest on the discretion of the member state, however. As can be read above, it has to be voted on by

2012 Treaty on European Union, art. 50.

the European Council, with prior consent from the European Parliament. With regard to this, the idea of a member state's sovereignty being absolute seems diminished, given that the member state could not even unilaterally decide on its own to leave an organization it has earlier consented to join.

b. Normative Principles

Other than the constitutional principles that governs legitimacy at the Union-level and governs the relationship between the supranational and national levels, there are also the normative values that constitute part of the fundamental principles of Union law.[2013] These values being "sustainable peace, freedom, democracy, human rights, rule of law, equality, social solidarity, sustainable development and good governance", they are not only to be considered as founding principles but also objectives to be attained by the Union in its actions and decisions.[2014] As such, the EU does not only internalize these values but promotes the same by virtue of the principles of "living by example"; by duty of its actions in "being reasonable"; and by consequence of its impact in "doing least harm".[2015] If one may recall the discussion on how the EU proceeds as an external actor, one can remember how the EU can also be described as a normative actor, promoting the values which it deems important, reasonable, and desirable. The same is evident in partnership programs, developmental programs, humanitarian aid, and the like, wherein one or more fundamental principle/norm is being promoted.[2016]

c. Decision-making principles

Having a supranational nature, the Union follows a carefully laid down procedure for decision making and legislation. As one may recall, the Commission, among the Union institutions, has the right to legislative initiative.[2017] The Council ought to make important decisions on the basis

---

2013 See *Craig/de Búrca*, EU Law (6th edition), p. 109.
2014 *Manners*, p. 46; *Von Bogdandy*, p. 106.
2015 *Manners*, p. 46.
2016 See for specifics *Manners*, p. 46.
2017 Treaty on the European Union, art. 17(2), *Manners*, pp. 46-59.

of the Commission's proposals.[2018] This is without prejudice however to the Council itself asking the Commission to conduct studies the former considers imperative to attaining common objectives, and to submit appropriate proposals concerning these common objectives.[2019] In the same vein, the EP may request the Commission to submit proposals on matters it believes the Union should act on to implement the Treaties, and the latter thereafter should make a prompt and sufficiently detailed response.[2020] Additionally, there is also a people's initiative in the EU decision-making framework notwithstanding the Commission's right of legislative initiative.[2021] Under said people's initiative, no fewer than one million citizens who are nationals of a significant number of member states may take the "initiative of inviting the European Commission, within the framework of its powers, to submit any appropriate proposal on matters which the citizens consider that a legal act of the Union is required for the purpose of implementing the Treaties."[2022]

Having mentioned the nuances of legislative initiative within the Union, one must know that there are two (2) types of legislative procedure: ordinary legislative procedure and special legislative procedure.[2023] On one hand, the ordinary legislative procedure consists of the joint adoption by the Parliament and Council of a regulation, directive, or decision on a proposal from the Commission.[2024] It is always important to know the particular treaty article as it would dictate the legislative procedure applicable to a certain area, though in most cases it is the ordinary legislative

2018 *Alesina/Perotti*, p. 29; *Craig/de Búrca*, EU Law (6th edition), p. 36; *Woods/Watson*, p. 38.

2019 *Woods/Watson*, p. 38.

2020 Framework Agreement on Relations between the European Parliament and the Commission, C5-349/2000[2001]; *Craig/de Búrca*, EU Law (6th edition), p. 125.

2021 Treaty on European Union, art. 11(4).

2022 Treaty on European Union, art. 11(4); Treaty on the Functioning of the European Union, art. 24.

2023 Treaty on Functioning of the European Union, art. 289; *Craig/de Búrca*, EU Law (6th edition), p. 125.

2024 Treaty on Functioning of the European Union, art. 289(1); *Woods/Watson*, p. 67.

procedure that shall apply.[2025] In this case, Article 294 TFEU provides for ordinary legislative procedure.[2026]

2025 *Craig/de Búrca,* EU Law (6th edition), p. 127.

2026 Said Article states:
"1. Where reference is made in the Treaties to the ordinary legislative procedure for the adoption of an act, the following procedure shall apply.
"2. The Commission shall submit a proposal to the European Parliament and the Council.
"3. The European Parliament shall adopt its position at first reading and communicate it to the Council.
"4. If the Council approves the European Parliament's position, the act concerned shall be adopted in the wording which corresponds to the position of the European Parliament.
"5. If the Council does not approve the European Parliament's position, it shall adopt its position at first reading and communicate it to the European Parliament.
"6. The Council shall inform the European Parliament fully of the reasons which led it to adopt its position at first reading. The Commission shall inform the European Parliament fully of its position.
"7. If, within three months of such communication, the European Parliament:
"(a) approves the Council's position at first reading or has not taken a decision, the act concerned shall be deemed to have been adopted in the wording which corresponds to the position of the Council;
"(b) rejects, by a majority of its component members, the Council's position at first reading, the proposed act shall be deemed not to have been adopted;
"(c) proposes, by a majority of its component members, amendments to the Council's position at first reading, the text thus amended shall be forwarded to the Council and to the Commission, which shall deliver an opinion on those amendments.
"8. If, within three months of receiving the European Parliament's amendments, the Council, acting by a qualified majority:
"(a) approves all those amendments, the act in question shall be deemed to have been adopted;
"(b) does not approve all the amendments, the President of the Council, in agreement with the President of the European Parliament, shall within six weeks convene a meeting of the Conciliation Committee.
"9. The Council shall act unanimously on the amendments on which the Commission has delivered a negative opinion.
"10. The Conciliation Committee, which shall be composed of the members of the Council or their representatives and an equal number of members representing the European Parliament, shall have the task of reaching agreement on a joint text, by a qualified majority of the members of the Council or their representatives and by a majority of the members representing the European Parliament within six weeks of its being convened, on the basis of the positions of the European Parliament and the Council at second reading.

There are three (3) things that can be noted from the provision on ordinary legislative procedure. First, there are stages in the process, including the first reading, second reading, conciliation, and if necessary, third reading.[2027] During the first reading, the Commission's proposal, at its simplest, may already be accepted by both the EP and the Council without amendments.[2028] But should there be no approval or amendments are proposed, then the procedure advances to second, and even third, reading, with efforts to conciliate positions and compromise.[2029]

The second thing one can take away from the ordinary legislative procedure is that even if it is formalistic in its rules, there is emphasis on compromise and dialogue, which is reflected in no less than the EP's Rules of Procedure, Joint Declaration, and Framework Agreement between the EP and Commission.[2030] Moreover, there is the institutionalization of

---

"11. The Commission shall take part in the Conciliation Committee's proceedings and shall take all necessary initiatives with a view to reconciling the positions of the European Parliament and the Council.

"12. If, within six weeks of its being convened, the Conciliation Committee does not approve the joint text, the proposed act shall be deemed not to have been adopted.

"13. If, within that period, the Conciliation Committee approves a joint text, the European Parliament, acting by a majority of the votes cast, and the Council, acting by a qualified majority, shall each have a period of six weeks from that approval in which to adopt the act in question in accordance with the joint text. If they fail to do so, the proposed act shall be deemed not to have been adopted.

"14. The periods of three months and six weeks referred to in this Article shall be extended by a maximum of one month and two weeks respectively at the initiative of the European Parliament or the Council.

"15. Where, in the cases provided for in the Treaties, a legislative act is submitted to the ordinary legislative procedure on the initiative of a group of Member States, on a recommendation by the European Central Bank, or at the request of the Court of Justice, paragraph 2, the second sentence of paragraph 6, and paragraph 9 shall not apply.

"In such cases, the European Parliament and the Council shall communicate the proposed act to the Commission with their positions at first and second readings. The European Parliament or the Council may request the opinion of the Commission throughout the procedure, which the Commission may also deliver on its own initiative. It may also, if it deems it necessary, take part in the Conciliation Committee in accordance with paragraph 11."

2027 *Craig/de Búrca,* EU Law (6th edition), p. 127.

2028 *Craig/de Búrca,* EU Law (6th edition), pp. 128-130.

2029 *Woods/Watson,* p. 68.

2030 Joint Declaration of the European Parliament, the Council, and the Commission of 13 June 2007 on practical arrangements for the co-decision procedure

trilogues, which are attended by representatives from the Council, Parliament, and Commission – normally not more than 10 from each institution – the aim being to facilitate compromise.[2031]

Lastly, one can take away from the ordinary legislative procedure an insight on power dynamics and normative foundations. The EP had always pushed for a co-equal role in the legislative process prior to the Lisbon Treaty and this has been achieved in the ordinary legislative procedure, which was priorly known as co-decision procedure.[2032] It has also been conferred a veto power, which although it has historically applied sparingly, there is a relative power that could be observed.[2033] Having said that, there is also power from the Commission itself in the entire process, being the main initiator of legislation: it is authorized to withdraw a proposal before it is adopted, submit a modified version, or refuse to proceed again, if it feels that the amendments to be proposed shall be fundamentally averse.[2034]

Aside from the ordinary legislative procedure, there is also the special legislative procedure, which is mainly a consultative procedure required by the Treaties for certain areas wherein a regulation, directive, or decision is adopted by the European Parliament with the participation of the Council, or by the latter with the participation of the European Parliament.[2035] In instances wherein special legislative procedure is applicable, the Council must consult the Parliament before it acts; otherwise, its actions may be annulled.[2036] This is the bare minimum requirement that ought to be complied with. There could also be instances wherein the Parliament ought to be consulted again should there have been important changes made

---

(Article 251 of the EC Treaty), [2007] OJ CI45/5; Rules of Procedure of the European Parliament, Annex XIX; *Craig/de Búrca*, EU Law (6th edition), pp. 129-130; *Woods/Watson*, pp. 69-71.

2031 *Craig/de Búrca*, EU Law (6th edition), pp. 130-131.

2032 *Craig/de Búrca*, EU Law (6th edition), p. 131; *Woods/Watson*, p. 71.

2033 *Craig/de Búrca*, EU Law (6th edition), p. 133.

2034 *Craig/de Búrca*, EU Law (6th edition), p. 132; *Woods/Watson*, p. 71.

2035 Treaty on Functioning of the European Union, art. 289(2); *Craig/de Búrca*, EU Law (6th edition), pp. 132-133.

2036 Case 138/79, Roquette Freres v. Council, [1980] ECR 333; Case C-65/93, European Parliament v. Council (Re Generalized Tariff Preferences), [1995] ECR I-643; Case C-156/93, European Parliament v. Commission (Re Genetically Modified Microorganisms in Organic Products, [1995] ECR I-2019; Case C-658/11, European Parliament v. Council, EC:C:2014:2025; as cited in *Woods/Watson*, p. 71.

to a measure previously consulted.[2037] It should be clarified though that consulting is one thing, but following what has been advised is another. The Council must take it into consideration but is under no obligation to follow the Parliament's view or even defend its position on the matter.[2038]

C. Cross-border movement of evidence: European Investigation Order

The following portion discusses the applicable regime of the European Union on mutual legal assistance in criminal matters. Before delving into the substantive and procedural provisions, there would be a preliminary discussion on its historical development of mutual legal assistance in the EU.

With respect to this, it would be easier to just enumerate the different regimes and policies the EU has implemented, but the same would only be half-baked. Therefore, this chapter also intends to show the reasons and motivations the EU has used in developing its mutual legal assistance regime, which would necessarily include a discussion on how the EU developed its policy on criminal matters and how the EU historically developed its legal cooperation on criminal matters as a response to the sign of the times. By going through this exercise, one could gain a better understanding on how the EU positions itself in matters of legal cooperation, what normally drives its decisions on these matters, and what changes, if ever, has it made through time. Afterwards, focus shall be given to the presently applicable mutual legal assistance in criminal matters regime, which shall include discussions on its substantive and procedural provisions.

1. Historical Development of Mutual Legal Assistance in the EU

The historical development of mutual legal assistance in criminal matters, or international and transnational cooperation in general, in the European Union is nothing short of interesting. International cooperation in general was not only influenced by the sign of the times, but its development also took into consideration the issues and concerns raised regarding said cooperation.

2037 *Craig/de Búrca*, EU Law (6th edition), p. 134.
2038 *Craig/de Búrca*, EU Law (6th edition), p. 134.

One must first understand that any criminal law policy or cooperation among member states on criminal matters historically was and remained purely intergovernmental, and often informal.[2039] For example, one of the earliest multilateral extradition treaties existed in 1802 through the Treaty of Amiens between France, Spain, Great Britain and Holland, Article 20 of which provided for the extradition of persons accused of murder, forgery or fraudulent bankrupt.[2040] The implementation of said treaty was only hindered by the war against Napoleonic France.[2041] The intergovernmental, and sometimes informal, characteristic remained even when the European Community took effect in January 1958.[2042] Community institutions were barely given any role to play in the negotiations of these type of criminal cooperation agreements or conventions, except for the Court of Justice to interpret civil law conventions, subject to restrictive jurisdictional rules then applied under the EEC treaty.[2043] In fact, developments in this area occurred in many fronts but almost, if not completely, without Community involvement. Developments occurred in the framework of the Council of Europe (which as one would recall is mainly intergovernmental in nature), within the framework of the European Political Cooperation (which addressed mostly criminal law issues), and the developed Schengen cooperation.[2044]

As regards the Council of Europe, it took the lead on multilateral agreements at the international level on cross-border cooperation, while the United Nations took the backseat.[2045] With cross-border cooperation traditionally encompassing six (6) elements of extradition, mutual legal assistance, transfer of prisoners, enforcement of sentences, transfer of proceedings, and confiscation of proceeds of crime, the Council of Europe was able to have conventions regarding the same, with the exception of the Conventions on enforcement of sentences and transfer of proceedings as having the least amount of support from member states.[2046] Among these conventions on cross-border cooperation, the 1957 European Convention on Extradition and 1959 European Convention on Mutual Legal Assis-

2039 *Woods/Watson*, p. 71.
2040 *Douglas-Scott*, p. 221; *Peers*, p. 269.
2041 *O'Higgins*, p. 492.
2042 *O'Higgins*, p. 492.
2043 *Peers*, p. 269.
2044 See *Peers*, p. 270.
2045 *Peers*, pp. 268-269, 270.
2046 *Peers*, pp. 6-7.

tance in Criminal Matters eventually became the key or core agreements in Europe.[2047]

On one hand, the 1957 Convention on Extradition provided that to implement extradition, the "requesting" state asks the "requested" state to "surrender" the fugitive to it, possibly after a provisional arrest to prevent flight.[2048] In view thereof, special extradition proceedings shall be held in accordance with what the national law of the requested state provides.[2049] The Convention however would provide that extradition should be granted should the subject person escaped from custodial sentence of over four months detention, or is accused of committing a crime punishable in at least one year detention in both the requesting and requested states (concept of dual criminality).[2050] This does not mean that there were no exceptions to granting extradition. Among others, extradition could be limited to a specific list of crimes and extradition could not be allowed should the subject offense is political, military, or sometimes, fiscal, or whether the purpose of the extradition is discriminatory in nature.[2051] Extradition is likewise not allowed should the subject person be a national of the requested state.[2052]

The 1959 Convention on Mutual Legal Assistance would apply to all offenses except political, military, and fiscal offenses, as well as those involving sovereignty, national interest or public order cases,[2053] and unlike the Extradition Convention, there is no sentencing threshold or dual criminality requirement except for search and seizure measures.[2054] Should a judge in the "home state" of the prosecution want a piece of evidence or any other relevant material, it should send a formal request called "letters rogatory" – usually through its own national ministry – to the relevant ministry of the "host state", which then forwards the request to a national judicial authority, i.e. a judge or prosecutor .[2055] Requests for mutual legal assistance could be denied should the home state think that it shall "preju-

2047 *Peers*, Mutual Recognition, pp. 6-7.
2048 *Peers*, p. 694.
2049 *Peers*, EU Justice and Home Affairs Law, p. 694.
2050 *Peers*, EU Justice and Home Affairs Law, p. 694.
2051 *Peers*, EU Justice and Home Affairs Law, p. 694.
2052 *Peers*, EU Justice and Home Affairs Law, p. 694.
2053 1959 European Convention on Mutual Legal Assistance, arts. 1(2) and 2.
2054 *Peers*, EU Justice and Home Affairs Law, p. 711.
2055 *Peers*, EU Justice and Home Affairs Law, p. 711.

dice the sovereignty, security, public order, and other essential interests of the country."[2056]

While being the key agreements on extradition and mutual legal assistance, the European Conventions were not without issue.[2057] The European Convention on Mutual Legal Assistance, as stated above, provides political, military and fiscal offenses, together with national interest as the only grounds for refusing a request for mutual legal assistance.[2058] Akin to the European Convention on Extradition, the European MLA Convention did not provide definitions of fundamental concepts and provisions such as what is "political offense" or "fiscal offense."[2059] These issues and concerns notwithstanding, the two instruments brought a crucial development in terms of legal/judicial cooperation in criminal matters as they did not only close a considerable gap in the present system of bilateral treaties among European States, but it successfully imparted an "important step forward in the doctrine of uniformity in the practice and procedure" of both extradition and mutual legal assistance in criminal matters.[2060]

Within the Community framework, which were mostly in the context of the European Political Cooperation, the established cooperation mechanisms were mostly informal or ad hoc.[2061] There was the establishment in 1975 of the Terrorism, Radicalism, Extremism, and International Violence ("TREVI") group and the European Convention on the Suppression of Terrorism ("ECST") in 1977, which could be said to be one of the intergovernmental arrangements that heralded the modern era of European counter-terrorism measures.[2062] Starting as a forum for exchanging information regarding organized crime and terrorism, the TREVI group was formed by European police officials to exchange information and provide mutual assistance on terrorism and related international crimes and in pur-

2056 *Peers*, EU Justice and Home Affairs Law, p. 711.

2057 *Peers*, Mutual Recognition, pp. 6-7.

2058 Article 2 of the Convention reads as follows: "Article 2. Assistance may be refused: (a) if the request concerns an offence which the requested Party considers a political offence, an offence connected with a political offence, or a fiscal offence; (b) if the requested Party considers that execution of the request is likely to prejudice the sovereignty, security, ordre public or other essential interests of its country." This is more or less the same grounds for refusal vis-à-vis political and fiscal offenses as provided for in the European Convention on Extradition. *O'Higgins*, p. 493.

2059 See *O'Higgins*, p. 493.

2060 *O'Higgins*, p. 493.

2061 *O'Higgins*, pp. 492,494.

2062 *Vermeulen/De Bondt*, p. 117.

suit thereof, high level meetings and gatherings were held among interior and justice ministers and top level security officials.[2063] It was only after a while when these cooperation activities were formally approved by the Ministers of Justice and Home Affairs and included within the European Economic Community.[2064] Given TREVI, there were other cooperative arrangements to combat terrorism, which included the Police Working Group on terrorism and the Counter-Terrorism Group.[2065]

The Schengen process among a small number of member states was ongoing coincidentally, which entailed the adoption of treaties and implementing measures vis-à-vis the adoption of internal border controls and parallel compensatory measures necessary to ensure and increase security.[2066] This started with a small agreement in 1985, to be followed by a longer Convention implementing the Schengen Agreement in 1990.[2067] While intergovernmentalism was the preferred approach, this move proved itself as a more effective measure as it was ratified in 1993 – or three years' time after signature, even if there was some opposition from some member states in the Community like the United Kingdom, Denmark, and Ireland.[2068] Considering that the 1959 Convention on Mutual Legal Assistance allowed additional bilateral or multilateral agreements to supplant or fill in details of its provisions, Schengen member states took the opportunity to integrate into the Schengen Framework additional requirements and/or obligation on mutual assistance.[2069] Accordingly, the grounds for refusal were reduced, the ground on double incrimination has been restricted, and simplified procedure on how requests for assistance are transmitted – allowing direct contact between judicial authorities and the executing state.[2070]

Things changed a bit after the Maastricht Treaty or between the years 1993 to 1998, which formalized the intergovernmentalism involved in Justice and Home Affairs.[2071] In 1993, the TREVI Group and other European institutions dealing with judicial, customs, and immigration issues were

---

2063 *Casale*, p. 50.
2064 *Casale*, p. 50.
2065 *Casale*, p. 50.
2066 *Casale*, p. 50.
2067 *Peers*, EU Justice and Home Affairs Law (Non-Civil), p. 270.
2068 *Peers*, EU Justice and Home Affairs Law (Non-Civil), p. 270.
2069 *Peers*, EU Justice and Home Affairs Law (Non-Civil), p. 270.
2070 *Winter*, pp. 580-581.
2071 *Klimek*, p. 15; *Peers*, EU Justice and Home Affairs Law (Non-Civil), pp. 292-293.

brought under the third pillar of the European Union.[2072] Occupying the third pillar in the original TEU structure, EC institutions together with the Council were assigned roles regarding the same but they were limited nonetheless.[2073] For instance, the European Parliament only had the right to be informed by the Council on any ongoing negotiations, while the European Commission did not have the right to initiate proposals on the areas of policing and criminal law.[2074] This mechanism ensured maximum control by the member states on these areas but it definitely hampered EU action.[2075]

There were admittedly moderate achievements notwithstanding the foregoing limitations on the Union structure. In terms of international cooperation in criminal matters, the relevant provisions of the Maastricht Treaty did not only provide for compensatory measures that would have to be taken once border controls between the member states have been removed. In addition to the consolidated TREVI and other European institutions dealing with crime, the Maastricht Treaty provided for the creation of the European Police Office ("EUROPOL"), for which, prior to being operational in 1998, a counter-terrorism preparatory group was established in 1997 to formulate the office's role in matters of counter-terrorism.[2076]

Additionally, the member states were not particularly shying away from introducing innovative ideas as regards formal modes of cooperation in criminal matters to improve the same, especially since they have long realized the need to improve its efficiency and effectiveness, particularly extradition.[2077] The European Union may be considered a "laboratory" at this moment in which several new ideas have developed and some "experiments" have been carried out in the field of international cooperation in criminal matters.[2078] These "experiments" admittedly ought to be not too drastic however and baby steps were imperative to make things work. To illustrate, the member states were able to agree within the Maastricht period on the 1995 Convention on simplified extradition process and the 1996 Convention relating to Extradition between Member States of the EU, both of which meant to accelerate and simplify the mechanisms of

2072 *Peers,* EU Justice and Home Affairs Law (Non-Civil), p. 270.

2073 *Casale,* p. 50.

2074 *Peers,* EU Justice and Home Affairs Law (Non-Civil), p. 271; *Vermeulen/De Bondt,* pp. 117-118.

2075 *Peers,* EU Justice and Home Affairs Law (Non-Civil), p. 271.

2076 *Peers,* EU Justice and Home Affairs Law (Non-Civil), p. 271.

2077 *Casale,* p. 50.

2078 *Plachta,* p. 179.

the 1957 European Convention on Extradition.[2079] While the new Conventions tackling extradition was laudable, it still contained a reservation clause that greatly diminished the practical mechanism of the provisions and at the same time, the two Conventions did not break free from the traditional extradition mechanism of being highly political and intergovernmental.[2080] With only a few member states ratifying these Conventions, they did not enter into force and consequently, disillusioning political figures in the EU from pursuing further innovations with regard judicial cooperation.[2081]

At this juncture, one may be compelled to ask why there was a need in the first place to undertake cross-border cooperation agreements when this has been covered quite extensively by the Council of Europe, even covering all six (6) traditional elements of the same.[2082] It was explained that member states wanted either to supplement widely ratified Council of Europe Conventions, like the one on Extradition, for instance by "reducing the number of exceptions to the rules as between EU member states," or "to find alternative routes to achieve the same ends where the Council of Europe measures had not attracted many ratifications."[2083] In view thereof, agreements regarding the same failed to enter into force even if the member states have made agreements and/or arrangements prior to the Maastricht Treaty.[2084]

Although it was not a complete win on extradition despite earnest efforts to be more efficient, one could notice agreements on corruption, fraud, and driving disqualification, as well as joint actions on efforts to harmonize substantive criminal law, as regards drug trafficking, racism, trafficking in persons, sexual exploitation, and organized crime.[2085] The EU realized that not only good and respectable citizens profit from the discontinuation of internal borders and freedom of passenger traffic, service traffic, and movement of goods.[2086] The centers of affluent societies of the EU member states provide a motivation for illegal products and services

2079 *Plachta*, p. 179.
2080 *Peers*, Mutual Recognition, p. 8; *Plachta*, p. 179; *Vermeulen/De Bondt*, p. 118.
2081 *Plachta*, p. 179.
2082 As mentioned earlier, this includes extradition, mutual legal assistance, transfer of prisoners, enforcement of sentences, transfer of proceedings, and confiscation of proceeds of crime.
2083 *Peers*, Mutual Recognition, p. 8; *Plachta*, p. 179.
2084 *Peers*, Mutual Recognition, p. 7.
2085 *Luchtman*, p. 74; *Peers*, Mutual Recognition, p. 7.
2086 *Luchtman*, p. 74; *Peers*, EU Justice and Home Affairs Law (Non-Civil), p. 293.

of all kinds as well as a target of criminal attacks on regular economic, finance, and competitive processes.[2087] Moreover, there is the ever looming threat of terrorism and the inherent problem of corruption and mafia-like structures.[2088] The potential menaces these threats and concerns brought influenced member states to discuss counter-measures, one of which is strengthening of cross-border cooperation.[2089]

In the 1997 Action Plan to combat organized crime, it became apparent that there is lack of knowledge on competent authorities in other member states and this consequently affects negatively efficient cooperation.[2090] Henceforward, the European Council adopted the Joint Action of 29 June 1998 on the creation of a European Judicial Network ("EJN") with the objective of creating a decentralized network of contact points, which were to play a crucial role in relation to international cooperation in criminal matters among member states.[2091] Included herein is a Joint Action on Good Practice in mutual legal assistance, promoting through said Joint Action the use of liaison magistrates and setting up so-called mutual "peer evaluation" where the first reports tackled the functioning of mutual legal assistance in Europe.[2092] The achievements of the Schengen framework could not be likewise ignored. As Vermeulen and De Bondt surmised, these achievements were perhaps attributable to the involvement of a lesser number of member states.[2093] The Schengen Convention was applied from 1995 and implemented by measures instituted by the Executive Committee, which was created by virtue of the Schengen Convention.[2094] It must be mentioned however that the scope of cooperation was growing more than expected and was exceeding the capacity of the Schengen institutional framework in terms of a dedicated administrative staff to oversee the process.[2095]

Changes were introduced during the Amsterdam Treaty, which covered the years 1999 to 2005, and more or less could be described as modified intergovernmentalism in terms of the Justice and Home Affairs: retaining key features of intergovernmentalism but acceding competencies to the

2087 *Hecker*, p. 65.
2088 *Hecker*, p. 65.
2089 *Hecker*, p. 65.
2090 *Hecker*, p. 65.
2091 *Vermeulen/De Bondt*, p. 118.
2092 *Nilsson*, p. 55.
2093 *Vermeulen/De Bondt*, p. 118.
2094 *Peers*, EU Justice and Home Affairs Law (Non-Civil), p. 272.
2095 *Peers*, EU Justice and Home Affairs Law (Non-Civil), p. 272.

Union on certain matters such as judicial cooperation, allowing the latter to take a conceptual approach in the development of said area.[2096] In this regard, the Amsterdam Treaty introduces the concept of the "area of freedom, security, and justice."[2097] To further develop this area, the content of the action taken on judicial cooperation included two (2) components: (1) the idea of approximating national law by providing minimum standards regarding definitions of crimes and their sanctions; and (2) the further development of a regulatory framework applicable to judicial cooperation.[2098] This eventually led to the 1998 Vienna Action Plan that called for an extensive use of the new possibility of harmonization and gradual adoption of minimum standards while prioritizing criminal acts linked to organized crime, terrorism, and illegal drug trafficking, as well as the speeding up and streamlining the judicial cooperation between member states and third countries.[2099]

Pursuant to the Amsterdam Treaty, concepts of "framework decisions" and "decisions" to supplant Conventions and common decisions were introduced: the first, to be used to approximate national law, with the same definition as directives; the latter: to be used for purposes other than approximating national law – with both ruling out direct effect.[2100] In practice, the Council favored the use of these instruments in the legislative process as they do not require ratification by national parliaments to take effect, which consequently phased out the need to use conventions and protocols.[2101] The Council eventually used the same instruments to replace pending pre-Amsterdam Treaty Joint Actions and conventions, which meant that national parliaments did not anymore have a power of approval over third pillar acts, even if some instances, they still tried to exert influence over them.[2102] For instance, a Decision was used to create the office of the Eurojust, which serves as the EU prosecutor's agency.[2103]

Moreover, the Treaty of Amsterdam introduced changes in relation to "closer cooperation" in AFSJ between certain member states. There was the integration of the Schengen *acquis* to the EC and EU legal order, while

2096 *Peers*, EU Justice and Home Affairs Law (Non-Civil), p. 272.
2097 Treaty on European Union, art. 29; *Klimek*, p. 16; *Peers*, EU Justice and Home Affairs Law (Non-Civil), p. 272; *Vermeulen/De Bondt*, p. 118.
2098 *Vermeulen/De Bondt*, p. 118.
2099 *Vermeulen/De Bondt*, p. 118.
2100 *Vermeulen/De Bondt*, pp. 118-119.
2101 *Peers*, EU Justice and Home Affairs Law (Non-Civil), p. 273.
2102 *Peers*, EU Justice and Home Affairs Law (Non-Civil), p. 273.
2103 *Peers*, EU Justice and Home Affairs Law (Non-Civil), p. 274.

granting UK, Ireland, and Denmark special status under the same, but nonetheless incorporating all Schengen measures, present and future, to the EC and EU system.[2104]

As regards the substantive measures adopted in criminal law during this period, the foundations were laid in 1999-2001 for the establishment of the principle of mutual recognition in criminal matters, which is sought to be the "cornerstone of judicial cooperation."[2105] Previously, cooperation in criminal matters was premised on "mutual assistance", which connoted flexibility and lack of stringency in cooperation.[2106] It was thought in the concepts of having a requesting state and requested state, wherein the latter retained a broad margin of appreciation on whether to give a request its due course and execution.[2107] The principle of mutual recognition, as proposed, is about acknowledging differences between the different legal and/or judicial systems of each member state and accepting them.[2108] Judicial decisions from another member state under the said principle are afforded the same effect and value as national judicial decisions "without any prior procedure needed for recognition and/or homologation."[2109] It is basically grounded on mutual trust as there is renunciation on the part of the executing state of any control upon the grounds that motivate the request for evidence of the issuing state, because the executing state can trust that the requesting authorities have already checked the legality, necessity, and proportionality of the measure requested.[2110]

One of the programmes the European Council undertook for the development of JHA law was the Tampere Programme of October 1999, which reflected the awareness of the European Council that revolutionary steps (and not just a mere evolutionary approach) ought to be taken by the EU should it want to succeed in innovating judicial cooperation in criminal matters and making the said mechanism more effective.[2111] This is more

---

2104 *Peers*, EU Justice and Home Affairs Law (Non-Civil), p. 293. The three (3) mentioned countries were also given special opt out status vis-à-vis Title IV legislation which could then be exercised during negotiations or adoption of the measure.

2105 *Alegre/Leaf*, p. 201; *Peers*, EU Justice and Home Affairs Law (Non-Civil), p. 274.

2106 *De Hert/Weis/Cloosen*, p. 55; *Plachta*, p. 180.

2107 *Vermeulen/De Bondt*, p. 119.

2108 *Vermeulen/De Bondt*, p. 119.

2109 *Luchtman*, p. 78; *Winter*, p. 581.

2110 *Winter*, p. 581.See also *Alegre/Leaf*, p. 201.

2111 *De Hert/Weis/Cloosen*, p. 56.

especially the case considering the perceived rise in cross-border crime.[2112] Consequently, the Tampere document included four (4) main points: (1) A common EU Asylum and Migration Policy, (2) a genuine European area of justice; (3) a unionwide fight against crime; and (4) stronger external action.[2113]

The principle on mutual recognition in criminal matters as mentioned above falls under the discussion on building an European area of justice. The European Council endorsed the said principle due to reasons that an "enhanced mutual recognition of judicial decisions and judgments and the necessary approximation of legislation would facilitate cooperation between authorities and the protection of individual rights."[2114] The European Council enjoined the Council and the Commission to adopt by December 2000 a programme to implement the mutual recognition principle, and additionally to work on an "European Enforcement Order and on those aspects of procedural law on which common minimum standards are considered necessary in order to facilitate the application of the principle of mutual recognition, respecting the fundamental principles of the member states."[2115] This has thereafter set into motion policies designed to enhance the free movement of criminal investigations, prosecutions, and sentences, across EU borders, by means of implementing the principle of mutual recognition to criminal matters.[2116]

Additionally, the Tampere Programme mentioned the need to step up the cooperation against crime. In relation thereto, the European Council states that "maximum benefit should be derived from cooperation between member state authorities when investigating cross-border crime in any member state."[2117] As a first step towards the realization of this goal, the European Council called for the setup of joint investigative teams to combat trafficking in drugs and human beings as well as terrorism.[2118]

2112 *Peers*, EU Justice and Home Affairs Law (Non-Civil), pp. 274, 293; *Plachta*, p. 179.

2113 Tampere European Council 15 and 16 October 1999 Presidency Conclusions.

2114 Tampere European Council 15 and 16 October 1999 Presidency Conclusions, Sec. B, Part VI, para. 33. See also *Peers*, Mutual Recognition, p. 5.

2115 Tampere European Council 15 and 16 October 1999 Presidency Conclusions, Sec. B, Part VI, para. 36.

2116 *Plachta*, p. 180.

2117 Tampere European Council 15 and 16 October 1999 Presidency Conclusions, Sec. B, Part IX, para. 43.

2118 Tampere European Council 15 and 16 October 1999 Presidency Conclusions, Sec. B, Part VI, para. 36.

Along the same timeline, one of the earlier developments was the 2000 Convention on Mutual Legal Assistance, meant to enter into force on August 2005.[2119] The Convention is said to have greatly expanded, simplified, and modernized the European Criminal Law on mutual assistance.[2120] At the outset, it must be clarified that the 2000 Mutual Legal Assistance Convention does not have elements relating to the principle of mutual recognition. Having clarified this, the 2000 MLA Convention is general in character and contracting parties ought to supplement and facilitate the application of the various agreements mentioned in the Convention.[2121] As Denza explained, the first point of the 2000 Convention is to recognize that mutual assistance was already grounded on the 1959 Convention and its additional protocol, the Schengen documents, and regional agreements such as those existing among the Benelux countries, and the purpose of the 2000 Convention is to modernize and further develop these provisions, taking into consideration technological advances.[2122]

The 2000 Convention introduced the principle of *forum regit actum* and the horizontalization of cooperation within the EU.[2123] First, the principle of *forum regit actum* relates to the law that is applicable to the execution of the request: the requesting state may now indicate the procedure and formalities that ought to be applied in the execution of a request, a concept otherwise not provided for in the 1959 European Convention on Mutual Legal Assistance.[2124] Second, the orientation of cooperation was changed from a vertical one, wherein requests are issued and received through central authorities, to generally a horizontal one wherein requests shall be made directly between judicial authorities with territorial competence for initiating and executing them.[2125]

2119 *Peers,* Mutual Recognition, p. 5. One can note herein that the 2000 Convention on Mutual Legal Assistance has been negotiated since the 1990's, albeit it has only been finally introduced during the same timeline as the Tampere Programme.

2120 *Douglas-Scott,* p. 227; *Peers,* Mutual Recognition, p. 8.

2121 *Denza,* p. 1048.

2122 See *Denza,* p. 1056.

2123 *Denza,* p. 1056.

2124 *Vermeulen/De Bondt,* p. 119. See also *Satzger,* p. 145.

2125 2000 Mutual Legal Assistance Convention, art. 6, para. 1. This is without prejudice to an exchange between central authorities or between a central authority and a judicial authority (para. 2). Also, the UK and Ireland are equivocally mentioned in the Convention as member states retaining the use of their respective central authorities (para. 3). See also *Vermeulen/De Bondt,* p. 120.

In relation to this, gaining familiarity with the other member states' practice on criminal matters remained an issue and thus the 2000 MLA Convention aimed to increase this, and at the same time, the subsequent uniformity in practice as more EU member states accede to the 2000 Convention.[2126] Providing for the different types of request a member state could make, which includes, but is not limited to, taking of testimonies or statements, interceptions of communication, the formation of joint investigation teams, etc., and allowing spontaneous exchange of information without a prior request,[2127] the 2000 Convention through its 2001 Protocol does not exclude political, military, and fiscal offenses, and parties are not allowed to exclude offenses which fail to satisfy the dual criminality test or are not extraditable under their own law.[2128]

It did not take long when Europe soon realized that aside from the modernization and simplification of mutual assistance, how urgently it needed to press the start button on the other endeavors laid down in the Tampere Programme.[2129] After the September 2001 attacks in the United States, the EU saw the bigger role it has to play.[2130] It dawned on Europe that it was not merely a target, or a contributor due to the growing number of radicalized, marginalized, and poorly integrated Muslims in European societies, but more importantly, it was a quintessential player that needed immediate response in countering and/or battling terrorism and transborder crime.[2131] As a way to respond, there was a change in many policy areas as well as new countermeasures and strategies to impede the increasing security threat of transnational crime and terrorism.[2132] In fact, the development of EU Criminal Law was at its high peak during 2001 to 2004.[2133] One could observe at the outset the substantial momentum gained with the nexus between internal and external security resulting in merging of police systems, judicial systems, special forces, and external military action.[2134] There was a reorganization of the security apparatus

---

2126 *Vermeulen/De Bondt*, p. 120.
2127 2000 Convention on Mutual Legal Assistance, arts. 8-20. See also *Denza*, p. 1056.
2128 *Vermeulen/De Bondt*, p. 120.
2129 See *Alegre/Leaf*, p. 202.
2130 See *Denza*, p. 1057.
2131 *Casale*, p. 51; *Eder/Senn*, p. 14.
2132 *Casale*, p. 51; *Eder/Senn*, p. 14; *Komárek*, p. 14.
2133 *Eder/Senn*, p. 13.
2134 *Peers*, EU Justice and Home Affairs Law (Non-Civil), p. 293. See also *Klimek*, pp. 17, 22-23.

at the local, national, and European level wherein one could see a closer cooperation between intelligence services, the police, and the military at the national and transatlantic levels.[2135]

This notwithstanding, the approach employed by Europe still retained a stark difference with the United States' on this matter. Compared to the United States which invoked "the first war of the 21st century" in its fight against terrorism and generally prefers military measures to stop the same, experience with domestic terrorism and other forms of "grass-roots" terrorism (e.g. left-wing terrorism in Germany, national terrorism in France, Spain, and the United Kingdom) has prompted Europe to adopt an all-encompassing approach, which included in particular an intensification in improving and/or innovating its law enforcement and judicial measures.[2136] Europe generally stayed on the path of a criminal justice model, and not the war model the United States espoused, even if several tensions admittedly would still be met in such a model.[2137] To start with, there was the deployment of the JHA policy making apparatus under the third pillar of the EU,[2138] from which there was the adoption on 21 September 2001 of the comprehensive EU Action Plan to Fight Terrorism.[2139] Accordingly, this received political approval in less than three months and key framework decisions were formally adopted by the European Council on 13 June 2002.[2140] These Framework Decisions on the European Arrest Warrant, Joint Investigation Teams, and Terrorism came at the advent of such action plans, which meant to expedite the extradition process among member states, allow the establishment of teams comprising law enforcement and judicial representatives jointly working in cross-border investigations involving two or more member states, and enumerate acts that could constitute terrorism, respectively.[2141] It can be

---

2135 *Bono*, p. 26.

2136 *Bono*, p. 26; *Walker*, p. 1145.

2137 See *Walker*, p. 1145.

2138 *Eder/Senn*, p. 14; *Peers*, EU Justice and Home Affairs Law (Non-Civil), p. 293.

2139 *Alegre/Leaf*, p. 202; *Bono*, p. 26; *Douglas-Scott*, p. 220.

2140 *Alegre/Leaf*, p. 202.

2141 Council Framework Decision 2002/584/JHA of 13 June 2002 on the European Arrest Warrant, OJ L190, 18.7.2002, p. 1-20; Council Framework Decision 2002/475/JHA of 13 June 2002 on Combating Terrorism, OJ L 164, 22.6.2002, p. 3-7; Council Framework Decision 2002/465/JHA of 13 June 2002 on Joint Investigation Teams, OJ L 162, 20.6.2002, p. 1-3; *Casale*, p. 51; *Douglas-Scott*, p. 220.

said that these three framework decisions overall meant to stress the importance of harmonizing the legislation of serious crimes.[2142]

One may notice at this point in time that due to the political need to respond, probably due to the heightened emotions brought by the 9/11 attacks, European policy makers "reached for recipes that they had decided upon two (2) years previously" because most of the foregoing, including the establishment of structures such as Eurojust, Police Chiefs Task Force, and the European Police College, and strengthening of the existing Europol, were all outputs of the Tampere programme.[2143] Inevitably, this leads to the notion that the policy changes being introduced were not from a careful study of the threat but instead, were only through a "reactive borrowing" from a list the EU policy makers thought sufficient to address the emerging issues.[2144] But then again, sunk costs might have been too high for policy makers to tailor fit policy changes to the existing threat and time constraints did not permit them to sit down and deliberate on the matters further.[2145]

The terrorist attacks in Madrid thereafter occurred in March 2004 and a look on the member states would show a dismal implementation record of the measures adopted on 21 September 2001.[2146] With the Madrid attacks providing a loud wake up call, the Justice and Home Affairs Ministers came up with the Declaration on Combating Terrorism, which was adopted by the European Council on 25 March 2004.[2147] Prior to this, the emergence of terrorism as a priority of the EU was mentioned in the 2003 European Security Strategy but still, implementation among member states has not been impressive.[2148] The Declaration to Combat Terrorism referred to the existing implementation flaws and urged member states to urgently and fully implement the measures on police and judicial cooperation.[2149] It called for new measures that would reinforce operational cooperation and intelligence exchange not only between national authorities but with European bodies such as Europol and Eurojust as well.[2150] It likewise provided clear guidelines for action by setting out seven (7) overarching

---

2142 *Argomaniz*, p. 7; *Eder/Senn*, p. 14; *Casale*, p. 51; *Douglas-Scott*, p. 220.
2143 *Argomaniz*, p. 7; *Casale*, p. 51.
2144 *Apap/Carrera*, p. 3; *Argomaniz*, pp. 7, 8; *Douglas-Scott*, p. 220.
2145 *Argomaniz*, p. 7.
2146 *Argomaniz*, p. 7.
2147 *Argomaniz*, p. 9.
2148 *Casale*, p. 51.
2149 *Argomaniz*, p. 8.
2150 *Argomaniz*, p. 10.

strategic objectives, which was accompanied thereafter by a "Solidarity Clause" – a symbolic "Europeanization" of the threat through the formal commitment of each member states to assist should another member state fall victim to a terrorist attack.[2151] A few days short of three months after the Declaration on Combating Terrorism, the European Council endorsed a revised EU Action Plan on Combating Terrorism on 18 June 2004, which elucidated the seven (7) strategic objectives mentioned in the March 2004 Declaration and presented measures in a scoreboard form, attributing tasks with clearly defined deadlines to monitor implementation, and without shying away from "naming and shaming" those which failed to satisfy their obligations.[2152]

Subsequently, one could witness the European Commission fulfilling its role as policy entrepreneur when it fielded months after the Declaration communications formulating policies on terrorism financing, infrastructure protection, and response management, all of which were within its competencies.[2153] Mindful of sensibilities it may touch should its proposals have supranational recipes considering that criminal matters still belonged to intergovernmentalism, the Commission focused on increasing information exchange and enhancing coordination with mechanisms such as the European Programme for Critical Infrastructure Protection ("EPCIP"), Critical Infrastructure Warning Information Network ("CIWIN") or the networking of rapid alert systems ("ARGUS").[2154]

The European Council accepted on 04-05 November 2004 the Hague Programme, reaffirming its priority to the development of an area of freedom, security, and justice.[2155] The approximation of substantive criminal law provisions should make it easier to apply the principle of mutual recognition of penal-judicial decisions, especially so in serious offense areas with an international dimension.[2156] At the same time, the European Council recognized the need or importance to improve international exchange of information about criminal prosecutions and to this end, introduced the "principle of availability of information", under which criminal prosecuting authorities of member states should be able to perform their duties unhindered, since all useful information would be universally

2151 *Argomaniz*, p. 10; *Douglas-Scott*, p. 220.
2152 *Argomaniz*, p. 10.
2153 *Argomaniz*, p. 11; *Casale*, p. 51.
2154 *Argomaniz*, p. 11.
2155 *Argomaniz*, p. 11.
2156 *Hecker*, p. 66.

accessible.[2157] The principle meant that data collected by one member state shall be made available to the others to same extent the collecting member state itself could access the data.[2158] Aside from this, one can witness institutional changes in general within the Union through either the creation of new offices or the revigorization of existing ones as regards counterterrorism measures.[2159]

Concurrent to the foregoing, the Framework Decision on the European Arrest Warrant ("EAW"), finally came into force on 01 January 2004 after much discussion among the EU institutions.[2160] Regarded as the "first and most striking example of extensive judicial cooperation in criminal matters within the EU Third Pillar," the EAW allows arrest warrants in one member state to be recognized and enforced in other EU states.[2161] Thus, it is basically "a judicial decision issued by a member state with a view to the arrest and surrender by another member state of a requested person, for the purposes of conducting a criminal prosecution or executing a custodial sentence or detention order" for a maximum period of at least 12 months or, where a sentence has been passed or a detention order has been made, for sentences of at least four months..[2162]

The purpose of the EAW then is "to simplify and expedite extradition procedures of persons convicted or accused of crimes between the EU member states."[2163] Noticeably, the extradition process, which was traditionally and mainly under executive discretion and subjected to intergovernmental processes, was now made into a purely judicial matter, whereby only the judicial authorities of the member states cooperate.[2164] This "judicialization" was necessitated to bring the extradition process within the ambits of mutual recognition and mutual trust.[2165] The EAW is the "first concrete measure implementing the principle of mutual recognition of judicial decisions in European Union Criminal law" and eventually provided the groundwork for other mutual recognition instruments, each setting

---

2157 *Hecker*, p. 67.
2158 *Satzger*, p. 162.
2159 *Hecker*, p. 67.
2160 *Argomaniz*, p. 11.
2161 *Casale*, p. 63; *Eder/Senn*, p. 14; *Peers*, EU Justice and Home Affairs Law (Non-Civil), p. 293.
2162 Framework Decision on European Arrest Warrant, art. 2(1); *Casale*, p. 63; *Douglas-Scott*, p. 223; *Komárek*, p. 14.
2163 *Douglas-Scott*, p. 223; *Plachta*, p. 184.
2164 *Casale*, p. 63; *Komárek*, p. 14.
2165 *Komárek*, p. 14.

out the principle that member states must recognize decisions of another member state's criminal authorities as regards a particular nature, subject to a limited number of grounds for refusal, detailed rules on procedures (such as time limits and standard forms), and vague provisions on human rights.[2166] These new measures, which included the Framework Decisions on freezing of assets and evidence in 2003 and on the recognition of criminal judgments in 2005,[2167] reduced the number of grounds a member state can use to refuse a request and abolished the applicability of the principle of dual criminality for a long list of crimes.[2168]

It bears to mention that while implementation of the EAW was somehow fast, the implementation of those which followed it, like the one on freezing of assets and evidence as well as recognition of (non-custodial) criminal judgments, was not.[2169] Revolutionary approaches, such as with the EAW and like instruments, would eventually meet opposition and the challenges to the EAW since its inception have caught up. It was not long after that there were intra-European debates that did not only question the implementation of these measures but also about the need to balance efficient measures and the necessity to secure civil and human rights of European citizens.[2170] To illustrate, the requested person has certain explicit rights under Article 11(2) EAW such the right to legal counsel and to an interpreter according to the law of the executing state but nowhere else could there be found in the EAW any concrete reference to the ECHR, especially to Articles 5 and 6 that ensure rights to liberty and fair trial, nor any explicit right to refuse on human rights consideration.[2171] Further, with working on a mutual recognition platform instead of the usual harmonization of laws among member states, the net effect (unwittingly or unwillingly) was the narrowing and reducing of the necessary guarantees of the right to defense, to the detriment of the principle of due process, among other things.[2172] Thus, constitutional courts, like those of Germany, went head to head against EU institutions because the Consti-

2166 *Klimek*, p. 1; *Plachta*, p. 184. See for details *Peers*, EU Justice and Home Affairs Law (Non-Civil), p. 293.

2167 OJ L196/45 2003 & OJ L76/16 2005, See *Plachta*, pp. 184-189.

2168 *Douglas-Scott*, p. 220.

2169 *Casale*, p. 64; *Peers*, EU Justice and Home Affairs Law (Non-Civil), p. 293.

2170 *Peers*, EU Justice and Home Affairs Law (Non-Civil), p. 294.

2171 *Douglas-Scott*, pp. 226-227; *Eder/Senn*, p. 14.

2172 *Douglas-Scott*, p. 226. See also for other concerns regarding mutual recognition and human rights, *Casale*, p. 65.

tutional Courts opined that with the EAW mechanism, constitutionally provided fundamental rights and guarantees are compromised.[2173]

There were contentions as well on the surrender of one's own nationals, which as one observed, was largely derived from a "jealously guarded conception of national sovereignty" that presupposes the existence of stark differences in the administration of criminal justice that might result to unfair treatment, something in contrast to the idea of mutual trust on which criminal justice cooperation within the Area of Freedom, Security and Justice ("AFSJ") is based.[2174] In addition, there was opposition regarding the abolition of the dual criminality principle, proposals to increase the allowed grounds for refusal, and contentions touching on conflicts of jurisdiction.[2175]

Such debates affected the slowdown in implementation of framework decisions that followed the EAW (all of which also incorporated the mutual recognition component espoused in the EAW), such as those on recognition of confiscation orders, transfer of custodial sentences, probation and parole, the European Evidence Warrant, and pretrial suspension orders, wherein there was admittedly great difficulty to find a concession with the lastly mentioned that consequently halted the framework decision on updating double jeopardy rules or regulating the transfer of proceedings from pushing any further.[2176] There was even a failure to agree on a framework decision on suspect's rights, which had been a high profile issue.[2177]

Among the aforementioned framework decisions that encountered stumbling blocks with regard implementation, the European Evidence Warrant ("EEW"), was meant to be the first stage in a two-stage process of replacing mutual legal assistance with mutual recognition.[2178] Created on 18 December 2008 and intended to be applied by 19 January 2011, the EEW was meant to be a judicial decision to obtain any object, document and data for use in proceedings in criminal matters for which it may be issued.[2179] One of first things noticeable in this framework decision is the use of "issuing" and "executing" authorities with regard the EEW instead

2173 *Douglas-Scott,* pp. 227-228. See further for decisions of Czech and Polish Constitutional Courts, *Casale,* p. 65.

2174 *Komárek,* pp. 11-14.

2175 *Komárek,* p. 15.

2176 *Peers,* EU Justice and Home Affairs Law (Non-Civil), pp. 294-295.

2177 *Peers,* EU Justice and Home Affairs Law (Non-Civil), p. 295.

2178 *Peers,* EU Justice and Home Affairs Law, p. 714.

2179 Framework Decision on the European Evidence Warrant, arts. 1(1) and 5; *Peers,* EU Justice and Home Affairs Law (Non-Civil), p. 295.

of the usual requesting and requested states and/or authority in mutual legal assistance instruments.[2180] As discussed earlier, cooperation in criminal matters grounded on requests often resulted in negative consequences on efficiency in cooperation. With the EEW, "the judicial decision will be recognized and executed directly by the executing state, without its having to be converted into a 'national' decision."[2181] Stating it otherwise, no further formality shall be required and the executing authority, which receives the EEW, shall forthwith take the necessary measures for the execution of the same in the same manner as an authority of the executing state would obtain objects, documents, or data in a similar domestic case, unless that authority invokes any of the grounds for non-recognition, non-execution, or postponement provided for.[2182]

In this case, the issuing authority then would be "a judge, a court, an investigating magistrate or a public prosecutor as defined by the issuing State and, in the specific case, acting in its capacity as an investigating authority in criminal proceedings with competence to order the obtaining of evidence in cross-border cases in accordance with national law."[2183] And should it be that the issuing authority is not anyone as previously mentioned, nor was the EEW validated by one of those authorities in the issuing state, the executing authority can decide in the specific case that no search or seizure can be carried out for the purpose of executing the EEW.[2184]

In light of this, the EEW does not concern itself with all movements of evidence and is issued in reference to objects, documents, and data which are "directly available" in the executing state, and may also include related objects, documents, and data which the executing authority may discover during the execution of the EEW.[2185] This means that evidence that could be only obtained by the holding of hearings or similar measures is not covered by the EEW.[2186] Other types of evidence such as for example, "DNA tests, obtaining information in real time, analysis, communications data retained by providers of a publicly available electronic communica-

2180 Framework Decision on the European Evidence Warrant, art. 2.

2181 *De Hert/Weis/Cloosen*, p. 57.

2182 Framework Decision on the European Evidence Warrant, arts. 1(2), 11; *De Hert/Weis/Cloosen*, p. 57.

2183 Framework Decision on the European Evidence Warrant, art. 2.

2184 Framework Decision on the European Evidence Warrant, art. 11(4).

2185 Framework Decision on the European Evidence Warrant, art. 4(5); *De Hert/Weis/Cloosen*, p. 61; *Peers*, EU Justice and Home Affairs Law, p. 714.

2186 *Peers*, EU Justice and Home Affairs Law, p. 714.

tions service or a public communications network and the exchange of information on criminal convictions extracted from the criminal record" are generally excluded from the scope of the EEW, except when they are already in the possession of the executing authority before the warrant was issued.[2187] Statements from persons present during the execution of the EEW and directly related to the subject of the warrant may equally fall within the scope of the EEW as long as it has been likewise requested by the issuing authority.[2188]

Additionally, the EEW provides a limited number of grounds by which execution may be refused by the executing authority. These include, but is not limited to, an incomplete EEW, double jeopardy, immunity or privilege, territoriality, proportionality, and national interests.[2189] As regards dual criminality, it is abolished as a requirement for searches and seizures for evidence falling within the scope of the Framework Decision, as long as the crime is enumerated in the list, drafted originally for the EAW, of 32 crime categories.[2190] As for remedies, the EEW provides different procedural safeguards for both the issuing and executing authorities although the substance of the EEW may only be challenged in the issuing state.[2191] The issuing state must be able to grant remedies "equivalent to those applicable in purely domestic proceedings," and both states would have to take into account "time limits and the facilitation of proceedings."[2192] Also, the EEW provides for *forum regit actum* arrangements to counteract human rights questions that may arise, e.g. admissibility rules, exclusion of evidence rules vis-à-vis substantive or procedural rights, on a purely mutual recognition application.[2193] In addition to this discretionary human rights safeguard, the EEW contains other standard human rights clauses with additional provisions that "any obligations incumbent on judicial author-

---

2187 Framework Decision on the European Evidence Warrant, art. 4, (2), (3), and (4); *De Hert/Weis/Cloosen*, p. 60.

2188 Framework Decision on the European Evidence Warrant, art. 4 (6); *De Hert/Weis/Cloosen*, p. 60.

2189 Framework Decision on the European Evidence Warrant, arts. 7, 13[1(f)], 14; *De Hert/Weis/Cloosen*, p. 60; *Peers*, EU Justice and Home Affairs Law, p. 714.

2190 *Peers*, EU Justice and Home Affairs Law, p. 714.

2191 *De Hert/Weis/Cloosen*, pp. 63-66.

2192 *Peers*, EU Justice and Home Affairs Law, p. 714.

2193 Framework Decision on European Evidence Warrant, art. 12(1) provides "The executing authority shall comply with the formalities and procedures expressly indicated by the issuing authority unless otherwise provided in this Framework Decision and provided that such formalities and procedures are not contrary to the fundamental principles of law of the executing State."

ities in this respect shall remain unaffected."[2194] This notwithstanding, the EEW was not meant to replace mutual legal assistance measures but will coexist with them in the transitional period until such time that the second stage happened.[2195]

Given the promising characteristics of the EEW, it may seem disappointing that the same and similar instruments with mutual recognition elements have undergone some issues and concerns. However, it was not all too bad in finding agreement among each other during this time period because on one hand, it was easier to agree on the Framework Decisions on the more populist subjects of crime victim's rights and national confiscation proceedings (in view of mutual recognition), and on the other hand, the Court of Justice has begun to engage further notwithstanding limits of its jurisdiction on issues regarding double jeopardy, the EAW, and crime victim's rights.[2196] There was also agreement, especially after the London terrorist attacks of 2005, to urgently strengthen Schengen and visa information systems, implement biometric details on passports, and exercise more control over the trade, storage, and transport of explosives.[2197] Furthermore, there have been substantive additions to the area of substantive criminal law wherein there have been many framework decisions on additional areas, including but not limited to counterfeiting the Euro, attacks on information systems, imposing rules on minimum penalties member states should impose, etc., as well as further steps to amend the Framework Decision on Terrorism by adding further crimes in line with a Council of Europe decision such as regards terrorism financing, recruitment, and radicalization, and amendments to the Framework Decisions on trafficking in persons and sexual offenses against children.[2198]

Given these, the London bombings in July 2005 could have prompted said agreements because this period was indeed instrumental in the institutionalization process as the immediate reaction to these attacks was to accelerate efforts and ongoing work on the existing framework.[2199] During this same time period, one can see the stronger link between internal and external security, with the EU bolstering their European Foreign and Security Policy ("EFSP") by intensifying their development programs, hu-

2194 *Peers*, EU Justice and Home Affairs Law, p. 714.
2195 *Peers*, EU Justice and Home Affairs Law, pp. 714-715.
2196 *De Hert/Weis/Cloosen*, pp. 67-77.
2197 *Peers*, EU Justice and Home Affairs Law (Non-Civil), p. 295.
2198 *Casale*, p. 51.
2199 *Casale*, p. 51; *Peers*, EU Justice and Home Affairs Law (Non-Civil), pp. 295-296.

manitarian aids, etc. to complement counter-terrorism measures on the premise that lack of development among non-European states posed a threat to European security.[2200] Also included herein are the inclusion of counter-terrorism measures and provisions in the European Neighborhood Policy ("ENP") agreements.[2201] With that being said, a reevaluation of the nature of threat and concomitant strategies occurred thereafter, which led to a realization that the threat is multifaceted and could not be handled in a linear manner.[2202] Coming up with the 01 December 2005 European Union Counter-Terrorism Strategy, one soon saw that among the four pillars of strategy, namely, prevent, protect, pursue, and respond, more attention was given to preventive measures.[2203]

Noticeably, there have been developments at the mid-point of the Amsterdam Treaty (2005-2009) that altered the institutional framework as regards JHA law.[2204] During this period, the Nice Treaty had already entered into force in February 2003 and one could observe the spilling over application of First Pillar principles to the Third Pillar, including indirect effect, scope of the Court of Justice's jurisdiction, and autonomous interpretation of Third Pillar measures, as well as the shifting of certain aspects of EU Criminal Law and policing policy to the First Pillar, particularly Community competence to determine criminal sanctions and rules applicable to cooperation between law enforcement authorities and the private sector.[2205]

Within this time period, the principle of availability of information, as introduced in the Hague Programme of 2004, was realized by a small group of member states by concluding the Prüm Convention on 27 May 2007.[2206] The Convention allows certain national authorities mutual access to DNA profiles and fingerprinting data.[2207] However, if there is a match, the personal information about identification is not automatically transferred.[2208] Further, it is the respective domestic law of the member

2200 *Argomaniz*, p. 14.
2201 *Bono*, p. 28.
2202 See for illustration *Bono*, p. 26.
2203 *Argomaniz*, p. 14.
2204 *Argomaniz*, p. 14.
2205 *Peers*, EU Justice and Home Affairs Law (Non-Civil), pp. 274-275.
2206 The member states were Belgium, Germany, Spain, France, Luxembourg, the Netherlands, and Austria. *Satzger*, p. 163.
2207 *Satzger*, p. 163.
2208 *Satzger*, p. 163.

states involved which governs the sharing of information.[2209] The Prüm Convention was later unionized through a Council Decision in 2008, at the request of nine (9) other member states which wanted to accede to the same.[2210]

In addition, the principle of availability was not limited to information but also evidence. It played a role in the framework decision on taking account of convictions in the member states of the European Union in the course of new criminal proceedings.[2211] Previous convictions of an accused in other member states are taken into consideration especially with respect to assessment of penalty in a new criminal proceeding.[2212]

With these developments, the European Council one year after adopted the Stockholm Programme on 10-11 December 2009 which expresses the conviction of strengthening measures at the European Union level vis-a-vis better coordination at regional and national levels to protect against the menaces and dangers brought by transnational crime, such as terrorism and organized crime, drug trafficking, human trafficking, etc.[2213] Included herewith is to consider pursuing further the setting up of a comprehensive system for obtaining evidence in cases with a cross-border dimension based on the principle of mutual recognition.[2214] There is acknowledgment that fragmentation exists among the existing instruments in this area and based on this, a new approach was needed.[2215] Therefore, there was a call for "a comprehensive system to replace all the existing instruments in this area, covering as far as possible all types of evidence, containing time-limits for enforcement, and limiting as far as possible the grounds for refusal."[2216] To this end, the European Council and Commission developed a comprehensive internal security strategy for the EU on 22 November 2010, which included serious and organized crime as one of the five (5) main issues the Union ought to address.[2217] Human trafficking, sexual exploitation of

---

2209 *Satzger*, p. 163.

2210 *Satzger*, p. 163.

2211 Council Framework Decision 2008/675/JHA, OJ (EU) 2008 No. L 220/32; *Satzger*, p. 163.

2212 *Satzger*, p. 163.

2213 *Peers*, EU Justice and Home Affairs Law (Non-Civil), pp. 276-277; *Riehle/Clozel*, 10 years after the roadmap: procedural rights in criminal proceedings in the EU today.

2214 Directive on European Investigation Order, recital 6.

2215 Directive on European Investigation Order, recital 5.

2216 Directive on European Investigation Order, recital 6.

2217 *Hecker*, p. 67.

children and child pornography, economic criminal activity, criminal drug activity, and terrorism were stated as priorities.[2218]

Any confusion that might have resulted from the commixtion between Third Pillar and First Pillar rules or procedures with respect to JHA areas has been resolved by the Lisbon Treaty. It is settled now that qualified majority voting and ordinary legislative procedure, i.e. regulation and directives, extended to JHA areas, particularly legal migration and most criminal law and policing issues.[2219] As a general rule, there is now a constitutional framework for decision-making in the Area of Freedom, Security and Justice, to which criminal matters belong.[2220] This structure warrants transparency, accountability, and participation from all concerned.[2221] Last minute agenda-setting by member states in view of quick European successes are thus proscribed, while the Council cannot ignore any amendment the Parliament may propose.[2222] Instead, transparency and democracy is highly promoted outside and (to a certain degree) inside the European Council.[2223] This notwithstanding, it is not exactly crack-proof because member states are still allowed to present initiatives to rival those of the Commission vis-à-vis policing and criminal law initiatives.[2224]

Also, the principle of mutual recognition on criminal matters was addressed in the provisions on the area of freedom, security, and justice, which was acknowledged to be one of the Union's tools in its endeavors to ensure a high level of security.[2225] The said applicable provision likewise addresses approximation, which is only allowed or justified if they are necessary to further the system of mutual recognition.[2226] In relation to this, the Lisbon Treaty provided for the possibility of having minimum requirements relating to criminal procedure, including enumerated aspects on (1) mutual admissibility of evidence between member states; (2) the rights of individuals in criminal proceedings; (3) the rights of victims of

2218 *Hecker*, p. 67.

2219 *Hecker*, p. 67.

2220 See *Klip*, pp. 115-123; *Vogel*, p. 125.

2221 *De Hert/Aguinaldo*, p. 5.

2222 *De Hert/Aguinaldo*, p. 5.

2223 See for the regime before Lisbon and its lack of constitutional features, *De Hert*, pp. 61-113.

2224 *Peers*, EU Justice and Home Affairs Law (Non-Civil), p. 278.

2225 Treaty on Functioning of the European Union, art. 67(3); *Peers*, EU Justice and Home Affairs Law (Non-Civil), p. 278; *Satzger*, p. 139.

2226 Treaty on Functioning of the European Union, art. 67(3); *Vermeulen/De Bondt*, p. 126.

crime; and (4) any other specific aspects of criminal procedure.[2227] These aspects are further intended to flank the development of the principle of mutual recognition in criminal matters.[2228]

Based on the aforementioned, the Council eventually came up with a Roadmap for Strengthening Procedural Rights of Suspected and Accused Persons in Criminal Proceedings in November 2009. Composed of six (6) measures, the Council via the Roadmap adopted a gradual approach with regard procedural rights due to the complexity of issues.[2229] These measures include translation and interpretation, information on rights and charge, legal advice and legal aid, right to communicate, special safeguards for vulnerable suspects and accused, and a green paper on pretrial detention.[2230] The Council thereafter endorsed this Roadmap to the European Council to make it a part of the Stockholm Programme.[2231] In the following years, agreements could be reached on six Directives outlining the rights to interpretation and translation (2010/64/EU), to information (2012/13/EU), to access to a lawyer (2013/48/EU), to legal aid (2016/1919/EU), the presumption of innocence (2016/343/EU), and procedural safeguards for children suspected or accused in criminal proceedings.[2232] The Commission also published a Green Paper on Pretrial Detention (COM [2011] 327 final) and a recommendation on procedural safeguards for vulnerable persons suspected or accused in criminal proceedings (2016/800/EU).[2233]

In the same vein, measures were adopted in terms of victims' rights and participation anew through the Directive of 25 October 2012, considering

2227 *Vermeulen/De Bondt*, p. 126. See Treaty on Functioning of the European Union, art. 82(2).

2228 *Vermeulen/De Bondt*, pp. 126-127.

2229 *Vermeulen/De Bondt*, pp. 126-127.

2230 *Vermeulen/De Bondt*, p. 127.

2231 *Riehle/Clozel*, p. 2.

2232 *Riehle/Clozel*, p. 2.

2233 *Riehle/Clozel*, p. 2.Riehle/Clozel notes that the Directives as herein mentioned are not still implemented by all member states. "Taking a look at the status of implementation of the Directives provided by the European Judicial Network (EJN),13 it shows that Directive 2010/64/EU is currently in force in 27 Member States; Directive 2012/13/EU still needs to be implemented in Belgium; Directive 2013/48/EU still needs to be implemented in four Member States (Bulgaria, Croatia, Cyprus, Romania). Only three Member States (Czech Republic, Hungary and Portugal) have implemented Directive 2016/343/EU in their domestic legal order. Finally, Directives 2016/800/EU and 2016/1919/EU have so far only been implemented in Poland."

that the previously adopted measures were thought to be outdated and minimum standards were provided as regards rights, support, and protection of victims of crime.[2234]

Given these changes, another development in the area of cross-border cooperation soon ensued. A group of member states proposed a Directive to establish the European Investigation Order ("EIO") in spring 2010.[2235] Said directive ("DEIO") was approved on 03 April 2014 and being more extensive in substance compared to the EEW, nullified the latter's practical significance.[2236] The EIO meant to replace earlier international law agreements on judicial assistance from 22 May 2017 onwards, as well as the different framework decisions on protective measures, i.e. freezing of evidence, and the European Evidence Warrant, resulting in the combination and compilation into a single act and unified legal framework governing the collection and transfer of evidence within the Union is crafted.[2237] It must be noted however that the Framework Decision 2002/46 on Joint Investigation Teams continues to be applicable despite the existence of the EIO.[2238] This is understandable that while the objectives of the EIO and joint investigation teams are generally the same, they differ on how they operate, what principles would apply, and what the scope of each one is.[2239] The applicable principle for example for the EIO is the principle of mutual recognition while the terms in the establishment of a joint investigation team depends on what would be agreed by the member states involved. Moreover, the joint investigation team to be constituted would be present in the forum state when evidence is to be collected, contrary to the situation of an EIO.[2240]

At this point of the discussion, one can identify distinguishing characteristics of the EIO as compared to the EEW. While the EEW only covers movements of evidence readily and directly available, the EIO provides for measures applicable to evidence collection.[2241] The EIO also strengthens the position of the issuing state pursuant to mutual recognition, wherein should there be uncertainties regarding a certain measure, it should be de-

---

2234 *Vermeulen/De Bondt*, p. 128.
2235 *Peers*, EU Justice and Home Affairs Law, p. 715.
2236 *Satzger*, p. 145; *Bachmaier-Winter*, p. 47.
2237 *Satzger*, p. 146; *Bachmaier-Winter*, p. 47.
2238 Directive on European Investigation Order, art. 3; *Bachmaier-Winter*, p. 47.
2239 *Bachmaier-Winter*, p. 48.
2240 *Bachmaier-Winter*, p. 48.
2241 Directive on European Investigation Order, art. 3; *Satzger*, p. 146.

termined by the law of the issuing state.[2242] As Satzger comments, the use of the wording "order" rather than "request" bolsters this, together with the arrangement of terms the executing authority is obliged to comply with.[2243] Further, the EIO differentiates itself from the EEW by adding the novel ground to refuse if the respective investigative measure is incompatible with the executing state's treaty obligations vis-à-vis Article 6 TEU and the CFR.[2244] Furthermore, to prevent conflicts arising from different procedural legal orders in the EU, the EIO now allows an executing state to replace the requested measure with another should less intrusive measures are available.[2245]

During the transposition period of the EIO directive, the EU undertook activities and policies that were meant to complement each other in terms of criminal justice, and maintaining security in the region in general. Not exactly to digress but the EU continues to adopt measures and policies applicable to different aspects of crime. One of these things are the post-Stockholm Programme strategic guidelines from June 2014, or the Renewed EU Internal Security Strategy.[2246] There was a need to revisit the Stockholm Programme especially after the January 2015 attacks in Paris, France.[2247] Running from 2015 to 2020, the programme focuses on consolidation and actual implementation of an already created *acquis communautaire*, including the aim of guaranteeing a genuine area of security for European citizens through "operational police cooperation and preventing and combating serious organized crime."[2248] In relation to this, one can witness the further use of the principle of availability of information among the more recent initiatives in this area, including the Directive on the use of passenger name record ("PNR") data for the prevention, detection, investigation, and prosecution of terrorist offenses and serious crimes, as well the exchange of information through the European Criminal Records Information System ("ECRIS") of third country nationals.[2249]

2242 *Satzger*, p. 146.
2243 *Satzger*, p. 146.
2244 *Satzger*, pp. 146-147.
2245 *Satzger*, p. 147.
2246 *De Busser/Riehle*, p. 39.
2247 *De Busser/Riehle*, p. 39.
2248 *Hecker*, p. 67.
2249 See Directive 2016/681/EU; *Satzger*, p. 163.

2. Substantive Provisions: European Investigation Order

The following discussion shall focus on the substantive and procedural provisions of the EIO, the applicable legal instrument with respect to the movement and securing of evidence in the EU.

a. Applicability of Assistance

Four (4) matters could be mentioned as regards the applicability of assistance vis-à-vis the EIO.

First, notwithstanding the general obligation to give the widest possible assistance that could be granted in traditional mutual legal assistance instruments, traditional mutual legal assistance instruments would still subject a request for cross-border movement of evidence to the discretion of a requested state.[2250] The EIO changes this dimension drastically. As defined, the EIO is a "a judicial decision which has been issued or validated by a judicial authority of a Member State ('the issuing State') to have one or several specific investigative measure(s) carried out in another Member State ('the executing State') to obtain evidence" in accordance with the Directive.[2251] And with the shifting to a demand-based system from one based on requests, the DEIO purports to give minimum (if not none at all) elbow room for the receiving state to enact the order.[2252]

Second, the DEIO does not necessarily define what constitutes matters (or criminal matters) covered by an EIO instrument. Instead, the DEIO enumerates the following as the types of proceedings to which the EIO may be used: "(1) with respect to criminal proceedings that are brought by, or that may be brought before, a judicial authority in respect of a criminal offence under the national State; (2) in proceedings brought by administrative authorities in respect of acts which are punishable under the national law of the issuing State by virtue of being infringements of the rules of law and where the decision may give rise to proceedings before a court having jurisdiction, in particular, in criminal matters; and (3) in proceedings brought by judicial authorities in respect of acts which are punishable under the national law of the issuing State by virtue of being infringements of the rules of law, and where the decision may give rise to

2250 *Heard/Mansell*, p. 354.
2251 Directive on European Investigation Order, art. 1(1).
2252 *Heard/Mansell*, p. 354.

proceedings before a court having jurisdiction, in particular, in criminal matters."[2253] Hence, "criminal proceedings" includes not only judicial proceedings but also those proceedings before an administrative authority that can be reviewed by a judicial authority.[2254]

Third, and in relation to the matters covered by the EIO, the EIO can be issued against both natural and legal persons.[2255] This contemplates situations wherein corporate criminal liability is an issue.

Fourth, one can mention the territorial application or geographical variability of the EIO within the European Union. Not all member states are implementing the EIO such as Denmark and Ireland.[2256] The UK for instance ought to opt in, which it did and opted to apply the EIO.[2257] The Directive shall be applicable to all EIO's received after 22 May 2017, the deadline for the transposition of the Directive by the member states.[2258]

b. Types of Assistance

The EIO does not only apply to information, documents, objects, or evidence in general that are readily or directly available. This is what distinguishes the EIO from the EEW. The EIO concerns itself not only with cross-border movement of evidence but also the collecting and securing of the same. In relation to this, the investigative measures contemplated by the EIO do not distinguish between coercive and non-coercive measures, with specific measures provided for the following measures: the temporary transfer to either the issuing or executing state of persons held in custody for the purpose of carrying out an investigative measure (art. 23); hearing by videoconference or other audiovisual transmission (art. 24); hearing by teleconference (art. 25); information on banks or other financial accounts (art. 26); information on banking and other financial operations (art. 27); investigative measures implying the gathering of evidence in real time, continuously and over a certain period of time (art. 28); covert operations (art. 29); and interception of communications (arts. 30 and 31).[2259]

2253 Directive on European Investigation Order, art. 4.

2254 *Bachmaier-Winter*, p. 48.

2255 See Directive on European Investigation Order, art. 4(d).

2256 Directive on European Investigation Order, recital 44 & 45, *Bachmaier-Winter*, p. 48.

2257 Directive on European Investigation Order, recital 43.

2258 *Bachmaier-Winter*, p. 48.

2259 See Directive on European Investigation Order, arts. 23-31.

c. Compatibility with other Arrangements

As already mentioned, the EIO was meant to be the single applicable legal framework to the cross-border movement of evidence among the member states. Effective 22 May 2017, it replaces the corresponding provisions of the following conventions applicable between the Member States bound by this Directive: (1) European Convention on Mutual Assistance in Criminal Matters of the Council of Europe of 20 April 1959, as well as its two additional protocols, and the bilateral agreements concluded pursuant to Article 26 thereof; (2) Convention implementing the Schengen Agreement, and (3) Convention on Mutual Assistance in Criminal Matters between the Member States of the European Union and its protocol.[2260] It also replaces the Framework Decision on Freezing of Evidence, and any reference to the same shall be construed as reference to the DEIO.[2261]

However, the DEIO member states are entitled to "conclude or continue to apply bilateral or multilateral agreements or arrangements with other Member States after 22 May 2017 only insofar as these make it possible to further strengthen the aims of this Directive and contribute to simplifying or further facilitating the procedures for gathering evidence and provided that the level of safeguards set out in this Directive is respected."[2262] It is incumbent upon member states to inform the Commission of which existing agreements and/or arrangements they still want to be applicable, and should also inform the Commission within three (3) months after entering into a new agreement/arrangement in relation to the DEIO.[2263]

Even with these provisions, one bears in mind that the EIO is not the only applicable instrument for the purpose of trans-border gathering of evidence within the EU. Not all EU Member States are bound by the EIO Directive.[2264] In fact, under certain circumstances, as Ramos highlighted, the Directive does not preclude the application of other international conventions on mutual legal assistance (MLA) by judicial authorities.[2265] Therefore, practitioners need a clear idea as to the situations in which it is compulsory to use an EIO, when it would be merely convenient to use it,

2260 Directive on European Investigation Order, art. 34(1).
2261 Directive on European Investigation Order, art. 34(2).
2262 Directive on European Investigation Order, art. 34(3).
2263 Directive on European Investigation Order, art. 34(4).
2264 *Ramos*, p. 1.
2265 *Ramos*, p. 1.

or when it would be impossible to gather evidence abroad by means of an EIO.[2266]

Aside from the foregoing, it must be remembered that the EIO is only a part of the entire existing EU Criminal Justice architecture. As discussed in the historical development of cross-border cooperation among EU member states, many programs and even information systems databases have been instilled within the EU to help and foster continued and strengthened cooperation among the EU member states. A quick example that can be cited is the formation of joint investigation teams, which the DEIO itself mentions as not being part of its coverage. Information lawfully obtained while being part of the joint investigation team may thereafter be used for purposes specified in the Framework Decision and the 2000 MLA convention.[2267]

Further, there could be use of the existing EU databases. Among many there is the Schengen Information System ("SIS"), which is available not only to immigration, border control, police, and custom authorities, but likewise accessible to judicial authorities.[2268] There is also the Customs Information System ("CIS") for use of customs authorities and the EU member states' access to the Visa Information System ("VIS") of information on visa applicants.[2269] Furthermore, there are the Prüm measures, which allow collection and exchange of DNA data, and the public-private partnerships in field of policing and surveillance as well as financial data surveillance such as the EU Passenger Name Records ("PNR") transfer system and Fourth EU Money Laundering Directive through national financial intelligence units ("FIU"), respectively.[2270]

In addition to these, one can mention the extensive legal framework the EU has as regards the exchange of information. There is the Framework Decision 2006/960 on Exchange of Information that regulates the exchange of information and intelligence between law enforcement authorities.[2271] There is moreover the framework as regards information exchange on criminal records through the Framework Decision 2009/315 on Criminal Records and the European Criminal Records Information System ("ECRIS"), the latter being a "decentralized information technolo-

2266 *Ramos*, p. 1.
2267 Framework Decision on Joint Investigation Teams, art. 1, § 11.
2268 *Peers*, EU Justice and Home Affairs Law, p. 907.
2269 *Peers*, EU Justice and Home Affairs Law, p. 907.
2270 See *Mitsilegas*, pp. 213-214.
2271 *Klip*, European Criminal Law, pp. 438-439.

gy system that should facilitate the exchange of information on criminal records."[2272]

Last but not the least, it must be mentioned that cooperation mechanisms could also be seen at the police, prosecutorial, and judicial level within the EU through the Europol, Eurojust, European Prosecutor's Office, and European Judicial Network.[2273] To further elucidate, the Europol is the official EU agency for law enforcement cooperation after its new regulation entered into force.[2274] The Europol acts as a support center for law enforcement operations, which includes providing or storing information on criminal activities, and acts as a center for law enforcement expertise.[2275] Its competence extends to organized crime, terrorism, and other forms of crime that affect a common interest covered by Union policy such as drug trafficking, immigrant smuggling, human trafficking, etc.[2276] The Eurojust (EU Agency for Criminal Justice Cooperation) is equally imperative in supporting and strengthening coordination and cooperation between national investigating and prosecuting authoritions in relation to serious crime affecting two or more member states.[2277] It mirrors more or less the Europol but in the judicial side.[2278] In November 2018, a Regulation on the European Union Agency for Criminal Justice Cooperation was adopted, which established a new governance system for Eurojust, provided clarifications on its relations to the European Public Prosecutors' Office, among other things. The Regulation shall be applied on 12 December 2019. Other than the Europol and Eurojust, the EJN as mentioned earlier in the study was created by Joint Action 98/428 JHA of 29 June 1998 and in December 2008, Council Decision 2008/976/JHA of 16 December 2008 became its new legal basis and/or framework. The EJN

2272 *Klip*, European Criminal Law, pp. 439-440.

2273 *Klip*, European Criminal Law, pp. 481-505.

2274 See Regulation (EU) 2016/794 on the European Union Agency for Law Enforcement Cooperation.

2275 See Regulation (EU) 2016/794 on the European Union Agency for Law Enforcement Cooperation, arts. 1 and 3. It must be understood that the Europol is not yet an operational police unit with executive authority. Member states allot or dedicate a national unit to form the sole connection with Europol for example. See *Satzger*, pp. 126-128.

2276 *Satzger*, p. 126.

2277 See Treaty on Functioning of the European Union, art. 85; *Satzger*, pp. 128-130.

2278 *Satzger*, p. 128.

was intended to be a network of national contact points for the facilitation of judicial cooperation in criminal matters.[2279]

d. Principles, Conditions, and Exceptions Applicable

i. Sufficiency of Evidence Requirement

Traditional mutual legal assistance instruments would have an integrated sufficiency of evidence requirement, wherein normally there is a direct relationship between how intrusive the investigative measure is and the amount of information to be given, including how relevant the evidence is to the criminal matter subject of the request. The requested state has the discretion to deny a request should the information be insufficient or irrelevant to merit the execution of the request. To a certain degree, this applies to the EIO.

As a general rule, the EIO ought to be recognized by the executing authority without any further formalities and executed in the same way and under the same modalities as if the investigative measure concerned had been ordered by an authority of the executing state.[2280] Based on this, the executing state should execute without question as if the investigative measure is related to its own domestic case and the order issued by one of its own.

However, it is simpler said than done. As provided also by the DEIO, the issuing state should ensure and subject to its own determination that the EIO issued is necessary and proportionate for the purpose of the subject proceedings, taking into consideration the fundamental rights of the suspected or accused person, and that the investigative measure "could have been ordered under the same conditions in a similar domestic case."[2281] It must be noted though that in instances wherein the executing authority reasonably believes that the issued EIO is not necessary and/or proportionate, the executing authority cannot deny recognition and/or execution of the same.[2282] Instead, it shall consult with the issuing authority on the importance of the EIO and the latter shall decide whether to withdraw the

2279 *Satzger*, p. 128.
2280 Directive on European Investigation Order, art. 9(1).
2281 Directive on European Investigation Order, art. 6(1).
2282 Directive on European Investigation Order, art. 6(3).

EIO or not.[2283] Alternatively, the executing authority may resort to another form of investigative measure should the purpose of the EIO still be met by less intrusive means, but the executing authority needs to consult or inform the issuing authority prior to doing this.[2284]

In connection with this, the specific procedures applicable to certain specific types of investigative measures within the ambits of the EIO still imbibe the sufficiency of evidence requirement by requiring more information to be provided, notwithstanding the general pieces of information already needed to be given in the EIO. To illustrate, with respect to information about bank and/or other financial accounts, the issuing authority should give reasons "why it considers that the requested information is likely to be of substantial value for the purpose of the criminal proceedings concerned and on what grounds it presumes that banks in the executing state hold the account and, to the extent available, which banks may be involved."[2285] Additional available information ought to be provided that could better facilitate execution of the EIO.[2286] With respect to information on bank and other financial operations, the issuing authority must be able to indicate the relevance of the information to the criminal proceedings subject of the EIO.[2287] The same equally applies should the investigative measure entail the gathering of evidence (whether real time, continuous, or for a specific period of time),[2288] establishment of covert operations,[2289] and interception of telecommunications.[2290]

ii. Dual Criminality

Mutual recognition, the applicable principle in the EIO instrument, is traditionally directly proportional to dual criminality: the more far-reaching mutual recognition is, the less far-reaching dual criminality requirement would likely be.[2291] It is said that this is closely linked to the rationale behind the dual criminality requirement: stemming from the principle

2283 Directive on European Investigation Order, art. 6(3).
2284 Directive on European Investigation Order, art. 10(3).
2285 Directive on European Investigation Order, art. 26(5).
2286 Directive on European Investigation Order, art. 26(5).
2287 Directive on European Investigation Order, art. 27(4).
2288 Directive on European Investigation Order, art. 28(3).
2289 Directive on European Investigation Order, art. 29(2).
2290 Directive on European Investigation Order, art. 30(4).
2291 *Vermeulen/De Bondt/Van Damme*, p. 63.

of legality (*nulla poena sine lege*) and closely linked to sovereignty and reciprocity,[2292] it is a protection mechanism aimed to protect member states to enforce something contrary to their own legal and criminal policy views.[2293] Interestingly, there is quite difficulty in defining the concept of dual criminality because it appears in many forms across the different existing EU instruments.[2294] As some commented, the definition that the behavior constitutes an offense in both states may sometimes not suffice in light of the diversity illustrated in some EU instruments like the EAW for example, wherein it is required that the act is an "offense under the law of the executing member state, whatever the constituent elements or however it is described", but no mention on territoriality and points to the irrelevance of how the offense could be labeled.[2295]

The many shapes and sizes of how dual criminality is defined across the many European instruments aside, there is nowadays a trend in the European Union to limit, if not totally abandon, the requirement of dual criminality.[2296] Although it could sometimes be discretionary, many believed that dual criminality constitutes an obstacle to effective cooperation and many argue that it is no longer necessary.[2297]

Interestingly, the limitation on the use of the dual criminality requirement really began with the European Arrest Warrant – wherein the requirement does not apply to a list of 32 offenses – and then for the European Evidence Warrant, its limitation was only applicable to search and seizure procedures similar to the 2000 Mutual Legal Assistance Convention.[2298] As regards the European Investigation Order, the requirement of dual criminality is present although it seems limited in application in the same manner as the EAW. Generally, the recognition and/or execution of the EIO may be denied "should the conduct for which the EIO has been issued does not constitute an offence under the law of the executing State." However, the dual criminality requirement does not apply if it concerns one of the 32 offenses provided in the DEIO, as indicated by the issuing authority in the EIO, "if it is punishable in the issuing State by a custodial sentence or a detention order for a maximum period of

2292 *Klimek*, p. 81.
2293 *Vermeulen/De Bondt/Van Damme*, p. 63.
2294 *Vermeulen/De Bondt/Ryckman*, p. 106.
2295 *Vermeulen/De Bondt/Ryckman*, p. 106.
2296 *Vermeulen/De Bondt/Van Damme*, p. 63.
2297 *Klimek*, pp. 81-82.
2298 See *Douglas-Scott*, p. 220; *Peers*, EU Justice and Home Affairs Law, p. 714.

at least three years."[2299] These offenses are the following: "(1) participation in a criminal organization; (2) terrorism; (3) trafficking in human beings; (4) sexual exploitation of children and child pornography; (5) illicit trafficking in narcotic drugs and psychotropic substances; (6) illicit trafficking in weapons, munitions and explosives; (7) corruption; (8) fraud, including that affecting the financial interests of the European Union within the meaning of the Convention of 26 July 1995 on the protection of the European Communities' financial interests; (9) laundering of the proceeds of crime; (10) counterfeiting currency, including of the euro; (11) computer-related crime; (12) environmental crime, including illicit trafficking in endangered animal species and in endangered plant species and varieties; (13) facilitation of unauthorized entry and residence; (14) murder, grievous bodily injury; (15) illicit trade in human organs and tissue; (16) kidnapping, illegal restraint and hostage-taking; (17) racism and xenophobia; (18) organized or armed robbery; (19) illicit trafficking in cultural goods, including antiques and works of art; (20) swindling; (21) racketeering and extortion; (22) counterfeiting and piracy of products; (23) forgery of administrative documents and trafficking therein; (24) forgery of means of payment; (25) illicit trafficking in hormonal substances and other growth promoters; (26) illicit trafficking in nuclear or radioactive materials; (27) trafficking in stolen vehicles; (28) rape; (29) arson; (30) crimes within the jurisdiction of the International Criminal Court: (31) unlawful seizure of aircraft/ships; and (32) sabotage.[2300]

iii. Double Jeopardy

The prohibition on double jeopardy or the rule of *ne bis in idem* is a ground for refusal under the EIO, wherein an executing authority may refuse to recognize and/or execute an EIO when "the execution of the EIO would be contrary to the principle of *ne bis in idem.*"[2301]

2299 Directive on European Investigation Order, art. 11(1)(g).

2300 Directive on European Investigation Order, Annex D.

2301 Directive on European Investigation Order, art. 11(1)(d). Based on the common understanding that *ne bis in idem* is a procedural side effect of *res juridicata pro veritatehabetur*, the present study agrees with Lelieur's conclusion that it is not a principle nor general principle of law but rather, *res judicata* is the principle and *ne bis in idem* is the rule drawn from said principle. See *Lelieur*, p. 198.

The prohibition on double jeopardy basically means that the offender, who has already been punished or finally acquitted, is protected against repeated prosecution and punishment due to the same act.[2302] It is a recognized fundamental principle of EU law and rooted in the laws of member states.[2303] It has also been codified under Article 50 in the Charter of Fundamental Rights, and which could be considered to apply to cases decided on the basis of EU rather than domestic law.[2304] Said Article 50 reads as follows:

> "No one shall be held liable to be tried or punished again in criminal proceedings for an offense for which he or she has already been acquitted or convicted within the Union in accordance with the law."

The general rule was that the rule of *ne bis in idem* only had internal effect and is relevant within the respective legal order, and is not applicable to judgments in other member states.[2305] At most, foreign punishment already executed is simply accredited to the new sentence, in view of which the Framework Decision on taking account of convictions in the member states in the course of new criminal proceedings has been helpful.[2306] Presently, member states have different rules on the territorial scope of its criminal law and there is no clear distribution of competences concerning the conduct of criminal proceedings in Europe.[2307] It also does not help that national definitions of the principle often differ from those propounded by the European Court of Justice.[2308] On account of these, there is the inherent risk of double punishment.[2309]

Worse, said risk is increased by virtue of member states needing to frame their transnational criminal law in favor of the Union to punish violations of EU law to the greatest possible extent.[2310] This leads consequently to questions on fair trial, due process of law, and the idea of personal legal certainty. As an author stated, individuals who undergo several prosecutions for the same facts are placed in a situation of unforeseeability because even if they have been tried already in one country, their legal situation

2302 *Satzger*, p. 148.
2303 *Suominen*, p. 224.
2304 *Satzger*, p. 149; *Suominen*, p. 225.
2305 *Satzger*, pp. 148-149.
2306 *Satzger*, pp. 149, 163.
2307 *Satzger*, p. 150.
2308 *Suominen*, p. 225.
2309 *Satzger*, p. 150.
2310 *Satzger*, p. 150.

can still be altered in the other.[2311] And if stronger EU sanctions have already been applied, then the individual could risk greater punishment for the same set of facts. It follows that the transnational application of the *ne bis in idem* rule is to be desired especially should the single Area of Freedom, Security, and Justice be truly implemented.[2312] This is also said to be consistent with the principle of mutual recognition, which following its definition, should also include decisions writing *finis* to criminal proceedings.[2313]

There have been previous efforts however to introduce a comprehensive prohibition on dual prosecution and punishment through treaties among EU member states. For example, ten years prior to the Charter of Fundamental Rights, there is the provision found in the Convention Implementing the Schengen Area ("CISA"), Part III of which regulates the principle in the Schengen Area.[2314] Having the most impact among all available provisions in EU law, Article 54 reads:

> "A person whose trial has been finally disposed off in one Contracting Party may not be prosecuted in another Contracting Party for the same acts provided that, if a penalty has been imposed, it has been enforced, is actually in the process of being enforced, or can no longer be enforced under the laws of the sentencing Contracting Party."[2315]

In view of the above-quoted provision, one could observe an objective legal interest – the efficiency of the transnational criminal justice – and a subjective one – the protection of the individual and freedom of movement.[2316] Moreover, there is an element of enforcement in addition to the final judgment, which does not later exist with Article 50 CFR.[2317] Despite such difference, Article 54 CISA and Article 50 CFR are held by the European Court of Justice in the Spacic judgment to co-exist with each

---

2311 *Lelieur*, p. 209.

2312 *Satzger*, p. 150.

2313 *Satzger*, p. 150.Lelieur cites what Schomburg said about the transnational application being a consequent extension of the principle of mutual recognition within the European Union and treating the individual as residing in a single area of justice. See *Lelieur*, p. 204.

2314 *Suominen*, p. 224.

2315 Convention implementing the Schengen Agreement, art. 54.

2316 *Suominen*, p. 224.

2317 *Satzger*, p. 150. For further discussion on these elements, see *Satzger*, pp. 153-161.

other and in light of the differences as regards the enforcement element, the CJEU held that the enforcement element must be abided with.[2318]

The Court in the abovementioned case referred to the freedom of movement of persons in its decision on the application of the *ne bis in idem* rule.[2319] The freedom of movement has direct effect and ought to be interpreted broadly given that it forms the "cornerstone of the EU legal order."[2320] As the CJEU ruled, the objective of the *ne bis in idem* rule in Article 54 CISA is to "ensure that no one is prosecuted on the same facts in several member states on account of his having exercised his right to freedom of movement."[2321] If European citizens are threatened with a new prosecution on the same facts because of a transnational offense, then their right to freely move in the European Union is not being respected.[2322] As such, Article 54 CISA and the case law on the provision continue to be the relevant law on the transnational application of the *ne bis in idem* principle in the EU.[2323]

The foregoing provisions notwithstanding, criticism still remains that there is actually no common standard in the EU for the *ne bis in idem* rule as the content and range of the foregoing provisions are "demonstrably unclear" especially taking into account the domestic perspectives.[2324] To illustrate, many countries historically recognize the transnational dimension of the principle subject to the requirement that the facts constituting the crime and judged by the foreign tribunal were not committed in whole or in part within their territory.[2325] Elements of the same can be found in Article 55 of CISA when said provision allows contracting parties to apply exceptions to Article 54 when the acts relating to the foreign judgment took place wholly or partially in the contracting party's own territory.[2326]

Furthermore, there has been application of the *ne bis in idem* rule to other situations, although normally it would be limited to final judgments.[2327] Moreover, defining the principle itself has been problematic in view of

---

2318 ECJ, Judgment of 27 May 2014, Case C-129/14 PPU, "Spasic", § 55; *Lelieur*, p. 209; *Satzger*, p. 151.
2319 *Lang*, pp. 182-183.
2320 *Lang*, p. 183.
2321 *Lang*, p. 183.
2322 *Lelieur*, p. 209.
2323 *Satzger*, p. 152.
2324 See *Suominen*, p. 225.
2325 *Lelieur*, p. 198.
2326 *Lelieur*, p. 198.
2327 *Suominen*, p. 225.

conflicts of jurisdiction within the EU, wherein it is hard to satisfy the "bis" (which criminal sanctions should be taken into consideration) and the "idem" (what constitutes the criminal act).[2328] Further, there are differing rules as regards issues closely related to the application of the rule of *ne bis in idem* such as the "revision of judgments, appeals after acquittal, how previous foreign judgments are taken into account when determining the penalty, whether administrative proceedings with a criminal law character but not formally classified as criminal, are effected, how decisions of prosecutors are taken into account, and on the effects of preliminary rulings and probation."[2329]

Applying the same to the EIO, the DEIO does not provide a detailed provision on how the rule of *ne bis in idem* applies. What it simply states is that the EIO may be refused execution should the same be incompatible with the principle. But as to how it would be incompatible, it was not provided for. This is unlike the EAW, which is said to be the clearest provision on the principle vis-à-vis cross-border cooperation, even to the point of distinguishing as regards member states and third states.[2330] It is a mandatory ground to refuse the EAW "if the executing judicial authority is informed that the requested person has been finally judged by a Member State in respect of the same acts provided that, where there has been sentence, the sentence has been served or is currently being served or may no longer be executed under the law of the sentencing member state."[2331] This interestingly resonates with the CISA provision. It is an optional ground for refusal on the other hand, "if the executing judicial authority is informed that the requested person has been finally judged by a third State in respect of the same acts provided that, where there has been sentence, the sentence has been served or is currently being served or may no longer be executed under the law of the sentencing country."[2332]

Taking into account that the DEIO considers compatibility with the *ne bis in idem* principle, then it is sound to consider the prevailing doctrine and/or provision found in the EAW instrument, CISA provision, and

2328 *Suominen*, p. 225.

2329 *Suominen*, p. 225.Questionsabouttheapplicabilityoftheprinciplearise also whenthefirstproceedingsdid not end with a traditional judgment but insteadwith a deal betweentheprosecutorandtheperpetratorthatbarsfurtherprosecutions on the same facts. Further, should the same bar apply when two different states have two different political approaches to the facts? See *Lelieur*, p. 199.

2330 *Suominen*, p. 225.

2331 Framework Decision on European Arrest Warrant, art. 3(2).

2332 Framework Decision on European Arrest Warrant, art. 4(5).

the CJEU Spasic judgment. It would be illustrative of prevailing doctrine and/or interpretation and would be further compatible to the *ratio decidendi* of the CJEU in ruling in favor of compatibility between Article 54 of the CISA and Article 50 of the CFR. Moving forward, member states which can either be an issuing or executing authority could take this into account: as an executing authority, to be equipped with a *ratio decidendi* to deny recognition or execution of an EIO; as an issuing authority, to prevent issuing the EIO at the outset to prevent triggering the principle.

Having mentioned the foregoing possible resolution, a preemptive measure actually exists in order for a member state not to raise *ne bis in idem* as a ground to refuse execution of an EIO. One can avoid in advance the *ne bis in idem* problem altogether by using the guidelines Eurojust issued as regards conflicts of jurisdiction, which suggests factors to be taken into account in multi-jurisdictional cases, especially given the increase in cross-border crime.[2333] Notwithstanding that the guidelines were published "to prevent and support the settling of conflicts of jurisdiction that could result in an infringement of the principle of *ne bis in idem*", and likewise ensure that the most effective practices are in place vis-à-vis criminal proceedings,[2334] they carry with it other issues that could possibly exarcerbate problems as regards implementation (e.g. competence issues, avoidance at the outset of exercising jurisdiction to avoid *ne bis in idem* situations).

Having observed that, the guidelines acknowledge that each case would be unique, and any decision made on jurisdiction issues should be based on the facts and merits of each individual case.[2335] All relevant factors ought to be taken into account and balanced carefully and fairly both for and against commencing a prosecution in each jurisdiction.[2336] As to what the factors that ought to be taken into consideration, Eurojust lists them as follows: territoriality; location of suspects/accused persons; availability and admissibility of evidence; obtaining evidence from witnesses, experts, and victims; protection of witnesses; interests of victims; stage of proceedings; length of proceedings; legal requirements; sentencing powers; proceeds of crime; costs and resources; and member state priorities.[2337]

Based on the sound Eurojust guidelines, any possible conundrum that could exist between member states as regards *ne bis in idem* as a ground

2333 *Eurojust*, p. 1.
2334 *Eurojust*, p. 1.
2335 *Eurojust*, p. 2.
2336 *Eurojust*, p. 2.
2337 *Eurojust*, pp. 3-4.

to refuse execution – notwithstanding the proposed resolution of adhering to how the EAW instrument or CJEU resolved the issue – can be already avoided at the outset. In the alternative, member states can invoke *ne bis in idem* as enunciated earlier above (i.e. based on EAW instrument and CJEU judgment, etc.) as the ground for refusal if needed.

iv. Substantive Considerations of Human Rights

In respect of human rights vis-à-vis the EIO, it can be discussed on both a substantive and procedural aspect. Substantively, human rights play a role with respect to grounds to refuse an EIO and in relation thereto, how obligations can play a role on whether to deny execution or not. There is correlatively an issue about taking into account severity of punishment.

1. Human Rights Obligation as Ground to Refuse Recognition or Execution

First, human rights considerations are evenly applicable with respect to grounds a requested state or executing state could use to refuse recognition and/or execution of an EIO. At the outset, there could be refusal of recognition or execution if the same shall violate the protection against double jeopardy, as discussed above. Moreover, the executing state can refuse recognition and/or execution should there be substantial grounds to believe that it would be incompatible with the executing state's obligations under Article 6 TEU (which relates to the different fundamental rights the EU and its member states abide with).[2338] An actual infringement of a fundamental right is not necessary before the executing authority can raise the ground for refusal. It is enough that there are substantial grounds to believe there could be an infringement, which concerns itself with fundamental rights the Union abides itself with.[2339] As to what these fundamental rights are, the fundamental rights provided for in Article 6 TEU refer to the Charter of Fundamental Rights and the European Convention on Human Rights, and the general principles of law applicable to the EU and its member states.[2340]

2338 Directive on European Investigation Order, art. 11(1)(f).
2339 Directive on European Investigation Order, art. 11(1)(f).
2340 Treaty on European Union, art. 6.

Although the EU member states are parties to the European Convention of Human Rights ("ECHR"), the EU is still in the process of being a party thereto.[2341] Correspondingly, the ECHR and jurisprudence of the European Court of Human Rights (ECtHR) has become indirectly applicable and binding through the Charter of Fundamental Rights wherein it is stated that the "meaning and scope of the rights of those rights in the Charter which correspond to rights in the ECHR shall be the same as those laid down in the Convention."[2342] The rights guaranteed in the ECHR were incorporated into EU law through Article 6 of the TEU as they are "constitutional traditions common to the member states" and the CJEU considers the same to be the common denominator for fundamental rights as it is applicable and legally binding to all member states.[2343]

In terms of criminal law, the fundamental rights that are related to it are the following: right to life; prohibition on torture and inhumane or degrading treatment and/or punishment; rights of arrested individuals; right to fair trial; presumption of innocence; no punishment without law; right to respect family and private life; limitations on use of restriction of rights or prevention of the misuse of power; right of appeal in criminal matters; and prohibition of double punishment.[2344] Fittingly, ECHR jurisprudence has time and time again emphasized a state's obligation to protect an individual against the probability of a serious breach of said individual's human rights in another state.[2345] In the case of Soering v. United Kingdom, the European Court of Human Rights established the principle that a state "would be in violation of its obligations under the ECHR if it extradited an individual to a state, in that case, the USA, where that individual was likely to suffer inhuman or degrading treatment or torture contrary to Article 3 ECHR."[2346] As the Court held:

> "The question remains whether the extradition of a fugitive to another State where he would be subjected or be likely to be subjected to torture or to inhuman or degrading treatment or punishment would itself engage the responsibility of a Contracting State under Article 3 (art. 3). That the abhorrence of torture has such implications is recognized in Article 3 of the United Nations Convention Against Torture

2341 See *Hecker*, pp. 67-68.
2342 *Satzger*, p. 176.
2343 *Satzger*, p. 176.
2344 *Satzger*, pp. 179, 180-214.
2345 *Alegre/Leaf*, p. 205.
2346 *Alegre/Leaf*, p. 205.

> and Other Cruel, Inhuman or Degrading Treatment or Punishment, which provides that "no State Party shall ... extradite a person where there are substantial grounds for believing that he would be in danger of being subjected to torture". The fact that a specialized treaty should spell out in detail a specific obligation attaching to the prohibition of torture does not mean that an essentially similar obligation is not already inherent in the general terms of Article 3 (art. 3) of the European Convention. It would hardly be compatible with the underlying values of the Convention, that "common heritage of political traditions, ideals, freedom and the rule of law" to which the Preamble refers, were a Contracting State knowingly to surrender a fugitive to another State where there were substantial grounds for believing that he would be in danger of being subjected to torture, however heinous the crime allegedly committed. Extradition in such circumstances, while not explicitly referred to in the brief and general wording of Article 3 (art. 3), would plainly be contrary to the spirit and intendment of the Article, and in the Court's view this inherent obligation not to extradite also extends to cases in which the fugitive would be faced in the receiving State by a real risk of exposure to inhuman or degrading treatment or punishment proscribed by that Article (art. 3)."[2347]

Obiter dicta in this case extended the principle to cover the possibility of a serious flagrant breach of one's right to a fair trial under Article 6 of the ECHR.[2348]

Given the aforementioned discussion, the same ground to refuse recognition and/or execution based on human rights consideration was not originally clear with respect to the EAW instrument, which if one would recall is the first true EU instrument adopting the principle of mutual recognition and mutual trust in criminal matters. While the relevant Framework Decision provides that "it respects fundamental rights and observes the principles recognized by Article 6 of the Treaty on European Union and reflected in the Charter of Fundamental Rights of the European Union, in particular Chapter VI thereof," and that nothing in said Framework Decision "may be interpreted as prohibiting refusal to surrender a person for whom a European Arrest Warrant has been issued when there are reasons to believe, on the basis of objective elements, that the said arrest warrant has been issued for the purpose of prosecuting or punishing a

2347 Soering v. United Kingdom, § 88; *Alegre/Leaf*, p. 205.
2348 *Alegre/Leaf*, p. 205.

person on the grounds of his or her sex, race, religion, ethnic origin, nationality, language, political opinions or sexual orientation, or that that person's position may be prejudiced for any of these reasons," and "no person should be removed, expelled or extradited to a State where there is a serious risk that he or she would be subjected to the death penalty, torture or other inhuman or degrading treatment or punishment," it was not ultimately clear if human rights concerns can be used to refuse recognition or execution of an EAW as no general ground for refusal has been given regarding this.[2349] At most, the CJEU in a series of cases in the area of criminal cooperation seemingly preferred the efficacy of the principle of mutual recognition based on mutual trust even if the same might have been to the detriment or infringement of fundamental rights.[2350] This is notwithstanding Article 1(3) which says that the Framework Decision "shall not have the effect of modifying the obligation to respect fundamental rights and fundamental legal principles as enshrined in Article 6 of the Treaty on European Union," a provision which most scholars advocated to be interpreted as a general ground to refuse for non-execution of an EAW should there be infringement of fundamental rights.[2351] It was only in the joined cases of Aranyosi and Căldăraru that the CJEU addressed these issues directly.[2352]

The facts of the case are as follows. European arrest warrants have been issued against Aranyosi and Căldăraru for the purposes of criminal investigation in relation to several accounts of burglary/theft and custodial sentence of one year and eight months for driving without a license, respectively.[2353] Both were arrested by Bremen authorities in Germany and placed in pretrial detention.[2354] Subsequently, the public prosecutor in Bremen declared the surrender is permissible given the lack of concrete evidence to show violation of detention conditions.[2355] However, the Higher

2349 *Bovend'Eerdt*, p. 113.

2350 *Gáspár-Szilágyi*, p. 210.

2351 *Bovend'Eerdt*, p. 113.

2352 Joint Cases C-404/15 and C-659/15 PPU PaiAranyosi and Robert Căldăraru, 05 April 2016; *Bovend'Eerdt*, p. 113.

2353 Joint Cases C-404/15 and C-659/15 PPU PaiAranyosi and Robert Căldăraru, 05 April 2016, §§ 29, 48; *Bovend'Eerdt*, p. 113; *Gáspár-Szilágyi*, p. 199.

2354 *Gáspár-Szilágyi*, p. 199.

2355 This was despite the findings of deplorable detention conditions in Hungary and Romainia. Further, in inquiring in which detention facilities the accused would be brought in, the Hungarian and Romanian authorities were not able to provide an answer. *Bovend'Eerdt*, pp. 114, 115; *Gáspár-Szilágyi*, p. 200.

Regional Court of Bremen (*Hanseatisches Oberlandesgericht in Bremen*) harbored a different opinion altogether, believing that in case of surrender, even if all formal requirements were satisfied to enable surrender, Aranyosi and Căldăraru would be exposed to detention circumstances in violation of Article 3 of the European Convention on Human Rights and the general principles laid down on Article 6 of the same Convention.[2356]

In deciding the matter, the Court took the occasion to explain that the Framework Decision on the EAW was meant to make surrender of persons simpler, more effective, and thereby be able to contribute to the objective of the EU to create an area of freedom, security, and justice between the member states.[2357] The principle of mutual recognition, which underlies the EAW instrument, is based on mutual trust that presumes all member states are complying with their respective human rights obligations.[2358] The EAW also mentions the obligation to respect rights and thus needs to be balanced with mutual recognition.[2359] In trying to hold this balance altogether, the Court held that compliance with the prohibition of inhuman or degrading treatment or punishment is binding on the Member States and, consequently, on their courts, where they are implementing EU law.[2360] Notably, this prohibition is absolute as it is closely linked with one's respect for human dignity and no less than Article 3 ECHR confirms this, wherein no derogation is allowed at any time.[2361] The values enshrined in these relevant provisions are fundamental to the Union and its member states and thus, regardless of the conduct of the person concerned, there is the absolute prohibition of torture and inhumane and degrading treatment or punishment.[2362]

Thus, in cases where there is evidence that shows that there is a real risk that detention conditions in the issuing member state infringe Article 4 of the Charter, there ought to be a two-step assessment as follows:

> "As a result, if an executing judicial authority has evidence which demonstrates that there is a real risk that detention conditions in the

---

2356 *Bovend'Eerdt*, pp. 114, 115; *Gáspár-Szilágyi*, p. 200.

2357 *Bovend'Eerdt*, p. 116.

2358 *Bovend'Eerdt*, p. 116.

2359 *Bovend'Eerdt*, p. 116.

2360 Joint Cases C-404/15 and C-659/15 PPU PaiAranyosi and Robert Căldăraru, 05 April 2016, § 84; *Gáspár-Szilágyi*, p. 207.

2361 Joint Cases C-404/15 and C-659/15 PPU PaiAranyosi and Robert Căldăraru, 05 April 2016, § 86; *Gáspár-Szilágyi*, p. 207.

2362 Joint Cases C-404/15 and C-659/15 PPU PaiAranyosi and Robert Căldăraru, 05 April 2016, § 87.

> issuing Member State infringe Article 4 of the Charter, the executing judicial authority must assess that risk using a two-stage test. First, the executing judicial authority must assess whether general detention circumstances in the issuing Member State constitute a real risk of an Article 4 violation. Such an assessment in itself is not sufficient to render surrender impermissible. During the second stage of its assessment the executing judicial authority judges whether there are substantial grounds for believing that the requested person in question will be subjected to a real risk of Article 4 violations. If, after its two-stage assessment, the executing judicial authority finds that there is a real risk of an Article 4 violation for the requested person once surrendered, the execution of the arrest warrant must be deferred until the executing judicial authority receives the information necessary to discount the existence of such a real risk. If this risk cannot be discounted within a reasonable time the executing judicial authority must then decide whether or not to terminate the procedure."[2363]

Therefore, the executing judicial authority must determine in "a specific and precise manner, whether there are substantial grounds for believing that the requested person faces a real risk of being subjected to inhuman or degrading treatment due to the detention conditions in the issuing state."[2364] The executing authority is obligated to request additional information from the issuing authority, which in turn must provide the additional information within the time fixed in such a demand.[2365] Any decision then must be postponed until such time additional information has been obtained that would enable a decision as to the existence of such risk.[2366] In cases that the risk cannot be ruled out in reasonable time, the executing authority must then decide whether it would terminate the surrender procedure.[2367]

Accordingly, the abovementioned case clarified that the presumption of mutual trust that all member states act in accordance with human rights is not absolute and unconditional.[2368] Effectuating mutual recognition in criminal matters is not inviolable especially in light of detriments or infringements to human rights. As such, even if there are no grounds for

2363 *Bovend'Eerdt*, p. 117.
2364 *Gáspár-Szilágyi*, p. 208.
2365 *Gáspár-Szilágyi*, p. 208.
2366 *Gáspár-Szilágyi*, p. 208.
2367 *Gáspár-Szilágyi*, p. 208.
2368 *Bovend'Eerdt*, p. 117.

refusal that exist per the list provided by the Framework Decision, the EAW could be denied recognition or execution should there be either a (1) real risk that detention conditions violate Article 4 of the CFR and/or (2) where there are "substantial grounds to believe that the person to be surrendered will be subjected to a real risk, execution can be deferred and eventually, terminated."[2369] Stating it differently, the CJEU seemed to have said in these joint cases that fundamental rights violations can constitute an exception to mutual trust.[2370] Secondly, the CJEU judgment in these joined cases seemed to be an effort to converge CJEU jurisprudence with that of the European Court of Human Rights.[2371] Sustaining a denial of the EAW resonates ECtHR jurisprudence such as Soering v. United Kingdom, among other case law, that imposes a positive duty upon member states to implement and protect human rights.[2372]

Having mentioned the foregoing, it is now clearly provided in the DEIO that an executing authority may refuse recognition or execution should there be substantial grounds to believe that "execution of the investigative measure indicated in the EIO would be incompatible with the executing State's obligations in accordance with Article 6 TEU and the Charter."[2373] While these principles were originally opined to be applicable to extradition between member states as well as between member states and third party states, and the EIO does not necessarily concern the arrest and surrender of persons, the same principles apparently were carried over to the concept of an EIO, which involve criminal matters as well.[2374]

2. Applicable Human Rights Obligations vis-à-vis Ground for refusal

Taking into account the abovementioned, one could look into the rights that can be engaged in an EIO situation that could trigger said ground for refusal. An example is the obligation on non-discrimination. Under Article 21 CFR, "any discrimination based on any ground such as sex, race, colour, ethnic or social origin, genetic features, language, religion or belief, political or any other opinion, membership of a national minority,

---

2369 *Bovend'Eerdt,* p. 117.
2370 *Bovend'Eerdt,* p. 118.
2371 *Bovend'Eerdt,* p. 118.
2372 *Bovend'Eerdt,* p. 118.
2373 Directive on European Investigative Order, art. 11, 1(f).
2374 See for human rights principles being applicable to extradition cases generally *Alegre/Leaf,* p. 205.

property, birth, disability, age or sexual orientation shall be prohibited." The same article likewise prohibits generally discrimination on ground of nationality. If a member state as executing authority receives an EIO it very well knows to be issued by reason of discrimination, then acting on the same would be incompatible with its obligations under Article 6 TEU and the CFR. Thus, it would be appropriate to engage the ground for refusal based on human rights obligations.

One can further cite the obligation vis-à-vis the principle of legality and proportionality of criminal offenses and penalties under Article 49 CFR. The first paragraph of said article provides that: "No one shall be held guilty of any criminal offence on account of any act or omission which did not constitute a criminal offence under national law or international law at the time when it was committed. Nor shall a heavier penalty be imposed than the one that was applicable at the time the criminal offence was committed. If, subsequent to the commission of a criminal offence, the law provides for a lighter penalty, that penalty shall be applicable." The second paragraph provides that "this Article shall not prejudice the trial and punishment of any person for any act or omission which, at the time when it was committed, was criminal according to the general principles recognised by the community of nations." There is thus a prohibition against *ex post facto* laws. Applying to an EIO context, it can be the case that the acts and/or omissions provided in the EIO did not constitute a criminal offense when it was committed and yet it came into light that the criminal charge is being applied retroactively to the suspect or accused person. Further, at the time of commission the act and/or omission is not criminal "according to the principles recognized by the community of nations." In such a scenario, there is a blatant violation of the prohibition. In the event that an executing authority receives such kind of EIO, which is incompatible with the obligation to uphold principles of legality and proportionality of criminal offenses and penalties, then under the DEIO the executing authority would be correct in denying recognition and/or execution.

Another example of a human rights obligation is in respect of the right to life and the prohibition of inhumane, degrading treatment, which was earlier mentioned to be in relation to criminal law. The right to life and prohibition of death penalty is found in the CFR under Article 2 and herein, the prohibition against death penalty and execution is equivocally provided.[2375] Comparing to the ECHR provision,[2376] the EU framework is more straightforward in prohibiting its member states to impose judicial execution.

In relation to this, there is the prohibition of torture as well as inhumane and degrading punishment or treatment which is provided in absolute terms (without qualifications) under Article 4 CFR and was mentioned in the Aranyosi and Căldăraru cases above.[2377] To put things in proper context, torture – as per United Nations General Assembly – connotes aggravated and deliberate forms of cruel, inhuman, and degrading treatment or punishment.[2378] It distinguishes itself from inhumane treatment or punishment in degree, wherein torture attaches a special stigma to deliberate inhuman treatment that causes serious and cruel suffering.[2379]

Inhuman treatment does not necessarily need to be deliberate, while degrading treatment does not necessarily require gross humiliation.[2380] The Strasbourg court repeatedly held:

> "Treatment has been held by the Court to be 'inhuman', because, *inter alia*, it was premeditated, was applied for hours at a stretch and caused either actual bodily injury or intense physical and mental suffering, and also 'degrading' because it was such as to arouse in the victims feelings of fear, anguish, and inferiority complex of humiliating and debasing them. In order for a punishment or treatment associated with it to be 'inhuman' or 'degrading', the suffering or humiliation involved must be in any event go beyond the inevitable element of suffering or humiliation connected with a given form of legitimate treatment or punishment. The question whether the purpose of the

---

2375 Charter of Fundamental Rights, art. 2(2).

2376 The CFR provision is in contrast to Article 2 ECHR, which initially reserved the right of contracting parties to subject convicted criminals to the death penalty, but has since then been overridden by protocols either abolishing death penalty during peacetime (Protocol 6) or during all circumstances (Protocol 13) for example. *White/Ovey*, p. 144.

2377 The same prohibition applies in the ECHR framework wherein the prohibition under Article 3 ECHR is in absolute terms and irrespective of the victim's conduct.Chahal v. United Kingdom, (App. 22414/93), 19 November 1996, (1997) 23 EHRR 413, ECHR 1996-V.

2378 Declaration on the protection of all persons from being subjected to torture and other cruel, inhumane, and degrading treatment or punishment, art. 1;*White/Ovey*, p. 170.

2379 Ireland v. United Kingdom, 18 January 1978, Series A No 25, (1979-80) 2 EHRR 25, § 167.

2380 *White/Ovey*, pp. 172, 173.

> treatment was to humiliate or debate the victim is a further factor to be taken into account but the absence of any such purpose cannot conclusively rule out a finding of violation of Article 3."[2381]

Within the ECHR framework, obligations under Article 2 and 3 ECHR on the right to life and the prohibition of torture, and other cruel, inhumane or degrading punishment or treatment, have extraterritorial effect. This extraterritorial application has generally been clarified and developed in case law.[2382] In the EU context however, what has been made clear through jurisprudence in the ECHR framework has been equivocally provided in Article 19 CFR wherein member states cannot remove, expel, or extradite an individual to a state where there is serious risk that he/she would be subjected to the death penalty, torture, or other inhumane or degrading punishment and treatment.

In the context of EIO situations, or even general MLA, these obligations still can find significance. At the outset, a criminal matter involving death penalty as punishment is obviously out of the question with respect to EU member states. Nonetheless, the extraterritorial application provided in Article 19 can still be kept in mind if one visualizes cross-border transfer of information and/or evidence in a broader context and involving EU member states. There ought to be then an undertaking from the issuing or executing state that the death penalty shall not be imposed. Otherwise, any request ought to be refused.

Further, situations could still exist among the member states themselves that reach the threshold on inhumane and degrading treatment or punishment such as exhibited in the Aranyosi and Căldăraru cases. An EIO

2381 T & V v. United Kingdom, (Apps. 24888/94 and 24724/94) 16 December 1999 [GC], (2000) 30 EHRR 121, ECHR 1999-IX, § 71; see also Jalloh v. Germany, (App. 54810/00), 11 July 2006 [GC], (2007) 44 EHRR 667, ECHR 1996-IX, § 68.

2382 Contracting parties ought to apply extraterritorially Article 2 on the right of life to protect those liable to expulsion not just from death penalty but also from any real risk of deliberate killing.Case law likewise ruled that if a contracting party acquiesced to Protocol 6 and extradited a person in risk of judicial execution, there would be a violation of the Protocol, and thus a commitment from the requesting state is necessitated that the death penalty shall not be applied. Akin to this, obligation under Article 3 are also given an extraterritorial effect in certain circumstances as illustrated in the Soering and Chahal judgments mentioned above. A contracting party may be held liable for violating Article 3 if its actions exposes a person to the likelihood of ill-treatment outside the jurisdiction of the contracting parties. *White/Ovey*, pp. 144, 179.

can cover transfers of persons in custody among other things. Allowing persons in custody to be transferred as an executing state to questionable facilities would violate one's obligation under Articles 4 and 19 of the CFR. It is also highly possible that in recognizing or executing an EIO, the suspect and/or accused is at risk of punishment that would expose him/her to either torture and other inhumane or degrading punishment or treatment. While no clear pronouncement is available as regards this scenario vis-à-vis the EIO, there remains the high plausibility that the threshold of "substantial grounds to believe that the investigative measure would violate obligations under Article 6 TEU and the CFR" would be met and there is sufficient reason to deny recognition or execution of an EIO.

Based on the foregoing, the ground for refusal based on human rights obligations has significance in an EIO situation. The non-discrimination obligation for example is straightforward in this regard. The same can be said for the obligation vis-à-vis the principle of legality and proportionality of criminal offenses and penalties. As regards Article 2 and 4 CFR obligations vis-à-vis Article 19 CFR, there is still the plausibility that executing or recognizing an EIO may lead to incompatibility with human right obligations. The nexus between investigative measure and punishment or treatment may not be as direct or straightforward all the time such as in arrest or extradition scenarios. Nevertheless, recognizing or executing an EIO could bring with it negative repercussions and the propensity to violate human rights undertakings provided in Article 6 TEU and the CFR.

v. Reciprocity

The principle of reciprocity is not equivocally mentioned in the EIO instrument, just like the EAW instrument.[2383] In its stead, one could see the principle of mutual recognition and mutual trust as applicable, wherein judicial decisions of a member state are accepted and recognized without further need to formalities and procedures.[2384] Despite not being explicitly mentioned, one could not help but ask whether reciprocity still exists in the context of the EIO.

2383 See *Klimek*, p. 83.
2384 See *Winter*, p. 581.

The principle of reciprocity is traditionally an important aspect of international relations.[2385] World politics, often referred to as archaic in structure, would only make cooperation achievable not through deference to a hierarchical authority or centralized enforcement but rather, through a mechanism consistent with sovereignty and self-help.[2386] Consistent with, if not originating from, the concept of sovereignty implies inter-state equality, the principle of reciprocity is a condition theoretically attached to every legal norm of international law.[2387]

In line with this, the principle of reciprocity can either have notions of specific reciprocity and diffuse reciprocity: on one hand, specific reciprocity refers to situations in which "specified partners exchange items of equivalent value in a strict delimited sequence", and existing obligations are clearly specified as rights and duties of the particular actors; on the other hand, diffuse reciprocity denotes less precise definition of equivalence, "wherein one's partners are rather viewed as a group rather than particular actors, and the sequence of events is less narrowly bounded", as well as stressing the importance of adhering to obligations and conforming to generally accepted standards of behavior.[2388]

Given these two notions, common elements of contingency and equivalence exist in the principle of reciprocity.[2389] As regards contingency, reciprocity is said to imply that "actions are contingent on rewarding reactions from others and that cease when these expected reactions are not forthcoming" – reciprocal behavior returns ill for ill as well as good for good.[2390] Equivalence, on the other hand, does not denote a strict equivalence of benefits but instead a rough equivalence: it can be characterized by changes of mutually valued but noncomparable goods and services.[2391] Thus, it is possible that there would not be any specific symmetry in performances but nonetheless both sides would gain equally valued benefits.[2392] Specific reciprocity would require bilateral balancing among actors while diffuse reciprocity focuses on an overall balance within the group.[2393]

2385 See *van der Wilt*, p. 80.
2386 *Keohane*, p. 1.
2387 *Keohane*, p. 1; *van der Wilt*, p. 71.
2388 *Keohane*, p. 4.
2389 *Keohane*, pp. 3, 5.
2390 *Keohane*, pp. 5-6.
2391 *Keohane*, p. 6.
2392 See *van der Wilt*, p. 73. See also *Klimek*, p. 83.
2393 *Keohane*, p. 7.

The principle of reciprocity has always been one of the principles on which classical judicial cooperation is based on, together with the principle of dual criminality, and of speciality, and firstly on the basis of cooperation between governments or the sovereign.[2394] They are predicated most of the time on a system of mutual performances and affording each other the widest possible assistance, while rarely containing unilateral obligations.[2395] It even can be a self-sufficient basis to grant assistance in the absence of any existing agreement.[2396]

It has been argued however that cooperation in Europe, although it began on "reciprocity in unequal obligations" or reciprocity in general,[2397] has started to abandon the said principle through the making of more and more bilateral treaties on matters such as mutual legal assistance and extradition.[2398] Within the context of the European Union, it underwent an evolution on extradition and mutual legal assistance instruments.[2399] And now with the principle of mutual recognition and mutual trust, there seems to be arguably a distortion, if not complete removal, of the principle of reciprocity.

At the outset, the principle of mutual recognition, especially with the EIO, might seem to promote the idea of reciprocity due to the mutual performance expected from both the issuing state and the executing state.[2400] But as pointed out by van der Wilt, the supposed congruity between the mutual recognition principle and reciprocity is deceptive.[2401] On a procedural aspect, if one would recall, the issuing authority in issuing an EIO needs to make sure it is necessary, adequate, and proportionate, and that the same is available in a similar domestic case.[2402] And when the executing authority receives the same, it shall recognize and/or execute the same without any further formalities.[2403] Like the EEW, the EIO completely depoliticizes the mutual assistance proceedings and judicial authorities would deal speedily with the recovery of evidence and handing over the

2394 *Nilsson*, p. 53; *van der Wilt*, p. 71.
2395 *van der Wilt*, p. 71.
2396 *van der Wilt*, p. 71.
2397 *Keohane*, pp. 6, 23.
2398 *Nilsson*, p. 54.
2399 See *Nilsson*, pp. 54-56.
2400 *Klimek*, p. 83; *van der Wilt*, p. 74.
2401 *van der Wilt*, p. 74.
2402 Directive on European Investigation Order, art. 6(1).
2403 Directive on European Investigation Order, art. 9(1).

same to the issuing authority.[2404] In the new setting of the EIO, ministers and ministries are ideally no longer involved in judicial proceedings and whether national interests would play a role vis-à-vis the EIO, the same would be reliant upon the judicial authorities' discretion.[2405] This in turn arguably distorts the principle of reciprocity or otherwise makes it difficult for member states to invoke it.[2406] More or less, the EIO and its application of the principle of mutual recognition has stood the traditional sovereign function of mutual legal assistance on its head: although the judicial authorities (executing authorities) may find that all the necessary conditions or requirements for recognition and/or execution have been fulfilled, it is a different concern altogether for the exercise of executive discretion to determine how far reciprocity on the part of the requesting state exists or is likely to exist.[2407]

On substantial issues, reciprocity is arguably equally distorted with respect to the EIO. The executing authority cannot refuse to recognize and/or execute the EIO should the latter have reasons to believe that the requirements of adequacy, necessity, and proportionality have not been met.[2408] At most, the executing authority may communicate with the issuing authority and the latter would decide whether to withdraw the EIO.[2409] While one can argue that both parties have obligations to fulfill in such a scenario, there still exists a disparity to the disadvantage of the executing authority because even if compliance to the requirements are questionable, it does not have the power to deny the EIO. Based on the tenets of the principle of reciprocity, one could conclude that its application becomes questionable in this regard. Additionally, the grounds to refuse recognition and/or execution are limited to precise causes.[2410] In connection to this, a question on reciprocity arises with respect to the limitation for dual criminality.[2411] Mirroring van der Wilt's arguments on the EAW because the same situation applies to the EIO, dual criminality was meant to assure perfect symmetry in bilateral and multilateral relations.[2412] The partial abolition of dual criminality and the introduction of a list

---

2404 *Nilsson*, p. 57.
2405 *Nilsson*, p. 57; *van der Wilt*, p. 77.
2406 See *van der Wilt*, pp. 76-80.
2407 See *van der Wilt*, p. 81.
2408 Directive on European Investigation Order, art. 6.
2409 Directive on European Investigation Order, art. 6(3).
2410 See *Bachmaier-Winter*, p. 53.
2411 See *van der Wilt*, p. 75.
2412 See *van der Wilt*, p. 75.

of 32 offenses with the EIO to which no refusal is allowed thwarts the symmetry in favor of those states with harsher penal law systems and to the detriment of those with more lenient penal law systems.[2413] This could result to a situation wherein some states may overall incur more obligations than others in this system.[2414] And reverting again to the principle of reciprocity, there is no reciprocity in this situation given the unequal sharing of obligations regardless if viewed from a specific or diffused reciprocity perspective.

This notwithstanding, all is not lost with the principle of reciprocity. The EIO still retains the same to a certain degree. While limited to precise causes, the different grounds for refusal, as well as grounds to postpone execution, or revert to other investigative measures, are testament to this. Reciprocity on an international level guarantees that states would not enter into unilateral obligations against their own will but national legislation often presents restrictions to satisfy the obligations a state accedes to.[2415] With regard to this, the inclusion of grounds for refusal or reservations serves as a middle ground that allows states with internal legal impediments to restrict their obligations accordingly but also allowing other states to limit their performance to the ones their counterparts are willing to engage.[2416] Thus, one can see in the EIO that an executing authority may refuse to recognize or execute an EIO, for example, either on the ground of territoriality,[2417] or when the investigative measure indicated in the EIO is restricted under the law of the executing state to a certain list of offenses, of which the subject criminal matter of the EIO is not included,[2418] or when there are substantial grounds to believe that executing the EIO would be incompatible with the executing state's obligation under Article 6 of the TEU.[2419] Moreover, the execution of the EIO may be postponed should it prejudice an ongoing criminal investigation or prosecution in the executing state, or that the objects, documents, and date requested is currently being utilized in other proceedings, unlike in the EAW wherein the executing state needs to execute an arrest warrant even in situations when it would be precluded from instituting criminal

---

2413 See *van der Wilt*, p. 75.
2414 *van der Wilt*, p. 75.
2415 *van der Wilt*, p. 73.
2416 *van der Wilt*, p. 73.
2417 Directive on European Investigation Order, art. 11(1)(e).
2418 Directive on European Investigation Order, art. 11(1)(h).
2419 Directive on European Investigation Order, art. 11(1)(f).

proceedings itself.[2420] Thus, a balance of performance is maintained in this situation more or less.[2421]

vi. Speciality or use limitation

The principle of speciality is one of the principles, as mentioned above, on which classical judicial cooperation has been developed.[2422] An application of the same means that the object, data, document, or any other evidence requested "can only be legally used for the request for which they are handed over."[2423] Accordingly, the DEIO is bereft of any exact general provision that the issuing authority is bound to limit its use of the evidence requested on the criminal matter indicated in the EIO. To this observation, an author notes that this raises two (2) possibilities: either the speciality rule does not apply any longer or it still tacitly applies.[2424] However, a closer look into the provisions of the DEIO would show facets of the principle are still present.

The use of the principle of speciality can be seen as regards personal data wherein it cannot be used other than the purpose to which it is requested. The DEIO provides that in its implementation, member states shall ensure that personal data are protected and processed only in accordance with Council Framework Decision 2008/977/JHA, which refers to the protection of personal data processed in the framework of police and judicial cooperation in criminal matters.[2425] This is now repealed by Directive (EU) 2016/680 of 27 April 2016 on the "protection of natural persons with regard to the processing of personal data by competent authorities for the purposes of the prevention, investigation, detection or prosecution of criminal offences or the execution of criminal penalties, and on the free movement of such data."[2426] Said Directive likewise covers processing of personal data in safeguarding against and the prevention of threats to

2420 Directive on European Investigation Order, art. 15(1). See also *van der Wilt*, p. 74.

2421 Cf. *van der Wilt*, p. 74.

2422 *Nilsson*, p. 53.

2423 *Boister*, p. 204.

2424 *de Silva*, p. 10.

2425 Directive on European Investigation Order, art. 20.

2426 Directive (EU) 2016/680 of 27 April 2016 on the "protection of natural persons with regard to the processing of personal data by competent authorities for the purposes of the prevention, investigation, detection or prosecution of criminal

public security.[2427] Accordingly, the Directive provides certain principles member states ought to follow with regard processing of personal data in criminal matters.[2428] Member states ought to observe within their respective jurisdictions time limits for storage and review.[2429] In the same way, the Directive provides minimum requirements and parameters member states ought to comply with as regards transfers of personal data to other member states, third states, or international organizations,[2430] whilst ensuring that processing is to be lawful only if and to the extent necessary for the performance carried out by a competent authority for purposes set forth in the Directive.[2431] Any member state law regulating processing shall specify at the least the objectives of processing, the personal data

offences or the execution of criminal penalties, and on the free movement of such data, art. 1(1).

2427 Directive (EU) 2016/680 of 27 April 2016 on the "protection of natural persons with regard to the processing of personal data by competent authorities for the purposes of the prevention, investigation, detection or prosecution of criminal offences or the execution of criminal penalties, and on the free movement of such data, art. 1(1).

2428 Directive (EU) 2016/680 of 27 April 2016 on the "protection of natural persons with regard to the processing of personal data by competent authorities for the purposes of the prevention, investigation, detection or prosecution of criminal offences or the execution of criminal penalties, and on the free movement of such data, art. 4. Such principles include but are not limited to, member states providing for personal data to be: (1) collected by the competent authorities for specified, explicit and legitimate purposes and not processed in a manner that is incompatible with those purposes (article 4.1.b); (2) adequate, relevant and not excessive in relation to the purposes to which they are processed (article 4.1.c); and (3) processed in a manner that ensures appropriate security of the personal data, including protection against unauthorised or unlawful processing and against accidental loss, destruction or damage, using appropriate technical or organisational measures (article 4.1.f).

2429 Directive (EU) 2016/680 of 27 April 2016 on the "protection of natural persons with regard to the processing of personal data by competent authorities for the purposes of the prevention, investigation, detection or prosecution of criminal offences or the execution of criminal penalties, and on the free movement of such data, art. 5.

2430 Directive (EU) 2016/680 of 27 April 2016 on the "protection of natural persons with regard to the processing of personal data by competent authorities for the purposes of the prevention, investigation, detection or prosecution of criminal offences or the execution of criminal penalties, and on the free movement of such data, arts. 9-10, 35-40.

2431 Directive (EU) 2016/680 of 27 April 2016 on the "protection of natural persons with regard to the processing of personal data by competent authorities for the purposes of the prevention, investigation, detection or prosecution of criminal

to be processed, and the purposes of processing.[2432] The rights of a data subject ought to be respected likewise.[2433]

Speciality also applies more or less to the transfer of evidence. On one hand, the executing authority shall indicate whether it requires the evidence to be returned to the executing state as soon as it is no longer required in the issuing state.[2434] However, there is no mention whether the further need of the evidence transferred by the issuing state is on the basis of the criminal matter it indicated in the EIO. On the other hand, when the objects, data, or documents subject of the EIO become relevant to another proceeding in the executing state, the executing authority may, after request and consultation with the issuing authority, arrange for a temporary transfer of evidence conditioned on the return of said evidence as soon as it is no longer required in the issuing state or at any other time agreed by the parties.[2435]

Elements of speciality are likewise present in the specific procedures provided for certain investigative measures. One example is the safe harbor provision or the general to immunity of a person in custody who is transferred from and to either the issuing state or executing state. As per the relevant provision, he/she shall not be prosecuted or detained or subjected to any other restriction of his/her personal liberty in the issuing State for acts committed or convictions handed down before his departure from the territory of the executing State and which are not specified in the EIO.[2436] Hence, there is a limitation to the criminal proceeding indicated in the EIO. Any further than that, to be used as a ground for prosecution, detention, or any other restriction of personal liberty, is not countenanced. In connection thereto, the transfer of a person in custody is for the purpose

---

offences or the execution of criminal penalties, and on the free movement of such data, art. 8(1).

2432 Directive (EU) 2016/680 of 27 April 2016 on the "protection of natural persons with regard to the processing of personal data by competent authorities for the purposes of the prevention, investigation, detection or prosecution of criminal offences or the execution of criminal penalties, and on the free movement of such data, art. 8(2).

2433 Directive (EU) 2016/680 of 27 April 2016 on the "protection of natural persons with regard to the processing of personal data by competent authorities for the purposes of the prevention, investigation, detection or prosecution of criminal offences or the execution of criminal penalties, and on the free movement of such data, arts. 12-18.

2434 Directive on European Investigation Order, art. 13(3).

2435 Directive on European Investigation Order, art. 13(4).

2436 Directive on European Investigation Order, art. 22(6).

of carrying out an investigative measure with a view to gather evidence for which the presence of the person in the subject territory is required.[2437] It follows that whatever practical arrangements are to be made between the issuing authority and executing authority,[2438] the pending criminal proceeding shall be taken into account, in which the assistance of the person in custody is needed.

vii. Special Offenses and National Interest Cases

The EIO provides for grounds to refuse the execution of an EIO on the basis of national or public interest of the executing authority. At the outset, one does not find the political, military, and fiscal offenses exception that one finds in the 1959 European Convention on Mutual Legal Assistance, for example. That being mentioned, there is a ground to refuse the execution of the EIO should there be an existing immunity or privilege under the law of the executing state which makes it impossible to execute the EIO or when there are rules on determination and limitation of criminal liability relating to freedom of the press and freedom of expression in other media, which make it impossible to execute the EIO.[2439] In relation to this, the DEIO additionally provides that should the power to waive the privilege or immunity lie with an authority of the executing state, "the executing authority shall request it to exercise that power forthwith." In cases where the power to waive the privilege or immunity lies with an authority of another state or international organization, it shall be for the issuing authority to request the authority concerned to exercise that power.[2440]

Secondly, the EIO may be refused should the execution of the same harm essential national security interests, jeopardize the source of the information, or relate to the use of classified information relating to specific intelligence activities.[2441] Thirdly, the execution of the EIO can be refused if the EIO was issued in proceedings brought by either administrative authorities or judicial authorities in respect of criminal infringements punishable under the national law of the issuing state, where the decision

---

2437 Directive on European Investigation Order, arts. 22(1); 23(1).
2438 Directive on European Investigation Order, arts. 22(5).
2439 Directive on European Investigation Order, art. 11(1)(a).
2440 Directive on European Investigation Order, art. 11(5).
2441 Directive on European Investigation Order, art. 11(1)(b).

may give rise to proceedings before a court having jurisdiction particularly on criminal matters, and the investigative measure included in said EIO would not be authorized under the law for a similar domestic case in the executing state.[2442] Fourthly, there is the territoriality ground to refuse recognition and/or execution, wherein an EIO can be refused when the criminal offense subject of the EIO was not committed in the issuing state but rather, partially or wholly in the executing state, and the subject conduct is not punishable under the national law of the executing state.[2443] Fifthly, national interests also play a role when the executing authority may decline the execution of the EIO when the same is with respect to the use of the investigative measure that is restricted under the law of the executing State to a list or category of offences or to offences punishable by a certain threshold, which does not include the offence covered by the EIO.[2444]

Previously, it was mentioned that the ground for refusing the recognition and/or execution of a request because there is substantial grounds to believe that doing so would be incompatible with obligations of the executing state under Article 6 TEU is based on fundamental human rights considerations and indeed, at first glance it is. However, upon closer scrutiny of the provision, it can equally be based on public order (or national interest in general) because, even if it takes account of fundamental rights, the same was formulated in broad terms wherein an infringement is not required but only a substantial ground to believe that it could happen.[2445]

It must be mentioned that should the aforementioned reasons be invoked in refusing an EIO, the executing authority must consult first with the issuing authority prior to refusing to recognize or execute an EIO and when appropriate, request the issuing authority to provide information as may be necessary.[2446]

In addition to how national interests play a role in denying the recognition and/or execution of an EIO, it also plays a role in the postponement of execution. The DEIO accordingly provides that the execution of the EIO may be postponed either when "(1) its execution might prejudice an on-going criminal investigation or prosecution, until such time as the executing state deems reasonable; or (2) the objects, documents, or data

2442 Directive on European Investigation Order, arts. 4(b)(c), 11(1)(c).
2443 Directive on European Investigation Order, art. 11(1)(e); *Heard/Mansell,* p. 360.
2444 Directive on European Investigation Order, art. 11(1)(g).
2445 *Bachmaier-Winter,* p. 54.
2446 Directive on European Investigation Order, art. 11(5).

concerned are already being used in other proceedings, until such time as they are no longer required for that purpose."[2447] When the ground for postponement ceases to exist, then the executing state must undertake the necessary measures for the execution of the EIO and inform the issuing authority by any means capable of producing a written record.[2448]

3. Procedural Provisions: European Investigation Order

a. Designation of Issuing and Executing Authorities

Traditional mutual legal assistance regimes would refer to a central authority which shall request and receive requests with regard mutual legal assistance. Such is built on a vertical construct of cooperation. Conversely, the DEIO provides for horizontal and decentralized cooperation via an issuing authority and an executing authority, wherein requests are not issued through and to a single authority. Thus, there is no longer a fixed 1:1 correspondence between member states in the receiving and transmitting of the EIO. The DEIO defines the issuing authority as one who is either a (1) "judge, a court, an investigating judge or a public prosecutor competent in the case concerned;" or (2) "any other competent authority as defined by the issuing State which, in the specific case, is acting in its capacity as an investigating authority in criminal proceedings with competence to order the gathering of evidence in accordance with national law."[2449] Should the EIO be issued by the latter, the EIO must be validated before it is transmitted to the executing authority, after examination of its conformity with the conditions for issuing an EIO under this Directive by a judge, court, investigating judge or a public prosecutor in the issuing State.[2450] Where the EIO has been validated by a judicial authority, that authority may also be regarded as an issuing authority for the purposes of transmission of the EIO.[2451]

As can be observed, the DEIO adopts a broad definition of "issuing authority" with the additional safety measure of requiring judicial validation should a court warrant be required in the executing state. This prevents

2447 Directive on European Investigation Order, art. 15(1).
2448 Directive on European Investigation Order, art. 15(2).
2449 Directive on European Investigation Order, art. 2(c).
2450 Directive on European Investigation Order, art. 2(c).
2451 Directive on European Investigation Order, art. 2(c).

complex issues such as needing to distinguish between investigating measures that might have actually needed judicial warrants because it could have infringed fundamental rights, and the need to enumerate and distinguish all the types of authorities on the national level that can request for investigative measures.[2452] Moreover, it takes into context the disparity among member states on coercive measures.[2453]

There might be issues arising as regards whether the requirements for being an issuing authority have been complied with. On this question the DEIO does not allow the EIO to be refused on grounds of lack of authority. At most, the executing authority is allowed to return the EIO should it not have the validation required.[2454]

On the other end of the spectrum there is the executing authority, which the DEIO provides as "an authority having competence to recognize an EIO and ensure its execution in accordance with this Directive and the procedures applicable in a similar domestic case."[2455] Accordingly, "such procedures may require a court authorization in the executing State where provided by its national law."[2456] As one would recall, a directive is meant for the member states to transpose to their respective national legal orders the provisions provided for in the directive. Subsequently, the member states would then need to determine who would have the competence to be an executing authority by either designating a central authority or authorities to receive and transmit the EIO's or allow the EIO's to be transmitted directly to the executing authority.[2457] As to how to best handle the same, each option has its pros and cons. On one hand, efficiency is better assured if the EIO is directly transmitted to the executing authority but there would be times wherein the issuing authority could be uncertain where the evidence needed is located and thus, having a central authority would be better.[2458] On the other hand, centralization could provide problems on delay and might not work properly with federal structures wherein there is no clear delineation of territorial competence.[2459]

2452 See *Bachmaier-Winter*, p. 48.
2453 *Bachmaier-Winter*, p. 48.
2454 Directive on European Investigation Order, art. 9(3); *Bachmaier-Winter*, p. 48.
2455 Directive on European Investigation Order, art. 2(d).
2456 Directive on European Investigation Order, art. 2(d).
2457 Directive on European Investigation Order, art. 7(3); *Bachmaier-Winter*, p. 49.
2458 *Bachmaier-Winter*, p. 49.
2459 *Bachmaier-Winter*, p. 49.

b. Preparation of Requests

i. Requirements for Requests

The EIO is transmitted "from the issuing authority to the executing authority by any means capable of producing a written record under conditions allowing the executing State to establish authenticity."[2460] Any subsequent communication shall then be made directly between the issuing and executing authorities.[2461] In connection to this, the DEIO allows transmittal of the EIO using the telecommunications system established by the EJN.[2462] In cases where the issuing authority is assisting the executing authority in the execution of the EIO, the former is allowed to address any supplementary EIO directly to the latter while being in the executing state.[2463] Likewise, in cases where the executing authority is unknown, "the issuing authority shall make all necessary inquiries, including via the EJN contact points, in order to obtain the information from the executing State."[2464] Additionally, where the authority in the executing state which receives the EIO has no competence to recognize the EIO or take the necessary measures for its execution, it shall, *ex officio*, transmit the EIO to the executing authority and so inform the issuing authority.[2465] Furthermore, should there be issues regarding transmission or authentication of documents in relation to the EIO, the parties are encouraged to discuss the same through direct communication with each other.[2466]

With respect to the formal requirements, the recognition of the fragmented framework for obtaining evidence while drafting the DEIO led to the creation of a single comprehensive instrument that should cover the process of obtaining evidence. The appropriate form[2467] provides that the EIO shall contain as a minimum "(1) data about the issuing authority and, where applicable, the validating authority; (2) the object of and reasons for the EIO; (3) the necessary information available on the person(s) concerned; (4) a description of the criminal act, which is the subject of the investigation or proceedings, and the applicable provisions of the criminal

2460 Directive on European Investigation Order, art. 7(1).
2461 Directive on European Investigation Order, art. 7(2).
2462 Directive on European Investigation Order, art. 7(3).
2463 Directive on European Investigation Order, art. 8(3).
2464 Directive on European Investigation Order, art. 7(4).
2465 Directive on European Investigation Order, art. 7(5).
2466 Directive on European Investigation Order, art. 7(6).
2467 Directive on European Investigation Order, Annex A.

law of the issuing State; (5) a description of the investigative measures(s) requested and the evidence to be obtained."[2468] In relation to this, member states have the obligation to indicate which official language of the Union and/or their official language(s) would be used vis-à-vis the EIO, should they be the executing state.[2469] Based on this, the issuing state shall endeavor to issue the EIO in the language(s) indicated by the applicable executing authority.[2470]

In addition to the foregoing, the issuing authority must disclose should the EIO it issues supplement a previously issued EIO.[2471] This ought to be certified, as required in the applicable provisions, and when needed, verified.[2472]

ii. Person or Authority Initiating EIO

As to whose instance an EIO can be issued, a suspected or accused person may now request the issuance of an EIO either by person or by a lawyer on his behalf.[2473] This would however be subject to the "framework of applicable defense rights in conformity with national criminal procedure."[2474] In other words, member states must ensure that any suspected or accused person has the right to avail of the EIO but it has the discretion to regulate how this would be exercised.[2475]

Although this measure is laudable as progressive with regard defense rights, there are lingering concerns that the same is problematic. Albeit the prosecution in an inquisitorial system of criminal procedure is impartial on paper, and that theoretically, a suspect or accused may apply for an EIO, in practice there had been instances of distorting the principle of equality of arms.[2476] It becomes more problematic in an accusatorial context wherein the request of the defense is subject to the discretion of an authority, which itself acts as the prosecution.[2477] Also, there are national

2468 Directive on European Investigation Order, art. 5(1).
2469 Directive on European Investigation Order, art. 5(2).
2470 Directive on European Investigation Order, art. 5(3).
2471 Directive on European Investigation Order, art. 8(1).
2472 Directive on European Investigation Order, art. 8(2).
2473 Directive on European Investigation Order, art. 1(3).
2474 Directive on European Investigation Order, art. 1(3).
2475 *Bachmaier-Winter*, p. 50.
2476 *Bachmaier-Winter*, p. 50.
2477 *Bachmaier-Winter*, p. 50.

systems that prohibit independent collection by evidence of the defense alone, thus again being subject to the discretion of the authority also in charge of prosecution.[2478]

As to whether the suspected or accused person could intervene in the issuance and/or execution of the EIO – a question that naturally arises given the foregoing imprimatur – the DEIO is actually silent and this is yet to be determined.[2479]

c. Execution of Requests

i. Applicable Law on Execution

The admissibility of evidence in the requesting state, or in terms of the EIO, the issuing state, may be determined by the rules that were applied in obtaining the same in a foreign state.[2480] Some legal systems would require that evidence should be obtained in accordance with the *lex fori*, while some would respect the admissibility as long as the *lex loci* has been followed.[2481] There are countries, on the other hand, which follow the so-called principle of non-inquiry and accept evidence coming from a foreign state without further question or inquiry.[2482]

Given this diversity, it is admittedly difficult to implement an unproblematic free circulation of evidence and ensure that defense rights would not be impaired.[2483] The EIO supposedly provides a solution to this issue. The EIO should be executed by the executing authority in accordance with the formalities and procedures expressly indicated by the issuing authority, unless the same are contrary to the fundamental principles of law of the executing state.[2484] Moreover, an issuing state may request that some of its representatives are allowed to assist in the execution of the EIO but only to the extent that they would be able to assist in the execution of the investigative measure in a similar domestic case.[2485] The executing authority is enjoined to comply with such request unless the same is contrary to

2478 *Bachmaier-Winter*, p. 50.
2479 See *Bachmaier-Winter*, p. 50.
2480 *Bachmaier-Winter*, p. 55.
2481 *Bachmaier-Winter*, p. 55.
2482 *Bachmaier-Winter*, p. 55.
2483 *Bachmaier-Winter*, p. 55.
2484 Directive on European Investigation Order, art. 9(2).
2485 Directive on European Investigation Order, art. 9(3).

its fundamental principles of law and would harm its essential national interests.[2486] Delegated authorities, if allowed, should keep in mind that they are bound by the laws of the executing state during the execution of the EIO. They would not have law enforcement powers in the territory of the executing state unless the execution of the law enforcement powers is in accordance with the law of the executing state and to the extent agreed between the issuing and executing authorities.[2487] And in effectuating the same, it is important that the issuing authority and executing authority consult each other by any appropriate means.[2488]

However, the requirement that the executing authority ought to act in accordance with the procedures and instructions given by the issuing authority in the EIO must be qualified. The DEIO equally provides that the executing authority is allowed to resort to another investigative measure should the investigative measure indicated in the EIO not be provided for in the domestic law of the executing state and/or does not apply in a similar domestic case.[2489] This is however not allowed for the following investigative measures that always need to be available under the national law of the executing authority: "(1) the obtaining of information or evidence which is already in the possession of the executing authority and the information or evidence could have been obtained, in accordance with the law of the executing State, in the framework of criminal proceedings or for the purposes of the EIO; (2) the obtaining of information contained in databases held by police or judicial authorities and directly accessible by the executing authority in the framework of criminal proceedings; (3) the hearing of a witness, expert, victim, suspected or accused person or third party in the territory of the executing State; (4) any non-coercive investigative measure as defined under the law of the executing State; (5) the identification of persons holding a subscription of a specified phone number or IP address."[2490]

The executing authority also has the option to resort to another investigative measure different from what the issuing authority provided for in the EIO when "the investigative measure selected by the executing

2486 Directive on European Investigation Order, art. 9(3).
2487 Directive on European Investigation Order, art. 9(5).
2488 Directive on European Investigation Order, art. 9(6).
2489 Directive on European Investigation Order, art. 10(1).
2490 Directive on European Investigation Order, art. 10(2).

authority would achieve the same result by less intrusive means than the investigative measure indicated in the EIO."[2491]

In either case, the executing authority needs to inform the issuing authority of these circumstances to give the latter the opportunity to decide on whether to accede or just withdraw the EIO.[2492] And in the event that the investigative measure requested in the EIO is not possible either because it does not exist under the law of the executing authority or not available in a similar case, and that no alternative measure exists, the executing authority needs to inform the issuing authority that the execution of the EIO is not possible.[2493]

ii. Applicable Procedural Rights

1. Importance of Defense Rights in the EIO

One of the aspects in which human rights are taken into account in the DEIO is its reference to defense rights vis-à-vis the applicable law in obtaining evidence by virtue of the EIO. There is acknowledgment that the transnational dimension of a proceeding must foster cooperation but the same should not be at the expense of infringing or reducing the rights of the defendant.[2494] And while there are no specific rules applicable to transnational criminal proceedings just yet, the EIO nonetheless provides that member states are obliged, without prejudice to national criminal proceedings, "to ensure that in criminal proceedings in the issuing state, the rights of the defense and fairness of proceedings are respected when assessing evidence obtained through the EIO."[2495] In other words, member states must ensure respect for defense rights and fairness of proceedings when assessing evidence obtained through an EIO, subject to their own national criminal proceedings.

In relation to this, the DEIO provides that the EIO should be implemented taking into account Directives 2010/64/EU, 2012/13/EU, and 2013/48/EU of the European Parliament and of the Council, which involve one's right to interpretation and translation, right to information,

2491 Directive on European Investigation Order, art. 10(3).
2492 Directive on European Investigation Order, art. 10(4).
2493 Directive on European Investigation Order, art.10(5).
2494 *Bachmaier-Winter*, p. 55.
2495 Directive on European Investigation Order, art. 14(7); *Bachmaier-Winter*, p. 55.

and right to access to a lawyer in criminal proceedings, respectively.[2496] Although the DEIO was silent as to how these directives ought to be operationalized in proceedings involving the EIO, these were notably the directives in place prior to the enactment of the DEIO and were geared towards the approximation of procedural law and rights in the European Union. After the DEIO, the European Parliament and Council also came up with the following Directives centering on procedural rights vis-à-vis the defense, such as Directive (EU) 2016/343 on strengthening certain aspects of the presumption of innocence and the right to be present at the trial in criminal proceedings, Directive (EU) 2016/800 on procedural safeguards for children who are suspects or accused persons in criminal proceedings, Directive (EU) 2016/1919 on legal aid for suspects and accused persons in criminal proceedings and for requested persons in European Arrest Warrant proceedings, which shall enter into force by 01 April 2018, 11 June 2019, and 25 May 2019, respectively.[2497] Given that these directives are part of EU law which member states ought to comply with, these directives should be read and applied *in pari materia* in the implementation of the EIO. Admittedly, no guidelines on how the same are operationalized vis-à-vis the EIO are readily available. What is currently available are guidelines and toolkits on the same in general initiated by the European Judicial Training Network ("EJTN") and organizations like Fair Trials International.[2498]

2. Human Rights Considerations in Procedures Provided in the Recognition or Execution of an EIO

Human rights considerations also play a role in the specific procedures provided by the DEIO on certain specific investigative measures. First, the transfer of persons from one state to another for purposes of giving evidence or assisting in the investigative measure as either suspect or witness.[2499] Although the person involved is already in the custody of either the issuing authority or executing authority, the person's consent is still

2496 Directive on European Investigation Order, Whereas recitals, § 15.

2497 Directive on the Right to Presumption of Innocence in Criminal Proceedings, art. 14, § 1; _Directive on Procedural Safeguards for Children who are Suspects or Accused Persons in Criminal Proceedings, art. 24, § 1; Directive on the Right to Legal Aid in Criminal Proceedings, art. 12, § 1.

2498 See Fair Trials International and Council website.

2499 Directive on European Investigation Order, arts. 22, 23.

vital before he/she could be transferred to assist in giving evidence.[2500] Any lack of consent is a ground for the executing authority to refuse execution of the EIO.[2501] As to how this consent shall be obtained, or in what form should it be, the DEIO does not provide however.[2502] The DEIO also does not provide what would happen should one withdraw consent after previously giving it.[2503] In addition to the importance of consent, the executing authority may refuse to recognize and/or execute the EIO should it tend to prolong the detention of the person in custody.[2504]

In connection to this, considerations ought to be given to the age, and physical and mental condition of the person involved, including the level of security required, in the practical arrangements to be made by both the issuing authority and executing authority, and when applicable, the member state in transit, in the transfer of said person.[2505] It follows that there is no provided time limit when a person may remain in the member state to which said person is transferred to.[2506] There is also no limitation as to the transfer of minors or when the transfer may result to detention in poor prison conditions.[2507] The same shall be dependent on the arrangements between the executing and issuing authorities, and as long as the transfer does not prolong the period of detention of the person in custody. Nonetheless, it is incumbent upon the authorities to take into consideration these factors in coming up with arrangements as regards this kind of investigative measure. And importantly, the period of custody in the state to which the person was transferred shall be considered part and parcel of the time period such person must serve in custody in detention.[2508] Safe harbor provisions also apply to the person involved, subject to exceptions, as such person has immunity from being prosecuted or detained in the state to which he/she transferred to in relation to acts committed or convictions handed down before his departure from the territory of the executing State and which are not specified in the EIO.[2509]

2500 Directive on European Investigation Order, arts. 22(2), 23(2).
2501 Directive on European Investigation Order, arts. 22(2), 23(2).
2502 *Heard/Mansell*, p. 363.
2503 *Heard/Mansell*, p. 363.
2504 Directive on European Investigation Order, art. 22(2).
2505 Directive on European Investigation Order, art. 22(3), (5).
2506 *Heard/Mansell*, p. 364.
2507 *Heard/Mansell*, p. 364.
2508 Directive on European Investigation Order, art. 22(7).
2509 Directive on European Investigation Order, art. 22(8).

The same consent element equally applies to hearings by virtue of teleconference or other audiovisual transmission, as well as by telephone conference, wherein the executing authority can deny to recognize or execute an EIO should the suspected or accused person refuse to give consent.[2510] At the same time, in the conduct of any hearing by teleconference or any other audiovisual transmission, the executing authority ought to "summon the suspected or accused persons to appear for the hearing in accordance with the detailed rules laid down in the law of the executing state and inform such persons about their rights under the law of the issuing state, in such a time as to allow them to exercise their rights of defense effectively."[2511] In view of this, the suspected or accused persons "shall be informed in advance of the hearing of the procedural rights which would accrue to them, including the right not to testify, under the law of the executing state and the issuing state."[2512] With respect to witnesses and/or experts, their rights are also taken into account when they are allowed to testify with an interpreter and when they "may claim the right not to testify which would accrue to them under the law of either the executing or the issuing state and shall be informed about this right in advance of the hearing."[2513]

Moreover, human rights consideration exists vis-à-vis the protection of personal data, wherein member states are enjoined to comply with the relevant framework decision on the same in implementation of frameworks relating to criminal matters.[2514] Access to such data shall be restricted, without prejudice to the rights of the data subject, and only authorized persons may have access to such data.[2515]

3. Defendant's Participation in the Recognition or Execution of an EIO

It was discussed beforehand that the defendant or third parties now have a greater opportunity to participate vis-à-vis the EIO and this was due to a lingering concern on the protection of a defendant's rights due to the risk of imbalance between the prosecution and defense with respect to gather-

---

2510 Directive on European Investigation Order, arts. 22(2), 23.
2511 Directive on European Investigation Order, arts. 22(3), 23(2).
2512 Directive on European Investigation Order, arts. 22(5)(e), 23(2).
2513 Directive on European Investigation Order, arts. 22(5)(d)(e), 23(2).
2514 Directive on European Investigation Order, art. 20.
2515 Directive on European Investigation Order, art. 20.

ing of evidence abroad, which violates the principle of equality of arms.[2516] To elucidate, equality of arms encapsulates fair administration of justice in both civil and criminal cases.[2517] This implies that each party must be given the reasonable opportunity to present one's case and evidence under conditions that do not place one at a substantial disadvantage vis-à-vis his opponent.[2518] In other words, there is a "mandate for partially symmetrical procedural treatment of adversaries in the preparation and presentation of their cases."[2519] Accordingly, equality of arms is often linked to considerations that proceedings ought to be adversarial.[2520] In order for the same to work effectively, however, it is imperative that relevant material is available to both parties to the extent that security consideration would not automatically excuse blanket restrictions on the availability of such evidence, where it affects the litigant's rights.[2521]

Likewise included within the concept's penumbra is the need to have a reasoned decision in both civil and criminal cases, the opportunity to appear in person or by representative during proceedings (subject to exceptions), and effective participation in the proceedings, the last not being easily satisfied by the presence of the litigant in court.[2522]

In light of the ongoing discussion, Sidhu nicely splits the concept of equality of arms into its four (4) rudimentary elements, namely, opponents, "arms", equality, and disadvantage, in able to make the concept further understandable. Firstly, in criminal cases, it would be the accused and prosecution that are predominantly the only parties, wherein the opponent status of the prosecution derives from its capacity to prosecute cases with the cooperation of law enforcement authorities and its capacity "to discredit merits of the case for the accused" to the point of impacting the court's decision, while the accused conversely is the subject of the criminal action and placed involuntarily at risk by the possible imposition of criminal sanctions, with his position mainly reactionary and effectively one of self-preservation.[2523] In civil law systems, the Advocate General could fill the opponent status in lieu of the prosecution at the appellate

2516 *Bachmaier-Winter*, p. 50.
2517 *White/Ovey*, p. 242.
2518 *Reid*, pp. 177-178; *White/Ovey*, p. 261.
2519 *Sidhu*, p. 91.
2520 *Reid*, p. 177; *Sidhu*, p. 97; *White/Ovey*, p. 261.
2521 *White/Ovey*, p. 261. See also Rowe and Davis v. United Kingdom (App 28901/95), 16 February 2000 [GC], (2000) 30 EHRR 1, ECHR 2000-II, § 60.
2522 *White/Ovey*, pp. 264-266.
2523 *Sidhu*, pp. 91-92.

level, when aside from acting as a mere independent and impartial adviser on the law, he becomes objectively speaking as an opponent when he recommends an accused's appeal to be dismissed, especially when he participates in deliberations that afforded him good opportunity to further his opinion to the detriment of the accused.[2524]

Secondly, "arms" refers to the opportunity to prepare and present one's case through the existence of procedural rights that enable the former.[2525] As once elucidated in a case, "while a criminal trial is not a game in which the participants are expected to enter the ring with a near match in skills, neither is a sacrifice of unarmed prisoners to gladiators."[2526]

Thirdly, the concept of equality of arms introduces a comparative element wherein it is weighed whether the procedural rights afforded one party is also afforded to the other.[2527] Reasonableness is coincidentally implicit wherein a reasonable man could discern whether procedural rights have been given in equal measure.[2528] To ascertain this, one can look into the integrated Directives on procedural rights as well as Articles 47 and 48 CFR.[2529]

The fourth element of the concept of equality of arms concerns the existence of a disadvantage for there to be an infringement to be registered.[2530] In connection to this, disadvantage in light of ECHR jurisprudence could refer to *de facto* prejudice and in some cases, inevitable prejudice.[2531] This is discerned through evaluating proceedings in its entirety and determining whether procedural inequality resulted in "an adverse and material effect on the defense's case and thus influenced the reliability of an outcome."[2532]

In light of this, it is clear that the DEIO pursuant to equality of arms gives the defense an opportunity to participate in the issuance of an EIO.

2524 See Borgers v. Belgium, (App 12005/86) (1991) Series A no. 214-B; *Sidhu*, pp. 92-93.

2525 *Sidhu*, p. 95.

2526 Williams v. Twomey, 510 F2d 634, 640 (7th Cir 1975) as cited in *Sidhu*, p. 95.

2527 *Sidhu*, p. 95.

2528 *Sidhu*, p. 95.

2529 See for the ECHR frameworkJespers v. Belgium, (App 8403/78) (1981) 27 DR 61 [55], as cited in *Sidhu*, p. 101.

2530 *Sidhu*, p. 103.

2531 *Sidhu*, p. 103.

2532 *Sidhu*, p. 103.See also for illustrative cases showing existence of counterbalancing procedures that ensure equality of arms, Matyjek v. Poland, (App 38184/03) ECHR 24 April 2007 [55]; Doorson v. The Netherlands (App 20524/92) ECHR 1996-II [72].

This has been tackled under preparation of requests. However, it is a different question altogether whether the suspected or accused person could question or intervene in the issuance and/or execution of the EIO – a question that naturally arises given the foregoing imprimatur. Issues may naturally arise during the proceedings that affect a suspect's or accused person's fair trial rights among other rights. The DEIO is actually silent and this is yet to be determined.[2533]

With said open-ended question, if one puts into complete fruition the concept of equality of arms, then the natural course to be taken is to allow complete participation for the suspect or accused person or affected person to question or interfere in the issuance or execution of an EIO. It would be easier said than done however, given issues may arise which are similar to the issue of allowing the defense to request the issuance of an EIO in the first place. Further, an EIO would most likely been issued prior to formal criminal cases are filed; thus in an inquisitorial process for example, there is a slim chance to gain knowledge of an EIO being issued or executed. This notwithstanding, the DEIO provides that it is important that member states ensure that within their own national legal orders, legal remedies equivalent to those available for similar domestic cases shall be provided for in the investigative measures to be indicated in the EIO.[2534] While substantive issues surrounding the EIO may only be challenged in the issuing state, this should be without prejudice to the guarantees of fundamental rights in the executing state.[2535] This could either mean that the executing state shall ensure fundamental rights are duly respected, or the possibility to refuse execution on substantial grounds that it could cause infringements of these rights, or the possibility to consult the issuing authority on doubts about the proportionality of the investigative measures included in the EIO.[2536]

iii. Applicable Time Element on Execution

One of the principal innovations of the EIO is imposing strict deadlines on the executing states regarding both the recognition/execution of the EIO, and the subsequent conducting of investigative measures. A decision

2533 See *Bachmaier-Winter*, p. 50.
2534 Directive on European Investigation Order, art. 15(1).
2535 Directive on European Investigation Order, art. 15(2).
2536 *Bachmaier-Winter*, p. 55.

on the execution of the EIO shall be taken "no later than 30 days after the receipt of the EIO",[2537] while investigative measures shall be taken "no later than 90 days following the taking of the decision to execute."[2538] The executing authority shall recognize the EIO without any further formality being required and shall ensure that it is executed in a way and under the same modalities as if the investigative measure concerned had been ordered by an authority belonging to the executing state, unless one of the allowable grounds for refusal or postponement is invoked.[2539] Upon receipt of the EIO, the competent authority in the executing state which receives the EIO has within a week from receipt, the obligation to inform and acknowledge receipt without delay by completing and sending the form set out in the DEIO.[2540] In cases wherein a central authority has likewise been designated by the executing state, both the central authority and the executing authority to whom the EIO is finally transmitted shall have the obligation to inform.[2541] In instances when the executing state determines that it has no competence to act and transmits the EIO to the relevant executing authority to be able to inform the issuing authority, it would be both the competent authority, which initially received the EIO, and the executing authority, which finally received it, that has the obligation to inform.[2542]

Furthermore, the executing authority shall inform "(1) if it is impossible for the executing authority to take a decision on the recognition or execution due to the fact that the form provided for in the DEIO is incomplete or manifestly incorrect; (2) if the executing authority, in the course of the execution of the EIO, considers without further enquiries that it may be appropriate to carry out investigative measures not initially foreseen, or which could not be specified when the EIO was issued, in order to enable the issuing authority to take further action in the specific case; or (3) if the executing authority establishes that, in the specific case, it cannot comply with formalities and procedures expressly indicated by the issuing authority."[2543] Upon request of the issuing authority, "the information

2537 Directive on European Investigation Order, art 12(3).
2538 Directive on European Investigation Order, art 12(4).
2539 Directive on European Investigation Order, art. 9(1).
2540 Directive on European Investigation Order, art. 16(1).
2541 Directive on European Investigation Order, art. 16(1).
2542 Directive on European Investigation Order, art. 16(1).
2543 Directive on European Investigation Order, art. 16(2).

shall be confirmed without delay by any means capable of producing a written record."[2544]

As regards recognition or execution, the decision on the same shall be taken and the investigative measure "shall be carried out with the same celerity and priority as for a similar domestic case" and, in any case, within the time limits provided for.[2545] It is imperative that the executing authority takes into account in its execution any shorter time period that would be indicated by the issuing authority in the EIO, "due to procedural deadlines, the seriousness of the offence or other particularly urgent circumstances."[2546] Consideration should equally be given should the issuing authority provide for a specific date by which the EIO needs to be executed.[2547]

Given the same circumstances, the executing authority generally is obliged to take a decision on recognition and/or execution as soon as possible and not later than 30 days from receipt of the EIO.[2548] Should it be impracticable to work within the specified date in the EIO or the time limit of 30 days to take a decision, the executing authority needs to inform without delay the issuing authority of these circumstances and the reasons behind it.[2549] The time period shall then be accordingly extended to not later than 30 days. Afterwards, should a decision to recognize and execute has been taken, the executing authority has not later than 90 days to execute the EIO without delay, unless there would be grounds to postpone the execution or the subject evidence is already in possession of the executing authority.[2550] It can also happen with this circumstance that it would not be practicable to execute within the time limit provided or the specific date given by the issuing authority, and in such a case the executing authority shall again inform by any means the issuing authority of these circumstances and they shall consult one another on the appropriate timing of executing the EIO.[2551]

In view of the foregoing, the executing authority shall without undue delay also transmit the required evidence to the issuing authority.[2552] If

2544 Directive on European Investigation Order, art. 16(2).
2545 Directive on European Investigation Order, art. 12(1).
2546 Directive on European Investigation Order, art. 12(2).
2547 Directive on European Investigation Order, art. 12(2).
2548 Directive on European Investigation Order, art. 12(3).
2549 Directive on European Investigation Order, art. 12(5).
2550 Directive on European Investigation Order, art. 12(4).
2551 Directive on European Investigation Order, art. 12(6).
2552 Directive on European Investigation Order, art. 13(1).

allowed by the domestic law of the issuing authority and the EIO states such request, the evidence may be handed over the designated authorities of the issuing state who are assisting in the execution of the EIO.[2553] Transmission of evidence may however be suspended, pending a decision on a legal remedy, unless "sufficient reasons are indicated in the EIO that an immediate transfer is essential for the proper conduct of its investigations or for the preservation of individual rights."[2554] This notwithstanding, suspending the transfer of evidence shall be in order if the same "would cause serious and irreversible damage to the person concerned."[2555]

In all the circumstances, the executing authority shall convey its decision by any means capable of producing a written record without delay.[2556]

iv. Authentication of Documents

Under the DEIO, the issuing authority needs to transmit the EIO to the executing authority by means capable of producing a written record to evince authenticity.[2557] And should there be issues regarding transmission and/or authenticity, it shall be dealt with direct communication between the issuing authority and executing authority, and where appropriate, with the involvement of their respective central authorities.[2558]

v. Importance of Confidentiality

Confidentiality and protection of personal data are a paramount consideration in the implementation of the EIO. Each member state shall take "the necessary measures to ensure that in the execution of an EIO the issuing authority and the executing authority take due account of the confidentiality of the investigation."[2559] Further, the executing authority shall guarantee the confidentiality of the facts and the substance of the EIO in accordance with its national law, except to the extent necessary

---

2553 Directive on European Investigation Order, art. 13(1).
2554 Directive on European Investigation Order, art. 13(2).
2555 Directive on European Investigation Order, art. 13(2).
2556 Directive on European Investigation Order, art. 16(3).
2557 Directive on European Investigation Order, art. 7(1).
2558 Directive on European Investigation Order, art. 7(7).
2559 Directive on European Investigation Order, art. 19(1).

to execute the investigative measure.[2560] Should confidentiality cannot be complied with, the executing authority shall notify the issuing authority without delay.[2561] On the other hand, the issuing authority shall also, in accordance with its national law and unless provided otherwise by the executing authority, maintain the confidentiality of any evidence and information provided by the executing authority, except as may be necessary to effectuate investigative measures described in the EIO.[2562] Additionally, it is imperative for member states to assure that banks do not disclose to the bank customer concerned or to other third persons that information has been transmitted to the issuing State in accordance with Articles 26 and 27 or that an investigation is being carried out.[2563]

The protection of personal data is related to the topic of confidentiality and in this respect, member states should ensure that personal data are protected and may only be processed in accordance with the Framework Decision on protection of personal data in processed in the framework of police and legal cooperation in criminal matters and the principles of the Council of Europe Convention for the protection of Individuals with regard to the Automatic Processing of Personal Data of 28 January 1981 and its Additional Protocol.[2564] Moreover, access to such data shall be restricted, without prejudice to the rights of the data subject. Only authorized persons may have access to such data.

vi. Return of Evidence

There is no provision in the DEIO stating that the issuing authority is obliged to return any evidence obtained through an EIO. It is incumbent upon the executing authority when transmission of evidence is made to indicate "whether it requires the evidence to be returned to the executing state as soon as it is no longer required in the issuing State."[2565] When the objects, documents, and information obtained are also relevant for other proceedings, the executing authority may, "at the explicit request of and after consultations with the issuing authority, temporarily transfer the

2560 Directive on European Investigation Order, art. 19(2).
2561 Directive on European Investigation Order, art. 19(2).
2562 Directive on European Investigation Order, art. 19(3).
2563 Directive on European Investigation Order, art. 19(4).
2564 Directive on European Investigation Order, art. 20.
2565 Directive on European Investigation Order, art. 13(3).

evidence on the condition that it be returned to the executing State as soon as it is no longer required in the issuing State or at any other time or occasion agreed between the competent authorities."[2566]

vii. Specific Procedures per Type of Assistance

As mentioned in the discussion, there are specific procedures provided by the DEIO as to specific types of assistance under Articles 23 to 31 (see above).

II. Implementation in Member State: United Kingdom

The two next portions in the study shall look into the respective member state frameworks of the United Kingdom and Germany as regards its implementation of international cooperation mechanisms, specifically the EIO which is the applicable instrument as regards mutual legal assistance between EU member states.

First in line for examination is the United Kingdom. The following discussion shall walk one through the historical development into the UK's cross-border cooperation mechanism, including its integration and implementation of the EIO, and the substantive and procedural provisions integral in understanding better the UK's existing mechanism. Included in the discussion herein are inputs from practitioners coming from different jurisdictions in the UK that shed light into how the law in practice sometimes differ from the law in the books.

A. Historical Development

1. Bilateral, Regional, and Multilateral Mutual Legal Assistance

The United Kingdom has many bilateral, regional, and multilateral mutual legal assistance treaties with other countries. For the bilateral MLA agreements, UK has existing agreements as of December 2019, Algeria, Antigua, Barbuda, Argentina, Australia, Bahamas, Bahrain, Barbados, Brazil,

2566 Directive on European Investigation Order, art. 13(4).

Canada, Chile, China, Colombia, Ecuador, Grenada, Guyana, Hong Kong SAR, India, Ireland, Italy, Jordan, Kazakhstan, Libya, Malaysia, Mexico, Morocco, Netherlands, Nigeria, Panama, Paraguay, Philippines, Romania, Saudi Arabia, Spain, Sweden, Thailand, Ukraine, United Arab Emirates, United States of America, Uruguay, Vietnam, some of which are restraint and confiscation and/or drug trafficking MLA's.[2567]

With respect to multilateral and regional agreements, one can give attention to key EU, Council of Europe, United Nations, and even Commonwealth instruments. With respect to the EU, the UK has adopted the following key EU measures related to MLA and extradition: European Arrest Warrant Framework Decision, 2000 Convention on Mutual Assistance in Criminal Matters between member states of the European Union and its corresponding protocol, Freezing Order Framework Decision, Confiscation Order Framework Decision, Schengen Acquis – UK Participation in Articles 48 to 53, EU-Japan Agreement on Mutual Legal Assistance Matters. Following however the exit of the UK from the European Union, as of 01 January 2021, the so-called Trade and Cooperation Agreement governs the relationship between the EU and the UK, including new applicable rules for judicial cooperation.[2568] Part of this Agreement provides the new legal basis in terms of surrender, mutual legal assistance, freezing and confiscation, and exchange of criminal record information.

With respect to the Council of Europe, the UK is part of the following Council of Europe multilateral agreements: 1957 Convention on Extradition including its additional protocols, 1959 Convention on Mutual Assistance in Criminal Matters, including its 1978 Additional Protocol and 2001 Second Additional Protocol, 1990 Convention on Laundering, Search, Seizure, and Confiscation of the Proceeds from Crime, 2001 Convention on Cybercrime ("Budapest Convention"), and the 2005 Convention on Laundering, Search, Seizure, and Confiscation of the Proceeds from Crime and on the Financing of Terrorism ("Warsaw Convention").[2569]

The UK is also part of many UN multilateral agreements which include MLA provisions, such as the 1988 UN Convention against Illicit Traffic in

---

2567 *UK Home Office International Criminal Unit*, p. 1.

2568 For specific provisions governing law enforcement and judicial cooperation in criminal matters, one can refer to Part Four of the Trade and Cooperation Agreement Between the European Union and the European Atomic Energy Community, of the One Part, And The United Kingdom Of Great Britain And Northern Ireland, of the Other Part dated 30 December 2020.

2569

Narcotic Drugs and Psychotropic Substances ("Vienna Convention"), 2000 UN Convention against Transnational Organized Crime, and 2003 UN Convention against Corruption.[2570] As regards Commonwealth schemes, the UK is part of the 2011 Commonwealth Scheme Relating to Mutual Assistance in Criminal Matters and the 2002 Commonwealth Scheme Relating to Extradition.[2571]

In relation to the abovementioned, one can note that the UK has extended some of its agreements to its crown dependencies and overseas territories, as follows:[2572]

Agreements extended by the UK	**Crown Dependencies**	**Overseas Territories**
1957 Convention on Extradition	Channel Islands; Isle of Man	None
1959 Convention on Mutual Assistance in Criminal Matters	Isle of Man; Jersey; Guernsey	None
1978 Additional Protocol to European Convention on Mutual Assistance in Criminal Matters	Jersey	
Vienna Convention	Isle of Man; Jersey; Guerney	British Virgin Islands; Cayman Islands; Bermuda; Turks and Caicos Islands; Anguilla; Montserrat
UNTOC	Isle of Man; Jersey; Guernsey	Gibraltar; British Virgin Islands; Cayman Islands; Falkland Islands; Bermuda; Anguilla; Turks and Caicos Islands
UNCAC	Isle of Man; Jersey; Guernsey	British Virgin Islands

2570 *UK Home Office International Criminal Unit*, p. 2.

2571 *UK Home Office International Criminal Unit*, p. 2.

2572 *UK Home Office International Criminal Unit*, p. 3.

Agreements extended by the UK	Crown Dependencies	Overseas Territories
Hong Kong SAR	Isle of Man	None
Mexico	Isle of Man	None
Thailand	Isle of Man	None
Ukraine	Isle of Man	None
USA	Isle of Man	None
USA-UK and Cayman Islands on Mutual Assistance in Criminal Matters	None	Anguilla; British Virgin Islands; Montserrat; Turks and Caicos Islands
USA-Bermuda Mutual Legal Assistance Treaty	None	None

Figure 3: List of Extended Agreements to Crown Dependencies and Overseas Territories

2. Domestic Legislation on International Cooperation

The Crime (International Cooperation) Act of 2003 ("CICA") is the applicable UK law to traditional mutual legal assistance requests. Prior to this 2003 Act, there was the Criminal Justice (International Co-operation) Act 1990(d), but was amended by the former "to make provision for furthering co-operation with other countries in respect of criminal proceedings and investigations; to extend jurisdiction to deal with terrorist acts or threats outside the United Kingdom; to amend section 5 of the Forgery and Counterfeiting Act 1981 and make corresponding provision in relation to Scotland; and for connected purposes."[2573]

The UK applied the European Investigation Order, which was meant to replace traditional MLA arrangements with member states in the EU such as the Council of Europe Mutual Legal Assistance and its protocols, the Convention implementing the Schengen Agreement, and the EU MLA Convention and its protocols.[2574] While the EIO was in force, the CICA was not the applicable domestic legislation but instead, it would be the Criminal Justice (European Investigation Order) Regulations 2017, which

2573 Crime (International Cooperation) Act of 2003, Preamble.
2574 *Mitsilegas*, p. 210.

came into effect last 31 July 2017.[2575] Said 2017 Regulations was necessitated by the Directive on European Investigation Order, which requires the member states to integrate into their respective domestic legal systems the EIO and likewise fill in details left wanting by the DEIO.[2576] The same 2017 Regulations covered the three jurisdictions of the United Kingdom, namely, England and Wales, Scotland, and Northern Ireland, though normally there would be different applicable laws and regulations in these jurisdictions depending on the subject matter.[2577]

In addition, one could also refer generally to the Criminal Procedure Rules and Criminal Practice Directions that govern the "practice and procedure to be followed in all criminal courts including magistrates' courts, Crown Courts, Court of Appeal (Criminal Division) and in extradition appeal cases before the High Court."[2578]

2575 Criminal Justice (European Investigation Order) Regulations 2017, Part I, 1.

2576 *Mitsilegas*, p. 211.

2577 In light of the withdrawal of the UK from the EU, the Criminal Justice (EIO) Regulations 2017 have been revoked and the CICA is now reinstated as the applicable legislation in respect to mutual legal assistance requests between the UK and EU member states. This primary legislation for mutual legal assistance has accordingly been amended by the European Union (Future Relationship) Act 2020 and Law Enforcement and Security (Amendment)(EU Exit) Regulations 2019 to accommodate the special partnership between the UK and the EU by virtue of its Withdrawal Agreement and Trade and Cooperation Agreement. Considering however the primary objective of the present contribution to look into how mutual legal assistance can be developed within and between the ASEAN and the EU, and how the regional EIO instrument was implemented among the member states, the focal points mainly used herein for the UK are mainly still the 2017 Criminal Justice EIO Regulations. It must be noted further, that despite the non-usage of the EIO by virtue of the new Trade and Cooperation Agreement and the new UK domestic legislation, the discussion herein remains relevant considering that the discussion herein is a good point for comparison against a continental legal system such as Germany but also, the principles and practices from the EIO Directive and the EU Criminal Justice Architecture still applies in the new arrangement.

2578 *Mitsilegas*, p. 211.

B. Substantive Provisions

1. Applicability of Assistance

Three (3) things could be mentioned as regards applicability of assistance with respect to the Regulations.

At the outset, the scope of the EIO Regulations generally applied to the entire UK and its territories. An exception to the rule however is as regards Regulation No. 32 or on European investigation orders relating to HMRC matters. An EIO issued and to be executed vis-à-vis HMRC matters (any matter in relation to which the Revenue Commissioners have functions) does not apply to Scotland.[2579]

Having said this, the Regulations first have a change in nomenclature following the DEIO. From "requests" towards "orders", issuing authorities and executing authorities, there was an apparent shift from what is known to be request-based mutual assistance to something demand-based in terms of evidence gathering and cross-border exchange by virtue of the Regulations. In light of this, the Regulations contemplated an EIO as an "order specifying one or more investigative measures that are to be carried out in a participating state for the purpose of obtaining evidence for use either in the investigation or the proceedings in question or both."[2580] The EIO accordingly applied whenever an offense has been committed or that there are reasonable grounds for suspecting that an offense has been committed, and that proceedings with respect to an offense have been instituted or it is being investigated.[2581]

In relation to this supposed shift from a "request-based" instrument to one which is "order-based" or "demand-based", it could be inferred from interviews made with UK authorities from Scotland, England, and Northern Ireland jurisdictions that even if the DEIO and the applicable domestic Regulations provide a clearer structure among other things, the shift in nomenclature from "request" to "order" did not bring anything new in practice. There was no momentous change brought by the change of terms used as regards requiring assistance vis-à-vis investigative measures.

Second, the Regulations equally applied to both natural and legal persons vis-à-vis criminal matters. As commented by an interviewee who was a former head of the Home Office, which deals with all mutual legal assis-

2579 Criminal Justice (European Investigation Order) Regulations 2017, Part I, 1(3).
2580 Criminal Justice (European Investigation Order) Regulations 2017, § 6(2).
2581 Criminal Justice (European Investigation Order) Regulations 2017, §§ 6, 7.

tance and extradition requests for England and Wales, this would be in line with the objectives of the Regulations and the DEIO. In light of this, corporate criminal liability exists in the United Kingdom, regardless of whether in England and Wales, Scotland, or Northern Ireland. Corporate criminal liability can arise from different kinds of crimes, depending on the applicable law of the applicable jurisdiction.

In light of this, corporate criminal liability does not exist in all EU member states and discrepancies could thus exist. As to whether this poses any problem in facilitating assistance via the EIO, all interviewees were not much concerned that a problem could arise due to the issue of corporate criminal liability. An interviewee involved in England and Wales, for example, believes that the DEIO reconciles any discrepancy and still allows assistance to be rendered.[2582] If any problems should arise, other interviewees, who this time are involved in outgoing requests and EIOs in Northern Ireland, said that these were resolved through open communication between authorities.[2583]

Interestingly, this is how discrepancies are generally treated by the practitioners interviewed, regardless of whether the discrepancies arise from differences with corporate criminal liability, grounds for refusal, or technicalities. As an interviewee mentioned, one could look for example at the EAW and how practitioners(prosecutors and/or judicial authorities) from different member states dealt with differences among each other. Any issue was dealt with on a practitioner level and without court intervention. There was a general tolerance that member states would be homogenous in treatment. Complete harmonization is a pipe dream, he explained. As long as there are principles, which states or people sign up to, and they are able to accommodate variations, then the process would work. Further, in practice, people understand the big points to make things work and how it is supposed to work. There might be small technicalities that only matter in individual cases but they are not enough to "bring the edifice down." Authorities, as can be inferred from the interviewee's answer, as well as from the answers from other interviewees, communicate with one another and do not exist in autarky. Indeed, the interviewees stress the importance or the helpfulness of the EJN because no cooperation would work without communication and coordination, even if one may have the best instruments.

2582 Interview with Nick Vamos.

2583 Interview with Elise McGrath and Catherine Hanna.

Third, it must be clarified – or more appropriately, reiterated – as this was mentioned *en passant* earlier that the United Kingdom was covered by a specific protocol on border controls, a specific protocol on the possibility of any measure involving Justice and Home Affairs in the EU, and to specific rules vis-à-vis the Schengen *acquis*.[2584] As regards JHA measures, the United Kingdom was granted an opt-out option, including on policing and criminal law.[2585] In relation to this, the UK can instead choose to "opt in" to each measure by giving notice within a period of three (3) months from receiving the JHA proposal that it wants to opt in.[2586] Applying this to the DEIO, the UK opted in and made the EIO Regulations apply. The EIO Regulation appropriately lists down the participating states for which the EIO shall be made applicable.[2587] It also provides when it shall apply. It entered into force on 31 July 2017.[2588] It would not apply in relation to cases before the Regulation came into force, wherein certain requests have been made or received pursuant to the 2003 Crime International Cooperation Act.[2589]

The EIO Regulations annex the schedule listing the participating states from which the UK may send or receive an EIO (this list constitutes other EU member states). It becomes imperative to mention now that the United Kingdom was the first EU member state to engage Article 50 TEU and exit the European Union.[2590] While it would be interesting to discuss the entire process that led to its exit, what is more important in the discussion is that said exit dubbed as "Brexit" marks a fundamental reorientation in law and policy internally and externally – internally when it comes to structures, processes, and outputs of domestic legal systems, and externally as regards the UK's relationship with and position in the European and international legal order.[2591] There were ongoing negotiations with the remaining EU member states of a withdrawal agreement whilst legislation is being prepared locally to prepare the UK legal system for the withdrawal of the supremacy and effectivity of EU law in the national level.[2592] A with-

2584 *Peers*, EU Justice and Home Affairs Law, p. 74.
2585 *Peers*, EU Justice and Home Affairs Law, p. 74.
2586 *Peers*, EU Justice and Home Affairs Law, p. 75.
2587 Criminal Justice (European Investigation Order) Regulations 2017, Schedule 2.
2588 Criminal Justice (European Investigation Order) Regulations 2017, § 1(1).
2589 Criminal Justice (European Investigation Order) Regulations 2017, § 3.
2590 *Gordon*, p. 21; *van Wijk*, p. 155.
2591 *Dougan*, p. 1; *Gordon*, p. 16.
2592 *Gordon*, p. 21.

drawal agreement entered into force on 01 February 2020, having been entered into last October 2019, and shall cover the transition period until 31 December 2020, during which the UK and EU could move towards an amicable partnership in the future.[2593] The Trade and Cooperation Agreement became effective on January 2021 and included new rules applicable to the judicial cooperation in criminal matters between the UK and the EU.

It becomes undeniable now that criminal justice policy is affected, which necessarily include cross-border cooperation.[2594] Admittedly, the future is still uncertain despite the new form of relationship, notwithstanding the UK government talking about the many benefits brought by the EU Criminal Justice Policies after it was called to justify opting back into a list of around 35 third pillar measures (the EIO included).[2595] The willingness to remain has been expressed numerous times, such as in the following statement:

> "As we exit, we will therefore look to negotiate the best deal we can with the EU to cooperate in the fight against crime and terrorism. We will seek a strong and close future relationship with the EU, with a focus on operational and practical cross-border cooperation. We will seek a relationship that is capable of responding to the changing threats we face together. Public safety in the UK and the rest of Europe will be at the heart of this aspect of our negotiation."[2596]

Prior to what has now been agreed upon, Mitsilegas discussed that there were three (3) possible consequences from the exit: (1) to enter into special agreements with the EU in the field of criminal justice matters; (2) to enter into different bilateral agreements with the different EU member states; and (3) in the absence of such agreements, fall back to admittedly outdated Council of Europe instruments to facilitate cross-border cooperation in criminal matters.[2597] It became thereafter clearer that the first option was pursued and not only that, but the same mechanism applied with the EIO shall be followed (e.g. pro-forma MLA request to be formed by specialized committee, principle of proportionality, time limits, etc.).

2593 For reference one can refer to the provisions of the EU-UK Withdrawal Agreement.
2594 *Mitsilegas,* p. 201.
2595 *Mitsilegas,* p. 216.
2596 *van Wijk,* p. 155.
2597 *Mitsilegas,* p. 217.

In consultation with practitioners on the possible impact Brexit can make on receiving from and rendering assistance in criminal matters to other EU member states, it can be generally inferred from their answers that they are all hoping for the best out of the Brexit situation. One interviewee believes that there would be not much difference in practice given that they would still afford the same kind of assistance that has been in place already.[2598] There might be changes once again in legal basis or nomenclatures but the widest possible assistance shall be given to whatever EU state that may require it.[2599] Another interviewee also believes that the positive changes in practice that the DEIO has brought for example shall continue to be used for more effectiveness and efficiency in rendering and receiving assistance in criminal matters.[2600]

In relation to the Brexit issue, UK took its commitment to the EIO seriously. As per interviews, UK wants to show that they can handle correctly the implementation of the EIO and handle its end of the bargain. By being a good partner in the implementation of the EIO, the interviewee opines that the UK acts rather on self-interest and not necessarily due to the fear of the enforcement mechanism of the European Commission. The UK is hopeful that by showing that it is working well with the EIO and other EU Criminal Justice Architecture, they can get a good deal with the EU upon finalization of Brexit.

2. Types of Assistance

The Regulations did not discriminate as to the types of assistance that can be provided. Assistance could be provided for both coercive and non-coercive investigative measures.[2601] Furthermore, the Regulations provided that the EIO shall also be applicable to those listed under the Investigative Powers Act 2016, which involves investigative measures such as interception of communications, access to communications data, and the like, that intrudes on the privacy of an individual.[2602] Given the same, the Regulations enumerated likewise specific investigative measures the UK

2598 Interview with David Dickson.
2599 Interview with David Dickson.
2600 Interview with Ellis McGrath and Catherina Hanna.
2601 See for mention of "non-coercive investigative measures", Criminal Justice (European Investigation Order) Regulations 2017, § 28(4).
2602 Criminal Justice (European Investigation Order) Regulations 2017, § 59.

may include in any EIO that shall have other requirements needed to be satisfied aside from the generally provided ones. The Regulations likewise provided for the specific investigative measures, which may be subject to an EIO, that UK authorities might execute should it be the executing state.

This notwithstanding, there were investigative measures not covered by an EIO. An example is the use of joint investigative teams. Another example are those which generally do not involve law enforcement authorities and/or prosecutors on both ends. There are investigative measures which solely involve police authorities on the requested end, such as suspect interrogations. Further, issues or discrepancies could arise between what may be provided as corporate criminal liability issues but treated as administrative in another member state. In the alternative, issues could also arise when the requested investigative measure is not provided under the domestic law. Following the Regulations, this was in itself a ground to refuse recognition or execution.

As to how these discrepancies are being handled, practitioners in their interviews (mainly involved in the respective central authorities of their respective jurisdictions) said that requests including investigative measures not quite covered by the EIO are as much as possible still executed.[2603] Open communication between authorities is also imperative.[2604] Authorities from the central authority in Northern Ireland mentioned the importance of having liaison magistrates to resolve any issue as regards the investigative measure(s) being requested. They cited for example an issue that arose with Portugal due to a discrepancy in the investigative measure being requested. The liaison magistrates were crucial in resolving the problem. Further, they cited an issue they resolved with Spain regarding an investigative measure not covered necessarily by the domestic law. At the end of the day, through the use of open communication and liaison magistrates (at some instances), they were able to hurdle over issues.

In connection with the foregoing, another thing taken from the interviews with different UK authorities is that the EIO instrument was a relatively new instrument and not well used yet compared to the traditional MLA request. Thus, birth pains and issues would be normal. There could also still be confusion as to its application and implementation. Authorities from Northern Ireland for example noted the need to always prepare arguments for the courts, if necessitated in EIO cases. Some judicial courts

2603 Interviews with Elise McGrath, David Dickson, and Nick Vamos...
2604 Interview with Elise McGrath and Catherina Hanna.

are not that well-versed with the EIO. Therefore, it is important to always prepare good arguments if court action is necessitated in the EIO.

3. Compatibility with other Arrangements

Even if the Regulations were silent as to the existence of other agreements and the compatibility of the Regulations with other arrangements, in practice there should not be any issue of the compatibility of the EIO with other arrangements the UK is part of, as its practice on traditional MLA shows. It must be noted though that the Regulations were meant to replace older MLA arrangements the UK has with other EU member states, as mentioned above. With this in mind, it was actually encouraged to consider police-to-police inquiries or other intelligence sharing networks prior to submitting a MLA request pursuant to the 2012 Step-by-Step Guide for Requesting Mutual Legal Assistance in Criminal Matters from G20 Countries.[2605] The same shall help improve the quality of the MLA request and any subsequent service received.[2606] Thus, MLA and police-to-police cooperation and cooperation between intelligence sharing networks and other agencies is not mutually exclusive to one another and can complement one another in the collection and/or exchange of information and/or evidence in criminal matters. In other words, whilst police cooperation and judicial cooperation operate on two different spheres, there is complementarity in the same in pursuit of a criminal investigation and/or prosecution.

This was equally expected in the EIO context, which is applicable between the UK and other member states. In connection to this, the UK was involved in many EU information systems and databases that form part of the EU Criminal Justice Architecture, such as for example, the second generation Schengen Information System ("SIS II"), in which the UK is heavily invested and has helped to facilitate effective operation of the European Arrest Warrant.[2607] Significantly, there is the entire infrastructure for exchange of information on criminal records consisting of two (2) parts: first, the Framework Decision 2009/315/JHA on the "organization and content of the exchange of information extracted from the criminal record between member states" calls for the establishment of central authorities in charge of managing criminal records in each member state, with the

2605 *G20*, p. 104.
2606 *G20*, p. 104.
2607 *Mitsilegas*, p. 212.

central authority of the convicting state obliged to inform other central authorities of any convictions handed down against nationals of other member states as entered in the criminal record; second, the establishment of the European Criminal Records Information System ("ECRIS") to have a decentralized information technology system based on the criminal records databases of each member state using interconnection software enabling exchange of information and a common communication infrastructure allowing an encrypted network.[2608]

Furthermore, the UK was part of the extended and sophisticated legal frameworks enabling collection and exchange of personal data and information for law enforcement purposes such as the Prüm measures, which allow collection and exchange of DNA data, the establishment of joint investigation teams (to which UK officers actively participate in), the public-private partnerships in field of policing and surveillance as well as financial data surveillance such as the EU Passenger Name Records ("PNR") transfer system and Fourth EU Money Laundering Directive through national financial intelligence units ("FIU"), respectively.[2609]

Resorting to the foregoing database systems was not precluded in an EIO context. There may be existing information in these database systems that are no longer needed to be obtained through an EIO. Alternatively, these database systems can provide stirring or leading information to judicial authorities that would allow them to define and delineate information and/or evidence they need to obtain through an EIO, or generally construct a criminal investigation and/or prosecution.

Adding to the different information systems/databases and frameworks allowing for collection and exchange of personal data for law enforcement purposes, the UK was also part of the Eurojust and Europol, in which they have extensive participation not only in taking leadership positions in the same but actively organizing and participating in coordination meetings and coordination centers.[2610] As mentioned earlier in this study, the Europol and Eurojust are vital agencies of the Union with regard criminal matters. They constitute the network between police and judicial authorities in the Union. Through the same, the UK could take the opportunity to cooperate with police authorities which have existing information as well as judicial authorities in discerning the appropriate investigation and/or prosecution of a criminal matter.

2608 *Mitsilegas*, pp. 212-213.
2609 *Mitsilegas*, pp. 213-214.
2610 *Mitsilegas*, pp. 215-216.

4. Principles, Conditions, and Exceptions Applicable

a. Sufficiency of Evidence Requirement

The sufficiency of evidence requirement could be seen to be existing with the Regulations' provisions. At the outset, a judicial authority or prosecutorial authority is allowed to issue an EIO in the UK if (1) an offense has been committed or that there are reasonable grounds for suspecting that an offense has been committed, and (2) proceedings have been instituted in respect of the offence in question or it is being investigated.[2611]

Furthermore, when it was the UK which issues the EIO, the sufficiency of evidence requirement could be seen in investigative measures such as banking and other financial information, gathering of evidence in real time – continuously and over a certain period of time, covert investigations, and interception of telecommunications where technical assistance is needed.

When the measure involves banking and other financial information, authorities must provide in addition to the general requirements (1) reasons why the requested information is likely to be of substantial value for the purposes of the investigation and/or proceedings the EIO relates to; (2) "grounds on which the issuing authority believes that the financial institutions in the executing state hold the account, and to the extent the information is available, specify the institutions concerned;" (3) and include any further information to be able to facilitate the execution.[2612] For the other investigative measures mentioned, the issuing authorities must be able to provide reasons why the requested information is relevant to the purposes of the investigation or proceedings to which the EIO relates.[2613]

On the other hand, when the UK was the requested state, the issue of sufficiency of evidence arises in terms of provided information by the issuing state, and it is impossible for the central authority to take a decision on the recognition or execution of the EIO because the information is "incomplete or manifestly incorrect."[2614] On this account, "the central authority must, without delay – (a) notify the issuing authority, (b) request

2611 EIO Regulations, Sec. 6, 7.
2612 Criminal Justice (European Investigation Order) Regulations 2017, § 15(2).
2613 See Criminal Justice (European Investigation Order) Regulations 2017, § 16(3), § 17(2), § 19(4).
2614 Criminal Justice (European Investigation Order) Regulations 2017, § 27.

that the issuing authority provide such further information as the central authority deems necessary for it to make a decision, specifying a reasonable period for the issuing authority to do so."[2615] Further, the central authority must not take its decision on the recognition and execution of the European investigation order until the period specified under paragraph (2)(b) as above-quoted has expired.[2616]

Based on interviews with some authorities, they do not have any recollection of experiences wherein an EIO or MLA request has been questioned on the issue of relevance of the requested investigative measure. Furthermore, there has been no exact barometer in practice as to what constitutes relevance. It occurs on a case-to-case basis especially on outgoing requests.[2617]

b. Dual Criminality

Generally, dual criminality is not required in making MLA requests except for search and seizures as well as restraint and confiscation of assets.[2618] As regards the EIO, dual criminality requirement had a qualified application. Accordingly, the Regulations allowed the UK to deny recognition or execution of an offense when the offense subject of the EIO (1) does not constitute an offense under the law of the relevant part of the United Kingdom; and (2) is not among the 32 listed offenses in the DEIO for which the dual criminality requirement does not apply and punishable in the issuing state with imprisonment or another form of detention for a maximum term of at least three years.[2619]

In relation to this, the dual criminality requirement played an indirect role when the UK may refuse to execute an EIO because the "use of the investigative measure indicated in the European investigation order is restricted under the law of the relevant part of the United Kingdom to a list or category of offenses or to offenses punishable by a certain threshold, which does not include the offense covered by the order."[2620]

2615 Criminal Justice (European Investigation Order) Regulations 2017, § 27(2).
2616 Criminal Justice (European Investigation Order) Regulations 2017, § 27(3).
2617 Interview with Catharine Hanna and Elise McGrath.
2618 *G20*, p. 102.
2619 Criminal Justice (European Investigation Order) Regulations 2017, § 28(1)(d).
2620 Criminal Justice (European Investigation Order) Regulations 2017, § 28(1)(e).

In connection to the dual criminality requirement, it could also be mentioned that the EIO could not be denied recognition or execution if the offense it relates to involves taxes or duties, customs, and exchange, and the law of the relevant part of the United Kingdom does not impose the same kind of tax or duty, or does not contain a tax, duty, customs, and exchange regulation of the same kind as the law of the issuing state.[2621]

In addition, the dual criminality requirement was present as a condition before a central authority authorizes the execution of an EIO entailing search warrants and production orders: "the conduct in relation to which the EIO was issued would, if it had occurred in the relevant part of the United Kingdom, constitute an indictable offense under the law of that part of the United Kingdom."[2622] Herein there is no exception provided for the catalog of 32 offenses found in the DEIO.

Despite the foregoing provisions, dual criminality is normally not an issue according to the interviews made with practitioners. No request for example from the Northern Ireland authorities have been denied on the basis of dual criminality.

c. Double Jeopardy

The UK was allowed by the Regulations to deny recognition or execution of an EIO if the execution of the EIO would be contrary to the principle of *ne bis in idem.*[2623] However, the Regulations did not provide how the principle would apply notwithstanding the specific investigative measures for which said principle is a ground to refuse. To illustrate, a nominated court may refuse to make a customer information order or account monitoring order, give effect to the EIO, or modify or revoke a search warrant, production order, customer information and account monitoring orders, if it is of the opinion that the execution of the same shall be contrary to the principle of *ne bis in idem.*[2624]

Admittedly, it is still unclear as per interview with an expert practitioner on how UK applies the principle of *ne bis in idem* to transnational

2621 Criminal Justice (European Investigation Order) Regulations 2017, § 28(3).
2622 Criminal Justice (European Investigation Order) Regulations 2017, § 38(3).
2623 Criminal Justice (European Investigation Order) Regulations 2017, Schedule 4, § 4.
2624 Criminal Justice (European Investigation Order) Regulations 2017, § 46(1), § 39(6), § 41(5), § 48(2).

criminal matters. It is not clear-cut whether the domestic meaning could apply, or the explanation provided by the CJEU. He opines that if it is cross-border matters, then it should be the CJEU case law that should apply. However, he mentions that the issue of Brexit "comes crashing in", which could entail the need to apply domestic meaning instead. Due to the continuous uncertainty, it has yet to be resolved. Having said these, said interviewee mentions that the UK courts would continuously use the so-called "cosmopolitan approach": one cannot point simply at a certain stage in the proceedings in another member state and simply find its counterpart in the UK court proceedings. One would need to evaluate the factors carefully.[2625]

Taking the abovementioned uncertainty into account, it would then be imperative to understand *ne bis in idem* on a completely domestic level. The prohibition on double jeopardy has been an ancient common law principle which accordingly "prohibits the prosecution of an accused for a criminal offense for which he has already been acquitted or convicted following a trial on the merits by a court of competent criminal jurisdiction."[2626] As an expert interviewee explained, there are two (2) rules in relation to this that produce the same results: there is first the "strict double jeopardy", which involves the same offense; while the second involves "abuse of process", which involves the same conduct regardless of indictment or charge.[2627]

Some cite different grounds on why the prohibition exist, such as the inequity that arises from permitting retrials as follows:

> "[i]n many cases an innocent person will not have the stamina or resources effectively to fight a second charge. And, knowing that a second proceeding is possible an innocent person may plead guilty at the first trial. But even if the accused vigorously fights the second charge he may be at a greater disadvantage than he was at the first trial because he will normally have disclosed his complete defense at the former trial. Moreover, he may have entered the witness-box himself. The prosecutor can study the transcript and may thereby find apparent defects and inconsistencies in the defense evidence to use at the second trial."[2628]

2625 Interview with Nick Vamos.

2626 *Coffey*, p. 36.

2627 Interview with Nick Vamos.

2628 *Coffey*, p. 38.

There is also the proscription of the state from using its resources to make repeated attempts to convict an individual:

> "[t]he underlying idea, one that is deeply ingrained in at least the Anglo-American systems of jurisprudence, is that the State with all its resources and power should not be allowed to make repeated attempts to convict an individual for an alleged offence, thereby subjecting him to embarrassment, expense and ordeal and compelling him to live in a continuing state of anxiety and insecurity, as well as enhancing the possibility that even though innocent he may be found guilty."[2629]

More often than not, the key principles identified to maintain a strict approach to double jeopardy are as follows: "(1) the increased risk of wrongful conviction; (2) issue of finality of criminal litigation; (3) need to have efficient investigations; (4) power imbalances and tactical advantages to the prosecution; and (5) the hardship associated with repeated prosecutions."[2630]

Given the different jurisdictions existing within the United Kingdom, which consequently have varying legal provisions and application on the prohibition on double jeopardy, each applicable law of each jurisdiction shall be discussed as follows.

As regards England and Wales, the protection against double jeopardy presently is not an absolute right and the same is subject to qualifications made through amendments mainly introduced by Criminal Justice Act 2003 ("CJA").[2631] The said law is considered the greatest reform of England's criminal justice system in years wherein it did not only abolish the right to a jury trial in complicated fraud cases, reformed evidentiary standards, abrogated common law rules to allow hearsay evidence, and bad character evidence, and extended the search power of the police.[2632] Such statutory modification later became the model for reform in several other common law jurisdictions, which allow post-acquittal retrials based on limited circumstances.[2633]

Traditionally, when one has been tried already and convicted or acquitted on the same, it shall be a bar to any subsequent proceedings.[2634] A

2629 *Coffey*, p. 38.
2630 *Coffey*, p. 38. See also *Taylor*, pp. 208-213.
2631 *Gillespie*, p. 385.
2632 *Taylor*, p. 190.
2633 *Coffey*, p. 37.
2634 *Gillespie*, pp. 385, 490.

prosecution appeal would be different however, wherein first, the prosecution believes that "the judge erred in law and that this resulted in termination of proceedings prior to the jury retiring, then the more appropriate response will be to use the powers under Part 9 CJA 2003;" the second is "that a person can be retried even if it was the decision of the jury to acquit the defendant whereas an appeal is only possible from decisions by a judge."[2635]

As it presently stands, the state by virtue of the CJA 2003 is allowed to retry a person previously acquitted of a "qualifying offense."[2636] These qualifying offenses include almost thirty crimes, including but not limited to, "murder, attempted murder, manslaughter, rape, attempted rape, unlawful importation, exportation, or production of Class A drug, arson endangering life, directing a terrorist organization, and conspiracy to commit any of the aforementioned crimes."[2637] Significantly, the CJA 2003 retroactively applies and anyone ever acquitted of the relevant crimes may be retried subject to the provisions of the law.[2638]

Retrial upon application by the prosecutor to the Court of Appeal is then allowed by the latter on two (2) conditions: (1) when there is new and compelling evidence that suggests that acquittal should be set aside; and (2) that it is in the interest of justice to quash the acquittal.[2639] It is important that before the prosecutor lodges an appeal of this kind before the Court of Appeal to secure a written consent from the Director of Public Prosecutions ("DPP").[2640] Consent in turn could only be given if one is satisfied that "new and compelling evidence" exists and that it is in "the public interest for the application to proceed."[2641] As to what constitutes "new and compelling evidence", the same law itself provides that it is evidence which was not adduced in the proceedings in which the person was acquitted, or if in appeal proceedings, in the prior proceedings to which the appeal was made.[2642] Notably, where the "new evidence" test is met, English courts held often that "there will be a *prima facie* case that a fresh prosecution is in the interests of justice and the question for the court

2635 *Gillespie*, p. 490.
2636 Criminal Justice Act, § 75(1); *Coffey*, p. 51; *Taylor*, p. 190.
2637 Criminal Justice Act, § 75 (Schedule 5); *Taylor*, p. 190.
2638 Criminal Justice Act, § 75(6); *Taylor*, p. 190.
2639 Criminal Justice Act, § 76(1); *Gillespie*, pp. 385, 491; *Taylor*, p. 190.
2640 Criminal Justice Act, c. 44, § 76(3); *Coffey*, p. 52; *Taylor*, p. 190.
2641 Criminal Justice Act, §§ 76(4)(b), 78(1); *Coffey*, pp. 52, 54.
2642 Criminal Justice Act, § 78(2); *Coffey*, pp. 52, 54.

is whether there are good reasons to refuse the application."[2643] It would seem to appear in the law, as an author noted, that once the Court of Appeal takes hold of the appeal, it would have little discretion on deciding to quash an acquittal because when the two aforementioned conditions exist, the court then "must make the order applied for."[2644] However, it would not be too straightforward because with the second condition, there remains elbow room for the Court of Appeal to exercise discretion.[2645]

The foregoing abrogation of the prohibition against double jeopardy – though arguably not a total abrogation – has garnered a lot of criticism and one of them is that this could undermine the finality of decisions, with those acquitted always with the fear that they would not be left alone by authorities.[2646] Given such risk, the Act provides for two (2) relevant standards against repeated investigations: (1) timing of any application to quash acquittal may only be done by the prosecution once; (2) investigations into the acquitted persons are constrained wherein the power of arrest, searches, and seizures are permitted only upon written application of the DPP.[2647] Further, in relation to the first standard, it must be noted that if application is rejected or when a retrial ends on acquittal, no further application is allowed.[2648]

The provisions on retrial for "qualified offenses", including the different parameters and standards on the same as provided in the Criminal Justice Act 2003, is applicable likewise to Northern Ireland.[2649] Thus, there ought to be satisfaction of the requirements on new and compelling evidence, as well as interests of justice, as provided by English law and jurisprudence on the matter.

As regards Scottish jurisdiction vis-à-vis how the prohibition against double jeopardy applies, provisions could be found in the Double Jeopardy (Scotland) Act 2011. While there is acknowledgment of the rule that once acquitted, an accused person cannot be prosecuted for the same offense on the basis of different rationales, the Double Jeopardy Act 2011 introduces in Scottish jurisdiction three (3) limited exceptions to the rule: "(1) where the acquittal was tainted because a person committed an of-

2643 *Leverick*, p. 406.
2644 *Coffey*, p. 54; *Gillespie*, p. 491.
2645 *Gillespie*, p. 491.
2646 *Gillespie*, p. 492.
2647 *Gillespie*, p. 492.
2648 *Gillespie*, p. 492.
2649 Criminal Justice Act 2003, § 96. See also The Criminal Justice Act 2003 (Retrial for Serious Offenses)(Northern Ireland) Order 2005.

fense against the course of justice in relation to the original proceedings; (2) where the acquitted person subsequently admits to committing the original offense; (3) and where there is new evidence that the acquitted person committed the original offense."[2650] The first two exceptions apply inconsequentially of the seriousness of the offense while the last exception applies only where the original prosecution was on indictment in the High Court.[2651]

As to what constitutes "new evidence" under the Scottish law, it is evidence that was not available and "could not with the exercise of due diligence have been made available" at the original trial.[2652] Moreover, such evidence must strengthen substantially the case against the acquitted person, and that the court must be satisfied that in light of this new evidence together with the evidence presented at the original trial, a reasonable jury properly instructed would have convicted the person of the original offense.[2653] It must be mentioned that this proviso is not present in the equivalent legislation of England and Wales, but instead provides that the evidence "appears highly probative of the case against the acquitted person".[2654]

It is further provided in the Scottish legislation that the new evidence upon which the application shall be made cannot be evidence which was inadmissible at the original trial but due to changes in rules of admissibility, has become subsequently admissible.[2655] This prohibition does not apply anymore should the fresh prosecution be granted. Instead, the prosecutor is not limited to lead or present (1) evidence during the original trial and (2) the new evidence on which the application was based, but also all other "available, competent evidence", including any evidence available during the original trial that either for any reason the Crown chose not to lead, or those which were inadmissible during the original trial but due to subsequent changes to admissibility rules, has become admissible at the time of re-prosecution.[2656] Stating it simply, while a prosecutor may not use subsequently admissible evidence (due to changes in admissibility rules) during an application for retrial, he/she can use evidence led during

2650 *Leverick*, p. 404.
2651 Double Jeopardy (Scotland) Act 2011, § 4(1); *Leverick*, p. 404.
2652 Double Jeopardy (Scotland) Act 2011, § 4(7)(b); *Leverick*, p. 405.
2653 Double Jeopardy (Scotland) Act 2011, §§ 4(7), 4(7)(c); *Leverick*, p. 405.
2654 See Criminal Justice Act, § 78(3)(c); *Leverick*, p. 405.
2655 Double Jeopardy (Scotland) Act 2011; § 4(4); *Leverick*, p. 405.
2656 *Leverick*, p. 407.

the original trial, new evidence on which his/her application was based, and subsequently admissible evidence, once his/her application is granted.

In addition to the abovementioned, an application for new prosecution should only be granted if it would be in the interests of justice but the Scottish law is silent as regards what factors ought to be taken into account in assessing the same.[2657] Nevertheless, the court in the landmark case of HM Magistrate v. Sinclair, which was the first case that tackled the issue of double jeopardy after the passing of the Double Jeopardy Act 2011, provided the factors that may be considered in weighing "interests of justice" as follows: "the fact of the acquittal, the effect any publicity attendant thereon might have on a subsequent trial, the importance of the rule against double jeopardy, the importance of finality, the stress which might be caused to an accused, to witnesses, to victims or their families, the seriousness of the crime(s), the nature and strengthening effect of the new evidence and the conduct of the Crown, both at the time of the original trial and since."[2658] Consequently, the Scottish court in light of these factors followed the English courts in ruling that when the "new evidence test" is met, a *prima facie* case for fresh prosecution is in the interests of justice.[2659]

In light of the abovementioned, it remains to be seen how *ne bis in idem* in transnational criminal matters would develop further and moreover, how it would be affected by the developments in UK's exit from the European Union. In the meantime, it would be prudent to take the development nationally into mind together with the developments in the EU level (CJEU judgment).

d. Substantive Considerations of Human Rights

i. Human Rights Obligation as Ground to Refuse Recognition or Execution of EIO

General human rights are considered in the UK EIO Regulations. First, it can be seen in the different grounds to refuse recognition or execution of an EIO. The UK may deny recognition or execution of an EIO if it

2657 HM Magistrate v. Sinclair, para. 124-131; Double Jeopardy (Scotland) Act 2011, § 4(7)(d); *Leverick*, p. 405.

2658 HM Magistrate v. Sinclair, para. 103; *Leverick*, p. 406.

2659 HM Magistrate v. Sinclair, para. 133; *Leverick*, p. 406.

violates the principle of double jeopardy or *ne bis in idem*, as previously discussed. The UK may further deny recognition or execution if the investigative measures involve either the hearing of persons in the UK through telephone conference, videoconference or other audiovisual transmission and temporary transfer of a prisoner, to which the person to be heard is a suspect or accused person and has not consented to be heard, or the person has not consented to be transferred, respectively.[2660]

Furthermore, an EIO could be denied recognition or execution when the investigative measure involves a UK prisoner to be transferred to an issuing state and said transfer is liable to prolong the detention of the person in custody.[2661]

In addition, denial of recognition or execution was allowed if the EIO has been issued for the purpose of prosecuting a person on account of that person's sex, race or ethnic origin, religion, sexual orientation, nationality, language, or political opinion; or that person's position vis-à-vis the investigation or proceeding the EIO relates might be prejudiced by reason of the person's sex, race or ethnic origin, religion, sexual orientation, nationality, language, or political opinions.[2662] This was reiterated in the provisions allowing denial by a nominated court to make a customer information or account monitoring order, give effect to an EIO or to revoke or vary a search warrant, production order, or customer information and account monitoring order.[2663]

In addition, denial of recognition or execution could be done if there are substantial grounds to believe that executing the EIO shall be incompatible with any of the Convention rights within the meaning of the UK's Human Rights Act 1998 ("HRA").[2664] For purposes of the study, the aforementioned Human Rights Act 1998 adopts and makes applicable under UK law the different rights mentioned in the European Convention on Human Rights and its Protocols.[2665] Accordingly, the preamble of the EIO Regulations stated that the presumption of compliance by other

2660 Criminal Justice (European Investigation Order) Regulations 2017, § 28(1)(i, j), § 37(4), § 54(3).
2661 Criminal Justice (European Investigation Order) Regulations 2017, § 28(1)(k).
2662 Criminal Justice (European Investigation Order) Regulations 2017, Schedule 4, § 7.
2663 Criminal Justice (European Investigation Order) Regulations 2017, § 46(2), § 39(6), § 41(5), § 48(2).
2664 Criminal Justice (European Investigation Order) Regulations 2017, Schedule 4, § 6.
2665 *Gillespie*, pp. 150-151; *Spencer*, p. 526.

member states to human rights obligations is only rebuttable.[2666] This is likewise reiterated as a ground for a nominated court to refuse making a customer information and/or account monitoring order, deny giving effect an EIO or revoke or vary a search warrant, production order, or customer information and account monitoring order in relation to the same.[2667]

ii. Applicable Human Rights Obligations vis-à-vis Ground for refusal

With regard how the abovementioned ground for refusal vis-à-vis convention rights (within the meaning of the Human Rights Act 1998) is operationalized, it can be mentioned at the outset that an exact reproduction of the subject ECHR rights is provided in the Schedule 1 of the HRA, e.g. right to life under Article 2 ECHR, prohibition of torture and other cruel, inhumane and degrading punishment or treatment under Article 3, etc. Specifically, HRA (as stated in Section 1) encompasses Articles 2 to 12 and 14 ECHR, Articles 1 to 3 of the First Protocol, Article 1 of Protocol 13 (i.e. abolition of death penalty in all circumstances), as read with Article 16 and 18 ECHR (i.e. derogation and reservations).

Applying the foregoing in the context of denying recognition or execution of an EIO, it can be said that the obligation under Article 14 ECHR vis-à-vis the HRA on non-discrimination is already provided in the Regulations as a ground to refuse recognition or execution of an EIO.[2668] For this reason, UK authorities acting as executing authorities can deny recognition or execution of an EIO if it is apparent that the EIO has been issued on grounds of discrimination.

Additionally, one can also refer to the right to life and the prohibition against torture and other cruel, inhumane, or degrading punishment or treatment, which have been reproduced or referenced in the HRA as well. If under the ECHR framework these obligations have extraterritorial application, it can be gainsaid to be equally applicable in EIO situations.[2669] Therefore, the positive obligation vis-à-vis the right to life in the context of the death penalty (as provided in Protocol 13 as above-stated) precludes the

---

2666 *Mitsilegas,* p. 211.

2667 Criminal Justice (European Investigation Order) Regulations 2017, § 46(2), § 39(6), § 41(5), § 46(1), § 48(2).

2668 In the UK framework, it has been argued that the principle of non-discrimination is applied together with the common law right of equality. See *Masterman*, p. 926.

2669 See *White/Ovey,* pp. 144, 179.

UK from extraditing, removing, or expelling a person outside its jurisdiction wherein there is inherent risk of judicial execution.[2670] There is also the positive duty when it involves torture, or cruel, inhumane, degrading punishment or treatment.[2671] This means the UK can deny recognition or execution of an EIO if it would violate these obligations, among other human rights obligations provided in the HRA. It can likewise be argued that pursuant to what the HRA provides, the extraterritorial application of these convention rights can go beyond the EIO and extend to general MLA situations as well. Human rights obligations would seemingly take precedent.

Additionally, the principle of proportionality can be mentioned as integral to the fruition of human rights obligations vis-à-vis recognition or execution of an EIO, wherein "any restriction of a Convention right must be proportionate to the legitimate aim to be achieved."[2672] As in the case of Soering v. United Kingdom, the Court held that it is inherent in the ECHR that "there is a search for a fair balance between the demands of the general public interest of the community and the requirements for the protection of an individual's rights."[2673] Needless to state, one must remember that even if he would have rights, these rights must be kept in context of society's rights and one should avoid being in a position creating undue problems for society.[2674] Initially, the question of assessing whether public bodies acted appropriately in accordance with proportionality was foreign to English courts, which traditionally only assessed whether a decision was illegal, procedurally improper, or irrational.[2675] Unlike Germany or France, the lack of proportionality is "not a ground upon which an administrative decision can be directly challenged" in the United Kingdom.[2676] And indeed so, proportionality differs considerably from traditional grounds, wherein (1) reviewing courts assess the balance which the decision maker has struck; (2) assessing proportionality goes beyond the four corners of traditional review as it needs to attend to the relative weight afforded values and interests; (3) the application of

2670 *White/Ovey*, pp. 144, 179.

2671 See Chahal v. United Kingdom, (App. 22414/93), 19 November 1996, (1997) 23 EHRR 413, ECHR 1996-V.

2672 *Wilson/Rutherford/Storey, et al.*, p. 219.

2673 Soering v. United Kingdom (1989) 11 EHRR 439; *Gillespie*, p. 164.

2674 *Gillespie*, p. 164.

2675 See Associated Provincial Picture Houses v. Wednesbury Corporation [1948] 1 KB 223; *Gillespie*, p. 165.

2676 *Booth QC*, p. 4.

the "heightened scrutiny test" might prove insufficient to protect human rights.[2677]

Interestingly, the "true coming" of the principle of proportionality, which was said to be only previously found on the "edges of administrative law", came in the advent of the HRA even though the word itself is not explicitly mentioned in the HRA text.[2678] With the advent of the HRA, there was an opportunity to consistently apply the doctrine especially in scenarios wherein there is conflict between rights, freedoms, and interests.[2679] Having said that, in assessing proportionality, three (3) questions had to be asked according to UK jurisprudence, namely: "(1) the legislative objective is sufficiently important to justify limiting a fundamental right; (2) the measures designed to meet the legislative objective are rationally connected to it; and (3) the means used to impair the right or freedom are no more than necessary to accomplish the objective."[2680] In Huang v. Secretary of State for the Home Department, a fourth – and overriding – requirement could be found: the need to balance interests of society with those of individuals and groups.[2681]

Being required to uphold the foregoing principle in line with its human rights obligations, UK authorities then could deny recognition or execution of an EIO if the same is incompatible with the principle. In the alternative, other investigative measures could be suggested that would be more proportionate to the objective of the EIO received (which the UK does in relation to execution of requests as discussed further below).

In summary, the Regulations were replete of human rights considerations vis-à-vis the substantive provisions. Specifically one can look into the grounds to refuse recognition or execution of an EIO. There is also the ground to refuse if it would be incompatible with human rights obligations found in the HRA. Further reading of the HRA would show a reproduction or reference of rights found in the ECHR. In an EIO framework these rights can find application vis-à-vis the investigative measures to be requested. And thus, if incompatibility exists or there are substantial grounds exist that incompatibility may arise, then an EIO may be denied

2677 R v. Secretary of State for the Home Department [2001] 2 AC 532; *Gillespie*, p. 165.

2678 *Booth QC*, p. 3.

2679 *Booth QC*, pp. 4, 5.

2680 De Freitas v. Permanent Secretary of Agriculture, Fisheries, Lands and Housing [1999] 1 AC 69; *Wilson/Rutherford/Storey, et al.*, p. 219.

2681 Huang v. Secretary of State for the Home Department [2007] UKHL 11; *Wilson/Rutherford/Storey, et al.*, p. 219.

recognition or execution. One of these human rights obligations involve considerations of severity of punishment that involves death penalty, torture, or inhumane or degrading punishment or treatment.

e. Reciprocity

It can be said that the UK application of the EIO through the implementation of its Regulations partially abrogated the principle of reciprocity on its procedural and substantive aspect.

At the outset, reciprocity was not stated in the Regulations itself as regards the issuance, recognition, and execution of an EIO. In its stead, the principles of mutual recognition and mutual trust could be found, which if one would recall, means the recognition and treatment of judgments of other jurisdictions with the same recognition and treatment as if it was issued domestically in one's own legal system. No additional treatment or step is necessary to assimilate such foreign judgment or order. Despite the lack of provision mentioning the principle of recripocity, it remains traditionally as a principle integral to international cooperation and the following discussion shows that the principle still exists more or less in its substantive and procedural aspects in the UK.

Taking a few steps back again to the discussion of reciprocity in light of the regional framework of the European Union, one learns that the principle of reciprocity, with all its aspects and different attributes, originates from the concept of sovereignty that implies inter-state equality and is traditionally imperative in the area of establishing good international relations. Also, the principle of reciprocity denotes a system of mutual performances and affording each other the widest possible assistance while rarely containing unilateral obligations, and given the same, reciprocity is often a self-sufficient basis to grant assistance in the absence of any existing agreement. The UK is an example of this, for being able to render both treaty-based and non-treaty based cooperation.

On a procedural aspect, the UK still provided for central authorities to receive an EIO while its judicial authorities and designated public prosecutors are authorized to send directly to other authorities an EIO as long as the requirements provided by the Regulations are met.[2682] Accordingly, the central authority made a referral to the executing authorities in terms

2682 In trying to make sense of the decision to retain central authorities, the interview with Nick Vamosmentioned that the unique nature of the UK criminal

of incoming EIO's. This is further distinguishable as discretionary and mandatory. Referral was discretionary when "(1) the executing authority is likely to give effect to the order," and "it is is expedient for the executing authority to give effect to the order;" whereas the referral is mandatory when "(1) the executing authority is likely to be able to give effect to the order; (2) recognition or execution of the European Investigation Order cannot be refused under the relevant provisions of the Regulations; (3) a referral is necessitated to give effect to the EIO."[2683] There is still admittedly an exercise of executive discretion, which as earlier mentioned, is integral in the concept of reciprocity.

Anent the substantive aspect of reciprocity, the Regulations did not allow refusal of recognition or execution should there be reasonable belief that the EIO was not necessary, adequate, and proportional. According to an interviewee, it would be difficult to challenge an EIO on these grounds as there is weak protection in the DEIO for such kind of argument.[2684] Furthermore, the dual criminality requirement remained applicable albeit with qualifications, wherein it shall not apply to the list of 32 offenses provided.[2685]

This notwithstanding, the Regulations enabled the UK the power to issue a variation or revocation order as well as to refrain transmission of any evidence requested via an EIO. This could be done on three (3) instances. First, as an issuing state, the judicial authority or public prosecutor who made or validated an EIO may vary or revoke said EIO at the instance of either the "(a) the person who applied for the order; (b) in relation to England and Wales and Northern Ireland, a prosecuting authority; (c) in relation to Scotland, the Lord Advocate or a procurator fiscal; (d) any other person affected by the order."[2686]

Second, there was the power to vary or revoke with respect to search warrants, production orders, and customer information and account monitoring orders on four stated grounds as follows: "(a) the execution of the European investigation order would be contrary to the principle of *ne bis in idem*; (b) there are substantial grounds for believing that executing the European investigation order would be incompatible with any of the

---

justice system and definition of judicial authorities was integral in its decision-making.

2683 Criminal Justice (European Investigation Order) Regulations 2017, § 51 (1) and (2).

2684 Interview with Nick Vamos.

2685 Criminal Justice (European Investigation Order) Regulations 2017, § 28(1)(d).

2686 Criminal Justice (European Investigation Order) Regulations 2017, § 10(1)-(3).

Convention rights (within the meaning of the Human Rights Act 1998); (c) there are substantial grounds for believing that the European investigation order has been issued for the purpose of prosecuting or punishing a person on account of that person's sex, racial or ethnic origin, religion, sexual orientation, nationality, language or political opinions; (d) there are substantial grounds for believing that a person's position in relation to the investigation or proceedings to which the European investigation order relates might be prejudiced by reason of that person's sex, racial or ethnic origin, religion, sexual orientation, nationality, language or political opinions."[2687]

It was notably explained by an interviewee that an application for the variation or production order mentioned herein could be made even if the subject evidence has been transmitted to the issuing authority already.[2688] In practice, the relevant central authority must be approached.[2689] Interestingly, even if the Regulations provide for the same, as of date of this writing, neither is there clear case law that elucidates this power further nor are there clear cut laws that govern said authority.[2690]

Third, the Regulations provided that transfer of evidence may be suspended on two (2) grounds. Firstly, it may be suspended "pending a decision regarding a legal remedy, unless sufficient reasons are indicated in the European investigation order that an immediate transfer is necessary for the proper conduct of the investigation or proceedings to which the order relates, or for the preservation of individual rights."[2691] Secondly, it may be suspended if "it appears to the transferring authority that the transfer would cause serious and irreversible damage to any person affected by the transfer."[2692]

In relation to the second ground to suspend, one interviewee told of the circumstances of his client who was subject of an EIO as a witness. Said witness is being treated as a hostile witness and all obtained information is being leaked to the press (albeit the same should be confidential). Given the disparaging situation the witness is being placed in, the interviewee is of the opinion that the same constitutes "serious and irreversible damage" as contemplated in the Regulations and thus has sought remedies from

2687 Criminal Justice (European Investigation Order) Regulations 2017, §§ 39, 41, 46, 48.

2688 Interview with Nick Vamos.

2689 Interview with Nick Vamos.

2690 Interview with Nick Vamos.

2691 Criminal Justice (European Investigation Order) Regulations 2017, § 31(2).

2692 Criminal Justice (European Investigation Order) Regulations 2017, § 31(3).

the relevant central authority and the court. It has yet to be known what decision has been made on this case.

Moreover, the UK still retained grounds to refuse the recognition and/or execution of an EIO. It had a list of grounds to refuse such as for example, territoriality, or when the investigative measure indicated in the EIO is restricted under the law of the executing state to a certain list of offenses, of which the subject criminal matter of the EIO is not includedr.[2693] Likewise, the Regulations provided that an EIO may be refused recognition or execution if there are substantial grounds to believe that "(a) the European investigation order has been issued for the purpose of investigating or prosecuting a person on account of that person's sex, racial or ethnic origin, religion, sexual orientation, nationality, language or political opinions;" or "(b) a person's position in relation to the investigation or proceedings to which the European investigation order relates might be prejudiced by reason of that person's sex, racial or ethnic origin, religion, sexual orientation, nationality, language or political opinions."[2694] Said ground for refusal grounded on non-discrimination is also one of the limited grounds for which a variation or revocation order could be issued.

Additionally, an EIO could be refused when there are substantial grounds to believe that executing the EIO would be incompatible with the executing state's obligation under Article 6 of the TEU. The UK only attaches a disputable presumption that an issuing authority has acted in accordance with human rights obligations under ECHR and CFR.

Moreover, the UK could postpone the execution should it prejudice an ongoing criminal investigation or prosecution in the executing state, or that the objects, documents, and date requested is currently being in other proceedings, unlike in the EAW wherein the executing state needs to execute an arrest warrant even in situations when it would be precluded from instituting criminal proceedings itself.[2695]

Based on the foregoing, it can be still said that a balance of performance is maintained in this situation more or less albeit an abrogation of reciprocity can be found.[2696] By retaining discretion, or a unilateral approach to handle issues that may arise from the recognition or execution of an

---

2693 Directive on European Investigation Order, art. 11(1)(f).

2694 Criminal Justice (European Investigation Order) Regulations 2017, Schedule 4, § 7.

2695 Directive on European Investigation Order, art. 15(1). See also *van der Wilt*, p. 74.

2696 Cf. *van der Wilt*, p. 74.

EIO, the UK might have abrogated reciprocity to a certain degree, but mostly retains it.

It must be mentioned that any unilateral approach the UK may have taken in relation to the EIO would not be anything new. Historically, the UK took the same kind of unilateral approach with respect to the European Arrest Warrant and added guidelines or provisions that were not found in the root Framework Decision. According to an interviewee, there was a time that people were being extradited even without a decision to proceed with trial.[2697] The UK then was of the opinion that said extraditions are premature. Thus, an amendment was made to the UK Extradition Act 2003 through the inclusion of Section 12(a) which states that extradition is barred unless there was both a decision to charge and to proceed to trial.[2698] While the effects of Section 12(a) were later neutralized according to the interviewee, this illustrates how UK deals with certain issues as regards international cooperation such as the EAW and EIO. UK does not completely waive or abandon its position on certain matters or how it finds its best to apply an international measure.

f. Speciality or Use Limitation

The Regulations were clear and unequivocal as regards the application of the principle of speciality or use limitation in terms of evidence obtained from a participating state pursuant to a made or validated EIO. The Regulations provided that the obtained evidence may be disclosed or used for the purposes of the investigation and/or proceedings in relation to which the EIO has been made or validated; and it might not be used or disclosed for any other purpose without the consent of the participating state from which it was obtained.[2699]

In connection to this, the UK has specific legislations called the Investigatory Powers Act of 2016, which sets out the extent to which certain investigatory powers may be used to interfere with privacy,[2700] and the Data Protection Act of 2018, part 3 of which implements Directive 2016/680 on "the protection of natural persons with regard to the processing of personal data by competent authorities for the purposes of the prevention,

2697 Interview with Nick Vamos.
2698 Interview with Nick Vamos; UK Extradition Act 2003, § 12(a).
2699 Criminal Justice (European Investigation Order) Regulations 2017, § 12.
2700 Investigatory Powers Act 2016, art. 1.

investigation, detection or prosecution of criminal offences or the execution of criminal penalties, and on the free movement of such data."[2701]

Under Section 10 of the Investigative Powers Act, an order is required to be secured in relation to mutual legal assistance requests within (i.e. EIO) and outside the EU context in relation to lawful interception. Speciality or use limitation finds application herein because the safeguards provided relating to retention and disclosure of material, mandate the destruction of the obtained or retrieved data as soon as there are no longer any relevant grounds for retaining it.[2702] Therefore in the event an EIO involves intrusion or interception of privacy or private data, then it cannot be used for any other purpose than what was mentioned in the EIO.

This limitation can be found equally in the relevant provisions of Part 3 of the Data Protection Act 2018. Data protection principles and rights are listed for the processing of personal information and data in law enforcement proceedings. For example, the purpose for which the personal data or information in the law enforcement process should be provided and in general, such data or information cannot be processed for any other purpose or transferred to another member state or third state unless certain conditions are met.[2703]

g. Special Offenses or National Interest Cases

One can notice from the EIO Regulations that there were a lot of grounds to refuse to recognize or execute an EIO more or less on the basis of national interest. The UK may refuse recognition or execution on the ground of national interest when (1) execution would be impossible by reason of an immunity or privilege under the law of the part of the UK in which the requested evidence is located; (2) execution would harm essential national security interests, jeopardize a source of information, or involve the use of classified information relating to specific intelligence activities; (3) the specified investigative measure in the EIO is not authorized in a similar domestic UK case; (4) on the basis of territoriality, wherein the conduct subject of the EIO was committed outside the territory of the issuing state and wholly or partially in the United Kingdom, and the conduct is not

2701 Data Protection Act of 2018, secs. 29-31.
2702 Investigative Powers Act of 2016, arts. 53(4) and 54.
2703 Data Protection Act of 2018, secs. 35-42 (data protection principles); secs. 72-78 (transfers to third countries).

punishable under the general criminal law of the part of the UK in which it occurred.[2704] One can note at this point that the ground for refusal based on the aforementioned was to curb arbitrary or unlawful action of both issuing and executing authorities.[2705]

Additionally, there was an integrated proportionality and necessity check as regards the issuing state wherein an EIO shall only be resorted to if the same is necessary and proportionate.[2706] Interestingly, this necessity and proportionality element has been importantly stressed in traditional MLA practice to ensure that the request for assistance is proportionate to the level of crime being investigated and there is necessity of the evidence in question to the investigation or proceedings, although they may have not been explicitly provided in the law.[2707] Law enforcement agencies are not only operationally independent and handle a gamut of domestic cases aside from handling requests but also have limited resources, hence, there should be consideration of whether resorting to MLA is needed.[2708] In addition to being necessary and proportionate, the requested information must also be relevant in certain cases such as the investigation or proceedings as regards banking or other financial information, gathering of evidence, covert investigations, and interception of telecommunications where technical assistance is needed.[2709] A natural consequence of this is that resort to an EIO is not always automatic in terms of a transborder kind of investigation. Given the same, one can note however that despite the positive duty imposed on issuing authorities to ensure necessity, proportionality – and sometimes relevance – in the issuance of an EIO, UK authorities did not have much room to refuse an EIO should these requirements not be satisfied.[2710] UK authorities could revert to and inform the issuing state and hopefully the latter would supply the lacking information needed to execute or recognize the EIO.[2711] In imperative situations and

---

2704 Criminal Justice (European Investigation Order) Regulations 2017, Schedule 4, §§ 1, 2, 3, 5.

2705 *Mitsilegas*, p. 211.

2706 *Mitsilegas*, p. 211. See also Criminal Justice (European Investigation Order) Regulations 2017, §§ 6(4), 7(4).

2707 *G20*, p. 104.

2708 *G20*, p. 104.

2709 Criminal Justice (European Investigation Order) Regulations 2017, §§ 16-19.

2710 Criminal Justice (European Investigation Order) Regulations 2017, § 28. See also Criminal Justice (European Investigation Order) Regulations 2017, Schedule 4.

2711 See Criminal Justice (European Investigation Order) Regulations 2017, § 27.

on limited grounds, authorities could opt for the variation or revocation order, or the application to the relevant central authority to suspend transmission of evidence.

In relation to this, the issuing authority may only issue an EIO when the investigative measure indicated therein could have been ordered under similar conditions in a similar domestic case.[2712] This was to avoid fishing expeditions or allowing one to do something indirectly what it could not do directly.[2713] Additionally, the UK may refuse recognition or execution if any of the following exist: "(1) the investigative measure indicated in the EIO does not exist under the law of the relevant part of the United Kingdom, and it appears to the central authority that there is no other investigative measure which would achieve the same result; (2) the investigative measure indicated in the EIO would not be available in a similar domestic case, and it appears to the central authority that there is no other investigative measure which would achieve the same result; (3) the use of the investigative measure indicated in the EIO is restricted under the law of the relevant part of the UK to a list or category of offenses or to offenses punishable by a certain threshold, which does not include the offenses covered by the order;" and (4) the investigative measure indicated in the EIO involves covert investigations, gathering of evidence in real time, continuously, and over a certain period of time, and/or interception of telecommunications, which would not be authorized in a similar domestic case.[2714]

Provided however, that the first three immediately previously mentioned grounds to refuse recognition or execution could not be made applicable to instances wherein (1) the evidence is already in possession of the central authority, or it appears to be in possession already of an executing authority, where "it appears to the central authority that the evidence could lawfully have been obtained in the framework of a criminal investigation or criminal proceedings or for the purposes of the EIO in the relevant part of the United Kingdom; (2) the obtaining of evidence contained in databases held by police or judicial authorities where it appears to the central authority that the evidence is directly accessible by the central authority or by an executing authority in the framework of a criminal investigation or criminal proceedings; (3) the hearing of a witness, expert, victim, suspect, accused person, or third party in the relevant part of the

2712 *Mitsilegas*, p. 211.
2713 *Mitsilegas*, p. 211.
2714 Criminal Justice (European Investigation Order) Regulations 2017, § 28(1).

United Kingdom; (4) any non-coercive investigative measure; (5) or the identification of a person holding a subscription of a telephone number or IP address specified in the order."[2715] These grounds on the basis of national interest could also be seen in allowing any nominated court to give effect to an EIO.[2716]

In the same vein, the Regulations allowed the UK to deny the request of the issuing state for its representative(s) to assist in the execution of an EIO if permitting the authority of the issuing state would be (1) contrary to a fundamental principle of law or (2) harmful to essential national security interests.[2717]

In addition to the foregoing, national interest also played a role on when the UK as an executing state may postpone recognition or execution of an EIO. There could be postponement of recognition or execution if the same would prejudice a criminal investigation or criminal proceedings taking place in the UK.[2718] There could also be postponement if the objects, documents, data, or information to which the EIO relates are already being used in a criminal investigation or criminal proceedings taking place in the UK.[2719] In any event, should there be denial or postponement of recognition or execution, the central authority and/or executing authority needs to consult with or inform the issuing authority the reasons for denial or postponement, and when postponement applies, the expected duration of the postponement.[2720] Once the expected duration lapses, the central authority or executing authority needed to inform the issuing authority accordingly and proceed with its decision to whether recognize or deny the EIO.[2721]

2715 Criminal Justice (European Investigation Order) Regulations 2017, § 28(2).
2716 Criminal Justice (European Investigation Order) Regulations 2017, § 37(7, 9, 12-13).
2717 Criminal Justice (European Investigation Order) Regulations 2017, § 34(2).
2718 Criminal Justice (European Investigation Order) Regulations 2017, § 29(2).
2719 Criminal Justice (European Investigation Order) Regulations 2017, § 29(2).
2720 Criminal Justice (European Investigation Order) Regulations 2017, § 28(5), § 29(3).
2721 Criminal Justice (European Investigation Order) Regulations 2017, § 29(4).

C. Procedural Provisions

1. Designation of Central Authority

The 2017 Regulations provided for executing authorities and issuing authorities. An "issuing authority" was an authority of the issuing state competent to make or validate an EIO.[2722] On the other hand, an "executing authority" means "an authority of the executing State having competence to recognize a European Investigation Order and ensure its execution in accordance with the Directive and the procedure applicable in a similar domestic case."[2723] Correspondingly, the issuing state was the source of the EIO.[2724]

As regards issuing authorities, the Regulations allowed both a judicial authority and designated public prosecutor to make or validate an EIO.[2725] On one hand, a "judicial authority" in the UK was defined as follows: "(1) in relation to England and Wales, means any judge or justice of the peace; (2) in relation to Northern Ireland, means any judge; (3) in relation to Scotland, means any judge of the High Court or sheriff."[2726] In relation to this, it was said that an application for an EIO may be made by the following: in England and Wales and Northern Ireland, by either a prosecuting authority or a constable (but with the consent of the prosecuting authority); in Scotland, by the Lord Advocate or prosecutor fiscal; and in any case where proceedings have been instituted, by or on behalf of a party to those proceedings.[2727] On the other hand, a designated public prosecutor may make an EIO under the same conditions as a judicial authority.[2728] Said public prosecutor in England and Wales and Northern Ireland may also, at the request of a designated investigating authority, validate an EIO should the same conditions are met.[2729]

On the other hand, the Regulations designated central authorities to receive EIO from other participating states in addition to executing authorities, which ought to execute the investigative measures requested in the

2722 Criminal Justice (European Investigation Order) Regulations 2017, § 25.
2723 Criminal Justice (European Investigation Order) Regulations 2017, § 5.
2724 Criminal Justice (European Investigation Order) Regulations 2017, § 25.
2725 Criminal Justice (European Investigation Order) Regulations 2017, §§ 6, 7.
2726 Criminal Justice (European Investigation Order) Regulations 2017, § 5.
2727 Criminal Justice (European Investigation Order) Regulations 2017, § 6(3).
2728 Criminal Justice (European Investigation Order) Regulations 2017, § 7(1).
2729 Criminal Justice (European Investigation Order) Regulations 2017, § 6(2).

EIO.[2730] For central authorities, there were three (3) for the UK: as regards England and Wales and Northern Ireland, the UK Central Authority ("UK-CA"); Crown Office, as regards Scotland; and Her Majesty's Revenue and Customs ("HMRC"), as regards tax and fiscal customs matters in England, Wales, and Northern Ireland.[2731] In view of this, the Revenue Commissioners may exercise the function of central authority on "HMRC matters", which involve matters the Revenue Commissioners have functions.[2732]

In relation to these central authorities, they may refer to an executing authority an EIO where the central authority considers either that: "(1) the executing authority is likely to be able to give effect to the order, and (2) it is expedient for the executing authority to give effect to the order."[2733] The central authority, however, must make the referral when "(1) the executing authority is likely to be able to give effect to the order; (2) recognition or execution of the European Investigation Order cannot be refused under the relevant provisions of the Regulation; (3) a referral is necessitated to give effect to the EIO."[2734] In any event, any referral should include a notice indicating the needed action from the executing authority in order to give effect to the EIO, the time period within which the executing authority must act in accordance with the provided time limits of the Regulations, and the details of any time period the central authority gives the executing authority to pose any objection to the former's decision to recognize or execute the EIO, or refer the same.[2735] In relation to referrals, one can further note that aside from the central authority being able to withdraw a previously made referral, the central authority was not allowed to refer to the Director of the Serious Fraud Office vis-à-vis England and Wales and Northern Ireland, unless the order relates to an offense involving serious or complex fraud. And in the event that indeed an EIO relates to a serious or complex fraud offense, then the Lord Advocate may give a direction under section 27 of the Criminal Law (Consolidation [Scotland] Act 1995 [Lord Advocate's direction] for the purposes of giving effect to the order.[2736]

2730 *European Judicial Network*, p. 23.
2731 *European Judicial Network*, p. 25.
2732 Criminal Justice (European Investigation Order) Regulations 2017, § 32(2), (5).
2733 Criminal Justice (European Investigation Order) Regulations 2017, § 51(1).
2734 Criminal Justice (European Investigation Order) Regulations 2017, § 51(2).
2735 Criminal Justice (European Investigation Order) Regulations 2017, § 51(3).
2736 Criminal Justice (European Investigation Order) Regulations 2017, § 51(5), § 52.

Given the foregoing provisions, the UK was one of, if not the only, the EU member states that retained the use of central authorities despite the aim of the DEIO to remove altogether the horizontal type of cooperation in mutual legal assistance. At first glance, this would be counter-intuitive to the objective of the DEIO to depoliticize the process of issuing and receiving EIOs as well as to hasten the entire process. According to an interviewee (who was former Head of Extradition, Head of the UK Central Authority for Mutual Legal Assistance, and liaison prosecutor in Washington DC, where he worked closely with the Department of Justice on UK/US investigations), there was a long discussion on whether the UK would in view of the DEIO retain the central authorities in receiving incoming EIOs and other MLA requests.[2737] UK decided finally to retain the central authorities not only because of the central expertise they have but also because of the different nature its courts have from other EU member states.[2738] UK follows a different criminal justice system: not only adversarial in nature (whilst most EU member states are inquisitorial), but also have a different take on what constitutes judicial authorities.[2739] Furthermore, UK courts do not want to be "administrative postboxes" as it is far from the nature of their arbitrary work.[2740] Thus, the retention of central authorities in practice and historically is the best option.[2741]

In addition, according to the head of the central authority in Scotland, having a central authority with respect to incoming requests still makes sense because of the small structure that their office has.[2742] Despite the retention of central authorities for incoming requests, UK authorities tried to act faster on incoming EIOs and execute the same as fast as possible. There is an effort to integrate the structural changes or improvements the EIO introduced, such as the time limits needed to be observed.[2743] The speed with which the central authorities work with has been seconded by an interviewee from Germany, who sits as representative in Eurojust.[2744]

2737 Interview with Nick Vamos.
2738 Interview with Nick Vamos.
2739 Interview with Nick Vamos.
2740 Interview with Nick Vamos.
2741 Interview with Nick Vamos.
2742 Interview with David Dickson.
2743 See Interview with Catharine Hanna and Elise McGrath.
2744 Interview with Gabriele Launhardt.

2. Preparation of Requests

a. Requisites for Request/EIO

When the UK acted as the issuing state, an EIO must (1) be set in the form set out in the DEIO; (2) contain the specified information; (3) contain any further information as may be required under the Regulations for specific investigative measures; (4) be signed by or on behalf of the person making or validating the EIO; and (5) include a statement certifying that the information given is accurate and correct.[2745] In connection to this, the authority making the EIO must make sure that the following conditions are met: "(1) it is necessary and proportionate to make the order for the purposes of the investigation and proceedings in question;" (2) "the investigative measures to be specified in the order could lawfully be ordered or undertaken under the same conditions in a similar domestic case;" (3) where the order is for an investigative measure in relation to which specific provisions apply, any imposed condition by virtue of said provision are satisfied.[2746] Regardless of who shall transmit the EIO to the executing state, it must be made sure that it is accompanied by a translation of the order into the language notified by the executing state under the Directive.[2747]

b. Person or Authority Initiating the EIO

The procedure of transmitting the same was dependent on which authority made or validated the EIO. In cases where the judicial authority made the EIO himself, then said judicial authority shall transmit directly to the central authority or appropriate executing authority of the executing state.[2748] Provided however, that should the judicial authority make the EIO upon application of the designated public prosecutor or constable (with consent of the designated public prosecutor), then the judicial authority shall give to the designated public prosecutor or constable, respectively, the EIO for transmission to the central authority or appropriate

2745 Criminal Justice (European Investigation Order) Regulations 2017, § 8.
2746 Criminal Justice (European Investigation Order) Regulations 2017, § 6(4), § 7(4).
2747 Criminal Justice (European Investigation Order) Regulations 2017, § 9(10).
2748 Criminal Justice (European Investigation Order) Regulations 2017, § 9(1)(c).

executing authority of the executing state.[2749] In cases where the designated public prosecutor made the EIO, he/she shall transmit the order to the central authority or designated executing authority of the executing state.[2750] In the event he/she validated an EIO on behalf of a designated investigating authority, the former could either transmit personally to the central authority or appropriate executing authority of the executing state, or give the order to the designated investigating authority to do the same.[2751]

In relation to this, the Regulations likewise provided for the variation or revocation of an EIO.[2752] Provided however, that a judicial authority may only vary or revoke upon application of either the (1) person who applied for the order; (2) the prosecuting authority in relation to England and Wales and Northern Ireland; (3) the Lord Advocate or a procurator fiscal in relation to Scotland; and (4) any person affected by the order.[2753] It must be noted that a constable by himself could not ask for the variation or revocation of the EIO. Said constable must first secure consent from the designated prosecuting authority.[2754] In any event, the amended EIO should still be in accordance with the requirements as regards form and contents and then transmitted to the central authority or appropriate executing authority of the executing state.[2755] And should the EIO be revoked instead after it has been transmitted already, the central authority or appropriate executing authority of the executing authority must be informed without delay.[2756]

In light of the foregoing, the Regulations took into account one's human rights in allowing a person to make an application for an EIO. Under the relevant provision, an application for an EIO may be made in any case where proceedings have been instituted, by or on behalf of a party to those proceedings.[2757] The applicable procedure is said to be well provided in the Regulations.[2758] Although an interviewee mentioned that he has yet

2749 Criminal Justice (European Investigation Order) Regulations 2017, § 9(1)(a), (b).
2750 Criminal Justice (European Investigation Order) Regulations 2017, § 9(2)(a).
2751 Criminal Justice (European Investigation Order) Regulations 2017, § 9(2)(b).
2752 Criminal Justice (European Investigation Order) Regulations 2017, § 10(1).
2753 Criminal Justice (European Investigation Order) Regulations 2017, § 10(3).
2754 Criminal Justice (European Investigation Order) Regulations 2017, § 10(4).
2755 Criminal Justice (European Investigation Order) Regulations 2017, § 10(6), (7).
2756 Criminal Justice (European Investigation Order) Regulations 2017, § 10(5).
2757 Criminal Justice (European Investigation Order) Regulations 2017, § 6(3)(a).
2758 Interview with Nick Vamos.

to see a case wherein the defendant requested for the issuance of an EIO, the interviewee opines that the defendant is better positioned with the EIO due to its "order" nature.[2759]

3. Execution of Requests

a. Applicable Law on Execution

There was no explicit mention in the Regulations as regards what the applicable law should be in the recognition or execution of an EIO received by the United Kingdom. It would seem however that on the basis of the specific procedures mentioned in the Regulations, the EIO should be executed by the UK in accordance with what has been provided for in the said EIO. For example, this is the case when the EIO refers to receiving evidence from a person, even if the same would entail hearing through telephone conference, or videoconference or other audiovisual transmission. The central authority in this case may nominate a court to receive the evidence for the purpose of giving effect to the EIO, provided that the person is not suspect or accused, or if one, has consented to giving evidence.[2760] However, the central authority must appoint if the person is unwilling to provide evidence in another form and if willing, the issuing state does not agree to receive the evidence in that form.[2761]

Interestingly, it would seem now given the immediately preceding sentence that the UK as an executing state has the possibility of suggesting an alternative form of taking evidence from a person even if the issuing state has provided the investigative measure it needs in the EIO. The judicial authority however must proceed as stated because first, no other grounds for refusal are present, and that the person from whom evidence shall be taken did not consent to any alternative form, or if person did, the issuing state does not want it in any other form as the one stated in the EIO. Stating it differently, even if the EIO is to be followed to the letter by the UK as an executing state, there was an elbow room for another form of taking evidence or investigative measure to be done under certain

---

2759 Interview with Nick Vamos.

2760 Criminal Justice (European Investigation Order) Regulations 2017, §§ 35(2), 36(2), 37(2).

2761 Criminal Justice (European Investigation Order) Regulations 2017, §§ 35(4), 36(4), 37(4).

circumstances. So even if there was no explicit mention that resort can be done to other forms of investigative measures, it can easily be read between the lines. The grounds for refusal mentioned in the Regulations themselves prove this point. The UK may refuse recognition or execution of an EIO if the investigative measure provided therein, for example, does not exist in the law of the relevant part of the UK, or does not apply to a similar domestic case.[2762] One can notice nonetheless that these grounds for refusal could only be invoked if "it appears to the central authority that there is no other investigative measure which would achieve the same result."[2763]

The applicable law could also be discussed in terms of an EIO which additionally requests an authority of the issuing state to assist in the execution of an EIO. This at the outset is generally always allowed unless permitting the same would be contrary to law or harmful to essential national security interests.[2764] Interestingly, once an authority of the issuing state is authorized to assist, certain laws shall have effect as to any liability arising from wrongful acts or omissions committed while executing the EIO: for those authorized by a chief officer of police for a police area in England and Wales, Section 88 of the Police Act 1996; by the Chief Constable of the Police Service of Northern Ireland: Sections 29 and 66 of the Police (Northern Ireland) Act 1998; by the Chief Constable of the Police Service of Scotland, Sections 24 and 90 of the Police and Fire Reform (Scotland) Act 2012; and by the Director of the National Crime Agency, paragraph 2 of Schedule 4 to the Crimes and Courts Act 2013.[2765]

b. Applicable Procedural Rights

i. Importance of Defense Rights; Principle of Equality of Arms

The principle of equality of arms generally applies vis-à-vis procedural rights. Herein procedural rights matter in the execution of the EIO and subject investigative measures. It also applies to the remedies one can take in view of the issuance or execution of an EIO. In light of this,

2762 See Criminal Justice (European Investigation Order) Regulations 2017, § 28.

2763 Criminal Justice (European Investigation Order) Regulations 2017, § 28(1)(b, c).

2764 Criminal Justice (European Investigation Order) Regulations 2017, § 34(2).

2765 Criminal Justice (European Investigation Order) Regulations 2017, § 34(5), (7), (9).

the principle of equality of arms is likewise formally incorporated in the UK legal order through the HRA.[2766] The concept in a predominantly adversarial system such as that of the UK enjoins that both the prosecution and defense should be able to "present their cases at trial by adducing their own evidence and by challenging the arguments of the opponent."[2767] It could also mean that the defense is able to adopt both a reactive and active approach in presenting its case wherein there is "more equality between the defense and its adversities once proceedings have been instituted, as the police have more powers to conduct investigations."[2768]

ii. Human Rights Considerations in Procedures Provided in the Recognition and Execution of an EIO

With the foregoing in mind, human rights elements could be seen on the parameters provided as to how certain investigative measures are to be executed, aside from being taken into account in the grounds to refuse recognition or execution of an EIO. First, in terms of transferring a UK prisoner to another state for purposes of a UK investigation, no transfer could be made if the subject prisoner does not have written consent to the same.[2769] With respect to requesting an EU prisoner to be transferred to the UK, consideration should be given to whether the said person shall consent or likely to consent to being transferred.[2770] At the same time, UK authorities needed to take into consideration the personal circumstances of the person to act on his or her own behalf.[2771] Whatever time spent by the UK prisoner in the executing state shall be counted to be as spent in custody in the place in the UK where the prisoner is liable to be detained pursuant to its sentence or order to which said prisoner is subject.[2772] Further, in relation to EU prisoners, there were safe harbor provisions applicable while said person is in the United Kingdom. This means that said person must not be prosecuted or detained or subjected to any other

2766 *van Wijk*, pp. 151-152.
2767 *van Wijk*, p. 152.
2768 *van Wijk*, p. 152.
2769 Criminal Justice (European Investigation Order) Regulations 2017, § 20(3), § 54(3), § 55(3); *Wilson/Rutherford/Storey, et al.*, p. 451.
2770 Criminal Justice (European Investigation Order) Regulations 2017, § 21(4).
2771 Criminal Justice (European Investigation Order) Regulations 2017, § 20(4), § 54(4).
2772 Criminal Justice (European Investigation Order) Regulations 2017, §§ 24, 57.

restriction of personal liberty in connection to conduct which occurred before the person's departure from the executing state and the same was not indicated in the EIO.[2773] This immunity shall not apply however should the transferred person be released from custody and refuses to leave the UK within a period of 15 days from release, or as said person left, returns to the UK.[2774]

Notwithstanding the specificities of human rights considerations mentioned above, it can be observed that there were aspects in the Regulations that lack mention or consideration of when certain procedural rights could come into play. To elucidate, some of the rights incorporated in UK Law which relate to mutual legal assistance and the application of the EIO involves rights on liberty and security and the right to a fair trial, as enunciated in Articles 5 and 6 of the ECHR and now incorporated in the Human Rights Law 1998. With respect to one's right to a fair trial, one has the right to a "fair and public hearing within a reasonable time by an independent and impartial tribunal established by law."[2775] As a minimum, one would have the right "(1) to be informed promptly, in a language which he understands and in detail, of the nature and cause of the accusation against him; (2) to have adequate time and facilities for the preparation of his offense; (3) to defend himself in person or through legal assistance of his own choosing or, if he has not sufficient means to pay for legal assistance, to be given it free when the interests of just so require; (4) to examine or have examined witnesses against him and to obtain the attendance and examination of witnesses on his behalf under the same conditions as witnesses against him; (5) to have free assistance of an interpreter if he cannot understand or speak the language used in court."[2776] Stating it differently, one should have the right to be informed, the right to adequately prepare for one's defense, the right to defend himself in person or through counsel, the right to confront witnesses against him, and the right to translation or interpretation.

On the basis of these rights, it was not clear when they could be engaged, even if they are said to be taken into account in the EIO Regulations. For example, in taking evidence from a person as a witness,

2773 Criminal Justice (European Investigation Order) Regulations 2017, § 23(2), § 56(2)

2774 Criminal Justice (European Investigation Order) Regulations 2017, § 23(3), (4), § 56(3), (4).

2775 Human Rights Law 1998, Schedule 1, Part 1, art. 6(1).

2776 Human Rights Law 1998, Schedule 1, Part 1, art. 6(3).

expert, suspect, or accused person, or hearing them through telephone, videoconference, or any other audiovisual means, there was no mention in the Regulations on whether one's right to counsel or legal representative would be applicable in such a case. What has been mentioned clearly is that should the person from whom evidence shall be heard or subjected to telephone conference, videoconference or other audiovisual means be a suspect or accused, said person cannot be examined until written consent is secured. There would then be possible scenarios that said person agrees but would be subjected to incriminating questions and issues that might need legal counseling. The same circumstances can apply to any other witness or expert, who might be at risk of being asked incriminating questions themselves. The Regulations is bereft of mentioning said protection.

Another example one can cite is the issuance of search warrants, production orders, and even customer information and account monitoring orders. There was no provision that would allow any interested person to intervene in such cases, or would be allowed to be present in the execution of search and seizures or production orders through himself or on his behalf through counsel. While the Regulations would provide that officers who unlawfully execute or purportedly execute an EIO can be held liable under the relevant laws, there was no clear-cut provision providing a person affected by such investigative measure, such as a suspect or accused, to file the case by himself/herself.

Moreover, one can look into the offense of disclosure should a financial institution or any of its employees disclose without authorization details about the EIO or any request for the issuance of customer information and/or account monitoring orders. One cannot help but inquire if the same unauthorized disclosure equally applied should the receiving end of the information be the person involved.

Based on these accounts, one can observe half-baked provisions vis-à-vis procedural rights considerations, wherein some are already automatically spelled out in the procedures to be undertaken in executing certain investigative measures while in other provisions, one needs to further read the rights into the law. An example of the latter is regarding competencies and compellability of witnesses. Relating the same to making, recognizing, and executing an EIO, this issue is important considering one of the investigative measures covered by an EIO was the taking of evidence from a person either as a witness, expert, suspect, or accused. The Regulations, as earlier noted, was silent as regards the applicability of this issue. Taking the same into account, persons who cannot understand questions and give understandable answers are considered as incompetent witnesses to testify.[2777] At the same time, a witness may refuse or be reluctant to testify but it needs to be determined if said witness is compellable to answer or testify.[2778]

Regarding the same, the basic rule is that all persons can be required to give evidence in criminal proceedings.[2779] Where there is a competent and compellable witness who refuses to attend court to give evidence – which could be the case in the context of an EIO – then a party may apply for the issuance of a witness summons to compel attendance.[2780] A witness who fails to appear in court to give evidence despite receiving a witness summons is liable for arrest and may be brought to court.[2781] One must note however that as regards compellability, the same does not apply to the defendant, who cannot even be compelled to give evidence on behalf of a co-defendant.[2782] The same non-compellability applies to a defendant's spouse or civil partner, who cannot be compelled to testify on behalf of the prosecution or co-defendant, although may be compelled on behalf of the defendant.[2783] An exception to the exception is that the spouse or civil partner cannot be compelled to be a witness on behalf of the defendant when the case involves assault, injury, or threat of injury to the spouse or to a child, wherein it is the legal nature of the offense with which the defendant is charged that determined if it is a specified offense.[2784]

In addition, parameters are also provided should the witness involved be under the age of 18, if the quality of the witness' evidence is likely to be diminished by reason of physical or mental incapacity, if the quality of evidence is likely to be diminished by reason of fear or distress about testifying, or if the witness is a complainant in a case involving a sexual offense.[2785] Before a trial takes place, either the prosecution or defense may apply for a "special measures" direction in relation to the aforementioned witnesses, wherein special measures could entail either of the following:

2777 Youth Justice and Criminal Evidence Act 1999, § 53; *Wilson/Rutherford/Storey, et al.*, p. 449.

2778 *Wilson/Rutherford/Storey, et al.*, p. 449.

2779 *Wilson/Rutherford/Storey, et al.*, p. 449.

2780 Criminal Procedure (Attendance of Witnesses) Act 1965, § 2; *Wilson/Rutherford/Storey, et al.*, p. 449.

2781 *Wilson/Rutherford/Storey, et al.*, p. 450.

2782 Criminal Procedure (Attendance of Witnesses) Act 1965, § 1.

2783 Police and Criminal Evidence Act, § 80; *Wilson/Rutherford/Storey, et al.*, p. 450.

2784 Police and Criminal Evidence Act, § 80(3); R v. A(B) [2012] EWCA Crim. 1529; *Wilson/Rutherford/Storey, et al.*, p. 450.

2785 Youth Justice and Criminal Evidence Act 1999 (as amended), § 16; *Wilson/Rutherford/Storey, et al.*, pp. 450-451.

"(1) screening the witness from defendant; (2) giving of evidence by live link; (3) giving of evidence in private; (4) removal of wigs and gowns; and (5) the playing of pre-recorded interview with the witness to replace examination in chief."[2786] Moreover, the law allows the pre-recording of cross-examination and re-direct examination, as well as examination being done through an intermediary or that the witness be provided the appropriate device to effectuate better communication.[2787] Given these parameters and special considerations given to ordinary witnesses, the same does surprisingly not apply to the defendant himself,[2788] notwithstanding that the European Convention on Human Rights enjoins the principle of equality of arms in such a scenario.[2789] Human rights jurisprudence provided what the legislation lacked however, wherein the inherent powers of the court varies in the manner defendants give evidence to ensure that they are not disadvantaged.[2790]

The abovementioned discussion evinces the need for one to be knowledgeable of the applicable procedural rights that are not necessarily mentioned specifically in the Regulations.

iii. Defendant's Participation in the Recognition or Execution of an EIO

Having mentioned this, a question arises as to the remedy an affected person, such as a suspect or accused person, could avail of vis-à-vis the issuance or execution of an EIO. Generally speaking, redress can be sought with UK courts by virtue of the HRA and one does not necessarily need to go to the European Court of Human Rights for any redress of any contravention of the ECHR.[2791] In other words, human rights obligations on the ECHR level are municipalized through the HRA.[2792]

But then again, specifically reading the Regulations would provide that any person affected by an EIO may make an application before a judicial

2786 Youth Justice and Criminal Evidence Act 1999 (as amended), §§ 23-27; *Wilson/Rutherford/Storey, et al.*, pp. 450-451.

2787 Youth Justice and Criminal Evidence Act 1999 (as amended), §§ 28-29.

2788 See Youth Justice and Criminal Evidence Act 1999, §§ 16, 17.

2789 *Gillespie*, pp. 180,183; *Wilson/Rutherford/Storey, et al.*, p. 451.

2790 R (on application of D) v. Camberwell Green Youth Court [2005] 1 WLR 393; R (on application of C) v. Sevenoaks Youth Court [2009] EWHC 3008.

2791 See *Gillespie*, pp. 152-160.

2792 *Masterman*, p. 907.

authority to revoke or vary the same.[2793] Albeit applicable only on limited grounds based on human rights, defense rights are opined to be strengthened due to the right to apply for a variation or revocation order.[2794] Prior to the EIO Regulations, courts were not involved and thus, the said application was impossible. With the Regulations, judicial review was made possible but according to the interviewees, has yet to be witnessed.

The foregoing can be consequently related to the concept of equality of arms by giving opportunity to the defense to use the EIO mechanism. This was previously absent from cross-border evidence gathering in the UK, when the defense could neither ask foreign authorities directly for evidence to be gathered abroad nor could local authorities act upon a request of a defense lawyer to do so.[2795] At most, the defense could challenge the decision that affects the defendant personally, such as the execution of an EAW for example, as well as being invited to be part of the execution of a request such as examination of witnesses.[2796]

The availability of going to the courts for redress of rights notwithstanding, it is a different question altogether if relief can be availed. There is a caveat that needs to be pointed out however vis-à-vis the municipalization of human rights obligations in the ECHR through the HRA. The HRA instrument itself provides for derogations and reservations on the convention rights. Other than this, how the rights should be properly operationalized is subject to the interpretation of the UK courts under Section 2 HRA.

In line with this, UK courts must also take into account insofar as it may be applicable to proceedings before it, "any judgment, decision, declaration, or advisory opinion of the European Court of Human Rights" as well as the views of the European Commission and Committee of Ministers.[2797] ECHR jurisprudence is not automatically binding but more of persuasive authority to the UK courts. Admittedly, there is some ongoing discussion as regards the degree UK judges must take into account ECHR jurisprudence in their decisions, with some saying it should be followed very closely while some say there should be a more flexible approach.[2798] As it presently stands however, the Supreme Court will feel itself bound

2793 Criminal Justice (European Investigation Order) Regulations 2017, § 10(2)(a).
2794 Interview with Nick Vamos.
2795 *van Wijk*, pp. 158-162.
2796 *van Wijk*, pp. 158-159.
2797 *Dickson*, p. 56.
2798 *Dickson*, p. 57.

to follow Strasbourg jurisprudence when (1) case law seems to suggest that when there has been a recent decision of the Grand Chamber expressly addressing the very issue at point; or (2) where there is a line of Chamber decisions – without any endorsement yet to the Grand Chamber – in which the attitude of the European Court to the very issue has been made clear.[2799] Otherwise, the Supreme Court shall persist in adopting a national approach and seek to justify the same authoritatively.[2800]

In connection to this, several factors or principles play a part in judicial decisions. At the outset, UK courts exercise judicial review in the domestic context– wherein there is deference to the Parliament and the executive over some issues.[2801] Allegedly, this has been extended to HRA 1998 actions, wherein courts shall defer to the executive where there is a "fair balance" between interests of society as a whole and individual's human rights.[2802] There is an ongoing debate however on to which rights the doctrine should apply – whether there should be a distinction among rights or if judicial deference (margin of appreciation in the ECHR context) applies to all rights.[2803] Referring to the ECHR jurisprudence, the margin of appreciation doctrine (which judicial review herein follows) was either applied liberally or restrictively, depending on the right involved.[2804] In a plethora of early cases, the English courts held that rights such as, for example, the right to silence and the privilege against self-incrimination "were not absolute but rather, depending on the degree to which they were violated, and the legitimacy of the goal pursued by doing so, be qualified."[2805]

Another doctrine worth mentioning is the derogation of Convention rights, which finds itself in the Human Rights Act 1998 as well. Like the aforementioned principles of judicial deference and (as stated in the discussion on human rights in substantive provisions) proportionality,

---

2799 *Dickson*, p. 59.

2800 Like in the Horncastle case, when the Court was confronted with the ECHR case of Al-Khawaja and Tahery v. UK, which seemed to undermine gravely the use of hearsay evidence in criminal cases, the seven-judge bench ruled that while the UK court would follow the European Court's decision when they applied clearly established principles, it would not do so where the decision insufficiently takes into consideration particular aspects of UK's domestic legal process. *Dickson*, p. 57.

2801 *Gillespie*, p. 163.

2802 *Gillespie*, p. 163.

2803 *Gillespie*, pp. 163-164.

2804 *Gillespie*, p. 164.

2805 *Booth QC*, p. 7.

derogation ought to be considered because it affects how UK courts would decide on a certain convention right obligation. Derogation – or the non-application of Convention rights – is allowed "in times of war or other public emergency threatening the life of the nation", provided however, that no derogation is allowed for Articles 2, 3, 4(1), and 7, as well as Protocol 1 Article 13.[2806] Finding the same in the UK human rights instrument, ECHR rights find application subject to derogation or reservation and the Secretary of State has the power to issue an order designating any derogation from an article of the ECHR or any of its protocols.[2807]

Courts would therefore take the foregoing into account in the event judicial relief is sought vis-à-vis the EIO. Interests are generally balanced with each other and automatic revocation of an EIO or denial of the same does not automatically follow for an affected person (suspect or otherwise) should his/her rights have been allegedly slighted or affected. It would be a different issue however for rights that are non-negotiable and subject to non-derogation. More stringent application would be applied in these cases.

c. Applicable Time Limits

There were time limits a central authority ought to comply with in recognizing and executing EIO's received from another EU state. At the outset, if one central authority receives an EIO which involves a request for evidence involving another central authority located in another part of the UK, the former is duty bound to forward the said EIO to the relevant UK central authority and notify the issuing authority, or when applicable, the central authority of the issuing state that the EIO has been forwarded.[2808] In relation to this, the applicable central authority must notify the issuing authority, or when appropriate, the central authority of the issuing state to confirm receipt of the EIO.[2809] This shall be without delay and in any case, must be within one week beginning with the day on which the EIO was received.[2810]

2806 See European Convention of Human Rights, art. 15; *Wilson/Rutherford/Storey, et al.*, p. 220.

2807 Human Rights Law 1998, §§ 2, 14(4); *Wilson/Rutherford/Storey, et al.*, p. 220.

2808 Criminal Justice (European Investigation Order) Regulations 2017, § 26(2).

2809 Criminal Justice (European Investigation Order) Regulations 2017, § 26(3).

2810 Criminal Justice (European Investigation Order) Regulations 2017, § 26(4).

Thereafter the central authority must take its decision as soon as possible, and in any case, "before the expiry of the period of 30 days beginning with the day after the day on which the order was received."[2811] It could however happen that it is impossible to take a decision to recognize or execute an EIO because the information provided is insufficient or manifestly incorrect.[2812] In such case, the central authority needed to inform the issuing authority without delay and request that the latter provide the lacking information deemed necessary to make a decision, specifying therewith a reasonable period for the issuing authority to do so.[2813]

In addition to insufficient or incorrect information, there might be other reasons that make it not practicable to comply with the time period to make a decision to recognize or execute the EIO. In such case, the central authority needed to inform without delay the issuing authority of the reasons for the delay and additionally, the central authority should specify a date, "within the period of 60 days beginning with the day after the day on which the EIO was received, by which the central authority expects to have taken its decision."[2814]

In the event that the central authority decided to recognize or execute an EIO it must have ensured that any investigative measure indicated therein is "carried out without delay and with the same celerity and priority as for a similar domestic case, and in any event, before the expiry of the period of 90 days beginning with the day after the day on which the central authority takes it decision on recognition or execution;" provided however that this shall not apply should the investigative measure relate to evidence already possessed by the central authority, or appearing to be in possession of an executing authority.[2815] The same 90-day period is reiterated across the Regulations' provisions in the execution of certain investigative measures, such as receiving evidence from a person, hearing by teleconference or other audiovisual means, etc.[2816]

The Regulations likewise took into consideration incidents when it is not practicable to carry out the investigative measure within the given time period of 90 days. In such case, it must notify the issuing authority

2811 Criminal Justice (European Investigation Order) Regulations 2017, § 30(1).
2812 Criminal Justice (European Investigation Order) Regulations 2017, § 27(1).
2813 Criminal Justice (European Investigation Order) Regulations 2017, § 27(2).
2814 Criminal Justice (European Investigation Order) Regulations 2017, § 30(2).
2815 Criminal Justice (European Investigation Order) Regulations 2017, § 30(3), (4).
2816 Criminal Justice (European Investigation Order) Regulations 2017, §§ 35, 36, 37.

of the reasons for the delay and consult with the latter on the appropriate timing to carry out the investigative measure.[2817]

Additionally, the time limits set out by the Regulations were without prejudice to any extension caused by the postponement of recognition or execution likewise provided for by the Regulations.[2818] The issuing authority was also allowed to propose shorter time limits due to procedural deadlines, the seriousness of the offense, or other particularly urgent matter; or that the investigative measure be conducted on a specified date.[2819] Accordingly, the central authority must take full consideration as much as possible.[2820]

Other than the time limits listed for acknowledgment of receipt of EIO and recognition or execution of the EIO, there was no exact time limit provided in the Regulations as regards transfer of evidence. What the Regulations ordered was that the transfer of either the evidence obtained by executing the EIO or evidence already in possession by the central authority or executing authority should be done without undue delay.[2821] Moreover, any transfer could be suspended should there be a pending incident involving a legal remedy, unless there were sufficient reasons indicated in the EIO requiring that immediate transfer was necessary for the proper conduct of an investigation or proceeding to which the order relates, or for the "preservation of individual rights."[2822] However, a transfer of evidence must be suspended if it appeared that there should be serious and irreversible damage caused to any person affected by the transfer.[2823]

The speed and/or time efficiency required by the Regulations, together with the defense rights they reinforce and the principle of mutual recognition, makes all the difference on practitioner level, according to an interviewee. He opines that speed affects the defense as well in the entire process given that any delay prejudices the defense one way or another. Other interviewees also mentioned the benefits of the structural changes the DEIO introduced. In practice, authorities exert the highest efforts to comply with the time limits provided by the Regulations. Further, they hope that the structural changes would be continuously in place regardless

2817 Criminal Justice (European Investigation Order) Regulations 2017, § 30(5).
2818 Criminal Justice (European Investigation Order) Regulations 2017, § 30(6).
2819 Criminal Justice (European Investigation Order) Regulations 2017, § 30(7).
2820 Criminal Justice (European Investigation Order) Regulations 2017, § 30(7).
2821 Criminal Justice (European Investigation Order) Regulations 2017, § 31(1).
2822 Criminal Justice (European Investigation Order) Regulations 2017, § 31(2).
2823 Criminal Justice (European Investigation Order) Regulations 2017, § 31(3).

of whether Brexit proceeds or not, given the positive results it has made in the UK overall system.

d. Authentication of Documents

The Regulations did not provide for the process of authentication should the issuing state require the same. What the Regulations provide is the need to transmit the EIO to a central authority or executing authority by means capable of producing a written record under conditions that allows the latter to establish authenticity.[2824]

e. Importance of Confidentiality

It seems that confidentiality is important as per the Regulations. To illustrate, any unauthorized disclosure was considered an offense in relation to customer information order and/or account monitoring orders made in the United Kingdom.[2825] Such unauthorized disclosure involves information that a request to obtain customer information and/or account monitoring order or the EIO itself is received; information on an ongoing investigation in relation to the request or order; and/or pursuant to a request or order, information has been given to the authority which made the request or order.[2826] This notwithstanding, the Rules of Court may make provisions as to the practice and procedure to be followed in relation to proceedings under these Regulations.[2827]

f. Return of Documents

It would seem that the return of objects, documents, or evidence requested via an EIO was not compulsory under the Regulations. Under the relevant provision, the transferring authority must indicate "whether it requires the

2824 Criminal Justice (European Investigation Order) Regulations 2017, § 5(3).
2825 Criminal Justice (European Investigation Order) Regulations 2017, § 50(2).
2826 Criminal Justice (European Investigation Order) Regulations 2017, § 50(3).
2827 Criminal Justice (European Investigation Order) Regulations 2017, § 60.

issuing authority to return the evidence as soon as it is no longer required in the issuing state."[2828]

g. Specific Procedures per Type of Assistance

The Regulations provided for additional requirements for certain investigative measures, in addition to the general requirements one must satisfy before an EIO could be made or validated. These additional requirements existed for scenarios when it is the UK which makes the EIO or the one that receives it. In relation to this, the Regulations provided additional requirements for specific investigation measures, may it be that the UK is the issuing state or executing one, such as hearing a person by videoconference or telephone; banking and other financial information; investigative measures requiring gathering of evidence in real time, continuous, or over a certain period of time; covert investigations; provisional measures; interception of telecommunications where technical assistance is required; temporary transfer of UK or EU prisoner to a participating state for the purpose of UK investigation.[2829]

III. Implementation in Member state: Germany

The next portion focuses on Germany as a member state of the European Union. Similar to the flow of discussion made about the United Kingdom, first, a historical development of international cooperation instruments or in particular, mutual legal assistance shall be discussed. Second, there would be a discussion of the different substantive and procedural provisions common to mutual legal assistance in criminal matters and the EIO, wherein certain characteristics or idiosyncrasies can be mentioned.

In connection to this, interviews were also made with German practitioners who are involved in international cooperation, mutual legal assistance, and the EIO. They provided insights as regards their practice and experience vis-à-vis mutual legal assistance and the EIO.

2828 Criminal Justice (European Investigation Order) Regulations 2017, § 31(4).

2829 Criminal Justice (European Investigation Order) Regulations 2017, §§ 14-24, 35-61.

A. Historical Development

1. Bilaterial, Regional, and Multilateral Mutual Legal Assistance

Germany is a signatory to many bilateral, regional, and multilateral mutual legal assistance agreements.

Bilaterally, Germany has agreements on mutual legal assistance in criminal matters with the United States (also data exchange treaty), Canada, Hong Kong, and Tunisia. On the other hand, Germany has a treaty for the transfer of offenders and cooperation in the enforcement of criminal judgments with Thailand and Taiwan.

On a multilateral level, one could look into the agreements within the European Union, Council of Europe, and the United Nations. As regards the Council of Europe for example, one can see that Germany is a signatory to the 1959 European Convention on Extradition and the 1959 European Convention on Mutual Legal Assistance, including its respective protocols. In relation to the latter, Germany has supplementary bilateral treaties with France, Israel, Italy, Netherlands, Austria, Czech Republic and Poland. Moreover, Germany is a signatory to the Budapest Convention on Cybercrime; Convention on Laundering, Search, Seizure, and Confiscation of the Proceeds of Crime; Agreement on Illicit Traffic by Sea, implementing Article 17 of the UN Convention against Illicit Traffic in Narcotic Substances and Psychotropic Substances; European Convention on the Compensation of Victims of Violent Crimes; European Criminal Law Convention on Corruption; European Convention on the International Validity of Criminal Judgments; European Convention on the Transfer of Proceedings in Criminal Matters; Council of Europe Convention on Action against Trafficking in Human Beings; Council of Europe Convention on the Protection of Children against Sexual Exploitation and Sexual Abuse; Council of Europe Convention on Preventing and Combating Violence against Women and Domestic Violence; Council of Europe Convention on the Counterfeiting of Medical Products and Similar Crimes Involving Threats to Public Health.

As regards the United Nations, Germany is a signatory to many conventions or treaties that include elements of international cooperation such as extradition, mutual legal assistance, etc. These include the UN Convention against Illicit Traffic in Narcotic Drugs and Psychotropic Substances; UN Convention against Transnational Organized Crime (including its protocols); International Convention for the Suppression of the Financing of Terrorism; International Convention for the Suppression of Acts of Nuclear Terrorism; UN Convention against Corruption; and the UN Convention on the Law of the Seas; Convention for the Suppression of Unlawful Acts against the Safety of Maritime Navigation.

Within the context of the European Union and with respect to mutual legal assistance, Germany is part of the following: the 2000 MLA Convention, including its 2001 Protocol; 2003 MLA Treaty between the European Union and the United States of America; 2007 Agreement between the European Union and the United States of America on the Processing and Transfer of Passenger Name Record Data by Air Carriers to the United States Department of Homeland Security; 2010 Agreement between the European Union and the United States of America on the Processing and Transfer of Financial Messaging Data from the European Union to the United States for the Purposes of the Terrorist Finance Tracking Program; 2004 Cooperation Agreement between the European Community and its Member States and the Swiss Confederation to Combat Fraud and Any Other Illegal Activity to the Detriment of Their Financial Interests; 2008 Agreement between the European Union and Australia on the Processing and Transfer of EU-sourced Passenger Name Record Data by Air Carriers to the Australian Customs Service; 2010 Agreement between the European Union and Japan on Mutual Legal Assistance in Criminal Matters; Council Framework Decision 2003/577/JHA of 22 July 2003 on the Execution in the European Union of Orders Freezing Property or Evidence; Council Framework Decision 2008/978/JHA of 18 December 2008 on the European Evidence Warrant; Council Framework Decision 2008/829/JHA of 23 October 2009 on the Application, between member states of the European Union, of the Principle of Mutual Recognition to Decisions on Supervision Measures as an Alternative to Provisional Detention; Council Framework Decision 2006/960/JHA of 18 December 2006 on Simplifying the Exchange of Information and Intelligence between Law Enforcement Authorities of the Member States of the European Union; Council Framework Decision 2009/315/JHA of 26 February 2009 on the Organization and Content of the Exchange of Information Extracted from the Criminal Record between Member States; Council Framework Decision 2009/316/JHA of 06 April 2009 on the Establishment of the European Criminal Records Information System ("ECRIS"); Council Framework Decision 2008/977/JHA of 27 November 2008 on the Protection of Personal Data Processed in the Framework of Police and Judicial Cooperation in Criminal Matters, which is now repealed by the Directive (EU) 2016/680 of 27 April 2016 on the protection of natural persons with regard to the processing of personal data by competent authorities for the purposes of the prevention, investigation, detection or prosecution of criminal offences or the execution of criminal penalties, and on the free movement of such data; and the Council Decision 2008/633/JHA of 23 June 2008 Concerning Access for Consultation of the Visa Information System by Designated Authorities of Member States and by Europol for the Purposes of the Prevention, Detection, Investigation of Terrorist Offenses and of other Serious Criminal Offenses.

2. Domestic Legislation on International Cooperation

Germany's governing law on international cooperation is the Act on International Cooperation in Criminal Matters ("AICCM" or Gesetz über die internationale Rechtshilfe in Strafsachen ["IRG"]), which has been last amended on 27 August 2017 (BGBl. I. S. 3295). By virtue of the DEIO and incorporating the EIO in German law, the fourth amendment of the AICCM happened on 05 January 2017.[2830]

B. Substantive Provisions

1. Applicability of Assistance

Three (3) things can be mentioned as regards applicability of assistance.

First, there is the change of nomenclature from being "request based" to being "order-based", which denotes the minimization of discretion to decide on the recognition or execution of an EIO.[2831] According to interviews made with practitioners and experts on this topic, the change of terminology from "request" to "order" is a big step theoretically. However, in practice, there is not much difference between the ordinary MLA request and an EIO.[2832] In fact, it is a common misconception that the EIO would mean automatic recognition or execution due to its terminology.[2833] The principle of mutual recognition has been existing more or

2830 See Act on International Cooperation in Criminal Matters, 1982, Federal Law Gazette I, p. 2071; *Schomburg/Lagodny*, p. 765.

2831 See *Heard/Mansell*, p. 354.

2832 Interview with Christian Schierholt. See also *Schomburg/Lagodny*, p. 766.

2833 Interview with Till Gut.

less in practice even before the EIO became applicable.[2834] Authorities are generally willing to afford each other the assistance required. Furthermore, as one interviewee mentioned, the obligations from MLA treaties and the EIO are similar when applied in practice. Despite the choice of "order" as terminology, there is still more or less discretion in play on whether the EIO received would be recognized or executed.[2835]

Second, it must be mentioned that the AICCM shall generally govern the relations with foreign states regarding legal assistance in criminal matters, which refer to include "proceedings relating from an offense which under German law would constitute a regulatory offense sanctionable by a fine or which pursuant to a foreign law is subject to a similar penalty, provided that a court of criminal jurisdiction determines the sentence."[2836] Provisions of international treaties shall accordingly take precedence over the provisions of the AICCM to the extent that they have become directly applicable national law.[2837] Part 10 of the same AICCM applies to the support in criminal proceedings involving EU member states, including the EIO which is covered by the law's Section 91.[2838] Sections 92 to 92b shall also apply in the context of legal assistance to those States who apply the provisions on the Schengen Acquis on the basis of an association agreement with the European Union on the implementation, application and development of the Schengen Acquis (Schengen-associated States).[2839]

Third, the EIO shall be applicable to both natural and legal persons. In relation to this, the issue of corporate criminal liability arises, which Germany does not have. Due to this, discrepancies may arise as regards how assistance shall apply. According to the interviews made, there would be no issue if the investigative measure subject of the EIO is non-coercive in nature. It would be allowed and executed. However, if coercive measures are involved, then one would need to look into the relevant law to see if the EIO can be executed notwithstanding involving legal persons and the matter is not necessarily a criminal matter in Germany due to the absence of corporate criminal liability.

2834 Interview with Christian Schierholt.
2835 See also *Schomburg/Lagodny*, p. 766.
2836 AICCM, § 1(1, 2).
2837 AICCM, § 1(1, 2).
2838 AICCM, §§ 91-98.
2839 AICCM, § 91(3).

2. Types of Assistance

It could be discerned that the EIO shall be applicable to both coercive and non-coercive measures, wherein measures not specifically mentioned in the sections implementing the DEIO shall be governed by the other applicable provisions of the AICCM.[2840] As an interviewee explained, it involves generally measures between two judicial authorities.[2841] It also does not contemplate for example scenarios wherein prosecutors are involved on one end but police authorities on the other, as well as police to police cooperation.[2842] And another interviewee mentioned that the present law does not use an enumerative list of measures.[2843] However, the EIO shall not apply to the formation and creation of joint investigation teams and any evidence that shall be obtained or secured through the same; cross-border observations; and the interrogations of the accused through telephone conference.[2844]

There are initial difficulties posed by the non-application of the EIO on certain investigative measures, for which practicioners often find solutions. Interviewees were asked in relation to the types of assistance that can be rendered or requested, what would happen if there is an overlap of coverage, wherein an investigative measure is included in the EIO although it is covered by another instrument or law; or situations where it is questionable whether the subject investigative measure is within the penumbra of the EIO (e.g. information exchange, voluntary disclosure of information, cross-border surveillance). In response, interviewees said that as much as possible, they would work with the relevant issuing authority to execute the EIO.[2845] Feedback from most practitioners according to an interviewee would show that they would cover everything being asked for.[2846] Instead of going back and forth with the EIO and any amendments it necessitates to accommodate the investigative measures requested, some believe it is better to execute the EIO concerned.[2847] Some practitioners would also in times of uncertainty communicate with the relevant issuing authority and see possible solutions or measures, if some of those requested investigative

2840 AICCM, § 91a(4).
2841 Interview with Christian Schierholt; Interview with Till Gut.
2842 Interview with Christian Schierholt.
2843 Interview with Till Gut.
2844 AICCM, § 91; *Schomburg/Lagodny*, pp. 773-774.
2845 Interview with Christian Schierholt; Interview with Till Gut.
2846 Interview with Till Gut.
2847 Interview with Till Gut.

measures are not possible through the EIO.[2848] This is a pragmatic measure being used by German authorities to facilitate the execution of EIOs received from other member states.[2849] In line with this, an interviewee mentioned that it only can become tricky when the investigative measure needs to course through the courts and the latter denies the request.[2850]

It is worth mentioning at this juncture that open channels of cooperation exist among authorities, even before the EIO was implemented.[2851] The existence of contact points through the EJN or Eurojust are helpful, as well as the existence of liaison magistrates for example between France and Germany.[2852] In connection to this, some practitioners would draft questions before making an EIO or MLA request. As an interviewee mentioned, it would be inefficient to go to the trouble of drafting an MLA request or EIO only to figure out that it would not work.

3. Compatibility with other Arrangements

The AICCM is silent on the compatibility of other arrangements with the use and implementation of the EIO. It would be safe to say however that the EIO is not mutually exclusive. Being part of the EU Criminal Justice architecture itself, it co-exists with other EU instruments that may be applicable in the investigation and prosecution of crimes. As mentioned already earlier, the EU would have cooperation mechanisms at the police, prosecutor, and judicial level through the existence of the Europol, Eurojust, European Prosecutors' Office, and European Judicial Network. There is also an existing legal framework for exchange of information and intelligence, including that of exchange of information about criminal records, as well as those involving border controls, etc. These are all readily available to German authorities in pursuit of an investigation and/or prosecution of criminal matters. Having said these, what has been previously highly recommended is to initiate contact with German authorities first, especially in high profile cases, to coordinate whether a particular measure is acceptable in German law.[2853] Based on interviews made, when German

2848 Interview with Christian Schierholt.
2849 Interview with Christian Schierholt.
2850 Interview with Till Gut.
2851 Interview with Till Gut. See also *Schomburg/Lagodny*, p. 769.
2852 See Interviews with Christian Schierholt, Till Gut, and Gabriele Launhardt.
2853 *G20*, p. 40.

authorities are on the requesting end, they utilize existing liaison points and other arrangements in fulfillment of their duties.[2854]

4. Principles, Conditions, and Exceptions Applicable

a. Sufficiency of Evidence Requirement

Sufficiency of evidence more or less exists in the German EIO framework. The law provides that judicial authorities in issuing an EIO must use the *pro forma* EIO provided in the DEIO.[2855] The issuing authority must be able to fill in the required information vis-à-vis the investigative measure and/or cross-border transfer of information or evidence stated in the EIO. The information must be sufficient enough to enable the executing authority to be able to decide on whether to recognize or execute the EIO. As illustrated by the EIO form, factual and legal basis ought to be provided. Likewise, the German law underlines the importance of proportionality: when it is an administrative authority making the request, the EIO must be approved by the public prosecutor's office before issuance.[2856] In its decision, one of the things the public prosecutor ought to consider is whether the request complies with the principle of proportionality.[2857] Hence, the facts of the case must be commensurate to the issuance of the EIO.

In connection to this, interviewees stated that there is no exact guide or barometer that determines what is relevant evidence.[2858] The same is determined by the issuing authority.[2859] German authorities follow a continental European approach wherein one does not need to lay down all the facts.[2860] According to an interviewee, the question on "relevance" is more common with Anglo-American countries.[2861] Thus, facts establishing probable cause, for example, only matters when German authorities deal with countries such as the United States of America.[2862] Significantly, there

2854 See for example Interview with Christian Schierholt.
2855 AICMM, § 91j(1).
2856 AICMM, § 91j(1).
2857 AICMM, § 91j(1); RiVASt, § 25(1)(3).
2858 Interview with Christian Schierholt; Interview with Till Gut.
2859 Interview with Christian Schierholt.
2860 Interview with Till Gut.
2861 Interview with Christian Schierholt.
2862 Interview with Till Gut.

are hardly raised questions on whether the investigative measure subject of the EIO is relevant.[2863] In practice, what is more considered as regards the execution of an EIO are three (3) matters: (1) legal provision for the investigative measure concerned is being used only for certain offenses; (2) there is strict or obligatory rule on investigating cases; and (3) mutual legal assistance or execution of EIO only happens if it is proportionate.[2864]

b. Dual Criminality

Generally, the dual criminality requirement shall apply as regards the surrender of objects and search and seizures.[2865] As regards surrender of objects, it could refer to objects that either (1) serve as evidence in foreign proceedings; (2) obtained by the person concerned or accomplice "for or through the offense which a request is based;" (3) obtained by the person concerned or accomplice "through the sale of such object, or as a replacement for it being destroyed, damaged, or taken away, or on the basis of a right accrued to them or as usufruct;" (4) which were created by or used or meant to be used in the commission or preparation of the offense on which the request is based."[2866] Surrender is generally not admissible, unless "the offense on which the request is based contains elements of the actus reus and mens rea of a criminal offense or of an offensepermitting the imposition of a fine under German law or unless mutatis mutandis it would be such an offense in German law."[2867]

With respect to the EIO, the dual criminality requirement does not need to be proven in the following offenses: "(1) participation in a criminal organization; (2) terrorism; (3) trafficking in human beings; (4) sexual exploitation of children and child pornography; (5) illicit trafficking in narcotic drugs and psychotropic substances; (6) illicit trafficking in weapons, munitions and explosives; (7) corruption; (8) fraud, including that affecting the financial interests of the European Union within the meaning of the Convention of 26 July 1995 on the protection of the European Communities' financial interests; (9) laundering of the proceeds of crime; (10) counterfeiting currency, including of the euro;

2863 Interview with Christian Schierholt.
2864 Interview with Christian Schierholt.
2865 AICCM, §§ 66(2)(1), 67(1).
2866 AICCM, § 66(1).
2867 AICCM, § 66(2)(1).

(11) computer-related crime; (12) environmental crime, including illicit trafficking in endangered animal species and in endangered plant species and varieties; (13) facilitation of unauthorized entry and residence; (14) murder, grievous bodily injury; (15) illicit trade in human organs and tissue; (16) kidnapping, illegal restraint and hostage-taking; (17) racism and xenophobia; (18) organized or armed robbery; (19) illicit trafficking in cultural goods, including antiques and works of art; (20) swindling; (21) racketeering and extortion; (22) counterfeiting and piracy of products; (23) forgery of administrative documents and trafficking therein; (24) forgery of means of payment; (25) illicit trafficking in hormonal substances and other growth promoters; (26) illicit trafficking in nuclear or radioactive materials; (27) trafficking in stolen vehicles; (28) rape; (29) arson; (30) crimes within the jurisdiction of the International Criminal Court; (31) unlawful seizure of aircraft/ships; and (32) sabotage."[2868] It is provided however that the double criminality requirement need not be checked in the aforementioned crimes if the same is punishable with a custodial sentence or freedom-restricting sentence of at least three (3) years."[2869] This same non-applicability of dual criminality can also be said as regards searches and seizures.[2870]

In relation to this, it can be mentioned that dual criminality plays an indirect role in limiting and/or refusing execution of an investigative measure subject of the EIO if such investigative measure is limited to a list of offenses to which the offense referred to in the EIO is not part of said list (*Grundsatz für Vergleichbarkeit*).

At this juncture it ought to be clarified that dual criminality does not require 1:1 equivalence of the elements defining the criminal offense in the issuing state and the requested state.[2871] The requirement is sufficiently satisfied when the conduct investigated can be sanctioned with either a criminal penalty or a regulatory fine.[2872]

It must also be mentioned that an EIO regarding the taxes, duties, customs or monetary affairs is allowed even if there would be no equivalent German law providing the same liability or offense subject of the EIO.[2873]

2868 AICCM, § 91b(4); *Schomburg/Lagodny*, pp. 782-784.
2869 AICCM, § 91b(4); *Schomburg/Lagodny*, pp. 782-784.
2870 AICCM, §§ 67(1), 91b(4), 94(1); *Schomburg/Lagodny*, p. 783.
2871 *G20*, p. 39. See in general *Schomburg/Lagodny*, pp. 782-784.
2872 *G20*, p. 39. See in general *Schomburg/Lagodny*, pp. 782-784.
2873 AICCM, §§ 91b(2), 94(1)(2).

In light of the foregoing, interviewees would give the idea that dual criminality is not much an issue in practice. They can generally execute notwithstanding the lack of dual criminality, except in cases wherein coercive measures are involved.

c. Double Jeopardy

The prohibition against double jeopardy is present in the AICCM. Accordingly, the AICCM provides that the EIO can be refused if the person subject of the EIO or legal assistance has been convicted in a state other than the issuing state, and the sentence has already been enforced, is being enforced, or by reason of the law of the sanctioning state can no longer be enforced.[2874] One can note from this provision that the double jeopardy requirement extends not only to convictions made and executed in Germany but also covers EU member states.

The same prohibition of double jeopardy has been mirrored in terms of freezing evidence, wherein the relevant provision provides that the recognition or execution of an EIO can be refused if the subject person under the same act on which the EIO or request was based, had already been judged in a state other than the issuing or requesting state, and said judgment has already been satisfied, about to be satisfied, or by reason of the judging state, cannot be satisfied or executed anymore.[2875]

In light of the foregoing, one must understand that the prohibition on double jeopardy, as enshrined in Article 103 (3) GG, is meant to protect an offender "who has been already punished or finally acquitted, against repeated prosecution and punishment for the same act."[2876] Accordingly, German constitutional law provides that the "first final criminal judgment creates a comprehensive bar to proceedings for any subsequent trial concerning the same fact."[2877] This is however limited to an internal effect within the respective legal order given the autonomy of legal systems.[2878] Due to the need to develop an European area of criminal justice, there was a consequent need to develop a transnationally applicable principle of *ne*

2874 AICCM, § 91e (1) 2.
2875 AICCM, § 94(3).
2876 *Satzger*, p. 148.
2877 *Satzger*, p. 148.
2878 *Satzger*, p. 149.

bis in idem.[2879] This occurred in the regional level through the integration of the provisions stated in Article 54 CISA and the Spasic judgment of the CJEU.[2880]

In relation to this, Germany has taken into account the provisions provided in Article 54 CISA, the CJEU judgments, and the decisions of its courts altogether. The transnationally applicable principle can now be found in the AICCM instrument under Section 91(e)(2) as an optional ground for refusal, when a request may be refused recognition or execution when the subject person has been convicted already in another state other than the requesting or issuing state and the corresponding execution element is met, wherein the judgment has been executed, about to be executed, or by reason of the law of the judging state, can no longer be executed.[2881] Accordingly, Germany based on an EU-legal approach, as the same cannot only affect decisions of German courts regarding grants or refusal of a mutual legal assistance, but also the decisions of other member states, insofar the person concerned will be affected by it.[2882]

Schomburg and Lagodny explain that as an optional ground to refuse recognition or execution of an EIO, the authorization should in principle not be refused if the procedure being carried out in the issuing state is also intended to determine whether a violation of this principle has occurred is present.[2883] In this case, it should not be the responsibility of the German executing authority to clarify (in a possibly complex procedure) whether an infringement has occurred.[2884] Rather, this decision is best left to the issuing authorities in the relevant procedure in the issuing state.[2885] In line with this, the information or evidence to be obtained by the measure for which it is requested can be of crucial importance to whatever decision the issuing authorities will make.[2886] Nonetheless, in cases where one's right against double jeopardy would be clearly affected, then the deferment of any discretion to the issuing authority can be reduced accordingly.[2887]

As to how the principle of *ne bis in idem* is applied in practice, this has been clarified through interviews with German authorities. Accordingly,

2879 *Satzger*, p. 149.
2880 *Schomburg/Lagodny*, p. 793.
2881 *Schomburg/Lagodny*, p. 792.
2882 *Schomburg/Lagodny*, p. 793.
2883 *Schomburg/Lagodny*, p. 793.
2884 *Schomburg/Lagodny*, p. 793.
2885 *Schomburg/Lagodny*, p. 793.
2886 *Schomburg/Lagodny*, p. 793.
2887 *Schomburg/Lagodny*, p. 793.

authorities disclosed that in applying the prohibition on double jeopardy, judicial authorities are given the discretion to decide whether the prohibition could be used to deny an EIO or mutual legal assistance request.[2888] A denial of the EIO or any mutual legal assistance request does not automatically follow should double jeopardy exist.[2889] In assessing whether double jeopardy exists however, an interviewee mentions issues as regards determining whether the execution element is met (as provided in the AICCM). There is uncertainty, for example, on whether an issued EAW or request for extradition prior to the issuance of an EIO, constitutes the execution element pertained to by the law, i.e. first part of executing a sentence or not.[2890] There is no clear-cut determination as regards this question.

In connection hereto, an interviewee mentioned that authorities act under the principle that no crime should go unpunished. There is the principle of mandatory prosecution and this is weighed against the principle of *ne bis in idem*. This could result to simultaneous proceedings in different EU member states concerning the same act or omission, or the same suspect or accused. Often the evidence needed in the German proceedings is found in another member state where similar proceedings are ongoing. This necessitates issuance of numerous EIO's to obtain the evidence or information required. To preempt this scenario or avoid the *ne bis in idem* principle altogether, certain factors are considered on whether to proceed with prosecution or investigation by German authorities. One needs to take into consideration the country where the victims are located, the pieces of evidence and where they could be found, etc.

Furthermore, one considers whether the case can be pursued and is connected to Germany. If there are many factors connected to Germany, then proceedings therein shall be initiated or continued. To illustrate, the interviewee cites a case involving the Mafia. Trial has already commenced in Germany but the accused was later extradited to Italy.[2891] More factors are connected to Italy thus deference was given to the proceedings there. However, since there is no legal basis to stop proceedings in Germany once a case started in another country, the trial proceedings in Germany only

2888 Interview with Till Gut.

2889 Interview with Till Gut.

2890 Interview with Christian Schierholt; see for explanation on the conviction element is in the principle of mutual recognition, *Schomburg/Lagodny*, p. 793.

2891 Interview with Christian Schierholt.

ended upon the cessation of trial proceedings in Italy by virtue of double jeopardy.

d. Substantive Considerations of Human Rights

i. Human Rights as a Ground to Refuse Recognition or Execution of an EIO

Human rights are considered and integrated in the AICCM substantive provisions vis-à-vis the EIO. At the outset, it is present as a basis to refuse recognition or execution of an EIO in five (5) instances. First, double jeopardy or the principle of *ne bis in idem*, as mentioned above, may be used to refuse recognition or execution of an EIO.

Second, consent of the person to be examined or transferred for foreign proceedings is a primordial consideration. Audiovisual examination as provided in Section 91(c) vis-à-vis Section 61c of the AICCM or temporary transfer from foreign country for foreign proceedings to Germany under Section 91(c)(3) vis-a-vis Section 62(1), respectively, shall not be allowed if the person to be examined refuses to give consent to the same.

Third, human right considerations are a factor likewise in the denial of requests involving the transmission of personal data information in relation to the Framework Decision on information and intelligence exchange between law enforcement authorities in the EU member states. Transmission of data is prohibited if the same would be disproportionate or unnecessary for the purposes for which they are to be transmitted.[2892]

Fourth, any request shall be denied if the same shall put the body, life, freedom of a person in danger.[2893]

Fifth, there is also the prohibition on recognition or execution of an EIO if there are reasonable grounds to believe that the investigative measure shall make Germany liable under Article 6 of the European Convention on Human Rights and the Charter of Fundamental Rights of the EU.[2894] This coincides with the limitation on assistance should the same conflict with the basic principles of the German legal system.[2895]

2892 AICCM, § 92(3).
2893 AICCM, § 92(4).
2894 AICCM, § 91b(2).
2895 AICCM, § 73.

Article 6 of the European Convention on Human Rights refers to one's right to a fair trial. Said right is found in the German Constitution under Article 103 as follows: "(1) in the courts every person shall be entitled to a hearing in accordance with law; (2) an act may be punished only if it was defined by a law as a criminal offense before the act was committed; and (3) no person may be punished for the same act more than once under the general criminal laws."[2896] Under one's right to fair trial, one can find the right also not to be punished by an *ex post facto* law and the abovementioned rule on *ne bis in idem*. In the same vein, the German Constitution also provides for rights as regards deprivation of liberty, wherein the liberty of a person may only be restricted pursuant to a formal law and in compliance with the prescribed procedures.[2897] Persons in custody may not be subjected to physical or mental maltreatment.[2898] Coincidentally, the Federal Constitution provides that it would be the judge who determines the permissibility and continuation of any deprivation of liberty in the sense that if deprivation was not in accordance with any judicial order, said judicial order must be obtained without delay.[2899] The same applies to persons provisionally detained for being suspected of committing an offense.[2900] In any event, a relative or person enjoying the confidence of the person taken into custody shall be notified without delay of any judicial decision imposing or continuing a deprivation of liberty.[2901] Aside from one's right to fair trial and on deprivation of liberty, the German Federal Constitution further gives guarantees in respect of the criminal process one's right to life and bodily integrity,[2902] inviolability of the home,[2903] prohibition of maltreatment of prisoners and detainees,[2904] freedom of movement,[2905] as well as the right to secrecy of communication.[2906]

2896 German Constitution, art. 103. For the applicability of the German Constitution or Basic Law in EIO proceedings, one can refer to the commentary in *Schomburg/Lagodny*, pp. 468-477.
2897 German Constitution, art. 104(1).
2898 German Constitution, art. 104(1).
2899 German Constitution, art. 104(2).
2900 German Constitution, art. 104(3).
2901 German Constitution, art. 104(4).
2902 German Constitution, art. 2.
2903 German Constitution, art. 13.
2904 German Constitution, art. 104.
2905 German Constitution, art. 2, § 2(2).
2906 German Constitution, art. 10.

ii. Applicable Human Rights Obligations vis-à-vis Ground for refusal

Anent the human rights obligations provided under the CFR, one can look into for example the obligation to the right to human dignity (Article 1), right of life vis-à-vis the death penalty (Article 2), the prohibition against torture and other cruel, inhumane or degrading punishment or treatment (Article 4), non-discrimination (Article 21), among others. The CFR accordingly provides the extraterritorial application of the right to life and prohibition of torture or inhumane or degrading punishment or treatment in Article 19 CFR wherein a member state is not allowed to remove, expel or extradite anyone to another state where there is a serious risk that he or she would be subjected to the death penalty, torture or other inhuman or degrading treatment or punishment.

Applying these human rights obligations to the context of the ground for refusal stated above, German authorities are obliged to deny recognition or execution of an EIO if the same involves an *ex post facto* law (the criminal offense was defined after the act or omission occurred) because German authorities would otherwise violate their obligation vis-à-vis rights to fair trial. Denial is also in order in cases where it is apparent that the EIO was only issued for purposes of discrimination against the subject person. As regards the prohibition of inhumane and degrading treatment or punishment, there is reason for denial if, for example, the investigative measure being sought is transfer of persons in custody to give assistance or information, and the said person shall be exposed to inhumane or degrading facilities and/or treatment.

In connection to the abovementioned, there is as well the well-ingrained principle of proportionality in the German legal order which finds great significance in criminal law.[2907] An important principle of constitutional law that was eventually developed through jurisprudence of the Constitutional Court, proportionality is said to be complied with as regards any measure that interferes with fundamental rights as long as the following conditions are met: "(1) it has to be based upon a legitimate purpose; (2) it must be suitable; (3) necessary; and (4) adequate (proportionate in the strict or narrower sense) to that end."[2908]

As regards criminal law, the Federal Constitutional Court has been able to develop yardsticks specifically applicable: on one hand, the principle of proportionality in respect of substantive criminal law mainly applies

2907 See *Albers/Beauvais/Bohnert, et al.*, pp. 213, 215.

2908 *Albers/Beauvais/Bohnert, et al.*, pp. 213-214.

to *Schuldprinzip*, wherein personal guilt and blameworthiness are determinants of liability and punishment, as well as to a necessary restrictive interpretation of elements of a crime; on the other hand, the principle of proportionality in procedural criminal law limits the ordering, enforcement, and duration of intrusive measures, such as remand detention, bodily intrusions, searches and seizures.[2909] In other words, one can see a balancing of interests with said principle.

Applying it to the German criminal justice system, the principle of mandatory prosecution ("*Legalitätsprinzip*"), which, although contemplates many exceptions ("*Opportunitätsprinzip*") that gives prosecutors elbow room to exercise discretion such as not pursuing minor cases, always need to adhere to the proportionality principle.[2910] The same rings true for the use of intrusive measures, where some provisions call out the need to assess if less intrusive measures are available, and that courts and law enforcement authorities need to always do a proportionality check on the use of the same; otherwise, any violation could lead to rendering evidence as inadmissible in trial.[2911]

It is imperative with how the EIO shall be operationalized given that proportionality is a constitutional principle and thus must apply to investigative measures contemplated in an issued or received EIO.[2912] The relevant AICCM provision notably provides that the procedural safeguards in domestic criminal proceedings equally apply.[2913] Furthermore, no less than the guidelines on international cooperation in criminal matters (*Richtlinien für den Verkehr mit dem Ausland in strafrechtlichen Angelegenheiten*), together with other parameters, provide that "mutual legal assistance is subject to the principle of proportionality."[2914] Hence, now it becomes clear that with respect to the EIO, it is important to take into consideration and follow accordingly the constitutional principle of proportionality. This applies to both incoming and outgoing EIO's.

2909 *Albers/Beauvais/Bohnert, et al.*, p. 215.

2910 *Albers/Beauvais/Bohnert, et al.*, p. 217.

2911 *Albers/Beauvais/Bohnert, et al.*, pp. 217-218.

2912 See *Albers/Beauvais/Bohnert, et al.*, p. 220.

2913 AICCM, § 91e(1). See also for applicability of procedural safeguards for domestic proceedings to the EAW *Albers/Beauvais/Bohnert, et al.*, p. 249.

2914 *Albers/Beauvais/Bohnert, et al.*, p. 220.

e. Reciprocity

The principle of reciprocity is generally applicable in Germany with respect to extradition. It is less applicable with respect to mutual legal assistance wherein Germany can provide MLA either based on treaty or non-treaty basis.[2915] Execution or recognition of incoming MLA requests without bilateral or multilateral agreements is allowed as long as the essential principles of German law are not violated.[2916] Specifically, Section 76 gives the assurance of reciprocity, when it mentions that in connection with German requests for legal assistance, a foreign state may be given an assurance that requests made by it shall be honored to the extent it would not be in conflict with the AICCM.[2917]

Given the abovementioned, an interviewee opined that the principle of reciprocity does not exist any longer due to the principle of mutual recognition.[2918] A closer look however would show that reciprocity more or less still exists in the German law as regards the EIO.

In previous chapters an argument was forwarded that the principle of mutual recognition distorts, if not completely removes, the principle of reciprocity on both procedural and substantive aspects. There is distortion through the lack of executive discretion to determine whether to deny or approve an EIO. There is likewise the apparent absence of prerogative on the part of an executing authority to determine the adequacy, necessity, or proportionality of an EIO. This remains a one-sided responsibility on the part of the issuing authority. That being said, Germany has on mostly a substantive level retained the rudiments of the reciprocity principle.[2919]

On a procedural aspect, German law provides the exchange of EIO's to be directly made between executive and issuing authorities. There is no central authorities to speak of with respect to the EIO, as explained earlier. Notwithstanding the fact that the executing and issuing authorities are mostly judicial authorities, in the German context exercise of executive discretion still exists.

In relation to Articles 1 and 2 of the DEIO, German law applies in general Article 32, para. 1 of the German Constitution, which states that

---

2915 *G20*, p. 39.

2916 *G20*, p. 39.

2917 AICCM, § 76.

2918 Interview with Till Gut.

2919 See for discussion of how mutual recognition in criminal matters distorts or removes reciprocity *Nilsson*, p. 57; *van der Wilt*, pp. 76-81.

relations with foreign states shall be conducted by the Federation. Accordingly, Section 74 (2) of the AICMM in connection with the agreement of exercise of jurisdiction (*"Zuständigkeitsvereinbarung"*) of 28 April 2004 between the German federal and state governments provides that the German federal government delegates its power to decide, with certain exceptions, on foreign requests for legal assistance and to request foreign state for legal assistance to the state governments.[2920] This power to request and decide on requests for legal assistance is then typically conferred by the state governments to the German public prosecutor's offices and to the courts; and henceforth it would be the public prosecutor's offices that usually act as recognition and execution authorities (*"Bewilligungs- und Ausführungsbehörde"*).[2921] Based on this, notwithstanding the lack of central authorities in respect to Germany (with direct contacts between judicial authorities being practiced), it would not be accurate to state that reciprocity on a procedural aspect has been abrogated due to lack of executive discretion.[2922] Executive discretion still exists albeit conferred and/or delegated to the judicial authorities themselves.

Having mentioned this, the fundamental aspects of reciprocity can be seen on the substantive aspect of cooperation. At the outset, Germany was one of the EU member states which did not automatically transpose the principle of mutual recognition completely as seen on how it implemented instruments with mutual recognition elements in their respective domestic laws.[2923] Germany is an example, wherein its Federal Constitutional Court held previously that the first German Act on the Implementation of the European Arrest Warrant ("EuHbG"), which integrated the Framework Decision on the EAW on its entirety, was unconstitutional and violated certain fundamental rights.[2924] Accordingly, the decision cited that the constitutional right that nationals should not be extradited was violated, wherein the said right is subject to reservation allowing extradition of Germans inside the EU or to an international court as long as fundamental constitutional principles are upheld.[2925] There ought to be consideration as a ground for refusal of those crimes with a "significant domestic factor" to protect the fundamental right against extradition. As the Court elucidated,

2920 *Schomburg/Lagodny*, p. 522.
2921 See in general *Schomburg/Lagodny*, pp. 521-526, 767. See also AICMM, § 91(d), para. 1, § 91(j), para. 2 to 4; RiVASt, §§ 7, 22, 27.
2922 See *Nilsson*, p. 57; *van der Wilt*, p. 77.
2923 *Satzger*, pp. 141-142.
2924 *Satzger*, p. 142.
2925 *Satzger*, p. 142.

the cooperation placed into practice in the third pillar of the EU as regards police and judicial cooperation in criminal matters in the shape of limited mutual recognition is a way of preserving national identity and statehood in a single European judicial area, particularly in accordance with the principle of subsidiarity.[2926] The German Constitutional Court believes that the principle of mutual recognition improves international cooperation in criminal matters but it cannot be without any limitations.[2927]

Furthermore, the Court held that the first implementing law was a violation of Article 19(4) – or the general right of access to courts – due to the lack of judicial review in Germany of the grant of extradition under the EuHbG.[2928] In light of this, a new EuHbG entered into force which took into account all of the Constitutional Court's findings such as integrating the reservation of a "significant domestic connecting factor."[2929]

Further, while the DEIO says that the EIO cannot be refused recognition or execution on the ground that there are reasonable grounds to believe that the EIO is not necessary, adequate, and proportional, German authorities cannot comply with the same as otherwise, it would be a violation of German fundamental principles. Accordingly, German law provides that not only can an EIO be denied recognition or execution if there are reasonable reasons to believe that the same shall cause Germany to violate its obligations under the ECHR or Charter of Fundamental Rights, but also when the same is violative of the fundamental principles of the country. Proportionality is a constitutional principle that all authorities, regardless of executive, judiciary, or legislative, should comply with and integrate into their decisions and actions. Any finding that this has not been complied with leads to negative consequences. As such, in the event that there is no proportionality in an EIO, German authorities ought to deny recognition or execution, or otherwise communicate with the relevant issuing authority about the same. Further, the requirement of dual criminality, which is inherent in the concept of reciprocity together with speciality, under German law on the EIO still applies albeit with qualifications that it shall not apply to offenses included in the list of offenses provided above.

Given these provisions that authorities ought to comply with, interviews with authorities reveal that should there be conflict, the resolution of the issue would depend on the receiving authority. Accordingly, should

2926 *Satzger*, p. 142; *Wahl*, p. 117.
2927 *Wahl*, p. 117.
2928 *Satzger*, p. 143.
2929 *Satzger*, p. 143.

the matter reach the German courts, the German courts would apply the national law in settling the same.

Based on the foregoing, it can be said that while the principle of mutual recognition in criminal matters is commonly believed to replace the principle of reciprocity, the German domestic law and principles themselves provide the buffer to not forego the same altogether. This matters on the substantive level wherein German authorities are mandated to consider proportionality among other things, if they are executing authorities.

f. Speciality or Use Limitation

Previously, the G20 guide on mutual legal assistance provided that generally, evidence that Germany provides may only be used for the specific purpose stated in the request.[2930] The exception is, as the G20 guide provides, when there is a special regulation stated in the subject bilateral or multilateral agreement that foregoes the use limitation.[2931] This more or less still applies in the context of the EIO. To illustrate, one could look into Bundesdatenschutzgesetz or the Federal Data Protection Act ("BDSG") on the processing of personal data and the implementing German law on Regulation (EU) 2016/679 and Directive (EU) 2016/680, the latter of which relates to the "processing of personal data by public bodies competent for the prevention, investigation, detection or prosecution of criminal or administrative offences or the execution of criminal or administrative penalties, as far as they process data for the purpose of carrying out these tasks," as well as the protection against and prevention of threats to public security."[2932]

Public bodies in general shall only be permitted to process personal data for the purpose for which it was collected and could only process the same for other purposes if it is necessary for public bodies to perform their duties and if certain conditions are further met.[2933] In case of criminal matters, processing for other purposes is only allowed if it is still within the purposes of criminal matters (as defined in Section 45 of the law) and the processing is necessary and proportionate to the purpose.[2934]

2930 *G20*, p. 42.
2931 *G20*, p. 42.
2932 Federal Data Protection Act, Section 45.
2933 Federal Data Protection Act, Section 23.
2934 Federal Data Protection Act, Section 49.

Moreover, Section 25 of the same law provides that the "transfer of personal data by public bodies to public bodies shall be permitted if it is necessary for the transferring body or the third party to whom the data are transferred to perform their duties and the conditions are met which would permit processing."[2935] The provisions continue to provide that "the third party to whom the data are transferred shall process the transferred data only for the purpose for which they were transferred."[2936] Furthermore, the law provides the parameters and conditions that must be met in cases of transfer of data to third countries and to international organizations,[2937] including the consent of the member state from which the personal data or information originally came from.[2938] Transfers ought to be made with appropriate safeguards,[2939] and in the absence of which, certain conditions are still ought to be complied with.[2940]

Additionally, certain principles for data processing vis-à-vis criminal matters and rights of the data subject ought to be respected and protected at all times.[2941] Rights specifically referring to processing of personal data in the context of criminal matters is likewise provided for.[2942]

The aforementioned parameters are consistent with other forms of cooperation Germany implements. To elucidate, information, including personal data, transmitted under Framework Decision on information and intelligence exchange between law enforcement authorities in the EU member states may only be used for purposes for which it was transmitted or to counter a current or significant public security risk.[2943] Any other use shall only be allowed upon consent of the executing or requested state and under conditions the same may determine.[2944]

As to how this is operationalized in practice, practitioners have mentioned in interviews that they would appreciate that should the evidence transmitted or given by virtue of a MLA request or EIO be used for another criminal matter, a short request be forwarded to them again re-

2935 Federal Data Protection Act, Section 23.
2936 Federal Data Protection Act, Section 23.
2937 Federal Data Protection Act, Section 78.
2938 Federal Data Protection Act, Section 78(3).
2939 Federal Data Protection Act, Section 79.
2940 Federal Data Protection Act, Section 80.
2941 Federal Data Protection Act, Sections 32-37.
2942 Federal Data Protection Act, Sections 47, 55-60.
2943 AICCM, § 92b.
2944 AICCM, § 92b.

garding the same.[2945] The same courtesy shall be given should German authorities be the issuing or requesting state. As to why another request is important, one interviewee explained that there is the possibility that the requirements shall be satisfied for one criminal matter may not be satisfied with another, for which the evidence transmitted or requested may also applicable. Thus, it is important to ensure that requirements are once again satisfied before any permission of using the evidence for another criminal matter is given.

g. Special Offenses or National Interest Cases

One can notice that there are grounds to refuse recognition or execution of an EIO, which are more or less based on special offenses or national interest or public order. First, there is the reason to refuse recognition or execution when the same is in conflict with principles of the German legal system, which, as mentioned in the immediately preceding section, goes hand-in-hand with a human rights-based ground for refusal of being in conflict with Article 6 ECHR and the Charter of Fundamental Rights.[2946] These principles could be found mainly in Articles 1, 20, and 20a of the German Federal Constitution and are accordingly protected against legal changes by Article 79 III of the same Constitution. One can take note that proportionality is one of the principles mentioned, which has been previously discussed above.

Second, the EIO or any request for assistance may not be recognized or executed if the same would compromise essential security interests, endanger sources of information, or require the use of classified information on specific intelligence activities.[2947] The same ground for refusal is also proferred as regards transmission of personal data by virtue of the Framework Decision on information exchange and intelligence between law enforcement authorities of the member states of the EU (so-called Swedish Initiative), wherein transmission of personal data shall not be allowed if the same shall compromise or impair essential security interests.[2948]

2945 Interview with Till Gut.
2946 AICCM, §§ 73, 91b(3).
2947 AICCM, § 91e(1)(2).
2948 AICCM, § 92(3); *Schomburg/Lagodny*, p. 792.

A refusal can be highly expected if essential security interests are endangered.[2949] Depending on the weight of the allegation on which the foreign proceedings are based, recognition or execution could also be considered especially if the threat to national security interests cannot be ruled out with certainty.[2950] Additionally, it is checked whether the risk can be mitigated or removed altogether through agreements with the issuing authority, e.g confidentiality of the findings.[2951] The same applies if the classified information from intelligence sources has to be used in processing the EIO.[2952] Interestingly, compromising essential security interests and requiring use of classified information on specific intelligence activities, in practice, is seldom used as a ground to refuse recognition or execution of an EIO, except in terrorism accounts.[2953]

In respect to endangering sources of information, this plays a huge role in practice especially in criminal proceedings involving organized crime as the same involves a transborder dimension.[2954] Hence, the Regulation serves the purpose of protecting sources either through the possibility of privileged information ("*Vertraulichkeitszusage*") or blocking declaration ("*Sperrerklärung*") in accordance with Section 96 of the Code of Criminal Procedure.[2955] Having said this, weighing of interests is done in practice through considering other investigative measures that could also meet the same result or obtain the needed information or evidence.[2956]

Third, in facilitating or effectuating legal assistance in general, which includes an EIO, it can only be provided "in those cases which German courts and executive authorities could render mutual legal assistance to each other,"[2957] which includes but not limited to, information on accounts held with a financial institution; information about individual account transactions or other transactions made in connection with an account; investigations for a certain duration, specifically requests for information on monitoring of individual account transactions, execution of controlled deliveries, use of undercover agents, and the surveillance of

2949 *Schomburg/Lagodny*, p. 792.
2950 *Schomburg/Lagodny*, p. 792.
2951 *Schomburg/Lagodny*, p. 792.
2952 *Schomburg/Lagodny*, p. 792.
2953 *Schomburg/Lagodny*, p. 792.
2954 *Schomburg/Lagodny*, p. 793.
2955 *Schomburg/Lagodny*, p. 793.
2956 *Schomburg/Lagodny*, p. 793.
2957 See AICCM, § 59(3); see also AICCM, § 91c(2).

telecommunication.[2958] In connection to this, the AICCM authorizes the use of another (if sometimes, less intrusive) investigative measure other than that indicated in the EIO if the same results can be obtained.[2959] Another investigative measure could also be used if the investigative measure indicated in the EIO or request does not exist in German law or the same is inapplicable in a similar domestic case.[2960] In any event, before any resort can be made to another investigative measure, the issuing or requesting state ought to be informed priorly.[2961]

Fourth, an EIO or any legal assistance in general, may be refused if the act(s) subject of the offense on which the EIO or legal assistance is based did not occur in the territory of the issuing state but partly within the German territorial jurisdiction, and the same is neither a criminal offense with punishment nor administrative offense with fine in German criminal law.[2962] Notably, German policy considers this territoriality clause compatible with the principle of mutual recognition,[2963] although said application of territoriality admittedly was not taken into account by German legislators in the EAW in the beginning.[2964] It finds itself now present in the AICCM as amended by virtue of the DEIO, which consequently allows "states to allocate prosecution to the best country which the seriousness of the offenses can be best assessed."[2965]

It bears mentioning likewise that in a previous paper tackling the same clause in its application in the EAW, it was noted that prosecutors and judges seem to apply this carefully and its application is not as big in practice as it was expected.[2966] Some adopt the view that possibilities to conduct own preliminary proceedings in Germany should not be stumbling blocks to the obligation to hinder extradition.[2967] Conversely, some case law acknowledges the possible hindrance caused if a case demands prosecution under German jurisdiction since the prosecutor must initiate prosecution under the principle of mandatory jurisdiction.[2968] In such

2958 AICCM § 91c(2).
2959 AICCM, § 91f(1).
2960 AICCM, § 91e(3).
2961 AICCM, § 91f(3), (5).
2962 AICCM, § 91e(3); *Schomburg/Lagodny*, p. 793.
2963 *Schomburg/Lagodny*, p. 793.
2964 See *Wahl*, p. 127.
2965 *Wahl*, p. 127.
2966 *Wahl*, pp. 127-128.
2967 *Wahl*, p. 128.
2968 *Wahl*, p. 128.

case, it is irrelevant whether formal proceedings have been initiated when the EAW was received, but rather, the facts of the EAW provides the basis for the proceedings.[2969] Nonetheless, clashes based on jurisdiction rarely happen in practice: interviewed practitioners did not feel the urge to initiate proceedings just to deny execution of an EAW.[2970]

With that being said, the fifth instance wherein national interests could be said to play a role is when the investigative measure indicated in the EIO is limited to certain offenses, and the offense subject of the EIO is not included as one of them.[2971] Sixth, recognition or execution of an EIO is not allowed if it violates diplomatic or consular immunity in accordance with the Vienna Convention on Diplomatic Relations and Vienna Convention on Consular Relations, respectively.[2972] Additionally, national interest plays a role in the request for the use of undercover agents wherein it may be refused recognition or execution if there is no agreement with respect to the duration of the operations, the precise conditions, and status of the investigators.[2973]

In addition to the abovementioned, national interest can also form the basis of asking the deferment of executing an EIO or any legal assistance: when the same could interfere with ongoing criminal investigations or the evidence requested is already being used in another procedure.[2974] One must note however, that should there be any postponement, the duration of the postponement should be specified and communicated duly to the issuing or requesting state.[2975] In relation to ongoing criminal investigation as a reason to postpone, one must note however that in respect to transmission of personal data information, the request shall be refused should it compromise the success of an ongoing investigation.[2976]

2969 *Wahl*, p. 128.
2970 *Wahl*, p. 128.
2971 AICCM, § 91b(1)(1).
2972 AICCM, § 91b(1)(2)(b).
2973 AICCM, § 91e(1)(5).
2974 AICCM, § 91e(2).
2975 AICCM, § 91e(4).
2976 AICCM, § 92(4).

C. Procedural Provisions

1. Designation of Central Authority

In Germany, the issuing authorities are the same authorities authorized to receive and execute an EIO. These authorities are as follows: "(1) any judicial authority (Federal Prosecutor General of the Federal Court of Justice, the prosecutor's offices, the prosecutor general's offices, the central authority in Ludwigsburg [for the investigation of National Socialist crimes], any criminal court) depending on the allocation of competences."[2977] Also, administrative authorities may also be issuing and executing authorities for prosecuting and punishing administrative offences. As regards independently conducted criminal investigations pursuant to section 386 (2) Tax Code, German fiscal authorities do not require validation by a judicial authority or a court.[2978] In the scenario that the fiscal authorities exercise the rights and responsibilities of a prosecutor's office in accordance with section 399 (1) Tax Code in conjunction with section 77 (1) of the Act on International Cooperation in Criminal Matters and themselves act as judicial authority within the meaning of article 2(c) EIO directive.

With respect to the designation of issuing and executing authorities, interviewees mentioned that it is more time-intensive if there are no direct contacts. Other than the issue of time, there is not much difference in dealing with vertical or horizontal cooperation, or coursing through central authorities in some jurisdictions. Interviewees understand as well that in some jurisdictions, while having direct contacts is more favorable, central authorities are retained in general due to the difference in criminal justice systems or architecture.

Moreover, an issue was mentioned in the interviews as regards the designation of issuing and executing authorities for the EIO. Interviewees mentioned the problem with the list Germany provided. Whilst under German domestic law, some authorities are considered "judicial authorities", they are not "judicial authorities" as contemplated in the DEIO. This leads to problems as regards EIOs issued by said "judicial authorities" and problems as to whether the same can be executed or not. Some member

2977 See Notification of the transposition of Directive 2014/41/EU by Germany, pp. 1-4.

2978 See Notification of the transposition of Directive 2014/41/EU by Germany, pp. 1-4.

states are more receptive than others. So according to the interviews, it would be dependent on the receiving authority.

2. Preparation of Requests

a. Requisites for the Request/EIO

At this juncture it must be mentioned that as regards when Germany is the issuing state, there was apparently a mixed response to the *pro forma* EIO that ought to be filled up when issuing one. According to one interviewee, there has been complaints from veteran MLA authorities because the relevant forms are too cumbersome and complex.[2979] Further, there is feedback that some practitioners felt constrained due to the forms.[2980] Comparing to the EAW, which is more concise as it involved only one (1) measure, the EIO form contains too many pages and too many measures, when generally, 80% of EIOs sent involve only witness statements and search and seizures.[2981]

Furthermore, with a MLA request before, it sufficed to send a letter plus an enclosed warrant.[2982] However, with the *pro forma* EIO, the same would not suffice any longer.[2983] Thus, the form may not be helpful especially in urgent cases. As illustrated by another interviewee, there was a witness that was flying from Madrid to Latin America and it was urgent to get the statement from said witness.[2984] Following the procedure laid down for the EIO, the authorities would not make it in time.[2985] Therefore, arrangements were made with the Madrid authorities to be able to secure the needed witness statement such as police cooperation, communicating through email, etc., which strictly speaking are against the requirements

2979 Interview with Till Gut.

2980 Interview with Till Gut. Prior to the prescribed form of the EIO, practice involves sending written requests, which would be sent with original papers; and in cases of urgent matters, there is the possibility to send the request by fax, email, or through phone. See RiVASt §§ 8, 10, 27(1).

2981 Interview with Till Gut.

2982 Interview with Till Gut.

2983 Interview with Till Gut; See for formal requirement to use the pro-forma EIO, AICCM, § 91(d)(1), (3).

2984 Interview with Christian Schierholt.

2985 Interview with Christian Schierholt.

for the preparation and issuance of an EIO.[2986] In other instances, there would be the possibility of sending the request already and send the EIO afterwards but this, according to the interviewee, would be dependent on the receiving end of the EIO.[2987] Stating it simply, practitioners needed to innovate to overcome stumbling blocks that the EIO procedural requirements presented during urgent cases. In light of the problems encountered such as the aforementioned, an interviewee mentioned that it might be a good idea to revise the certificates and forms.

On the other hand, there would be some practitioners who appreciate the *pro forma* EIO, especially those who are new to MLA practice.[2988] Moreover, the *pro forma* EIO is beneficial for those who are at the receiving end of the EIO.[2989] Previously, it has been diversified and the same posed sometimes problems for practitioners who needed to execute a request.[2990]

Another requirement ought to be satisfied in the preparation of requests to Germany is a German translation.[2991] Outgoing requests or EIOs on the other hand require that it be in the official language of the country concerned. Failure to include the required translation can be considered "incomplete" in the meaning of Article 16, paragraph 2 of the DEIO. This language requirement poses a problem sometimes for German authorities, especially in urgent cases that need to be dealt with. Although they may have readily made translations for the common types of EIOs, translation in general requires time and effort. The same could affect the efficiency of the entire process. Some interviewees were of the opinion that the language requirement should not be a hard and fast rule given that most EU member states are perfectly comfortable in using the English language.

In addition to the foregoing, Germany has additional requirements vis-à-vis an EIO involving transit of a person in custody. Based on the provisions of its national law, Germany likewise requires the following documents : "(1) the document which forms basis for the detention in the executing state, as this is the basis for the German arrest warrant; (2) a document stating that a temporary transfer will be recognized and enforced by the executing state, as Germany will only act as a transit state provided there is such recognition; (3) a document calculating the period of detention, since

2986 Interview with Christian Schierholt.
2987 Interview with Christian Schierholt.
2988 Interview with Till Gut.
2989 Interview with Till Gut.
2990 Interview with Till Gut.
2991 See EIO Form; *G20*, p. 42.

if the detention period has exceeded the person in custody may have to be released."[2992]

b. Person or Authority Initiating the EIO

Requests to Germany shall be made by a judicial authority or any other authorized issuing authority in accordance with the form(s) provided for in the DEIO.[2993] In the event that the EIO is incomplete or lacks the information that would enable the executing state to recognize or execute the EIO, then the issuing state shall be informed as soon as possible in a manner that enables it to produce a written record.[2994]

As to whose instance the EIO can be issued, the AICCM or other applicable German laws are bereft of provisions allowing the defense to file a motion or request for the issuance of an EIO on his/her behalf. According to interviews made with practitioners, this is not possible in a continental legal system such as Germany. At most, victims or third persons could suggest and/or give leads to prosecuting authorities, although this is more likely for the benefit of the prosecution rather than the defense. This notwithstanding, the defense can participate in the proceedings in general, according to interviewees, but this is of course in accordance with the parameters provided by law. In an inquisitorial system and in accordance with German Criminal Procedure, the defense, as a general rule, could only challenge some instances. With respect to the EIO, most of the time, the defense is not apprised of whether an EIO has been issued. In this case, the most the defense could challenge is the evidence itself obtained through an EIO.

3. Execution of Requests

a. Applicable Law on Execution

The AICCM provides that the investigative measures, including any coercive measure, subject of the EIO or any request for legal assistance shall

2992 See Notification of the transposition of Directive 2014/41/EU by Germany, p. 2.
2993 AICCM, § 91d(1).
2994 AICCM, § 91d(3); RiVASt, Nr. 18.

be carried out using the same rules as if the request has been made by a German authority.[2995] Stating it differently, there shall be no distinction under procedural law whether the hearing of a witness, for example, is conducted on the basis of a MLA request or EIO, or in the context of a national criminal investigation.[2996] Further, as long as the DEIO does not provide for anything else to be followed, and there is nothing that would violate the fundamental principles of the German legal system, the formalities provided for by the issuing state in making and executing an EIO shall be followed and that all responsible authorities are requested to comply.[2997] Should the special formalities or requirements cannot be satisfied, the corresponding authority of the requesting state shall be accordingly notified.[2998] In addition, there is the possibility of requesting the presence of the issuing state's authorities during the execution of the EIO.[2999] Notably, there are no readily available measures regarding this but German authorities would instead act or decide on the basis of the request by the issuing state.[3000]

As regards audiovisual interrogations, it shall be made under the direction of the competent body and on the basis of the right of the requesting/issuing state.[3001] The German authority shall participate in the hearing, take notes on the person's identity and must take note of compliance of the hearing with the essential principles of German law.[3002] Further, the accused shall be advised or told of his rights at the beginning of the hearing, which shall be according to the law of the requesting/issuing state and under German procedural law.[3003] Witnesses or experts shall on the other hand be advised on their right to refuse to give evidence ("*Zeugnisverweigerungsrecht*") and/or right to remain silent ("*Auskunftsverweigungsrecht*").[3004] The same standards apply to hearings of persons through telephone.[3005]

2995 AICCM, § 91e(1).
2996 *G20*, p. 39.
2997 AICCM, § 91h(2); *Schomburg/Lagodny*, pp. 806-807.
2998 AICCM, § 91h(2).
2999 *Schomburg/Lagodny*, p. 807.
3000 *Schomburg/Lagodny*, p. 807.
3001 AICCM, § 91h(3).
3002 AICCM, § 91h(3).
3003 AICCM, § 91h(3).
3004 AICCM, § 91h(3).
3005 AICCM, § 91h(4).

b. Applicable Procedural Rights

i. Defense Rights in the Context of Fair Trial Rights

Human rights are also considered in the procedural aspects of the EIO. As mentioned earlier in the discussion of human rights vis-à-vis substantive aspects, Article 6 ECHR obligations are taken into account as regards grounds to refuse recognition or execution of an EIO. These same fair trial rights also have a part in ensuring that procedural rights are upheld. To recall, there is the right to hearing in accordance with law, prohibition against physical or mental maltreatment, etc. In relation to criminal matters, the Article 6 ECHR and CFR obligations must be read together with the rights provided by the Federal Constitution as regards right to life and bodily integrity, inviolability of the home, prohibition of maltreatment of prisoners and detainees, freedom of movement, as well as the right to secrecy of communication.

Not all significant rights are provided by the Federal Constitution and one would need to make a cross-reference to other significant rights that could be found in the Code of Criminal Procedure, such as but not limited to the following: right to refuse testimony on personal or professional grounds,[3006] right of professional assistants to refuse testimony,[3007] refusal of information,[3008] right to examine or confront witnesses,[3009] right to refuse to give testimony under oath,[3010] assignment of legal counsel for witnesses.[3011] In addition to whatever may be provided as standards in the implementation of investigative measures vis-à-vis the EIO, these rights ought to be equally taken into consideration.

To illustrate, the lastly mentioned right about assigning counsel for witnesses gains significance in relation to EIO's calling for taking of testimonies or statements from a witness. According to the relevant provision, witnesses may avail themselves of an assistance of legal counsel, who shall be permitted to be present in general, unless there are reasons to believe that the latter's presence shall negligibly hinder the orderly taking of evidence.[3012] As regards witnesses who do not have the assistance of legal

---

3006 German Code of Criminal Procedure, §§ 52, 53.
3007 German Code of Criminal Procedure, § 53(b).
3008 German Code of Criminal Procedure, § 55.
3009 German Code of Criminal Procedure, § 58.
3010 German Code of Criminal Procedure, § 61.
3011 German Code of Criminal Procedure, § 68b.
3012 German Code of Criminal Procedure, § 68b.

counsel at his/her examination and whose interests needing protection cannot be done any other way, shall be assigned a counsel for such duration of the examination if it becomes apparent that the witness is unable to exercise his rights himself at the examination.[3013]

Furthermore, something also interesting can be said as regards the right to refuse to give evidence or right to remain silent as not all kinds of examination is subject to this right. According to the relevant provision of the Code of Criminal Procedure, it is allowed to subject an accused (and an ordinary witness) to physical examination or bodily intrusions such as a blood test if the same is for the purpose of establishing certain facts in relation to proceedings.[3014] The said examination is ordered by either the judge or under exigent circumstances, by the public prosecution service, and shall be admissible even without the consent of the accused.[3015] Nonetheless, any results shall only be used for the purpose of the criminal proceedings for which they were taken.[3016] Molecular and genetic examinations, photographs, fingerprints, measurements and other similar measures can also be taken against the accused (and any other witness).[3017] These exceptions notwithstanding, the right to remain silent or refuse to give evidence would still apply as for example, the AICCM mentions that the EIO or any request in general for legal assistance shall be denied in the event it relates to the right to refuse to give evidence or remain silent.[3018]

Human rights are also taken into account in the preparation of requests or EIO. To illustrate, in terms of search and seizures and the items to be seized need to be surrendered there ought to be an assurance that the rights of third parties shall remain unaffected by reason of said surrender.[3019] The same goes with the enforcement of orders allowing confiscation of criminal proceeds, wherein one of the requirements is proof that in the proceedings on which the foreign decision was based to confiscate, the sentenced person had both the opportunity to be heard and adequate defense, and the decision must have been taken by an independent judicia-

3013 German Code of Criminal Procedure, § 68b(2).
3014 German Code of Criminal Procedure, §§ 81a(1), 81c.
3015 German Code of Criminal Procedure, § 81a(1), (2).
3016 German Code of Criminal Procedure, § 81a(3).
3017 German Code of Criminal Procedure, §§ 81b, 81e, 81f, 81g, 81h.
3018 AICCM, § 91b(1)(2)(a).
3019 *G20*, p. 41. Several other safeguards are provided for searches and seizures in the Code of Criminal Procedure, see for example StPO, §§ 101-110.

ry.[3020] Further, as an interviewee mentioned, should the investigative measure subject of a request or EIO would relate to conditions of detention for example, authorities would require guarantees regarding the same.[3021]

It is interesting to note that the human rights considerations vis-à-vis preparation of requests are not one-sided and only applicable to incoming requests and EIO. The same safeguards are provided for outgoing requests or EIO. With respect to outgoing EIO or requests, German issuing authorities ought to ensure that the request complies with the proportionality principle and that the investigative measure indicated in the EIO could be ordered under the same conditions in a comparable domestic case.[3022] This could be thought of as a protection against arbitrary action as well as prevention of undertaking something indirectly what cannot be done directly. In the same vein, the *Oberlandesgericht* or higher regional court may revisit or remand an EIO should it think that the requirements for providing legal assistance, or in the case of the EIO, executing the investigating measure, has not been complied with, or that there has been a misuse of powers.[3023] Pending any decision on the same, any transmission of evidence may be suspended.[3024]

ii. Human Rights Considerations in the Procedures Provided

Considerations of human rights are equally present in the execution of the investigative measure(s) requested in the EIO. For example, there is an applicable safe harbor provision for temporary transfer to a foreign country for foreign proceedings, wherein under the relevant provision, a person in pretrial detention or serving a prison sentence or detained under custodial measure of rehabilitation and incapacitation on German territory may be transferred upon request to the issuing state's territory in order to testify as a witness or for the purpose of identification or inspection by the court in pending proceedings, provided that said person shall not "during the period of transfer, be punished or subjected to any sanction

3020 *G20*, p. 41. One can likewise see relevant provisions on freezing of assets in view of Council Framework Decision 2003/577 / JHA of 22 July 2003 on the enforcement of decisions to freeze property or evidence in the European Union, AICCM, §§ 94-95.

3021 Interview with Christian Schierholt.

3022 AICCM, § 91j(3); *Schomburg/Lagodny*, pp. 815-816.

3023 AICCM, §§ 61(1),(2); 91i. See also *Schomburg/Lagodny*, pp. 811-813.

3024 AICCM, § 91i.

that cannot be issued in absentia, and that in the case of his release, he may leave the issuing state" and it should be ensured that the person shall be returned immediately after evidence has been taken, unless said requirement has been waived.[3025] The safe harbor provision shall not apply, however, when the person has left but has returned to the issuing state, or after not being needed any further, has failed to left the territory of the issuing state within 15 consecutive days.[3026]

iii. Defendant's Participation in the Recognition or Execution of an EIO

As mentioned in the section tackling preparation of requests, the AICCM is bereft of provisions tackling participation of a suspect or accused person in the issuance of an EIO. Following what the interviewed persons said, there are limitations to what the defense could do vis-à-vis an EIO, especially when the EIO is normally issued and executed without knowledge of the defense or prior to the commencement of formal proceedings. At most, the AICCM provides that the transmission of evidence to the issuing state may be placed on hold pending appeal in the issuing state against the EIO, or within the scope of the AICCM.[3027] As to how this kind of appeal is lodged by a suspect or accused persons in German proceedings, no further details are provided.

Notwithstanding no clear-cut provisions as to remedies vis-à-vis the EIO, the accused is not without further relief. It also does not mean that the principle of equality of arms does not exist. On the contrary, a defense counsel in behalf of the suspect or accused is given certain rights to not only safeguard his/her position but also to adhere to equality of arms. Among other rights, a defense counsel has the right to be present in judicial and public prosecution hearings, as well as in judicial witness hearings (StPO § 168); right to request evidence in preliminary and main proceedings, the right to inspect files (StPO § 147) and the right to appeal, however, not against the will of the accused (StPO § 297).

Moreover, the issuance or execution of an EIO does not preclude the accused from questioning the admissibility of evidence in the trial itself. The Code of Criminal Procedure provides for certain rules that apply thereto. For purposes of this discussion, evidence under criminal procedure can

3025 AICCM, § 62(1)(3, 4).
3026 AICCM, § 91c(3).
3027 AICCM, §§ 61, 66, 91i; *Schomburg/Lagodny*, pp. 811-813.

be prohibited based on its nature, the method of how it was obtained, or when certain evidence is prohibited to be used to clarify certain facts.[3028]

c. Applicable Time Limits

Time limits are provided for in the applicable German law for the EIO. And while the time limits the law provided are stated in mandatory terms ("*Sollfristen*"),[3029] according to interviews, these time limits are not mandatory but they are beneficial and there is an effort to recognize or execute in accordance with said time limits.[3030]

First, the executing state ought to confirm receipt of the EIO not later than one week from receipt of said EIO by the appropriate executing authority.[3031] When the EIO has been sent to the wrong authority, then the receiving authority needs to send it to the appropriate one, and the same should be indicated in the confirmation receipt to be sent to the issuing authority.[3032] In connection to this, an interviewee mentioned that confirmation of receipt is one of the new features introduced by the EIO. According to feedback received by said interviewee from other prosecutors or judicial authorities, confirmation of receipt of an EIO is a big relief because there would be some requested states or executing authorities which did not give any confirmation or acknowledgment of receipt prior to the EIO's implementation.[3033] This was likewise confirmed by other interviewees who were practitioners: at least they know the other party has received the EIO they sent and easily follow up, if necessary.[3034]

Furthermore, German authorities ought to decide on whether to recognize or execute an EIO or any other form of legal assistance not later than

3028 StPO, §§ 52, 53, 54, 81c, 136; BZRG, § 51 I. It might also be interesting to note herein that there is judicial review of admissibility of mutual legal assistance in the respective criminal matter by the District Court by the Federal Constitutional Court Decision of 24 June 1997, 2 BvR 1581/95, for instance: court decisions with respect to order of seizure (Section 98, para. 2), court decision with respect to covert measures (Section 101), or appeal against an issued search and seizure order of a court (Section 304).

3029 See AICCM, § 91g; see also *Schomburg/Lagodny*, p. 802.

3030 Interviews with Till Gut, Christian Schierholt, and Klaus Hoffman.

3031 AICCM, § 91d(2), *Schomburg/Lagodny*, pp. 788-789.

3032 AICCM, § 91d(2).

3033 Interview with Till Gut.

3034 See Interviews with Christian Schierholt and Klaus Hoffman.

30 days from receipt of the EIO or request.[3035] When the subject of the EIO or legal assistance request involves securing or obtaining evidence, it should be decided on as much as possible within 24 hours from receipt of said EIO or legal assistance request.[3036] Provided further, when there is no reason to postpone execution or recognition, the investigative measure subject of the EIO (or legal assistance request) ought to be done not later than 90 days from date when decision to recognize or execute has been made.[3037] These stated time periods are without prejudice to the issuing state requesting for a different time period for practical reasons.[3038] Further, should it be not practical to work within the stated time periods or the requested shorter time by the issuing state, German authorities are obliged to inform the issuing state of the same and the foreseen period of time, within which the investigative measure subject of the EIO or request can be executed.[3039] The same required disclosure applies when there are any grounds to refuse recognition or execution, or postpone the same.[3040] In any event, any decision to grant, execute, or postpone ought to be justified.[3041]

A time period is also provided for when the EIO or request calls for the cross-border surveillance of telecommunications without the need for technical assistance from German authorities. When the same is not provided in a comparable domestic case, German authorities ought to inform within 96 hours from receipt of EIO or request the issuing state that the monitoring cannot be done, and that any findings already collected while the person under surveillance is within the territorial jurisdiction of Germany, cannot be used or could only be used under certain conditions, which shall be accordingly communicated.[3042]

In addition to the foregoing, the transmission of evidence may be postponed until such time that a legal remedy has been decided in cases when an application or submission has been made in the requesting state against the issuance of EIO or within the scope of the applicable law.[3043] In any

---

3035 AICCM, § 91g(1).
3036 AICCM, § 91g(1).
3037 AICCM, § 91g(2).
3038 AICCM, § 91g(3); see also *Schomburg/Lagodny*, p. 769.
3039 AICCM, § 91g(4), (5).
3040 AICCM, § 91e(4).
3041 AICCM, § 91e(3).See for discussion *Schomburg/Lagodny*, pp. 802-803.
3042 AICCM, § 91g(6).
3043 AICCM, § 91i(1).

event that the question is about the scope of the applicable law, then the requesting state shall be accordingly notified of the same.[3044]

d. Authentication of Documents

Although the German law does not provide specific provisions about authentication, it provides that the EIO or any request for legal assistance shall be made in a manner capable of producing a written record. At the outset, one must accomplish the same kind of form provided in the DEIO. It is also important in German law and practice that should there be inquiries vis-à-vis the EIO being incomplete or lacking the information that would enable the executing state to recognize or execute the EIO, then the issuing state shall be informed as soon as possible in a manner that enables it to produce a written record.[3045]

e. Importance of Confidentiality

The existence and nature of requests for assistance, the EIO included herein, are subject to confidentiality in Germany.[3046] It is possible however that disclosure would be necessary, especially in cases involving compulsory measures.[3047] The requesting or issuing state ought to expressly state in the request or EIO that the case is particularly sensitive, should the same be the situation.[3048]

Outside the EU, Germany has asked for guarantees of confidentiality from countries such as Turkey and the United States in some MLA cases, according to one interviewee.

f. Return of Documents

It seems that evidence seized should be returned should the surrender of the same be included in any MLA request or EIO. In such case, there

3044 AICCM, § 91i(2).
3045 AICCM, § 91d(3).
3046 *G20*, p. 42.
3047 *G20*, p. 42.
3048 *G20*, p. 42.

ought to be an assurance that not only rights of third parties will remain unaffected, but also that the objects surrendered subject to reservation shall be returned immediately upon request.[3049]

g. Specific Procedures per Type of Assistance

The relevant German law contains specific provisions tackling specific forms of investigative measures, including the transmission of information, including personal data;[3050] application of the framework decision on information and intelligence exchange between law enforcement authorities in EU member states;[3051] transmission of data without formal requests;[3052] telecommunications surveillance without technical assistance from German authorities;[3053] joint investigation teams (for which the DEIO shall not apply);[3054] and search and seizures, which includes freezing or confiscation orders.[3055]

It must be noted herein that not all of the abovementioned are covered by the EIO, such as the information exchange (Council Framework Decision 2006/960/JHA on simplifying the exchange of information and intelligence between law enforcement authorities of the Member States of the European Union) and transmission of data without formal requests, which the DEIO does not mention.

IV. Comparing the United Kingdom and Germany with the Regional Framework

A. Historical Development of Mutual Legal Assistance: Existence of Domestic Legislation

One could notice with respect to historical development the continuous development of cross-border cooperation in the regional framework, which is part and parcel of the criminal justice infrastructure the EU is

3049 RiVASt, Nr. 76.
3050 AICCM, § 92.
3051 AICCM, § 92b.
3052 AICCM, § 92c.
3053 AICCM, § 92d.
3054 AICCM, § 93.
3055 AICCM, §§ 94, 95.

building and developing. Notably, this criminal justice infrastructure did not have its roots in the EU organization. Traces of cross-border cooperation agreements could already have been seen in the beginning among the EU member states even before the First and Second World Wars. These however were mostly intergovernmental in nature and informal. During this time period, the conditions have not yet been met to merit acquiescence and willingness from the nation states to head towards supranationalism or a singular framework for criminal matters and international cooperation in relation to the same. There was the prevalent thought that criminal matters are a matter of sovereignty and individual decision making.

The Council of Europe was historically responsible, if not the most favored forum, in producing different agreements involving the different aspects of cross-border cooperation such as the European Conventions on Extradition and Mutual Legal Assistance in Criminal Matters. These eventually became core European instruments and paved way to different new agreements rooted on their provisions.

One can look into the Schengen Agreement and the extradition and MLA agreements later agreed within the Union's framework. Additionally, one can look into the shifting from intergovernmental to supranational handling of criminal justice affairs in the regional framework, happening at each phase of development the EU since the Maastricht Treaty.

The European Union became an active and participative forum for matters involving international cooperation in criminal matters after the Amsterdam Treaty. Now, in the era of the Lisbon Treaty, more developments can be attributed to the criminal justice architecture of the EU. In connection to this, the EU has developed and continues to develop a sophisticated infrastructure that not only spans information sharing through different database systems, but also includes the establishment or revamping of Union agencies such as the Europol, Eurojust, and EJN that are all integral EU machineries in cross-border cooperation in criminal matters. There is also development along the alley of substantive and procedural rights through the different EU enactments, directives, regulations, etc.

Additionally, there is the existing principle of mutual recognition in criminal matters. Such mutual recognition is grounded on the mutual trust among EU member states that they are complying with their obligations as members of the EU such as regards the protection of human rights. The European Arrest Warrant is the first international cooperation instrument that applied this principle. As to how this principle is operationalized in international cooperation matters, there is supposedly no extra step necessary to determine the contents of a request, etc. – there is a trust that what is contained in a request or European Investigation Order (as the applicable instrument for mutual legal assistance among the member states) was issued in compliance with the requirements of sufficiency, necessity, and proportionality and more importantly, human rights obligations as defined in Article 6 of the TEU. In fact, the EAW reflects the principle of mutual recognition in criminal matters by changing the nomenclature from "requests" to "orders" giving the idea that regional cooperation has shifted from a request-based system to an order-based one. This later caused confusion that an EAW means automatic extradition. It became later apparent that this was not the case as member states are beholden to certain obligations under their respective constitutional systems. Thus, the EAW instrument was later amended to cater to national constitution court judgments tackling certain issues such as extradition of own nationals, etc.

The principle on mutual recognition underlies also the current European Investigation Order. Notably, the UK and Germany are two EU member states which integrated into their respective domestic legal systems the EIO by legislating or amending existing law accordingly. One could note in light of this development that even before the DEIO, both the UK and Germany have not only been concluding treaties with other states, and being participative in the EU Criminal Justice Architecture, but they also have their own domestic legislation on international cooperation in criminal matters, which includes mutual legal assistance. With the DEIO and then integrating it to their respective legal systems, the UK came up with a new law such as the EIO Regulations to implement the EIO while Germany made amended the AICMM to integrate therein the applicable provisions relating to the EIO.

B. Substantive Provisions

1. Applicability of Assistance

With respect to applicability of assistance, four (4) main points can be identified.

First, as regards the obligation to render assistance, there was theoretically a shift from a request-based to demand-based system in both the regional and member state frameworks by virtue of the EIO. Before, traditional mutual assistance contemplates the sending of requests and although states would have the obligation to render the widest possible assistance, it is pretty much still discretionary on the receiving state whether to extend mutual legal assistance or not. However, nowadays with the EIO the regional and member state frameworks provide theoretically a more limited elbow room to deny any request. As it should theoretically be applied, there should be a paradigm shift. If before the question sounded more like "may I have this evidence from your country?", then now it is more like "I need the evidence from your country so hand it over to me. Trust that I have done everything in order." Practitioners in the UK and Germany who were interviewed would however say that despite such a change in nomenclature and in theory, the practice of cross-border collection and exchange of evidence remains the same. The EIO may have introduced fundamental structural changes, to which practitioners are grateful for, the change of terminology from "request" to "order" did not affect much as historically, practitioners would make sure to extend the assistance required from them.

Second, criminal matters to which the EIO applies are not defined. Instead, the proceedings that the DEIO covers are enumerated as follows: (1) with respect to criminal proceedings that are brought by, or that may be brought before, a judicial authority in respect of a criminal offence under the national law of the issuing State; (2) in proceedings brought by administrative authorities in respect of acts which are punishable under the national law of the issuing State by virtue of being infringements of the rules of law and where the decision may give rise to proceedings before a court having jurisdiction, in particular, in criminal matters; and (3) in proceedings brought by judicial authorities in respect of acts which are punishable under the national law of the issuing State by virtue of being infringements of the rules of law, and where the decision may give rise to proceedings before a court having jurisdiction, in particular, in criminal matters. Germany provides additionally a definitive list in its law of what is not covered by the EIO, e.g. joint investigation teams, cross-border surveillance, hearing by teleconference.

Third, the EIO applies to both natural and legal persons. The regional and member state instruments explicitly provide this. Said provision could raise questions however as regards corporate criminal liability. Germany for example does not follow this concept. Should discrepancies arise however, practicioners are able to smooth out and resolve any concerns. Some opine that the EIO can still be effectuated notwithstanding any difference in viewpoint with respect to corporate criminal liability.

Fourth, there was the going concern about the UK leaving the EU and the consequences it shall bring. As mentioned earlier, the UK was the first country to decide to leave the EU. And even if the UK authorities intimated their desire to stay in the justice and home affairs of the EU, it is too soon to determine the future of the new relationship forged between the EU and the UK as regards judicial cooperation in criminal matters. This is notwithstanding the fact that certain elements, principles, and practices from the EIO are carried over to the new partnership. Having said this, the UK is said to be politically motivated to perform well in its commitments such as with the EIO. Not necessarily because it is wary of the enforcement mechanism of the European Commission but because the UK needs to show they can make good their endeavors to get the best possible withdrawal agreement with the EU.

2. Types of Assistance

Given the shift to a demands-based system of cross-border obtaining and transferring of information and evidence, there is no distinction as to what types of assistance can be provided. This was the intention of the EU with the EIO instrument. Regardless of whether it is coercive or non-coercive, or whether the evidence is readily available or not, it can be the subject of an EIO. In spite thereof, this does not readily happen because even the DEIO allows parties to conclude agreements with each other as regards mutual legal assistance or what could be the subject thereof. Further, there are not only exceptions to which the EIO is not applicable, such as joint investigative teams for example or exchange of information on personal data, but there are also no clear-cut demarcations or even guidelines regarding how the DEIO replaces older mutual legal assistance instruments.

Indeed, there could be instances wherein an investigative measure is not covered by the EIO but could still be requested, or alternatively, the EIO includes investigative measures that are not all covered by the instrument. The member state legal frameworks would provide investigative measures that they can extend in mutual legal assistance or cross-border exchange and transfer of evidence, but some of these types of assistance are not subject of the EIO. Addressing these concerns of possible overlaps or confusion as regards applicability of the EIO for such kind of investigative measure, authorities from Germany and the UK have been consistent in answering that they would still as much as possible execute the EIO even if there is uncertainty or a question on whether a particular investigative measure is covered or not. They are more inclined to executing an EIO as much as possible. And when they are the issuing states, interviews reveal that this would be dependent on the receiving authority or party. Herein the contact points and liaison persons of each member state or the networking system provided by the European Judicial Network or Eurojust become useful.

Additionally, something could be mentioned about the birth pains connected with the EIO instrument. The EIO is relatively new and issues could arise as to how it applies or is implemented. There was experience for example with Northern Ireland authorities who needed to prepare argumentations and explanations as regards EIOs which go through the courts.

In line with the abovementioned, there might also be discrepancies that could arise due to certain investigative measures being unavailable in an executing member state. In connection to this, discrepancies could also arise due to the application of the DEIO to both natural and legal persons and not all EU member states, like Germany for example, espouse corporate criminal liability. In settling discrepancies in general, which includes the aforementioned incompatibilities, it was learned through interviews that open communication is imperative and the existence of liaison magistrates to smooth out any issues is helpful in resolving stumbling blocks. Additionally, there could be issues that might arise as regards the EIO and corporate criminal liability matters in Germany if the investigative measure involved is coercive in nature. As per advice of an interviewee, it would be wise to check the relevant domestic law or procedure to determine if the same is allowed. Otherwise, there would be no issue encountered as regards non-coercive measures, even if Germany does not have corporate criminal liability.

3. Compatibility with Other Agreements

As regards the compatibility of the EIO with other existing arrangements, the EIO was meant to replace a lot of earlier EU instruments on cross-border cooperation vis-à-vis exchange of information and evidence, to the exception of some instruments such as the one on joint investigation teams. Despite this, as mentioned above, problems and issues arise regarding possible overlaps or inapplicability that are addressed by practicioners.

Further, it must be remembered that the EIO is only a part of the big criminal justice infrastructure scheme the EU has for itself now, and the

EIO is envisaged to be one of the useable tools but not mutually exclusive to the other tools available to authorities, i.e. SIS, Eurojust, EJN, Europol, and other parts of the criminal justice infrastructure of the EU. Both the UK and Germany are included in said criminal justice architecture, and the UK has opted in many of its related measures – even actively participating in most – albeit it must be remembered that the UK has a special opt-out status in the EU vis-à-vis the area of freedom, security, and justice.

In light of this, it must be stressed herein the importance of the EJN, Europol, and Eurojust for the efficacious handling of criminal matters. As mentioned earlier, the liaison persons or contact points through the EJN are helpful in practice. The Europol might be the network of the police units of the member states but it likewise has useful database systems that can be helpful in the investigation and prosecution of criminal offenses. Whilst the EIO is an exchange between judicial authorities, this does not preempt information or evidence to be obtained through other means. The Eurojust as well is integral for being the coordination hub and network of judicial authorities for cooperation in criminal matters. In respect to these, earlier guides vis-à-vis MLA encourage the use of other forms of cooperation alongside MLA or in the EIO context. This is meant to improve the efficiency and effectiveness of investigations and prosecutions.

4. Principles, Conditions, and Exceptions

A lot of principles, conditions, and exceptions exist within the EIO regime, which traditionally were also part of the traditional MLA regime. For purposes of this study, focus is given to seven, to wit: (1) sufficiency of evidence requirement; (2) dual criminality; (3) double jeopardy; (4) substantive considerations of human rights; (5) reciprocity; (6) speciality or use limitation; and (7) special offenses or national interest.

One can begin with the principle involving a sufficiency of evidence requirement which exists in both the regional and member state framework. It can be seen that in general, the more coercive or intrusive a measure is, the more requirements are needed to be provided by the issuing authority. One can cite as examples investigative measures involving search and seizures and surveillance methods, which require the issuing state to provide information as to the necessity and relevance of the information or evidence to be obtained.

In relation to this, both member state frameworks through interviews show that there is no exact barometer in determining "relevance" of a certain information or evidence that maybe subject of an EIO. This would happen in a case-to-case basis and is determined personally by the issuing authority. Germany, for example, is different from Anglo-American jurisdictions which need to abide with certain evidentiary requirements such as probable cause, for example. In light of these revelations, interviewees from both Germany and UK cannot recall any particular incident wherein an EIO or MLA request has been questioned on grounds of relevance.

Second, there is the dual criminality requirement which on a regional-level, is meant to be retained although with serious limitations. It does not apply to a list of 32 offenses. This is applied in UK and Germany as well in their respective domestic laws prior to the EIO, they more or less forego the dual criminality requirement depending on the investigative measure and/or criminal offense involved. Dual criminality in Germany, for example, applies in search and seizures in general. The dual criminality likewise plays a role when one reads through different sanctions to which a catalog of offenses is made available. Like Germany, the UK traditionally applies the requirement to search and seizure cases, as well as restraints and confiscation of assets. Also like Germany, dual criminality plays an (indirect) role in terms of denying the EIO because the investigative measure is limited to a catalog of offenses, to which the subject matter in the EIO is not included in.

Third, the protection against double jeopardy can be added to the existing principles or conditions involving the EIO. At the outset, it was a bit questionable how the same applies on transborder cases especially since the protection traditionally had an internal effect within the relevant legal system, may it be national or EU level. At most, there was only consideration of prior judgments in imposition of punishment or penalties. There was however the dire need to set in motion the transborder application of the principle of *ne bis in idem* given the desire to build an own area of justice and home affairs within the EU and with this, there was the greater risk for a person to suffer double, if not more, punishment based on the same set of facts. In view of the CJEU Spasic judgment, it was held that Article 54 of the CISA and Article 50 of the CFR are compatible with each other. The enforcement element is considered in the transnational application of the *ne bis in idem* principle.

Despite this resolution however, there are certain issues that still remained vis-à-vis the principle of *ne bis in idem*. Some of these pertain to application of the principle to other matters, albeit only with regard final judgments. There are other member states likewise that adhere to the transnational application as stated above but also take into account whether there are elements of the crime committed wholly or partly in their respective territories.

Having mentioned this, the DEIO considers compatibility with the *ne bis in idem* principle but does not provide anything further. This is in stark contrast to the EAW instrument, which is consistent with Article 54 CISA and the CJEU judgment, albeit the EAW instrument distinguishes between a mandatory and optional ground to refuse: mandatory, if the other state is another member state; optional, if a third state. In terms of the EIO it is henceforth sound to consider the prevailing doctrine and/or provision found in the EAW instrument, CISA provision, and the CJEU Spasic judgment. It would be illustrative of prevailing doctrine and/or interpretation and would be further compatible to the *ratio decidendi* of the CJEU. Moving forward, member states which can either be an issuing or executing authority could take this into account: as an executing authority, to be equipped with a *ratio decidendi* to deny recognition or execution of an EIO; as an issuing authority, to prevent issuing the EIO at the outset to prevent triggering the principle.

As it should then stand, the transborder element of double jeopardy involves an enforcement element wherein no one shall be prosecuted or punished twice for the same offense based on same facts and the judgment therein has been executed, to be executed, or there is something in the national law that disallows execution. The same enforcement element is applied in the German law in its protection against double jeopardy vis-à-vis the EIO while it is not so clearly provided for in the UK law. Germany has done so in integrating the *ne bis in idem* principle in its implementing law as an optional ground for refusal. Accordingly, Germany decided to follow the EU legal approach as it recognizes that this can influence not only the decisions of German authorities as regards legal assistance but likewise those of other member states in relation to persons to whom the principle may apply vis-à-vis legal assistance requests. On the other hand, it becomes more questionable or uncertain for the UK on how the transnational application would be given the issue of its exit from the EU. One has yet to determine whether the UK should apply the jurisprudence of the CJEU or follow its own domestic application. It was opined that should the proceedings be held in the UK, then it might be prudent to apply UK domestic law and jurisprudence while EU legal approach would apply in proceedings or criminal matters in other member states.

As an optional ground to refuse recognition or execution of an EIO for Germany, German authorities do not automatically refuse should the principle apply. Instead, German authorities in practice would need to weigh the application of the principle with the principle of mandatory prosecution, or whether the crime was partially or wholly committed in Germany, with evidence readily available therein. Furthermore, German authorities would refrain from refusal should there be already an issue of whether the principle applies (or there is a violation of the prohibition) in the proceedings being held in the issuing state. It is posited that German authorities should not be the ones determining whether the prohibition exists, but rather, the matter is better left to the discretion of the issuing authorities, especially in cases when the requested information or evidence is highly determinant of the issue. Nonetheless, if there is an apparent risk to the person involved of his/her right being violated, then this delegation of discretion to the issuing authorities can be said to be reduced.

Given these concerns, there is a way to preempt or avoid in advance *ne bis in idem*. Eurojust released guidelines as to how to resolve matters involving conflicts of jurisdiction. It is interesting to note that in practice, judicial authorities from Germany for example are aware of the possibility of simultaneous proceedings in different member states for the same criminal offense or same accused. In deliberating whether to initiate or continue proceedngs that also involve other member states, different factors are taken into account, which more or less follow the factors provided in the Eurojust guidelines. In relation to this, the existence of *ne bis in idem* does not automatically result to inaction or cessation of investigation or criminal proceedings in Germany. This needs to be balanced with the principle of mandatory prosecution.

Fourth, there are substantive considerations of human rights in an EIO framework. Human rights are considered in many grounds for refusal that the DEIO provides. An example is if the EIO violates the principle of *ne bis in idem* or the protection against double jeopardy, as earlier discussed. UK and German laws also provide specifically the denial of recognition or execution of an EIO when there is no consent from the person being requested to give information or evidence. Additionally, UK law provides violation of non-discrimination as a ground to refuse recognition or execution of an EIO.

Likewise, the executing state can refuse recognition and/or execution should there be substantial grounds to believe that it would be incompatible with the executing state's obligations under Article 6 TEU (which relates to the different fundamental rights the EU and its member states abide with). The operative phrase herein is "substantial grounds to believe", which means that an actual infringement of a fundamental right is not necessary before the executing authority can raise the ground for refusal. In connection thereto, German law would provide the same ground for refusal but in terms of human rights obligation under Article 6 ECHR and the CFR. UK on the other hand provides human rights obligations vis-à-vis the HRA.

Interestingly, the said ground for refusal based on human rights obligations was not available in the EAW instrument. Being a mutual recognition instrument, there was no mention of human rights obligations as a ground for refusal but then again, the EAW instrument also mentions the need to protect human rights. Thus, it was posited by many that it ought to be considered as a ground for refusal. The CJEU in the Aranyosi and Căldăraru cases made it clear that the principle of mutual recognition ought to be balanced with human rights obligations. Even if not explicitly provided, executing authorities were duty-bound to deny the EAW against Aranyosi and Căldăraru as there was the serious risk that both would be exposed to inhumane and degrading treatment in the facilities of the issuing authorities.

Having said this, certain human rights obligations come into play in the EIO framework that could merit denial of recognition or execution of an EIO. Common in both regional and member state frameworks for example is the principle of non-discrimination. If the EIO is apparently issued for purposes of discrimination, then denial of the same is in order. The same can be said for violating principles of legality and proportionality of criminal offenses and punishment (in German law, this falls under fair trial rights) or the prohibition against *ex post facto* laws. If the acts or omissions covered by the EIO are not criminal offenses at the time of its commission or omission, or the criminal offense was defined by law after the acts/omissions were done, then executing authorities are duty bound to refuse recognition or execution of the EIO.

One could look into the obligations in relation to the right to life vis-à-vis death penalty and the prohibition against torture, or cruel, inhumane, degrading punishment or treatment which have extraterritorial application. The CFR makes it clear that no person shall be removed, expelled or extradited to another state to which there is serious risk of death penalty, torture, or inhumane or degrading punishment or treatment. In terms of an EIO, an investigative measure could entail the transfer of persons in custody to give information or evidence. If the detention facilities are questionable and there is a risk of exposing the person to inhumane or degrading treatment or punishment, then like in the cases of Aranyosi and Căldăraru, there ought to be denial of recognition or execution of the EIO.

It can likewise be mentioned at this juncture that due to the prohibition of death penalty in the EU and among its member states, and the extraterritorial application as mentioned above, then they are likewise duty bound not to cooperate in a general MLA framework as a requested or executing state if doing so would expose the affected person to serious risk of death penalty, torture, or inhumane and degrading punishment or treatment. A commitment is then necessary, for example, that the death penalty shall not be imposed by the requesting state. Alternatively, transfer of persons in custody would not be allowed if it would subject them to deplorable prison conditions bordering inhumane or degrading treatment or punishment.

Additionally, proportionality matters as a human rights obligation, especially in respect of Germany which considers it as a constitutional principle imperative to all government actions and decisions. It is integral in both instances of issuing and executing EIO's. Considering this, violations of the same can trigger the ground for refusal based on human rights obligations as well. In the alternative, another measure could be suggested, like what is provided in German law, that would be less intrusive and proportionate to the information required.

Fifth, reciprocity has been a traditional principle in mutual legal assistance and as regards the EIO, its application is not quite easily discernible anymore given the existence of the principle of mutual recognition in criminal matters. On a member state level, the UK and Germany would be able to provide assistance even without any existing treaty or agreement. With the introduction of instruments like the EIO, which are based on the principle of mutual recognition, it is argued that reciprocity is lost or seriously abrogated. The removal of executive discretion is a reason, as well as the lack of opportunity to deny an EIO should the same not be necessary and proportionate, and the limitation of the grounds to refuse recognition or execution. In light of this discussion, it must be said that UK and Germany still apply the principle of reciprocity with the way they handled the EIO's implementation domestically. UK still retains executive discretion, which the EIO instrument intended to take away from the equation of mutual legal assistance between EU member states by stressing the nature of an EIO as a judicial decision. The UK applies a lot of grounds for refusal, which arguably are more than what the regional instrument provides (the UK includes discrimination for example which is not in the DEIO), and retains the use of central authorities which have conditions to be satisfied before it being allowed to transmit the EIO further to an executing authority. Mutual legal assistance or the EIO in the context of the UK is thus not completely depoliticized.

On the other hand, executive discretion in Germany still exists although it allows direct contacts between judicial authorities. The executive discretion that generally belongs to the Federal Government has been delegated to state governments, which then delegated the same to the public prosecutors' offices and courts. As it currently stands, public prosecutors' offices are the authorities imbued with this discretion through delegation. Germany then illustrates a point wherein executive discretion can still exist albeit there is non-usage of central authorities. Moreover, Germany retains the substantive aspects of reciprocity by not transposing the principle of mutual recognition in its entirety domestically. Well, its authorities tried to do in the beginning with the EAW but were quickly reprimanded by the German Federal Constitutional Court, whose inputs were taken into consideration into the new amendments. Accordingly, the principle of mutual recognition is good but it cannot be done without limitations. Authorities need to look into the domestic effect and the rights that may be infringed, as well as the consideration of the different constitutional principles such as proportionality, for example.

Sixth, speciality or use limitation is another traditional principle or condition in mutual legal assistance or international cooperation in general, together with the abovementioned reciprocity and dual criminality. At first glance, the DEIO is bereft of any mention of this rule. Although a further reading of the specific provisions of the DEIO would show that speciality still applies. Moreover, the EU framework has Directive (EU) 2016/680 of 27 April 2016 on the protection of natural persons with regard to the processing of personal data by competent authorities for the purposes of the prevention, investigation, detection or prosecution of criminal offences or the execution of criminal penalties, and on the free movement of such data, which is relevant in the discussion of use limitation.

As to how the UK and German laws take this into account, they provide clearly for its existence. The evidence or information requested ought to be only used in respect of the subject matter indicated in the EIO, nothing more and nothing less. German authorities for example would appreciate that another request be made should the evidence or information obtained from them need to be used for another criminal matter. This is to ensure that there is still compliance with the requirements for the EIO and parameters provided by German law. Significantly, both Germany and the UK apply the Directive 2016/680 domestically, wherein the UK integrated its provisions in Part 3 of its Data Protection Act 2018 while Germany has its own Federal Data Protection Act. Both laws provide the conditions, parameters, and requirements that ought to be followed in relation to processing of personal data as regards criminal matters and the transfer thereof to fellow member states, third states, and other international organizations. Further, the UK has specific legislation called the Investigative Powers Act of 2016 which covers investigative measures of law enforcement authorities that intrude on the privacy of individuals or private persons. The Investigative Powers Act of 2016 provides the needed safeguards and parameters anent interception of communications and data, as well as the retention and disclosure of such overseas by virtue of an EIO or MLA. It mandates the destruction of data if the purpose for the same has been fulfilled or there is no longer need for the information obtained. This finds application as in light of speciality and use limitations it means that data or communications vis-à-vis privacy obtained between the UK and another state, need to be destroyed unless meritorious grounds exist for its continuous use and custody. Similar principles are reflected in the Data Protection Act 2018, which applies data protection principles and rights to law enforcement proceedings, including general restrictions and requirements ought to be met before any processing and/or transfer is allowed.

The last principle, condition, or exception that can be mentioned is the existence of special offenses and national interest. While the EIO in both the regional framework and member states like the UK and Germany is over the idea of raising political offenses, military offenses, and the like as grounds to refuse, public order or national interest still does play a role in allowing a country to refuse an EIO. Both the DEIO and its implementing member state legislations provide for grounds to refuse the execution of an EIO on the basis of national or public interest of the executing authority. These include, but not limited to, immunity or privilege (under the law of the executing state that makes execution impossible), essential national security interests, territoriality, etc.

In relation to the foregoing, the ground of refusing the recognition and/or execution of a request because there are substantial grounds to believe that doing so would be incompatible with obligations of the executing state under Article 6 TEU could be considered equally as grounded on state interest. Even if it is easy to classify the same as slowly based on fundamental human rights considerations, it can equally be based on public order (or national interest in general) because, even if it takes account of fundamental rights, the same was formulated in broad terms wherein an infringement is not required but only a substantial ground to believe that it could happen. Hence, it might as well be a political judgment call.

National interests also play a role in the postponement of recognition and/or execution of an EIO, when its execution might prejudice an ongoing criminal investigation or prosecution, or the objects, documents, or data concerned are already being used in other proceedings, until such time as they are no longer required for that purpose.

In addition to substantive provisions, there are procedural ones like the preparation of requests and execution of requests, the latter of which involve the applicable law, time limits, confidentiality, return of documents, and specific procedures for specific investigative measures.

C. Procedural Provisions

1. Usage of Horizontal Cooperation; Designation of Authorities

Interestingly, DEIO follows through with the paradigm shift from normal vertical cooperation and use of central authorities that occurs within a traditional MLA regime to a more horizontal form of cooperation, wherein issuing authorities and executing authorities directly correspond to one another as regard the EIO. The use of horizontal cooperation and direct contacts between authorities was first seen with the 2000 MLA Convention. In connection to this, there is as such no fixed 1:1 correspondence and instead exchange of EIO's occur directly between judicial authorities, which decide by themselves to recognize or execute the EIO. It removes the involvement of ministers or the use of executive discretion.

As to how this was brought in the respective legal systems of the UK and Germany, which both have central authorities for MLA requests, the UK designated issuing authorities (judicial authorities and prosecutors) and then central authorities to receive EIO's and decide on whether to transmit the same to the executing authorities; while Germany foregoes the central authorities vis-à-vis the EIO altogether and those designated authorities can be either issuing or executing ones. As to why the UK decided to retain central authorities for the EIO, this was in tune with the unique system it has compared to other EU member states. Its courts serve a different function and were hesitant to become administrative postboxes that would handle incoming EIOs or MLA requests. Moreover, the retention of central authorities work better traditionally for the UK as they have the needed expertise to handle both MLA requests and the EIO.

2. Preparation of Requests

As per the preparation of the requests, the DEIO provides minimum requirements to what information ought to be provided, which shall be accomplished in the official language indicated in the registry of the respective executing state and transmitted accordingly to the executing authority or central authority, when applicable, in a manner capable of producing a written record. The member states are also allowed to make use of the EJN to determine the appropriate executing or central authority. In cases wherein the receiving authority does not have competence to act on the EIO, the DEIO provides that the said authority transmits it *ex officio* to the authority-in-charge. Furthermore, open communication among authorities is encouraged to facilitate inquiries regarding the issued EIO. Additionally, the DEIO provides that the issuing authority ought to indicate whether the EIO issued is a supplement of an earlier EIO. The member state frameworks more or less mirror these, wherein the UK and Germany require that an EIO be issued in accordance with the form included in the DEIO, among other things.

In light of this, UK law gave out a reminder that issuing authorities ought to make sure of the EIO's necessity, as well as its applicability in a similar domestic case, and that should special requirements need to be met, that these have been accordingly complied with. In practice, UK benefits from liaison magistrates and the use of available networks between authorities in handling the preparation and issuance of requests. As regards German law and practice, it was clarified by interviewees that a complete set of facts is not required but sufficient information to allow recognition or execution of the EIO.

Moreover, German interviewees made interesting inputs as regards the prescribed form of the EIO. Given the *pro forma* EIO, it can sometimes be a stumbling block to the speediness required in a request or EIO. Most of the time, an EIO would involve taking of witness statements or searches and seizures and yet the form would contain matters that are not necessarily needed. For most old-timer MLA practitioners, the prescribed form is constraining when previously, MLA requests could simply constitute an email or a simple letter with the attached warrant. Further, the prescribed procedure for issuing requests might not be compatible with urgent cases as some interviewees experienced. This notwithstanding, practitioners found a way through open communication and coordination with the other authorities to make urgent cases work. There is also a possibility of having the formal EIO transmitted later on, although this would depend on the receiving authority.

On the other hand, there are some who are appreciative of the prescribed EIO form. This is especially true for new practitioners and those who are in the receiving end of EIOs. It makes it easier to know and understand what the EIO constitutes.

Another thing which could be mentioned under this section is the participation of a private person, suspect or accused in the preparation of an EIO. In the advent of the EIO, there is a greater opportunity to participate given to the defendant and third parties, who may be affected by the issuance, recognition, or execution of an EIO. There has been a lingering concern on the protection of a defendant's rights due to the risk of imbalance between the prosecution and defense with respect to gathering of evidence abroad, which violates the principle of equality of arms.

Through the DEIO, a suspected or accused person may now request the issuance of an EIO either by person or by a lawyer on his behalf. This would however still be subject to the "framework of applicable defense rights in conformity with national criminal procedure." As regards how this is implemented, the UK criminal proceedings would allow the defense to file a motion for the issuance of an EIO on its behalf. According to some interviewees, this has been long existing in UK practice wherein one could request for the issuance of an MLA request. Having said this, interviewees have yet to encounter a situation wherein the same has actually been done. It is different however with Germany because as interviewees explained, a defendant or accused requesting that an EIO to be issued cannot be accommodated in an inquisitorial kind of system. The relevant law or the Code of Criminal Procedure also does not provide any provision regarding this. At most, one could expect victims or third persons requesting or suggesting the issuance of an EIO for a particular kind of evidence. But of course, there is no guarantee that their requests shall be accommodated. In line with this, one can then say that Germany is falling short of its positive duty by not giving the defense the rightful participation it arguably deserves in the issuance of an EIO. If one would recall the principle of sincere cooperation, adherence of Germany to its obligation would be then questionable because the aim of the DEIO is not being realized. But then again, Germany cannot be completely faulted in this regard due to the underlying incompatibility of its existing inquisitorial system with the aim of the DEIO. Whilst participation of the defense is ideal and ought to be realized in pursuit of defense rights, there ought to be a reevaluation of how it would truly be put into fruition while considering differences in criminal justice systems and proceedings per member state.

3. Execution of Requests

a. Applicable Law on Execution

As regards execution of requests, the DEIO seeks to provide a solution to the diversified requirements for cross-border evidence to be admissible among member states. Some would follow *lex fori*, some *lex loci*, while some follow the principle of non-inquiry, which makes it difficult to put in place a uniform system as regards admissibility of evidence obtained elsewhere. The DEIO, as a solution, now provides that the EIO should be executed by the executing authority in accordance with the formalities and procedures expressly indicated by the issuing authority, unless the same are contrary to the fundamental principles or laws of the executing state. Additionally, the DEIO allows an issuing state to request for the presence of its own authorities in the execution of an EIO. This is however subject to the provision that the executing state may suggest other investigative measures should the requested investigative measure and/or formalities be unavailable in the executing state.

This notwithstanding, member states ought to have investigative measures on the following: (1) the obtaining of information or evidence which is already in the possession of the executing authority and the information or evidence could have been obtained, in accordance with the law of the executing state, in the framework of criminal proceedings or for the purposes of the EIO; (2) the obtaining of information contained in databases held by police or judicial authorities and directly accessible by the executing authority in the framework of criminal proceedings; (3) the hearing of a witness, expert, victim, suspected or accused person or third party in the territory of the executing state; (4) any non-coercive investigative measure as defined under the law of the executing state; and (5) the identification of persons holding a subscription of a specified phone number or IP address.

As to how the foregoing is transposed in the member state level, there was no explicit mention in the Regulations as regards what the applicable law should be in the recognition or execution of an EIO received by the United Kingdom but it would seem however that on the basis of the specific procedures mentioned in the Regulations, the EIO shall be executed by the UK in accordance with what has been provided for in the said EIO. This notwithstanding, the UK authorities had the elbow room to suggest other investigative measures which could be less-intrusive but would still get the job done, provided there is permission from the issuing state, among other requirements to be satisfied. It must be noted further that UK law allowed authorities from issuing states to be present under certain conditions, including that these authorities can be held liable under the applicable police laws in the applicable jurisdiction the execution of an EIO takes place. Thus, for all intents and purposes, authorities from issuing states allowed to be present in the UK should abide by applicable UK law and act accordingly.

German law provides that the investigative measures, including any coercive measure, subject of the EIO or any request for legal assistance shall be carried out in the same rules as if the request has been made by a German authority, which means, there shall be no distinction under procedural law whether the hearing of a witness, for example, is conducted on the basis of a request or EIO, or in the context of a national criminal investigation. Given the same, the issuing state may provide the formalities that ought to be followed in the execution of the EIO and as long as the same would not violate the fundamental principles of the German legal system, the formalities provided for in making and executing an EIO shall be followed and that all responsible authorities are requested to comply with. Should the special formalities or requirements be not satisfied, the corresponding authority of the requesting state shall be accordingly notified. Additionally, the presence of the issuing authorities during the execution of the EIO may be requested.

This mirrors the solution forwarded by the DEIO. German law moreover provides for specific investigative measures and the intricacies that ought to be followed. As regards audiovisual interrogations, for example, it shall be made under the direction of the competent body and on the basis of the right of the requesting/issuing state. At most, the German authority shall participate in the hearing by taking notes on the person's identity and of the compliance of the hearing with the essential principles of German law. It is imperative likewise to advise the accused as well as the witnesses at the beginning of the hearing of their respective rights, which shall be according to the law of the requesting/issuing state and under German procedural law. The same standards apply to hearings of persons through telephone.

b. Applicable Procedural Rights

Human rights are equally considered with regard the procedures in an EIO framework. At the outset, the DEIO gives the idea that defense rights are given paramount consideration in obtaining evidence through the EIO. The DEIO acknowledges that the transnational dimension of a proceeding must foster cooperation but it should not compromise the rights of the defendant. Member states also have the positive duty "to ensure that in criminal proceedings in the issuing state, the rights of the defense and fairness of proceedings are respected when assessing evidence obtained through the EIO" but without prejudice to what the national criminal proceedings shall provide.

This positive duty is fleshed out and specified even further at the many aspects of implementing the EIO. First, the DEIO integrates the directives on procedural rights, in particular, the one on the right to interpretation, right to information, and the right to access a lawyer in criminal proceedings. While the DEIO was silent as to how these directives would come into play, these directives were meant to approximate procedural law and rights among the member states. In addition to these directives, there are also directives focusing on one's presumption of innocence, the right to be present during trial in criminal proceedings, the right to legal aid for suspects and persons included in criminal proceedings and those subject to the EAW. In relation hereto, the European Judicial Training Network and Fair Trials International came up with toolkits and guidelines as to how these directives should apply in practice.

As to how these directives and the respective procedural safeguards they tackle apply on a member state framework, there are human rights considerations in the specific procedures provided by the DEIO on specific investigative measures and the execution of the same. To illustrate, one could look into provisions involving the transfer of persons from one state to another for purposes of giving evidence or assisting in the investigative measure as either suspect or witness and hearings by virtue of teleconference or other audiovisual transmission, as well as by telephone conference. There is also the primordial consideration of protecting personal data, wherein member states are enjoined to comply with the relevant framework decision on the same in implementation of frameworks relating to criminal matters. Access to such data shall be restricted, without prejudice to the rights of the data subject, and only authorized persons may have access to such data. Notably, the foregoing considerations vis-à-vis specific investigative measures are carried over in the member state frameworks of the UK and Germany. Simultaneously, the UK and German legislations would provide for what needs to be taken into account as regards preparing the EIO itself and issuing the same.

Nonetheless, there are other procedural rights considerations that are not explicitly mentioned in the UK and German laws that ought to be taken into account. One would need to look into other sources of their respective laws such as the basic law, code of procedures, or other legislation to find out how the aforementioned procedural rights could apply. To illustrate, UK has laws in respect of competency and compellability of witnesses that matter in an EIO framework. Having said this, there is generally no 1:1 congruity between the UK and Germany as regards how procedural rights play out in their respective criminal law systems. This is understandable because while the UK follows an adversarial kind of system, Germany follows an inquisitorial one. In line with this, one comment from an interviewee comes to mind wherein he mentioned how the UK follows a cosmopolitan approach in determining whether procedural rights have been respected or infringed. One cannot simply look into the counterpart proceedings of another member state and say that this is the equivalent of a certain stage in UK criminal proceedings. One needs to weigh certain factors to determine and cannot haphazardly conclude.

In connection to this, there is the question on whether the suspected or accused person could intervene in the issuance and/or execution of the EIO – a question that naturally arises given the foregoing imprimatur. The DEIO mostly provides provisions that require remedies to be taken up in the issuing state and not the executing state. This would be consistent with the principle of mutual recognition that limits executing states to further inquire or question the propriety of an EIO issued. To illustrate, one could only ask a remedy from the issuing state in issues of necessity, adequacy, and/or proportionality. Not even the executing state can refuse recognition or execution on these issues. At most, it could communicate with the issuing state regarding the same.

In connection to this, member states must ensure that within their own national legal orders, legal remedies equivalent to those available for similar domestic cases shall be provided for in the investigative measures to be indicated in the EIO. While substantive issues surrounding the EIO may only be challenged in the issuing state, this should be without prejudice to the guarantees of fundamental rights in the executing state. This could either mean that the executing state shall ensure fundamental rights are duly respected, or the possibility to refuse execution on substantial grounds that it could cause infringements of these rights, or the possibility to consult the issuing authority on doubts about the proportionality of the investigative measures included in the EIO.

Despite the DEIO provision that states that remedies ought to be taken in the issuing state, one could seek remedies in UK proceedings vis-à-vis issuance and/or execution of the EIO. As an executing state, one may not have the remedy of questioning the necessity, proportionality, or adequacy of an EIO issued but as learned from interviewees, it might still be possible to raise questions on the same, or on the general propriety of the said EIO with the UK courts or the UK central authority involved. There has yet to be a case law on it but one expert states this scenario is possible, though he believes that courts would probably take a strict approach and decide on stringent circumstances.

Furthermore, the UK law allowed the suspension of transmittal of evidence or information subject of an EIO pending resolution of a legal remedy or the existence of serious and irreparable damage. Interestingly, the UK traditionally allowed authorities to revoke consent to transmit evidence, albeit the said evidence has been transmitted already. It has yet to be determined whether this applies further in the context of the EIO.

This notwithstanding, one can find something similar in the EIO Regulations of the UK, which provides for a so-called application for a variation or revocation order. This is based on a limited number of grounds, which are grounded on human rights. Said application is available to a suspect, accused, or any other affected person. An interviewee mentioned that there is no exact legal basis for this variation or revocation order and one has yet to encounter case law about it. Nonetheless, it is a remedy not equally found in German proceedings. Moreover, an EIO is normally issued without the knowledge of the suspect, accused, or any other person. It happens usually during the investigation stage and thus, the defense would not be apprised. It follows that it would be difficult, if not impossible, for the defense to question the issuance of the EIO. Based on interviews, it was learned that what would be possible for the defense is to question the evidence acquired through the EIO later on.

c. Applicable Time Limits

In addition to the abovementioned, there are time limits placed on both the regional and member state instruments as regards the confirmation of receipt, decision to recognize or execute an EIO, executing the investigative measure indicated in the EIO, and delivering the evidence to the issuing authority and/or state. There is consistency as to the number of days the executing authority ought to abide with, as well as the reasonable grounds and circumstances wherein postponement of making a decision to recognize or execute, as well as the time to execute the EIO and delivering the information or evidence. Should there be non-compliance or undue delays, it is possible for member states to inform the Eurojust, although the Eurojust does not have adjudicatory powers. At most, it would send reminders or notices to the member state in question or help in finding a solution to the delays. So far, authorities who were interviewed have not encountered a situation wherein they raised concerns on delay with the Eurojust. Significantly, this brings into light what one interviewee from the UK mentioned about practitioners fixing generally issues among themselves and without court interventions. Practitioners would generally look into the bigger picture and while small details or certain questions would be relevant for certain cases, they would try to make the system work.

With this remark in mind, both UK and German authorities acknowledge that while these time limits are not mandatory, they provide good motivation to act swiftly on requests or EIOs. Interviewees have been consistent in pointing out that the speed element the EIO has structurally introduced in MLA practice as something positive. Interestingly, the UK is said to act speedily or at least make an effort to make good its endeavors. As mentioned earlier, there is allegedly a political aspect to this and promotion of self-interest.

Other than this, there is appreciation from German authorities for example, that the EIO requires the requested authority to confirm receipt of the EIO. Prior to this, they would sometimes need to second guess whether the other authority received its EIO. With a confirmation of receipt, one can discern the amount of time an EIO has been with the executed authority and gauge when a follow up is needed.

d. Authentication of Documents

The regional and member state frameworks are in agreement as to the requirement of transmitting the EIO in a manner producing a written record. German practice further requires that should there be inquiries post-transmission as to the correctness of the EIO or the incompleteness of the same to enable execution or recognition, then it should be made also in the same manner of being able to produce a written record.

e. Confidentiality

It can also be said procedural-wise that confidentiality, including protection of personal data, is of paramount importance in dealing with EIO or general mutual legal assistance requests on both regional and member state levels. Parameters and safeguards are in place to ensure protection of the same. The UK, for example, penalized unauthorized disclosure in relation to account monitoring orders, etc. German law acknowledges however that while confidentiality is essential and needs to be protected, there would be instances that disclosures might be needed in furtherance of the execution of an EIO or request.

f. Return of Documents

Adding to the procedural provisions is the return of documents, which is related to the substantive principle of speciality or use limitation. Accordingly, the regional and member state frameworks do not provide for such requirement, unless the executing authority or state communicates to the issuing authority the need to return of the evidence to the former once the criminal matter has been resolved or finished. Should the return of evidence be required, the German law additionally requires an assurance that not only rights of third parties will remain unaffected, but also that the objects surrendered subject to reservation shall be returned immediately upon request.

g. Specific Procedures

Lastly, the regional and member state legal frameworks are replete of specific provisions addressing specific investigative measures. These specific provisions provide the additional requirements that ought to be satisfied as well as how the same should be carried out in execution.

Part 3: Comparing and Contrasting the ASEAN and the EU

During the previous parts of this study, one has been able to learn the respective regional and member state frameworks of the ASEAN and the EU and their respective member states Philippines, Malaysia, United Kingdom, and Germany with respect to mutual legal assistance in criminal matters. Through learning the different regional and member state frameworks, one has been able to compare and contrast each one with other. The study began with comparing the regional frameworks of the ASEAN and the EU, respectively, to the applicable frameworks of two of their member states.

The following discussion shall be a comparison and contrast of the two (2) regional blocs. Divided into two (2) components, the first one shall focus on the regional frameworks themselves, wherein the development of (1) their respective principles, norms, and practices, (2) existing cooperation mechanisms, (3) approach to regional security, (4) and mutual legal assistance in criminal matters shall be compared and contrasted with each other to flesh out interesting points and matters ought to be taken into account should the study proceed in answering its main research question.

The second component of the discussion shall integrate into the discussion the respective member states within the respective regional organizations, mainly underscoring (1) how regional decision and policymaking and legal instruments are translated and transposed in the respective domestic orders of the member states, (2) efficiency, and (3) protection of human rights.

I. Comparing the Regional Frameworks

As mentioned above, the first step in the entire process of this portion of the study is an evaluation of the regional framework. First, an evaluation or analysis would be done of how principles, norms, and practices have developed. The study finds this imperative because it influences more or less what direction the regional frameworks would take in their respective decision making, as well as provide a gauge of how effective they would be able to influence and implement regional decisions on a member state level.

Second, there would be a discussion of cooperation mechanisms and third, approach to regional security and international cooperation in criminal matters. These are relevant to know how the ASEAN and the EU so far have molded their respective criminal justice architecture and the same shall provide an idea once again how they would take action.

Lastly, the elements of the respective MLA arrangements among the respective member states shall be discussed. These include idiosyncrasies that might be existing per regional framework and the reasons that might explain the same.

A. Development of Principles, Norms and Practices

One of the materials the present study encountered in attempting to build the historical development of the ASEAN, the EU, and their respective regions is Victor Lieberman's two-volume book entitled "Strange Parallels".[3056] Whilst said work was not exactly cited in the present study due to differing subject matters, what one can mainly take away from his work is the prevailing theme of existing parallels occurring in history between Asia and Europe and the thesis that these parallels reflect each other one way or another and consequently affect the development of both regions.[3057] What one was undergoing is not mutually exclusive to itself. Instead, it could have a spillover effect to another part of the world, or alternatively, the same kind of event or similar circumstance is happening simultaneously. Grippingly, the comparison of the historical developments of the ASEAN and the EU would indeed show strange parallels that mirrors how one acted and reacted as against the other. There were common experiences, although at different points in time one may be found on one end of the situation, while another may be found at the opposite end of it. There were likewise common problems and conundrums faced, especially in light of how their respective member states coalesced towards each other, but with different turnarounds on how each decided to go forward. Indeed, the historical development of both the ASEAN and the EU, as well as the regions they represent, has admittedly a huge impact on how each organization developed their principles, norms, practices, and their overall daily business. To some extent, it was also reactionary to the circumstances their respective regions went through.

3056 See for reference *Lieberman*, pp. 1-6.
3057 See for reference *Lieberman*, pp. 1-6.

The Southeast Asian region and its countries, of which ASEAN represents, are not homogenous. Topography and geography was a factor, wherein Southeast Asia would have a mainland portion and also a maritime one. Furthermore, there are different religions or influences that each country within said region underwent. The ASEAN countries might have in the early stages developed their own cultures and ideals together with their respective kingdoms, groups, and tribes, but they did not exist in autarky. Instead, there was an ebb and flow of ideas and other cultural influences through the intensive agricultural and maritime trade that was happening among the different nations. Included herein is the influence from other cultures not part of the Southeast Asian region, such as the Indians and Chinese. This led consequently to the assimilation of ideas and beliefs that enriched the socio-political aspect of the Southeast Asian countries. Thus, while culture and tradition was homegrown, it was not to the exclusion of other influences.

On the other hand, one could notice a sort of homogeneity with the European region. Its topography and geography, compared to the Southeast Asian region, allows closer or easier proximity from one country to another. Further, in the European region, a homogenous aspect grew through the influences of the Ancient Antiquities, the spread and influence of the Christian Church, and the Germanic warriors who took over the western part of the Roman Empire. Through the spread of the Ancient Antiquities, when the Ancient Greeks occupied several territories and states in Europe, and then later on, when the Roman Empire placed the entire region under its power and authority, there was a diffusion of ideals, knowledge, culture, and overall socio-political structure among the European states. Although the same was not linear and the same for everyone and every state, there was still a common denominator amongst them in the experience that later on shaped their overall identity.

In addition to this, there was the influence from the Christian Church, which influenced not only the Roman Empire but was also authoritative and influential enough in dictating European affairs during the early and modern ages. Its influence was far-reaching and existing in all European states. The experience from the Christian Church might not be exactly the same for all parts of Europe but then again, there was a common experiences in how it shaped European civilization and identity later on. To illustrate, there was the influence of how the Christian Church planted the seeds of being the supreme religion to the detriment of other religions in the region. There were incidents of forced migrations or conversions, etc. There were likewise incidents wherein the Christian Church was instrumental in instigating armed conflicts with other parts of the region due to encounters with other religions. At the same time, the Christian Church was instrumental in preserving the knowledge from the Ancient Antiquities that led to formation of new forms of knowledge, etc. Further, there was no separation between church and state during the peak of the Christian Church's influence. They were instrumental in influencing sovereign decisions and kings during these times also had influence in the leadership of the Church. It was only later on, when things were too complicated and problematic that the entanglement was severed.

At this point of the discussion, it bears to mention that Southeast Asia is an artificial construct during the First World War, created to define the Allied's command area. There was no predetermined Southeast Asia prior to this time albeit the countries constituting said region were already connected somehow to one another prior to the period of the First World War. In the same respect, Europe was also an artificial construct. It was not a given, pre-constructed definition and delineation. In this regard, it can be said there was no regional identity during this time and the above-mentioned narrative evinces this. At most, what could be witnessed is the individual identities of the different countries constituting the respective Southeast Asian and European regions, which through trade would bounce off each other's socio-political and cultural influences, or otherwise engage sometimes in conflict due to territorial issues and other disputes. There were common factors here and there but overall, the regional identity has yet to be developed during the early to modern ages of both regions.

The first major interaction between the Europeans and Southeast Asians would probably be the time during which empires were being built and expanded and then later were embarking in colonialism and imperialism. This could also be said as the point wherein both regions were starting to build a regional identity centered on similarly shared experiences and circumstances.

Based on each one's historical development, Asia and Europe both entered the early modern age at the same time: there was the golden age of commerce when Asia and Europe's interaction with the world was arguably at its peak. During the same time period, European states and sovereigns started to explore and colonize states in both Africa and Asia.

Notably, one of the influences the Roman Empire had on European colonization or imperialism is the concept of hegemonic rhetoric: they are experts in sugar-coating their interventionalist expansionism as something with an altruistic and humanitarian purpose, although the same is far from the truth. There was also an ideal during the Roman Empire of superiority and that anything outside the Roman Empire was barbaric or second-class. The same rang true with the use of Christianity in conquests, explorations, and the like through the use of violence and forced conversions: wherein non-Christians ought to be saved (e.g. crusades, etc.) from their paganic or "evil" ways. Said kind of ideal was likely shown by the European colonizers when they colonized and ruled over states in Africa and Asia. This consequently elicited a response or reaction from their colonized states on how their non-negotiables would be, which is mainly to be self-governing and detach themselves from the shackles of colonialism and any other form of foreign intervention. Significantly, these non-negotiables presently still applies.

Prior to the colonization of the Southeast Asian states, as mentioned earlier, they had their own social, political, and cultural systems. This may be influenced by other states such as India, China, or even Arab states (which were trading partners of Asian countries). There was also good relations among the different states through the trade they fostered with one another. However, when the Europeans came and conquered the states in Asia, the Europeans introduced different changes resulting in the abrogation of pre-existing customs and practices. Technically speaking, European colonizers came in and tried to mold their colonies into their own images. There was intervention in the self-determination of the colonized. This eventually led to positive, and mostly, negative effects. A curtain was placed among the Southeast Asian nations and the once-appreciated interaction between communications was taken away. There was a disruption of the social strata and income inequality was apparent. Worse, there were accounts of violence against those colonized and the harsh taking of their respective resources. This eventually led to the brewing resentment among the colonized, in Africa and Asia alike, against their colonizers. The seeds for nationalism movements were planted to be eventually harvested later on.

Despite these negative effects, there was a rationalization the Europeans used for their actions. They were not truly honest about the motives for economic and political gains. Some were of the position that they are being altruistic in their efforts. The colonized were the "others" that needed to be educated or assisted to learn the more civilized ways of the westerners. One can notice the so-called "white man superiority" mentality. In this regard, European colonizers were also normative powers in trying to influence norms and practices. The colonized however, were not easily persuaded to buy into these rationalizations because their experience told them differently. To a certain degree, the norms and practices they brought in were assimilated and taken in by their colonized states. However, the process was not one-way as the colonized also were influential of the socio-political and cultural development of the colonizers.

When the First and Second World Wars happened, the ideal of European superiority crumbled into pieces, especially in the eyes of the colonized. Some of the European states lost during the World Wars their colonies and even if they wanted them back, the resistance was much stronger at this point. The seeds of nationalism and self-determination have grown and was ready to be reaped. Furthermore, the European states' own citizens were not anymore willing to support financially (through taxes) the upkeep of colonies, especially when they were not anymore convinced that there are benefits to the same.

After the peak of colonization and the World Wars, both Asian and European regions needed to rebuild themselves. Asian nations, like those in Southeast Asia, were struggling however given that after colonization, they were basically depleted of resources and incapacitated to build a nation from the ground up. One thing was for sure though. They were keen not to allow any further intervention in their affairs and this ideal was generally brought into the present. The ideas for open communication and regional collaboration also flourished given the common experiences and circumstances they were living in. On the other hand, European nations were also finding themselves in a bad situation. Taking too much damage, they needed to find ways to resolve the issues left by the First and Second World Wars. There were also ideas to foster regional cooperation on their end.

Notwithstanding the desire to communicate, collaborate, and cooperate, it was not an easy path to take for the Southeast Asian nations. The earlier attempts to form regional cooperation neither went beyond the negotiation stages nor lasted very long. Many reasons could be cited as to why they did not succeed and these were also litmus tests as to what may or may not work for the region. These factors include but are not limited to, the idea being promoted is not the *zeitgeist* of the period, i.e. the non-acceptance of pan-Asian sentiments which was among the many things promoted during the ARC, the lack of neutrality (which led to the breakdown of the Bandung Conference), the rejection of anything constituted of foreign power intervention or domination, the efforts of some to manipulate the discussion (or put themselves as leaders), as well as the fact that the Southeast Asian nations themselves were embroiled in (sometimes violent) conflict with one another. After the world wars and during the critical period of nation building, there was still a sense of distrust among some nations as well as unresolved issues such as for example, differences in ideologies and territorial disputes. This led later to armed conflicts or tensions with each other. Should there be for a regional organization that would be acceptable and properly work for everyone, the aforementioned factors must be taken into consideration. There is also the need to be able to work despite differences among each other.

Europe was not so much different in terms of conflict and tension among its states. Right after the First and Second World Wars, Europe was still picking up the broken pieces of war when it was embroiled in the Cold War between the US and the Soviet Union. Like in Southeast Asia but on a bigger scale, the difference in ideologies led to the European continent being divided into two sides (i.e. communist and democratic states). There were also European states which were under dictatorship or fascist rulers. Furthermore, there was the general push of regional cooperation but there were competing ideas on how this should proceed. There was also a question on where would be its starting point and which state should lead. There were also parties which were preoccupied with their own self-interests. France, for example, took a hard line against Germany and wanted to impose as many restrictions to the latter for its own gains. Regional cooperation took off only when a third state like the United States took efforts to play on countries' interests that regional cooperation became promising: anchoring on the coal and steel productions of both Germany and France. This led to the formation of the European Coal and Steel Community.

The ASEAN was later formed by Indonesia, Singapore, Malaysia, Philippines, and Thailand. It was a regional organization with no Pan-Asian sentiments. It would remain neutral and proscribe anything constituting foreign power intervention and domination. Member states are on equal footing, with neither one member state having the upperhand in discussions and/or agreements nor an authority that would dictate to the member states. These considerations were necessary to address the historical circumstances of the region, urgently consolidate the independence of the former colonies, and preserve the national sovereignty against external influences. These considerations underlie the different constitutional, normative, and decision-making principles and overall institutional design of the regional organization. First, with constitutional principles, the principle of non-intervention could be found at the heart of it all. It influences the different legal-rationalistic norms the ASEAN has: (1) prohibition against the use of force and a commitment to pacific settlement of disputes, (2) regional autonomy, (3) doctrine of non-interference, and (4) no military pacts and a preference for bilateral defense cooperation.

As to how the principle of intervention is interpreted, it does not only contemplate one's right to self-determination or the prohibition of entering into great power-led military arrangement, but in operative terms, it likewise covers the following aspects: (1) refraining from criticizing the actions of a member government towards its own people, including violation of human rights, and from making the domestic political system of states and the political styles of government as basis for deciding membership in ASEAN; (2) criticizing the actions of states, which were deemed to have breached the non-interference principle; (3) denying recognition, sanctuary, or other forms of support to any rebel group seeking to destabilize or overthrow the government of a neighboring state; (4) providing political support and material assistance to member states in their campaign against subversive and destabilizing activities.

Admittedly, there were attempts to revisit the principle of intervention the ASEAN lives by especially during the crises the region has experienced. However, as a collective, ASEAN member states decided to maintain the status quo. The principle of non-intervention even applies to the functioning of the different ASEAN bodies, which are solely preoccupied with their area of expertise. To illustrate, the ASEAN Law Ministers' Meeting would not intervene with the works of the ASEAN Finance Ministers' Meeting or the AICHR. At most, there is an enhanced interaction: a process wherein individual member states could comment on domestic policies of another, should the same have regional repercussions, but would leave ASEAN out of the equation. The same was consequently used in establishing the ASEAN Surveillance Process and ministerial troika, and eventually found itself in the ASEAN Charter. Should there be instances when it would seem that the "flexible engagement" concept has been accepted (rejected variation of the principle of non-intervention), like for instance in how ASEAN member states dealt with the leaders of the military junta in Burma, recent institutional changes in ASEAN, overall, are evolutionary rather than a break from established principles and norms, like as it how with the principle of non-intervention.

In addition to the principle of non-intervention, or the constitutional principles and legal-rationalistic norms of ASEAN, much can be said about the decision-making principles of the regional organization. Not having any pan-Asian sentiments nor the desire for one to dictate to the member states what to do, the ASEAN remains intergovernmental. It does not have any enforcement mechanism that would reinforce agreements among each other. There may be rotation of chairmanship of the ASEAN each year but decision-making is still not led by one member state but instead, it is done through the so-called ASEAN way.

The ASEAN Way constitutes working guidelines by which conflicts could be managed and also describe the means of carrying out actions, not specific ends, within ASEAN, which include the following principles: principle of seeking agreement and harmony, the principle of sensitivity, politeness, non-confrontation and agreeability, the principle of quiet, private, and elitist diplomacy versus the public washing of dirty linen, and the principle of being non-Cartesian, non-legalistic. The ASEAN Way was instrumental during the formative years of the ASEAN when the member states themselves were embroiled in different conflicts with one another. Despite underlying issues, they were able to move forward through the ASEAN Way. The ASEAN Way, as earlier discussed, in any case should not be taken as being the same as unanimity. Instead, this decision-making process allows common ground to be found among member states without being aversive to one another. It is a pragmatic approach that allows the ASEAN to run its daily business without hurting sensibilities and sensitivities that might result from disagreements that could arise from decision and policymaking.

It bears mentioning that while the ASEAN came up later on with an ASEAN Charter, as well as it is e*n route* to its vision of creating the ASEAN Communities and being more institutionalized, the principles, norms, and overall framework it adopts basically stayed the same. These core values or non-negotiables have stood the test of time albeit there might have been evolutions or progressions witnessed of the same.

On the other hand, the western European states were able to find what would pique their interest further in having regional cooperation. One could first look into how the European Coal and Steel Community was formed, as mentioned above, and then evolved to the European Economic Communities, the European Communities, and thereafter, the European Union. The historical development likewise evinced, akin to the ASEAN, that certain efforts did not take off because of the absence of a similar *zeitgeist* during the time of proposals (e.g. European Political Community, European Defense Community). Later, one can also notice a common mindset among the founding member states when things were agreeable to each one of them. Moreover, historical experience likewise shed light on the positions of certain member states: some were cooperative and initiated the negotiations toward more cooperation (for example, Benelux countries) while some, like the United Kingdom, which were not into the idea of supranationalism and did not want to wholly dip its feet into the water and expecting concessions to be given to it in the process. If one would recall, the United States in the formative years of the European Communities expected the UK to take the lead but the latter was adamant to do so. It even sought concessions from the United States during the Marshall Plan but still was not 100% committed to the propositions. It was only later on that the UK agreed. But like how history unfolded, the UK was in the stage of leaving the EU but still negotiated its position towards the Union and its member states.

Despite the common appreciation of regional cooperation, tension between being intergovernmental and supranational in nature soon arised. This led to divisiveness among the member states and impasse on certain points of the agenda that needed to be addressed (e.g empty chair policy). It can be gainsaid that everything was a slow and sure process and eventually, with the European Union, there are more supranational features than intergovernmental. Competences are clearly defined and delineated as to what exclusively belongs to the Union or the member states, and what is shared between each other. There are also principles such as conferral, subsidiary, proportionality, institutional balance, among others that underlie the functioning of the European Union.

It can be pointed out in light of this discussion that the European Union maintains the ideal of being a normative power, although in a more positive way. Through its endeavors such as the European Neighborhood Policy agreements, among other things, it has been able to influence others of its own ideals, policies, etc., with the aim of assimilating the same among its partners. Its agreements further embody the ideals, principles, and norms it lives by given the conditions or provisions the EU includes in its partnerships or agreements with other countries or partners.

B. Existing Cooperation Mechanism

The nature of the ASEAN and the EU as regional organizations would explain the difference in their respective cooperation mechanisms. As mentioned *en passant* earlier, the ASEAN is an intergovernmental organization whilst the EU is supranational (albeit there are still matters within the EU that more or less remain intergovernmental in nature).

By being mainly supranational in nature, the existence of the EU is more or less independent and separate from its member states. Hence, even if it was not always the case and only after the Lisbon Treaty, the

EU can decide on its own on different matters belonging to its exclusive competence or those matters falling under the shared competence with its member states (under certain conditions). To recall, the EU has exclusive competence on matters involving the following: (1) the customs union; (2) the establishing of the competition rules necessary for the functioning of the internal market and monetary policy for the member states whose currency is the euro; (3) the conservation of marine biological resources under the common fisheries policy; (4) Common Commercial Policy; and (5) conclusion of certain international agreements. Shared competence, on the other hand, could include areas member states cannot exercise competence where the EU has done so such as the internal market, area of freedom, security, and justice, etc. Shared competence includes likewise areas where member states are not precluded from exercising competence such as in terms of humanitarian aid, research and technological development, and common foreign, security, and defense policies. Based on these, the EU could not only develop Union-wide policies but likewise enter into soft law agreements, treaties, or international agreements on behalf of its member states. Thus, there are agreements such as the ENPs or international treaties involving economic and trade policies.

Its policy making includes the use of directives, regulations, and decisions. In turn, member states are beholden to the principle of sincere cooperation and ensure that they abide with the decisions and policies of the EU. Furthermore, there is an enforcement mechanism through the European Commission, which acts as the EU watchdog and ensures that member states are complying with their respective commitments and responsibilities. In relation to this, the EU is unique with its legislative policy and overall constitutional mechanism. Given the same, there is the unique principle of institutional balance that keeps the EU institutions working well with each other. This is not the same as the principle of checks and balances existing in national jurisdictions. Instead, it allows proper delegation of duties and responsibilities among the EU institutions. One may not act in excess of its authority.

Anent such legislative policy, it is formalistic but still encourages at some points the consensus approach, which is similar to the ASEAN process. Should there be for example no agreement among the Parliament, Council, or Commission, then the TEU and TFEU would encourage taking consensus and open communication to resolve any existing issues. Further, the EU institutions would have agreements among each other in fostering good working relations. While they do not necessarily need to agree on everything (which would be counter-intuitive to the principle of institutional balance for example), there is an effort to have amiability among each other.

Additionally, it can be mentioned that the member states can forge agreements with each other under the concept of enhanced (formerly, close) cooperation, which was introduced in the Amsterdam Treaty. Under the said concept, member states which are interested to forge cooperation with one another can use the existing mechanisms and procedures available as long as they are consistent with the spirit and letter of the existing treaties.

The ASEAN by virtue of the provisions of its ASEAN Charter could also act on its own as an international organization and legally speaking, can enter into agreements on behalf of its member states. To a certain extent, this might be misleading. The ASEAN remains still as an intergovernmental organization. Its decision-making processes and the overall functioning of the organization and its respective bodies are dependent on the member states. Hence, it is a condition *sine qua non* that member states agree to the agreements or treaties the ASEAN would enter into on their behalf.

In light of this, the consensus approach remains at all levels, even at the highest authoritative body in the organization which is the ASEAN Summit. There is neither an authority which demands or enforces compliance among the member states, nor an authority which would dictate what member states need to do. In this respect, there would be no principle of sincere cooperation nor principle of institutional balance to speak of, albeit member states sworn themselves to politeness and being cooperative in the declarations and agreements concluded in the organization. In fact, the principle of non-intervention prohibits member states to be critical of each other with regard the respective national affairs of each one within the ASEAN framework. Having said this, the main legislative output in the ASEAN are the declarations (soft law agreements) and treaties. There have been no framework decisions, decisions, directives, nor regulations that would need to be transposed to the domestic law. One can note that in most years of the organization, the member states limited themselves into declarations. This is because the ASEAN is less formalistic and more into soft law endeavors. There has been a paradigm shift nowadays, depending on the area of policy subject of the agreement, wherein ASEAN member states use treaties and international agreements. Most of these treaties could be observed in economic and trade policies as well as the building blocks for the ASEAN Economic Community.

Member states can then opt to enter into bilateral treaties (even with each other) or use the ASEAN mechanism to conclude agreements with one another. As mentioned above, there ought to be acquiescence or agreement from all to be binding and valid. The ASEAN Way in this respect enters the picture and further, the concept of "ASEAN-X". Should there be an agreement that one or some of the member states are not agreeable to, then such member state(s) shall not be forced to do something it does not want to. Such member state(s) may of course be convinced to decide otherwise but without the compulsion or enforcement the EU, for example, can do. Given the same, only those which were agreeable to the agreement shall be included, with the option of the non-agreeing member states to join in later on. An example of this is the Agreement on Information Exchange, which was entered into under the ASEAN framework but not all member states are parties to.

Another matter that could be mentioned about cooperation mechanism with respect its member states and respective bodies and institutions is the difference between the ASEAN and the EU as regards having an adjudicatory body. The ASEAN does not have a similar body such as the CJEU in the European Union. There is no regional adjudicatory body that would be instrumental in developing regional doctrines or themes. Further, any conflicts are resolved among the member states with the same kind of ASEAN Way. Significantly, the same kind of conflict resolution in ASEAN has been consistent even from the beginning. Before Vietnam, Cambodia, Laos, and Myanmar joined the ASEAN, there were conflicts and mistrust from these countries of the organization. There were also the conflicts within the said countries that ought to be resolved. One can look back as well into the territorial dispute over Sabah for example between Malaysia and the Philippines, or the expulsion of Singapore from the Federation of Malaysia, or the *konfrontasi* done by Indonesia, which all existed prior to the decision to form the ASEAN. Through consensus approach, and not being antagonistic in general, the ASEAN was instrumental in resolving conflicts and later convincing Vietnam, Cambodia, Laos, and Myanmar to join the organization, which consequently led to its expansion. This notwithstanding, the ASEAN has been criticized for being a talk shop and being a failure as a regional organization. It was criticized for allegedly mishandling the Asian Financial Crisis in 1997, the conflict in East Timor, and the military junta in Myanmar, among other things. Part of the criticism involves the ASEAN Way as a manner of avoiding problems and not solving them outright. Nonetheless, the ASEAN as a regional organization persists and able to maintain its cooperation mechanism with its member states dealing with issues when they are ready to do so.

The topic of existing cooperative mechanisms is not limited to the member states. It also includes external partnerships and the external actions the respective organizations engage in. The ASEAN believes in being inclusive and outward-looking. It is receptive to constructive relations with other countries or regional organizations. At the same time, it is inclusive in its approach to regional endeavors should one want stability and security in the Southeast Asian region. It follows that the ASEAN is open to trade, economic links, and security dialogues with other countries and groups of countries and with other international organizations. Based on this, ASEAN was actually the pioneer of dialogue partnerships with numerous countries and the European Union (which nowadays has been elevated to an "enhanced partnership" that calls for stronger cooperation in different areas). Such dialogue partnerships revolved initially around economic issues but later on evolved to include political and security ones. Significantly, the dialogue partnerships paved way to so-called post ministerial conferences, which allow bilateral discussions to be made between ASEAN member states and partner countries every after ASEAN Summit. Likewise, ASEAN also established the ASEAN Regional Forum, East Asia Summit, and the ASEAN+3. Following the ASEAN Way of consensus-based decision-making, the ASEAN Regional Forum provides the venue for political and security talks while the latter mentioned two forums/groupings focus on fostering cooperation between ASEAN and its neighbors.

Underlying the foregoing processes is the use of dialogues in fostering cooperation in and on behalf of the ASEAN member states. To a certain extent, the value of ASEAN as a normative power could be highlighted because it has been instrumental in sharing the advantages of a consensus approach as regards certain issues and problems that ought to be addressed. In fact, it was through the ASEAN that other non-ASEAN countries acquiesced to the Treaty of Amity and Cooperation, which among other things disavows the use of weapons or violence in the region. While treaties or agreements may not automatically result from these dialogues or discussions between ASEAN, its member states, and external partners, it could still end in undertakings between countries, or between ASEAN, its member states, and other countries or regional organizations. The ARF is a good example of the same, which includes influential countries such the United States and EU member states. Certain problems and issues could be raised during meetings of the same without being adversarial and antagonistic with each other. Further, there is the avenue for more understanding among each other without necessarily being controversial.

The EU, on the other hand, is equally engaged in external relations. Admittedly, concluding agreements and arrangements with other countries and organizations form a big chunk of the organization's dealings. In light of this, the external action the EU partakes in illustrates the range of ambitious, global roles for the EU, including increasing its global clout and influence. Simultaneously, the EU promotes through its external actions the ideals and values it holds dearly, such as those involving peace and security, democracy and human rights, and aid to less privileged countries, defending the social model, establishing its position in world markets, preventing environmental damage, and ensure sustainable growth.

The normative power of the EU, which was earlier mentioned, is also apparent in its global politics. To illustrate, there are the numerous developmental programs it endeavors on. Another example is much closer to home: the European Neighborhood Policy, wherein the EU and its neighbor-partners agree on action plans grounded on incentives, which more or less caters to the EU standards and values within the socio-, economic, and political planes. This common observation notwithstanding, it was mentioned in previous chapters that not all analysts however buy into the idea of the EU as solely a normative power. They believe that the EU does not act so benignly all-time but also as a "soft imperialism power": the emphasis on democratization projects, strategies for "new abroad" are seen as examples of the EU's hegemonic power driven by both normative and strategic interests such as the need for stability. The same examples cited earlier equally apply: a look into the historical development of the ENP, for example, was initiated at the first place to secure the EU's borders, believing that what happens with its neighbors might spill over to its affairs. The provisions of the ENP were fashioned more or less to cater to EU's stability and not only to influence the Union's neighbors to internalize EU values and policies.

If these observations are truly accurate, then it would be reflective of the influence the historical development of the EU has. "Soft imperialism power" would be toned down version of what the Roman Empire espoused and the colonizers which came after in during the early modern era. One could then see how the EU and its member states are convinced of their own truths and how the same should be assimilated elsewhere. Moreover, it becomes doubtful of true underlying intentions behind its endeavors.

C. Approach to Regional Security and International Cooperation

The European integration project has been since its inception a security project, with its key output being a powerful security community. The EU slowly eased towards the nomenclature of "security policy", which focuses on mechanisms for ensuring security both among its member states and between them and the wider world, and influences thereafter the "fluctuating balance between the EU's position as consumer and producer of security."

The EU is unique as regards how security and defense policy is handled given that the EU commits itself in its external action to "effective multilateralism" and prevention as a means of conflict management. Accordingly, the EU deepened and broadened the reach of its foreign and security policy, but it likewise adheres to a more comprehensive concept of security. The EU is equally devoted to it vis-à-vis the "area of freedom, security, and justice". During the period involving the 11 September 2001 attacks in the United States, one could see the overlapping or interconnectedness between criminal law policies and security and foreign policy in the EU. While not necessarily following the steps of the United States in handling the matter of terrorism, etc., the EU had the realization that the success of one area of policy is enhanced or determined by the other. In connection therewith, the EU has enacted a substantial number of measures, including, if not particularly, on police and judicial cooperation in criminal matters.

Compared to the EU, the ASEAN is more of a regional security partnership. It may be envisioned to be a security community at its establishment but it was not within the penumbra of a traditional security community. Instead, the ASEAN illustrates an arrangement created by a majority of states in the region and by extraregional powers, who act as partners in upholding plurality of means to manage regional security. What does not make it a traditional security community is its realization that it is preferable, if not practical, to construct a security system based on jointly managed mechanisms and programs, rather than one entirely founded on relative strength of a military alliance. Thus, one could notice an encouragement within the ASEAN for capacity-building on a member state level. Strength among the member states would translate to strength of he organization.

Further, the ASEAN organization's view of regional security and stability is not myopic. Rather, it adheres to comprehensive security and takes into consideration at the outset non-traditional security threats as well.

Although the ASEAN is still criticized due to the processes of dialogues and consensus among its member states and with its external partners, the ASEAN has normalized informal processes for regional issues to be resolved in non-violent ways. It has also provided a regional context within which peaceful negotiations could be conducted. As observed, there have been occasional tensions among member states due to centrifugal tendencies brought by diversity of membership, or otherwise some remaining degree of mutual suspicion, but at the same time, no conflict has erupted in Southeast Asia. Based thereon, the ASEAN espouses regional security on the basis of mutual confidence, consensus, and balance of interests.

Both organizations are open to the idea of forging agreements or arrangements as regards international cooperation in criminal matters. Internally, or among the ASEAN member states, the process towards the same might be more laborious considering that no one is taking a lead within said organization that would otherwise set the needed agenda, plans, roadmaps, etc. The EU conversely has the mechanism for making agendas and laying down roadmaps that ought to be followed by virtue of its supranational nature and the Commission fills in the role of initiating legislative output. The Parliament and the European Council could also make suggestions or ask for inputs regarding a particular point. Though having its own process, which could likewise be laborious, there would be a responsible body in the EU to stir the course of the organization. .

This obviously does not occur within the ASEAN, although sometimes they have agendas set for each meeting they organized at all levels of the organization. To illustrate, the ASEAN, since its establishment, had proposals laid down to establish an extradition treaty. However, more than 50 years have passed and yet there has been no extradition treaty. ASEAN member states are still in the drawing table for said treaty. While this is understandable given the nature of how decision-making is done within the ASEAN, the time consumed might be unproductive in addressing certain issues, especially in exigent or urgent circumstances. What ASEAN member states could do then is to address these issues individually or domestically, bilaterally, with the other country involved. In the alternative, the lack of concrete, detailed, or preemptive arrangements can enable ad hoc measures and flexibility among the ASEAN member states. For example, some ASEAN member states have the Agreement on Information Exchange and Establishment of Communication Procedures. Looking into the provisions herein however, the cooperation or sharing of databases for example, happens at as needed basis. To elucidate, there is no automatic sharing of passenger name records between the contracting states. Instead, it is indicated as "as needed" or "as appropriate".

So far, the EU criminal justice architecture is more complex, intensive, and sophisticated than what the ASEAN has. Noticeably, the EU member states historically took seriously the importance of fostering cross-border cooperation in criminal matters, regardless of whether it is police-to-police cooperation (which notably TREVI illustrates) or judicial cooperation. Their commitment was manifested through their participation in the different treaties in the Council of Europe on judicial cooperation. To recall, the Council of Europe (to which EU member states were also a part of) was the progenitor of landmark judicial cooperation agreements in Europe such as the 1959 European Convention on Extradition and the Convention on Mutual Legal Assistance. The Council of Europe has interestingly covered all aspects of international cooperation in criminal matters such as transfer of persons in custody to serve sentences, enforcement of sentences, and transfer of criminal proceedings.

It has now admittedly the expertise, the well-financed institutions, databases, and base agreements needed to fuel any criminal justice architecture it has built thus far. To illustrate, it has the benefits of the Schengen Agreement, the Prüm Convention for sharing and exchange of DNA databases, sharing of passenger name records, among many things, to make the investigation, prosecution, and prevention of (transnational) crime efficacious. The EU is also quick at its feet compared to the ASEAN given that there are the EU institutions tasked in addressing imperative issues. There are available networks and integration on a police, prosecutorial, and judicial level through the existence of the Europol, Eurojust, and the EJN that allows close coordination and cooperation among member states. In other words, the EU possesses the required architecture to operationalize and function while the ASEAN due to its intergovernmental nature depends on the capacities of its member states to succeed. Additionally, like the ASEAN the EU allows member states to conclude agreements or arrangements with each other on certain policy areas as long as the same is in line with the vision and ideals of the EU.

It must be mentioned though that cooperation in criminal matters in the EU was not instantly supranational in nature. In the beginning, cooperation and coordination in tackling issues surrounding criminal matters was done intergovernmentally. Predominantly decisions and policymaking were done by the member states in the Council of Europe. Thus, at one point in time, the EU was akin to the ASEAN in being intergovernmental as regards decision-making and crafting mechanisms among its member states for more effective crime control. To illustrate, the efforts made by the ASEAN member states against drug trafficking in the Southeast Asian region, which is one of, if not the most, serious transnational crime problem in the region, is reminiscent of the TREVI cooperation and the formative years of the Europol (Drug Monitoring Center).

Comparing this to the ASEAN, it must be mentioned at the outset that the ASEAN member states take transnational crime seriously. It understood that in Southeast Asia the problem of transnational crime is severe and pervasive. It consists of illicit drug trafficking, human trafficking, money laundering, transnational prostitution, piracy, arms smuggling, international economic crimes, cybercrime, and corruption. Three ASEAN member states (e.g. Myanmar, Laos, and Thailand) are major producers of narcotics and transit points for drugs sent to North America, Europe, and other parts of Asia. At the same time, some of the largest and most dangerous criminal organizations operate in the region (e.g. Chinese triads, Japanese yakuza, Vietnamese gangs). Hence, there were efforts to combat drug trafficking and transnational crime since the inception of the ASEAN.

The ASEAN however adopted a different approach than the EU member states. The ASEAN member states were mainly into the establishment of expert group meetings or forums where experts and ministers could meet and exchange ideas and possible proposals, as well as declarations and soft law agreements, which arguably have little to no enforceability compared to a treaty obligation. In these declarations, the ASEAN member states would declare respectively their commitments to the cause and exert efforts to fight drug trafficking or transnational crime. More often than not, these declarations would include the salient points that ought to be addressed in the respective national systems of the member states. While member states would nevertheless act despite such non-formalistic arrangements, there is no enforcement mechanism that would ensure compliance. Rather, the nature of a gentlemen's agreement exists among the member states. Member states are preempted by the principle of non-intervention to call out each other on implementation flaws. If non-compliance indeed exists, the most another member state can do is to engage the other into dialogues bilaterally, and outside the ASEAN framework. This is allowed by enhanced interaction, especially if non-compliance or the problem touches on the regional security or stability, or otherwise having regional repercussions if not addressed.

The ASEAN likewise distinguishes itself from the EU with regard the judicial cooperation mechanisms. Aside from the ASEAN MLAT, within the ASEAN framework there were no other forms of judicial or legal cooperation like with the EU member states vis-à-vis the Council of Europe. There are no agreements on transfer of persons in custody to serve sentences, enforcement of sentences, or transfer of criminal proceedings to speak of.

Notwithstanding the different approaches taken in this regard, both regional organizations and their respective member states were not spared from complexities arising from transnational crime. In the ASEAN for example, globalization, technological advancement, greater mobility of people and resources through national borders has enabled transnational crime to become more pervasive, diversified, and organized. The region had to acknowledge and deal with many new forms of organized crimes that transcend national borders and political sovereignty such as terrorism, new types of drug abuse and trafficking, innovative forms of money laundering activities, arms smuggling, trafficking in women and children, and piracy. This pervasiveness does not only occur in the Southeast Asian region alone but European states are likewise susceptible to these problems.

Moreover, both the ASEAN and the EU were besieged with problems related to terrorism. In 11 September 2001, the entire world was caught in surprise by the terrorist attacks in the United States. The United States thereafter announced that the Southeast Asian region was the second front on the global war on terror, while Europe also experienced terrorist attacks like in Madrid, Spain on March 2004. In response, the ASEAN member states continued cooperation and coordination as regards regional counterterrorism measures, considering that terrorism problems in many Southeast Asian countries are localized and terrorist networks might be operating in the region (e.g. Abu Sayyaf Group in the Philippines, Jema'ah Islamiyah in Indonesia). The ASEAN came up as well with a Declaration on Joint Action to Counter Terrorism, wherein they expressed their joint commitment to combat terrorism, including initiating cooperative joint practical counterterrorism measures that are in line with a member state's specific circumstances. It bears mentioning that the counterterrorism measures laid down in said Declaration were meant to increase the capacity of existing frameworks in combating transnational crime.

In addition, the ASEAN member states (Philippines, Malaysia, Indonesia, Cambodia, Brunei, and Thailand) under the ASEAN framework entered into an Agreement on Information Exchange and Establishment of Communication Procedures on 07 May 2002 to promote cooperation in combating transnational crime, including terrorism through the establishment of communication networks, logistical arrangements, combined training, and border controls, among others. Likewise, counter-terrorism measures were initiated in the ASEAN-led ARF including workshops on capacity building.

With the response given by the ASEAN, terrorism threw challenges towards its existing regional mechanisms. Despite the member states being agreeable to a united front, efforts have been hampered by domestic politics and public sensitivities, especially in Muslim-majority countries such as Malaysia and Indonesia, or those with large Muslim-minorities such as the Philippines and Thailand. This notwithstanding, ASEAN equivocally rejected any identification of terrorism with religion and was clear in saying that "terrorist elements" refer to Islamic extremists.

As mentioned above, the EU also encountered its share of terrorist attacks. After the September 2001 attacks in the United States, Europe realized that it was not merely a target, or a contributor due to the growing number of radicalized, marginalized, and poorly integrated Muslims in European societies, but more importantly, it was a quintessential player that needed immediate response in countering and/or battling terrorism and transborder crime. As a way to respond, there was a change in many policy areas as well as new countermeasures and strategies to impede the increasing security threat of transnational crime and terrorism. In fact, the development of EU Criminal Law was at its high peak during 2001 to 2004. One could observe further the substantial momentum gained with the nexus between internal and external security resulting in merging of police systems, judicial systems, special forces, and external military action. There was a reorganization of the security apparatus at the local, national, and European level wherein one could see a closer cooperation between intelligence services, the police, and the military at the national and transatlantic levels.

Experience with domestic terrorism and other forms of "grassroots" terrorism (e.g. left-wing terrorism in Germany, national terrorism in France, Spain, and the United Kingdom) has prompted Europe to adopt an all-encompassing approach, which included in particular, an intensification in improving and/or innovating its law enforcement and judicial measures. Europe generally stayed on the path of a criminal justice model, which included among others, an action plan to fight terrorism. Framework Decisions on the European Arrest Warrant, Joint Investigation Teams, and Terrorism came at the advent of such action plans, which meant to expedite the extradition process among member states, allow the establishment of teams comprising law enforcement and judicial representatives jointly working in cross-border investigations involving two or more member states, and enumerate acts that could constitute terrorism, respectively. It can be said that these three framework decisions overall meant to stress the importance of harmonizing the legislation of serious crimes.

Then the terrorist attacks in Madrid occurred in March 2004 which showed a poor implementation of EU policies on a domestic level. Prior to this, the EU came up with the 2003 European Security Strategy but implementation on a domestic level was not impressive. Thereafter a Declaration on Combating Terrorism was made on 25 March 2004 that identifies implementation flaws that member states needed to address, such as police and judicial cooperation, as well as lists strategic objectives and the "Europanization" of the threat through a formal commitment of each member state to assist should another member state fall victim to a terrorist attack.

Subsequently, the European Commission was fulfilling its role as policy entrepreneur when it fielded months after the Declaration communications formulating policies on terrorism financing, infrastructure protection, and response management, all of which were within its competencies. Careful about the supranational recipes it was formulating and proposing, the Commission focused on increasing information exchange and enhancing coordination through different mechanisms. This occurred simultaneously with the acceptance of the European Council of the 2004 Hague Programme that called for approximation of substantive criminal law provisions, which should make it easier to apply the principle of mutual recognition of penal-judicial decisions, especially so in serious offense areas with an international dimension. At the same time, the European Council recognized the need or importance to improve international exchange of information about criminal prosecutions and to this end, introduced the "principle of availability of information", under which criminal prosecuting authorities of member states should be able to perform their duties unhindered, since all useful information would be universally accessible. Aside from this, one can witness institutional changes in general within the Union through either the creation of new offices or the revigorization of existing ones as regards counterterrorism measures.

In light of the foregoing, the difference in approaches is further highlighted. Furthermore, a few observations can be mentioned regarding to the pace by which the two regional organizations function:

When the EU entered into modified intergovernmentalism with regard criminal matters, specifically on judicial cooperation, through the Amsterdam Treaty, one could notice more aggressive endeavors to foster cooperation in criminal matters. Certain developments can be mentioned in this respect. First, there were the aspirations for an EU Area of Freedom, Security, and Justice. The EU was at one point described to be a "laboratory" for experimental criminal law policies. Second, there was the criminalization of certain offenses and the development of substantive criminal law on a regional level. As mentioned above, the peak was during the response of the EU against terrorism in the region. Third, there was the introduction of Framework Decisions (which later changed to Directives and Regulations during the Lisbon Treaty) that hastened policies and mechanisms vis-à-vis judicial cooperation in criminal matters, without necessarily requiring the consent of the member states. Fourth, there was the introduction of the principle of mutual recognition in criminal matters, which was grounded on mutual trust among the EU member states. An example of this is the European Arrrest Warrant, which as mentioned above was integral to counter-terrorism measures. Fifth, there was a simultaneous establishment or strengthening of EU institutions on a police, prosecutorial, and judicial levels such as the Europol, Eurojust, and EJN, that are all integral in the efficacious cooperation among member states in criminal matters. Taking the foregoing into account, the EU has been able to follow through in general its roadmaps and plans of actions as regards criminal matters resulting in the sophisticated architecture it has now.

In comparison, the developments in the ASEAN are less grand and far-reaching. It also appeared to be on a slower pace. The ASEAN did not meddle into the national policies and affairs of each member state notwithstanding the call for enhanced cooperative efforts and closer cooperation in tackling cross-border crime. They shared the view that it is important to address transnational issues to prevent negative consequences to the organization and the member states but formal cooperation mechanisms like in the EU can barely be found. Instead, there was the establishment for example of the ASEAN Ministers Meeting on Transnational Crime, which signals the securitization of transnational crime in the region. Moreover, there is no integration or close cooperation within the ASEAN framework vis-à-vis the police, prosecutorial, or judicial authorities. The ASEANAPOL may be the national police organization for the ASEAN but it is not within the ASEAN framework. Further, the ASEAN does not have the same kind of sophisticated database systems that the EU has started to promote, establish, and integrate in its criminal justice architecture.

Albeit the ASEAN member states within themselves did not have concretized formal treaties on cooperation in criminal matters, the ASEAN did not waste time and thereafter entered into joint declarations and/or agreements with other countries in efforts to combat transnational crime. Significantly, terrorism was designated by the ASEAN ministers as early as 1997 as a prevalent issue that needs to be addressed and after the 11 September 2001 attacks in the United States, the ASEAN member states engaged in cooperative measures that are not necessarily covered by treaty obligations. The ASEAN eventually came up with a Convention on Counter-Terrorism, ASEAN Convention against the Trafficking of Persons, ASEAN Mutual Legal Assistance Treaty, among other declarations and agreements.

In comparison to the EU, it would be easy to dismiss the ASEAN as having no efforts within the organization and among its member states to have a roadmap or plan of action it can stick with and implement. It would also be easy to criticize the ASEAN for not following through on its political will and commitments. Measuring its achievements and developments with the policies of the EU could lead someone to believe that the ASEAN is a failure in its efforts. However, these criticisms arise from the lack of understanding the ASEAN and the mechanisms it has. It cannot be measured with parameters of what it is not or what it is not trying to be. As discussed earlier, the ASEAN is a different organization than the EU. It does not likewise aspire to be the EU as a supranational authority.

Having mentioned this, the ASEAN also came up with plans of action to combat terrorism and transnational crime for example. Commitments were also made with other countries for joint efforts to address these problems. Admittedly however, developments in the regional level work at a slower pace than in the EU. This has been especially the case when judicial cooperation and criminal matters in general fell under the supranational authority of the EU. The EU has designated bodies that handle legislative policy and there is a good working mechanism towards decision and policymaking. Hence, the EU has been able to establish database systems, measures such as the European Arrest Warrant and the European Investigation Order, and other infrastructures helpful to cooperation in criminal matters.

Notwithstanding the seemingly faster pace by which the EU works in its decisions and policymaking in relation to criminal matters, the EU was not immune to criticisms and challenges. To elucidate, one may notice that due to the urgent need to respond to the terrorist attacks and quell heightened emotions of its citizens, European policy makers used ready-made recipes in the Tampere Programme to address issues (i.e. establishment of structures such as Eurojust, Police Chiefs Task Force, and the

European Police College, and strengthening of the existing Europol). Inevitably, this leads to the notion that the policy changes being introduced were not from a careful study of the threat but instead, were only through a "reactive borrowing" from a list the EU policy makers thought sufficient to address the emerging issues.

Further, implementation on a regional level does not necessarily translate to smooth and effective implementation on a member state level. While the EU policymakers were busy in crafting regional policies, it dawned on them after the Madrid attacks in 2004 that there has been dismal implementation on a member state level. There were many implementation flaws that needed to be addressed. And although implementation flaws are better avoided or handled with the supranational authority over criminal matters through approximation, there could still be differences in degree and manner of implementation. In connection to this, implementation problems could also arise due to incompatibility with the fundamental principles and norms of the member state. This was for example experienced when the European Arrest Warrant was first introduced. The idea behind it was initially for "automatic execution" without further inquiry on the basis of the principle of mutual recognition in criminal matters. It soon became apparent that this cannot be the case due to constitutional principles some member states must adhere to, such as the non-surrender or extradition of own nationals by Germany. Thus, on the EU level adjustments were made to adhere to certain intricacies.

Taking the above discussion into account, the ASEAN and the EU as regards criminal law policy and/or international cooperation in criminal matters more or less are on the same page. Any difference lies in approach and execution. Differences in approach however did not mean that one would be in a better situation than the other. Both the ASEAN and the EU encountered challenges and difficulties in relation to their respective responses to terrorism and transnational crime.

D. Mutual Legal Assistance in Criminal Matters

Both the ASEAN and the EU have mutual legal assistance agreements among its member states. As mentioned in the previous chapters, the ASEAN would have the 2004 Mutual Legal Assistance Treaty whilst the EU would have the European Investigative Order among its member states.

As to how these came about, the EIO was not the first EU instrument tackling mutual legal assistance. Its member states started with the 1959 Council of Europe MLA Convention, which is the mother instrument on mutual legal assistance in criminal matters among European states. There are also the mutual legal assistance provisions one can find in the Convention Implementing the Schengen Agreement. Then there was the 2000 MLA Convention, which introduced new features that aim to make the MLA system among member states more efficient. Thereafter, the principle of mutual recognition based on mutual trust was applied equally to criminal law policy. There was likewise a shift from how the cooperation mechanism is based on treaty to being based on a directive that ought to be transposed domestically by the member states. A product of this in relation to MLA would be the European Evidence Warrant, which would then apply to evidence already collected and readily available to be transmitted to another member state. This became however moot and academic by virtue of the applicability of the EIO later on.

Compared to the EU, the ASEAN only has its 2004 MLA treaty as the singular ASEAN agreement tackling mutual legal assistance. It is not a directive or anything similar imposed by the ASEAN on its member states. Rather, it is an international agreement agreed upon by the member states. Further, there was no historical development wherein there were older treaties in existence. Interestingly, its member states would exercise reciprocity and provide mutual legal assistance without basis on treaty.

It can be said that the respective agreements of the ASEAN and the EU would have similar structures, maintaining the usual elements that could be found in a MLA arrangement or treaty. The difference instead lies on the applicability of the principle of mutual recognition in the EU instrument, the importance of the respective values and ideals of each organization, the applicability of other instruments and arrangements within the respective organizations, and the consideration of other issues such as technological advancements. These would be apparent in the substantive and procedural provisions of the respective mutual legal assistance arrangements.

For the substantive provisions, there are four (4) circumstances which were looked into in this present study. First, there is the applicability of assistance. As mentioned above, the EIO is based on a directive while the ASEAN MLAT is based on treaty. Assistance based on the EIO lies more on the principle of mutual recognition based on mutual trust, and the overall principle of sincere cooperation that member states need to abide with. Having said this, both the ASEAN and the EU enjoin their respective member states to provide the widest possible assistance to each other. Although the ASEAN instrument does not specifically state, both the EIO and the said ASEAN MLAT applies indiscriminately to both natural and legal persons. As regards discrepancies that could arise due to differences on liabilities of legal persons, for example, the ASEAN and the EU accommodate open communication among the relevant member states and its authorities to address the issue.

At this point, this study notes that it is easier to attribute the existence of open communication channels among authorities to the ASEAN than the EU due to the existence of the ASEAN Way notwithstanding the shift towards formalistic agreements such as those involving criminal matters such as the ASEAN MLAT. Interviews and personal communication with authorities from the ASEAN member states give the sense that the openness, courtesy, and respect prevalent in the ASEAN organizational culture continuously exist and is instrumental in the carrying out of tasks and responsibilities. It is revealed however that the same kind of congeniality and open communication generally exists as well for EU authorities. In general, the EU is driven by its formalistic and legalistic way of operations. There is in the organization itself a well built and oiled bureaucratic structure necessitated by its supranational nature.

This bureaucratic nature notwithstanding, there are snippets of the consensus approach scattered across its institutions and the implementation of its policies and legal framework, such as the case of international cooperation in criminal matters herein. Backtracking a bit, the consensus approach has found its way for example in the interactions between the European Parliament, European Commission, and the European Council vis-à-vis the EU ordinary legislative procedure. While not exactly falling within the four corners of how the ASEAN Way works, the rudiments of consensus-building and its benefits are still there. As regards the mechanism for regional cooperation in criminal matters, such as the EIO, despite the very formalistic requirement of filling up a pro-forma EIO, for example, practitioners are not prejudiced to contact the receiving end of its request and consult if needed. Consensus is likewise encouraged for certain issues that may be met in the EIO framework. Significantly, aspects of this open communication and networking has been institutionalized in the EU already. The EJN, Eurojust, and the EUROPOL are some of the components of the EU Criminal Justice Architecture that allows this kind of connectivity and networking to flourish. And attested to by some practitioners interviewed for this study, liaison officers and contact persons make it possible to effectuate needed requests and/or EIO's and apply the needed assistance to the requesting member state.

Another aspect that can be mentioned as regards applicability of assistance is on territorial application. The EIO does not apply to all EU member states such as Denmark and Ireland. The EU Criminal Justice Architecture is unique in this sense wherein some member states can opt out of a particular measure and should they decide to apply said measure, like the UK vis-à-vis the EIO, they ought to manifest their intention to opt in.

In relation to this, there is the pending issue nowadays with the EU due to the exit of the United Kingdom, which opted in earlier to the EIO and other arrangements constituting the EU Criminal Justice Architecture. Albeit agreement has been reached, there is still uncertainty given the change of status of the relationship between the UK and the EU.

In comparison, the territorial application of the ASEAN MLAT applies to all member states of the ASEAN, which are signatories to the said treaty. The member states were all on board the MLA treaty. More recently, the ASEAN MLAT was made into a true regional instrument that allows contracting parties that are not ASEAN member states. While many expressed their intention to accede, the contracting parties of the ASEAN MLAT at the date of this writing has still been limited to the ASEAN member states.

Second, one could look into the types of assistance the respective MLA instruments cover. Both would apply to coercive and non-coercive measures alike. The EIO would not however apply to joint investigative teams and cross-border surveillance, for example, as these measures are covered by different EU instruments. The ASEAN MLAT, on the other hand, provides a specific list of measures, with a catch-all provision that allows other measures to be entertained, depending on what is agreed upon by the relevant member states. It follows that joint investigative teams might be possible, for example, under the ASEAN context, should the same be agreed upon by the member states involved. Further, there is the possibility of exchange of online evidence on the basis of said catch-all provision, albeit specific provisions on the same are not provided for in the ASEAN MLAT.

Third, there is the compatibility of their respective MLA instruments with other arrangements. For the EU, one could look into the overall criminal justice architecture it has developed throughout the years. There is also possible resort to informal forms of cooperation using the networks that could be provided by the Eurojust, Europol, and the EJN, for example. As regards the ASEAN, this could mainly contemplate as well existing arrangements such as using the Agreement on Information Exchange and Establishment of Communication Procedures as another legal basis. There is also the existence of formal and informal channels of cooperation among ASEAN member states. The ASEANAPOL, albeit independent of the organization, is vastly used and available in establishing contacts as per informal cooperation. In respect to this comparison, the importance of using both forms of informal and formal cooperation in the criminal justice process cannot be underestimated. Hence, one can look into the integration and cooperation models occurring in the EU not only on a judicial cooperation level but also in the infrastructures on the police, prosecutorial, and judicial levels.

Fourth, the ASEAN and the EU both have a baseline of principles, conditions, and exceptions applicable in their respective instruments. Firstly, one could cite the sufficiency of evidence requirement both have in respect of the investigative measures that could be covered by their respective instruments. This requirement is best understood by stating that in the event of more intrusive measures, more information or relevance of the investigative measure should be provided for. This is understandable given the harder scrutiny domestic courts would require as regards coercive measures. Thus, this requirement is meant to easier facilitate the execution of an EIO or MLA request, respectively.

Another requirement apparent in both the ASEAN and EU instruments is on dual criminality. Both provide the same as a ground to refuse a request. However, the EU differentiates itself by qualifying said requirement. While it would apply in general, it would not apply to a list of 32 offenses under certain conditions. Dual criminality is one of the requirements existing with speciality and reciprocity in traditional mutual legal assistance instruments. Although the ASEAN MLAT retains the same in its purest form, the difference in the EU context can be attributed to the principle of mutual recognition.

The prohibition on double jeopardy or the application of the principle on *ne bis in idem* applies in both the ASEAN and EU instruments as a mandatory ground for refusal. There is no congruence on how the concepts are defined and applied however. As regards the ASEAN, there is the prohibition of double jeopardy under the ASEAN MLAT and it is a mandatory ground to refuse a request: a requested state shall deny assistance when the request relates to an investigation, prosecution, or punishment of a person for an offense where the person either has been convicted, acquitted, or pardoned by a competent court or other authority in the requesting or requested member state; or has undergone the punishment provided by law of that requesting or requested member state, in respect of that offense or of another offense constitute by the same act or omission as the first-mentioned offense. The same has arguably a transnational element in application (although limited between the requesting and requested states) and is reasonably consistent with the provisions provided in the ASEAN Human Rights Declaration regarding double jeopardy, to wit, "no person shall be liable to be tried or punished for an offense he or she has already been finally convicted or acquitted in accordance with the law and penal procedure of each ASEAN member state."

Considering the foregoing, the definition of the prohibition in the ASEAN Human Rights Declaration is made dependent on domestic law and procedure. There is also no ASEAN counterpart to any European Court of Human Rights or European Court of Justice that could further provide clarification and definition to the matter. Thus, there would be reliance on the application of the member states and how they would understand the concept. This further illustrates a quasi-formality, wherein member states can determine by themselves a policy, a definition, or a procedure, albeit the general details or the needed commitment may be provided in the regional instrument.

Moreover, the transnational element being espoused in the ASEAN MLAT provision is not consistent with the much later ASEAN Human Rights Declaration. There is seemingly no harmonization between two similar ASEAN instruments. Furthermore, the transnational element introduced in the ASEAN MLAT provision restricts itself between the requesting and requested state. Yet, there could be instances when the conviction, acquittal, pardon, or service of punishment occurring in another ASEAN member state or third state. If one follows the strict wording of the ASEAN MLAT, then the ground to refuse would not apply. However, if one is true to the spirit of the prohibition and the transnational element the ASEAN MLAT provision imbibes, then it would be proper for the MLA request to be denied should the conviction, acquittal, pardon, or service of punishment occurred in another ASEAN member state or third state.

The foregoing observations about the ASEAN context notwithstanding, this does not mean that the EU has perfectly determined and settled the principle of *ne bis in idem*. At the outset, the prohibition on double jeopardy is provided for in the European Convention on Human Rights and later on, in the Charter of Fundamental Rights. Notably, the existence of these instruments maybe similar to the ASEAN instrument on human rights but unlike ASEAN, the EU has an adjudicatory body.

Before, the principle's application only had an internal effect but there had been efforts to give it a transnational effect in light of the formation of an area of freedom, security, and justice as well as the principle of free movement of persons. Efforts towards the same include Article 54 of the CISA, which includes an enforcement element. This enforcement element in turn has been declared by the CJEU as compatible with the principle and should be therefore applied. Despite this, there are still questions on the coverage and range of the principle due to domestic differences in application. It does not help that the EIO does not provide an exact definition compared to the European Arrest Warrant, which more or less adopts the CISA definition of the principle. The lack of detailed provision in the DEIO notwithstanding, it was suggested earlier that it is proper to follow the *ne bis in idem* principle as found in the CJEU judgment and the European Arrest Warrant. In the alternative, one could resort to avoiding *ne bis in idem* situations at the outset. The Eurojust in line with this issued guidelines in handling conflicts of jurisdiction, which can be used in preempting or avoiding problems that may arise due to the *ne bis in idem* principle.

One of the principles, conditions, and exceptions likewise tackled in mutual legal assistance and EIO in the ASEAN and the EU respectively, is the substantive consideration of human rights. In this respect, the use of human rights considerations exist as grounds for refusal can be highlighted. The prohibition on double jeopardy is included herein as well as one's right to refuse on the basis of substantial grounds to believe that obligations under Article 6 TEU shall be violated. This provision clarifies that member states can deny recognition or execution of an EIO on the basis of its human rights obligations as provided for in the ECHR, CFR, and the TEU. Interestingly, this is an offshoot of a question raised in a case involving the EAW: on whether human rights obligations of a member state could be used as a ground to refuse recognition or execution. With the CJEU clarifying the matter, the said clarification was transposed in respect to the EIO.

These human rights obligations could involve the principle of non-discrimination, right to life, prohibition of torture or cruel, inhumane, or degrading punishment or treatment, which could be triggered in EIO situations. Obligations as regards the right to life and the prohibition of torture and cruel, inhumane, or degrading punishment or treatment have extraterritorial application, wherein EU member states are not allowed to extradite, remove, or expel any person to another state where there is serious risk of death penalty, torture, or cruel, inhumane, degrading punishment or treatment. Within the EU the issue of death penalty would not be an issue but on a broader context this extraterritorial application requires that either the member state ought to demand an undertaking that the death penalty shall not be imposed or deny any request altogether.

On the contrary, the ASEAN MLAT may provide that certain rights come into play with respect to the substantive provisions of valid and mandatory grounds for refusal (i.e. double jeopardy, non-discrimination, attendance of person in requesting state), but it does not have the same ground for refusal with regard human rights obligations akin to the EIO instrument. Thus, it becomes questionable whether an ASEAN member state can raise extraterritorial application of its human right obligations to deny a MLA request. Again, if one follows the strict letter of the law, then the limited grounds for refusal listed in the ASEAN MLAT must be enforced to the exclusion of other existing human rights obligations. This would also be consistent to the prior position of the ASEAN vis-à-vis Myanmar's membership notwithstanding its past political instability and alleged human rights violations: the ASEAN believed these matters are domestic in nature and should not be interfered with in accordance with the principle of non-intervention. Alternatively, an option in the ASEAN MLAT would be to use national interest as a ground to refuse a MLA request, which is generally subjective.

Another principle or condition involved in mutual legal assistance is reciprocity, which forms the triumvirate of principles in mutual legal assistance together with speciality and dual criminality. Accordingly, the ASEAN MLAT retains the importance of reciprocity. Substantive and procedural-wise, the principle exists. There is the exercise of executive discretion through the central authorities whilst the grounds for refusal illustrate the existence of the procedural aspect of reciprocity.

On the other hand, the principle of mutual recognition might seem to have congruence with reciprocity but in truth, it abrogates the principle one way or another. As mentioned earlier, there is the taking away of executive discretion by allowing direct contacts to be made. Procedural-wise, the grounds for refusal have been minimized with respect to the EIO and even if there might be questions as to the necessity, proportionality, or adequacy of an EIO, it is to be determined by the issuing authority itself. The executing authority does not have the ground to refuse execution of the EIO on this ground, based on the DEIO.

As mentioned, speciality or use limitation is one of the core principles applied to mutual legal assistance. The ASEAN MLAT specifically requires this and concomitantly, requires the return of evidence upon the cessation of proceedings the requested evidence or information was requested for. The DEIO does not explicitly provide this, and this certainly raised the question on whether it still applies within the context of the principle of mutual recognition. However, should one look into the specific provisions of the DEIO one could observe that there is a use limitation provided in the EU framework. Furthermore, the EU framework has data protection considerations, wherein certain parameters and requirements ought to be followed in relation to the processing of personal data and information for the purposes of the prevention, investigation, detection or prosecution of criminal offences or the execution of criminal penalties, including the safeguarding against and the prevention of threats to public security. Generally, personal data shall be processed for the purpose for which it was collected and it ought to be ensured that processing shall be for a lawful purpose. Accordingly, transfer of personal data and information has concomitant requisites and parameters to be followed. Adequate standards or conditions ought to be satisfied most especially if information is to be transferred to non-EU member states and international organizations.

Another substantive principle that finds application in the ASEAN MLAT which differs with the EIO is the existence of national interest matters and specific offenses. National interests play a significant role in denying execution of a MLA request under the ASEAN MLAT. Specifically, the request must be denied if any of the following exist: "the provision of the assistance would affect the sovereignty, security, public order, public interest or essential interests of the requested member state;" "the provision of the assistance could prejudice a criminal matter in the requested member state;" or "the provision of the assistance would require steps to be taken that would be contrary to the laws of the requested member state." As to what constitutes national interest, etc., it would seem that the requested state does not need to explain itself. Further, there is no provision detailing what the same means.

At the same time, the ASEAN MLAT still maintains the political and military offenses exception, albeit it limits the same to specific circumstances. On the contrary, the EIO foregoes the political and military offenses exception. This does not mean however that national interests do not provide grounds to refuse any longer. There is a right to refuse execution if on grounds of territoriality, national interests, privilege, etc. Furthermore, an executing authority is given the right to postpone execution if the same would compromise an existing criminal matter or the evidence and information required is being used for a pending matter.

Anent the procedural provisions important to MLA or the EIO, three main observations can be made as regards designation of central authorities or the type of cooperation the ASEAN and the EU respectively apply, preparation of requests, and execution of requests.

First, in respect of cooperation mechanism, there is a stark difference between the two organizations on how they envision the cooperation between authorities in their respective MLA instruments. The EU uses horizontal cooperation that allows for direct contacts among authorities whilst the ASEAN still retains the vertical form of cooperation wherein central authorities are involved. In this regard, direct contacts expedite theoretically the processing and executing of requests. There could be issues however in determining to which executing authority a request needs to be sent. This is where open communication as well as the relevant role the EJN and contacts such as liaison magistrates could come into play.

Furthermore, the horizontal form of cooperation illustrates an application of the principle of mutual recognition based on mutual trust. It depoliticizes the mutual legal assistance process by taking away executive discretion and mainly entrusting judicial authorities to decide on the recognition or execution of an EIO. This consequently affects the substantive aspect of reciprocity, which, as discussed in the earlier chapters, is being considered abrogated partially, if not wholly, by the principle of mutual recognition.

In comparison, the retention of vertical cooperation through central authorities retain the needed central expertise and control from the member states. Reciprocity is something the ASEAN holds in high value and thus, the political and executive discretion remains. This is especially highlighted by stating the use of diplomatic channels in the ASEAN MLAT to transmit and send MLA requests. Moreover, the retention of central authorities optimizes the control and monitoring of international cooperation requests. It makes it easier to know where one needs to go to as regards information on international cooperation, and more or less the authorities would have the needed knowledge on the same.

Second, as regards preparation of requests, the EIO innovates through the introduction of a prescribed form to be complied with by the member states. There is a pro-forma EIO whilst the ASEAN MLAT would only provide what is necessarily included in a particular request. The prescribed EIO may affect flexibility but issues that could arise from the same are dealt with on a practitioner-level, the same with the ASEAN.

As to in whose instance an EIO or MLA request can be issued, one of the unique selling points of the EIO was that it supposedly allows participation from the defense vis-à-vis the EIO. Accordingly, the DEIO provides that the defendant himself can ask for the issuance of an EIO on its behalf but the same could be problematic because in inquisitorial proceedings, the participation of the defense is different as it could be in an adversarial one. Included in assessing this issue is the difficulty in the first place for the defense to know whether an EIO has been issued or not as the same is normally resulted in during investigations and prior to the case being filed in court. At most, in inquisitorial proceedings, the defense would only be apprised during the court proceedings already.

Contrariwise, the ASEAN MLAT is prosecution-centric. It is a law enforcement or prosecutorial tool to the exclusion of any participation from the defense to request that a MLA request be issued on its behalf. In fact, the ASEAN MLAT provisions would provide that nothing in said treaty would give any rights to the suspect or accused person subject of the MLAT to intrude in the execution of the same. It can be therefore said that the ASEAN instrument is centered on the government-to-government interaction and cooperation with lesser consideration of defense rights that can be affected by the same, albeit there are provisions handling general human rights considerations.

Third, as to the execution of a MLA request or EIO, there would be specific procedures provided for specific investigative measures under both the ASEAN and EU context. As regards the applicable law, both the ASEAN and EU frameworks can accommodate the procedures and formalities provided by the requesting or issuing state that ought to be followed in the investigative measure to be executed or implemented. As long as this would not be contrary to fundamental principles of the requested or executing state, or in violation of its domestic laws, said requested procedures shall be followed. On the part of the EU, this solution was thought to address issues arising from admissibility of evidence and human rights concerns. In addition to this, both the ASEAN and EU frameworks introduced the possibility of including in an EIO or MLA request for authorities of the requesting or issuing state to be present during the investigative measure to be implemented or executed. Furthermore, the EU framework provides the safeguard of allowing the executing state to suggest another investigative measure should the one requested is not allowed or provided for in the domestic legal system of the executing state, or in cases the same would violate the fundamental principles and laws. This is nonetheless subject to exceptions, wherein the EU framework enumerates instances wherein an investigative measure ought to be available in the member states such as regards the hearing of a witness, expert, victim, suspected or accused person or third party in the territory of the executing State, for example (five instances in total are provided).

At this point it must be mentioned however that in comparing the provisions of both the ASEAN and EU in their respective frameworks, the general rule provided in the ASEAN MLAT is more of a *locus regit actum* arrangement because generally, the request ought to be executed in accordance with the laws and procedures of the requested state. Any accommodation for a *forum regit actum* arrangement is the exception because the ASEAN MLAT then allows the requesting state to provide the formalities needed to be taken into account during execution, although this should not be contrary to the domestic laws of the requested state. Comparing this to the DEIO, it goes straight away to the general rule of a *forum regit actum* arrangement. Notwithstanding this difference in phrasing, both the ASEAN and EU frameworks would have the same net effect: formalities and procedures provided by the requesting or issuing state can be accommodated as long as not in contradiction or violation of domestic laws of the requested or executing state. In cases of violation, *lex loci* would prevail.

With regard the applicability of procedural rights, both the ASEAN MLAT and the DEIO integrated in their provisions procedural rights vis-à-vis the rights of an accused, suspect, or affected person. Specific procedures for specific investigative measures likewise take these rights into account. Additionally, there is the integration of the directives of procedural rights in the DEIO, which intends to approximate more or less procedural rights in criminal proceedings across the EU. The integration of the directives on procedural rights could still be admittedly problematic given the existence of different types of criminal proceedings among the member states. On the other hand, the ASEAN MLAT integrates procedural rights in its provisions albeit the same procedural rights are not present in the ASEAN Human Rights Declaration. This is admittedly a weird phenomenon considering that the ASEAN Human Rights Declaration was enacted after the ASEAN MLAT. Thus, the later instrument should have reflected already the procedural rights being respected among the member states.

Concomitant to the issue of procedural rights is the question on whether the suspected or accused person could intervene in the issuance and/or execution of the EIO or MLA request. The DEIO mostly provide provisions that require remedies to be taken up in the issuing state and not the executing state. In line with this, member states must ensure that within their own national legal orders, legal remedies equivalent to those available for similar domestic cases shall be provided for in the investigative measures to be indicated in the EIO. While substantive issues surrounding the EIO may only be challenged in the issuing state, the executing state must ensure that fundamental rights are respected, e.g. possibility to refuse execution on substantial grounds that it could cause infringements of these rights, or the possibility to consult the issuing authority on doubts about the proportionality of the investigative measures included in the EIO.

This same kind of remedy is not provided in the ASEAN MLAT. As earlier noted, the ASEAN framework is prosecutor-centric and more focused on a government-to-government exchange. The ASEAN MLAT is deplete of any provisions concerning judicial relief(s) that a suspect, accused person, or any other affected person.

One of the important factors that affect the execution of requests would be the time limits applicable. This is one of the improvements introduced by the EIO, which does not exist with the ASEAN MLAT. At most, the widest possible assistance exercised by ASEAN member states can be cited as an applicable provision, as well as the need for practitioners to act "promptly". Although the time limits the EIO provides are not mandatory, the time limits provide guidelines as to the speediness authorities ought to take when accepting requests. In connection to this, there are requirements to confirm receipt of an EIO. This gives a clear confirmation to issuing authorities that receipt was in order and could thus count the number of days an EIO has remained with an executing authority. In light of this, there is possible resort to the Eurojust should there be unreasonable delays or non-response on EIOs. While not an adjudicatory body, the Eurojust is authorized to help in the resolution of issues and/or disputes as regards the execution of an EIO. Conversely, the ASEAN does not have the same kind of body a member state can run to in case of delays. Hence, they would be limited in settling the issue among themselves.

To conclude, while the basic elements constituting a MLA system exist for both the ASEAN and the EU, the instruments that apply are different in origin and nomenclature. Moreover, there are differences in certain aspects due to differences in treatments by the ASEAN and the EU. Salient differences as regards substantive provisions include the horizontal vs. vertical cooperation practiced by the respective organizations, the application of the principle of mutual recognition, the right to participate by the defense rights, and the different human rights obligations member states ought to comply with. With respect to the procedural provisions, salient differences could be found with the prescribed forms of the EIO and the time limits member states are encouraged to abide with.

II. Comparing the Member State Frameworks with Each Other

After the evaluation of the regional frameworks themselves, the member state frameworks shall now be entered into the equation, in particular knowing how the respective member state frameworks are able to translate or apply to their respective domestic orders what the regional framework has provided. This is constituted of three steps, all in furtherance of the research question as to how mutual legal assistance in criminal matters can be developed between and within the ASEAN and the EU.

First, there is the question on transposition of law in the member states. This includes the law in the books and the law in practice. It is important to know this because it can provide an idea as to how member states are willing and able to implement in their own domestic jurisdictions agreements or arrangements concluded in the regional level. By seeing how strong compliance is, one would gain insights as to how this can translate to strengthening cooperation further not only within the member states themselves but moreover, between the regional frameworks they are a part of.

Second, there is the question of efficiency. By identifying efficiency concerns, solutions could be thought of to address the problems.

Third, there is the protection of human rights. This would be important given that both the ASEAN and the EU endeavors to uphold the promotion and protection of human rights. While this rhetoric exists on a regional level, it is interesting to know how the same is considered on a domestic level and how committed member states are to this endeavor.

A. Transposition of law in member states including law in practice

In respect to the transposition of the regional instrument or its implementation in the member states, including the law in practice, ten insights could be gained as follows:

First, the Philippines, Malaysia, United Kingdom, and Germany have been generally faithful to their respective regional instruments covering mutual legal assistance and the EIO. Their adoption of the regional instruments, including its implementation into their respective domestic jurisdictions, is in line with the objective of the respective instruments in fostering international cooperation in criminal matters. Substantive and procedural provisions remain true in general to the intent and provisions of the respective regional instruments, although there might be instances that deviations or additional requirements could be cited that were included in the domestic law.

It must be mentioned at the outset that despite the existence of the ASEAN MLAT, the Philippines does not have domestic legislation dedicated to mutual legal assistance in criminal matters. This highlights somehow the lack of enforcement mechanism on the part of the ASEAN to elicit compliance from its member states to enact the necessary legislation to put into fruition what has been agreed upon on a regional level. Notwithstanding this, the Philippines has proven itself as an agreeable and cooperative partner in mutual legal assistance in the region and with its fellow ASEAN member states. The lack of domestic legislation has not stopped the member state from providing the widest possible measure of mutual legal assistance with the ASEAN MLAT being enough domestic basis to provide the same. As a general rule, it would not deny requests it receives from fellow member states. The said member state uses the ASEAN MLAT together with applicable provisions of its criminal law and procedure to execute requests in the fastest possible time. Further, it ensures that execution is made promptly although issues of delay are normally met if the investigative measure requires court approval to do so.

Despite the aforementioned, one could think of issues that could arise out of the lack of domestic legislation. These include not knowing which procedures or provisions are needed to take into account in making a request, including what would be prohibited, etc. There is no readily available information on the same and the regional agreement could only provide to a certain extent. Details are normally left out to the discretion of the member states. And although the ASEAN member state authorities would have open channels of communication with each other, allowing for preliminary consultations or clarifications, no less than the Philippine authorities themselves have been candid about the benefits of having domestic legislation. There have been proposals and draft legislation on international cooperation in criminal matters but a law has yet to be passed.

On the other hand, Malaysia has the domestic legislation tackling international cooperation in criminal matters, including legislation on mutual legal assistance in criminal matters. Under said law, the Malaysian government confers special status to so-called preferred foreign states to which mutual legal assistance in criminal matters and to which the provisions of the law would apply. In the event the requesting state is not a preferred foreign state, special accommodation could still be given but subject to the discretion of the relevant authorities.

With this being mentioned, the domestic law on mutual legal assistance is arguably complete and equivocal in its provisions. Compared to the Philippines wherein one needs to navigate through different substantial and procedural laws to know which is applicable, the Malaysian law provides the needed guidance as to how MLA should proceed.

The Malaysian law would provide that the widest possible assistance shall be provided for criminal matters and ancillary criminal matters, which include situations of needed freezing, confiscation, etc. of properties in relation to a crime. This notwithstanding, not all criminal matters shall be allowed mutual legal assistance because Malaysia only allows the same for serious offenses and serious foreign offenses. This means in general that the offense must be punishable by at least one year. In relation to this, the MLA request could be denied for reasons of "insufficient importance" or "insufficient relevance to the investigation". Even if this seems to delimit the assistance that Malaysia gives to its fellow ASEAN member states or other states requesting its assistance, it is understandable because it avoids fishing expeditions and the allotment of resources that could have been allotted elsewhere.

Anent the member state frameworks of the EU such as in Germany and the United Kingdom, the sword of Damocles finally dropped on United Kingdom as regards the issue of Brexit due to the now applicable Trade and Cooperation Agreement as well as the amendments made domestically to encapsulate the new relationship between the UK and the EU. It is yet to be seen though what the actual future impact this new relationship brings to UK cooperation in criminal matters with other EU member states. Interestingly, in considering what would happen with the participation of the UK in the various parts of the EU criminal justice architecture, some opined that ideally the cooperation should continue, etc. and in practice, the learnings of the EIO and the application of the principle of mutual recognition should continue. Taking the new amendments and revisions brought by the new arrangement between the UK and the EU into account however would show that while the EIO is no longer applicable, its essence, principles, and practices have been adopted in the new rules. Thus, it can be surmised more or less that how EIO was carried out during its applicability would be carried forward albeit in another name and form.

Second, the member state frameworks provide assistance on all kinds of investigative measures, coercive and non-coercive alike. There would be investigative measures excluded on the part of Germany and the United Kingdom on the basis of the DEIO such as joint investigative teams, but in the event that there would be questions on whether a particular investigative measure is covered by the EIO or not, and whether the EIO should be accepted in respect to such investigative measure; in practice, authorities would execute the same more often than not. There would also be no issues as much as possible if the investigative measure concerned is non-coercive in nature. Further, should there be issues or problems on a particular EIO or MLA request, practitioners generally resolve the same in efforts to effectuate the EIO or MLA request as much as possible.

Third, there are discrepancies as to what the regional framework provides as regards designation of authorities and how the United Kingdom implemented the same. Although the EIO promotes the use of direct contacts or horizontal cooperation through the use of issuing and executing authorities, the UK opted to retain its central authorities in receiving EIOs from other member states and then forwarding the same to the relevant executing authorities for execution. This keeps more or less the essence of traditional mutual legal assistance, like both the Philippines and Malaysia practice in their respective jurisdictions, and the tenets of the substantive aspect of reciprocity as it keeps the executive discretion exercised by the state.

Albeit what the UK prompted to do vis-à-vis retention of central authorities (like in the Philippines and Malaysia) can easily be dismissed to be incongruent with the spirit and aim of the EIO directive, the retention of central authorities actually makes total sense because of the unique function the courts in the UK, the Philippines, and Malaysia have. As UK authorities explained, you cannot expect UK courts to act in the same manner as other judicial authorities in other EU member states. Together with the Philippines and Malaysia, UK espouses adversarial proceedings and do not have the same system as one can find for example in Germany and most EU member states (inquisitorial proceedings). Thus, the idea of judicial authorities would be different between each kind of proceedings. With respect to the UK, it would be incompatible with the function of its courts should it be designated as administrative postboxes for incoming EIOs.

Fourth, there are insights one could gain from the so-called sufficiency of evidence requirement and how the respective member state frameworks apply the same. There is a direct proportional relationship between the information to be provided in a MLA request or an EIO and the intrusiveness of the investigative measure being requested. Stating it otherwise, one must provide more information or explain the relevance of the MLA request or EIO should coercive measures or more intrusive measures are required. In light of this, the completeness of the set of facts is not required for Germany but only such as that would enable the proper recognition and execution of the EIO. As German authorities pointed out, it is different from the Anglo-American tradition that requires probable cause to be established, which the Philippines interestingly applies as regards coercive measures such as searches and seizures and/or interceptions of communications, for example. Probable cause, as contemplated herein, is more than reasonable suspicion. It is the existence of substantial grounds for a reasonable man to believe that a crime has been committed and that the place needs to be searched or the items or objects to be seized is related thereto. Probable cause is ingrained in the legal fiber of the Philippine system and thus, any request to be sent to the Philippines involving coercive measures would need to comply with this requirement because the same would course through the Philippine courts for the issuance of the needed court order authorizing the relevant coercive measure.

Fifth, it can be discerned from all the member state frameworks that dual criminality has not been an actual issue in the execution of either MLA requests or EIOs in practice. The lack of dual criminality is not even a ground to refuse a request vis-à-vis the Philippine Cybercrime Act. In relation to the EU member states, there has been an effort to minimize the application of the requirement by making it inapplicable to a list of 32 offenses under certain conditions. Both Germany and the UK has implemented the same. Having said these, in practice, no issue has been encountered on the same.

Sixth, there is something interesting about the implementation or application of the prohibition of double jeopardy in the respective member state frameworks. At the outset, all of the Constitutions (or basic laws) and code of criminal procedure of the respective member state frameworks have provisions tackling the same. Germany is unique among the rest as its law is clear with respect to the transnational application of the prohibition. Following Article 54 CISA, the CJEU judgment, and the provision found in the EAW, Germany includes an execution element in addition to the objective and subjective elements of the principle of *ne bis in idem*. Furthermore, the existence of double jeopardy does not necessarily translate to outright denial of an EIO. It would be discretionary on the authority involved. A yardstick for discretion for local authorities is their duty to prosecute: no crime should remain unpunished. Another yardstick is whether the purpose of the proceedings in the issuing state is mainly to determine whether the prohibition has been violated. Thus, it would be a weighing of factors despite the existence of any double jeopardy in an EIO.

The German definition on *ne bis in idem* deviates however from the general (but undetailed) provision found in the regional instrument. UK conversely provides the same undetailed provision in its domestic legislation. In connection hereto, there is uncertainty as regards the cross-border or transnational application of the principle (or prohibition) in the UK, especially with the looming resolution of the issue of Brexit. It could simply follow its domestic interpretation or follow the judicial pronouncements of the CJEU.

As regards the Philippines and Malaysia, the ASEAN MLAT limits the transnational element of the prohibition against double jeopardy between the requested and requesting state. Malaysian law limits it to the requesting state, i.e. conviction, acquittal, pardon, or service of punishment occurred in the requesting state. This paved way to the question as to when the conviction, acquittal, pardon or service of punishment occurred in another ASEAN member state or third state. As mentioned in the earlier discussions, two conclusions can be derived and it also depends on whether the state involved is the requested or requesting state. First, when either the Philippines and Malaysia are the requesting states, the evidence or information requested through the MLA request would naturally be used within their respective domestic courts, which concomitantly should apply domestic laws and principles. Thus, the prohibition against double jeopardy as applied domestically ought to be applied.

Second, the conclusion is altered when the subject state is the requested state and with different possible outcomes for both the Philippines and Malaysia. The Philippines ought to proceed with the request notwithstanding a circumstance wherein the conviction, acquittal, pardon, or service of punishment occurred in a third state, because the provision in the treaty only considers the requested or requesting state. Following strictly the MACMA provision, on the other hand, would limit Malaysia to deny a request only when the conviction, acquittal, pardon, or service of punishment occurred in the requesting state. Malaysia would not concern itself if the circumstances occurred on its own domestic soil.

Conversely, the spirit of the prohibition in its transnational sense should result to a denial of the request, or at the least make the requested state wary of granting the request, in both cases wherein the circumstances occurred in Malaysia or in a third state. Interestingly, these conundrums have yet to be encountered in practice. A pragmatic solution would probably lie on the need to balance interests on a case-to-case basis and the usage of preliminary consultation and open communication between authorities in the ASEAN.

Seventh, the speciality or use limitation applies in the member state frameworks in both ASEAN and the EU, albeit the speciality principle was not directly mentioned in the DEIO. All member states uphold this principle and consequently, would demand the return of documents or evidence upon cessation of proceedings for which the EIO or MLA request was made. Moreover, the UK and Germany have data protection laws vis-à-vis the protection of natural persons with regard to the processing of personal data by competent authorities for the purposes of the prevention, investigation, detection or prosecution of criminal offences or the execution of criminal penalties, including the safeguarding against and the prevention of threats to public security. These particular laws require personal data or information to be processed for lawful and specific purposes, among other requirements that ought to be satisfied should said data or information be transferred or processed further. Having mentioned this, in the event that the evidence or information is discerned usable for another criminal matter, it would be imperative for the requesting state or issuing state to issue another EIO or send another MLA request. Depending on the receiving end, an advance notice could be made with the EIO to formally follow, according to an interviewee. As regards the ASEAN member states, this is allowed in practice as long as there has been prior communication.

Eighth, the prominence of national interests and special offenses as an exception to the execution of an EIO or a MLA request is apparent among the different member state frameworks examined. For Malaysia, for example, a MLA request shall be denied if it shall contravene sovereignty, security, public order, or any other essential public interest of Malaysia. It shall also be denied if the Attorney General opines that the said request shall impose an excessive burden upon the resources of Malaysia. Included herein as well are the political and military offenses exceptions. Furthermore, criminal proceedings or a pending criminal investigation in Malaysia shall take precedence over MLA requests involving the same evidence or information.

On the other hand, snippets of national interest could be found in Philippine legislation with MLA provisions. Whilst there is no general legislation for MLA in the Philippines, national interest could still play a part in the denial or execution of MLA requests. This is due to the significance the country places on reciprocity, wherein procedurally, a country should not be made to do something against its will. Thus, in traditional MLA agreements such as the ASEAN MLAT, there are grounds for refusal to ensure that there is equality in footing between cooperating states and that one is not forced to do something against its interest or will.

With respect to the EU member states, the same national interest-based grounds for refusal are retained in their respective domestic legislation. These include the existence of privilege, territoriality, pending criminal matters, etc. Further, Germany and the UK included in their respective laws the ground to refuse based on substantial grounds to believe that executing the EIO would violate their obligations under Article 6 of the TEU. While this has a human rights element, it embodies as well a national interest.

Ninth, the EU member states follow the designated form provided for by the EIO. The pro forma EIO is implemented and ought to be complied with by Germany and the UK. This pro forma EIO would have its pros and cons but it is still being implemented. On the other hand, the ASEAN member states do not have the same kind of pro forma EIO but they would need to provide the needed information as required in their respective legislations. In the case of the Philippines, authorities were the ones who provided the minimum information required in a request, but the ASEAN MLAT could also be a good starting point. In all member states, additional information can be asked from the requesting/issuing member state to be able to effectuate properly a MLA request or EIO.

Tenth, the time limits provided for in the DEIO are equally found in the domestic laws of the UK and Germany. Authorities would admit that these are not mandatory. Nonetheless, they promote efficiency and effectiveness of the procedure. Should the investigative measure be non-coercive, compliance would be faster. However, issues could be met if the coercive measure needs to go through the courts.

On the other hand, there may be no time limits in the ASEAN regional instrument and member states are only encouraged to act "promptly", but authorities tend to act swiftly on requests. Further, both Malaysia and the Philippines require themselves as requesting states and those which may send MLA requests to them to provide information about the time element involved in their requests, so the requested states will be aware of any urgency involved.

B. Efficiency

Assessing the respective member state frameworks, including the law in practice, one could state that there have been no alarming problems of efficiency among practitioners. As much as possible the member states are able to give the needed assistance in the collection and transmittal of required information and evidence. There is a willingness among them to work with each other. In the event that there are problems or issues encountered, or there are uncertainties as to a certain procedure or investigative measure to be included in a MLA request or EIO, practitioners maintain open channels of communication that allows for preliminary consultations among each other. This is regardless of the ASEAN or the EU member states. Germany and the UK also benefit from the support the entire EU Criminal Justice architecture gives to them through the Eurojust, the EJN, and other infrastructures or databases the EU provides. There is also the existence of liaison magistrates.

In relation to this, the time constraints member states encounter in the recognition or execution of a MLA request or an EIO can also be considered as regards efficiency. While the EIO would provide for time limits, the ASEAN MLAT does not. Despite this, ASEAN member states exert efforts to execute requests as soon as possible. Delays are commonly encountered when a request is coursed through the courts for the issuance of the required order for a coercive measure. This issue is not however mutually exclusive to the Philippines and Malaysia. Stumbling blocks could also be encountered in Germany and the United Kingdom. Thus, while providing time limits can encourage member states to work faster, there could be inevitable issues that would delay execution, especially those outside the control of the executing authorities.

Third aspect that affects efficiency is the designation of central authorities. To the exception of Germany, all member state frameworks maintain central authorities. Theoretically, direct contacts enable faster and more efficient exchange of EIOs among authorities. However, with the structural changes introduced by the EIO, the UK is still able to work faster than expected and execute the needed investigative measure. The central authorities of both the Philippines and Malaysia are also on the same page. Thus, while direct contacts make matters theoretically faster, the speed or efficiency would highly depend on the willingness of the authorities themselves to cooperate. If authorities are self-motivated, then mutual legal assistance regardless of name or deviation would work.

C. Protection of Human Rights and Defense Rights

In comparing and assessing the protection of human rights and defense rights in the context of mutual legal assistance, three aspects could be looked into. First, one ought to consider the general stance of the member states as regards human rights in their respective domestic policies. Second, there is the integration of human rights protection in their respective domestic laws tackling MLA or the EIO. This includes consideration of human rights in the grounds to refuse a MLA request or an EIO, preparation and execution of the request, as well as the specific procedures for the investigative measures that could be subject of the MLA request or EIO. Third, one needs to consider how strong defense rights are being promoted, protected, or defended on the member state level.

First, as regards the general stance of the member states pertaining to human rights, all member state frameworks have an avowed commitment to the protection of human rights. Their respective Constitutions or basic laws would provide these different human rights that ought to be respected, promoted, and protected. This is reflective of the constitutional principles of their respective regional organizations.

Both Germany and the UK are duty-bound to uphold their human rights obligations under Article 6 of the TEU vis-à-vis the EIO, which both the Philippines and Malaysia do not equivocally provide. These include obligations found in the Charter of Fundamental Rights and the European Convention on Human Rights. Thus, should they have substantial grounds to believe that their obligations under said provision shall be violated, they could deny the recognition or execution of an EIO.

One of the obligations that Germany and the UK need to comply with is the prohibition of the death penalty and the imposition of torture, or cruel, inhumane, and degrading punishment. Thus, these member states cannot entertain requests if the punishment involves the death penalty, torture, or cruel, inhumane, and degrading punishment. This is a non-negotiable. In connection to this, Malaysia imposes the death penalty and whipping as two forms of punishment. The Philippines does not completely prohibit the death penalty and limits its imposition on heinous crimes as may be determined by law, although nowadays the imposition of the death penalty has been suspended.

Additionally, there is significant value in the determination of what is necessary, proportional, and adequate as regards issuing an EIO. Proportionality is one of the fundamental principles of Germany that ought to be respected and upheld. Otherwise, there could be negative consequences for non-compliance. For example, should this not be followed in issuing an EIO, the admissibility of the evidence obtained through it shall be affected. The UK considers likewise the concept of proportionality, albeit in a different manner from Germany, in its decisions especially those involving human rights. As regards the Philippines and Malaysia, however, this principle is not explicitly provided or otherwise defined under a different nomenclature (e.g. substantive due process, procedural due process, substantial fairness, etc.).

In relation to the foregoing, it can be said that non-observance of human rights obligations by each member state would have negative repercussions. The Philippines has for example the fruit of poisonous tree doctrine and exclusionary rule. To elucidate, searches and seizures under the Philippine Constitution is prohibited unless the same is with a lawful warrant issued by the court. Any evidence obtained in violation of the same, including anything obtained in relation to it, is considered inadmissible as evidence.

Second, as regards how human rights are integrated in the respective domestic laws on MLA or the EIO, the Philippines stands out uniquely given the lack of domestic law that would spell out the human rights needed to be taken into account. This notwithstanding, a reading of the other relevant laws and procedure would show that human rights are of primordial consideration in the Philippine jurisdiction. Authorities ought to act respectfully and any violation of human rights (even in extradition or MLA proceedings which only have earmarks of a criminal process) deserve redress. In connection to this, the probable cause requirement relates to the protection of human rights. The Philippine Constitution prohibits fishing expeditions and abuse of the use of searches and seizures. Thus, there is the probable cause requirement that avoids unscrupulous or frivolous searches and seizures, or the otherwise interruption of one's right to privacy. To be personally determined by the judge, this protects anyone subjected to a coercive measure from abuse. Further, authorities are duty bound to make a return to the judge of what has happened with any warrant issued. For those involving communications, including online evidence, they would be later required to destroy any record or data involving the same.

The other examined member states, on the other hand, take into account human rights across the different provisions of their respective domestic laws tackling either the EIO or MLA. There is clear explanation on what ought to be considered in the execution of requests, the grounds to refuse, and the specific procedures needed to be followed as per investigative measure. Though it must be mentioned at this juncture that one still needs to read in the UK Regulations certain human rights safeguards or parameters that have not been explicitly mentioned in the law, e.g. examination of witnesses, when right to representation is engaged, etc. The same can be said with Germany through the need to be aware of intricacies in certain investigative measures such as search and seizures that can be found in its Code of Criminal Procedure.

Having said this, one can go back to the discussion on the prohibition against double jeopardy or the *ne bis in idem* principle. As mentioned earlier, all member states would have in their respective frameworks an elucidation and application of said prohibition. They were able to transpose in their respective frameworks the principle and its concomitant prohibition. This can be considered a win already vis-à-vis the principle. However, if one would look into the transnational nature of the *ne bis in idem* principle being promoted in the regional frameworks, Malaysia, Philippines, and the UK have their shortcomings because they do not have respective laws or jurisprudences tackling the same. Looking into their respective MLA or EIO related domestic laws does not help as well. The MACMA of Malaysia limits the prohibition to the conviction, acquittal, pardon or service of sentence in the requesting state. It does not consider any similar circumstance occurring in its own jurisdiction, another member state, or a third state. The UK, on the other hand, only provided a general provision on *ne bis in idem* without elucidating or defining its scope or parameters. As to how these gaps in their respective frameworks can be addressed, resolution would depend on whether they are a requesting or requested state (as discussed earlier). There would still be unforeseeability however as to how a subjected person can be protected against double jeopardy.

Germany, on the other hand, has integrated in its domestic framework the transnational nature of the principle in line with the EU legal approach. Being an optional ground for refusal, Germany's position is sound. In following the regional approach, it recognizes how the same can affect the decisions of its own authorities as well as those of other member state authorities in relation to legal assistance requests, wherein the subject person may be subjected to the prohibition. As to how this human rights consideration is operationalized, refusal is not automatic. Instead, authorities in Germany consider whether the EIO refers to the issue of determining whether the prohibition has been violated in the first place. Generally, German authorities would apply a hands-off approach and allow the issuing authorities to determine the issue within their own proceedings. Delegation of this discernment is however decreased if there is an apparent risk to the person involved as regards such person's rights.

It can further be mentioned that the UK specifically provides non-discrimination as a ground to refuse execution of an EIO, which is not found in the regional instrument. An EIO may be refused execution if the same was issued on discriminatory grounds. While not having a direct counterpart in the German law, non-discrimination is one of the human rights obligations Germany adheres to. Thus, if substantial grounds exist that the EIO would be incompatible with its human rights obligations as defined in Article 6 ECHR and the CFR, then Germany can also deny recognition or execution of the EIO based on non-discrimination.

Moreover, even if theoretically speaking, the UK could not deny an EIO on grounds of necessity, proportionality, or adequacy, it is still possible to find relief with UK authorities as an executing state. There is the option of referring the matter to the relevant central authority or going to the courts for redress. This is especially possible if the issuance was made unbeknownst to the suspect, accused, or other interested person in the issuing state. As for asking the courts for relief, courts would probably take a strict approach on the matter and thus, arguments ought to be convincing and clear as to any violation to one's rights.

Furthermore, the UK law provided for a so-called variation or revocation order. Issued under limited grounds based on human rights (such as discrimination), this order may be issued to vary or revoke the execution of the EIO or transmittal of the requested evidence or information. Traditionally, UK could revoke consent to the transmittal of evidence, regardless of being sent already, if it finds reasonable grounds to do so, including grounds based on the protection of human rights. While there is no test case yet, there was the plausibility of this kind of relief in the UK. What is currently provided is the suspension of transmitting the requested evidence under the EIO Regulations pending resolution of a legal remedy and/or the existence of serious and irreparable remedy. As to whether this exists in Germany, there is no variation or revocation order in German law. At most, there would be the provision that allows suggesting the use of another investigative measure.

It must be mentioned at this point that the Philippines and Malaysia do not share the same ground for refusal as that of Germany and the UK wherein they could deny a request if there are "substantial grounds to believe" that it would be incompatible with Article 6 CFR obligations – or general human rights obligations in the context of the Philippines and Malaysia. It became imperative earlier to inquire whether they could invoke other general human rights considerations in order to deny a MLA request, i.e. domestic human rights principles, values, prohibitions, and international human rights obligations, which may conflict with a request received. The answer is in the negative if one follows the strict letter of the ASEAN MLAT and the MACMA. No ground for refusal is provided wherein a requested state can deny a request if the same conflicts with an existing human rights obligation. This is further supported by existing rule of non-inquiry the Philippines follows as regards international cooperation requests. The same applies to Malaysia as well, by not only excluding any circumstance occurring in Malaysia vis-à-vis double jeopardy when it is the requested state, but more importantly, by not providing the ground for refusal itself in its domestic law.

Alternatively, should the member state be placed in a position of strong urgency to uphold its human rights obligations over a MLA request received, for example in cases when the human rights involved are constitutionally provided or falling under customary international law obligations, then both Malaysia and the Philippines could resort to the use of the "national interest" ground for refusal as a form of catch-all exemption that takes into account public interest. Having mentioned this, both Malaysia and the Philippines have yet to encounter this in practice. Thus, it remains to be tested whether using national interest as a ground to refuse a MLA request due to a human rights obligation will succeed. At most, the member states would openly communicate and consult with one another about any issue that would arise in respect of any human rights issues or problems that may arise due to a MLA request. This comes however with the caveat that open lines of communication might prove insufficient in addressing imperative human rights issues that may arise. Thus, it might be prudent to clearly delineate and define boundaries.

Third, as regards how defense rights play a role, this could be analyzed on three aspects. One, there is the participation of the defense in the issuance of a MLA request or EIO in its behalf. Two, one could look as to whether the suspect, accused, or interested person could interfere in the issuance or execution of a MLA request or an EIO. Three, one could look into how defense rights play a role in the execution of investigative measures subject of the MLA request or the EIO.

Anent the participation of the defense for the issuance of a MLA request or an EIO, there is seemingly no legal basis in the Philippines and Malaysia for the defense to do this. Albeit they both have adversarial proceedings, the MACMA itself does not provide the right for the defense to request the issuance of a MLA request for its benefit in a case. As regards the Philippines, the same applies given that it has no domestic legislation on mutual legal assistance and only uses the ASEAN MLAT as legal basis. The ASEAN MLAT, as one may recall, does not contain a provision providing said right or any other provision of similar import. Further, Philippine criminal procedure is of similar fashion. Philippine Rules of Court provides for the filing of motions that ask for judicial relief or the use of modes of discovery but the Rules of Court lack provisions that tackle international cooperation instruments such as a MLA request. Although the Supreme Court itself recognized that modes of discovery are in congruence with the aim of the ASEAN MLAT in more recent case law, this would not be sufficient to excuse the lack of procedural law that allows issuance of a MLA request at the instance of the defense or any other interested person. Therefore, MLA remains a prosecution or investigative tool mainly among the ASEAN member states.

On the other hand, participation of the defense to ask the issuance of an EIO in its behalf is one of the selling points of the EIO. The UK law would accommodate this as a possibility, not only according to authorities but given as well its adversarial proceedings, wherein prosecution and defense have equality of arms. However, there is no case law yet nor test case yet. This conversely does not exist in Germany or it otherwise hard to fathom how it will be made possible. Within the penumbra of inquisitorial proceedings, authorities mention the impossibility of the defense asking for an EIO to be issued in its behalf. In light of this, it can be gainsaid that if one considers the principle of sincere cooperation and the aim of the DEIO to generally empower the defense or accused in criminal proceedings vis-à-vis the issuance of an EIO, then Germany is seemingly lacking or otherwise failing in its obligations to put this into motion. Nevertheless, as discussed in an earlier chapter, Germany cannot truly be fully faulted for its shortcomings because there has already been an observed incompatibility between an inquisitorial kind of proceeding and what the DEIO wishes to uphold vis-à-vis participation of the defense. Stating it differently, the idea of allowing the defense to participate in the issuance of an EIO or MLA request is appreciated and should be upheld pursuant to defense rights, but ought to be reevaluated perhaps as regards how it can be truly put in fruition in the difference in proceedings (such as inquisitorial or adversarial) among the EU member states.

This mentioned impossibility further relates to the second aspect of defense rights vis-à-vis MLA requests or the EIO. In an inquisitorial proceeding, such as in Germany, there is the impossibility for a suspect, accused, or interested person to question the issuance of the EIO. The EIO is normally issued during the investigation phase of the proceedings and thus, the collection of evidence is not known to the suspect or accused person involved. At most, the remedy lies in the evidence or information obtained in relation to the EIO, which is for all intents and purposes incompatible with what the regional framework seeks to implement. The UK provided contrariwise remedies for the defense vis-à-vis the issuance or execution of the EIO. As mentioned earlier, there is the variation and/or revocation order that could be applied for. There is likewise the suspension of transmitting evidence due to the resolution of a legal remedy. Admittedly though, it remains unclear what exactly these legal remedies would constitute.

Alternatively, both the Philippines and Malaysia would provide a remedy for the defense in respect to the issuance and/or execution of an EIO, but in a limited approach. For the Philippines, mutual legal assistance has earmarks of a criminal process to which certain rights would apply. Judicial review can also be availed of especially if proven that there is grave abuse of discretion leading to lack or excess of jurisdiction. Akin to the Philippines, Malaysia provides for judicial review by virtue of Order 53 under the Rules of Court 2012 to question any government order or issuance vis-à-vis fundamental rights in its Federal Constitution. As to the issue on whether relief could be granted, one can note from more recent Philippine case law that while it is still left unclear whether an affected person may question the validity of the MLA request itself and/or the grant thereof, he/she is not precluded from questioning the resulting investigative measure from such a request, the implementation of said measure, as well as the admissibility of any evidence obtained therefrom. Furthermore, the needed relief can be granted for any violation of rights as long as circumstances may warrant it. As *People of the Philippines v. Sergio* illustrated, the Court shall not avoid the question on whether a constitutional right is infringed. This is especially the case when the Philippines is the requesting state, the criminal proceedings are situated in the Philippines, and the evidence obtained through MLA is used in Philippine courts.

Third, one can mention the integration of defense rights in the specific investigative measures contemplated in the respective member state frameworks. This is generally apparent in all the member state frameworks examined. One could look into the right of representation, the right against self-incrimination, and the general considerations of one's consent before being asked to participate in an investigative measure requested. There might be discrepancies as to when the respective applicable rights would be engaged, but they nevertheless exist and respected in practice.

Part 4: Developing Mutual Legal Assistance between and within the ASEAN and the EU

The following discussion evaluates and analyzes the salient points of the comparison made in the immediately preceding part of the study to highlight certain lessons that could be learned as well as the factors that would be important to take into consideration in suggesting and recommending how mutual legal assistance in criminal matters could be developed (further) within and between the ASEAN and the EU. The present study focuses on the following values: (1) intergovernmental v. supranational nature or formal v. informal, which refers to the nature or institutional design of the two regional organizations subject of the study; (2) principle of non-intervention v. soft imperialism power, which highlights the workings and/or principles and practices of the two regional organizations; and (3) harmonization v. approximation, which refers to the question of standardization of laws among member states or the need to provide baseline rules and regulations to which member states ought to follow and implement to make policies and decisions in the regional level work.

In light of this, these chosen values may not be complete and exact in determining the best route the possible development and/or strengthening of mutual legal assistance in criminal matters between and within the ASEAN and the EU should take but these values provide good starting points.

I. Lessons Learned

A. Intergovernmental v. Supranational; Formal v. Informal

Based on the foregoing discussion, there are certain lessons learned that could be further considered in providing suggestions as to how mutual legal assistance in criminal matters could be improved within and developed between the ASEAN and the EU.

First, one could look into the lessons that could be learned from the evaluation of the regional framework.

The difference in nature of the two regional organizations dictates how decision-making, compliance, and enforcement would proceed. Because of its intergovernmental nature, and mostly informal manner of decision-making, the ASEAN cannot decide on its own and impose to its member states a decision or agreement it has entered into. Contrariwise, the member states ought to agree or acquiesce to a certain agreement or arrangement before the same can be legally binding on them. This notwithstanding, there is more to being legally binding on the member states. There is no compliance or enforcement mechanism within the framework that would elicit compliance among the member states. At most, one can expect self-regulation among the member states. This is apparent in the ASEAN MLAT. Despite having this treaty, one can find countries such as the Philippines without any domestic legislation on the same. And while it can be commendable that the Philippines is making the system work without specific domestic legislation on the matter, there is no positive reinforcement or nudging from the part of ASEAN to push the Philippines to come up with the required law. In fact, it would be the principles of ASEAN that hinder other member states to require the Philippines (or Cambodia) to legislate because all have a commitment not to intervene in the national affairs of their fellow member states.

Additionally, the mainly informalistic nature of the ASEAN accounts for the lack of preemptive, specific measures as regards cooperative mechanisms. The bulk of the legislative output of ASEAN are declarations or gentlemen's agreements on how to deal with certain issues. Whilst there is commitment on the part of the member states to deal with the problems tackled in their respective jurisdictions, there is the lack of the needed bite for member states to earnestly or promptly act on their commitments. Again, one can cite the Philippines for its lack of legislation. The Philippine situation is made worse by the startling revelation that absent any standardization on international cooperation such as MLA, the domestic framework itself is muddled and lacks harmonization. While statutory construction or judicial interpretation might be useful toolkits to solve the issue – or by the practitioners who would normally fill in the gaps in the law – the fact remains that almost 16 years since the ASEAN MLAT was agreed on, no legislative output has been made domestically by the Philippines. This notwithstanding, the ASEAN or its member states cannot call out the Philippines (and even Cambodia) on this inadequacy due to reasons discussed in the next following section.

The same kind of observation applies to treaties and agreements concluded within the ASEAN framework such as the one on trafficking in persons, or the agreement on information exchange, for example. The Agreement on Information Exchange mandates the sharing of databases or even the sharing of airline list of passengers, but only "as appropriate", or on a "as needed" basis. Thus, there are no readily available mechanisms or infrastructure ASEAN-wide that one can resort to when the need arises. This encourages consequently flexibility and ad hoc cooperation procedures.

Flexibility and application of ad hoc procedures are not necessarily bad but it is not completely good. While flexibility is beneficial to a certain extent because there is room to improvise and adapt to the situations that arise, and that ASEAN member states are actually doing a great job practice-wise as regards mutual legal assistance, tackling international co-operation in criminal matters, especially in the prevention, investigation, and prosecution of transnational crime and terrorism requires existing efficient and working infrastructures at a minimum. Tools and the needed structure ought to be readily available when needed by authorities.

This notwithstanding, the advancement this requires might be disproportional to the capabilities of the member states themselves. Compared to most members of the European Union, the ASEAN member states are not only few in number but their economic and socio-political capacity is admittedly lesser. This might explain the lack of readily available and running infrastructures within ASEAN. Despite this, the resilience shown by the ASEAN member states throughout the region's historical development is still reflected in their dealings with one another. The lack of formal arrangements does not hinder them from affording the assistance another member state needs. There would be rooms for improvement as regards concretizing and implementing arrangements, agreements, and other commitments, but for now, they are trying their best to do good in their respective endeavors.

Having said this, an effective cooperation mechanism needs to take into account the difference in nature of both regional organizations. The ASEAN does not have the same infrastructure as the EU and issues might arise in facilitating implementation and compliance to any agreement. Therefore, the relevant agencies on the member state level ought to be involved in any cooperation mechanism. These include necessarily the existing central authorities and their attached agencies. In relation to this, capacity building within the ASEAN itself can be explored. The EU and its existing agencies and bodies could help in the manner wherein a two-way learning, information sharing, and capacity-buidling can be fostered. This has already been made possible by the ASEAN and its member states in the past. If one would recall the height of the 2001 terrorist attacks and the joint endeavors entered into by the ASEAN with other countries, as well as the other times the ASEAN member states joined other states in coordinated efforts, this could very well be entertained especially in view of international cooperation in criminal matters with one another. No less than the EU has been a partner by the ASEAN and its member states in different endeavors. Thus, if truly committed, capacity building in terms of building the needed infrastructure between and within the two regional organizations can be pursued.

Additionally, the ASEAN could explore the possibility of creating its equivalent of the existing EU bodies vis-à-vis cooperation in criminal matters. Still intergovernmental in nature but would serve the same coordination and cooperation functions as its EU counterparts, the ASEAN can explore the establishment of its own ASEAN Judicial Network and ASEAN Agency for Criminal Justice Cooperation, and/or consider taking within its framework the ASEANAPOL and strengthen its capacity to be an effective agency for law enforcement cooperation. No less than the ASEAN Secretariat has recognized the importance within the ASEAN of having both informal and formal channels of cooperation in criminal matters. The ASEAN member states such as the Philippines and Malaysia are also already benefiting from the use of both informal and formal channels of cooperation. Thus, streamlining and improving the network in this regard would be advantageous for all concerned. Furthermore, should this idea be explored, then there would be more or less 1:1 correspondence in networking and communicating with each other towards an efficient and effective cooperation mechanism.

Considering the foregoing insights, the balance between rigidity and flexibility cannot be stressed enough in terms of fostering cooperation in criminal matters between and within the ASEAN and the EU. Ideally, for an effective cooperation mechanism to work between the ASEAN and the EU, both must respect the more informalistic nature of one and the more formalistic nature of the other. The formal arrangement comes into the picture by having a treaty obligation between the two regional organizations (with the caveat that ASEAN member states must agree). A treaty obligation would reinforce more or less compliance by all signatories. As regards the aspect of flexibility, the existence of EU bodies such as the Europol, Eurojust, and EJN together with possible ASEAN counterparts would promote the use of informal channels of cooperation, which is equally important in cooperation in criminal matters. In line with this, any formal cooperation should be compatible with existing other arrangements.

B. Principle of Non-Intervention and the ASEAN Way v. EU Normative Power

As learned from the historical development of both regional frameworks, the history of both had an impact in molding what the respective organizations are today. Due to the experience and learnings of each regional organization and their respective member states, principles, ideals, and norms have been formed in each one.

One could look into the development in ASEAN of its constitutional principles (including legal rationalistic norms), normative principles, and decision-making principles. At the center of these norms and principles are the tenets of non-intervention. Member states are not allowed to interfere in the domestic affairs of their fellow member states. One member state cannot tell another how to run its business on its own backyard. This is notwithstanding "enhanced interaction", wherein a member state can comment on another's national affairs if the same would affect the regional security or stability, because even with the same, commenting or talking to the other member state could be done only outside the ASEAN framework. So technically speaking, the ASEAN would remain a hands off policy as regards how the member states run their respective domestic affairs.

Given that member states cannot interfere in each other's domestic affairs, the same rings all the more true with regard foreign intervention. Learning from the bitter experiences of the past, the ASEAN detests foreign intervention or the alignment of its member states to foreign powers for defense, etc. While some member states have been friendlier to foreign powers, the general consensus or attitude existing in the ASEAN is against any foreign intervention.

In light of this, one cannot help but think of the normative power the EU tries to exercise in its internal and external affairs. It has also been said that the EU does not act so benignly all time. It is also a "soft imperialism power": the emphasis on democratization projects, strategies for "new abroad" are seen as examples of the EU's hegemonic power driven by both normative and strategic interests such as the need for stability. Taking this into consideration, the EU could then have the tendency to impose itself and its ideals and principles to others.

Interestingly, the EU has a track record of imposing or attempting to impose this "soft imperialism power" towards the ASEAN and its member states. When the two organizations started their dialogue partnership, the beginning fared well for both organizations but later on the differences between the two became apparent. After the Cold War and when a new form of partnership took place between the EU and the ASEAN, the EU tried to impose its democratization projects on the ASEAN and the member states. The EU insisted on discussing human rights and democratization with the aid and economic cooperation it has with the ASEAN and its member states. And although one would expect the ASEAN and its member states to waver and submit to the whims of the EU due to the supposedly weaker position it has, the ASEAN and its member states stayed adamant and insisted on the regional order it abides with – dismissing the plot of the EU as undue interference. This notwithstanding, as discussed in the Introduction, the EC/EU did not see anything wrong in what it was doing. It had this self-imposed obligation to promote and protect human rights in accordance with its obligations under the TEU even to the point that it will not hesitate to interfere in the domestic order if the need arises. Due to this clash of values and non-negotiables, the ASEAN and the EU experienced at one point in time an impasse in their relations due to issues relating to the membership of Myanmar in the ASEAN, to which the EU and its member states were against.

If one looks into the historical context from which the ASEAN operates, it must have been obvious to the EU at the very beginning that what it was trying to do would not fare well to the ASEAN and its member states. This is especially the case when it was widely observed that the EU itself was not only failing in its commitments towards the ASEAN in several occasions but also failing in certain issues in its own backyard. Should there be any hint or inkling that the EU is imposing itself and its ideals and principles to the ASEAN and its member states, then the latter would turn its head away from the discussion. Now in the advent of a strategic partnership and recently agreed upon EU-ASEAN Plan of Action that seeks to enhance cooperation in security and criminal matters, the EU should have learned its lesson by now on how to tread carefully in trying to impose its hegemonic or soft imperialism power on the ASEAN and its member states. If the EU hesitates or overlooks the tenets of the principle of non-intervention and the ASEAN Way, then perhaps this strategic partnership would not progress and any planned meaningful and deeper relationship between the two regional organizations would not prosper. Criticism or finding of faults should be avoided. Instead, by focusing on the problems and issues ought to be addressed, solutions are mutually found by both organizations through consensus-building, without necessarily imposing one's will on the other.

C. Harmonization v. Approximation; Minimum Standards

It is settled that there are still differences among the member state frameworks as regards how each implements or interprets a particular substantial or procedural provision vis-à-vis mutual legal assistance in criminal matters. Further, one can internalize that the kind of proceedings each member state espouses have a resonating effect on how a particular provision in the regional instrument is applied domestically. For example, there is the difference of treatment as regards defense rights when one follows adversarial proceedings or inquisitorial proceedings.

Given the differences that exist between member states or contracting states, the process or the overall mechanism is still made to work. The authorities interviewed would give the idea that they are able to cooperate with each other properly most of the time and whatever issues, problems, or discrepancies they have with one another, it is settled most of the time through open channels of communication or preliminary consultation with each other. They do not exist and operate to the exclusion of other authorities in other member states but the networks they build are vital to the success of making the international cooperation work.

In this regard one could learn that despite the differences or lack of harmonization among the member states themselves, the system could work. This resonates with a comment an interviewee made as to harmonization being a pipe dream. Harmonization is then not a necessary step to make cooperation work. Instead, what is needed – as seen in the regional instruments – is a minimum set of principles each member state ought to abide with to build a minimum level of understanding and workable environment among the member states. While some provisions may be too generalized, and must be determined by the respective domestic laws, it could still work if one follows a certain standard.

Furthermore, should the same minimum standards or sets of principles be self-internalized by the respective contracting states, or member states in this matter, then this also provides the motivation to become a good partner in the overall mechanism. This of course contributes to the success of the cooperation mechanism in place.

II. Suggestions for Developing Mutual Legal Assistance: Least Common Denominators

A. Mutual Legal Assistance Within the Regional Frameworks

In line with the idea above-stated, finding the least common denominators would be the best way to approach the development of mutual legal assistance, regardless of the same being between or within the ASEAN and the EU. These least common denominators shall determine the minimum amount of understanding required for the cooperative mechanism to work.

Anent the development within the ASEAN and the EU, this has been more or less settled and the mechanism has been working with seldom problems. As regards the ASEAN, one can see the learnings of the ASEAN Way finding its way to formal channels of cooperation because despite the formalistic requirements, which could often be dismissed as too stringent, the ASEAN member states are still able to find ways to resolve problems and issues that could be encountered vis-à-vis mutual legal assistance. There is focus on the interests of the entire community. They are able to make things work without necessarily imposing one's will to another. If one also takes into consideration the trainings, meetings, etc. they conduct regularly among themselves in tackling best practices, etc., in international cooperation, then the existence of consensus and openness to one another helps in making the cooperation mechanism efficient.

At this juncture, one could contemplate on whether the imposition of time limits, the use of a pro forma MLA request, and the use of direct contacts prove useful within the ASEAN framework. Among these three features learned from the EU framework, it would be the use of time limits that could be adopted, albeit might not make any significant change to the speed the ASEAN member states work with.

The use of a prescribed form might prove itself counter-intuitive to the flexibility the ASEAN member states generally exercise among themselves as regards mutual legal assistance. It might rather be limiting and constraining rather than allowing member states to send requests freely in whatever format they think is best. This has been seen admittedly as a flaw of the pro forma EIO with the EU member states. What could have been achieved through a simple letter with an attached warrant is not anymore allowed in the EIO context. Rather, authorities would need to fill up several pages of forms.

Further, a prescribed form could prohibit the use of draft copies or advance copies being sent by authorities to one another should they need clarifications on how the MLA request should be drafted, or during urgent matters, when the MLA is needed as fast as possible to be made. Having the prescribed form then would run counter to the manner or culture ASEAN member states have developed amongst each other vis-à-vis MLA.

Additionally, the use of direct contacts in lieu of central authorities for the issuing and executing authorities might also not be advisable, even if the same has proven useful and effective for EU member states. One ought to remember that direct contacts in the EU work generally because of the existing working infrastructures and networks it has such as the EJN and Eurojust. These networks are well established and contact points are readily known and available.

While the ASEAN member states' authorities would have their own established contact points, the ASEAN is bereft of any comparable formal network or infrastructure like that in the EU. Unless the ASEAN endeavors to establish similar bodies, problems may be encountered in searching for particular executing authorities in any particular matter requiring mutual legal assistance.

Furthermore, the central authorities have traditionally worked best in the sending and receiving of MLA requests. They have developed the needed expertise to handle situations relating to mutual legal assistance. Likewise, the model of having central authorities as shown by Malaysia and the Philippines, and in the EU, by the UK, proves more effective given the difference in structures these countries have, the use of adversarial proceedings, and the functions their respective courts perform. Therefore, the use of central authorities or the retention of horizontal cooperation might work best.

With respect to the use of time limits, it may theoretically improve the efficiency of the ASEAN member states as well as provide good rules of thumb for member states to abide with, but one must not forget that the imposition of time limits is underscored by the principle of mutual recognition based on mutual trust more or less. There are determined time limits due to the notion in the EU that no further step is needed to recognize the EIO being issued. For purposes of emphasis, the principle of mutual recognition does not exist in the ASEAN nor is there a similar provision of similar import. Thus, the additional steps of inquiring into the request, etc. theoretically still exists within the ASEAN context.

In addition to this, the ASEAN member states are in general effective already in effectuating MLA requests. Should one believe the statements of the Malaysian and Philippine authorities, ASEAN member states do not encounter much problems in dealing with each other and in fastly providing the needed mutual legal assistance. If there is any delay encountered, most of the time this is not attributable to the concerned authorities themselves but could be attributed to delays caused by court processes, which these authorities can only influence to a certain extent.

Based on the foregoing, the time limits could be put into place but could end up as having no significant positive change nor practical value anymore. At most, it can serve the function of positive reinforcement for authorities to act promptly, efficiently, and effectively.

Similar to the ASEAN, the EU is generally effective in its cooperation mechanism, and in this case, the EIO. At the outset, there is the principle of sincere cooperation and the enforcement mechanism that enjoins member states to be compliant in their duties and responsibilities. Further, there is adherence to and internalization by member states of the principle of mutual recognition and the application of this principle makes it easier for an EIO to be recognized or executed. Together with this, there is a common acceptance of European values and/or human rights obligations that needs to be realized, which put the member states already on the same page. Moreover, open communication exists among the different authorities. The existence of the Eurojust, EJN, and other channels of communication and cooperation, as well as the principle of availability of information, help also in making the cooperation mechanism work between EU member states. Further, there are the structural changes in the EIO which member states applied to their domestic jurisdictions. These include time limits, the prescribed form that theoretically should ease the issuance and execution of an EIO, use of direct contacts, among other things.

Stating it simply, the EU was able to form a sophisticated form of MLA among its member states. As to whether there is added value should the learnings from the ASEAN be applied, it would be the flexibility and openness the ASEAN member states have in relating to one another. While the EIO prescribed form has its advantages of being easily understandable, it could be more or less restricting and limiting as to how an EIO can be issued to another executing authority. Hurdles could be met when one is confronted with exigent or urgent circumstances that handling a pro forma EIO might be counter-productive and not time-efficient. While practitioners make adjustments in practice in addressing these kinds of issues, it would have been practicable and efficacious if urgent situations are contemplated within the EIO context that excuses the use of, or the delay in transmitting, the pro forma EIO. This would then foster flexibility and likewise account for urgent matters that need to be met by authorities.

As regards the other learnings from the ASEAN framework, it would not make sense for the EU member states to fall back to the traditional MLA framework especially given the higher caliber the EIO framework now has. It offers more protection for human rights by, for example, integrating defense rights more into the instrument; lessens the grounds to refuse recognition or execution; establishes direct contacts between authorities; integrates the principle of mutual recognition; and provides time limits to encourage faster executions of EIOs, among other things. Further, there are principles that apply equally to the member states that makes the provisions of the EIO meaningful. Given these innovations that so far work for the EU member states, it defies common sense and logic to abandon the same to go back to the traditional notions of mutual legal assistance.

Having mentioned the foregoing, and identifying how the regional and their member state frameworks work respectively, it would be prudent to identify the least common denominators as well as the non-negotiables of each one to identify the building blocks that could constitute an interregional framework.

B. Groundwork for the Cooperation Mechanism between the ASEAN and the EU

At the outset, both regional organizations should be on equal footing with each other. No regional organization should act with ascendancy over the other. Any observed soft hegemonic power or imperialism from the EU should be toned down in negotiating and acceding to any interregional mutual legal assistance treaty. Any interregional mutual legal assistance treaty or development of a cooperation mechanism is not hinged on human rights conditions, which the EU places normally on development aids, the ENP, and other external actions it undertakes. Any treaty would be pure and simple about interregional mutual legal assistance and/or international cooperation in criminal matters with no strings attached. In other words, any interregional mutual legal assistance treaty should not be a "carrot" on a stick for democratization and human rights concerns. This would in fact be in line with the tenets of reciprocity and would adhere to the principle of non-intervention of the ASEAN.

Second, in line with the least common denominators suggestion, there should be consideration of the willingness of the respective member states to enter into such an arrangement. The ASEAN could then opt for the ASEAN Way among themselves and/or the "ASEAN minus X" rule, that would allow those member states ready, willing, and able to enter already into the arrangement or agreement while those which need time are given the time and space they need. On the other hand, the EU can act with exclusive competence to enter into any agreement with the ASEAN and its member states. Alternatively, resort to "enhanced cooperation" can be explored albeit the concept is originally limited to agreements between EU member states.

C. Suggestions for Substantive Provisions

A discussion of the least common denominators or non-negotiables with respect to substantive provisions of a mutual legal assistance agreement is imperative.

First, said interregional mutual legal assistance between the ASEAN and the EU should remain – or start – with being request-based, rather than demand-based or order-based as one sees in the EIO. The principle of mutual recognition based on mutual trust is mutually exclusive to the EU and its member states. The same principle or something of similar import does not exist in the ASEAN and its member states. Following the tenets of traditional mutual legal assistance, the nomenclature therefore ought to be followed are requests. Besides, the ASEAN and its member states might not appreciate it should its possible EU member state partners impose upon them through "orders". This is notwithstanding the fact that in practice, the change in nomenclature did not mean an automatic, no-questions-asked kind of implementation. However, one could still entertain said possibility should such kind of "order-based" mechanism be applicable both ways and that all ASEAN member states agree to the idea.

Second, it is proper that whatever interregional mutual legal assistance shall be developed, it shall be applicable to all criminal matters. This would be the minimum or otherwise standard requirement in traditional mutual legal assistance. If further explanation or clarification is required, then the DEIO example could be followed. An enumeration of certain matters wherein the MLA shall be applicable could be provided.

In relation to this, clarificatory provisions might be in order as regards the applicability to natural and legal persons as provided by the EU example. There might be issues arising out of corporate criminal liability in ASEAN and EU member states alike. Thus, a clarification might help in defining and delineating the applicability of assistance.

Third, it is advisable that any mutual legal assistance to be developed between the ASEAN and the EU contemplates all kinds of assistance. This would make the agreement more flexible to changing times as well as technological advancements. In this respect, the catch-all provision provided in the ASEAN MLAT may be included as a safety net provision. The EU could likewise consider including in the scope those measures not originally included in the DEIO such as joint investigation teams, cross-border surveillance, etc., to avoid future possible conundrums on whether a particular investigative measure is included or not. Also, while mutual legal assistance would normally contemplate a judicial to judicial kind of cooperation, there might be instances wherein there are investigative measures that do not have the same kind of correspondence but are likewise included in a MLA request. In such cases, it is suggested that the MLA request is construed in favor of approval rather than denial of the request. In other words, contracting parties should act towards effectuating a request rather than denying it.

Fourth, there are the different principles, conditions, and exceptions. As regards the sufficiency of information requirement, since both the EU and the ASEAN have the same direct proportionality between the information to be provided and the intrusiveness of the investigative measure, this should then be maintained. Thus, the more information shall be required, the more intrusive the measure involved is. In relation to this, since both the ASEAN and the EU would need to provide the widest possible measure of assistance, the lack of provided information should not be a ground to refuse recognition or execution.

With respect to the dual criminality requirement, the exclusion of the 32 offenses from the applicability of the requirement could be attempted. However, if one looks into the origins of why these 32 offenses have been excluded in the first place, it might be hard to convince the ASEAN member states to agree. Alternatively, the ASEAN and the EU could agree on a particular list – not necessarily encompassing the full list of 32 offenses, but doing it in a step-by-step basis. But then again, the dual criminality requirement is losing significance in practice so the interregional MLA between the ASEAN and the EU might be the needed jump board to exclude the requirement altogether.

With regard the double jeopardy requirement, there ought to be a proper definition that embodies the transnational nature both the ASEAN and the EU aim for but still fall short in their respective applicable provisions. This is suggested considering the lack of transnational definition in the ASEAN (very restricted application) and its member states, as well as the issues found still in the EU context. By establishing a proper delineation and definition at the outset, problems would be avoided in the future. In light of this, it would be ideal to consider a double jeopardy or *ne bis in idem* provision that embodies a true transnational nature or puts it into fruition: a provision that does not only consider either the requested state, the requesting state (i.e. Malaysian law), or both, but instead considers likewise third states where a conviction, acquittal, pardon, or service of sentence has already occurred vis-à-vis the facts constituting the offense included in the request. In relation to this, a request shall be denied if the person subject of the request has been convicted, acquitted, or pardoned in a state other than the requesting state for the same facts constituting the offense; and in case of conviction, the sentence has already been enforced, is being enforced, or by reason of the law of the sanctioning state can no longer be enforced. This reflects more or less the ASEAN MLAT provision (as it already tackles service or execution of sentence) but expands it beyond the requesting and requested state.

Significantly, this proposed provision is progressive in nature. It captures transnationality as how it should be: it would not only take note of judgments elsewhere in determining one's sentence but would free one altogether from the risk of being placed in jeopardy one way or another. It would mitigate, if not remove, any risk that has been increased by virtue of EU member states needing to frame their transnational criminal law in favor of the Union to punish violations of EU law to the greatest possible extent, which,as mentioned earlier in this study, consequently carries with it issues on fair trial, due process of law, and the idea of personal legal certainty. In the context of the EU, there is the high risk of being placed in a situation of unforeseeability because even if they have been tried already in one country, their legal situation can still be altered in the other. This is arguably counter-intuitive to the intent of having an area of justice and home affairs. The same can be gainsaid about the ASEAN member states. They have agreed on an ASEAN Security Community and are moving toward the same direction of penalizing the same criminal offenses, especially terrorism and transnational crimes (and even started to formalize international agreements among themselves regarding criminal matters such as these), which are often the subject matter of MLA requests. It also offers the opportunity to operationalize the prohibition found in the ASEAN Human Rights Declaration without waiting for developments to occur at a member state level.

It is understandable however if the suggested provision would not be fully acceptable as a mandatory ground for refusal, especially if it involves a third state, which is not a contracting party to the interregional treaty. One can follow the route done in the German framework wherein the ground for refusal, irrespective of fellow EU member state or third state, is optional in nature. The existence of double jeopardy does not equate to automatic refusal of a MLA request. Instead, authorities are given the needed space for discerning whether to proceed or not in granting a request. Indeed, scenarios could occur wherein the issue being determined in the requesting state is about the existence of double jeopardy itself and the requested information and evidence is integral to its determination. Further, this puts into consideration the possibility that the criminal matter has been committed wholly or partially in the territory of the requested state. Therefore, there might be an interest for it to pursue its own criminal proceeding.

With regard reciprocity and speciality requirements, this should be maintained in any interregional mutual legal assistance agreement between the ASEAN and the EU. These are cornerstones of mutual legal assistance and other international cooperation mechanisms. Further, a look into the law in practice and how the regional instruments are applied domestically show the importance of these values. Thus, it is suggested that these should be considered to be included. This necessarily includes the provision requiring the return of documents or evidence once the proceedings for which it was requested has ceased. In addition to this, data protection considerations should be taken into account. As mentioned above, the EU has a data protection framework that equally applies to the protection of natural persons with regard to the processing of personal data by competent authorities for the purposes of the prevention, investigation, detection or prosecution of criminal offences or the execution of criminal penalties, including the safeguarding against and the prevention of threats to public security. While there is no ASEAN framework on data protection standards especially in criminal and security matters, any interregional treaty ought to consider the conditions needed to be satisfied in transfers of personal information and data to and from EU member states. In respect thereto, an additional provision or annexed schedule can be provided tackling data protection issues and further down the road, data protection agreements or arrangements can be explored by both regional organizations.

In respect of special offenses or national interests, the political and military offenses exception found in the ASEAN MLAT may be retained. However, it is suggested that these exceptions be treated as discretionary grounds for refusal rather than mandatory. This would accommodate the non-existence of these grounds for refusal in the EU instruments. Further, it should be within the discretion of the contracting parties on whether to proceed in the execution of a MLA request should this exist or not.

In relation to this, one could converge the other grounds to refuse execution based on national interests found in both the ASEAN MLAT and the EIO. These include, but is not limited to those that might affect sovereignty, public order, or other essential public interest; territoriality; privilege; pending criminal investigation; etc.

The last substantive provision in consideration are regarding human rights. As regards grounds to refuse a request, one could take into account for example existing provisions that enforce the prohibition against non-discrimination, prohibition against *ex post facto* laws, or denials grounded on consent of the individual concerned. One could also integrate the ground for refusal found in the DEIO regarding the human rights obligations of the EU member states under Article 6 TEU, which embodies the provisions in the Charter of Fundamental Rights, European Convention of Human Rights, etc. This is a non-negotiable for EU member states, especially those which relate to conditions of detention, rights to fair trial, and prohibition of death penalty and the imposition of torture, and cruel, degrading and inhumane punishment. Interestingly, rights of similar import can already be found in the ASEAN Human Rights Declaration but are not operationalized as a basis to refuse a MLA request in the ASEAN MLAT due to non-intervention considerations. If one would then integrate a similar provision found in the DEIO regarding "the human rights obligations of the EU member states under Article 6 TEU," this would provide ASEAN member states a basis in treaty to deny requests if the same is incompatible with their own human rights obligations, especially those which have extraterritorial application. There would be no need to find a loophole any further in invoking "state interest" as a ground for refusal.

Anent the issue of conditions of detention that relate to the prohibition against torture or other cruel, inhumane, degrading punishment or treatment, the standards of ASEAN member states would need to be assessed as there might be stark differences to what the EU member states espouse. Standards or doctrines found in ECHR or CJEU jurisprudence may be incompatible with the ASEAN member states' situation. Mutual legal assistance could include requests for the transfer of persons in custody to give information or evidence. Thus, tackling conditions of detention is imperative. What could be done to address this concern initially is for EU member states to get commitments from ASEAN member states should there be issues relating to conditions of detention.

On this note, it becomes interesting to resolve the issue of the imposition of the death penalty, torture, and/or cruel, inhumane, and degrading punishment at this juncture. These human rights obligations have extraterritorial application and therefore, as mentioned above, are indeed non-negotiables. Provided that some ASEAN member states still impose the death penalty and other forms of corporal punishment such as whipping in Malaysia, a ground to refuse could be included in the interregional treaty tackling the same. Alternatively, the same kind of commitment can be taken from those concerned.

D. Suggestions for Procedural Provisions

The substantive provisions constituting any possible mutual legal assistance treaty between the ASEAN and the EU aside, there are also some suggestions that could be made in relation to the procedural ones.

First, it might be prudent to retain central authorities for the time being. While direct contacts would have its advantages, one of the reasons it works for the EU member states, as already mentioned before, are established networks and contacts among them. There is also the Eurojust and the EJN that helps in facilitating these contacts and channels of communication. The same formalized network does not exist unfortunately in the ASEAN infrastructure. So unless the ASEAN develops similar counterpart agencies within its framework such as an ASEAN Criminal Justice Network or similarly structured coordinating bodies, authorities might be constrained in not knowing who to contact or to whom a request should be sent to. So while direct contacts may speed up the process, it might not work between the ASEAN and the EU. At least with the central authorities, they would traditionally have the expertise needed to address the requests. Point persons are also easier identifiable. Moreover, should trainings and consultations be required, one would be apprised already of whom to contact and the point persons would be easily identifiable. This of course is without prejudice to exploring again the idea of direct contacts when the needed corresponding infrastructures are present between and within the ASEAN and the EU.

Second, there would be the aspect of the preparation and issuance of a MLA request. At this point, there is no need to impose a prescribed or pro forma MLA request like the EIO. Instead, at a minimum, there ought to be flexibility among the contracting states to the form and format of the MLA request. At most, the interregional treaty could copy the provision in the DEIO that requires parties to acknowledge receipt of the MLA request. This reinforces or promotes good MLA practice among the contracting states and would also give an idea on when to follow up with a requested state regarding a particular request.

In connection to preparations of requests, one ought to consider at whose instance it can be issued. Given the lack of participation of the defense in the ASEAN MLAT and in the domestic legislations of its member states, it might be prudent at the first stages of the interregional treaty to provide that the participation of the defense in the issuance and execution of a MLA request is highly encouraged and shall be determined in the respective domestic laws of the contracting states. By drafting the provision as such vis-à-vis the right to participate by the defense or request the issuance of a MLA request on its behalf, it does not only accommodate the promotion of the right found in the DEIO, but more importantly, it gives ASEAN member states the opportunity to internalize and/or reconsider the participation they give to the defense in the process, as well as reassess that the MLA framework is not limited to being a prosecution tool. In the alternative, should ASEAN member states continue to view MLA as a process exclusively meant for investigators and prosecutors, or the inclusion of defense participation is a way of the EU to impose its ideals to the ASEAN, there would still be no harm in retaining such a provision. Through additional talks, consensus-finding processes, etc., provisions tackling the same could be included in additional protocols to any interregional treaty.

Third, the interregional treaty could combine the provisions of both the ASEAN MLAT and the DEIO on the applicable law vis-à-vis execution of requests: the MLA request could be recognized or executed in accordance with the laws and/or formalities of the requesting state, subject to the domestic laws of the requested state (or unless it violates the fundamental principles or domestic laws of the requested state). Thus, the general rule would be automatically be a *forum regit actum* arrangement and this could overcome the issues relating to human rights as well as evidentiary and admissibility rules, while maintaining respect to the domestic laws and fundamental principles of the requested state. Understandably, if the request does not indicate any procedure or formality to be followed, then the law of the requested state shall prevail. Additionally, the interregional treaty can include provisions of allowing the presence of authorities from the requesting state during the execution of the investigative measure requested. Furthermore, a requested state can suggest other investigative measures if the investigative measure requested is not available or not allowed for the particular criminal matter in the domestic legal system of the requested state.

In relation to the last mentioned suggestion, one must bear in mind that while suggesting another investigative measure is allowed in the EU framework, there are five (5) instances to which an investigative measure should be available in an EU member state, namely, (1) the obtaining of information or evidence which is already in the possession of the executing authority and the information or evidence could have been obtained, in accordance with the law of the executing state, in the framework of criminal proceedings or for the purposes of the EIO; (2) the obtaining of information contained in databases held by police or judicial authorities and directly accessible by the executing authority in the framework of criminal proceedings; (3) the hearing of a witness, expert, victim, suspected or accused person or third party in the territory of the executing State; (4) any non-coercive investigative measure as defined under the law of the executing State; (5) the identification of persons holding a subscription of a specified phone number or IP address. These five instances can be taken further into consideration on the relevant provision on applicable law on execution.

Fourth, it is likewise important to consider that human rights protection is present in the execution of the investigative measures that are subject of a MLA request between the ASEAN and the EU member states. This is already apparent in the respective regional instruments and domestic instruments tackling mutual legal assistance. While participation of a suspect, accused, or the defense in general would still need to be negotiated, the basic protection of human rights vis-à-vis investigative measures should be a non-negotiable. This includes the integration of procedural rights and the availability of remedies should redress be needed.

Fifth, there is the option to include time limits in the provisions of the possible interregional treaty. This would be like the provisions in the DEIO which are not mandatory but could provide good barometers on speed and efficiency. More or less, there is a commitment from the contracting parties to act fast as they could on MLA requests that would foster strong interregional cooperation in criminal matters.

Sixth, a standard provision could be provided as regards authentication in general. Not only are requests needed to be accomplished or issued in a manner that produces a written record, but all the evidence or information to be obtained via a MLA request does not require further authentication.

Seventh, there could be specific provisions tackling specific investigative measures, akin to the provisions found in all regional and member state instruments tackled so far. This would highlight any specificities needed to be addressed as well as idiosyncrasies that could exist with a particular measure. Bearing this in mind, the contracting parties may also opt to include those that touch on technological advances such as those involving online evidence or cyberdata. What is more imperative is that the instrument, whilst maintaining traditional MLA characteristics, would be able to stand the test of time in relevance and application.

Summary, Conclusion and Further Recommendations

Based on the renewed commitment the ASEAN and the EU gave each other in pursuing stronger cooperation in combating terrorism and transnational crime, as well as the present structures of each one in tackling the same, the present study was mainly interested in knowing how mutual legal assistance in criminal matters could develop between and within the Association of Southeast Asian Nations and the European Union. This present study focused only on mutual legal assistance in criminal matters because the ASEAN does not presently have yet a regional extradition treaty among its member states that one could compare to the European Arrest Warrant of the European Union.

This notwithstanding, the present study mainly had five (5) objectives. The first one was to know the historical development of the ASEAN and the EU, including the historical development of their respective regions that influenced the establishment of these regional organizations, the historical development of the two regional organizations' international cooperation mechanisms in criminal matters, specifically on mutual legal assistance, and the respective legal frameworks applicable to these mechanisms. The second was to know the historical development of international cooperation in criminal matters, specifically mutual legal assistance, as well as the legal framework (including substantive and procedural provisions) for it in selected member states of the ASEAN and the EU, which includes a study of how a sample member state from each region implements mutual legal assistance through law and practical information (law in the books v. law in practice). The third was to compare and contrast the mutual legal assistance frameworks of ASEAN and EU on criminal matters with their respective member state frameworks by knowing the present state of the mutual legal assistance framework on criminal matters and its application in the ASEAN and the EU, including a study of how a sample member state from each region is implementing the same, formally and informally, through law and practical application. The fourth was to compare and contrast the ASEAN and the EU regional frameworks with each other, including a comparison of their respective historical developments, institutional frameworks, fundamental principles, norms, and practices, and their existing mechanisms of mutual legal assistance vis-à-vis how the same is implemented in their respective member state frameworks. Lastly, the fifth objective is to evaluate, analyze, and anticipate the problematic issues and problems with respect to the respective frameworks and provide recommendations for improvement, harmonization, revision, etc., when appropriate, and whether there could be a (further) development of mutual legal assistance in criminal matters between and within the ASEAN and the EU.

With respect to the first and second objectives, it was learned that the ASEAN and EU are more alike than different with their respective historical developments. The regions in which these organizations have shared experiences and strange parallels – albeit sometimes they are found on different ends of the experience – that ultimately shaped the principles, ideals, norms, and beliefs each regional organization espouses. The historical development also dictated the development of each one's nature, thought and decision-making process.

In the same vein, this influenced their existing infrastructures, cooperation mechanisms, and criminal justice architecture. In line with this, EU has admittedly been able to create more sophisticated, detailed, and complex structures in fostering cooperation among its member states, including those related to international cooperation in criminal matters. Conversely, the ASEAN has yet to come up with an ASEAN extradition treaty whilst already having a treaty tackling mutual legal assistance in criminal matters.

Anent mutual legal assistance in criminal matters, which exists in both regional frameworks, one could look into the different substantive and procedural provisions of each. The present study utilized interviews and communications with practitioners and experts in the member states to gain insight on how mutual legal assistance and general cooperation occurs between them. Any information then gained from the abovementioned is used to meet the third objective of the study, which is to compare and contrast the regional frameworks and member state frameworks with each other.

It was discovered that member state frameworks remain true in general to the regional instruments on mutual legal assistance. They implement as much as possible to the letter the provisions of the ASEAN MLAT and the DEIO, respectively. Should there be nuances, differences, or additions to how the regional instrument is transposed and applied domestically, this was understandable given the differences in national legal systems, principles, and existing laws of each member state. This notwithstanding, member states and their respective practitioners, authorities, and experts, are able to run the mechanism smoothly in general. It was learned that albeit there are discrepancies, unsettled issues, or overall lack of harmonization of laws, these never hindered the member states from effectively and efficiently working with each other. It helps that there are open channels of cooperation among authorities, which helps in solving any issue or problem that arises in relation to mutual legal assistance.

In connection with the third objective, the regional frameworks are then compared with each other to highlight certain issues as the fourth objective of the study. In evaluating the regional frameworks themselves for instance, one could observe a strange parallel situation between the ASEAN and the EU as regards their historical developments and how they developed their own principles, norms, and practices. Next, one could look into how they compared as regards their existing cooperation mechanisms, approach to regional security and international cooperation, and mutual legal assistance matters. Further in pursuit of the fourth objective, the member state frameworks vis-à-vis the regional frameworks were analyzed and three distinct aspects stood out: the transposition or translation of the law in the member states, the efficiency in implementing the MLA frameworks, and the protection of human rights.

This now leads to the fifth and final objective of the study which is to thresh out the lessons that could definitely be learned. With regard to this, there is considerable weight that should be given the distinguishing features of the two regional organizations which then becomes the basis to understand how they are as international actors in terms of their decision and policymaking. One of these lessons is the compliance or enforcement mechanism that the EU has, which helps in the faster implementation or policy-making in said regional organization, whereas the ASEAN is mainly driven through informal, consensus-based approaches in their everyday business.

Another lesson that could be learned is with respect to the ASEAN principle of non-intervention and the general characteristic of the EU of being normative and hegemonic (soft imperialism). This must definitely be taken into account in deciding for a mutual legal assistance regime between the ASEAN and the EU. Neither party should dominate the determination of terms.

The last lesson that is interesting to point out is the fact that the lack of harmonization does not necessarily result to inefficiency of the cooperation mechanism. Admittedly, the ASEAN member states do not have harmonization of laws and the same maybe forever a pipe dream given the intergovernmental nature of the ASEAN. The same lack of harmonization occurs in the EU, although in a smaller scale perhaps. Nonetheless, member states are able to make the cooperation mechanism or mutual legal assistance work. There is approximation or the acceptance of minimum standards that help in building and maintaining (almost) smooth operations with each other.

Given these lessons, the present study then came up with different suggestions ranging from the MLA within the regional frameworks (involving their own member states), the groundwork for the development of MLA, and suggestions for both substantial and procedural provisions that could be included in the possible MLA regime between the ASEAN and the EU. These suggestions mainly start with least common denominators and non-negotiables of each regional organization in efforts to find agreement between the regional and member state frameworks.

In summary, the comparative criminal approach used by the present study in comparing the regional frameworks of the ASEAN and the EU, and the respective member state frameworks of the Philippines, Malaysia, the UK, and Germany, including a comparison of the law in books and the law of practice, would ultimately show that a mutual legal assistance regime could indeed be developed between and within the ASEAN and the EU. There is no need for the imposition of will of one regional organization to the other on what it thinks the other should do or practice. Instead, by building a common understanding of their respective frameworks and that of the other, as well as a common acceptance of the minimum principles, ideals, and norms based on their differences, a formal international cooperation mechanism is highly plausible.

Understandably, the ASEAN and the EU made a renewed commitment during the ASEAN 50th Anniversary celebrations to strengthen their cooperation with one another in the ASEAN-led ASEAN Political-Security Community, including fostering cooperation in fighting terrorism and transnational crime. The building of a mutual legal assistance regime between the two now-strategic partners would then be a step towards fulfilling this reciprocal commitment. It would not only enrich the criminal law policy of the regional organizations and their respective member states, but more importantly, show a strong political and security statement that both regional organizations are ready, willing, and able to commit to their respective endeavors and are willing to set their differences aside for the common good.

Admittedly however, the present study is not enough. It is suggested that other member states of each regional organization be compared, analyzed, and evaluated for a better well-grounded understanding of the existing frameworks. There is a possibility that the sample member states in the present study were not able to show all needed information. There is the possibility of underlying issues that were not completely fleshed out.

Also, there is the need for more interviews, observations, and communications with authorities and experts on the field to gain more insights on the situation. Empirical studies could thus be undertaken, without prejudice to studies using different approaches to discern if the prognosis would still be the same.

Further, there is the possibility to undertake studies specifically comparing the security and criminal law policy of the ASEAN and the EU, including the possibility of looking into each one's member states. These studies could later on involve the possibility of developing closer cooperation between and within the ASEAN and the EU in criminal matters other than mutual legal assistance. For example, the development of a regional extradition treaty in ASEAN could be studied in furtherance of an interregional treaty with EU, as part of a set of international cooperation mechanisms between the two regional organizations. Another option for exploration is building data protection arrangements for transfers of personal data and information in criminal matters.

By undertaking the foregoing recommendations, one then could foresee the promotion and establishment of stronger toolkits, arrangements, and agreements between and within the regional organizations to combat transnational crime and build effective cooperation mechanisms in criminal law.

Bibliography

Laws

ASEAN

Agreement on Information Exchange and Establishment of Communication Procedures; Putrajaya, Malaysia, 2002

ASEAN Action Plan on Social Safety Nets, 2012

ASEAN Convention Against Trafficking in Persons, Especially Women and Children; Kuala Lumpur, Malaysia, 2015

ASEAN Convention on Counter-Terrorism; Cebu, Philippines, 2007

ASEAN Declaration on Joint Action to Counter Terrorism; Bandar Seri Begawan, Brunei Darussalam, 2001

ASEAN Declaration on Transnational Crime: Manila, Philippines, 1997

ASEAN Human Rights Declaration; Phnom Penh, Cambodia, 2012

ASEAN Treaty on Mutual Legal Assistance in Criminal Matters; Kuala Lumpur, Malaysia, 2004

Declaration of ASEAN Concord, Bali, Indonesia, 1976.

Joint Communiqué of the Second ASEAN Ministerial Meeting on Transnational Crime; Yangon, Myanmar, 1999

Southeast Asian Nuclear-Weapon-Free Zone Treaty; Bangkok, Thailand, 1995

Treaty of Amity and Cooperation in Southeast Asia Indonesia, Denpansar, Bali, 1976

Vientiane Action Programme; Vientiane, Laos, 2004

Zone of Peace, Freedom and Neutrality Declaration; Kuala Lumpur, Malaysia, 1971

EU

Consolidated version of the Treaty on European Union, OJ C 326, 26.10.2012, p. 13–46

Consolidated version of the Treaty on the Functioning of the European Union, OJ L. 326, 26.10.2012, p. 47-326.

Convention implementing the Schengen Agreement, OJ L 239, 22.9.2000, p. 19-62

Convention on Mutual Assistance in Criminal Matters between the Member States of the European Union; Brussels, Belgium, 2000

Council Framework Decision 2002/465/JHA of 13 June 2002 on joint investigation teams, OJ L 162, 20.6.2002, p. 1–3

Council Framework Decision 2002/584/JHA of 13 June 2002 on the European arrest warrant and the surrender procedures between Member States, OJ L 190, 18.7.2002, p. 1–20

Council Framework Decision 2006/960/JHA of 18 December 2006 on simplifying the exchange of information and intelligence between law enforcement authorities of the Member States of the European Union, OJ L 386, 29.12.2006, p. 89–100

Council Framework Decision 2008/675/JHA of 24 July 2008 on taking account of convictions in the Member States of the European Union in the course of new criminal proceedings, OJ L 220, 15.8.2008, p. 32-34

Council Framework Decision 2008/977/JHA of 27 November 2008 on the protection of personal data processed in the framework of police and judicial cooperation in criminal matters, OJ L 350, 30.12.2008, p. 60–71

Council Framework Decision 2008/978/JHA of 18 December 2008 on the European evidence warrant for the purpose of obtaining objects, documents and data for use in proceedings in criminal matters, OJ L 350, 30.12.2008, p. 72–92

Council Framework Decision of 13 June 2002 on combating terrorism, OJ L 164, 22.6.2002, p. 3–7

Directive (EU) 2016/1919 of the European Parliament and of the Council of 26 October 2016 on legal aid for suspects and accused persons in criminal proceedings and for requested persons in European arrest warrant proceedings, OJ L 297, 4.11.2016, p. 1-2

Directive (EU) 2016/343 of the European Parliament and of the Council of 9 March 2016 on the strengthening of certain aspects of the presumption of innocence and of the right to be present at the trial in criminal proceedings, OJ L 65, 11.3.2016, p. 1–11

Directive (EU) 2016/680 of the European Parliament and of the Council of 27 April 2016 on the protection of natural persons with regard to the processing of personal data by competent authorities for the purposes of the prevention, investigation, detection or prosecution of criminal offences or the execution of criminal penalties, and on the free movement of such data, and repealing Council Framework Decision 2008/977/JHA, OJ L 119, 4.5.2016, p. 89–131

Directive (EU) 2016/681 of the European Parliament and of the Council of 27 April 2016 on the use of passenger name record (PNR) data for the prevention, detection, investigation and prosecution of terrorist offences and serious crime, OJ L 119, 4.5.2016, p. 132-149

Directive (EU) 2016/800 of the European Parliament and of the Council of 11 May 2016 on procedural safeguards for children who are suspects or accused persons in criminal proceedings, OJ L 132, 21.5.2016, p. 1–20

Directive (EU) 2017/541 of the European Parliament and of the Council of 15 March 2017 on combating terrorism and replacing Council Framework Decision 2002/475/JHA and amending Council Decision 2005/671/JHA, OJ L 88, 31.3.2017, p. 6-21

Directive 2012/29/EU of the European Parliament and of the Council of 25 October 2012 establishing minimum standards on the rights, support and protection of victims of crime, and replacing Council Framework Decision 2001/220/JHA, OJ L 315, 14.11.2012, p. 51-73

Directive 2014/41/EU of the European Parliament and of the Council of 3 April 2014 regarding the European Investigation Order in criminal matters, OJ L 130, 1.5.2014, p. 1-4

European Convention of Human Rights; Rome, Italy, 1950

European Convention on Mutual Assistance in Criminal Matters; Strasbourg, France, 1959

EU-UK Trade and Cooperation Agreement, OJ L 444, 31.12.2020, p. 1486–1487.

EU-UK Withdrawal Agreement (2019/C 384 I/01), entered into force 01 February 2020.

Framework Agreement on Relations between the European Parliament and the Commission C5-349/2000, OJ C 121/122, 24.4.2001, p. 122

Protocol (No 25) on the exercise of shared competence, OJ 115, 9.5.2008, p. 0307

Protocol (No 3) on the statute of the Court of Justice of the European Union, OJ 115, 9.5.2008, p. 0210-0229

Germany

Act on International Cooperation in Criminal Matters, 1982, Federal Law Gazette I page 2071

Basic Law for the Federal Republic of Germany, 1949

German Code of Criminal Procedure, 1987, Federal Law Gazette Part I p. 1074-1319

Federal Data Protection Act, 2017, Federal Law Gazette I p. 2097), as last amended by Article 12 of the Act of 20 November 2019, Federal Law Gazette I, p. 1626

Guidelines for International Proceedings in CriminalMatters (Richtlinien für den Verkehr mit dem Ausland in strafrechtlichen Angelegenheiten), (BAnz. S. 10550)

Malaysia

Court of Juridicature Act 1964

Federal Constitution of Malaysia, 1957

Interpretation Act of 1967, Act 388

Malaysian Child Act of 2001, Act 611

Malaysian Criminal Procedure Code of 1937, Act 593

Malaysian Extradition Act 1992, Act 479

Malaysian Rules of Court 2012

Malaysian Subordinate Court Act of 1948, Act 92

Mutual Assistance in Criminal Matters Act of 2002, Act 621

Philippines

Executive Order No. 292, Administrative Code of the Philippines of 1987
Constitution of the Republic of the Philippines, 1987
Philippine Revised Rules of Court, 2000
Philippine Rules of Civil Procedure, 1997
Philippine Rules of Criminal Procedure, 2000
Philippine Rules on Electronic Evidence, 2001
Republic Act No. 10071, Prosecutor Service Act of 2010
Republic Act No. 10168, Terrorism Financing Prevention and Suppression Act of 2012
Republic Act No. 10175, Cybercrime Prevention Act of 2012
Republic Act No. 157, Act Creating Bureau of Investgation of 1947
Republic Act No. 4200, Anti-Wiretapping Law of 1965
Republic Act No. 8792, Electronic Commerce Act of 2000
Republic Act No. 9160, Anti-Money Laundering Act of 2001
Republic Act No. 9372, Human Security Act of 2007

UK

Anti-Terrorism, Crime, and Security Act 2001, 2001 c. 24
Crime (International Co-operation) Act 2003, 2003 c. 32
Criminal Justice (European Investigation Order) Regulations 2017, 2017 No. 730
Criminal Justice Act 2003, 2003 c. 44
Criminal Justice and Public Order Act 1994, 1994 c.33
Criminal Procedure (Attendance of Witnesses) Act 1965, 1965 c. 69
Double Jeopardy (Scotland) Act 2011, 2011 asp 16
Human Rights Act 1998, 1998 c. 42
Police and Criminal Evidence Act 1984, 1984 c. 60
Youth Justice and Criminal Evidence Act 1999, 1999 c. 23

UN

Economic and Social Council resolutions, Resolution 1984/50 of 25 May 1984
International Covenant on Civil and Political Rights, Resolution 2200A (XXI) of 16 December 1966

Juriprudence

Amion v. Chiongson, AM No. RTJ-97-1371, 22 January 1999.
Animal Defenders v. UK (GC), 22 April 2013.
Arceta v. Mangrobang, G.R. No. 152895, 15 June 2004.

Asian Terminals v. Philam Life Insurance, G.R. Nos. 181163, 181262, 181319, 24 July 2013.

Associated Provincial Picture Houses v. Wednesbury Corporation [1948] 1 KB 223.

Bakar bin Ahmad v. Public Prosecutor [1968] 4 MC 294.

Bangayan v. Bangayan, G.R. Nos. 172777 and 172792, 19 October 2011.

Beltran v. Samson, G.R. No. 32025, 23 September 1929.

Borgers v. Belgium, (App 12005/86) (1991) Series A no. 214-B.

Brannigan and McBride v. United Kingdom, (Apps 14553/89, and 14554/89), 26 May 1993, Series A No. 258-B, (1994) 17 EHRR 539.

Brunner v. European Union Treaty, [1994] 1 CMLR 57.

Case C-156/93, European Parliament v. Commission (Re Genetically Modified Microorganisms in Organic Products, [1995] ECR I-2019.

Case C-65/93, European Parliament v. Council (Re Generalized Tariff Preferences), [1995] ECR I-643.

Case C-129/14 PPU, Spasic judgment (Re Ne Bis In Idem Principle).

Case C-658/11, European Parliament v. Council, EC:C:2014:2025.

Cerezo v. People of the Philippines, G.R. No. 185230, 01 June 2011.

Chahal v. United Kingdom, (App. 22414/93), 19 November 1996, (1997) 23 EHRR 413, ECHR 1996-V.

Chai Ah Kau v. Public Prosecutor, [1974] MLJ 2 191, 192, [1972-1974] SLR 609.

Chang Liang Sang &Ors v. Public Prosecutor, [1982] 2 MLJ 231, FC.

Chavez v. Court of Appeals, G.R. No. L-29169, 19 August 1968.

Clay and Feather International v. Lichaytoo, G.R. No. 193105, 30 May 2011.

Commissioner of Internal Revenue v. Court of Tax Appeals, G.R. No. 203403, 14 November 2018.

Congressman Garcia v. Executive Secretary, G.R. 157584, 02 April 2009.

Chua v. People of the Philippnes, G.R. No. 195248, 22 November 2017.

Danaharta Urus SdnBhd v. KekatongSdnBhd, [2004] 2 MLJ at 257.

Dato' Mohamed Hashim Shamsuddin v. Attorney General, Hong Kong [1986] 2 MLJ 112.

Datuk James Wong Kim Min [1976] MLJ 245.

De Freitas v. Permanent Secretary of Agriculture, Fisheries, Lands and Housing [1999] 1 AC 69.

Disini v. Secretary of Justice, G.R. No. 203335, 18 February 2014.

Doorson v. The Netherlands (App 20524/92) ECHR 1996-II [72].

Editions Plon v. France, 18 May 2004.

Esquillo v. People of the Philippines, G.R. No. 182010, 25 August 2010 (J. Bersamin, dissenting), citing Walder v. US, 347 US 62, 64-65 (1954).

Estrada v. Sandiganbayan, 421 Phil. 290, 430, 19 November 2001.

Go v. BangkoSentral ng Pilipinas, G.R. No. 178429, 23 October 2009.

Gonzales v. Hechanova, G.R. No. L-21897, 22 October 1963.

Government of the United States of America v. Purgunan, G.R. No. 148571, 24 September 2002.

Grimaldi v. Fonds des Maladies Professionelles, Case C-322/88, [1989] ECR 4407.

Gutang v. People of the Philippines, G.R. No. 135406, 11 July 2000.

Hashim Bin Saud v. Yahaya Bin Hashim [1977] 2 MLJ 116.

HM Magistrate v. Sinclair, [2014] HCJAC 131, para. 124-131.

Ho Wai Pang v. People of the Philippines, G.R. No. 176229, 19 October 2011.

Hon Ne Chan v. Honda Motor Co., G.R. No. 172775, 19 December 2007.

Huang v. Secretary of State for the Home Department [2007] UKHL 11.

Ichong v. Hernandez, 101 Phil. 1155 (1957).

Inacay v. People of the Philippines, G.R. 223506, 28 November 2016.

Integrated Bar of the Philippines v. Zamora, G.R. No. 141284, August 15, 2000, 338 SCRA 81.

Ireland v. United Kingdom, 18 January 1978, Series A No 25, (1979-80) 2 EHRR 25.

Jaa'far&Ors v. Public Prosecutor, [1961] MLJ 186.

Jalloh v. Germany, (App. 54810/00), 11 July 2006 [GC], (2007) 44 EHRR 667, ECHR 1996-IX.

Jamali bin Adnan v. Public Prosecutor [1986] 1 MLJ 162; [1985] CLJ (Rep) 167.

Jespers v. Belgium, (App 8403/78) (1981) 27 DR 61 [55].

Joint Cases C-404/15 and C-659/15 PPU PaiAranyosi and Robert Căldăraru, 05 April 2016.

KekatongSdnBhd v. DanahartaUrusSdnBhd, [2003] 3 MLJ 1.

Kuroda v. Jalandoni, 83 Phil. 171, 178 (1949).

Lee Gee Lam v. Timbalan Menteri Hal EhwalDalamNegeri, Malaysia and Anor [1993] 3 MLJ 265.

LiawKwaiWah v. Public Prosecutor, [1987] 2 MLJ 69, 71, SC.

Lo Ching v. Archbishop of Manila, 81 Phil. 101; Borovsky of Immigration, G.R. No. L-4362 (1951).

Loc Hock Seng v. Anor and Public Prosecutor, [1980] 2 MLJ 13, FC.

Lorrain Esme Osman v Attorney General of Malaysia [1986] 2 MLJ 288.

Matyjek v. Poland, (App 38184/03) ECHR 24 April 2007 [55].

Microsoft Corporation and Lotus Development Corporation v. Maxicorp, Inc., G.R. No. 140946, 13 September 2004, 438 SCRA 224, 225.

Miranda v. Arizona, 384 U.S. 436, 467-468 (1966).

Nolasco v. Paño, G.R. No. L-69803, 08 October 1985 (J. Teehankee, separate).

Okabe v. Gutierrez, G.R. No. 150185, 27 May 2004.

Ong Lai Kim v. Public Prosecutor, [1991] 3 MLJ 111, 115.

Ooi Ah Phua v. Officer-in-Charge of Criminal Investigations, Kedah/Perlis [1975] 2 MLJ 198.

PalaniappaChettiar v. ArunasalamChettiar, FM Civil Appeal No. 34 of 1958, [1961] MLJ ■■■ii.

Parliament v. Council (case C-65/93).

Paulin v. Gimenez, G.R. No. 103323, 21 January 1993, 217 SCRA 386, 389.

People of the Philippines v. Alicando, G.R. No. 117487, 12 December 1995.

People of the Philippines v. Bandin, G.R. No. 104494, 10 September 1993.

People of the Philippines v. Barasina, G.R. No. 109993, 21 January 1994.

People of the Philippines v. Canton, G.R. No. 148825, 27 December 2002.

People of the Philippines v. Cogaed, G.R. No. 200334, 30 July 2014.

People of the Philippines v. Cogaed, G.R. No. 200334, 30 July 2014.

People of the Philippines v. de la Cruz, G.R. No. 118866-68, 17 September 1997.

People of the Philippines v. Flores, G. R. No. 128823-24, 27 December 2002.

People of the Philippines v. Gamboa, G.R. No. 91374, 25 February 1991.

People of the Philippines v. Holgado, G.R. No. L-2809, 22 March 1950.

People of the Philippines v. Mariacos, G.R. No. 188611, 16 June 2010.

People of the Philippines v. Nicandro, G.R. No. L-59378, 11 February 1986.

People of the Philippines v. Nicolas, G.R. No. 135877, 22 August 2002.

People of the Philippines v. Pavillare, G.R. No. 129970, 05 April 2000.

People of the Philippines v. Pavillare, G.R. No. 129970, 05 April 2000.

People of the Philippines v. Paynor, G.R. No. 116222, 9 September 1996

People of the Philippines v. Piedad, G.R. No. 131923, 05 December 2002.

People of the Philippines v. Pinlac, G.R. Nos. 74123-24, 26 September 1988.

People of the Philippines v. Romualdez, G.R. No. 166510, 23 July 2008.

People of the Philippines v. Sergio, G.R. No. 240053, 09 October 2019.

People of the Philippines v. Tan, G.R. No. 117321, 11 February 1998.

People of the Philippines v. Tan, G.R. No. 117321, 11 February 1998.

People v. Aruta, 351 Phil. 868, 880 (1998).

People v. dela Piedra, G.R. No. 121777, 24 January 2001, 350 SCRA 163.

People v. Echegaray, G.R. No. 117472, 25 June 1996.

People v. Tee, G.R. Nos. 140546-47, 20 January 2003.

Pharmaceutical and Health Care Association of the Philippines v. Duque, G.R. No. 173034, 09 October 2007.

PihakBerkuasaNegeri Sabah v. Sugumar Balakrishnan, [2002] 3 MLJ 72.

Pollo v. Constantino-David, G.R. No. 181881, 18 October 2011, 659 SCRA 189, 204-205.

Prudente v. Dayrit, G.R. No. 82870, 14 December 1989.

Public Prosecutor v. Chan Chuan and Amor, [1991] 2 MLJ 538, 540.

Public Prosecutor v. Lau KeeHoo, [1983] 1 MLJ 157, FC.
Public Prosecutor v. Lau Ngiik Yin, [2007] MLJU 668 at [4].
Public Prosecutor v. OttavioQuattrocchi, [2003] 2 CLJ 613.
Public Prosecutor v. Tan SweeHoon, [1993] 3 SLR 758, 762.
Public Prosecutor v. Teh Cheng Poh, [1978] 1 MLJ 68.
R (on application of C) v. Sevenoaks Youth Court [2009] EWHC 3008.
R (on application of D) v. Camberwell Green Youth Court [2005] 1 WLR 393.
R v. Lemsatef [1977] 2 All ER 835; Abdul Rahman v. Tan Jo Koh [1968] 1 MLJ 25, FC.
R v. Secretary of State for the Home Department [2001] 2 AC 532.
Ramli Bin Salleh v. Yahaya Bin Hashim [1973] 1 MLJ 54.
Republic v. Sandiganbayan, G.R. Nos. 112708-09, 29 March 1996.
Romualdez v. Sandiganbayan, G.R. No. 152259, 29 July 2004.
Roquette Freres v. Council (case 138/79); Maizena GmbH v. Council (case C-21/94).
Rowe and Davis v. United Kingdom (App 28901/95), 16 February 2000 [GC], (2000) 30 EHRR 1, ECHR 2000-II.
Sabio v. Senator Gordon, 535 Phil. 687, 714-715 (2006).
Salas v. Sta. Mesa Market Corporation, G.R. No. 157766, 12 July 2007.
Sarigumba v. Sandiganbayan, G.R. Nos. 154239-41, 16 February 2005.
Sau Soo Kim v. Public Prosecutor [1975] 2 MLJ 134; Fan Yew Teng v. Public Prosecutor, [1975] 2 MLJ 235.
Sebastian v. Garchitorena, G.R. No. 114028, 18 October 2000.
Secretary of Justice v. Lantion, G.R. No. 139465, 18 January 2000.
Sinnathurai Subramaniam v. Public Prosecutor, [2011] 5 CLJ 56, CA.
Soering v. United Kingdom [1989] 161 Eur. Ct. H.R.
Sugumar Balakrishnan v. PengarahImigresenNegeri Sabah, [1998] 3 MLJ 289.
Suruhanjaya Sekuriti v. Datuk Ishak Ismail [2016] 3 CLJ 19 FC.
T & V v. United Kingdom, (Apps. 24888/94 and 24724/94) 16 December 1999 [GC], (2000) 30 EHRR 121, ECHR 1999-IX.
Tan Sri Eric Chia Eng Hock v. PP [2007] 1 CLJ 565.
The Government of the State of Kelantan v. the Government of the Federation of Malaya and Tunku Abdul Rahman Putra Al-Haj, [1963] MLJ 355 (Federation of Malaya High Court).
Variola v. Amministrazione delle Finanze, Case 34/73, [1973] ECR 981.
Williams v. Twomey, 510 F2d 634, 640 (7th Cir 1975).

Other references

Abdulgani, Roeslan, The Bandung Connection: the Asia-Africa Conference in Bandung in 1955, Bandung, 1981.

Abraham, Itty, From Bandung to NAM: Non-Alignment and Indian Foreign Policy, 1947–65, in: Commonwealth & Comparative Politics 46 (2008) 2, pp. 195-219.

Acharya, Amitav, Asia is Not One, in: The Journal of Asian Studies 69 (2010) 04, pp. 1001-1013.

Acharya, Amitav, Bandung Revisited: The Legacy of the 1955 Asian-African Conference for International Order, Singapore, 2008.

Acharya, Amitav, Constructing a Security Community in Southeast Asia: ASEAN and the Problem of Regional Order, 3, London, 2014.

Acharya, Amitav, Ideas, Identity and Institution-Building: Making Sense of the Asia-Pacific Way, in: The Pacific Review 10 (1997) 3, pp. 319-346.

Acharya, Amitav, Regionalism and the Emerging World Order, in: New Regionalism in the Global Political Economy: Theories and Cases, 2003, pp. 20-32.

Acharya, Amitav, Whose Ideas Matter?: Agency and Power in Asian Regionalism, New York, 2011.

Acharya, Amitav/Tan, See Seng, The Normative Relevance of the Bandung Conference for Contemporary Asian and International Order, in: Acharya, Amitav/Tan, See Seng (Ed.), Bandung Revisited: The Legacy of the 1955 Asian-African Conference for International Order, Bd. 5, Singapore, 2008, pp. 1-16.

Albers, Pim/Beauvais, Pascal/Bohnert, Jean-François /Böse, Martin/Langbroek, Philip/Renier, Alain/Wahl, Thomas, Towards a Common Evaluation Framework to Assess Mutual Trust in the Field of EU Judicial Cooperation in Criminal Matters, Hague, 2013.

Alegre, Susan/Leaf, Marisa, Mutual Recognition in European Judicial Cooperation: A Step Too Far Too Soon? Case Study on the European Arrest Warrant, in: European Law Journal 10 (2004) 2, pp. 200-217.

Alesina, Alberto/Perotti, Roberto, The European Union: a Politically Incorrect View, in: Journal of Economic Perspectives 18 (2004) 4, pp. 27-48.

Amer, Ramses, Conflict Management and Constructive Engagement in ASEAN's Expansion, in: Third World Quarterly 20 (1999) 5, pp. 1031-1048.

Anderson, Jeffrey, The European Union, the Soviet Union, and the End of the Cold War, in: Dinan, Desmond (Ed.), Origins and Evolution of the European Union, Second Edition, Oxford, 2014, pp. 255-273.

Ang, Cheng Guan, The Bandung Conference and the Cold War International History of Southeast Asia, in: Acharya, Amitav/Tan, See Seng (Ed.), Bandung Revisited: The Legacy of the 1955 Asian-African Conference for International Order, Singapore, 2008, pp. 27-47.

Anwar, Dewi Fortuna, Indonesia in ASEAN: Foreign Policy and Regionalism, Singapore, 1994.

Apap, Joanna/Carrera, Sergio, Judicial Cooperation in Criminal Matters-European Arrest Warrant–A Good Testing Ground for Mutual Recognition in an Enlarged EU? CEPS Policy Briefs No. 46, February 2004, in: (2004), pp. 1-26.

Appadorai, Angadipuram, The Asian Relations Conference in Perspective, in: International Studies 18 (1979) 3, pp. 275-285.

Appadorai, Angadipuram, The Bandung Conference, in: India Quarterly: A Journal of International Affairs 11 (1955) 3, pp. 207-235.

Argomaniz, Javier, Post-9/11 Institutionalisation of European Union Counter-Terrorism: Emergence, Acceleration and Inertia, in: European Security 18 (2009) 2, pp. 151-172.

ASEAN Political-Security Department, Security Cooperation Division, ASEAN Documents on Combating Transnational Crime and Terrorism, Indonesia 2012.

Aston, Nigel, Christianity and Revolutionary Europe, 1750-1830, Cambridge, 2002.

Bachmaier Winter, Lorena, European Investigation Order For Obtaining Evidence in the Criminal Proceedings, in: Zeitschrift für Internationale Strafrechtsdogmatik 9 (2010), pp. 580-589.

Bachmaier-Winter, Lorena, Transnational Evidence: Towards the Transposition of Directive 2014/41 Regarding the European Investigation Order in Criminal Matters, in: EUCrim 2015 (2015) 2, pp. 47-59.

Bahrampour, Firouzeh, The Caning of Michael Fay: Can Singapore's Punishment Withstand the Scrutiny of International Law, in: Am. UJ Int'l L. & Pol'y 10 (1994), pp. 1075-1108.

Barbé, Esther/Johansson-Nogués, Elisabeth, The EU as a Modest 'Force for Good': the European Neighbourhood Policy, in: International Affairs 84 (2008) 1, pp. 81-96.

Bassiouni, M Cherif, International Criminal Law, Volume 2 Multilateral and Bilateral Enforcement Mechanisms, Leiden, 2008.

Bassiouni, M Cherif, The Modalities of International Cooperation in Penal Matters, in: Bassiouni, M Cherif (Ed.), International Criminal Law, Bd. 2, Leiden, 2008, pp. 3-34.

Becker, Elizabeth, When the War was Over: Cambodia and the Khmer Rouge Revolution, New York, 1998.

Beeson, Mark, Institutions of the Asia Pacific: ASEAN, APEC, and Beyond, Oxon, 2008.

Benda, Harry, The Structure of Southeast Asian History: Some Preliminary Observations, in: Journal of Southeast Asian History 3 (1962) 1, pp. 106-138.

Bentele, Ursula, Back to an International Perspective on the Death Penalty as a Cruel Punishment: The Example of South Africa, in: Tul. L. Rev. 73 (1998), pp. 251-271.

Best, Edward, The European Integration Process: An Example for Other Regions?, in: Ott, Andrea/Vos, Ellen (Ed.), Fifty Years of European Integration: Foundations and Perspectives, Cambridge, 2009, pp. 333-348.

bin Musa, Dato'Abdul Razak/bin Jaafar, Dato' Umar Saifuddin, Mutual Legal Assistance and Recovery of Proceeds of Corruption, in: Ninth Regional Seminar on Good Governance for Southeast Asian Countries, Tokyo, 2016.

Boister, Neil, An Introduction to Transnational Criminal Law, Oxford, 2012.

Bono, Giovanni, The Impact of 11 September 2001 and the "War on Terror" on European Foreign and Social Policy: Key Issues and Debates, in: Bono, Giovanni (Ed.), The Impact of 9/11 on European Foreign and Security Policy, Brussels, 2006, pp. 7-26.

Booth QC, Cherie, Proportionality and the Human Rights Act: A Year in Reflection, in: Amicus Curiae (2001) 38, pp. 3-11.

Bose, Sarmila, Fading Echoes: Legacy of Empire and Democracy in India, in: Nicolaïdis, Kalypso/Sèbe, Berny/Maas, Gabrielle (Ed.), Echoes of Empire: Memory, Identity, and Colonial Legacies, London, 2017, pp. 47-62.

Bovend'Eerdt, Koen, The Joined Cases Aranyosi and Caldararu: A New Limit to the Mutual Trust Presumption in the Area of Freedom, Security, and Justice, in: Utrecht J. Int'l & Eur. L. 32 (2016), pp. 112-121.

Brands, Henry, Jr, From ANZUS to SEATO: United States Strategic Policy towards Australia and New Zealand, 1952–1954, in: The International History Review 9 (1987) 2, pp. 250-270.

Bretherton, Charlotte/Vogler, John, The European Union as a Global Actor, London, 1999.

Burke, Roland, "The Compelling Dialogue of Freedom": Human Rights at the Bandung Conference, in: Human Rights Quarterly 28 (2006) 4, pp. 947-965.

Caballero-Anthony, Mely, The ASEAN Charter: An Opportunity Missed or One that Cannot Be Missed, in: Southeast Asian Affairs (2008), pp. 71-85.

Caballero-Anthony, Mely, Regional Security in Southeast Asia: Beyond the ASEAN Way, Singapore, 2005.

Casale, Davide, EU Institutional and Legal Counter-Terrorism Framework, in: Defence Against Terrorism Review 1 (2008) 1, pp. 49-78.

Chesterman, Simon, Does ASEAN Exist? The Association of Southeast Asian Nations as an International Legal Person, in: Singapore Yearbook of International Law and Contributors 12 (2008), pp. 199-211.

Chongkittavorn, Kavi, Covering ASEAN for Three Decades, in: Lee, Yoong Yoong (Ed.), ASEAN Matters! Reflecting on the Association of Southeast Asian Nations, Singapore, 2011, pp. 39-42.

Christie, Clive A Modern History of Southeast Asia: Decolonization, Nationalism and Separatism, New York, 1998.

Christie, Jan Wisseman, State Formation in Early Maritime Southeast Asia, in: Bijdragen tot de Taal-, Land- en Volkenkunde 151 (1995) 2, pp. 235-288.

Cini, Michelle, From the Marshall Plan to EEC: Direct and Indirect Influences, in: Schain, Martin (Ed.), The Marshall Plan Fifty Years After, New York, 2001, pp. 13-37.

Ciorciari, John, The Limits of Alignment: Southeast Asia and the Great Powers Since 1975, Washington D.C., 2010.

Cockerham, Geoffrey B., Regional Integration in ASEAN: Institutional Design and the ASEAN Way, in: East Asia 27 (2009) 2, pp. 165-185.

Coffey, Gerard, Post-Acquittal Retrials for Serious Offences in the Irish Criminal Justice Process: Lessons from England and Wales, in: (2013), pp.

Collins, Roger, Early Medieval Europe 300–1000, 1999.

Collins S.J, David, The Christian Church, 1370-1550, in: Scott, Hamish (Ed.), Oxford Handbook on Early Modern European History, 1350-1750, Volume 1: People and Places, Bd. 1, Oxford, 2015, pp. 543-570.

Cooper, Frederick, Colonialism in Question: Theory, Knowledge, History, Berkley, 2005.

Cotterell, Arthur, A History of Southeast Asia, Singapore, 2014.

Couperus, Stefan/Kaal, Harm, Introduction: (Re) constructing Communities in Europe, 1918-1968, in: Couperus, Stefan/Kaal, Harm (Ed.), (Re) constructing Communities in Europe, 1918-1968: Senses of Belonging Below, Beyond and Within the Nation-state, New York, 2016, pp. 1-13.

Craig, Paul, Institutions, Power, and Institutional Balance, in: Craig, Paul/De Burca, Grainne (Ed.), The Evolution of EU Law, Oxford, 2011, pp. 41-84.

Craig, Paul/de Búrca, Grainne, EU Law: Text, Cases, and Materials, Fourth Edition, Oxford, 2008.

Craig, Paul/de Búrca, Grainne, EU Law: Text, Cases, and Materials, Sixth Edition, Oxford, 2015.

Craig, Paul/de Búrca, Grainne (Ed.), The Evolution of EU Law, Oxford, 2011.

Cremona, Marise, External Relations and External Competence of the European Union, in: Craig, Paul/De Burca, Grainne (Ed.), The Evolution of EU Law, Oxford, 2011, pp. 217-268.

Crozier, Andrew, Festina Lente: An Introductory Sketch of the History of ASEAN, in: Welfens, Paul/Knipping, Franz/Chirathivat, Suthiphand (Ed.), Integration in Asia and Europe: Historical Dynamics, Political Issues, and Economic Perspectives, Heidelberg, 2006, pp. 13-29.

Curtin, Deirdre M/Dekker, Ige F, The European Union from Maastricht to Lisbon: Institutional and Legal Unity Out of the Shadows, in: Craig, Paul/De Burca, Grainne (Ed.), The Evolution of EU Law, Oxford, 2011, pp. 155-186.

Davidson, Jamie/Kammen, Douglas, Indonesia's Unknown War and the Lineages of Violence in West Kalimantan, in: Indonesia (2002) 73, pp. 53-87.

Davidson, Paul, ASEAN Features: The ASEAN Way and the Role of Law in ASEAN Economic Cooperation, in: Singapore Yearbook of International Law and Contributors 8 (2004), pp. 165-176.

De Busser, Els/Riehle, Cornelia, News, in: EUCrim 2015 (2015) 2, pp. 34-46.

De Hert, Paul, Division of Competencies Between National and European Levels with Regard to Justice & Home Affairs', in: Apap, Joanna (Ed.), Justice and Home Affairs in the EU. Liberty and Security Issues after Enlargement, Cheltenham (UK), 2004, pp. 55-102.

De Hert, Paul/Aguinaldo, Angela, A leading role for the EU in drafting criminal law powers? Use of the Council of Europe for policy laundering, in: New Journal of European Criminal Law 10 (2019) 2, pp. 99-106.

De Hert, Paul/Weis, Karen/Cloosen, Nathalie, The Framework Decision of 18 December 2008 on the European Evidence Warrant for the Purpose of Obtaining Objects, Documents and Data for Use in Proceedings in Criminal Matters – A Critical Assessment, in: New Journal of European Criminal Law 1 (2009) 1, pp. 55-78.

de Silva, Júlio Barbosa, The Speciality Rule in Cross-Border Evidence Gathering and in the European Investigation Order—Let's Clear the Air, in: ERA Forum 19 (2019) 3, pp. 485-504.

Denza, Eileen, 2000 Convention on Mutual Assistance in Criminal Matters, The, in: Common Market L. Rev. 40 (2003), pp. 1047-1074.

Department of Foreign Affairs, DFA statement on the stay of execution of Mary Jane Veloso, 2015, accessible via https://www.officialgazette.gov.ph/2015/04/29/dfa-statement-on-the-stay-of-execution-of-mary-jane-veloso/.

Department of Foreign Affairs, Philippine Treaties Online, 2017, accessible via http://210.5.104.56/treaty/index.php?r=treaty/listalltreaties&Treaty_page=2&Treaty_sort=category_id.

Deutsch, Jan-Georg, Colonial Modernities: A View from the Imperial Verandah, c. 1880-1960, in: Nicolaïdis, Kalypso/Sèbe, Berny/Maas, Gabrielle (Ed.), Echoes of Empire: Memory, Identity, and Colonial Legacies, London 2017, pp. 35-46.

Dewanto, Wisnu Aryo, Implementing Treaties in Municipal Courts, in: Mimbar Hukum-Fakultas Hukum Universitas Gadjah Mada 23 (2011) 1, pp. 1-18.

Di Floristella, Angela Pennisi, The ASEAN Regional Security Partnership: Strengths and Limits of a Cooperative System, London, 2015.

Di Floristella, Angela Pennisi Are Non Traditional Security Challenges Leading Regional Organizations Towards Greater Convergences – The EU and ASEAN Security Systems in Comparative Perspective, in: A. Asia Eur J 11 (2013), pp. 21-38.

Dickson, Brice, Human Rights and the United Kingdom Supreme Court, Oxford, 2013.

Dinan, Desmond (Ed.), Origins and Evolution of the European Union, Second Edition, Oxford, 2014.

Dingman, Roger, John Foster Dulles and the Creation of the South-East Asia Treaty Organization in 1954, in: The International History Review 11 (1989) 3, pp. 457-477.

Dougan, Michael, Editor's Introduction, in: Dougan, Michael (Ed.), The UK After Brexit: Legal and Policy Challenges, Cambridge, 2017, pp. 1-12.

Douglas-Scott, Sionaidh, The Rule of Law in the European Union--Putting the Security into the Area of Freedom, Security and Justice, in: 29 European Law Review (2004), pp. 219-238.

Eder, Franz/Senn, Martin, Europe and Transnational Terrorism: An Introduction, in: Eder, Franz/Senn, Martin (Ed.), Europe and Transnational Terrorism: Assessing Threats and Countermeasures, Baden-Baden, 2008, pp. 13-20.

Emmers, Ralf, ASEAN and the securitization of transnational crime in Southeast Asia, in: The Pacific Review 16 (2003) 3, pp. 419-438.

Emmers, Ralf, The Securitization of Transnational Crime in ASEAN, Singapore, 2002.

Emmerson, Donald, ASEAN's" Black Swans", in: Journal of Democracy 19 (2008) 3, pp. 70-84.

Emmerson, Donald, "Southeast Asia": What's in a Name?, in: Journal of Southeast Asian Studies 15 (1984) 1, pp. 1-21.

Esmaquel, Paterno II, ASEAN treaty helps save Mary Jane Veloso, Metro Manila 2015.

Eurojust, Guidelines for "Which Jurisdiction Should Prosecute?", 2016.

European Council, ASEAN-EU Plan of Action (2018-2022), Brussels, 2018.

European Council, Joint statement of the 22nd EU-ASEAN ministerial meeting, Brussels 2010.

European Judicial Network, Directive 2014/41/EU of 03 April 2014 regarding the European Investigation Order in Criminal Matters – Competent Authorities and Languages, 15 December 2017, Brussel 2017.

Evans, Paul, The Dialogue Process on Asia Pacific Security Issues: Inventory and Analysis, in: Studying Asia Pacific Security (Toronto and Jakarta: University of Toronto-York University Joint Centre for Asia Pacific Studies and Centre for Strategic and International Studies, 1994) (1994), pp. 297-318.

Evans, Paul M, Human security and East Asia: In the beginning, in: Journal of East Asian Studies 4 (2004) 2, pp. 263-284.

Faruqi, Shad Saleem, Exceptions to Double Jeopardy Protection, 2017, accessible via http://www.thestar.com.my/opinion/columnists/reflecting-on-the-law/2017/02/16/exceptions-to-double-jeopardy-protection-no-persons-should-be-imperilled-by-subsequent-criminal-pros/.

Fernández-Armesto, Felipe, Exploration and Navigation, in: Scott, Hamish (Ed.), Oxford Handbook on Early Modern European History, 1350-1750, Volume 2: Cultures & Power, Oxford, 2015, pp. 173-199.

Fifield, Russell The Five Principles of Peaceful Co-Existence, in: The American Journal of International Law 52 (1958) 3, pp. 504-510.

Fifield, Russell Hunt, National and Regional Interests in ASEAN: Competition and Cooperation in International Politics, Singapore, 1979.

Flers, Nicole, EU-ASEAN Relations: The Importance of Values, Norms and Culture, in: EU Center Singapore Working Paper No. 1 (2010), pp. 2-10.

Fook, Lee Chong/Mansoor, Mazlifah/Hassan, Che Audah, Process of Criminal Justice Part II (Second Edition): Trial Proceedings, Sentencing, and Appeals, Singapore, 2010.

Frost, Frank, Introduction: ASEAN since 1967—origins, evolution and recent developments, in: ASEAN into the 1990s, 1990, pp. 1-31.

Funston, John, Challenges Facing ASEAN in a More Complex Age, in: Contemporary Southeast Asia (1999), pp. 205-219.

G20, A Step-by-Step Guide for Requesting Mutual Legal Assistance in Criminal Matters from G20 Countries, 2012.

Gaddis, John Lewis, Was the Truman Doctrine a Real Turning Point?, in: Foreign Affairs 52 (1974) 2, pp. 386-402.

Gana Jr, Severino, Extradition and Legal Assistance: The Philippine Experience, in: 114th International Senior Seminar, Tokyo (2001).

Ganesan, Narayanan, Rethinking ASEAN as a Security Community in Southeast Asia, in: Asian Affairs: An American Review 21 (1994) 4, pp. 210-226.

Gáspár-Szilágyi, Szilárd, Joined Cases Aranyosi and Căldăraru: Converging Human Rights Standards, Mutual Trust and a New Ground for Postponing a European Arrest Warrant, in: European Journal of Crime, Criminal Law and Criminal Justice 24 (2016) 2-3, pp. 197-219.

Gillespie, Alisdair, The English Legal System, Fifth Edition, Oxford, 2015.

Glaubitz, Joachim, Anti-Hegemony Formulas in Chinese Foreign Policy, in: Asian Survey 16 (1976) 3, pp. 205-215.

Goh, Gillian, The 'ASEAN Way', in: Stanford Journal of East Asian Affairs 3 (2003), pp. 113-118.

Gordon, Michael, Brexit: The Relationship Between the UK Parliament and the UK Government, in: Dougan, Michael (Ed.), The UK After Brexit: Legal and Policy Challenges, Cambridge, 2017, pp. 15-33.

Gregoratti, Leonardo, Roman Traders as a Factor of Romanization in Noricum and in the Easter Transalpine Region, in: Roselaar, Saskia (Ed.), Processes of Cultural Change and Integration in the Roman World, Leiden, 2015, pp. 239-252.

Griffiths, Robert, Under the Shadow of Stagflation: European Integration in the 1970s, in: Dinan, Desmond (Ed.), Origins and Evolution of the European Union, Oxford, 2014, pp. 165-188.

Gupta, Akhil, The Song of the Nonaligned World: Transnational Identities and the Reinscription of Space in Late Capitalism, in: Cultural Anthropology 7 (1992) 1, pp. 63-79.

Haacke, Jürgen, ASEAN's Diplomatic and Security Culture: a Constructivist Assessment, in: International Relations of the Asia-Pacific 3 (2003) 1, pp. 57-87.

Hamid, Abdul Ghafur/Sein, Khin Maung, Judicial Application of International Law in Malaysia: An Analysis, in: APYIHL 1 (2005), pp. 196.

Harding, Andrew, The Constitution of Malaysia: A Contextual Analysis, Oxford, 2012.

Harding, Andrew, Law, Government, and the Constitution of Malaysia, Oxford, 1996.

Hartley, Trevor, European Union Law in a Global Context: Text, Cases and Materials, Cambridge, 2005.

Healy, Róisín/Dal Lago, Enrico, Investigating Colonialism within Europe, in: Healy, Róisín/Dal Lago, Enrico (Ed.), The Shadow of Colonialism on Europe's Modern Past, London, 2014, pp. 3-22.

Heard, Catherine/Mansell, Daniel, The European Investigation Order: Changing the Face of Evidence-Gathering in EU Cross-Border Cases, in: New Journal of European Criminal Law 2 (2011) 4, pp. 353-367.

Hecker, Bernd, The EU and the Fight Against Organized Crime, in: Hauck, Pierre/ Peterke, Sven (Ed.), International Law and Transnational Organized Crime, Oxford, 2016, pp. 63-83.

Heisenberg, Dorothee, From the Single Market to the Single Currency, in: Dinan, Desmond (Ed.), Origins and Evolution of the European Union, Oxford, 2014, pp. 233-254.

Hemmer, Christopher/Katzenstein, Peter J, Why Is There No NATO In Asia? Collective Identity, Regionalism, And The Origins Of Multilateralism, in: International Organization 56 (2002) 03, pp. 575-607.

Hensengerth, Oliver, Regionalism in China-Vietnam Relations: Institution-Building in the Greater Mekong Subregion, Oxon, 2009.

Hirst, John, Die Kürzeste Geschichte Europas, Hamburg, 2015.

Horváth, Zoltán Handbook on the European Union, Budapest, 2005.

Human Rights in ASEAN, DFA, DOJ officials to meet with Indon execs over Mary Jane Veloso case, 2015, accessible via https://humanrightsinasean.info/news/dfa-doj-officials-to-meet-with-indon-execs-over-mary-jane-veloso-case/.

International Bar Association, The Death Penalty under International Law: A Background Paper to the IBAHRI Resolution on the Abolition of the Death Penalty, 2008, accessible via https://www.google.com/url?sa=t&rct=j&q=&esrc=s&source=web&cd=14&ved=2ahUKEwjr3qr17czmAhWPh1wKHfUXASQQFjANegQIAhAC&url=https%3A%2F%2Fwww.ibanet.org%2FDocument%2FDefault.aspx%3FDocumentUid%3D5482860B-B9BC-4671-A60F-7B236AB9A1A0&usg=AOvVaw2g7bTBqeSkq62jVXMkA3QX 23 December 2019.

Ioannou-Naoum-Wokoun, Karin/Ruelling, Martin Helmuth, The European Union: History, Institutions, Law, Politics, Bremen, 2010.

Jacqué, Jean-Paul, Principle of Institutional Balance, The, in: Common Market L. Rev. 41 (2004), pp. 383-391.

Jian, Chen, The Tibetan Rebellion of 1959 and China's Changing relations with India and the Soviet Union, in: Journal of Cold War Studies 8 (2006) 3, pp. 54-101.

Kamal, Baizura, International Cooperation: Mutual Legal Assistance and Extradition, in: Sixth Good Governance Seminar for Southeast Asian Countries, Tokyo, 2012.

Kelsall, Michell Staggs, The New ASEAN Intergovernmental Commission on Human Rights: Toothless Tiger or Tentative First Step, Honolulu, 2009.

Kennedy, Dane, Imperial Parasitism: British Explorers and African Empires, in: Nicolaïdis, Kalypso/Sèbe, Berny/Maas, Gabrielle (Ed.), Echoes of Empire: Memory, Identity, and Colonial Legacies, London, 2017, pp. 17-28.

Keohane, Robert O, Reciprocity in international relations, in: International organization 40 (1986) 1, pp. 1-27.

King, Margaret, A Return to the Ancient World?, in: Scott, Hamish (Ed.), Oxford Handbook on Early Modern European History, 1350-1750, Volume 2: Cultures & Power, Oxford 2015, pp. 3-28.

Kivimäki, Timo, The Long Peace of ASEAN, in: Journal of Peace Research 38 (2001) 1, pp. 5-25.

Klimek, Libor, European Arrest Warrant, Cham, 2016.

Klip, André, The Constitution for Europe and Criminal Law: a Step Not Far Enough, London, 2005.

Klip, André, European Criminal Law, An Integrative Approach, 3rd, Cambridge, 2016.

Komárek, Jan, European Constitutionalism and the European Arrest Warrant: In Search of the Limits of "Contrapunctual Principles", in: Common Mark. Law Rev. 44 (2007), pp. 9-40.

Krstić, Tijana, Islam and Muslims in Europe, in: Scott, Hamish (Ed.), Oxford Handbook on Early Modern European History, 1350-1750, Volume 1: People and Places, Bd. 1, Oxford, 2015, pp. 670-693.

Ku, Khemlin, International Cooperation: Mutual Legal Assistance and Extradition in Cambodia, in: Sixth Regional Seminar on Good Governance for Southeast Asian Countries, Fukuoka, 2013.

Kulsudjarit, Kongpetch, Drug Problem in Southeast and Southwest Asia, in: Annals of the New York Academy of Sciences 1025 (2004) 1, pp. 446-457.

Lang, Alessandra, Mutual Recognition and Mutual Trust, in: Pedrazzi, Marco/Viarengo, Ilaria/Lang, Alessandra (Ed.), Individual Guarantees in the European Judicial Area in Criminal Matters, Brussels, 2011, pp. 181-188.

Le Quéré, Enora, The "Opportunistic Exploitation" of Melos: A Case Study of Economic Integration and Cultural Change in the Roman Cyclades, in: Roselaar, Saskia (Ed.), Processes of Cultural Change and Integration in the Roman World, Leiden, 2015, pp. 222-238.

Lee, Yoong Yoong (Ed.), ASEAN Matters! Reflecting on the Association of Southeast Asian Nations, Singapore, 2011.

Lelieur, Juliette, 'Transnationalising' Ne Bis In Idem: How the Rule of Ne Bis In Idem Reveals the Principle of Personal Legal Certainty, in: Utrecht Law Review 9 (2013) 4, pp. 198-210.

Leverick, Fiona, "Legal History" in the Making: HM Advocate v Sinclair and the Double Jeopardy (Scotland) Act 2011, in: Edinburgh Law Review 19 (2015) 3, pp. 403-408.

Lieberman, Victor, Strange parallels: Volume 1, Integration on the mainland: Southeast Asia in global context, c. 800–1830, Cambridge, 2003.

Lim, Bandol, ASEAN: The Challenge is Upon Us, in: Lee, Yoong Yoong (Ed.), ASEAN Matters! Reflecting on the Association of Southeast Asian Nations, Singapore, 2011, pp. 33-38.

Liu, Yanling, The Promises and Contradictions of ASEAN, in: Lee, Yoong Yoong (Ed.), ASEAN Matters! Reflecting on the Association of Southeast Asian Nations, Singapore, 2011, pp. 19-21.

Luchtman, Michiel, Choice of Forum in an Area of Freedom, Security and Justice, in: Utrecht L. Rev. 7 (2011), pp. 74-101.

Ludlow, N. Piers, From Deadlock to Dynamism: The European Community in the 1980s, in: Dinan, Desmond (Ed.), Origins and Evolution of the European Union, Second Edition, Oxford, 2014, pp. 218-232.

Ludlow, N. Piers, Value, Flexibility, and Openness: The Treaty of Rome's Success in Historical Perspective, in: Baquero Cruz, Julio/Closa Montero, Carlo (Ed.), European Integration from Rome to Berlin: 1957-2007, Frankfurt, 2009, pp. 17-32.

Lulić, Josipa, Theorizing Romanization. Cognition and Cultural Change in Roman Provinces: A Case of Religious Change in Roman Dalmatia, in: Roselaar, Saskia (Ed.), Processes of Cultural Change and Integration in the Roman World, Leiden, 2015, pp. 20-38.

Maier-Knapp, Naila, A friend in need. A friend in deed? ASEAN-EU interregionalism in the light of non-traditional security crises in South-East Asia, in: ASEAS-Austrian Journal of South-East Asian Studies 3 (2010) 1, pp. 76-100.

Malaya, J. Eduardo/Monedero-Arnesto, Sheila, Enhancing International Legal Cooperation: Extradition, Mutual Legal Assistance, Transfer of Sentenced Persons, and Cooperation on Transnational Organized Crimes and Narcotic Drugs (Treaties, Laws, and Procedures), Manila, 2019.

Malaya, J. Eduardo/Monedero-Arnesto, Sheila/Paras, Ricardo III, Enhancing International Legal Cooperation: Extradition, Mutual Legal Assistance, Transfer of Sentenced Persons, and Cooperation on Transnational Organized Crimes and Narcotic Drugs (Treaties, Laws, and Procedures), Manila, 2019.

Manners, Ian, The Normative Ethics of the European Union, in: International Affairs 84 (2008) 1, pp. 45-60.

Masterman, Roger, Taking the Strasbourg jurisprudence into account: Developing a 'municipal law of human rights' under the Human Rights Act, in: International & Comparative Law Quarterly 54 (2005) 4, pp. 907-931.

McCallum, JA, The Asian Relations Conference, in: The Australian Quarterly 19 (1947) 2, pp. 13-17.

Merriman, John, A History of Modern Europe, Bd. 1, New York, 1996.

Messenger, David, Dividing Europe: The Cold War and European Integration, in: Dinan, Desmond (Ed.), Origins and Evolution of the European Union, Second Edition, Oxford, 2014, pp. 32-54.

Michalski, Anna, The Enlarging European Union, in: Dinan, Desmond (Ed.), Origins and Evolution of the European Union, Second Edition, Oxford, 2014, pp. 271-293.

Mitsilegas, Valsamis, Cross-Border Cooperation after Brexit, in: Dougan, Michael (Ed.), The UK After Brexit: Legal and Policy Challenges, Cambridge, 2017, pp. 203-224.

Muntarbhorn, Vitit, The Challenge of Law: Legal Cooperation among ASEAN Countries, Bangkok, 1987.

Narine, Shaun, ASEAN in the Twenty-First Century: A Sceptical Review, in: Cambridge Review of International Affairs 22 (2009) 3, pp. 369-386.

Narine, Shaun, Forty Years of ASEAN: a Historical Review, in: The Pacific Review 21 (2008) 4, pp. 411-429.

Narine, Shaun, The New ASEAN in Asia Pacific and Beyond, Boulder, 2018.

Nguyen, Chat Le, Towards the Effective ASEAN Mutual Legal Assistance in Combating Money Laundering, in: Journal of Money Laundering Control 15 (2012) 4, pp. 383-395.

Nilsson, Hans, From Classical Judicial Cooperation to Mutual Recognition, in: Revue internationale de droit pénal 77 (2006) 1, pp. 53-58.

Nixon, Richard, Asia After Viet Nam, in: Foreign Affairs 46 (1967) 1, pp. 111-125.

Nowak, Manfred, Report of the Special Rapporteur on Torture and Other Cruel, Inhuman, or Degrading Treatment or Punishment, 2005.

O'Higgins, Paul, European Convention on Extradition, in: The International and Comparative Law Quarterly 9 (1960) 3, pp. 491-494.

Office of the Attorney General, Introduction to Mutual Assistance in Criminal Matters Act, 2016, accessible via http://www.agc.gov.my/agcportal/index.php?r=portal2/left&menu_id=OVBtWnBvWEo3MlhNZ0RtNGF0QzBBUT09.

Osborne, Milton, Southeast Asia: An Introductory History, Sydney, 2013.

Pacquette, Gabrielle, Colonial Societies, in: Scott, Hamish (Ed.), Oxford Handbook on Early Modern European History, 1350-1750, Volume 2: Cultures & Power, Oxford 2015, pp. 280-306.

Parchami, Ali, The Echoes of Rome in British and American Hegemonic Ideology, in: Nicolaïdis, Kalypso/Sèbe, Berny/Maas, Gabrielle (Ed.), Echoes of Empire: Memory, Identity, and Colonial Legacies, London, 2017, pp. 105-122.

Park, No-Hyoung, The Third World as an International Legal System, in: BC Third World LJ 7 (1987), pp. 37-60.

Parsons, Craig, The Truimph of Community Europe, in: Dinan, Desmond (Ed.), Origins and Evolution of the European Union, Second Edition, Oxford, 2014, pp. 115-135.

Pasadilla, Gloria, East Asian Cooperation: The ASEAN View, Makati, 2004.

Patrick, Stewart, Embedded Liberalism in France?, in: Schain, Martin (Ed.), The Marshall Plan Fifty Years After, New York, 2001, pp. 205-249.

Peers, Steve, EU Justice and Home Affairs Law, Third Edition, Oxford, 2011.

Peers, Steve, EU Justice and Home Affairs Law (Non-Civil), in: Craig, Paul/De Burca, Grainne (Ed.), The Evolution of EU Law, Oxford, 2011, pp. 269-299.

Peers, Steve, Mutual Recognition and Criminal Law in the European Union: Has the Council Got It Wrong, in: Common Market L. Rev. 41 (2004), pp. 5-36.

Plachta, Michael, European Arrest Warrant: Revolution in Extradition?, in: European Journal of Crime, Criminal Law and Criminal Justice 11 (2003) 2, pp. 178-194.

Pushpanathan, S, Combating Transnational Crime in ASEAN, in: 7th ACPF World Conference on Crime Prevention and Criminal Justice, New Delhi, 1999

Quintana, Mary Grace, International Cooperation: Mutual Legal Assistance and Extradition, in: Sixth Good Governance Seminar for Southeast Asian Countries, Tokyo, 2012

Ramcharan, Robin, ASEAN and Non-interference: A Principle Maintained, in: Contemporary Southeast Asia 22 (2000) 1, pp. 60-88.

Ramos, Jorge Angel Espina, The European Investigation Order and its relationship with other judicial cooperation instruments: establishing rules on the scope and possibilities of application, in: Eucrim: the European Criminal Law Associations' fórum (2019) 1, pp. 53-60.

Reeves, Jeffrey, Transnational Organised Crime in Asia: Norms, Principles and Regimes, in: Pardo, Ricardo Pacheco/Reeves, Jeffrey (Ed.), Non-Traditional Security in East Asia: A Regime Approach, London, 2015, pp. 73-92.

Reid, Anthony, The Bandung Conference and Southeast Asian Regionalism, in: Acharya, Amitav/Tan, See Seng (Ed.), Bandung Revisited: The Legacy of the 1955 Afro–Asian Conference, Singapore, 2008, pp. 19-26.

Reid, Anthony, A History of Southeast Asia, Chichester, 2015.

Reid, Karen, A Practitioner's Guide to the European Convention on Human Rights, London, 2015.

Richardson, Sophie, China, Cambodia, and the Five Principles of Peaceful Coexistence, New York, 2013.

Ricklefs, Merle Calvin/Lockhart, Bruce/Lau, Albert/Reyes, Portia/Aung-Thwin, Maitrii, A New History of Southeast Asia, London, 2010.

Riehle, Cornelia/Clozel, Allison, 10 Years After the Roadmap: Procedural Rights in Criminal Proceedings in the EU Today, in: ERA Forum 2019, pp. 321-325.

Robertson, John, Europe's Enlightenment, in: Scott, Hamish (Ed.), Oxford Handbook on Early Modern European History, 1350-1750, Volume 2: Cultures & Power, Oxford 2015, pp. 141-172.

Rollason, David, Early Medieval Europe 300-1050: The Birth of Western Society, London, 2014.

Roselaar, Saskia, Introduction: Processes of Cultural Change and Integration in the Roman World, in: Roselaar, Saskia (Ed.), Processes of Cultural Change and Integration in the Roman World, Leiden, 2015, pp. 1-19.

Rublack, Ulinka, Protestantism and Its Adherents, in: Scott, Hamish (Ed.), Oxford Handbook on Early Modern European History, 1350-1750, Volume 1: People and Places, Bd. 1, Oxford, 2015, pp. 571-600.

Rüland, Jürgen/Jetschke, Anja, 40 Years of ASEAN: Perspectives, Performance and Lessons for Change, in: The Pacific Review 21 (2008) 4, pp. 397-409.

Saravanamuttu, Johan, ASEAN Security for the 1980s: The Case for a Revitalized ZOPFAN, in: Contemporary Southeast Asia 6 (1984) 2, pp. 186-196.

SarDesai, Damodar Ramaji, Southeast Asia: Past and Present, Boulder, 2012.

Satzger, Helmut, International and European Criminal Law, Second Edition, Munich, 2018.

Schomburg, Wolfgang/Lagodny, Otto, Internationale Rechtshilfe in Strafsachen= International Cooperation in Criminal Matters, 6th Edition, Munich, 2020.

Scopacasa, Rafael, An Allied View of Integration: Italian Elites and Consumption in the Second Century BC, in: Roselaar, Saskia (Ed.), Processes of Cultural Change and Integration in the Roman World, Leiden, 2015, pp. 39-57.

Scott, Hamish, Introduction, in: Scott, Hamish (Ed.), Oxford Handbook of Early Modern European History, 1350-1750, Volume 1: Peoples and Places, Oxford, 2015, pp. 1-36.

Sèbe, Berny, Towards Cosmopolitan Perspectives on Empires and their Echoes? The Case for a European Framework, in: Nicolaïdis, Kalypso/Sèbe, Berny/Maas, Gabrielle (Ed.), Echoes of Empire: Memory, Identity, and Colonial Legacies, London, 2017, pp. 123-140.

Secretariat, ASEAN, ASEAN Handbook on International Legal Cooperation in Trafficking in Persons Cases Indonesia, 2010.

Service, Robert, The End of the Cold War, London, 2016.

Severino, Rodolfo, ASEAN, Singapore, 2008.

Severino, Rodolfo, ASEAN Today and Tomorrow: Selected Speeches of Rodolfo C. Severino, Jr., Secretary-General of the Association of Southeast Asian Nations, Jakarta, 2002.

Severino, Rodolfo, ASEAN: What It Cannot Do, What It Can and Should Do, in: Lee, Yoong Yoong (Ed.), ASEAN Matters! Reflecting on the Association of Southeast Asian Nations, Singapore, 2011, pp. 3-7.

Sidek, Roziza, International Cooperation: Mutual Legal Assistance and Extradition, in: Sixth Good Governance Seminar for Southeast Asian Countries, Tokyo, 2012.

Sidhu, Omkar, The Concept of Equality of Arms in Criminal Proceedings under Article 6 of the European Convention on Human Rights, Cambridge, 2017.

Smith, Karen E, The Outsiders: the European Neighbourhood Policy, in: International affairs 81 (2005) 4, pp. 757-773.

Smith, Michael, The Shock of the Real? Trends in European Foreign and Security Policy since September 2001, in: Studia Diplomatica (2006), pp. 27-44.

Soesilowati, Sartika, ASEAN's Response to the Challenge of Terrorism, in: Masyarakat, Kebudayaan dan Politik (Society, Culture and Politics) 24 (2011), pp. 228-241.

Solidum, Estrella, The Politics of ASEAN: An Introduction to Southeast Asian Regionalism, Singapore, 2003.

Soriano, Manuel, International Cooperation: Extradition and Mutual Legal Assistance, in: Sixth Good Governance Seminar for Southeast Asian Countries, Tokyo, 2012

Sovannasam, Un, The ASEAN Efforts in Dealing with Transnational Crime, in: Lee, Yoong Yoong (Ed.), ASEAN Matters! Reflecting on the Association of Southeast Asian Nations, Singapore, 2005, pp. 77-84.

Spencer, John R, Mutual Recognition of Decisions in Criminal Justice and the United Kingdom, in: Vernimmen-Van Tiggelen, Gisele/Surano, Laura/Weyembergh, Anne (Ed.), The Future of Mutual Recognition in Criminal Matters in the European Union, Brussels, 2009, pp. 523-548.

Stavrou, Protesilaos Five Constitutional Principles of EU Law, 2015, accessible via https://protesilaos.com/five-principles-eu-law/.

Stirk, Peter, Integration and Disintegration Before 1945, in: Dinan, Desmond (Ed.), Origins and Evolution of the European Union, Second Edition, Oxford, 2014, pp. 11-33.

Stråth, Bo/Wagner, Peter, European Modernity: A Global Approach, London, 2017.

Stubbs, Richard, The ASEAN alternative? Ideas, Institutions and the Challenge to 'Global' Governance, in: The Pacific Review 21 (2008) 4, pp. 451-468.

Suominen, Annika, The Principle of Mutual Recognition in Cooperation in Criminal Matters: A Study of the Principle in Four Framework Decisions and in the Implementation Legislation in Nordic Member States, Cambridge, 2011.

Takagi, Isao, The Process of ASEANisation and its Characteristics (The 15th Anniversary of the Department of Economics, Soka University), in: 創価経済論集 15 (1986) 2, pp. 267-282.

Tan, Hsien-Li, The ASEAN Intergovernmental Commission on Human Rights: Institutionalising Human Rights in Southeast Asia, Cambridge, 2011.

Tarling, Nicholas, Southeast Asia: A Modern History, Oxford, 2001.

Taylor, Nyssa, England and Australia Relax the Double Jeopardy Privilege for Those Convicted of Serious Crimes, in: Temp. Int'l & Comp. LJ 19 (2005), pp. 189-218.

Terpstra, Nicholas, Early Modern Catholicsm, in: Scott, Hamish (Ed.), Oxford Handbook on Early Modern European History, 1350-1750, Volume 1: People and Places, Bd. 1, Oxford, 2015, pp. 601-625.

Thambipillai, Pushpa, Three Decades of ASEAN Linkage: Brunei Darussalam, From 1984 Towards 2015, in: Lee, Yoong Yoong (Ed.), ASEAN Matters! Reflecting on the Association of Southeast Asian Nations, Singapore, 2011, pp. 43-52.

Tilman, Robert, Southeast Asia and the Enemy Beyond: ASEAN Perceptions of External Threats, Boulder, 1987.

Timmermans, Frans, An Introduction to the Lisbon Treaty: Another Dan Brown Mystery Solved, in: Ott, Andrea/Vos, Ellen (Ed.), Fifty Years of European Integration: Foundations and Perspectives, The Hague, 2009, pp. 105-108.

Tiwari, Sivakant, ASEAN'S Perception Problem, in: Lee, Yoong Yoong (Ed.), ASEAN Matters! Reflecting on the Association of Southeast Asian Nations, Singapore, 2011, pp. 29-32.

Tuan, Hoang Anh, ASEAN Dispute Management: Implications for Vietnam and an Expanded ASEAN, in: Contemporary Southeast Asia (1996), pp. 61-80.

UK Home Office International Criminal Unit, International MLA and Extradition Agreements the UK is Party to, London, 2016.

United Nations, United Nations Treaty Collection, 2017, accessible via https://treaties.un.org/pages/ViewDetails.aspx?src=TREATY&mtdsg_no=XVIII-12&chapter=18&clang=_en.

United Nations Office on Drugs and Crime, United Nations Convention against Corruption Signature and Ratification Status as of 12 December 2016, 2016, accessible via https://www.unodc.org/unodc/en/treaties/CAC/signatories.html.

van der Wilt, Harmen, The Principle of Reciprocity, in: Blekxtoon, Rob (Ed.), Handbook on the European Arrest Warrant, The Hague, 2005, pp. 71-81.

van Wijk, Marloes, Cross-Border Evidence Gathering: Equality of Arms in the EU?, The Hague, 2017.

Vanke, John, Charles De Gaulle's Uncertain Idea of Europe, in: Dinan, Desmond (Ed.), Origins and Evolution of the European Union, Second Edition, Oxford, 2014, pp. 136-164.

Vermeulen, Gert/De Bondt, Wendy, Justice, Home Affairs, and Security. European and International Institutional and Policy Development, Antwerp, 2015.

Vermeulen, Gert/De Bondt, Wendy/Ryckman, Charlotte, Rethinking International Co-operation in Criminal Matters in the EU: Moving Beyond Actors, Bringing Logic Back, Footed in Reality, Antwerp, 2012.

Vermeulen, Gert/De Bondt, Wendy/Van Damme, Yasmin, EU Cross-Border Gathering and Use of Evidence in Criminal Matters. Towards Mutual Recognition of Investigative Measures and Free Movement of Evidence?, Antwerp, 2010.

Vogel, Joachim, The European Integrated Criminal Justice System and Its Constitutional Framework, in: Maastricht Journal of European and Comparative Law 12 (2005) 2, pp. 125-147.

Von Bogdandy, Armin, Founding Principles of EU Law: a Theoretical and Doctrinal Sketch, in: European Law Journal 16 (2010) 2, pp. 95-111.

Wahl, Thomas, The Perception of the Principle of Mutual Recognition of Judicial Decisions in Criminal Matters in Germany, in: Vernimmen-Van Tiggelen, Gisele/Surano, Laura/Weyembergh, Anne (Ed.), The Future of Mutual Recognition in Criminal Matters in the European Union, Brussels, 2009, pp. 115-146.

Walker, Clive, Clamping Down on Terrorism in the United Kingdom, in: Journal of International Criminal Justice 4 (2006) 5, pp. 1137-1151.

Weatherbee, Donald E, International Relations in Southeast Asia: the Struggle for Autonomy, Lanham, 2014.

Weatherbee, Donald E, Southeast Asia and ASEAN: Running in Place, in: Southeast Asian Affairs 2012 (2012) 1, pp. 3-22.

White, Robin C A/Ovey, Clare, Jacobs, White, and Ovey European Convention on Human Rights, Fifth Edition, Oxford, 2010.

Wickham, Chris, Medieval Europe, Yale, 2016.

Wilson, Steve/Rutherford, Helen/Storey, Tony/Wortley, Natalie, English Legal System, Oxford, 2014.

Wolters, Oliver William, History, Culture, and Region in Southeast Asian Perspectives, Singapore, 1999.

Woods, Lorna/Watson, Philippa, Steiner and Woods EU Law, Twelfth Edition, Oxford, 2012.

Yoshimatsu, Hidetaka, Collective Action Problems and Regional Integration in ASEAN, in: Contemporary Southeast Asia: A Journal of International and Strategic Affairs 28 (2006) 1, pp. 115-140.

Zagaris, Bruce, United States Treaties on Mutual Assistance in Criminal Matters, in: Bassiouni, M Cherif (Ed.), International Criminal Law, Bd. 2, Leiden, 2008, pp. 385-402.

Zhang, Shu Guang, Constructing 'Peaceful Coexistence': China's Diplomacy toward the Geneva and Bandung Conferences, 1954–55, in: Cold War History 7 (2007) 4, pp. 509-528.

Zmora, Hillay, Monarchy, Aristocracy and State in Europe 1300-1800, London, 2002.